Embedded Racism

Embedded Racism

Japan's Visible Minorities and Racial Discrimination

Second Edition

Debito Arudou

LEXINGTON BOOKS
Lanham • Boulder • New York • London

Published by Lexington Books
An imprint of The Rowman & Littlefield Publishing Group, Inc.
4501 Forbes Boulevard, Suite 200, Lanham, Maryland 20706
www.rowman.com

6 Tinworth Street, London SE11 5AL, United Kingdom

British Library Cataloguing in Publication Information Available

Library of Congress Cataloging-in-Publication Data

Names: Arudō, Debito, 1965- author.
Title: Embedded racism : Japan's visible minorities and racial discrimination / Debito Arudou.
Description: Second edition. | Lanham, Maryland : Lexington Books, [2022] | Includes bibliographical references and index. | Summary: "Revised and updated for this Second Edition, Embedded Racism is the product of three decades of work by a scholar living in Japan as a naturalized Japanese citizen. It offers a perspective into how Japan's overlooked racial discrimination not only undermines Japan's economic future but also emboldens white supremacists worldwide"—Provided by publisher.
Identifiers: LCCN 2021039012 (print) | LCCN 2021039013 (ebook) | ISBN 9781793653956 (cloth) | ISBN 9781793653970 (paperback) | ISBN 9781793653963 (ebook)
Subjects: LCSH: Japan—Race relations. | Racism—Japan. | Minorities—Japan—Social conditions. | Aliens—Japan—Social conditions. | Race discrimination—Japan. | Race discrimination—Law and legislation—Japan. | Physical-appearance-based bias—Japan. | Social isolation—Japan. | Nationalism—Social aspects—Japan.
Classification: LCC DS832.7.A1 A78 2022 (print) | LCC DS832.7.A1 (ebook) | DDC 305.800952—dc23
LC record available at https://lccn.loc.gov/2021039012
LC ebook record available at https://lccn.loc.gov/2021039013

∞™ The paper used in this publication meets the minimum requirements of American National Standard for Information Sciences—Permanence of Paper for Printed Library Materials, ANSI/NISO Z39.48-1992.

Contents

Preface to the Second Edition

As this book is updated for its Second Edition, it remains the culmination of nearly thirty-five years of researching and living in Japan—from around the time I first visited in 1986 to the present day. I have always been intrigued by how some normalized images of Japan did not square with what I was experiencing in everyday life. Despite being friendly and hospitable to guests, very progressive in unexpected ways, and open enough to outside things to co-opt them (even the music for Japan's national anthem was written by a foreigner), Japan has a palpable undercurrent of exclusionism. It is both subtle (e.g., ideas and proposals dismissed due to their "lack of precedent") and overt (e.g., "No Foreigners Allowed" signs—the subject of my related book *"Japanese Only": The Otaru Hot Springs Case and Racial Discrimination in Japan*). As I stayed longer, became fluent in Japanese, and felt acculturated and comfortable in Japanese society (to the point of taking Japanese citizenship and giving up my American), I saw the exclusionism more and more—and wanted to understand it.

As a social scientist, I like figuring out why societies behave in patterns, that is, "why people generally do this and not that." I eventually arrived at answers that transcended the tautological "cultural" explanations, that is, "Japanese do this because they are Japanese." That mattered to me. I never liked "culture" as an explanation for human behavior, since (a) "culture" is hard to define, and eclipses individual choice and foible, (b) it is often a "black box" that encages researcher curiosity, and (c) I assume that people anywhere are generally rational: they do things because those things are in their best interests. I do not think people are unthinking "prisoners of culture." In most cases there is a system—a collection of logics and incentives—that occasions behavior, and in this research one that encourages people to behave inclusively or exclusively. Even if those belief systems initially made no sense to me, they made sense to *someone*. My quest in this book was to find out how they made sense to people, and to quantify how they were underpinned by rules, customs, mores, and procedures.

Exclusionism in Japan (especially that of the racialized ilk) has been one big puzzle, taking me decades to deconstruct, then reconstruct a coherent picture of why a society as kind and conscientious as Japan's can be so cold and unsympathetic toward people perceived as outsiders. But as we consider in this book how racism takes shape in Japanese society, one conclusion I would like readers to internalize immediately is that Japan should not be treated as "special"—again, that "Japanese do this because they are uniquely Japanese" thing.[1] That generally leads to the conclusion of "Japanese racism isn't *really* racism as we know it in the West—it's just something that the Japanese reflexively do as cultural practices." Succumbing to that narrative invites all sorts of exceptionalism that is ungrounded—and it causes enormous cognitive dissonance when Japan is called upon to observe the international standards of human rights set forth under the international treaties it signed. (As we shall see later in this book, Japan officially takes advantage of this "unique" exceptionalist narrative to avoid addressing its own racism.) Avoiding this logical pitfall is not just a matter of normative principle. As I argue in the last chapter, Japan's racialized nation-state membership processes are so exclusionary that they are undermining the very fabric of Japanese society: Japan is strangling itself demographically on its Embedded Racism. And as I argue in the new chapter 11 for this Second Edition, Japan's Embedded Racism is in fact undermining the world's democracies.

In sum, Japan is no exception, especially to the world's racialization processes, and it deserves similar critique for racism. I believe that Japanese society behaves like any other—it just does it with an internal logic that is "special" and "unique" in ways that all societies are special and unique. This book seeks to unspool the internal logic that justifies and embeds racism. I hope you find its arguments compelling.

What's new to this Second Edition? This book has been completely updated and revised. The previous edition covered up to 2015, and a lot has happened to make the situation for Japan's Visible Minorities and foreign residents both better and worse:

- The ultraconservative Abe Shinzō government (2012–2020) became Japan's longest-running postwar administration, and with it the cementing of "status quo politics" that imported even more foreign labor under exploitative visa statuses; yet Japan continues to avoid a clear immigration policy encouraging permanent settlement and naturalization.
- Carlos Ghosn, the high-profile CEO of car manufacturer Nissan, was arrested and perpetually detained without trial, leading to his daring escape

from Japan, with much international attention drawn to Japan's "hostage justice" system of criminal jurisprudence.

- The Japanese government conducted unprecedented surveys on discrimination nationwide, revealing concrete numbers on just how widespread racist practices are in scale and form. Meanwhile, hate speech laws went into effect, driving public displays of bigotry and calls for violence against foreigners further underground and online.
- The Alien Registration system that officially segregated foreigners from their Japanese families was shut down, but registered foreign residents continue to be racially profiled by police and excluded from Japan's official population tallies.
- The COVID-19 pandemic devastated Japan's booming tourist economy and led to a painful postponement of the 2020 Tokyo Olympics. In response, the government instituted racist policies that banned border reentry not only to all foreign tourists but also registered foreign residents. (Japanese citizens reentering under the same conditions, however, were allowed in.) As the disease spread regardless (imported by unquarantined Japanese citizens), government and media nevertheless targeted domestic "foreign clusters" as hotbeds of contagion.
- The rise to prominence of Japan's Visible Minorities included Miss Japan beauty queens and athletes, most notably world tennis champion Ōsaka Naomi. Yet local governments segregated children of international marriages into "low-IQ" classes in compulsory education, utilized terminology categorizing anyone with international connections (including Wajin Japanese) as "foreign citizens," and continued to treat Japanese citizens with international roots as suspicious both in the political realm and the job market.
- Japan's "lost decades" of economic doldrums since the economic bubble burst in 1993 officially became the "lost quarter century" in the 2020s as China further outdistanced Japan as Asia's representative regional power.
- And much more, including updates and conclusions to cases mentioned in the previous edition.

A quick note before continuing: Claims have been assiduously footnoted with evidence throughout the book, including hundreds of links to my twenty-five-year online archive, *Debito.org*. Please note that this archive is not merely a blog of my opinions. In almost all cases it contains the full text of newspaper articles in multiple languages, primary-source documents and images, first-person accounts and testimonials, and outside links to references so you can see and double-check the exact sources for yourself. Good science requires verification and replication of results. *Debito.org* exists to make sure the historical record does not disappear into the ether.

It's time to give thanks. I would like to express my gratitude to the many people who have been helpful in this research. Deservedly first, I would like to thank my doctoral dissertation committee at Meiji Gakuin University: Dr. M. G. Sheftall, Dr. Sven Saaler, Dr. Ōiwa Keinosuke, Dr. Ōki Akira, and most of all Dr. Tom Gill for never giving up on me even when the project was in its (several) embryonic stages.

Next, there are colleagues who over the decades provided assistance ranging from the palliative (thanks) to the ego-bruising (ouch, but thanks): Ivan Hall, Chris Pitts, Michael Penn, David Johnson, Eric Johnston, Sakanaka Hidenori, Yuma Totani, Mark Levin, Christine Yano, Chalmers Johnson, Mark Selden, Ben Stubbings, James and Kumiko Eriksson, Karen Stafford, Chad Edwards, Michael H. Fox, Bern Mulvey, "Rube" Redfield, Goetz Heermann, Nick Hill, Tim Greer, Eric Kalmus, Christopher and Amy Savoie, Paul Toland, Paul Kallender-Umezu, Steve van Dresser, Mark Schreiber, Kaoru Miki, Jeff Kingston, David Edgington, Okamoto Masataka, Ōmura Satoshi, Dave Spector, Higashizawa Yasushi, Shiba-ike Toshiteru, Moro-oka Yasuko, Doudou Diene, Ana Bortz, Tom Goetz, Pat O'Brien, Robert Aspinall, Kirk Masden, Farrell Cleary, Joe Tomei, Alan Rosen, Cynthia Worthington, Daniel Kirk, Paul Beaufait, Gavin Anderson, Shawn Clankie, Simon Jackson, Richard Hopkins, Shouya Grigg, Mark Rosa, Ben Goodyear, Steven Herman, Colin Jones, Edward Y. Sumoto, Louis Carlet, Alex Kerr, Tilman Koenig and Daniel Kremers, David Hearn and Matt Antell, Tyler Lynch, Rue Birch, Heinrich Koechlin, Tokyo Sam, Stefan Stosik, Carl Polley and Beryl Yang, Kyle Cleveland, Rick Gundlach, Caroline Pover, Jon Heese, Anthony Bianchi, Susan Duggan, Edward and Aki Haig, Evan Heimlich, Randal Irwin, Chris Mackenzie, Daniel Walsh, Dave Gutteridge, Jens Wilkinson, Imtiaz Chaudhry, Mark Mino-Thompson, Ryan Hagglund, Ben Shearon, Elliott Samuels, Barry Brophy, Barbara Bayer, Monty DiPietro, Paul Murphy, Jay Klaphake, Douglas Shukert, Charles Kowalski, Jon Letman, Isabelle, David McNeill, Jim O'Neill, Martin Fackler, Pio d'Emilia, Larry Repeta, Skipp Orr, Ronald E. Hall, Shin Hae Bong, John Lie, T. J. Pempel, John Maher, Ralph Ittonen Hosoki, Robert Whiting, Jim Brooke, Jeff Alexander, Mark West, Robert Pekkanen, Lonny Carlyle, Bob Huey, Dick Minear, Trent Maxey, Frank Upham, Keiko Yamanaka, In Ha Lee, Gabriele Vogt, Julian Dierkes, Curtis Millhaupt, John McLaughlin, Kawakami Sonoko, Thom Simmons, Gene van Troyer, Dan Carolin, Peter Firkola, Steven Fylypchuk, Chris Gunson, Mark Smith, Steve Silver, Albrecht Stahmer, Garrett DeOrio, Ken Worsley, Bob Sanderson, Jon Dujmovich, Chris Flynn, John Lawrence, Murray Wood, Tony McNicol, Tim Hornyak, Steven Parr, Jim diGriz, Rich Fassler, John Evans, Ken Sutherland, U. G. Valentine, Scott Hards, Steve McGowan, Fukushima Mizuho, Tsurunen Marutei, FRANCA, The Community in Japan, UMJ, The Buraku Liberation League, IMADR,

Mindan, the JCLU, W. E. B. Du Bois, and my editors for the Second Edition at Lexington Books Courtney Morales and Matthew Valades. Also deep thanks to the commentators at *Debito.org* for their quarter-century of critiques and encouragement of my rough drafts since 1996.

Also, to those who kept me human and grounded: Magica De Spell, Olaf Karthaus, my daughters, Sugawara Ayako, Don and Lynne, Christine and Jodi, Todd and Shingo, Aldwonker, Roddy, Tim and Wendy, Sacha and Linka, and my fearless drinking buddies at Sapporo Off-Kai (especially Meros, Nonchan, Saori, Kubotchi, and Mr. Joke).

The final line goes to my best friend, Jen. Thank you for always being there.

Debito Arudou, PhD
July 1, 2021

NOTE

1. See, for example, Samuel P. Huntington's influential *Clash of Civilizations and the Remaking of World Order* (1996: 26–7), where he classifies the world's major civilizations as "Western, Orthodox, Islamic, African, Latin American, Sinic, Hindu, Buddhist," and "Japanese." Only Japan gets its own "special" civilization without influences spilling across its borders.

Introduction

WHY SUCH A LONG INTRODUCTION?

Racism is a difficult subject to discuss. Everyone seems to have an opinion about it, but few seem to agree on exactly what it is. That makes short books about racism practically impossible. If this book were about, say, Japanese beer, it would not have to devote much space defining what "beer" is, and few would claim that being terse about beer's origins would be giving short shrift to a social force that fundamentally underpins the order of whole societies.[1] That is why this book must devote due space in the introductory stages to defining terms and recounting important debates, otherwise it will surely be faulted for not mentioning them.

This introduction will first establish "race" and "racism" as a social (not biological) construct, put it in context with historical origins and causes of racism, talk about why Japanese society is no exception to worldwide racialization processes, and demonstrate how Japanese Studies has been wrongly exceptionalistic about racism in Japan. If this is TMI for some undergraduate readers, or old hat for the old hands, then by all means please skip to chapter 1.

WHY "RACISM" IS AN ISSUE OF SOCIAL POWER RELATIONS, NOT BIOLOGY

To better understand the effects of racism on a society, let us begin with a brief review of the debate over the origins and causes of racism.

First, regarding the concept of "race": Current schools of thought in the social sciences generally reject the traditional notion of "race" as an objective, scientifically substantiated biological construct, where inherited characteristics of *Homo sapiens* as a species enable humankind to sort itself into groups of traits, tendencies, and types.[2] Historically, scientists (and later policymakers) have categorized people as "Black," "White," "Yellow," "Brown," "Red," "Colored," and so on based upon their phenotype, organizing them into taxonomies of "Caucasoid," "Mongoloid," "Negroid," and so on with further subdivisions.[3] However, since then history and science have generally concluded that this classification is neither scientific in rigor (because taxonomic boundaries are blurry, and people are similar regardless of their skin color), nor apolitical in purpose (because the differentiation of peoples inevitably leads to differentiation in their treatment by society).[4] As Kowner (2013) puts it, "[B]iology has never been the core issue of racial ideologies, and, needless to say, racism."[5]

For example, "biological determinism," the argument that "shared behavioral norms, and the social and economic differences between human groups—primarily races, classes, and sexes—arise from inherited, inborn distinctions and that society, in this sense, is an accurate reflection of biology," has been thoroughly debunked by Gould et al. (using examples of discredited sciences such as polygeny, craniology, inherited and innate intelligence, etc.) as unscientific "mismeasurements."[6] If "race" were truly an objective biological concept, like a taxonomy of animal species, you would likely see a strict classification system in the field applied worldwide. But as Spickard (1992) argues convincingly, that system simply does not exist. Comparing official racial classifications in the American, British, South African, and Brazilian nation-states (which are overtly political in creation and application), Spickard points out that they are all different in terminology and scope—adapted because the "sociopolitical landscape [in each country] demanded different divisions."[7]

Thus, a caution for "newbies" to the debate couching racism in terms of biology: you are not only about a century behind the times in terms of social science but also likely to wind up using a psychological escape hatch—wrongheaded overgeneralization. Even the most shrewd critical thinker who has not been trained in the social science of racism may (a) feel less need to consider and investigate the individuality of a subject (for if categorizations of people are ironclad, people become prisoners of their biology from birth); or (b) fail to consider the socialization and sociopolitical aspects behind the racialization of people—that is, seeing "racism(s)" as a sociopolitical construct. History clearly demonstrates how socially constructed racism incorporates political dynamics, and how people born into the dominant social group dexterously manipulate the status quo to perpetuate their dominance and privilege.[8]

In sum, the concept of "race" is more about social science than physical science. Inserting biology where it doesn't belong generates assumptions that "race" is a static concept free of politics, without grounding in a social process of racialization. It also tends to legitimize assumptions that differences in behavior and social status can be reduced to innate biological factors; to quote Spickard succinctly, "races are not types."[9] As J. C. King, himself a geneticist, aptly notes:

> Both what constitutes a race and how one recognizes a racial difference are culturally determined. Whether two individuals regard themselves as of the same or of different races depends not on the degree of similarity of their genetic material but on whether history, tradition, and personal training and experiences have brought them to regard themselves as belonging to the same groups or to different groups . . . there are no objective boundaries to set off one subspecies from another.[10]

"RACE" AND THE PROCESSES OF "RACIALIZATION" AS A SOCIAL CONSTRUCT

So let us now turn to the sociological, performative aspect of race: the "racial formation process"—or for the purposes of this research, "racialization."[11]

Racialization involves dividing people into groups based upon phenotype, by (a) differentiating "us" from "them" as "Self" vs. "The Other," then (b) ascribing predictive behavioral aspects to their character, and finally (c) subordinating them in terms of the locus of power within a society. Clearly this is an intensely political process beyond mere issues of "economic determinism, sociological or biological reductionism" and into the realm of social power relations.[12] Postmodern scholarship since the mid-1980s has gone even further: seeing social "othering" as a byproduct of artificial community formation (i.e., "imagined communities") in the form of the modern nation-state.[13] In other words, the dynamics that foster racism are found everywhere, as they are innate to the very political organization of human society.

In essence, racialization is but one process of condensing social relationships down to elemental decisions based upon first impressions, without having to take the time and effort to investigate and familiarize oneself with the vast array of people one encounters over a lifetime as individuals.[14] It can also be a fundamental way for people to determine allegiances, for example, who is "a member" of your group and who is not, who shares "your interests" and who does not, who is "an insider" and who is not. This differentiation has been at the root of the creation of teams, clans, tribes, fiefdoms, kingdoms, nations, nationalisms, interest and pressure groups, political parties, self-justifying value systems and ideologies, "uniqueness" schools of thought, civil wars, wars, and even pogroms and genocides. To some schools of thought, racism is so fundamentally "embedded" in human machinations that it underpins the historical roots of protocapitalism, colonialism, and the Westphalian system of government; and to this day remains at the very core of current international labor migration policy, globalization, and capitalism as a system.[15]

Thus, racism is not a trivial topic within the social sciences. In the analytical paradigms I will be using in this book, race is the fundamental factor (whether conscious and unconscious) behind political activity involving the creation of law, public policy, and social order within a society. In Japan's case, I refer to this process in chapter 1 as "Embedded Racism."

The Social Construct in Historical Context

However, a brief disclaimer about "race," "racism," and "racialization" must be made in terms of historical contingency. As mentioned earlier, "race" is not an "objective condition," as it has a very different meaning historically than it does today.[16] For example, as Miles (1993) points out, at the turn of the nineteenth century the term "race" was even applied to Irish immigrants as formal policy under the British Empire, even though "Irish" people under modern conceits are not biologically or even visually differentiable from "British" people.[17] "Race" less than a century ago was essentially shorthand for "a different people due to birth circumstances," that is, not being "born British." It was a political distinction based not on phenotype (as opposed to, for example, slaves in the British and American systems being identifiable and trackable as "Negroes"), rather based on the political borders of the nation-state. As Miles further notes, this racial distinction changed over time, when other "people of color" (such as Indians, Pakistanis, and Hong Kong Chinese who were [former] British imperial subjects) began to claim their right to reside in Great Britain as residents under the Commonwealth; then public policy changed to no longer identify the Irish as racially different, and instead identified people (ostensibly by difference in nationality, but in practice by difference in visibly identifiable biological markers) as "colored" and "culturally different" to restrict their entry into Great Britain; from there developed the complex and problematic social science called "race relations."[18]

Thus, because the concept of "race" and the act of racialization has not been a fixed concept over time, it is necessary for the scholar of racism to be aware of how the dynamic of racism has fundamentally influenced the development of political policy toward minorities in the modern nation-state. This will universalize the phenomenon of racism, and, for the purposes of this book, allow the transposition of well-developed theories of how racism "works" in terms of power relationships in one society (e.g., theories of "Whiteness Studies" in the American example) into demonstrating how it "works" in another society (i.e., creating "Wajin Studies" for the Japanese example; more on this later).

Deconstructing "Racism": The Merits and Shortcomings of Postmodernism and Postcolonialism

Although this book does not have the space to offer a thorough historical sociology of racism, the deconstructions of the status quo offered by postmodernist/postcolonialist thought have been powerful in demonstrating how racism has been consciously and unconsciously integral to a society's public discourse and public policy. Some authors have focused upon analysis of discursive formations to parse out the "genealogy" and "ontology" of national narratives, uncovering latent racialized biases and conscious and unconscious agenda-setting.[19]

For example, Saïd (1978), in his postulation of "Orientalism," has demonstrated how the voices of minorities within a society, and the majority of the world outside the world's major media and historical academe, tend to be "othered" and underrepresented in the narrative (if not ignored).[20] In terms of this research, Saïd's contribution to the canon is the awareness of how the underrepresentation of minority voices leads to distortions in worldviews of peoples, where "White" views of, for example, Arabs and Arabic culture influence how other White and even non-White consumers of "White" discourses see Arabs and Arabic culture. This process, profoundly influenced by colonial superior/subordinate "civilizing" conceits of differentiation, has led to not just mere "othering," but also *scholarly ignorance* of foreign cultures, subordination of civilizations, and even dehumanization.[21]

I acknowledge my deep debt to these scholars and disciplines (see appendix 2) for demonstrating the power of unquestioned hegemonic national discourses and nation-state narratives but will now discuss two shortcomings in their analysis.

One shortcoming with postmodernist/postcolonialist critiques of racism, as they seek to break down social phenomena to its elements, sources, causes, and origins, is that they problematize the very terms of debate: Not that "race" is being seen once again as an objective biological construct, but rather that the very expression of debate on racism in words tends to invite criticism. As Farber and Sherry (1997) point out, postmodernism by its very nature politicizes and even polemicizes debate about its topic;[22] for example, if the discussants are not as self-aware as the "experts" qualified to discuss postmodernism, postmodernist critiques can wind up stifling public discussion similar to the ways hegemonic discourses stifle public discussion.

How Issues of Racial Discrimination Have Been Elided in Postcolonial Japanese Studies

The other shortcoming is a fundamental assumption of European/White hegemony in the ordering of the world's colonial/imperial systems. This is where Japan comes in. For example, Saïd's "Orientalist" thesis is generally predicated upon the influences and hegemony of "Western" culture over the world's view of itself and history. While I am not questioning this phenomenon's existence, it leads to generalizations that tend to ignore one major party at the colonial/imperial bargaining table who was *not* "Western"—Japan.[23]

Although I agree that Japan was (a) a relative latecomer to the economic carving up of the world, and (b) followed quite "Western" models of creation of its own nation-state, industrialization, and colonization, it also predicated itself on quite different models of differentiation and subjugation of "less civilized peoples" (more below).[24] Also, by leaving Japan out of the "Orientalist" model, there is a significant political dimension to the discussion that warrants mention: Japan's academe has never engaged in the thorough postcolonialist debate that the "West" has had regarding its own role as a colonial power.[25]

For example, Japan's public discourse and historical narrative frequently portray Japan more as a "victim" (less as an aggressor, or if so as a justified aggressor) during World War II, waxing nostalgically about "the good things" a more-civilized Japan imparted to its less-civilized Asian brethren under the Greater East Asia Co-Prosperity Sphere.[26] "Imperialist" attitudes such as these have been thoroughly debunked by postmodernist/postcolonialist scholars in other former colonial powers, but not in Japan. Japan's dominant discourse of latent Japanese "uniqueness" and colonialism-influenced superiority over other people to this day has a profound effect upon Japan's attitudes (and thus public policies) toward foreigners both inside and outside Japan.[27] This discourse and dynamic are what this research will now begin to uncover and discuss.

OVERVIEW OF THE DEBATE REGARDING RACISM IN JAPAN

Why Japan Is Not a "Special Case" in the World Discussion of "Racism"

Does "racism," as seen and defined in other societies, exist in Japan? Racism in Japan is often seen as exceptional, for example, portrayed as *ethnic* (not racial), or less extreme (because it does not involve the same expressions of racially motivated hatred: there are relatively few cases of, for example, overt physical violence toward minorities).[28] Regardless, scholars of racism in Japan concentrate on the differentiation and separation of peoples within its borders (a practice that, of course, happens in all societies). For them, however, the question is one of source: Is differentiation really due to biological characteristics? Or is this differentiation due to globalization's socioeconomic or cultural effects on Japan, i.e., Japan's response to an internationalizing domestic labor market due to the labor shortage of the 1980s, or just *sui generis* due to Japan's politico-historical or innate practices of defining oneself in comparison to the Other?[29]

I argue that one need not focus overmuch on the *biology* (because how it is seen and defined is very subjective and, as mentioned above, grounded in historical/sociopolitical contexts) but rather on the *process* of differentiation (which demonstrates a surprising degree of universal patterns). The common denominator is the act of the nation-state deciding its membership—that is, who is part of the "Self" and who of the "Other"—making nonmembers outsiders as part of the "grammar" of a culture. As Clammer (2001) succinctly puts it, "There cannot be inclusion without exclusion."[30] Clearly Japan is no exception to this process. Japanese society, as in every society, has a majority group (ethnic and/or cultural) and minority groups. It may be due to, for example, the economic ultracentrifuge of capitalism, the vestiges of a colonial past, and/or the social self-enforcement of diffuse power found in every society in order to protect the corpus of the nation from deviance.[31] But nevertheless there is a majority that dominates the national discourse and shapes the national identity. This is why Japan should not be treated as a "unique" or even "special" case in terms of racism.

This research acknowledges that Japan is unusual historically in that (a) it has never been colonized from abroad since becoming a civilization (except arguably for a brief period after World War II), instead becoming an industrial and imperial power to escape being colonized by other imperial powers; (b) Japan colonized its neighbors of similar Asian ethnicities, not distant "peoples of color" as seen in Western colonialism, and did so under a rhetoric of Pan-Asian equality, family, and (ironically) resistance to racial discrimination (see chapter 2); (c) Japan colonized in a unified and speedy manner not seen elsewhere; and (d) Japan's "family state" (*kazoku kokka*) structure and rhetoric (more below) was (and remains) quite different than Western statist structures based upon the sense of contract between lord and serf.[32] As Oguma (2002) notes, "The Great Japanese Empire was the last example of imperialism by an advanced nation, and at the same time was the first example of imperialism by a third-world nation."[33] That said, in regard to the processes of nation-state formation and racialization of society, this research will now argue that Japan falls within established patterns.[34]

Universal Processes of Racialization and Nation-State Formation in Japan

For example, let us compare Japan to an established and well-analyzed pattern of societal racialization: Great Britain's categorization of Irish, then Jews, into a racially different Other, as a means of defining law and social policy in the early twentieth century.

The process, according to Miles (1993), had six steps[35]:

(1) *Bring people into proximity either physically (through labor migration) or in discourse space (through the official promotion of a group or tribe of "outsiders" beyond the established borders of the nation-state).* Japan did this: Meiji-Era policies established very clearly who were "insiders" and "outsiders" through, for example, its promotion of slogans[36] in the emerging national narrative to make people aware that there were "Others," even physically different "Others," far beyond the next village.

(2) *Make distinctions between these people on the basis of origin, language, phenotype, and so on, and ground them in law and invented traditions.* Japan did this too. Even as an empire preaching brotherhood among Asian peoples, it still made clear distinctions between "Japanese" and "colonists" and "foreigners" in regular discourse (more below).

3) *Assert that these differences are natural, based upon blood or ideology.* Japan still does this, with legally codified blood requirements for Japanese citizenship (see chapter 4); and, as will be discussed in later chapters, culture/ideology still influences Japanese public policy and social science regarding how people who are "different" are to be treated.

(4) *Assign negative attributes to these differences.* Volumes of pre- and postimperial scholarship, not to mention the postwar nativist discourse of *Nihonjinron* (theories of Japanese uniqueness in cultural and national identity) have been dedicated to how Japan's tropes of difference and uniqueness mean superiority over the "Other."[37]

(5) *Assume that the "Other" is inassimilable into the national body*, and

(6) *Assert the "Other" presents and represents a threat to the national order by its very existence.* Japan has done this very effectively: as will be described in future chapters, Meiji-Era slogans and policies made it clear that Japanese (as nationals of the nation-state) need to be protected against those foreign "Others." Meiji-Era policies kept its foreign scholars and advisors on short-term work statuses. Japan's perpetual subordination of colonial subjects within Japan ultimately made its postwar self-cleansing of empire easier. Japan's Bubble-Era "internationalization" (*kokusaika*) policies still kept "outsiders" disenfranchised, and even present-day visa regimes keep foreign and migrant labor on a "revolving door" status—justified (as we shall see in later chapters) under an official invective of "foreigners are a threat to Japan's social order."

In sum, Japan's history and social processes must of course be carefully studied to avoid conflating them with facile theories that Japanese society behaves like every other. However, Japan's *processes* of attribution, inclusion, and exclusion in order to establish and crystalize *racisms* within its society have patterns found worldwide. Nevertheless, the problem remains that many scholars and analysts treat Japan's racism as somehow "different" or "milder" than that found in other countries. This has resulted in prominent scholarship within Japanese Studies ignoring certain minorities, if not all minorities. This book aims to remedy that.

For example, as researchers search for a superlative about Japan and the apparent uniformity of its people (e.g., Befu's "homogeneous Japanese society"), "the Japanese" have often been analyzed as a homogeneous bloc, with events, phenomena, and domestic discourse in Japan being portrayed as if they affected *all* people (regardless of origin) living in Japan; this results in minorities going under-researched, if not even portrayed as "invisible."[38] The result has been a worldwide normalization (if not justification) of Japan's discourse of "Self" ("Japanese") and "Other" ("not Japanese") as part of Japan's "unique culture" and social order maintenance. Thus, "Foreigners" by definition have become not part of "Japan," meaning *they too have been "othered" within the field of Japanese Studies*.[39] Again, the problem is that the lessons of Saïd's Orientalism are not being sufficiently applied to Japan: little scholarship is devoted to how *domestic discourse in Japan and on Japan sets the agenda for scholarship on Japan,* in a way that favors and reinforces "the Japanese" as the dominant discoursers crowding out minority voices.

Therefore, what is also necessary is a discourse on the discourse itself, which is the objective of this introduction. Let us now address the research gap in the field of Japanese Studies, that is, how racism and racialized paradigms within Japanese society normalize "othering" to the point where not only are the racialization processes invisible, but the people being racialized themselves are also rendered invisible. This especially applies to the Visible Minorities who, as the "Japanese Only" exclusions in chapter 3 demonstrate, do exist in Japan.[40]

JAPAN'S UNDER-RESEARCHED VISIBLE MINORITIES: "BLIND SPOTS" WITHIN JAPANESE STUDIES

Let's look at some examples of research gaps. Scholarship on discrimination in Japan generally focuses on groups including the *Burakumin* historical underclass, *Zainichi* Koreans, Ainu, Okinawans, women, the physically and mentally infirm, ethnic and historical minorities, the elderly, children, former leprosy victims, crime victims, HIV sufferers, the homeless, ex-convicts, foreigners, and victims of human trafficking, North Korean kidnappings, and other forms of bullying and social abuse.[41] This is, of course, a viable categorization of groups who face discrimination in Japanese society.

However, the categorization of "foreigners" within Japan, and the research on discrimination against them in Japan, is often flawed because it is not always inclusive of all minorities in Japan. For example, scholarship on Japan's minorities tends to focus on *Zainichi* Koreans and Chinese "Oldcomers," and Chinese/Nikkei migrant/immigrant labor "Newcomers."[42] That research focuses more upon discrimination as a function of nationality and legal status, not as a racialization process, which leads to some odd conclusions: "In contrast with the dominance of racial categories as in the United States, the Japanese/foreigner binary is salient in Japan"; "Legally, Japanese ancestry is a purely civil, not racial status."[43]

This sometimes engenders a hierarchical mindset toward "foreigners" that disadvantages people in our Visible Minority category (e.g., Caucasians, non-Asian naturalized citizens, etc.), as they allegedly (a) are not *as* discriminated against as other minority groups (such as the Zainichi, who have been in Japan longer),[44] (b) are only temporary workers, not long-term residents or immigrants (again in contrast to the Zainichi), or (c) are in numbers small enough to be negligible; in other words, they simply don't count.[45] This approach results in hundreds of thousands of people living in Japan, including Japanese citizens, being overlooked or omitted from studies of racism in Japan.

Researchers also tend to overlook issues of racialized discrimination by focusing on the international migration of labor into Japan vis-à-vis national migration policies and legal issues. These analyses do offer valuable observations from a comparative international perspective, instructive for scholars and policymakers of international migration.[46] However, this tends to overlook how the determination of nationality/citizenship (and the barriers to becoming "Japanese") is not only a matter of legal status but also an issue of visual identification at the "Micro," more interpersonal levels of society. They also underplay the discourses at the systemic "Macro" level, that is, how racialization is a natural function of the general maintenance of imagined communities and nation-states. As Zachmann (2013) notes, "Racism is a venom that poisons the very sources of law."[47] Thus, studies of discrimination in Japan by legal status alone are insufficient and must go deeper.

"Blind Spots" vis-à-vis Racism by Visual Identification in Japan

Furthermore, research that does manage to recognize discrimination against "foreigners" beyond purely legal status still tends to overlook (if not dismiss) racialized visual identification as a factor, focusing instead on ethnic identification, ethnic self-identification, and/or broader issues of culture and belief systems.

Clammer (2001) includes in his analysis of Japan's "Others" even "cognitive minorities" (e.g., discrimination against *Sōka Gakkai* members), and avoids visual identification altogether—stating tersely that "ethnic differentiation is in many ways simply an epiphenomenon."[48] Komai (1993, 1995, 1999, 2001), despite extensive research on the lives of non-Japanese minorities in Japan, offers no rigorous treatment or even a clear definition of "racism" in his earlier analysis of Japan's treatment of migrant workers; his later work eschews "race relations" in favor of "ethnic relations." Lie (2004) rightly eschews "race" as a scientific concept (preferring instead to focus upon the existence of ethnicities and the interplay of multiethnic groups in Japan), but then under-analyzes how visual identification plays a part in separating people into those multiethnic groups (or, more to the point of this research, how it separates people, including multiethnic Japanese children, into the binary of Japanese and Gaijin).[49] Befu's (2001) influential work on Japanese identity also construes "racism" in Japan as a matter of ethnicity rather than visual identification: "Because the large numbers of Koreans and Chinese who live in Japan are racially indistinguishable from Japanese, the prejudicial attitude Japanese have toward them is more a case of ethnic prejudice and discrimination, that is, ethnocentrism, rather than racial prejudice."[50]

Although all of the above analyses have correctly identified root causes of several types of discrimination in Japan, they still do not pass what this book will call a "Yunohana Test." That is to say, they overlook what happened at "Japanese Only" establishments (in this case, an exclusionary public bathhouse in Otaru called "Yunohana") that let in customers who "looked Japanese" and kicked out those who did not. More in chapter 3, but consider the dynamics being ignored by these scholars: Their concepts of ethnocentrism, ethnic self-identification, or even legal status were not factors in the sorting of customers at places like Yunohana. Managers undertook no "ethnocentric" survey of customers' ethnicity—they just summarily kicked out the Gaijin based upon instant visual identification of biological markers. Thus, the canon remains blind to this strand of discrimination toward Visible Minorities, with deleterious effects on otherwise solid research.

Case in Point: Weiner's Book *Japan's Minorities*

To demonstrate how these scholarly "blind spots" detract from otherwise sound research on racism and minorities in Japan, let us focus on a highly cited compendium of research in this field: Michael Weiner's *Japan's Minorities* (1997; 2nd Ed. 2009).

Weiner's introduction refers to Japan's "principal minority populations" (xvii), specifically as Ainu, Koreans, Burakumin, Chinese, Okinawans, and Nikkei South Americans. Although indeed minorities in Japan, tellingly they are not Visible Minorities, that is, they are generally of "Asian" roots and can "pass" as "Japanese" in many social interactions, including the "Yunohana Test" at an exclusionary Otaru bathhouse.[51] This raises the question: What of the people of darker skins or differently colored physical characteristics in Japan?

Moreover, in a book covering "discrimination in Japan, racial and ethnic," *there is no reference either to the Ana Bortz Case (1998–1999) or Otaru Onsens Case (1993–2005)*, two significant lawsuits covered in chapter 3 that describe the Japanese judiciary's position on the constitutionality of racial discrimination in Japan. Instead, Weiner argues that Japan, unlike other nations, has been able to carry on racism "without reference to the colour stigmata" (xiv: which logically should have precluded the Russell chapter on "Blacks"). Thus, especially after more than two decades of influx of visually distinct migrant/immigrant laborers, increased international marriage, and unprecedented levels of "Newcomer" Permanent Residents, it is a serious oversight of scholarship to omit examples of racialized stigmata that have been repeatedly certified in Japan's judiciary, in an updated edition long after those landmark court cases have concluded.

Other scholars in Weiner's book, even when acknowledging color stigmata in Japan, tend to overlook or downplay the racialization process both interpersonally and in the public policy arena. For example, Robert Fish in his section on "mixed-blood Japanese," offers an excellent overview of Japan's national debate on how Japanese children created and abandoned by American soldiers in Japan during the Occupation (1945–1952) were to be "treated" as they reached school age in Japan, that is, as official objects of pity, as "cute" (48), or as potential bullying cases in school that required attention for special policies for proper care and assimilation.

However, Fish states that this is not a racialization process, saying, "'race,' *per se*, did not create consistent problems for students" (55). Instead, he argues inter alia that the behavior of the students themselves was to blame: "Overwhelmingly, the children who had difficulties in school had extreme difficulties in their home life, and those who found themselves isolated often behaved in relatively antisocial ways that would have created problems for the children regardless of physical appearance" (ibid.). He cites Ministry of Education data that much of the bullying was "because of their rough personalities" (54)), or due to socioeconomic issues, such as parental connections with Japan's sex trades, or being raised by single mothers with unstable father figures (51–52). Fish also claims Japan was in fact "ahead of the curve at actively encouraging equality" (53) compared to, for example, the contemporary United States with segregation.

However, this analysis demonstrates a fundamental misunderstanding of the racialization processes in every society. What of the perennial and cyclical bullying problems (still in existence today) that drive enormous numbers of students to mental illness and suicide in Japan?[52] What of the "microaggressions"[53] that alienate, psychologically drain, and grind people down because they are seen as "different"? Could these constant alienations and "otherings" conceivably be the cause of the so-called rough personalities, not an effect?[54]

What Fish overlooks is Japan's policymaking process of embedding racism through "typifying race," thereby veering dangerously close to the abovementioned realm of "biological determinism." That is to say, how the acceptance and normalization of differentiation (i.e., the assumption that "mixed-blood children" *are* different because they *look* different) in fact legitimizes and systematizes racism. (This is why scholars of racism generally do not use racial categorizations without proper problematization.) In fact, as argued above, the racialization process need not involve a biological concept of "race" *at all*: The act of differentiating, "othering," and subordinating can be due to any physical marker that has a social stigma attached to it (e.g., hair textures, narrower eyes, cleft palates, skin blemishes, etc.; see Japan's school "hair police" that stigmatize even Japanese citizens in chapter 5).

Notwithstanding the Japanese government's (constructive) postwar attempts to enforce equality for "mixed-blood children" at the Japanese elementary school level, the fact that "mixed-blood children" were officially categorized, "othered," and singled out for differential treatment on an official level in fact invited more attention by Fish to the issue of legal and social constructions of blood stigmata in Japanese society.[55] In effect, especially in an atmosphere of impressionable youths like a schoolyard, this typification could in fact have reinforced mixed-bloodedness as a stigma, creating a self-fulfilling prophecy that encouraged the very racialization that government policies were trying to avoid. Thus, the sociology of racialization processes should have been more fully problematized and discussed in research by Fish and many other scholars of discrimination in Japan.

That has been the point of this introduction. The rest of this book will argue that Japan's treatment of its Visible Minorities is in fact the acid test of, as Clammer puts it, the "racial porosity" within the "social grammar" of Japanese society; Visible Minorities are the "canary in the coal mine" regarding Japan's openness to "outsiders." It will also introduce a new paradigm—"Embedded Racism"—for the field of Japanese Studies to analyze it. It will outline the contours of Japan's racialization dynamic, showing how Japan's structuralized social patterns contain racialization processes so embedded in space and time that they contribute to the differentiation, "othering," and subordination of people by phenotype—even when it is, as I shall argue in the concluding chapter, detrimental to Japanese society and the world as a whole.

Thank you for bearing with me through this long introduction. I hope newcomers to the issues have not been drowned in information (welcome to our realm—it is indeed a rich vein for perpetual debate), and that veterans of the field feel that their concerns have been satisfactorily raised, considered, and addressed. Let us now commence with the largely unprecedented spadework on the issues of Visible Minorities in Japan.

NOTES

1. With apologies and respect to colleague Jeff Alexander, author of *Brewed in Japan: The Evolution of the Japanese Beer Industry* (University of Washington Press, 2013).

2. Appiah in Goldberg, ed. 1990: 4–5, Du Bois 1905, Montagu 1942, Anderson 1993, Gould 1981, Root 1992, Winant 2003: 51–62, and so on.

3. Demel 2013, Kowner 2013, Omi & Winant 1986, Winant 2003, Spickard 1992: 14, and so on.

4. *Taxonomize*: Demel 2013, Gould 1981, Spickard 1992: 22, Footnote 4. *Blurriness*: King 1981, Witherspoon 2007. *Neither Scientific Nor Apolitical*: Goldberg 1990, Root 1992, Miles 1993, Balibar & Wallerstein 1995, and so on.

5. Kowner (2013: 124–125). Regarding power relations, Kowner continues:

> The rise of scientific thought had little impact on this development, and so the race idea remains first and foremost a paradigm of distinction and self-enhancement. The emphasis on distinction since 1800 encompassed virtually any domain, from the physical, cultural, and intellectual, to the spiritual, but it essentially dealt with two groups: "us" and "them," Europeans (and their descendants in other continents) and all others. By providing a justification for economic exploitation and political dominance while alleviating fears of losing power, this paradigm also enhanced the confidence and morale of those who conceived it. (125)

6. Gould (1981: 20).

7. Ibid.: 18.

8. Spickard (1992: 19). *See also* Yoshino (1992: 115–116).

9. Spickard: 20–22.

10. King (1981: 156–157), quoted in Spickard ibid.: 16. *See also* Witherspoon et al. (2007) who say in their abstract, "The proportion of human genetic variation due to differences between populations is modest, and individuals from different populations can be genetically more similar than individuals from the same population." Although the article does later say that with enough data there can be some patterning along genotypical lines, the science is gray and exceptions legion enough to warrant a disavowal of biology as a meaningful determinant of a people's position in society.

11. Winant (2003: 51, 56).

12. *Self vs. The Other*: Dixon & Durrheim 2000, Habermas 1993, Neumann 1996, Tajfel & Turner 1979, and so on. *Intensely Political Process*: Anderson 1993, Gellner 1983, Hobsbawm & Ranger 1983, Kowner 2013, Omi & Winant 1986, Outlaw 1990, Spickard 1992. *Beyond Economic Determinism*: Goldberg (1990: 298).

13. Gellner 1983, Hobsbawm & Ranger 1983, Omi & Winant 1986, Anderson 1993, Balibar & Wallerstein 1993.

14. Spickard (1992: 19).

15. *Labor Migration Policy*: cf. Balibar & Wallerstein 1993, Miles 1999, Sharma 2006. *Globalization:* cf. Eades, Gill, & Befu 2000. *Capitalism*: cf. Sharma 2006.

16. Winant (2003: 55–56). *See also* Dikötter (1997: 3–4).

17. Miles (1993).

18. In more candid speeches delivered by British leaders (cf. Enoch Powell's inter alia use of "pickaninny" in his "Rivers of Blood" speech, 1968, etc.), public identifications of peoples also resorted to connecting skin color and an apparent lack of "civilization."

19. Goldberg (1990: 297–298).

20. Saïd (1978).

21. As discussed thoroughly by theorists such as Gellner, Foucault, Anderson, Balibar and Wallerstein, and so on.

22. Farber & Sherry (1997).

23. Cf. Iida 2002: 271–273, Minear 1980, Vlastos 1998.

24. *Western Models of the Nation-State*: cf. Gluck 1985, Sterling 2010, and so on. *Differentiation and Subjugation*: Oguma 2002, Kowner & Demel 2013: 9–10, and so on. Kowner & Demel underscore how issues of racism are being elided in scholarship of Asia and Japan:

> An otherwise very well-written and penetrating recent textbook on racism published by Oxford University Press [Ali Rattansi, *Racism: A Very Short Introduction* (2007)], may serve as an example. Incredibly, the entire text devotes no more than 11 lines to China, three to Japan [on youth subcultures emulating African-American fashion], and none to Korea. Another recent book published by Harvard University Press does not fare any better. Entitled *The Problem of Race in the Twenty-First Century,* it contains virtually no references to issues of race or racism in either of these nations. There is no justification for this oversight. (10)

25. Cf. Arnason & Sugimoto (1995), and so on.

26. Cf. Iida 2002, Oguma 2002.

27. Cf. Befu (2001).

28. *Ethnic, Not Racial:* cf. Befu (2001). *Less Extreme*: cf. Fish (2009).

29. *Globalization's Effects:* cf. Clammer (1995, 2000). *Domestic Labor Shortage:* cf. Tsuda 2003, Roth 2002, Lesser 2003. *Sui generis:* cf. Oguma 2002, Befu 2001, Takezawa 2011.

30. Clammer (2001: 18).

31. *Ultracentrifuge of Capitalism:* cf. Marx 1867, Balibar & Wallerstein 1991. *Colonial Vestiges:* Miles 1993; Stoler 1995. *Protection from Social Deviance:* Foucault (1970).

32. *Colonized in a Uniquely Unified Speedy Manner:* Reischauer 1995, Oguma 2002. *Different from Western Statist Structures:* cf. Gluck 1985, Oguma 2002, Fukuoka 2000, Mark Levin, lecture, University of Hawai'i at Mānoa, April 11, 2012.

33. Oguma (2002: 334).

34. As Kowner & Demel (2013) note, "Without exception, East Asians . . . tended to adopt the idea of race after they developed a natural awareness and once they realized it was instrumental in the construction of national identities" (24). This makes the "blind spots" regarding Japan's racialization processes within Japanese Studies even more surprising.

35. Miles (1993: 137).

36. For example, *sonnō jōi*, "revere the Emperor, expel the barbarians"; *wakon yōsai*, "maintain Japanese spirit by adapting Western technology"; *datsu-A nyū-O*, "leave Japan and join the West," and so on (*See* Iida 2002: 12, Frühstück in Ashkenazi & Clammer eds. 2000: 144).

37. Cf. Oguma 2002, Myers & Peattie 1987.

38. Cf. Reischauer 1970, Hane 1972, Menton et al. 2003. *Invisible*: Cleveland 2014.

39. This discourse has even affected research discussing racialized identification in Japan: For example, Iida (2002) portrays "modern Japan's identity" as sui generis and reacting toward external stimuli, devoid of any domestic foreign influence whatsoever.

40. On the other hand, attempts to generate a more inclusive discourse may have encouraged scholarship that overcompensated, by overemphasizing Japan's multiculturality and multiethnicity. As Gill (2001) essentially argued in critiques of works by Murphy-Shigematsu (1993), Denoon et al. (1996), Maher & MacDonald (1995), and Lie (edition 2001). Either way, scholarship on discrimination in Japan has been distorted by conscious and unconscious oversights within the dominant discourse of the canon.

41. Cf. Sugimoto 1997, Clammer 2001, Neary in Weiner ed. 2009, Aoki in Sugimoto ed. 2009, Weiner 2009, Ministry of Justice, Bureau of Human Rights 2009, and so on.

42. Cf. Cary 2000, Chung 2000, Fukuoka 2000, Linger 2001, Roth 2002, Higuchi & Tannō 2003, Lesser 2003, Tsuda 2003, Tanaka & Kim 2006, Shipper 2008, Ryang & Lie 2009, Nantais 2011, and so on.

43. *Japanese/foreigner binary:* Kashiwazaki (2009: 144). *Civil, not racial*: Wetherall (2008: 281).

44. An example of this mindset was expressed as a question during an interview with the author: "You have described yourself as a 'human rights' activist. The term evokes images of previous activists such as Martin Luther King, Jr., Desmond Tutu and Gandhi, to name a few—all disenfranchised that were born and raised as such. Isn't your descriptive taking it a bit far considering that you are an Ivy-educated, middle-class, white male from the United States who is only feeling a sliver of the discrimination today?" *Japan Review.net*, November 17, 2001, at http://www.japanreview.net/interview_dave.htm (dead link).

45. Befu (2001: 75).

46. For example, how long-term "foreigners" face significant barriers to becoming citizens and/or more enfranchised members of Japanese society, in contrast to other developed democratic nations tending to enfranchise its permanent-resident noncitizens as "denizens." Cf. Hammar 1990, Kajita 1994, 1998, Kondō 1996, Hanami 1998, Kashiwazaki 1998, 2000, 2009, Komai 1999, 2001, Asakawa 2007. Morris-Suzuki (2015) also conceptualizes recent official movements of inclusion and exclusion of minorities in terms of "semi-citizenship," which is a powerful tool for analysis but still overlooks, again, full citizens who are discriminated against for not looking "Japanese" enough.

47. Zachmann (2013: 453).

48. Clammer (2001: 7).

49. Lie (2004: 1–5).

50. Befu (2001: 75). There of course are many other books on specific ethnic and social origin minorities in Japan, including works authored and edited by Chung, Denoon et al., Ryang & Lie, Lie, Linger, Maher & MacDonald, Sugimoto, Tsuda, Roth, Shipper, and so on. While each of these works merits inclusion in terms of its approach to racism in Japan, for the sake of brevity, this chapter shall let the examples above and below suffice to illustrate some basic analytical shortcomings in the canon. Later chapters shall cite and analyze other authors' findings as appropriate.

51. Although Weiner's Second Edition includes a new chapter by John Russell on "Blacks" in Japan and their "otherness," Blacks are neither included under Weiner's "principal minority population" nor made a part of the non-Asian minority population in Japan. In other words, neither Black Japanese citizens from international unions, nor Japan's residents of African descent, count.

52. Cf. McVeigh (2000: 88–9), Kingston (2012).

53. Sue (2010).

54. Regarding Fish's comparison with the United States, I agree that the element of "hypodescent" in the American example (e.g., *Plessey v. Ferguson* and the "one drop rule," meaning a person who had one drop of African-descent blood was classified as a "black person" (Omi & Winant 1986)) was not present in Japan's policymaking—"mixed-blood" children were still officially "Japanese" in public policy (Nakashima 1992: 175). However, I would not agree that the existence of racism in a society is deniable if it is allegedly less pronounced than in other societies.

55. As Fish denotes, ibid.: 42.

Part I

THE CONTEXT OF RACISM IN JAPAN

Chapter 1

Racial Discrimination in Japan

Contextualizing the Issue

Let us open this book with a quote, one that neatly summarizes the fundamental issue covered in this book. It is from a manager at a Japanese public bathhouse (*onsen*) called Yunohana, in the city of Otaru, Hokkaidō, Japan. It was said to the author (a Caucasian male, who happens to be a naturalized Japanese citizen) on October 31, 2000, as he tried to enter the establishment: "We understand that you have Japanese citizenship. But you do not look Japanese. So, to avoid misunderstandings, we will have to refuse you entry."

Japan portrays itself as "a society predicated upon the rule of law" (e.g., *hō no shihai suru shakai, hōchi kokka*).[1] Yet Japan has a curious legal contradiction: racial discrimination is unconstitutional but not illegal. The Constitution of Japan (Article 14) explicitly guarantees protection against racial discrimination, but Japan has no law in its Criminal or Civil Code (*keihō* or *minpō*) that makes "discrimination by race" (*jinshu sabetsu*) an illegal activity or a criminal offense.

This has invited much criticism. United Nations (UN) reports and Japanese judicial decisions have explicitly called certain situations "racially discriminatory"; one UN human rights official remarked, "Racial discrimination in Japan is deep and profound . . . and practiced undisturbed."[2] For example, apartment owners and realtors in Japan frequently refuse accommodation to noncitizens because they are "foreign";[3] signs saying "Japanese Only" or "Foreigners Refused" (*gaikokujin okotowari*) can be found on businesses open to the public.[4]

Discrimination of course exists in all societies, but as this book will discuss, in Japan it is systemic as well as informal. For example, the Government of Japan (GOJ) has official registration systems that until 2012 did not include foreign denizens with valid visas as "residents" (*jūmin*)—and to this day do not include foreigners as, for example, spouses.[5] The GOJ also does not include registered foreign residents in official tallies of Japan's total population.[6] Further, the GOJ drafts public policies that are officially written (and sometimes enforced) as only applying to "citizens" (*kokumin*), despite the equal status of noncitizens as taxpayers. Nevertheless, the GOJ has repeatedly argued to UN human rights committees that Japan does not need an explicit law against racial discrimination.[7]

In the *Otaru Onsens* Case (1993–2005), the fieldwork that launched this research, Japan's courts twice acknowledged that "Japanese Only" signs on public bathhouses (*onsen*) constitute clear and present racial discrimination. The courts also ruled, however, that despite Japan's signatory status to the UN Convention on the Elimination all forms of Racial Discrimination (CERD), that international treaty was inapplicable.[8] Underscoring the weak legal status of foreigners in Japan vis-à-vis discrimination, Japan's Supreme Court in 2008 acknowledged that a lack of Japanese citizenship *necessarily* leads to discriminatory treatment in Japan.[9]

This legal gray area permits extreme cases of exclusionism in Japan. Consider the following examples.

In December 2006, the Setaka Town Assembly in Fukuoka Prefecture, under pressure from fearful local residents, passed a resolution (*seigan*) without debate granting permission to build a new university in town, but only if it had no exchange students (*ryūgakusei*). The reported reason given was a fear of "foreign crime" that foreign students might cause.[10]

In June 2009, parents from a "Southeast Asian nation" tried twice to enroll their twelve-year-old daughter in a public junior high school in Ōsaka, but teachers at faculty meetings tried to block her enrollment due to worries about their "lack of preparations" and her "insufficient Japanese language ability." Faculty demands that the girl attend language school elsewhere were eventually rejected by the Ōsaka municipal Board of Education, and the school was told the student was to be enrolled, pending outside lessons at a Japanese language school or the provision of an interpreter. Due to the imbroglio, however, the student was forced to miss the first six weeks of school.[11]

In September 2007, it was reported that a pregnant "foreign woman," who had given birth at home, was refused postnatal medical care seven times by five hospitals in Tsu, Mie Prefecture. This was reportedly due to hospital claims of a "lack of proper facilities" and because "her Japanese wasn't good enough." Despite the life-threatening conditions, a hospital only admitted her after she had "begged to be treated over two hours" and been rejected by two of the hospitals twice.[12]

In June 2007, local residents unlawfully blocked a realtor from selling a plot of land for house building to a Brazilian of Japanese descent (Nikkei) in Nakamizo, Fukuroi, Shizuoka Prefecture, citing residents' fears of "Brazilians being prone to committing crimes." "The head of the Nakamizo community association stated bluntly that Non-Japanese were not welcome in the neighborhood. 'Honestly speaking, we don't want [Brazilians] to move into the neighborhood if possible.'"[13]

In May 2014, media reported that a confectionary vocational school (*senmon gakkō*), Konshō Gakuen in Kumagaya, Saitama Prefecture, had a formal school regulation (*hōshin*) that explicitly refused admission to all "foreign" students since it opened in 1976. Although a Peruvian student had lodged a complaint with Saitama Prefecture in November 2012, educational authorities claimed to have no mandate to force the school to repeal the regulation. The school claimed it was necessary to avoid being responsible for "illegal foreign students," adding reasons such as "other schools are doing the same," "it's no big deal," and "we didn't know it was wrong." However, on May 23, due to media pressure, the school formally withdrew its restriction, although as of this writing it is still unclear if foreigners have been admitted in practice.[14]

On February 23, 2010, Japan's Sumō Association (*sumō kyōkai*) announced that it would further narrow opportunities for "foreign" wrestlers in the sport (already fixed at only one foreign wrestler per stable). It would now count any wrestler with "foreign roots" (*gaikoku shusshin*) as "foreign," even if he had obtained Japanese citizenship through naturalization—in direct contravention of Japan's Nationality Law regarding the legal status of naturalized citizens. Similarly, in September 2020, the Japan Rugby Football Union announced that they would also deny Japanese-citizen eligibility to its foreign-born naturalized players.[15]

On February 11, 2015, a column in the prominent daily newspaper *Sankei Shinbun* by Sono Ayako, a famous novelist and former adviser to Prime Minister Abe Shinzō on education reform, cited the alleged behaviors of "black people" (*kokujin*) in South Africa after the fall of Apartheid and advocated racial segregation in Japan: "Since learning about the situation in South Africa twenty or thirty years ago, I've come to think that whites, Asians and blacks should live separately." Despite widespread domestic and international criticism, including a formal letter of protest from the South African ambassador to Japan, neither the author nor the newspaper retracted the article.[16]

From 2018, local governments began using the term *gaikokujin shimin* (foreign city citizens) to classify people in their jurisdictions as "foreign" not only if they had foreign nationalities, but also if they were "people like those who obtained Japanese citizenship, children born from international marriages, people with foreign cultures in their backgrounds, and people who have foreign roots." This effectively not only reclassified naturalized citizens as "foreign," but also essentially categorized as "foreign" anyone with foreign connections, including Japanese citizens.[17]

In 2019, it was reported that non-Japanese children were being put into "special education" schools (headlined as "prison camps for Brazilians" in the Mainichi Shinbun) for years against their wishes, at rates more than twice the rate for Japanese schoolchildren. Assigned manual labor such as digging potatoes instead of learning math, these non-Japanese children were assumed to be low IQ because they were not proficient in Japanese. This policy was justified by a school vice principal claiming, "When foreigners increase in number, the learning process of Japanese students is delayed."[18]

From March 2020, due to the COVID-19 pandemic, Japan instituted a ban on all noncitizens (including Permanent Residents) reentering Japan, effectively treating all foreigners regardless of visa status in Japan the same as tourists. However, Japanese citizens traveling under the same conditions were exempted from this ban. This led to hundreds of thousands of non-Japanese residents being stranded abroad for months, unable to work their jobs, pay their bills, continue their studies, or be with their Japanese families in Japan; conversely, non-Japanese residents in Japan found themselves stranded within Japan, unable to leave the country to take care of family matters and tend to ailing or deceased relatives overseas. *Japan Times* noted that no other G7 developed country instituted this kind of "Japanese Only" border control policy, banning all foreign residents with legal visas but letting in all citizens.[19]

These examples should startle. How does a society as peaceful, orderly, developed, educated, cosmopolitan, and law abiding as Japan's reconcile its constitutional guarantees of equal protection under the law with institutionalized practices that discriminate, often explicitly and egregiously, by nationality and race? What key elements create and justify the exclusions of people perceived to be "foreign"? What creates, reinforces, and perpetuates the mindset that people who do not "look Japanese" are "not Japanese," including *Japanese citizens* being treated as foreigners with fewer legal rights?

This root of this issue is how a person is determined to be "Japanese." As this book will now argue, this is often done by how "Japanese" a person *looks*. Let me give you an example:

A HYPOTHETICAL AND A CONCRETE EXAMPLE OF PREJUDICE AND UNEQUAL TREATMENT

Consider a hypothetical Japanese person walking down the street in Japan one morning who sees two people: (1) a homeless Asian man (who to him "looks Japanese") lying on the sidewalk in a drunken stupor, and (2) a Caucasian man in a suit and tie hurrying to work. That hypothetical Japanese viewer is likely to see the homeless person in terms of, for example, economic or social class (as in, perhaps, *kitanakute kusai yatsu da*—"what a dirty, stinking guy"). On the other hand, that viewer is likely to see the Caucasian person in terms of *gaijin da* (a racialized epithet for outsider or foreigner),[20] perhaps as an English teacher due to his non-Asian physical attributes.

There is nothing unusual or Japan specific in this encounter: Every day, people in every society make instant decisions about people's backgrounds, education, occupation, intelligence, class and economic status, life opportunities, and so on based upon "first impressions." It is a natural if not necessary way for individuals to organize and order the various inputs and interactions constantly taking place in a society. Further, making assessments about similarities and differences between oneself and others is not unusual or necessarily discriminatory.

However, note that the above encounter had a fundamentally important process of categorizing those two people. Our witness in the first case made judgments about the homeless man on the basis of probable difference in class, economics, cleanliness, and so on. In the second case, however, our witness made judgments (positive or negative) about the man on his way to work on the basis of a racialized visual identification of physical appearance (in this case, represented by the word *gaijin*).

Since a *gaijin* is generally understood in Japan as a person who is an outsider, almost always "not Japanese," this assessment by our witness may in fact be quite inaccurate: The Caucasian man could be, for example, a naturalized Japanese citizen. Although this may seem statistically unlikely (although not impossible, the author is one, and on average about a thousand people naturalize every year),[21] the process of visual identification and differentiation nevertheless went one step beyond mere "difference by outward appearance" and into elements of "othering." Our witness decided on first glance that the Gaijin, unlike the Drunk, was *not* Japanese because he did not *look* Japanese. That is to say, issues of physical appearance were being linked to issues of *citizenship* and therefore legal status in Japanese society. Thus, in both cases, even though our hypothetical witness was making spot assessments about the Drunk or the Gaijin, in one case the basis of the judgment was more *economic*, while the other was more *biological*.

To make this discussion less hypothetical, let us take the Drunk and the Gaijin to a public bathhouse in Otaru in 1999 during the abovementioned Otaru Onsens Case. One *onsen* bathhouse, called Yunohana, had a "Japanese Only" sign outside its front door. Our witness in this case, Yunohana's manager, had the power to decide who came in, and decided this not on the basis of an extended conversation or a rigorous test of each customer's "Japaneseness" at the door, but rather on *how customers looked to him at first glance*. In the case of the Drunk, even if the manager thought the Drunk was too intoxicated or smelly to enter and denied him service, all the Drunk would need to do is sober up, change clothes, and perhaps bathe elsewhere first; then he would later likely be admitted simply on the basis that he was not visibly identifiable as "foreign." In fact, as we shall see in chapter 3, Yunohana allowed service to a Chinese woman (who was not drunk but was in fact a foreigner) because she simply did not *look* "gaijin."

The Gaijin, however, could not have passed this visual identification test under any circumstances at Yunohana. He could have been dressed in his Sunday Best, lived his whole life in Japan, spoken native or flawless Japanese, and even carried a Japanese passport as proof of "Japaneseness," but regardless he would be refused service at Yunohana because to the manager he did not "look Japanese."

This "Yunohana Test" has happened in practice repeatedly both to the author and to one of his two Japanese daughters. This was based solely on being visually identified as a Gaijin: Both daughters had been born and raised in Japan as Japanese citizens and were native speakers of Japanese. But one looked more "Japanese" because she had her Japanese mother's hair and eye color, and she was permitted entry. The other looked "gaijin" (Yunohana's express term) because she had her Caucasian father's hair and eye color, and she was not permitted entry. These and other cases outlined in the fieldwork of chapter 3 demonstrate the power of biologically based "visual identification" in Japan.

To return to the point that opened this chapter, a racialized categorizing of people into "Japanese" and "not Japanese" is being enforced at the service-sector level because of a lack of civil or criminal laws in Japan to prevent it. Although social grouping and discrimination by physical appearance occur in all societies, an important distinction here is that people being grouped into a "foreign" category *also include Japanese citizens.*

SCOPE AND CONTRIBUTIONS OF THIS BOOK

The cases presented above illustrate the necessity for scholars of discrimination in Japan to consider a new category of discriminated minority group: "Visible Minorities." As chapter 2 will demonstrate, most research focuses on groups discriminated against for their ethnicity or historical/social origin, such as the Burakumin, Ryūkyūans, Ainu, Zainichi Koreans and Chinese, and an overlapping but ill-defined set of resident "foreigners" (such as Nikkei South Americans).[22] However, many of these "foreigners" are in practice Japanese citizens, with the bad luck of being "visibly" discriminated against on sight alone. As such, this visually distinguished minority in Japanese society is an understudied area in the research canon, to which this book will contribute.

WHAT IS A "VISIBLE MINORITY"?

"Visible Minority" is already an established term for societal analysis.[23] Approved by the Canadian Government as an official legal status in 2009, Visible Minorities refer to people who belong to a visually identifiable group as defined by Canada's Employment Equity Act, that is, "persons, other than Aboriginal peoples, who are non-Caucasian in race or non-white in colour." In Canada, Visible Minorities are mainly of people of Chinese, South Asian, Black, Arab, West Asian, Filipino, Southeast Asian, Latin American, Japanese, and Korean heritage; in other words, from a performative perspective, these are people who on first glance may not look like a "Canadian" in terms of physical appearance and "visual identification." Although this governmental definition does not extend beyond Canada's borders, "Visible Minority" has also become an accepted term for rigorous analysis in Canadian academia.[24] This book will apply it to Japanese Studies.

For the purposes of this research, *"Visible Minorities" are residents of Japan who are visually identified as not "looking Japanese"* (e.g., Subcontinental Indians, the African Diaspora, Caucasians, Middle Easterners, non-Nikkei South Americans, some Asians, etc.) *and are thus treated as "not Japanese."*

Note that this research has limited its scope of judging "Japanese" or "not Japanese" to "visual identification." This leaves out other potential qualifications of "Japaneseness," such as culture, native language, primary education, and so on. This has been done in order to analyze the power and legitimacy of "first impressions" and judgments from people in positions of power or public service (e.g., bathhouse owner, shopkeeper, hotelier, landlord, police officer, politician, or bureaucrat). These positions in society deal with people on a daily basis and make decisions affecting people visually identified as Gaijin on the most fundamental levels. As we shall see below, this includes the denial of basic customer services, intrusive questioning of identity and intent by authorities, and even the creation of rules and public policies that deny equal treatment under the law.

In sum, the data set gathered under the fieldwork in chapter 3 is strictly confined to cases of clear denials of customer service to "foreigners," based not upon a business owner's nuanced assessments of individual qualification as a "Japanese" (e.g., length of time in Japanese society, acculturation, Japanese language ability, or familiarity with the specific rules of the business establishment), but on an owner's instant visual identification of whether a customer "looks Japanese." In sum, if the person in question "looks Japanese," he or she is granted service; if not, denied.

DISCLAIMER: THIS BOOK IS A CRITICAL ANALYSIS OF JAPANESE SOCIETY BUT NOT A POLEMIC

Critical analyses of Japan are often done with a degree of cultural relativism and disclaimer, to stave off opposing claims and criticisms that the analyst is engaging in "Japan bashing" or "cultural insensitivity."[25] Being overly cautious, however, tends to blunt analysis (as we shall see in chapter 2), resulting in conclusions that a somehow misunderstood Japanese society has its own unique cultural milieu and therefore unique standards to be judged by, if it is to be judged at all. However, I wish to argue that being analytical (if not critical) is not necessarily being judgmental. Consider it part of critical thinking. To some degree, judgments will be made in this book, as it is discussing a difficult subject—racism—and judgments are the nature of the beast in this field: After all, people are themselves in the process of being judged inter alia on the color of their skin and how it allegedly contributes to the content of their character.

So I wish to stress at the outset that this research is a critical analysis of an important social issue in Japan. But it is not a polemic. It is done in the spirit of the genre of "critical research," which endeavors to think about the relationships between knowledge, society, politics, and established structural frameworks embedded both in institutions and in language, thereby challenging research, policy, and other forms of human activity in meaning and method.[26]

In addressing issues of racism, this research neither intends to be a general denouncement of the people of Japan as "racists," nor does it intend to show that most people in Japan are even conscious "racists." Instead, this research will outline the contours of the conscious and unconscious rules of interaction, and the tacit, "embedded" understandings within Japanese society that lead to differentiated, "othering," and subordinated treatment of peoples by physical appearance. It will also outline how those rules and understandings are systemically created, normalized, and perpetuated by Japan's social structures (e.g., laws and public policies, and especially in their interpretation and enforcement) and a national discourse (e.g., messages in the media).

These dynamics within the social construction of community are found in all societies and are of course not limited to Japan. However, in Japan's case, the racialized linkage between physical appearance and legally enforced rights as a "Japanese" has a direct impact on Japan's future, particularly on its ability to tolerate and co-opt diversity. I call this theoretical dynamic "Embedded Racism."

INTRODUCING A THEORY OF "EMBEDDED RACISM"

This term has been adapted from Goldberg and Essed[27] and defined as, "*The overt, covert, subtle, or implicit expression of a normalized, hegemonic racialized discourse, one that is hidden and anchored in daily interpersonal interactions, laws and law enforcement, media, and other public dialogue, which has the effect of differentiating, 'othering', and subordinating people into a predetermined group or social status within a social order.*" This research focuses upon how an "Embedded Racism" affects "Visible Minorities" in Japanese society.

The Research Focus Not on What "Racism" *Is*, But on What "Racism" *Does*

I wish to avoid a prolonged discussion of two topics: (1) a discussion of "race" and the politically charged processes of "racial" categorizations (which differ by nation and society), and (2) a discussion of how to quantify how someone "looks Japanese." Regarding (1), I have already given a brief overview of race and racism over time and place in the Introduction of this book. Regarding (2), the criteria by which someone judges someone as "looking Japanese" are completely subjective. Nevertheless, it is clear that people engage in the process of visually identifying and grouping people as a *process* of racialization in society, as seen in the Otaru Onsens Case where people were grouped into or outside of a Gaijin category. Thus, in this book, racism and racial discrimination in Japan will be discussed in the *performative* context, that is, as Du Bois accomplished in his analysis of the American example, shifting the focus from "what Black *is*" to "what Black *means*" in practice.[28]

In the Japanese example, I will demonstrate performatively two things: (1) How racialized physical appearance is a defining factor in choosing who is to be treated as "a Japanese" and who is not (I call this practice at the interpersonal, "Micro" level); and (2) how these racialized notions of "Japaneseness" are "embedded" as part of social norms and rules through the national discourse (I call this practice at the institutionalized and systemic "Macro" level). In sum, this book will discuss how people in Japan not only see people who "look" different *as* different, but also how racialized social constructs in Japan, based upon visual identification, categorize people into the "Other" for differentiated and subordinated treatment in a legalized and lawful sense.

I will then argue that a hegemonic discourse in Japan permits and encourages the visual "othering" of peoples into a societal mindset justifying the unequal treatment of people differentiated as "foreign." This will be seen in Japan's enforcement of its laws, in its policymaking, and its media messages. I will conclude that Japan's self-description of identity is a racialized one, predicated upon an "Embedded Racism" grounded in visual identification, thus making it extremely difficult for people who "look different" to be included and treated as "Japanese."

I acknowledge that this phenomenon is not limited to Japan. In fact, the Introduction argues that Japan is no exception from racialization processes worldwide. I hope this book will provide insights into how societies and nation-states in general maintain domestic narratives that sponsor, regardless of stated intentions, differentiation between peoples that lead to systemic racialized power dynamics.

OUTLINE OF THIS BOOK

Chapter 2 offers an overview of how racism "works" in Japan, giving a historical development of Japan's racialization processes, and the long-standing aversion in academia, media, and public debate to calling unequal treatment of Japan's minorities "racial discrimination." Chapter 3 gives concrete examples of cases of racial discrimination—my fieldwork on hundreds of places with "Japanese Only" signs and rules. It uncovers the contours of performative racism in Japan at the "Micro" level, finding common themes and justifications for visually identifying "Japanese" and refusing "Gaijin" entry and service.

The subsequent chapters in part III give findings at the "Macro" level, based upon government reports and White Papers, public policies as interpreted and enforced by law enforcement officials, Japanese judicial rulings, and Japanese media reports. It will unpack how nation-state policies systematize, embed, and reify a national narrative that constructs a racialized self-image of "Japaneseness."

Chapter 4 gives the legal underpinnings of this racialized identity, describing how "Japanese bloodlines" are interwoven within Japan's legal definitions of a "Japanese citizen," that is, laws dealing with nationality, family registry, resident registry, and policing that ultimately encourage systemic racial profiling in public.

Chapter 5 describes how "Japaneseness" is enforced, developing how racialized definitions of "citizen" are applied to law enactment and interpretation, and enforcement of public policy dealing with education, visa regimes, and security issues. It shows how the presumptive expression of "Japanese bloodline" results in uneven and unequal legal protection of people according to how "Japanese" they look.

Chapter 6 offers a seminal study at how the lack of Japanese nationality affects legal outcomes in the Japanese judiciary. It discusses several cases demonstrating that in "Japanese vs. foreigner" criminal cases, people who are seen as "Japanese" have advantages in jurisprudence and justice, while people who are seen as "foreign" are systematically given harsher punishments, afforded less assistance as victims, or have their testimony corrupted, ignored, or voided. This chapter in particular has become less "seminal" due to the landmark Carlos Ghosn Case, which confirmed many findings of the First Edition.

Chapter 7 is the most ambitious of the book, tying together the above patterns that underpin the national narrative, and showing how they are popularized through media representations of "foreigners" and "Japanese." For example, the "peaceful Japan" narrative is contrasted with a "foreign crime wave" campaign by police forces and political leaders (to the point of official distortion of data); or, for another example, the "stable Japan" narrative is constantly contrasted with the potential disquiet and confusion of incoming resident "foreign cultures." This is all reinforced by an increasingly sensational domestic media, shifting its message from fetishization of "foreigners" to fear of them. By the end of the 2000s, xenophobia not only sells consumer goods, but also encourages public expressions of racialized hatred both on the street and online. Throughout the 2010s, particularly under the ultraconservative Abe administration, this resonates in expressions of belligerency between Japan and its neighboring countries in the Asian Region, as well as a very public questioning of the national loyalties of Japanese residents with visibly "foreign roots." Likewise, this trend has made it politically impossible for domestic actors to defend the human rights of "foreigners" without having their loyalties questioned.

Chapter 8 describes the public challenges being made to the binary "Japanese" vs. "foreigner" narrative, by domestic grassroots human rights groups and the UN, as well as by domestic advocates for greater tolerance and legal/societal protections against racial discrimination. Nevertheless, the GOJ maintains that the system needs no fundamental changes. In UN hearings, Japan repeatedly argues that a law against racial discrimination and/or hate speech is unnecessary, not only because of issues of freedom of speech, but also because, axiomatically, "foreigners" do not have the same rights as "Japanese." Continuously elided within the debate is the fact that Japan's Visible Minorities, including Japanese citizens, are also affected by this abrogation of civil and human rights. The rise of Visible Minorities as Japan's international representatives (in, for example, sports and beauty contests) during the 2010s has not altered this course significantly. Thus, the racialized system that differentiates "others," and subordinates putative outsiders becomes reinforced and hegemonic, weathering changing times because it is embedded in the very roots of "Japanese" identity.

Chapter 9 takes the concept of "Embedded Racism" out for a test drive, applying it both to the data set in this research and to the conclusions of other researchers in the field. Finally, chapter 10 answers the essential "So What?" question, describing why these unresolved issues of racial discrimination matter to Japan's future. It gives statistics and arguments on how the racialized concept of "Japaneseness" is hurting Japan as a society and an economy, arguing that Japan needs radical changes in its very self-image in order to survive as a society. It offers potential solutions for unraveling its entanglement of bloodline and legal status.

A new chapter 11 for this Second Edition discusses the damage done to democracies worldwide from online promoters of racial discrimination, modeled on Japan's unfettered *Netto Uyoku* (far-right netizens), with White supremacists worldwide pedestaling Japan as a viable model of an "ethnostate."

The book concludes that Japan's "Embedded Racism" is a fundamental obstacle to its future prosperity amid the world's increasingly globalized international economies. A phenotypically based rubric for defining "citizens" creates a societal inability to turn migrants into immigrants. With an aging society and a birthrate well below population maintenance levels, on this present course, Japan will be unable to create "new Japanese," and its quarter-century (and counting) of economic malaise will only continue.

Let us now turn to chapter 2 and describe how racism "works" as part of the grammar of Japanese society.

NOTES

1. *See*, for example, the Ministry of Justice website at www.moj.go.jp/shingi1/kanbou_houkyo_gaiyou02-02.html.

2. *See*, for example, United Nations (2001, 2006); for judicial decisions, *see*, for example, Webster (2007a, b, c). *See also* "UN independent investigator raps Japan for discrimination." *Voice of America*, July 11, 2005; "Japan racism 'deep and profound.'" *BBC News*, July 11, 2005; "U.N. calls for antidiscrimination law." *Japan Times*, July 12, 2005; "Antidiscrimination law needed: Racism rapporteur repeats criticism." *Japan Times*, May 18, 2006.

3. "Japan's foreign residents offer up insights in unprecedented survey on discrimination." *Japan Times*, March 31, 2017, which cites a figure of 39.3 percent of foreigners nationwide having their rent applications dismissed by realtors and landlords because they are not Japanese. Before this, a 2014 local survey by the 2014 Tōkyō Metropolitan Government indicated that close to half of all the 1,573 respondents (45.6 percent) cited "the difficulty renting apartments or other residences" as their most common issue of discrimination. *See also* "Discrimination against foreigners in renting apartments highlighted in survey." *Mainichi Shinbun*, April 10, 2014.

For a case study of refusal policies, *see*, for example, "Tokyo Sharehouse, with its new Tōkyō-wide system of Japanese-Only rentals." *Debito.org*, April 14, 2014, at www.debito.org/?p=12282.

4. Arudou (2011); *see also* Debito.org, "The Rogues' Gallery of Exclusionary Establishments" at www.debito.org/roguesgallery.html.

5. www.debito.org/activistspage.html#juuminhyou. More information passim in later chapters.

6. *See*, for example, "Population drops for fifth year as migration to cities continues." *Yomiuri Shinbun*, June 25, 2014, archived at www.debito.org/?p=12482.

7. United Nations ibid.

8. Arudou (2006a, b).

9. "Top court says marriage requirement for nationality unconstitutional." *Kyodo News*, June 4, 2008.

10. "*Setakachō ryūgakusei haijo seigan mondai: 'Futekisetsu' to shūsei saitaku: Chōgikai honkaigi.*" [The resolution to exclude exchange students from Setaka Town: A town council meeting calls it adopts an amended version after being called "improper"]. *Nishi Nihon Shinbun*, December 21, 2006; "Town opts for isolation policy." *Japan Times*, January 17, 2007.

11. "Foreign schoolgirl's admittance delayed due to teachers' opposition." *Kyodo News*, July 28, 2009.

12. "Foreign woman rejected 7 times by hospitals in western Japan after childbirth." *Mainichi Shinbun*, September 27, 2007; "Woman has miscarriage after waiting 3 hours to be transferred for emergency birth." *Mainichi Shinbun*, September 27, 2007.

13. "Racism surfaces over bid by foreigner to buy land, settle." *Asahi Shinbun*, June 29, 2007.

14. "*Saitama no senmon gakkō ga gaikokujin no nyūgaku kyohi*" [Saitama vocational school refuses entry to foreigners]. *NHK*, May 23, 2014; "*Saitama no senmon gakkō: gaikokujin o nyūgaku kyohi*" [Saitama vocational school refuses entry to foreigners]. *Mainichi Shinbun*, May 23, 2014; "School axes policy of barring foreigners." *Japan Times*, May 23, 2014; "'No foreigners allowed' cooking school backtracks, will accept foreign applicants." *Mainichi Japan*, May 23, 2014.

15. "*Gaikokujin rikishi hitoheya hitori o saikakunin.*" [Reconfirmed: Foreign sumō wrestlers are to be one per stable] *Asahi Shinbun*, February 23, 2010; "*Kika de mo dame, gaikokujin rikishi 'hitoheya hitori tettei tsūtatsu.'*" [Even naturalization is out: Full notification that foreign wrestlers are one to a stable] *Yomiuri Shinbun*, February 23, 2010; "JSA to change rule on foreign sumo wrestlers." *Kyodo News*, February 24, 2010; "JRFU rules certain Japan passport holders will be regarded as non-Japanese." *Japan Today*, September 26, 2020.

16. Sono Ayako, "*Tekido na kyori' tamochi uke'ire o*" [Bring them in but maintain an appropriate distance]. *Sankei Shinbun*, February 11, 2015; "*Sono Ayako san 'Imin o uke'ire, jinshu de wakete kyojō saserubeki' Sankei Shinbun de shuchō*" [Sono Ayako advocates in the Sankei Shinbun that 'immigrants should be accepted but forced to live separated by race']. *Huffington Post Japan*, February 11, 2015; "Author Sono calls for racial segregation in op-ed piece." *Japan Times*, February 12, 2015; "Japan

PM ex-adviser praises apartheid in embarrassment for Abe." *Reuters*, February 13, 2015; "*Sankei Shinbun Sono Ayako koramu, Minami-A taishi kōgibun, jinshu kakuri seido kyoyō*" [Sankei Shinbun's Sono Ayako column: South African Ambassador protest letter on the tolerance of racial segregation]. *Yahoo News*, February 14, 2015; "South African ambassador slams Sankei op-ed by Sono praising apartheid." *Japan Times*, February 15, 2015; "Outrage as top author backs racial segregation." *South China Morning Post*, February 15, 2015; "Outrage grows over Sono 'apartheid' column." *Japan Times*, February 20, 2015; and so on.

17. Definition from Nagoya City pamphlet, "*Nagoya-shi jiki sōgō keikaku—chūkanan*" [Nagoya City Next Term Comprehensive Plan, Intermediate Proposal], August 2018: 62, translation mine. More information about other local governments using this terminology verbatim at www.debito.org/?p=15820.

18. "'Prison camps for Brazilians': Foreign kids in Japan being ushered into special education." *Mainichi Shinbun*, September 4, 2019; "High ratio of foreign students put in special education after sitting IQ tests in Japanese." *Mainichi Shinbun*, September 3, 2019, both archived with commentary at www.debito.org/?p=15734.

19. *See*, for example, "Foreign residents stranded abroad by Japan's coronavirus controls Japan is the only Group of Seven member denying entry to long-term and permanent residents." *Japan Times*, May 19, 2020.

20. For a discussion on why "gaijin" is a racialized word, *see* Arudou, "Once a gaijin, always a gaijin." *Japan Times*, August 5, 2008.

21. "*Kika kyoka shinseisha sū tō no sui'i*" [Change in the number of applicants granted permission to naturalize]. Ministry of Justice website, at www.moj.go.jp/MINJI/toukei_t_minj03.html. As of March 2021, numbers naturalizing are on a downward trend.

22. *See*, for example, Fukuoka 1993, Sugimoto 1997, Clammer 2001, Neary in Weiner ed. 2009, Aoki in Sugimoto ed. 2009, Weiner 2009, and so on.

23. www.statcan.gc.ca/concepts/definitions/minority-minorite1-eng.htm.

24. *See*, for example, Stafford et al. (2010).

25. *See*, for example, the concluding chapter of Ian Buruma, *Behind the Mask* (1984); "Beyond Japan-bashing: The 'gang of four' defends the revisionist line (James Fallows, Chalmers, Clyde Prestowitz, Karel van Wolferen)." *US News & World Report*, May 7, 1990.

26. Thomas (1993). *See also* appendix 2.

27. Goldberg (1990: xv); Essed (2002).

28. Du Bois (1903).

Chapter 2

How Racism "Works" in Japan

Let us open this chapter[1] with another quote—one that demonstrates the embeddedness and hegemony of Japan's racialized membership narratives—even in overseas societies. This is a paraphrased email from a friend in Honolulu, dated May 30, 2013:

> Our neighbor, an attorney in Hawai'i's most prominent law school, is a Caucasian with a Japanese wife who spends considerable time in Japan doing business. I brought up the Otaru Onsens Case, but he was unaware of it. Even though he said he had experienced discrimination in Japan, his attitude was still, "Why didn't he just go to another onsen?" When I pointed out to him that it would not be nice to have an "Americans Only" sign in Hawai'i, he changed his tack. He mentioned that some years ago, there was a Japanese developer in Waikiki who had a "Japanese Only" offer of condos in a real estate project he was offering. But that lasted about a day, because over here that behavior won't sell.

This illustrates an interesting double standard: in the United States, a victim of discrimination is seen to have recourse—state intervention. But in Japan, the victim is expected to accept discrimination as normal and go elsewhere. Of course, the legal difference is that the United States has civil rights laws preventing racial discrimination and Japan does not; discrimination is also a factor of being part of Japan's image, that is, "It's not acceptable in America, but in Japan it's just how they do business."[2] This cognitive dissonance happens despite Japan's status as a rich-country participant in global standards of human rights.

Moreover, the vignette from Hawai'i shows how "blind spots" about racism in Japan (or in Japanese business practices trying to export it)[3] can even be seen in experts well educated about Japan and the law. This matters, because experts and specialists in Japanese Studies inform the scholarly literature, create syllabi, get cited in media, and devise foreign policy. Being blind to Japan's normalized racist practices is an essential reason why Japan gets away with them.

This chapter will focus on how this "exclusionary normal" has been constructed in Japan. It will discuss how Visible Minorities—people who do not "look Japanese"—are treated in Japanese society, particularly by businesses with "Japanese Only" signs, a government that refuses to stop them, and a field of study that ignores them.

Although it is difficult to quantify specifically how one "looks Japanese" (e.g., skin color, shape of epicanthic fold of the eye, contours of facial features (*rinkaku*), acculturated behaviors, fashion sense, etc.), the dynamic of how physical appearance fundamentally defines membership in Japan is well researched even in the canon of Japanese Studies.[4] Notions of "Self" in any society are crafted by sociological factors without a great deal of individual agency and are fundamental in deciding who becomes part of the "Other." So let us now turn our attention to these sociological factors, particularly the historical roots of Japan's racialization processes:

THE HISTORICAL ROOTS OF JAPAN'S ENDOGENOUS RACIALIZED APPROACH TO "OUTSIDERS"— AS A COLONIZER, NOT A COPYCAT

Much research on "race" and its conceits in Japan has focused on how Western concepts of racism were exported to Asia, due to contact with and replication/fetishization of "foreignness" in Japan's mass media or subcultures, or due to the influences on Japan being a colonial power.[5] However, this research does not subscribe to the argument that Japan has racism because it copied exogenous Western-style racism, for example, "Japan's very birth as a nation was largely defined by the adoption of Western institutions and ideologies—including racial ones—that remain with Japan even today."[6] Not only is this inaccurate, it also inadvertently tends to excuse Japan's racism as somehow "not Japan's fault." Instead, this research will argue that Japan's racialization processes are the result of something more endogenous—rooted in history, and embedded at the structural level through Japan's construction of nation-state narratives and national policymaking.

As in all societies with membership systems, the construction of an "Other" has always been part of Japan's past, and being considered an "outsider" did not always involve "foreigners" or even people who could be considered "racially distinct." Even before modern countries existed, Japan had devised its own formal caste system (the *Ryōsensei*, eventually called the *Mibun Seido* or *Shinōkōshō*—Warriors, Farmers, Craftsmen, and Merchants) with social hierarchies assigned from birth, including a perpetually "othered" outcaste group of "untouchables" (the Burakumin).[7] On more informal levels, an "outsider" back then could conceivably be anyone not from, say, one's family or village; according to Meiji-Era dictionaries, the standard "othering" word *gaijin* (or *guwaijin*) was applied to Wajin Japanese.[8]

As Japan morphed into a nation-state to make all "Japanese" into "insiders," the concept of Gaijin was then applied to extranationals as a template for modernization and a contrast to confirm Wajin national identity. Gluck (1985) has noted how Meiji Japan used "foreigners" (including the metaphorical sense) as a perpetual means of contrast to justify its national unification and catch-up industrialization programs.[9] Its programs for "modernizing" as a nation-state and an industrial power were based upon contemporary Western models of education—creating notions of citizenship as a civic duty, fostering a media to constantly reify it, and constructing a military-industrial complex to enrich and protect it. But to create, define, and unite the "Japanese people" behind the imperial system, discourses within national narratives (Gluck describes them as "modern myths") were promoted which at their core defined "Japaneseness" in contrast with the outsider; even social deviance and other thoughts inimical to current state goals (such as individuality and socialism) were attributed to being "foreign" (as in, significantly, "not Japanese"), thereby discounted or excluded.[10]

As discussed in the Introduction, this was in fact a racialization process. As Dikötter (1997) notes, "Racial discourse . . . in Japan thrived and evolved over time because it reconfigured pre-existing notions of identity and simultaneously appealed to a variety of groups, from popular audiences to groups of scientists."[11] However, this discourse was not exactly copied from the West. As Koshiro (2013) notes, "the Japanese colonial empire operated within its own racial constructions."[12] In fact, Japan's goal of becoming a colonial power meant *expanding "Japaneseness" to include the foreign*, in order to assimilate non-Japanese subjects into the empire. When Japan became a colonial power between 1905 and 1945, it advocated a "multicultural, hybrid" model, in order to proclaim a universalist approach toward the Asian brethren it wished to colonize.[13] Koshiro writes, "The Japanese as colonial masters also understood that they were not a 'pure' race but rather an amalgam of races of Asia and the Pacific."[14] Oguma (2002) notes that Japan even claimed, in contrast to the other colonial powers in the early twentieth century, that it was *ideologically unable to practice racial discrimination* because it was unifying its neighboring brethren of the same Asian race (as opposed to the Europeans, who were colonizing faraway places of non-White peoples).[15] This narrative made an international impact when Japan, as the first non-White imperial power, was the first country in the League of Nations to advocate a proposal for a racial equality clause in its Covenant (1919), albeit unsuccessfully.[16]

Japan's Historical Roots of Social Hierarchy and Skin Color

That said, this new "modern myth" of hybridity would still keep Japan's assimilated peoples performatively "othered" and subordinated in ways different from "Western-style racism." As Oguma et al. note, the fundamentals of Japan's racialized approach toward outsiders still existed even under officially universalist antiracism stances. For example, Fukuzawa Yūkichi, a Meiji-Era intellectual with great influence over Japan's development as an imperial power (he still graces Japan's ¥10,000 note), wrote *An Outline of a Theory of Civilization* (*Bunmei-ron no Gairyaku*, 1875).[17] Within it, Fukuzawa borrowed from contemporary Western eugenics science on racial hierarchies while diverging from the classical definition of "civilization" to offer an updated, static concept including a spiritual element, that is, one where a society attains "both material well-being and the elevation of the human spirit . . . abundance of daily necessities and esteem for human refinement."[18] Fukuzawa also offered Japan's nascent post-feudal society (a time when Japanese systems for universal literacy and tertiary education were being established) an overall political purpose: establishing a Japan that could deal with the outside world on its own terms. *Outline* was an argument for societies as a whole to emulate and learn from more "civilized" lands, in this case a model upon which Japan would create a sovereign nation-state.[19]

However, undergirding Fukuzawa's philosophy was a biologically based racism. He couches his analysis of social behavior in terms of skin color, for example, "young men of the Caucasian race (persons of white skin)," with hierarchical rankings. According to Fukuzawa, societies composed of "persons of white skin" (i.e., the United States and Europe) were at the highest stage of fully developed "civilization," followed by Asian countries ("semi-civilized" (*hankai*), e.g., Turkey, China, and Japan, with Japan unsurprisingly ranked highest), and at the bottom ("barbaric" (*yaban*)) were people of dark skin, such as Africans or Australian aborigines.[20] This philosophy grounded in contemporary imported Western science justified not only a further "othering" of minorities but also the forced assimilation of "lesser" peoples. As Russell (2009) notes, "The ascription of barbarity, backwardness and squalor to Japan's minorities served these ambitions [of a forging of national identity] well, since it not only confirmed the relative closeness of Japan to the West but also provided Japanese with a civilizing mission of their own, one that aimed both to elevate the primitive Other and themselves as well."[21] These racialization and subordination processes were seen as a means to reproduce the conditions that were presumed necessary by Japan's Meiji oligarchs for a rise to power as seen in the West.[22]

Fukuzawa's memes of racialized hierarchy and mission were soon visible within Japan's empire.[23] People within Japan's colonies (Taiwan, Korea, and later parts of China, Russia, and Oceania) faced a very uneven approach to their legal status within Japan.[24] For example, Koreans, Chinese, and Taiwanese during Japan's administration of their societies were considered Japanese subjects with Japanese citizenship.[25] They were granted certain Japanese-citizen privileges, such as the option to reside and work in Japan indefinitely without a visa (notwithstanding those who came to Japan or its colonies as forced labor) and to serve in the Japanese military.[26] However, these were not full Japanese-subject privileges. Taiwanese and Koreans did not, for example, have the right to move their Family Registry (*honseki*) to Japan Proper (*naichi*); vote their own colonial representatives to the Diet; create their own legislatures, standing militaries, or police forces; or administratively become an additional prefecture of Japan as, for example, Hokkaidō did.[27]

Further, this colonial experience would establish a template for systematic treatment of "Others" and foreigners (including the newfound "foreigners" as Japan shed its empire and abandoned the narratives of universalism) during the immediate postwar Era and beyond.[28] Today's "modern myth" of Japan as a "homogeneous race" (*tan'itsu minzoku*), with an "insular spirit" (*shimaguni konjō*) from Japan's ocean-bounded geography and Tokugawa-Era isolation (*sakoku*),[29] has not in fact existed from time immemorial. According to abundant scholarship, Japan's pure blood narrative is in fact a post–World War II creation.[30]

Postwar Decolonization and the New "Homogeneous Japan" Discourse

The postwar GOJ found reversing their prewar inclusive narratives surprisingly easy. In the immediate years following Japan's defeat in World War II and under the eye of the American Occupation (hereinafter SCAP, for Supreme Command Allied Powers), McVeigh et al. note how American reforms of Japan left essential parts of nation-state generating apparatus fundamentally unaltered, due to the exigencies of smooth bureaucratic maintenance of public order, and due to the contemporary political vicissitudes ensuring Japan did not fall into the Communist Bloc after revolutions in China and North Korea.[31] Crucial to Japan's future course was the status of education of Japan's youth, and McVeigh (2000) pays particular attention to "educational nationalism."[32] SCAP's failure to fundamentally reform the Ministry of Education (*Monbushō*, now *Monkashō*) allowed an extremely centralized "monopoly of legitimate education" to promote exclusivist notions of "Japaneseness."[33] Establishing the hegemony of Japan's "homogeneous society" national narrative from primary school age, and then leaving it fundamentally unreformed to the present day, McVeigh portrays the postwar regime of inculcated "Japaneseness" as a "stealth ideology," one with unclear goals and concepts, yet so pervasive that it became hard to see other alternatives in Japanese society.

The "Japaneseness" described by McVeigh merges three types of national identity—"ethnocultural, statist, and racial"—into "habitual and unconscious sentiments" that became tautological and mutually defining.[34] Simply put: "The merging of these concepts forms a logic of tautological equivalencies: *'one looks Japanese because one is ethnically Japanese because one possesses Japanese citizenship'*" (emphasis mine).[35] This phenotypically based requirement for national membership in Japanese society would thus become an inescapable doctrine for the overwhelming majority of people living in Japan, because compulsory education in Japan is fundamental to social mobility, acculturation, and even normatively being seen as a "good Japanese."[36] Fukuoka (2000) would probably agree, as he uses Japanese schooling as a qualification for "Japaneseness" in his groundbreaking scholarship on racialization processes in Japan (more below).[37]

Thus, the compulsory education system was fundamental to how "good Japanese" were to be socially conditioned as part of the "Self" in Postwar Japan. However, regarding the "Other," the GOJ immediately enacted policies that would perpetually influence its policy toward "foreign" residents.[38] First, under the terms of surrender, former imperial subjects in Japan's colonies lost their Japanese citizenship.[39] Under pressure from SCAP, Japan gave former subjects (seen as potential enemy nationals under emerging Cold War polarities) who were still within Japan's borders a choice: (a) to return to their homelands as non-Japanese or (b) go through the (often humiliating) process of naturalization to become Japanese citizens.[40] In either case, only Japanese of "Japanese blood" (and only if inherited from a Japanese male) were permitted to retain their Japanese citizenship after World War II (with the exception of aborigines within Japan's current sovereign borders, that is, the Ainu of Hokkaidō, and later the Ryūkyūans of Okinawa). This made the postwar narrative of "homogeneous Japan" easier to accomplish.[41] Intellectuals and policymakers stressed the need for Japan's "reconstruction" by demolishing Japan's former colonial tendencies, enabling the government to "reinforce their exclusionary policy against colonial immigrants during their postwar transition."[42]

Thus, the ethnically hybrid Pan-Asian empire narrative was quickly replaced by an ethnically homogeneous one. According to Shin, "This postwar self-image in turn justified further exclusion and discrimination against their remaining colonial subjects."[43] New national policies established foreign registry systems for all resident nonnationals to track their whereabouts *as* "foreigners" (1947, put into effect in 1952), with measures that were not otherwise enforced upon law-abiding Japanese citizens, for example, fingerprinting and identification cards that to the present day must be carried at all times under criminal penalty, enabling lawful police identity checks and racial profiling that did not require probable cause (more in chapter 5). This would set the agenda for future treatment of all "foreigners" and "migrant workers" to Japan, controlling possible future choices both for policymakers and for incoming foreign residents of Japan.[44]

POSTWAR MINORITIES IN JAPAN: CREATING A NARRATIVE OF INVISIBILITY THROUGH "HOMOGENEITY"

As will be described in chapter 8, the GOJ has long claimed that there are no "minorities" (*shōsū minzoku*) at all within its borders, and for a long period of its history did not see "race" (*jinshu*) as the ultracentrifuge of human classification. Unfortunately, scholarship on Japan also shared this view. Let us focus on one representative example.

According to Fish (2009), during the worldwide expansion of empires through the Tokugawa Era, conceits regarding issues of "race" were not of the "light/dark" polarity, but rather of the "we Japanese/others" binary, that is, who is "Japanese" and who is not. Phenotype-based racism in Japan, Fish believes, was exogenous, coming from the Western Enlightenment and the intellectual need to categorize and classify everything (41–3). According to Fish, during the Meiji, Taishō, and early Shōwa Eras, this would change little: People adjudged as "mixed blood" (*konketsu*, defined as "people who appear to be the offspring of one parent of East Asian origin and one parent of non-East Asian origin" (42)) belonged at the time to well-regarded classes (e.g., children of missionaries, leading businessmen, teachers, and scholars) and were small in number so as to have little need to be "othered" (44).

However, despite Fish's otherwise excellent scholarship, it should be noted that other less visually identifiable (therefore "invisible") minorities were being brought into the Japanese Empire and were nonetheless being "othered" and treated significantly differently. As mentioned above, during Japan's Meiji-Era Imperial expansion, Japan's colonized peoples were officially seen as fellow members of the same Japanese race under Pan-Asian tenets of Asian brotherhood. But people who were not considered part of the group of "dominant Japanese," be they a historical underclass (the Burakumin), citizens of empire (e.g., Koreans, Taiwanese, or Chinese), or indigenous peoples of new Japanese territory (the Ainu and Ryūkyūans), were under government policy to be forcibly assimilated (*dōka*) into cultural invisibility—or even isolated and eradicated (e.g., native Formosans) as subjects to the emperor.[45] Therefore, despite Fish's claims that Japan's concepts of "race" were exogenously influenced by the Western Enlightenment, this racialization process was clearly performatively endogenous to the formation of this particular nation-state as a colonizer.[46]

Thus, Japan's Invisible Minorities, by definition, were phenotypically similar enough to Japanese in most cases to "pass" as "Japanese." As Fish (45) himself acknowledges, "Japan had dealt with issues of diversity throughout its colonial period, but rarely involving people with such stark phenotypical difference [as 'mixed-blood' children]. After all when looking at a pre-war photograph, one would often be hard-pressed to pick out the Chinese or Korean living in Japan based on facial features alone." However, as seen above, arguments that because Japan's minorities were not visible, therefore there was no "color stigmata"—meaning Japan's discrimination was ethnic, not racial—also encouraged scholarship that fundamentally misunderstood established modern nation-state racialization processes (i.e., as described in the Introduction, that racism is a matter of social power relations, not biology).

Postwar racial discrimination continued toward Japan's minorities even if they could phenotypically "pass" in Japanese society: Most Zainichi Koreans and Chinese adopted Japanese *tsūshōmei* (names for public use), while others, such as entertainers, "passed" as Japanese in order to establish and maintain careers in Japan.[47] Burakumin were often not uncovered and discriminated against until background checks were carried out before employment of or marriage to a non-Burakumin.[48] Some minority children did not consider themselves "foreign" until they were required to register as *gaikokujin* with the ward office at the age of fourteen (later sixteen), to give their fingerprints like potential criminal suspects, and to carry their registry cards on their person at all times—thus being socially "othered" from their peers at a delicate age.[49] Thus, most minorities in Japan were not only phenotypically "invisible," they were also *officially "invisible" within the national discourse and research narratives* of *Japan as a society*: "homogeneous" and minority free.

This "modern myth" of homogeneity was further reified and made hegemonic by superiority complexes created by the pseudoscience genre of *Nihonjinron* (Japanese distinctiveness studies), which gained widespread currency in Japan's intellectual and popular debates about what caused the "Japanese miracle" of record economic high-speed growth in the 1960s, 1970s, and 1980s. These triumphalist narratives eventually percolated worldwide through scholarship and media discourse on Japanese society as an economic giant.[50]

*Maintaining the New Postwar "Homogeneity" Narrative: The "*Konketsuji *Problem"*

As a case study of how new national narratives are maintained, and how they affect worldwide scholarship on Japan, it is instructive to discuss how Japanese society handled an early challenge to the postwar domestic discourse of homogeneity: the existence of mixed-blood children (*konketsuji*). During and after the American Occupation, Invisible Minorities were suddenly becoming visible. Although Yoshino (1992) declares, "one will always be Japanese by virtue of blood," Japanese were having international children with the requisite Japanese blood that were visually identifiable as "foreign."[51] They were quickly linguistically differentiated through racialized epithets: *konketsuji*, *ainoko*, *hāfu*, *daburu*, *kuwātā*, and so on.[52] As Fish notes, "most people could identify a 'mixed-blood' child with relative ease," and "the emphasis on and perception of difference is not at all surprising."[53]

Shin (2010) notes how GOJ policymaking to deal with Visible Minorities during the immediate postwar years (1945–1953) would become the template for the social treatment of how people who "look foreign" would be treated to the present day. Back then, people who "looked American" yet were "mixed-blood Japanese" (*konketsuji*) were seen as abandoned byproducts of liaisons with the oldest profession, and the GOJ devised policies treating them as a "problem" to "fix" by assimilation, so they could be overlooked within the "homogeneous" narrative.[54] Fish (2009) describes this process step-by-step:[55]

Step One: Politicians and bureaucrats drew attention to a looming "problem" (*mondai*) that would soon need addressing; in the case of the *konketsuji*, Japan's postwar national narrative involved a return to Japan's "peaceful, tranquil homogeneous state," and that homogeneity would allegedly create problems for those children who were not themselves "homogeneous" (by lacking "pure" Japanese blood).[56]

Step Two: The GOJ drew up a policy proposal itemizing specific problems to be addressed, with high-level inputs from intellectuals, politicians, bureaucrats, and specialists in special deliberation councils (*shingikai*). The *shingikai* policy conclusions were constructive: make sure that these children were educated properly in the Japanese school system as any other Japanese, and treat them equally as "Japanese." In this case, the "problems" explicitly stated included (a) the apparent shame of *konketsuji* being visibly identifiable as sired by American soldiers, (b) the apparent disabilities of being raised in a single-mother family (under a phenotypically based presumption of a mother being involved in prostitution), (c) the anticipation of probable stigmatization and nonacceptance by one's school peers, and (d) the inability to function in Japanese society due to phenotype.

Step Three was public debate: Politicians in the Diet and prefectural level offered ponderous musings on how Japan's "character" and "Japaneseness" would be affected by this apparent dilution of Japan's race/ethnicity. The media and the public discourse repeatedly cited (according to Fish, inaccurate) statistics of 100,000 (and growing) *konketsuji* "children of assignations" (*ainoko*), offering a metaphor of the remnants of the American Occupation through its prostitutes. This stereotype would be propagated through popular culture, including films, newspapers, memoirs, poetry, and even school speeches and essays.

However, instead of an original, inclusive narrative (i.e., that these heterogeneous children were a positive part of Japan's future), the homogeneous society narrative (under which these heterogeneous children were a remaining aberration of Japan's past) became predominant. Nevertheless, since these heterogeneous children were blameless for their existence, official dictum from the Ministry of Education et al. portrayed *konketsuji* as objects of pity, as children "who carry the destiny of misfortune on their backs" (53). The national narrative concluded that these unfortunate children were from irresponsible relationships on the parents' level.

Step Four, the collection of data that substantiated the anticipated status quo, was soon completed and disseminated through the media to confirm the expectation that *konketsuji* in fact did not do as well in school as their "regular" "pure-blooded" counterparts (54).

Finally, over time, Step Five embedded the racialized mindset into the national narrative. As the stigmatized and unstigmatized children grew up together, the perpetually conjectured causes of their putative blood-based differences would be attributed to, for example, actual racism and racial discrimination, socioeconomics, difficulties fitting into Japan's homogeneous society, social opprobrium associated with being abandoned by foreign fathers, or, as the Ministry of Education officially claimed, the "rough personalities" of the differentiated children themselves.

Thus, phenotype as a potential cause of social stigmatization has been systematically overlooked within the discussion by officials, by media normalizing officialdom's discourse, and even by scholars later disinterring and reinterpreting that historical discourse as something relatively benign. (Further discussion of Fish's research, and how this book's theory of Embedded Racism offers a more accurate assessment of the situation, is at the end of the Introduction and in chapter 9, respectively.) In this way, the "*Konketsuji* Problem" was covered up as a postwar aberration, and the hegemony of homogeneity resumed.

However, as the decades passed, new generations of Visible Minorities, as children of licit international marriages, again began to blur the allegedly clear lines between Japanese and Gaijin.[57] They were further blurred by future work visa programs, where Visible Minorities who were "fully foreign" (i.e., without "Japanese blood" or citizenship, e.g., Caucasians, Middle Easterners, South Americans, Africans and African Americans, Subcontinental Indians, and South Asians) were born and raised in Japan. Nevertheless, the GOJ kept the binary between Japanese and Gaijin intact by "othering" these children of diversity, allowing them to be treated as "foreign" depending upon how "Japanese" they looked. To accomplish this, public debate overlooked any "problem" with "racial discrimination" by basically denying that it exists.

PRESENT-DAY TREATMENT OF "FOREIGNERS" IN JAPAN: THE DISCOURSE OF DIFFERENTIATING "JAPANESE" FROM GAIJIN AND NOT CALLING IT "RACIAL DISCRIMINATION"

One problem with any social problem is that if it gets ignored, it remains unaddressed in public policy. In the case of Japan's racial discrimination, this is not accidental. The current public discourse has been muted by semantics that play down racialization processes.[58] GOJ statements officially couch domestic discrimination (*sabetsu*) in terms of discrimination toward women, Burakumin, Ainu, Zainichi Koreans, the physically handicapped, gays and lesbians, homeless and day laborers, and even the less economically well-off in Japanese society (*uākingu puā*, i.e., "the working poor").[59] There are also mentions of discrimination toward "foreigners" (*gaikokujin sabetsu*), toward specific nationalities (Nikkei South Americans, Koreans, Chinese, Filipinas, etc.), and toward ethnicities in general (*minzoku sabetsu*). However, "racism" under the more specific form of discrimination by *race* (*jinshu sabetsu*) is avoided as a term of reference.[60] For example, as chapter 3 will discuss, media and public discussion of the Otaru Onsens Case lawsuit almost always refused to use the term *jinshu sabetsu* as a "fact of the case" in any context. However, as Dikötter notes, "It is not a necessary to use the word 'race' in order to construct racial categories of thought."[61] Therefore, a discussion hobbled by linguistic barriers or editorial constraints should not obscure the importance of power and hierarchy behind Japan's articulation of racial taxonomies.

This is where the "Japanese Only" establishments surveyed in chapter 3 offer insight into the embedded nature of Japan's racial discrimination. Exclusionary managers did not formally say at the front door, "You do not pass my standardized racial test to qualify as a Japanese customer." They just picked out the Gaijin from the Japanese by whatever arbitrary means they desired, and Japanese society let them get away with it—through negligence if not legitimized mindsets treating anyone who "looked foreign" as "different." That is why chapters 4–8 focus upon the public discourse creating that mindset. Chapter 3's cases of "Japanese Only" exclusionism are not only a powerful bellwether of a society's ideological tendencies and dominant social discourses but also of structural power relations in the public arena. Exclusionary mindsets cause people not only to be excluded from public establishments but also to be *excluded from the public discussion regarding the exclusions*. What is lacking in Japanese social science is sufficient reference to visual identification when answering the question, "What is a Japanese?" Although much research on discrimination in Japan rightly refers to the performative process of differentiation, othering, and subordinating people in terms of social origin, ethnicity, and "race," some of it nevertheless ignores discrimination by skin color.

This will not do. Skin color in Japan, as in all societies that make visual distinctions between people depending on melanin content, is also a defining factor as to how one "looks Japanese."[62] For example, according to much research, one skin tone held in high social esteem in Japan is Whiteness.[63] Ashikari's study (2005) of the material culture of the Japanese cosmetics industry argues that skin is an avenue for conveying "Japaneseness," because Japan's middle class believes that "Japanese as a race share the same skin tone, and the notion of Japanese skin works as one medium to express and represent Japaneseness."[64] Being "white" is a common symbol of culturally valued "purity" and "cleanliness," thus lighter skin is preferable to darker as it looks "cleaner," meaning darker skin is considered "less Japanese."[65] Although the material culture of Japanese cosmetics and fashion reproduces and reinforces this high value toward lightness and beauty, there is a racial component, according to Ashikari: "The preference for white skin, linked to consumer culture, appears to be a matter of both beauty and race."[66]

Sterling (2010) might concur, noting that the omnipresence and normalization of "Whiteness" (in contrast to the "objectification" of Blackness) in Japanese society has perhaps "made it possible to miss the presence of racial thinking in Japan."[67] To Sterling, the focus on skin color may explain why so much emphasis is placed upon a Japanese self-image as "Caucasian," as seen in the historical "body projects" for the "improvement of the [Japanese] race" via interbreeding with Occidentals, and the "ideal body" as "Western."[68] Whiteness may be used to substantiate theories that the Japanese are in fact, among other far-flung peoples, "Aryan"—given that contemporary historical rankings of the "races" (cf. "Social Darwinism") put White people on top.[69] It may also explain why Japan lobbied for (and received) "honorary white" status in Apartheid South Africa.[70]

The point is that skin color is indubitably a factor within the rubric of "looking Japanese," and research that overlooks discrimination by skin color is complicit in ignoring an entire class of minorities being discriminated against.

Prominent Japanese Research on Discrimination in Japan without Reference to Skin Color

For example, let us briefly consider three prominent Japanese researchers who have written at great length on racial discrimination in Japan: Fukuoka Yasunori, Sugimoto Yoshio, and Aoki Hideo.

A major authority on Zainichi Koreans in Japan, Fukuoka (1993, trans. 2000, xxix–xxxviii) offers in his introduction a "typological framework of 'Japanese' and 'non-Japanese' attributes" as an intellectual experiment to debunk the "myth of [Japan as] the 'homogeneous society'" (xxxv). A well-intentioned and thorough attempt to demonstrate how diverse Japanese society is, in contrast to the national narrative's binary of "Japanese" vs. "Non-Japanese," it deserves a brief mention here to show how surprising the "blind spot" is.

Fukuoka offered eight different "types" of people in Japan organized under three different constructs: "Lineage," "Culture," and "Nationality." Fukuoka's definition of "Lineage" referred to whether or not a person has Japanese blood, using a simple binary plus or minus (hereinafter "yes" or "no") qualification. More details in endnote.[71] However, after all Fukuoka's effort, no construct mentions skin color. Fukuoka's typology inspired Sugimoto to come up with an expanded grid of qualifications for his extremely influential book *An Introduction to Japanese Society* (1997: 172; updated 2014). Again, within fourteen elaborate typologies, nowhere was skin color mentioned. More than a decade later, Aoki created within Sugimoto's next influential reference work on Japanese culture (2009: 185) a more scaled-down version in his grouping of Japanese and ethnic minorities in Japan, with a schematic of dominant Japanese, Koreans in Japan, Okinawans, Ainu, and Burakumin. Again, nowhere was skin color.

In other words, without the element of visibly distinguishing characteristics, all of the people included in their typologies would probably be able to pass the "Yunohana Test" and enter an Otaru bathhouse. No academic schematic accounts for the behaviors in chapter three.

These researchers are in good company. Similar oversights can be found in Cleveland (2014: 218, calling Japanese minorities "invisible"), and, as discussed in the Introduction, in just about all scholarship on discrimination toward minorities in Japan.[72] The funny thing is that even though the Otaru Onsens lawsuit received national and international attention from 1999 onward, none of these academics include cases of discrimination based upon skin color, or mention the Otaru, Bortz, or other court cases in their research. Visible Minorities (i.e., Gaijin) are not only an unacknowledged minority in Japan, but also unacknowledged as a distinct group in Japan being discriminated against in a very distinct way. Thus, the gap in Japanese Studies being addressed by this research is an analysis of how a new category, Gaijin, is treated in Japan as "foreign," regardless of nationality, acculturation, language ability, or all the other qualities that are mentioned by Fukuoka and Sugimoto as qualifiers for "Japanese" status. "Japaneseness" is based upon phenotypical first impressions alone.

SUMMARY

This chapter outlined the research gaps in the study of racism in Japan which this book is trying to fill. It complemented the Introduction, which discussed how Japanese society has been insufficiently analyzed within worldwide postcolonial debates. Arguing that racialized power relationships within all societies have been constructed through the formation and maintenance of nation-states, the Introduction concluded that Japan's nation-state formation conforms to racialization parameters seen elsewhere in the world, ergo racism in Japan should not be seen as "different" or comparatively "benign." Nevertheless, this chapter argued, scholarship has demonstrated enormous "blind spots" toward seeing racial discrimination in Japan as "racial" like anywhere else, particularly in terms of skin color.

This book argues that academic "blind spots" occur because their research definitions of "foreign" are flawed. "Foreignness" is seen as a function of "ethnicity" within an Asian-phenotype community only (overlooking Visible Minorities, who are clearly "foreign" yet not "Asian" in terms of visual identification). Or "foreignness" is seen as a function of legal status (meaning that if you took Japanese citizenship, it shouldn't matter anymore if you don't "look Japanese"; this has been proven untrue by the "Japanese Only" establishments in the next chapter). Or that "Japaneseness" requires lineage, language ability, cultural literacy, birth status, or nationality (all of which are irrelevant to "Japanese Only" establishments). Or scholars simply ignored evidence that "Japanese Only" establishments exist, or exist in numbers large enough to matter.

Even the research that does not ignore the "Japanese Only" dynamic, and thoroughly dissects the expressions of discriminatory treatment toward historical, ethnic, and social minorities, still ignores skin color as a factor. Some even conclude that "foreigner discrimination" is not "racial discrimination." This chapter argued that this is a misinterpretation of history, as Japan's "othering" processes evolved over time: proto-state Japan first viewed locals as "The Other," then as it developed a nation-state identity, foreigners became "The Other." Imperial Japan then amended "The Other" when it advocated a multicultural "Pan-Asianism" (even though Japan's colonies were still "othered" through legal subordination), then Postwar Japan reverted to seeing "foreigners" as "The Other," claiming that Japan's "homogeneous" society has no domestic minorities. These are all racialization processes as defined in the Introduction. Unfortunately, this history has been misinterpreted by scholars as evidence of Japan's lack of a "color stigmata," and of Japan's milder "ethnic" (not "racial") discrimination.

Under these flawed assumptions, scholars overlooked Japan's racialized self-image in terms of physical appearance, that is, that you're only Japanese if you "look Japanese" (which would be quickly called "racism" if it happened in other societies). This dynamic continued even as more migrant and immigrant workers from non-Asian countries came to work in Japan and were immediately through visual identification rendered into Gaijin, never to become "Japanese." So prominent researchers refused to see them as actual "minorities" in Japan (rather, more as temporary workers or guests), or else tended to overlook their existence (and their multiethnic children's existence). Within all the copious scholarship on discrimination covered in this research, Japan allegedly has no "Visible Minorities."

At the heart of all of these "blind spots" is a lack of scholarly focus on the structural racialization processes within Japan's laws, institutions, media, and national discourse, which is what this book will examine through a theory of Embedded Racism to understand racialized power structures within Japan's social structures. Through this lens, observers can better comprehend why "Japanese," using dichotomous racial paradigms to define themselves as phenotypically "different" from "foreigners," remain structurally unable to create public policies that will protect even their fellow citizens from racism—resulting in a cognitive dissonance where racial discrimination is unconstitutional yet not illegal. As noted in the beginning of this chapter, this dissonance is so strong that the rest of the world accepts it as normal.

Let us now consider concrete examples of racial discrimination in the next chapter: "Japanese Only" exclusionary establishments.

NOTES

1. Portions of this chapter have been published as "Japan's under-researched visible minorities: Applying critical race theory to racialization dynamics in a non-white society." *Washington University Global Studies Law Review* 4 (14), Fall, 2015. Used with permission.

2. A good example of "how Japan does business" was when an American realtor in Japan, Century 21, was found "unintentionally" adopting Japan's discriminatory apartment rental policies. In 2021, a Saitama branch offered specialized "Foreign nationalities OK" (*gaikokuseki* OK) apartment listings, meaning the default for regular apartments is that non-Japanese applicants were *not* OK. When Century 21 USA

was notified, a representative at Century 21 Japan excused it by citing Japan's lack of discrimination laws:

> CENTURY 21 offices in Japan are franchisees and not branches of C21 Japan nor C21 US. Our franchisees in Japan are all independently owned and operated. . . . There are certainly cases where an "expectation gap" arises between the prospective customer and the agent, and oftentimes this gap grows wider during the course of interaction between the two. This is particularly true when different cultural norms, sets of regulations, and industry practices exist. For example, in the US there is the wide-reaching Fair Housing Act (FHA) that bans pretty much all forms of discrimination. Japan does not. Therefore, what could be a violation of the FHA in the US would not necessarily be one in Japan. Having said this, however, C21 Japan HQ believes it is never good for business to practice and kind of [*sic*] intentional discrimination and caution our franchisees accordingly. We will, therefore, request the office you have identified to remove the subject bin to avoid any semblance of discrimination, no matter how unintentional the original reason might have been.

See "'Foreign nationalities OK' apartments bin at Century 21 Saitama realty." *Debito .org*, March 28, 2021, www.debito.org/?p=16541.

3. For an example where overseas regulations stopped the export of normalized workplace harassment in Japanese companies as "the Japanese way of doing business," *see* "'Japanese way' costs $190,000." *New Zealand Herald*, May 30, 2010, at www.debito.org/?p=6810. For an example where local regulations did not stop the export of exclusionary Japanese business practices, consider the case where Japanese tour groups overseas offered online arrangements for participants to join the Standard Chartered Hong Kong Marathon 2016, but refused all customers without Japanese citizenship: "This website is designed exclusively for Japanese people. Applications from other nationalities are not acceptable. Applications from non-Japanese runners will be treated as 'invalid' and any deposit payment would not be refunded." After activist protests to sponsors Hong Kong Amateur Athletic Association, Standard Chartered Bank, and the Hong Kong Tourist Association, the site was amended to say, "This tour is designed exclusively for people residing in Japan. Applications from other countries are not acceptable. Applications from runners who are not residing in Japan will be treated as 'invalid' and any deposit payment would not be refunded." However, the site still maintained the wording that Japanese citizenship was required to register. On-site photographic evidence also depicted the presumption that "people residing in Japan" did not include foreigners. *See* "20th Standard Charted Hong Kong Marathon Japan tour registration is 'Japanese Only': Applications from non-Japanese runners 'invalid,' deposit payment not refunded." *Debito.org*, November 9 and 13, 2015, at www.debito.org/?p=13627 and www.debito.org/?p=13640.

4. Cf. Ashikari 2005, Clammer 2001, Oguma 1995, Siddle 1997, Weiner 1997, Yoshino 1992, 1997.

5. *Western concepts of racism exported to Asia*: Dikötter 1997, Wagatsuma 1967, Wagatsuma & DeVos 1967. *Replication and fetishization of Westernness*: Atkins 2001, Condry 2006, Kelsky 2001, Russell 1991, 2009, Sterling 2010. *Influence of colonialism itself*: cf. Doak 2001, Eskildsen 2002, Tamanoi 2000, Weiner 1995.

6. Sterling (2010: 24).

7. There is a rich literature on the Burakumin and Japan's historical caste systems in both English and Japanese, and as such should not be focused overmuch in this book breaking ground on Visible Minorities. Start with Amos 2011 and 2019.

8. Arudou, "Once a 'gaijin,' always a gaijin." *Japan Times*, August 5, 2008. It notes that there were other words (e.g., *ijin*) used for extranationals before *guwaijin* was redefined specifically for use for "foreigners." *See also* "The 'gaijin' debate: Arudou responds." *Japan Times*, September 2, 2008. More on how the performative aspect of the word is still affecting Wajin Japanese in "'Gaijin' mindset is killing rural Japan." *Japan Times*, October 7, 2008.

9. Gluck (1985: 38–9, 135).

10. Ibid.: 38.

11. Dikötter (1997: 8).

12. Koshiro (2013: 475). *See also* Kawai (2015: 5–8).

13. Iida (2002: 142–143); Oguma ibid.; Saaler & Koschmann (2007: 6–14); Shin (2010: 328).

14. Koshiro (2013: 476).

15. Oguma ibid.: 332–333. Fujitani also put it eloquently when he noted how Koreans within the Japanese Empire faced a rhetoric that was "a transformation in the type of racist discrimination . . . a movement from what might be called an unabashed and exclusionary 'vulgar racism' to a new type and inclusionary and 'polite racism' that denied itself as racism even as it operated as such." *See* Fujitani Takashi, "Right to kill, right to make live: Koreans as Japanese and Japanese as Americans during WWII." *Representations* 99(1) 2007: 17, 33.

16. Cf. Lauren 1988, Kearney 1998, Dikötter 2006. Even then, as Russell (in Weiner, ed. 2009: 99) notes,

> [Japan's] rhetoric of racial equality left much to be desired, for not only did Japan's racial equality clause not question the right of League members to possess colonies (at the time Japan was also seeking [a new colony in China]) but its demand for "fair and equal treatment" applied only to "civilized nations" (*bunmei koku*) and League member states—not to their colonies and subject peoples. Japan's ruling elites were less interested in securing equality for non-whites than in ensuring that Japan, as a sovereign nation and member of the League, would be afforded the same privileges as Western nations.

17. Dilworth 2009, Russell in Weiner ed. 2009.

18. *Fukuzawa borrowed from Western eugenics*: Russell ibid.: 95. *Elevation of the human spirit*: Dilworth (2009: 48). Regarding the concept of "civilization," the classical definition of it to writers of this time period probably meant a society with a written language—as seen in the very word for "civilization" (*bunmei*) in Chinese and later Japanese, with characters meaning "clear script"—through which its history is recorded for posterity (cf. Webster's Dictionary, etc.)

19. Dilworth ibid.: xv and xxv.

20. *White-skinned people at the top*: ibid.: 57. *Dark skin at the bottom*: Fukuzawa ibid.: 24. This hierarchy is claimed to continue into present-day Japanese society,

with the ranking as "Western/Asian/Black/guest worker/Nikkeijin" (Clammer 1995), with Japan in second place below "Western" but above "Asian" (Befu 2001: 75).

21. Russell ibid.: 95. *See also* Fish (2009: 43).

22. Russell ibid.: 96.

23. A thorough history of Japan's linkage of nationality and ethnonational identity, and how it differs from the European colonial experience, may be found in Kashiwazaki (2000, 2009). A thorough history of how case-by-case bureaucratic reactions to individual foreign applicants for Japanese naturalization (before provisions were formally encoded in Japan's Nationality Law) may be found in Asakawa (2007), with particular emphasis on the precedent-setting treatment of "foreign" residents in the newly annexed Ogasawara Islands in 1878.

24. Cf. Myers & Peattie 1987, Ching 2001.

25. Myers & Peattie 1987, Morris-Suzuki 2010.

26. *See* Ching ibid.; Oguma (2002: 321–341); Chen (1987) notes: "Holding a virtual monopoly of higher positions in the colonial government [of Taiwan and Korea] and managerial and skilled positions in colonial finance and industry, Japanese opposed integration, fearing that it would eventually wipe out the political and economic advantages they enjoyed. To protect their interests, Japanese turned to the colonial government, a move which often resorted to such measures that can only be construed as a thinly disguised form of racial discrimination" (273).

27. Although eventually the express goal of Japan's colonization programs was full assimilation (*dōka*), Japan's fifty years as a colonial power was perhaps insufficient time for the colonizer to overcome the reflexive self-preservation of their privilege over the colonized, experience an "interest convergence" (such as a civil war) that would compel colonizer to cede privileges to the colonized, or develop a concept of the colonized as having equal rights as the colonizer.

Nevertheless, Oguma would probably argue that equality between Japanese and colonial subjects would not have happened under any circumstances, since Japan's concept of "brotherly relations" was built upon hierarchical concepts within the *Ie Seido* (Family System) (334–341). Under this hierarchy, Japanese would reserve the "elder brother" status (with near-absolute rights of family title, inheritance, etc.) whereas the "younger brother" colony would be subordinated, waiting for a theoretical equality that would in reality never come (this is, of course, where the "family" metaphor breaks down, as people are more mortal than nation-states, meaning the power relations are perpetual). Oguma (338–339) cites an illustrative speech from the Korean governor-general Minami Jirō dated 1942 to a Korean audience, when he was advocating Korean conscription in the Japanese war effort. Oguma notes that Koreans expected the trade-off would be political enfranchisement in return for possibly sacrificing their lives for the empire. However, Minami was clear that demanding one's rights was a "selfish" Western conceit, anathema to the essence of being loyal imperial subjects:

> Generally speaking, the essence of imperial subjects is fundamentally different from the Western belief that one should "start" by demanding one's rights. All imperial subjects are part of a great family that consists of a single sovereign (*ikkun banmin*), where the relationship is that between liege and lord but where the emotional ties are those of a

> father and his children. In interacting with the family head, family members do not talk in terms of rights and obligations. Rather, the elder brother acts as befits an elder brother, while the younger brother acts as befits a younger brother. It is natural and fundamental that all should cooperate in harmony to help the family flourish and move up in the world.
>
> In any family, parents look forward to their children growing up and, when they are old enough, they take all the steps that are needed to ensure that they are educated. This is a consequence of the parents' feelings and love. It is not the custom in Japanese families for children to start ranting about their right to an education simply because they are old enough to attend school. Those who shamelessly practice what is not the custom in Japanese families are delinquents, and it must be said that this in and of itself disqualifies them from becoming imperial subjects.

Thus, the political dimension of the "nation as family" structure (Gluck 1985: 189) is quite clear: The child never becomes a "father" (because the father never dies), and the child's expecting a say (or even raising the very question about a say) in the way "the family" is run is neither "loyal" nor even "Japanese." It was a perpetual status of differentiation and subordination based upon borders delineated under Japan's nation-state, and, despite Japan's "brotherhood" rhetoric, was at the core anti-equality and performatively racializing.

28. Oguma 2002, Shin 2010: 327.
29. Hobsbawm (1983: 2). *See also* Befu (2001).
30. Cf. Oguma 2002, Weiner 2009.
31. McVeigh in Eades et al. eds. (2000).
32. Ibid.: 78.
33. *Monopoly of legitimate education*: Gellner (1983: 34).
34. McVeigh ibid.: 89–92.
35. McVeigh ibid.: 90.
36. McVeigh ibid.: 91–92.
37. Fukuoka (2000).
38. Shin (2010).
39. Morris-Suzuki 2010, Myers & Peattie 1987, Ching 2001.
40. *Pressure from SCAP:* Shin: 328. *Humiliating naturalization processes:* cf. Morris-Suzuki 2010; and the author's own experience with naturalization 1997–2000. Historians differ as to whether Japan "stripped" citizenship from or enforced a "voluntary de-naturalization" upon its former colonists, or whether it was a matter of "lapsing out of an ambiguous state," due to the terms of the 1952 San Francisco Peace Treaty, and a lack of mutual recognition of the rights of sovereign nationalities. Cf. Iwasawa 1998, Levin 2001: 500, Oguma 2002: 341, Shin 2010. Nantais (2011) would argue that the "othering" of Japan's Non-Wajin former imperial subjects was not entirely due to the Japanese government. Barely two months after the Japanese surrender and American Occupation, the former imperial subjects, as *Sangokujin*, were already designated (under SCAP's JCS 1380/15, November 3, 1945) as "liberated peoples," therefore not Wajin, but they were given the choice of being "repatriated" as foreigners or remaining in Japan as enemy nationals. Many of the Sangokujin chose to side with the victors and receive preferential treatment, driving wedges that would be exploited by Japanese in authority when the Occupation ended. However,

with the onset of the Cold War in China and the Korean Peninsula, the Occupation's view dramatically shifted to view Sangokujin as potential communist "subversives"; this intensified SCAP's push for "repatriation," which was problematic until the Sangokujin had their status of registered Japanese national formally removed. That was accomplished by the GOJ by 1950, shortly before the Occupation ended, although the "repatriation" remained voluntary: The *Zainichi* were still allowed to voluntarily remain in Japan—as noncitizens—instead of being forcefully sent "home" to war-torn lands.

41. Oguma ibid.; Shin ibid.

42. Shin ibid.: 328.

43. Shin ibid.: 328.

44. Shin ibid.

45. *"Dominant Japanese"*: Aoki (2009: 185). *Isolated and eradicated*: cf. Huang 2010: 52, Shih 2008: 60.

46. I am stressing this point because much scholarship takes the tone of "Japan was merely copying the Western Enlightenment's concepts and attitudes towards race and people of color." This is often used as a means of excusing Japan from Postcolonialism/Postmodernism critique, rendering its racialization processes as somehow exceptional or more benign (*see* Introduction). As I will stress throughout this book, Japan's racialization processes are neither exceptional nor benign, and the insinuation that goes with this tone is that Japan is somehow not responsible for its own actions because it is merely copying others. This is both belittling to Japan as a society and wrongheaded from a social science perspective.

47. *Tsūshōmei*: cf. Cary in Noguchi & Fotos, eds. (2000: 98). *"Passed" as Japanese:* cf. Lie 2004, Sterling 2010: 51.

48. Cf. Neary in Weiner ed. (2009: 59, 80–81).

49. Fukuoka (2000: 46, 230–231).

50. Befu 2001, Iida 2002, Oguma 2002, Sterling 2010: 48–50.

51. Yoshino (1992: 211).

52. Dower (1999), and so on.

53. Fish (2009: 45).

54. Shin (2010). Fish ibid.: 44, 55.

55. Fish ibid.: 45–53.

56. *Peaceful, tranquil homogeneous state*: Oguma (2002: 299).

57. There have of course been many people in Japan's media who would be classified as *konketsuji* (albeit called "half"), including currently baseball star Yū Darvish, Enka singer Jerome Charles White Jr. (aka Jero), and TV stars Rebecca Eri Ray Vaughan (aka Bekkī), Umemiya Anna, and Miyazawa Rie. Although all are famous and acclaimed for their Japanese roots (in a phenomenon called "They'll claim us if we're famous" in Whiteness Studies), they are still socially asterisked as "half" Japanese if they are visually identifiable as "Gaijin." A case in point is Miyazawa Rie, who is so completely identifiable as "Japanese" only (despite her selling point as a "half" in a 1991 nude pictorial) that she can "pass": contemporary youth (according to my classroom surveys 2008–2011) were largely unaware of her foreign roots.

58. Dikötter 1997: 2–3, Befu 2001: 75–76, Sterling 2010: 24.

59. Ministry of Justice, Bureau of Human Rights 2009.

60. Kawai (2015: 2) argues that this distinction between *minzoku* and *jinshu* is a racialized construct of Japan's place as an Asian power linguistically distancing itself from its fellow Asians: "Put simply, in the concept of *jinshu* the Japanese shared 'a common fate' with people in Asia as a non-white and thus 'inferior' race; reading the Japanese as a *minzoku* made it possible to change this fate by leaving the Western racial order while retaining a racialised notion of the Japanese nation. . . . They used the words *jinshu* and *minzoku* mainly for groups other than the Japanese themselves and for discussing racial/ethnic discrimination and conflicts outside Japan."

61. Dikötter (1997: 8).

62. Cf. Yoshino 1992: 115–121, Arudou 2012.

63. Cf. Yoshino 1992: 115–121, Arudou 2012.

64. Ashikari (2005: 79).

65. Ibid. *See also* Assogba 2012, Kowner & Demel 2013: 20–21, Matsutani 1989.

66. Ashikari ibid.: 76.

67. Sterling (2010: 25).

68. *Japan's Caucasian Self-Image*: Oguma (2002: 143–155). *Body Projects:* Frühstück in Ashkenazi & Clammer eds. (2000: 143–148). *Ideal body as Western:* ibid.: 144; Russell in Weiner ed. (2009: 97).

69. Frühstück: 147–148.

70. Osada (2002).

71. Fukuoka of course problematizes these terms in his chart and devotes many pages to deconstructing them. Under Fukuoka's definition of "Culture," a "yes" meant the person in question "has internalized Japanese culture," that is, speaks Japanese, "has the kind of values, customs, and lifestyles generally thought of as 'Japanese'" (xxix–xxx). A "no" indicated the subject has "internalized a different culture." "Nationality" was clearer as it is a legal status: you either had citizenship under Japan's Nationality Law or you did not. Fukuoka's definition of "Lineage" refers to whether or not a person has Japanese blood. Fukuoka's definition of "Culture" refers to whether "has internalized Japanese culture," that is, speaks Japanese; "has the kind of values, customs, and lifestyles generally thought of as 'Japanese'" (xxix–xxx); or has "internalized a different culture." "Nationality" is clearer as it is a legal status—either the person has Japanese nationality as defined under Japan's Nationality Law or does not. Fukuoka purposely renders "Lineage" and "Culture" in quotation marks, as they are "constructs as conceived in Japanese society, not in any absolute sense of the word" (xxix). He also shows due diligence regarding Japan's latent diversity. He footnotes that "there is nothing 'pure' about the concept of the Japanese race itself," as there was "no such thing as a single, clearly defined ethnic group that has inhabited the Japanese archipelago since antiquity," and that both "culture" and "blood stock" have absorbed "countless foreign influences over the centuries" (both 276).

As for the typologies, Fukuoka gives examples of people who fall into each category:

Type 1: Mainstream "Pure" Japanese.

Type 2: First-generation Japanese migrants abroad.

Type 3: Japanese raised abroad: *kikoku shijo*.

Type 4: Naturalized Japanese, for example, Zainichi Koreans with Japanese nationality.

Type 5: Third-generation Japanese migrants abroad and 'war orphans' (*zanryū koji*)

Type 6: Zainichi Koreans with Japanese upbringing, Korean passport, Japanese culture.

Type 7: Some Ainu. Japanese passport, Ainu lineage and culture.

Type 8: "Pure non-Japanese."

Under Mainstream "pure" Japanese, the person has all three attributes, with Japanese blood, "acculturation," and nationality. Fukuoka asserts "this is the widely-held image of . . . the person most people in Japanese society believe themselves to be" (xxxi). Under *Issei* (first-generation) Japanese migrants, the person is a "Pure" Japanese who has emigrated abroad (e.g., to Hawai'i or North or South America) and presumably given up his or her Japanese nationality. Under Japanese raised abroad, the person has Japanese blood and nationality, but has internalized a foreign culture "more than Japan's" by being born overseas, or spending "several years" abroad growing up and going to school before returning to Japan. The example given is "returnee children" (*kikoku shijo*). Under Naturalized Japanese, the person has internalized "Japanese culture" and holds Japanese nationality, but lacks Japanese blood. The example cited is of naturalized *Zainichi* generational foreigners born in Japan, such as former Koreans, and they are not set apart in Japanese society except as "potential marriage partners" (xxxii). Under *Nisei* and *Sansei* (second- and third-generation) Japanese immigrants and War Orphans (*zanryū koji*) would fall people who have Japanese blood but neither the "culture" (as they have spent the bulk of their lives overseas, were born overseas, or in the case of the "War Orphans," were "abandoned in China" after World War II (xxiii)) nor Japanese nationality. Under Zainichi Koreans with Japanese upbringing, these are Koreans who "pass" (xxxiv) as Japanese, having internalized Japanese culture through Japanese schools to the point of taking Japanese aliases (*tsūshōmei*), but who lack Japanese nationality and blood. Under Ainu would fall Hokkaidō's indigenous people, who, according to Fukuoka, have internalized an "independent culture" (xxxiv) and lack Japanese blood but have Japanese nationality due to Japan's colonialism and Meiji-Era assimilation policies. Finally, people falling under the category "Pure Non-Japanese" lack all three attributes. Fukuoka says that although other types of people above (*Issei*, *Nisei*, *Sansei*, War Orphans, *Zainichi*) are also "classified as foreigners, as understood by most members of Japanese society" (xxxiv), this type of people conjures "an image of unambiguous foreignness to place in mental counterpoint opposite the image of unambiguous Japaneseness with which most Japanese identify themselves" (xxxv). He attaches the word *gaijin* to them (which he unproblematically defines as "an abbreviation of *gaikokujin*") and says that they are visible these days as migrant labor in Japan's public spaces.

Although Fukuoka offers a nuanced analysis of how Japan divides its society up into types of people, the point of reiterating all this in endnote is to show that "blind spot": that after all this granular detail and painstaking analysis, Fukuoka still overlooks the element of skin color.

72. Exceptions are emerging, which may be signaling a welcome break in the moratorium. *See*, for example, Kawai (2015), which mentions the issue of skin color in relation to racialized constructions of Japaneseness.

Part II

"JAPANESE ONLY"

EXAMPLES OF RACIAL DISCRIMINATION

Chapter 3

"We Refuse Foreigners"

Case Studies of "Japanese Only" Exclusionary Businesses

In 1946, shortly after the end of World War II, the Emperor Shōwa (better known as Hirohito in the West) was quoted as saying, "Japan's Racial Equality Clause was denied by the Western powers, and racial discrimination such as the Japanese exclusion in California still remains, which is enough insult to raise the wrath among the Japanese."[1]

It is instructive not only of the anger that racial discrimination brings out in its victims (thus affecting an emperor otherwise famous for his silence in public), but also of another angle of Japan's cognitive dissonance regarding racial discrimination: self-victimization, but not perpetration.[2] Racial discrimination is seen as something that happens to foreigners and minorities outside Japan (including to Japanese people), but, as will be discussed in chapter 8, not within Japan.[3]

That view is incorrect. This chapter will offer hundreds of case studies of exclusionary businesses in Japan that refuse service to "foreigners" on sight. It will also outline four cases that resulted in a civil court lawsuit. Then, all of these cases will be analyzed in terms of themes and patterns, concluding that the fundamental problem lies within the social construct of "What is a Japanese." It will reveal that "Japaneseness" is determined by racialized paradigms, for example, physical appearance, meaning that people in these cases must "look Japanese" to be treated as "Japanese."

Subsequent chapters in part III of this book will uncover what creates and perpetuates this social construct, citing cases in the national discourse that reify and perpetuate an Embedded Racism—the systematic disenfranchisement of peoples based not only on legal status (i.e., citizen vs. noncitizen) but also physical appearance (as Visible Minorities).

A NOTE ABOUT THE CASE STUDIES

Many of these cases were the fieldwork for my doctorate degree, based on primary-source interviews by the author, reports from other eyewitnesses, or secondary sources reported in the mass media. Updated for this Second Edition, they focus on racialized refusals of entry and of service to customers in Japan's private sector. These cases are not merely actions between individuals; they involve actions between individuals/groups and corporate/institutional/business entities offering legally sanctioned and licensed services to the general public.[4] For the sake of brevity and inclusiveness, this chapter offers only summaries of the investigations (and not, for example, the text of full interviews). More details about names, places, interactions, and discussions between excluder and excluded, and photos (mostly not included due to the prohibitive cost of reproducing book images) may be found at the online archives for each section (see endnotes). Readers are strongly advised to view them for the full visual impact of "Japanese Only" signposted discrimination in Japan.

Case Studies of Private-Sector "Japanese Only" Signs and Rules That Did not Result in a Civil Lawsuit

What follows are capsule summaries of approximately 484 establishments that have a history of explicitly barring entry or service to "foreigners."[5] Although many (but not all) cases were informally called "racial discrimination" (*jinshu sabetsu*) by government officials, activists, or even the excluders themselves, they did not result in a civil suit claiming racial discrimination in the Japanese judiciary.

Arranged from north to south on the Japanese archipelago, each section offers (a) the location of the exclusionary establishment with links to evidence, (b) background information on the causes and justifications behind the exclusionism, (c) actions taken by activists to get said exclusionary establishments to change their rules, and (d) current status as of 2021.

WAKKANAI, HOKKAIDŌ[6]

Places: "Super Sentō" Yuransen (a public/private-sector hot springs bathhouse), a barbershop, a sports store, and a hotel (*minshuku*) in Wakkanai City.

Background: First confirmed as having "Japanese Only" signs up in English and Russian in 2000. Yuransen management claimed that visiting Russians were driving away their regular Japanese clients. Yuransen also had a separate "foreigner bath" (unsegregated by gender, in violation of ordinances covering public bathing facilities)[7] and charged 2,500 yen for entry (whereas the entry fee for Japanese in the regular public-sector bathing facilities was then 360 yen). During three interviews conducted by the author, management cited "Japanese Only" signs on private-sector bathhouses in Otaru (see lawsuit section below) as justification for their exclusionary rules, and claimed that having segregated baths was better than Otaru's bathhouses refusing "foreigners" outright. Further investigation of the area, and interviews by the author of local residents and businesses, revealed similar exclusionary rules in a local barbershop and a sports store, both claiming that Russian clientele had adversely affected their business. Minshuku Itsuki wrote on its Rakuten hotel entry and on its personal reservation site (in English): "We are unable to accept any foreign people," and, "Any reservations from foreign people will be cancelled."

Action taken by observers/activists: Activists including the author contacted the city government and local authorities in charge of bathhouse administration numerous times, and were told that the latter only had authority over hygiene issues, not discrimination issues. A petition (*chinjō*) submitted by activists in 2004 to pass a local antidiscrimination ordinance (*jōrei*) died in committee. A phone call to Minshuku Itsuki in November 2009 received a stern rebuke from the manager, and a reiterated conviction that now even naturalized Japanese citizens would be refused service.

Current status (as of 2021): The sports store took its exclusionary sign down after media attention, while the barbershop indicated that it would accept the author as a customer, as per follow-up interviews in 2000. Yuransen never changed its exclusionary rules and went bankrupt in March 2006. Minshuku Itsuki no longer displays text refusing all "foreign people" on its reservations website. Wakkanai still has no antidiscrimination ordinance. Sporadic but unconfirmed reports occasionally reach the author of "foreigner" refusals at Wakkanai ramen and barber shops.

MONBETSU, HOKKAIDŌ

Place: Miscellaneous places around Monbetsu City (Hokkaidō) (two public/private-sector bathhouses, a ramen shop, a restaurant, a karaoke parlor, and more than 100 bars).

Background: According to newspaper articles, plus several visits and interviews between 2000 and 2009 by the author and other activists, since 1995 Monbetsu's local restaurateurs' association (*inshokuten kumiai*) created and sold standardized signs in Cyrillic saying "Japanese Only Store" (*Nihonjin sen'yō ten*). These signs graced the front of over 100 bars and restaurants in the Hamanasu Dōri nightlife district. Interviews with bars

МАГАЗИН ТОЛЬКО
ДЛЯ ЯПОНЦЕВ.

Figure 3.1 Example of One of More than 100 Exclusionary Signs Found in Monbetsu, Hokkaidō Prefecture, All of Which Say in One Version or Another, "Store Only for Japanese" in Russian. *Source:* Photo courtesy of author.

displaying the signs revealed fears of Russian sailors' custom, including the language barrier, drunken unruliness, nonpayment of bills, rumors of rape, surrounding Japanese customer dissatisfaction, and ties to Russian organized crime (although many interviewees said they had no actual experience with any of these issues—the sign was a preventive measure); some refused the author's business even though he is not Russian and was accompanied by other Japanese. Three restaurants and a karaoke parlor expressed similar sentiments, and said they would have refused the author had he not been a fluent Japanese speaker. Two bathhouses (one private sector, one public/private (*dai-san sekutā*)) claimed drunk and unruly Russian bathers were driving away Japanese customers.

Action taken by observers/activists: In July 2000, the Japanese Ministry of Justice (MOJ), Bureau of Human Rights (BOHR) (*jinken yōgobu*) Asahikawa Branch wrote a letter (see chapter 8) to the restaurateurs' association calling their activities "clear racial discrimination against foreigners," demanding they remove their exclusionary signs. In an interview with the author in April 2001, the *kumiai* head claimed that these signs were now the property of their respective purchasers, and what they did with them was not their concern. After extensive media exposure of the situation in local newspapers and national TV between 2000 and 2005, signs began coming down, and further interviews and media exposure of the restaurants, karaoke parlor, and the bathhouses resulted in exclusionary rules being rescinded in the karaoke parlor, one restaurant, and the public/private-sector bathhouse. In 2006, an interview with another restaurant enabled the author to take down one of the Cyrillic signs with permission. In 2004, the author and one other activist submitted a petition (*chinjō*) to pass a local antidiscrimination ordinance (*jōrei*), which subsequently died in committee.

Current status (as of 2021): Confirmed by a local resident in March 2021, the Cyrillic signs in Hamanasu Dōri have disappeared (only one sign was still visible), now twenty-two years after they first went up. The private-sector bathhouse took down its exclusionary sign after its owner died and his sons faced competition from public-private consortium bathhouses in and out of town. One of the former exclusionary restaurants went bankrupt in 2007. Monbetsu still has no antidiscrimination ordinance.

SAPPORO, HOKKAIDŌ[8]

Place: Miscellaneous places around Sapporo City during the 2002 World Cup and onward (nightlife enterprises, one ramen shop, and one pachinko parlor).

Background: During the "anti-hooligan" media and policy drives (2001–2002; see chapters 5 and 7) on the eve of the 2002 Soccer World Cup, Sapporo, host to the England-Argentina match, went on alert[9] (due to the anticipated acrimonious relations between these teams' fans). Amid other exclusionary signs and rules, a standardized multilingual sign (in English, Spanish, Italian, German, and Russian, but not Japanese) saying "Members Only: Please present your member's card" appeared on several "soaplands" (houses of near-prostitution) and one ramen shop. These places, according to interviews by the author, had no member system—it was their version of a "Japanese Only" sign (although many displayers said they could not read any of the foreign languages on it).

Action taken by observers/activists: Following prompting from activists, media exposure by local newspaper reporters forced some of the signs to come down. The author interviewed the ramen shop manager, who did not understand the sign but put it up anyway, claiming she was afraid of "soccer hooligans" and was using it to protect her business. Once advised of sign's meaning and effect, the ramen shop manager allowed the author to take it down. Activists brought this issue before the Sapporo City Assembly in 2004, submitting a petition (*chinjō*) for the passage of an antidiscrimination ordinance (*jōrei*); this petition died in committee.[10]

Current status (as of 2021): Although most of the "Japanese Only" signs and rules disappeared with the passing of the World Cup, and after nearly two decades the Susukino "Members Only" signs (which were on color photocopy paper) have biodegraded. Sapporo still has no antidiscrimination ordinance.

MISAWA, AOMORI[11]

Place: Miscellaneous places around Misawa City (Aomori Prefecture), 2002–2003 (bars).

Background: At least seven hostess bars were discovered in 2002 by the author with "Japanese Only" signs up in the entertainment district outside the

US Misawa Air Force Base main gate (near their main business thoroughfare, dubbed "White Pole Road"). Several interviews by the author of all seven places indicated that management had experienced, or was afraid of experiencing, communication and behavioral problems with US servicemen; others stated that their Japanese customers did not want US servicemen drinking in their bar, as it would disrupt the atmosphere. All sign displayers initially refused the author entry, despite his lack of connection to the US servicemen and his proof of Japanese citizenship. One bar's manager (Globe) admitted that he had copied his "Japanese Only" sign from Otaru Onsen Osupa's sign (see lawsuit section below) down to the font, citing the Otaru Case as a justification and a template for refusing all "foreigners" entry. Other excluders in Misawa then copied this.

Action taken by observers/activists: The author attempted to meet with all places with signs up to explain issues of racial discrimination connected with the signs, but all places in 2002 refused to change their rules. Three of the bars were found to be owned by the same matron, who refused to meet with the author on three separate occasions. The author wrote letters to the local newspaper (which did not cover the story), the US base (which did not answer), the Aomori MOJ, BOHR (which wrote a letter to all seven bars but did not report results back to the author), the Misawa City government (which did not answer), and the US Consulate Sapporo (which refused to comment or take any action, moreover strongly warned the author against continuing any further activism in the Misawa Case).[12] Follow-up interviews in 2003 indicated that four of the seven establishments had taken their signs down, and one let the author in for a drink—because they said they had received a letter from the BOHR advising them to. The remaining three, owned by the abovementioned matron, kept the sign up and continued to refuse to meet with the author.

Current status (as of 2021): A Google street view crawl along "White Pole Road" and environs, as of May 2018 and November 2019, found rusted storefronts, shuttered businesses, and a general feeling of economic malaise. Although exclusionary signs may still be lurking behind the shutters, the author was unable to find any online presence of the abovementioned exclusionary bars.

AKITA

Place: Akita City, Akita Prefecture (a disco).[13]

Background: Between 2002 and 2003, a disco named Honey Bee had a "foreigners are not admitted" sign taped to their front door. Accompanied by a local newspaper reporter, the author was admitted into the premises to interview the management regarding their reasons for the exclusionary sign: "Foreign" clients had allegedly been drunk, rowdy, and vandalistic; had brought their own alcohol onto the premises; had talked loudly outside and disturbed the neighbors; and had tried to instigate love triangles with other Japanese clients. Repeated warnings were allegedly ineffective, so "foreigners" were banned from entry to protect the atmosphere for Japanese clientele.

Action taken by observers/activists: The author asked what rules the disco wished to enforce, and once explained to him in Japanese, provided a culturally sensitive English translation. As follows: (front door) "We prefer Non-Japanese customers who follow our rules. If you don't, we call the police. This is not a bluff." (interior) "RULES: 1) No loitering outside (it causes neighborhood complaints); 2) No bringing in drinks from elsewhere (if you come here, kindly support our business); 3) No causing trouble with other customers here (any complaints, you're out); 4) Our prices are our prices. Other people pay with no complaints. Don't like it? Go elsewhere, please. Any trouble, we call the police." After this, the author received permission to remove the "Japanese Only" sign from the front door.

Current status (as of 2021): Honey Bee is still open to all customers.

FUKUSHIMA

Place: Fukushima Prefecture (35 hotels, later 318 hotels).[14]

Background: In September 2007, the author was advised that the Fukushima Prefecture's Tourist Information website in English listed and advertised thirty-five hotels in the region that officially refused "foreign" clients.

Action taken by observers/activists: In September 2007, the author contacted the Fukushima Tourist Information Agency (FTIA) and advised them this practice of refusing "foreigners" is unlawful under the Hotel Management Law (see Tōkyō Shinjuku section immediately below). A FTIA bureaucrat who contacted all thirty-five hotels responded in October, stating, "Most of the answers were, 'We do not explicitly refuse foreigners,'" as they had never had a "foreign" client. However, eight hotels of the thirty-two they were able to contact stated they would continue to refuse "foreigners" because they did "not have staff who spoke English," therefore "they could not positively (*sekkyokuteki ni*) receive foreigners." The FTIA said they advised them of the unlawfulness of this practice and would be clarifying their website questions in future.

Current status (as of 2021): A January 2010 search of the Japanese website using search terms "*gaikokujin no ukeire: fuka*" revealed 318 lodgings refusing "foreign" lodgers; amending the search terms revealed 335 other places accepting “foreigners.” It would appear that the prefectural tourist agency website enabled the exclusionism by officially offering member hotels a pre-set option to refuse foreign lodgers, an option hundreds of those hotels clearly chose.[15] After activists lodged another complaint with the FTIA, the FTIA amended the “foreigners refused” to “reception cannot be done in foreign languages” (*gaikokugo taiō fuka*) as of January 5, 2010. That said, as of July 2012, reentering search terms 外国人の受入：不可 into the キーワード section at revealed several exclusionary hotels. By February 15, 2015, no hotels on the fukushima.tabi-kura.com website indicated that they refuse “foreigners.”

Perhaps learning a lesson from their own residents being refused entry at hotels and shops around Japan following the Fukushima nuclear meltdown, a 2021 search of www.tif.ne.jp revealed no refusing hotels.[16]

SHINJUKU, TŌKYŌ

Place: Shinjuku-ku (Ōkubo Hyakuninchō, Kabukichō) (hotels and nightlife).[17, 18]

Background: In interviews both by phone and in person in 2005, the author confirmed that two hotels in the Ōkubo area of Shinjuku had signs up in English and Japanese refusing all “foreigners” or “foreign women.” The justification in the former case was that “foreign” clients had refused to follow Japanese hotel decorum, pilfered items from rooms, and could not be reasoned with because management does not speak foreign languages. In the latter case, the “love hotel” in question refused “foreign” women because they were assumed to be prostitutes accompanying their clients to hotels. In the Kabukichō area, surveyed between 2006 and 2008, various nightlife enterprises had homemade “Japanese Only” signs displayed.[19]

Action taken by observers/activists: The author visited the hotels in question in 2005 and asked managers to remove the signs. They refused, although they acknowledged that they would allow in “foreign” clients who spoke Japanese; however, they refused to amend their signs to reflect this. The author then took some photos of the signs, went to the nearest Police Box (*kōban*), and showed them the signs and a copy of the Hotel Management Law (*ryokan gyōhō*), Article 5, which says that hotels may not refuse customers unless (1) rooms are full, (2) there is a threat of contagious disease, or (3) there is a threat to “public morals” (*fūki*).[20] The police officers on duty refused to take any action and told the author to take the issue up instead with Shinjuku Police Headquarters.

During a separate research trip,[21] the author confirmed with a nightlife establishment that their “Japanese Only” sign had been created by an untraceable (i.e., neither online nor in the phone book) “Tōkyō Crime Prevention and

Health Cooperative"[22] (*Tōkyō bōhan kenzen kyōryoku kai*). When asked if they had health or crime issues with foreigners up to now, they indicated that they had not. When asked if the author may enter, the management refused, then asked for proof of Japanese citizenship. Upon seeing that proof, the management said the author may enter as he is a naturalized Japanese. (For the record, the author declined.)

Current status (as of 2021): Web searches of the establishments still in business indicate no rules still refusing foreigners. A 2021 google street view search of the Kabukichō nightlife addresses in question revealed no exclusionary signs.

SHINJUKU, TŌKYŌ

Place: Takadanobaba (a job placement agency).[23]

Background: Takadanobaba is Tōkyō's most famous college town, with establishments catering to many foreign students. A job placement agency in the area printed on the corporate sign outside their front door, "People with foreign nationalities cannot register for our services" in Japanese.

Action taken by observers/activists: The author phoned the agency and confirmed that their "no foreigner" rules existed and applied to all of their branches. When pointed out that this practice violated the Japan Labor Standards Law Article 3 and the Worker Dispatch Law, the manager said he would "try harder" (*doryoku shimasu*) but would not change his rules. The author then notified labor unions. Nothing further was reported.

Current status (as of 2021): The company remains in business with several branches nationwide. It is unclear from their website if they still refuse foreign workers.

SHIBUYA, TŌKYŌ

Place: Tōkyō Aoyama-Dōri (aesthetic salon for women's beautification and relaxation).[24]

Background: In 2005, the author was sent confirmation that a Hawaiian-motif women's salon, in one of Japan's most trendy and high-rent consumer locations, had "Japanese Women Only" signs and advertising flyers outside their establishment.

Action taken by observers/activists: The author phoned the salon on February 24, 2005, and confirmed the exclusionary rules. The manager's justification was that she did not speak any foreign languages, and that "foreign" (*gaijin*) women's feet were too big for their footbaths. When asked if these exclusionary rules also applied to Asian foreigners, or to the *Zainichi* Korean and Chinese generational "foreigners" who have no language barrier or apparent foot size issues, the manager hung up.

Current status (as of 2021): A web search could no longer find the establishment in business.

ASAKUSA, TŌKYŌ[25]

Place: Tōkyō Asakusa (tempura restaurant).

Background: In April 2014, foreign tourists brought by their Japanese hosts to an Asakusa tempura restaurant reported a "Japanese Only" sign at the front door. Managers reportedly said they would refuse entry to any "foreigner," regardless of their language ability or length of stay in Japan.

Action taken by observers/activists: The author telephoned the restaurant directly and confirmed they do refuse all foreigners entry. Reasons given were as follows: (a) foreigners are unhygienic (*eiseimen*; specifically, they don't take off their shoes), (b) foreigners cause inconvenience (*meiwaku*) to other customers, and (c) foreigners don't speak Japanese. When asked if these were not merely his prejudices against foreigners, the manager said repeatedly that he "just can't deal with them" (*taiō o shikirenai*) and hung up. Then other online activists began phoning, dropping by, contacting local government officials and Japanese media outlets (*Asahi Shinbun* reportedly visited), and issuing negative online reviews.

Current status (as of 2021): The sign was taken down within two weeks of being reported. A web search does not indicate that exclusionary rules have resurfaced, but the restaurant (despite a detailed online presence) at this writing appears to be closed.

OGIKUBO, TŌKYŌ

Place: Tōkyō Ogikubo (Suminami-ku) (hostess bar).[26]

Background: In January and March 2004, the author confirmed with the management of one Filipina hostess bar that "foreign" customers were not accepted unless they were accompanied with Japanese. The justifications were language barriers and ambience control for Japanese clientele.

Action taken by observers/activists: The author showed the management his proof as a Japanese citizen and asked if he could bring in a "foreign" friend. Confirming that both could speak Japanese, the bar allowed both in for beverages.

Current status (as of 2021): A web search could no longer find the establishment in business.

AZABU, TŌKYŌ

Place: Tōkyō Minami Azabu (ballet school).[27]

Background: Over 2007–2008, the Hon. Rahman Hamid, commercial secretary of the Embassy of Pakistan, Tōkyō, forwarded the author some official letters of protest (on Pakistan Embassy letterhead) that he had sent to a ballet school, which allegedly had refused his three-year-old daughter membership and instruction due to, inter alia, "classes being full."

Action taken by observers/activists: The author confirmed by email that the client had been refused service. After some negotiation, the ballet school formally apologized to the clients for "miscommunication" and admitted the student.

Current status (as of 2021): The ballet school's bilingual website indicates that it is open to foreign clients.

AKIHABARA, TŌKYŌ

Place: Tōkyō Akihabara (knickknacks and weapons store).[28]

Background: Between 2007 and 2008, the author received reports of a store with a sign saying "Not for sightseeing. Japanese Only. Sorry, an order by the authorities we can't selling our knives and weapons for the foreigner [*sic*]" in parts English, Japanese, and Chinese. The author confirmed in 2008 by phone and in interviews that the management believed that their goods (which were not all weapons—there were also numerous novelty items of a peaceful nature) could not be sold to "foreigners" due to official laws forbidding transportation of weapons onto airplanes, plus a recent local multiple stabbing incident by a Japanese.

Action taken by observers/activists: The author and a newspaper reporter confirmed that the sign was up before the 2008 Akihabara stabbing incident,[29] that "foreigners" were not involved in any weapons-use incident in the area, and that not all "foreign" clients would be boarding airplanes after purchase. The manager also confirmed that a blanket exclusion from seeing all goods in the store was probably unnecessary. The author was then allowed to amend the sign to clarify the laws regarding weapons purchases, that is, all clients must have traceable addresses in Japan. The new sign read: "Not for sightseeing. Knife & weapon sales require ID and address in Japan." The management then allowed the author to replace the exclusionary sign.

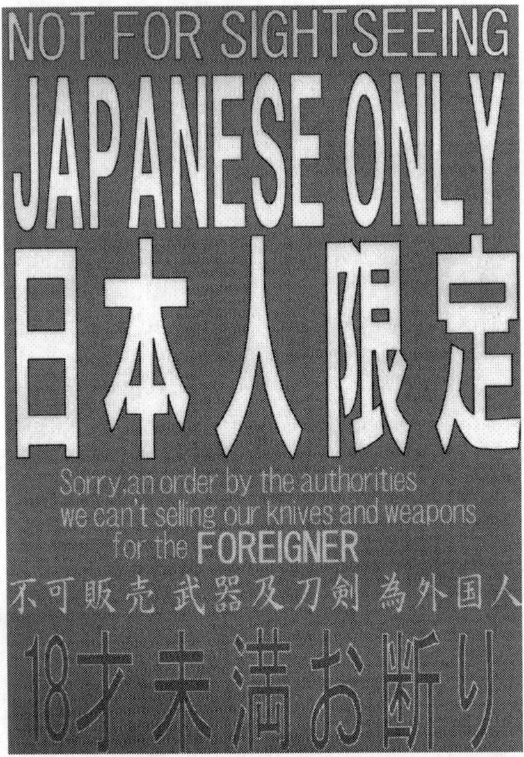

Figure 3.2 Exclusionary Sign Outside Akihabara Store MAD. Original photo as of May 14, 2007, courtesy of anonymous contributor. Revised photo after author's consultation with store owner, as of June 17, 2008, archived online with images and fieldwork notes, at www.debito.org/roguesgallery.html#Akihabara. *Source:* Photo courtesy of author.

Current status (as of 2021): The store's website in June 2015 still indicated that "foreigners" may not buy knives. A follow-up visit in September 2014 indicated the owner remained unhappy with the behavior of his "foreign" clients but acknowledged that his Japanese clients were also unruly at times, so no blanket exclusionary policy would be reinstated. A 2021 web search revealed that the store had pulled up stakes from Akihabara because it was "riddled with gaijin" (*gaijin darake*), indicating that the owner still felt "foreigners" were essentially to blame for his troubles.[30]

KŌFU, YAMANASHI

Place[31]: Kōfu, Yamanashi Prefecture (several public/private-sector "sentō" bathhouses and "super sentō" Isawa Kenkō Land).

Background: According to contemporary newspaper articles and on-site interviews, in the late 1980s–early 1990s Kōfu City had a noticeable increase in the number of "foreigners" (particularly from Southeast Asian countries) working in local menial-labor (3K) and sexually oriented (*mizu shōbai*) industries, many of whom frequented local bathhouses (*sentō*) to get clean and relax during their off-hours. Concurrently, however, there was a large media campaign in Japan regarding the spread of AIDS worldwide, and connections were made between "foreigners" and that disease. At least one customer complained to a bathhouse named Kami-Ishida that she did not want to share bathwater with a Thai customer, so the management decided to exclude all "foreign" customers. Further concerns arose with allegations that "foreigners" were not following Japanese bathhouse manners, and with allegations that the "lazy" (*taiman*) nature of "foreign workers" was unappealing to the Japanese customer base. Further reports of similar exclusionary establishments (a games arcade and a hotel bathhouse) in Nagano and Tōkyō were cited to lend legitimacy to other bathhouses in Kōfu establishing their own "Japanese Only" rules. A declining bathing industry in the area (local bathhouses had decreased from around seventy establishments to twenty-eight over two decades)[32] was also seen as a cause for desperate measures by bathhouses to maintain their customer base. One bathhouse, however, steadfastly remained open to "foreign" clientele and weathered the temporary drop in business. Bathhouse management citywide then received pamphlets from the city Department of Public Health (*hokensho*) stating that AIDS was not transmittable by sharing bathwater. These were forwarded to frequent Japanese customers. The 1992 public panic associating "foreigners" with AIDS passed, and eventually all baths in Kōfu opened their doors again.

Action taken by observers/activists: In 2004, the author received a report from a bather who visited a newer establishment called Isawa Kenkō Land, which had signs up excluding clients who have tattoos or are inebriated, and also "foreigners" who are illegal visa overstayers or who insufficiently understand the Japanese language. Visiting the premises on June 7, 2004, the author confirmed that spot checks of Alien Registration Cards (ARCs) (see chapters 4 and 5) were mandatory for anyone the management considered to be "foreign" (including the author), although this was waived after protest and management's satisfaction at the author's Japanese language ability. An interview revealed management's motivation for demanding a "foreigner" visa check (a job otherwise reserved for people empowered by the MOJ, such as Immigration or the police): crime prevention (see chapter 5). They also felt the need to verify language ability because management claimed they might not be able to communicate with "foreigners" in the event of an emergency (although a query on how communication would occur with blind or deaf clientele remained unanswered). Management's final expressed concern was about the reaction of elderly Japanese clientele who have wartime memories and might have some trepidation at bathing with "foreigners" (although a query about what would happen to German customers remained unanswered).

Current status (as of 2021): The signs at Isawa Kenkō Land are no longer visible out front, and the website indicates no policies subjecting foreign customers to extra visa scrutiny.

AZUMA-MURA, GUNMA

Place[33]: Azuma-mura, Gunma Prefecture (public swimming pool).

Background: According to press reports and activists' investigation, in 1998 a swimming pool allegedly had incidents of "foreigners" roughhousing in the pool area, including throwing a young Japanese swimmer in the pool, and touching a young Japanese girl's posterior. A sign was posted forbidding all "foreigners" from entry.

Action taken by observers/activists: An activist group including the author investigated and released information to the media. After public pressure and exposure, the exclusionary sign was quickly replaced by one warning against horseplay. The justification given to the activist group was that a public-sector building cannot refuse taxpayers, which also includes "foreign" taxpayers.

Current status (as of 2021): The pool remains open to the public.

KOSHIGAYA, SAITAMA

Place[34]: Koshigaya City, Saitama Prefecture (bars and adult video store).

Background: As of 2004–2007, three Filipina hostess bars had "Japanese Only" signs up. One sign required (in English) "foreigners" to have a Japanese escort to qualify for entry, while text below it in Japanese refused all "foreigners" without exception. The adult video store's exclusionary sign (in Japanese) was the most sophisticated the author has yet seen: "Not allowed in store: Chinese and naturalized citizens, Chinese war orphans, people with Chinese blood are absolutely refused entry. Only pure-blooded Japanese males" (*nyūten kyohi: Chūgokujin & kikajin, zanryū koji, Chūgoku-kei konketsu jinji, zettai nyūten kinshi, junketsu Nihonjin danji nomi*).

Action taken by observers/activists: The author tried to confirm conditions and justifications by phone, but two places had no listing and two others did not answer the phone.

Current status (as of 2021): The bars in question and the adult video store are no longer visible on online searches.

Figure 3.3 Sign in Koshigaya, Saitama Prefecture, Outside Nightlife Store EDEN Which Limits Entry to "Pure-Blooded Japanese Males" Only. Photo taken March 2007, submitted by a reporter of a major international magazine who requests anonymity. *Source:* Photo courtesy of author.

CENTRAL JAPAN

Place[35]: Miscellaneous bars/"relaxation clubs" in Toda City (Saitama Prefecture), Isesaki City and Ōta City (Gunma Prefecture), Kurashiki City (Okayama Prefecture), and Hiroshima City (Hiroshima Prefecture).

Background: Between 1998 and 2008, the author received by email snapshots of signs contributed by local noncitizen residents who had either been refused entry at the premises or had found them in their neighborhoods. Signs or management either said "Japanese Only" or required "foreigners" to have Japanese escorts.

Action taken by observers/activists: The author visited the Kurashiki bar with proof of citizenship and was still refused entry by management. Management declined to give their justifications. The Hiroshima bar told "foreign" excluded people that Americans from a nearby military base were intimidating its Japanese clientele, attracted by an international bar run by "foreigners" next door. The other places were unreachable for comment.

Current status (as of 2021): Most of the enterprises in question cannot be found in a web search. Those found do not indicate they refuse foreigners.

NONOICHI, ISHIKAWA

Place[36]: Nonoichi City, Ishikawa Prefecture (newspaper distribution company).

Background: In 2007, a noncitizen resident of Nonoichi was approached by an independent newspaper distribution company (*seiruzu*) representative and offered a subscription to the *Hokkoku Shinbun*, the regional newspaper. The day after signing a contract, the client received a postcard from the distributor canceling the subscription, saying in English, "Boss didn't accept foreigner's subscription. I am sorry."

Action taken by observers/activists: After receiving copies of the contract receipt and the postcard, the author contacted the distributor and received no comprehensible reason for the cancellation, except that there was allegedly something wrong with the contract so the company unilaterally cancelled it, with no follow-up to renew it with the "foreign" customer. *Hokkoku Shinbun* was also contacted and denied any knowledge of or connection with this independent distributor.

Current status (as of 2021): The subscription remains cancelled.

NAGASAKI, NAGASAKI PREFECTURE

Place[37]: Nagasaki Yorozuya-machi (an American-style steakhouse restaurant).

Background: In 2021, citizen and noncitizen Nagasaki residents noticed an American-styled steakhouse (named "Bronco," with a wood-paneled American West-esque motif, including exterior decor of revolvers, horses, tiki heads, and exterior signs saying "Open" and "Welcome" in English), located in Nagasaki's main downtown shopping area. It had several handwritten signs in its stairwell saying, "Foreign people are forbidden to enter this restaurant to prevent infection," echoing the contemporary fear of COVID-contagious foreigners only (see chapter 4). Other interior decor included a US Confederate flag.

Action taken by observers/activists: Photos of the establishment were sent across the internet and to the author for display on Debito.org. Nagasaki residents began phoning the owner and putting negative reviews online. Government agencies and the local chamber of commerce were contacted.

Current status (as of 2021): The signs came down within two weeks of discovery, activists suspect, because of pressure from the local shop owners' association and MICE (Meeting Incentive travel, Convention, Exhibition/Event), a local government organization promoting Nagasaki's new "Dejima Messe Nagasaki" as an international convention center.

MISCELLANEOUS PLACES

Place[38]: Otaru, Hokkaidō (a dining bar), Yūfutsu, Hokkaidō Prefecture (a golf course), Shintoku, Hokkaidō (an orthopedic clinic), Tōkyō Takadanobaba (a job placement agency), Tōkyō Tsukiji Fish Market (a restaurant), Tōkyō Asakusa (an *izakaya* tavern and a tempura restaurant), Tōkyō Shibaura (*Japan Times* "Japanese Only" newspaper want ads), Tōkyō citywide (an exercise gym chain), Ōmiya (Saitama Prefecture; a capsule hotel), Nagoya (Aichi Prefecture; a nightclub), Okazaki City (Aichi Prefecture; an internet café), Kyōto City (Kyōto Prefecture; a *ryokan* hotel), Ōsaka City (a realtor), Kōbe City (a soul bar), Kitakyūshū City (Fukuoka Prefecture; a restaurant), Uruma City (Okinawa Prefecture; a billiards hall and a karaoke hall), and Tokashiki Village (Okinawa Prefecture; a diving and hiking tour company).

Background: A dining bar in Otaru verbally refused service to former *Yomiuri Shinbun* reporter Mark Austin for being a foreigner; when he asked the manager if refusing him was not racial discrimination, he replied "Yeah it is, can't be helped" (*shiyō ga nai*). The Hokkaidō golf course in 2018 reportedly turned away Jay Bothroyd, a Sapporo Consadole soccer player who once played for England's national team, expressly for being a foreigner; their website stated that "non-Japanese players must be accompanied by a club member" and it is unclear whether Bothroyd came unaccompanied. The orthopedic clinic, despite having links to international medical tourism sponsored by the government, refused in 2012 to treat a foreign teacher employed by a local government; the doctor cited language barriers, despite the teacher coming with a translator. The Tsukiji restaurant in 2007 had a very complicated system for how clients should dine, with elaborate rules written in Japanese; according to queries, the management assumed that "foreigners" would not be able to read or follow these rules and refused them service outright by appending "Japanese People Only" to its billboards. The Asakusa *izakaya* put up a "Japanese Only" sign in 2018, explaining in Japanese, "Our staff do not speak foreign languages, so we refuse all overseas people." The *Japan Times* has put up multiple advertisements requiring job applicants to be "Japanese only." The Tōkyō gym chain barred "foreigners" if they could not read or write their name and address in Japanese. The Ōmiya capsule hotel wrote on its Rakuten hotels entry in 2015 that it simply accepted no reservations from foreigners. The Nagoya nightclub in 2005 had a sign up saying "All foreigners must be members" and then, according to witnesses, Japanese were let in without checking membership (while all "foreigners" based upon appearance were barred from entry). The internet café in Okazaki in 2006 claimed that a "foreigner" had sent spam from their premises, and an antispam bot had locked up their server. The Ōsaka realtor had a symbol (rendered as "gaijin" in kanji) in its brochures indicating "foreigners allowed" (the default being that they are not). The manager of the Kyōto *ryokan* in 2005 said he had temporarily segregated his facilities by nationality (but not by gender) because of a large inrush of "foreign" clients, and alleged their bigger bodies deserved a separate bath. The hotel in Kyōto in 2009 had "Japanese speakers only" on its Rakuten Travel website listing. The soul bar in Kōbe had a sign up saying "Excuse me, Japanese people only," despite featuring the music of people they would probably exclude. The manager of the restaurant in Kitakyūshū said in 2006 that he was personally afraid of "foreigners," moreover he neither spoke any foreign languages nor had menus in English. The Okinawa billiards hall in 2006 justified their "Japanese Only" sign due to the staff's lack of English proficiency, despite never having any trouble with "foreign" clients; the manager claimed his actions were not discriminatory because allegedly his American relative by marriage had suggested he put the exclusionary sign up to "avoid any trouble." The karaoke hall had a sign up in good English that they were admitting only Japanese speakers because their staff has "limited English skill"; how the staff would gauge sufficient language ability in customers was unclear. The diving and hiking tour company had a notice on its website saying, "Dear foreign customer, we don't give you service due to safety reason and regulation. We are appreciated your understanding [*sic*]."

Action taken by observers/activists: Austin contacted both the Otaru Tourism Association and Debito.org to publicize the event; activists contacted the shop and the owner denied refusing Austin for being foreign; no reply was heard from the Otaru Tourist Association. Bothroyd tweeted out his discontent, and English sports media picked up the issue; nothing of consequence was reported afterward and Bothroyd deleted his tweet. The author contacted the Hokkaidō orthopedic clinic and confirmed that no foreigners would be treated, then reported it to the *Hokkaidō Shinbun*; the newspaper followed up with interviews with the teacher, the city government, and the clinic. Concerned parties contacted the Tsukiji restaurant and the "Japanese People Only" wording was soon removed from their elaborate rules. The person discovering the Asakusa bar sign in 2018 pulled it down, but it was replaced the next day; consumers then put up negative online reviews. The author writes for the *Japan Times* and brought this violation of the Labor Standards Law (and of their own guidelines against ads that "are, or may easily be construed to be illegal, misleading, fraudulent, indecent, suggestive, or offensive") to their attention multiple times, but received no answer. The Tōkyō gym chain was reported to website Debito.org, whereon commenters advised the reporter of other gym chains without restrictions. The capsule hotel and Rakuten were contacted, and rules were soon amended to say, "This hotel has no staff who speak foreign languages. If you don't understand Japanese, please bring someone who does." The nightclub in Nagoya would not comment, connect the author to the manager, or return calls. The Okazaki internet café withdrew its exclusionary sign after a phone call from the author, agreeing that their original decision had been hasty and intemperate. The realtor's problematic labeling was sent to the Land, Infrastructure, and Transport Ministry and the Japan Property Management Association, as well as to media, but no answer from any party was forthcoming. The Kyōto *ryokan* said that they would take the same request from the author under advisement. The other Kyōto hotel did not refuse the author lodging thanks to his sufficient Japanese language ability,[39] but refused to rescind its exclusionary rules claiming they were doing nothing unlawful; it was later contacted by the Kyōto Tourist Association (at the author's behest), who disagreed and told them to amend its exclusionary rules. The Kōbe soul bar was contacted by activists and the sign was soon taken down, although the manager allegedly later claimed that despite a sign specifically saying "Japanese people only," he actually meant "Japanese *language* only." The restaurant in Kitakyūshū served the author and his friends after ascertaining their sufficient Japanese language ability, but the Fukuoka Bureau of Human Rights refused to entertain a request from the author for investigation of the restaurant (the Kitakyūshū City Tourist Board, however, did contact the restaurant at the author's behest and advised the restaurant to cease refusing "foreigners"). The billiards hall would only take into advisement requests from a local activist to remove their sign and never returned calls from the author. Online activists contacted the Okinawan diving and hiking tour company to point out how there was no "safety reason and regulation" for refusing foreigners from hikes and put pressure on the owners to change their rules; however, other online activists apparently intervened to make the English of their exclusionary message more grammatically correct and plausibly deniable.

Current status (as of 2021): The internet café, billiards hall, Kyōto *ryokan*, Kyōto hotel, karaoke hall, soul bar, Otaru dining bar, and Kitakyushu restaurant are still open and according to web searches accept all customers. The Ōsaka realtor no longer has a visible net presence, and the Tsukiji restaurant was impossible to track down. The Asakusa tavern no longer has the exclusionary sign out front, according to Google street view dated March 2020. The Ōmiya capsule hotel has no language excluding foreigners or people who don't speak Japanese on their website or Rakuten entry. The Nagoya nightclub website still has a membership system but indicates no policy excluding foreigners. The Hokkaidō orthopedic clinic lost its website, as it was being hosted by a local general hospital; it is unclear if the clinic itself is still in business, but the general hospital does not refuse foreigners; and since the orthopedist in question is still listed on the general hospital's roster, it is unlikely his medical license was affected by any violation of the Hippocratic Oath. The Hokkaidō golf course has an elaborate website in English, prominently advertising its course as being designed by Jack Nicklaus, but still saying "Non-resident of Japan has to be accompanied by membership."[40] A 2021 web search indicates the *Japan Times* still displays discriminatory ads, with some requiring "native speakers of Japanese" (日本語ネイティブ限定, etc.) as a way of getting around "Japanese Only."[41] The Tōkyō gym chain's website indicates no exclusionary rules regarding foreign clients. The diving and hiking tour company still has a notice refusing all foreigners on its website, except this time in better English: "Dear global customers, Since we are not yet prepared and for safety reasons, we are afraid that we are unable to accept you. We apologize for this inconvenience and would appreciate your kind understanding."[42]

ONLINE EXCLUSIONS

This section briefly talks about online websites that have exclusionary rules built into their search terms. A surprising number can be found with a simple Google search,[43] so let's focus on the basic essential of finding accommodation. A 2021 cursory Google search of the "shares, house" website returned 39 discrete sites and 111 individual "sharehouse" rental properties nationwide saying "*Gaikokujin fuka.* Must have Japanese citizenship" as part of their conditions for entry. A similar search of GuestHouseBank.com returns about 1,150 discrete sites (many with multiple apartments listed) of sharehouses saying exactly the same thing ("*Gaikokujin fuka.* Must have Japanese citizenship").[44] Another Google of Rakuten, Japan's Amazon.com, returned 301 sites of hotels, rental car agencies, and the like that expressly refuse foreign customers.[45] Notwithstanding the possibility of duplicate results within searches, this may indicate a widespread, codified system of exclusions throughout Japan's online hospitality industry.[46]

Interim Observations and Discussion of Generalizability

In sum, actions taken by activists that resulted in a confirmed successful full elimination of exclusionary rules happened in twenty-seven cases. Actions that were clearly unsuccessful in eliminating exclusionary rules numbered thirty-eight. Situations where the outcome was mixed or unclear total approximately 420. These numbers do not include the potentially hundreds of exclusionary apartments, job listings, and various services also found online.[47]

A potential criticism of this data set is, "How representative is the sampling?" Compared to the hundreds of thousands of other businesses open to the public in Japan that do not refuse "foreigners" entry, is it possible to generalize these cases as somehow representative of Japanese society?

I would argue that this is the wrong way to frame the research question. As mentioned in previous chapters, the question is not about a matter of degree, but rather about a matter of process. These are verified cases of exclusionary practices by physical appearance in Japan, and in this research they are not being cited to represent business practices across whole industries; they are being cited to show how the process of discrimination in Japan is manifested in specific examples. Thus, the question being answered by this chapter is not, "How *many* examples of discrimination are there in Japan?" but rather "*How* do people discriminate in Japan?" Once that is answered with sufficient sampling, then trends and justifications for discrimination can be analyzed for patterns that are, by definition, not representative of society as a whole, but instead for the purposes of this research are representative of how a society as a whole treats minorities. But before we begin this analysis, let us turn to the few examples of Japan's judiciary in cases where civil suits were brought against exclusionary businesses (or, in one case, against the government), for racial discrimination in specific.

CASE STUDIES OF CIVIL COURT LAWSUITS AGAINST DISCRIMINATORY BUSINESSES IN JAPAN

The next section gives three legal suits brought by excluded "foreigners" and/or naturalized Japanese citizens, with backgrounds of the case, the judicial decision, and precedents set:

The Ana Bortz Case, Hamamatsu, Shizuoka Prefecture (1998–1999)

Background[48]: On June 16, 1998, Ana Bortz, a Brazilian TV journalist, walked into a Hamamatsu jewelry store called Sebido to browse. The manager, Itsuyama Goro, asked her nationality, and upon hearing "Brazil," he came from behind the counter and physically (according to antitheft camera records of the event) tried to eject her from the premises.[49] When Bortz asked why, the manager went behind the counter, pulled from the wall an obscured notice indicating that his store was off-limits to "foreigners," and forcefully thrust it in her face. Bortz refused to move. The manager called the police, who then asked Bortz to leave, indicating that they could legally do nothing to stop the management refusing her service. Indignant at this treatment, Bortz decided to sue.

Result: On October 12, 1999, the Shizuoka District Court ruled in favor of Plaintiff Bortz, awarding her 1.5 million yen in damages for damages to honor (*meiyo kison*) and for mental anguish (*seishin kutsū*). Citing inter alia the CERD, presiding judge Sō Tetsuro ruled that Defendant Itsuyama refusing Bortz solely on the basis of being "foreign" was in violation of the treaty. TV Asahi announced with surprise that there are no civil or criminal laws against racial discrimination in Japan, so for the first time a case of discrimination specifically by race (not nationality)[50] was adjudged as illegal by applying international treaty as domestic law. Sebido did not appeal.

Postscript: The Ana Bortz Case became a positive precedent for people refused service for "looking foreign." The CERD could be enforced and result in a sizeable (by Japanese standards) court award. Moreover, "Japanese Only" signs that were proliferating around Hamamatsu at the time, according to Bortz in subsequent interviews (2000–2002), began to disappear (as of January 2010, the author has confirmed with local residents that there are apparently no visible signs up in Hamamatsu). Subsequently, the City of Hamamatsu, citing its status as the site of the Bortz Case, sponsored the *Hamamatsu Sengen* (Hamamatsu Declaration) in 2001, a joint communiqué between various local towns and cities, asking the national government to ensure better social welfare benefits and to ease visa restrictions for "foreigners" (since repeated in the similar *Toyoda Sengen* (2004), *Yokkaichi Sengen* (2006), and another lobbying effort by twenty-eight municipalities in 2009).

The Otaru Onsens Case, Otaru, Hokkaidō Prefecture (1993–2005)

Background[51]: From 1993, hot spring Otaru Onsen "Osupa" had "Japanese Only" signs up at its front doors, claiming that Russian sailors (who, at the time, were increasingly frequent visitors bringing business to the Hokkaidō port city of Otaru) were not following Japanese bathhouse rules. After alleged complaints from Japanese customers threatening to take their business elsewhere, Osupa put up exclusionary signs and refused all foreigners entry, regardless of whether or not they were Russian sailors, including the author on more than one occasion.

From 1995, a similar situation arose in a portside bathhouse named Panorama, and they took a similar path of putting up exclusionary signs.

Figure 3.4 Example of Trilingual Exclusionary Sign from Otaru Onsen Yunohana, September 19, 1999, Saying, "We refuse entry to foreigners." In online archive with field notes at www.debito.org/roguesgallery.html#Otaru are amended versions of this sign, and Otaru Onsen Osupa's "Japanese only" sign that became a template for other exclusionary businesses (see Misawa above). *Source:* Photo courtesy of author.

Management indicated in interviews that they were of two minds about enforcement, so sometimes the rules were enforced, other times not, depending on the level of Japanese language and whether or not the foreign-looking clientele were accompanied by Japanese.

From 1998, new "super *sentō*" bathhouse Yunohana opened with a "Japanese Only" sign on its front door. Management's claim in several interviews was that they had a similar experience with Russian sailors, and their previous sauna, located in a downtown nightlife district of Otaru, had allegedly been driven bankrupt by ill-mannered Russian bathers scaring away Japanese clientele. Although this account is disputed,[52] an undisputed fact of the case is that Yunohana had refused several customers (including some Japanese children of international marriages) whom they considered by physical appearance to be "foreigners," including the author numerous times.

More detail is necessary in this chapter because this is a firsthand account observed by the author: On September 19, 1999, the author and several friends, including Japanese families and their foreign spouses, visited Osupa, Panorama, and Yunohana to take a bath. The group included one phenotypically "White" German adult (Olaf Karthaus) and his Japanese-citizen family of four, one phenotypically "Asian" mainland Chinese citizen adult and her two Japanese-citizen children, two phenotypically "White" American-citizen adults (including the author) and their families (total five Japanese citizens), and several other Japanese-citizen friends.

Upon entry into Yunohana, the customers were immediately differentiated into "Japanese" and "Gaijin," with the latter "othered" and subordinated. The Visible Minorities (i.e., the German and two American adults) were immediately told they could not enter the premises, while their "Japanese" family members, including the Invisible Minority Chinese who could "pass," were allowed in. When it was later disclosed that the Chinese woman was Chinese (*chūgokujin*), Yunohana then refused her entry.

Discussion then ensued about Yunohana's guidelines for refusal. Although Yunohana continued to claim that they were refusing "foreigners" by nationality, the customers counterargued that it was in fact an issue of discrimination by race (*jinshu*), since Yunohana's admitting the Chinese woman clearly involved refusing "foreigners" on sight. My wife then queried about our young daughters, one of whom phenotypically looks more "Asian," the other more "Caucasian," respectively (see chapter 1). Yunohana replied that my older daughter could come in, but my younger daughter could not because she looked too much "like a foreigner" (*gaijin ppoi*). As both sisters were born and raised in Japan, spoke Japanese as their first language, and had Japanese bloodline and citizenship, "foreignness" was thus being determined by physical appearance, substantiating the argument that "Japanese Only" rules and signs were racial discrimination regardless of nationality.

Later that day, two other Otaru Onsens had mixed responses to the next visit of the group of international adults. (NB: The children, tired by this experience, did not attend further.) Onsen Panorama opened their doors to the "foreigners" after confirming that the "Japanese" in the group would "look after" (*mendō o miru*) their foreign counterparts. However, they still performatively differentiated between "Japanese" and "Gaijin" and would refuse all Gaijin entry unless there were extenuating circumstances.

More similar to Yunohana, Onsen Osupa unconditionally refused entry to the people who "looked foreign." However, to further investigate their treatment of Visible and Invisible Minorities, the author returned to Osupa on February 23, 2000, with Ainu activist Kayano Shiro (son of the late former Diet Member Kayano Shigeru) to see how Ainu would be treated. Osupa managers said that Kayano would of course be permitted entry because he has Japanese citizenship (*Nihon kokuseki*) (NB: the word *Nihonjin* for "Japanese" was not used in this context), but the author could not because he did not. Thus, further differentiation was made between Japan's Invisible and Visible Minorities, with the Visible Minority subordinated.

On October 31, 2000, the author, having received his Japanese citizenship two weeks earlier, went back to Yunohana with two Wajin Japanese friends (A-San and B-San), where the following exchange took place with the evening manager (transcript of an audio recording, excerpted)[53]:

DEBITO: Good evening.

CLERK IN LOBBY [to A-san and B-san]: Sorry, but we refuse service to all foreigners (*gaijin*).

DEBITO: I'm not a foreigner. I'm a Japanese . . .

[Manager appears after 2 minutes.]

MANAGER: Uh, I'm sorry to have to say this, well, I understand that you've naturalized. But the fact is that our policy is to refuse service to all foreigners (*gaikokujin*).

DEBITO: I'm not a foreigner. I'm a Japanese.

MANAGER: I understand that you've naturalized. Still, other foreigners (*gaikokujin*) have come here and we've refused service to all of them.

DEBITO: I'm not a foreigner. I am a Japanese (*Nihonjin*). I have Japanese citizenship. That means I'm not a foreigner.

MANAGER: I understand that, but . . . What I'm trying to say is that we Japanese (*wareware Nihonjin*) [*rest unintelligible*] . . .

DEBITO: . . . when you say "we," I also am part of that "we." I'll show you proof. [Brings out driver license.] . . . So even though you have seen my proof that I am a Japanese, does this mean that you are refusing me entry even though you are acknowledging that I am a Japanese?

MANAGER: As far as we go, uh, we understand what's going on, and we are not refusing you on the basis of that.

DEBITO: So does this mean that the problem is one of race? (*jinshu to iu mondai*)

MANAGER: There are lots of things involved here, but, uh, there is some understanding of that. You see, the problem is our customers . . . there's this thing about the Russians . . .

A-SAN: But he's naturalized . . .

DEBITO: So by my outward appearance (*gaiken*), I am refused entry.

MANAGER: Outward appearance, uh, well. I saw your proof and I acknowledge it. But when our other customers are here, meaning our other Japanese customers who hate [foreigners] . . . if "hate" is the appropriate word. But anyway if the numbers of our customers were to go down, we'd be in a tight situation, now, wouldn't we . . .?

DEBITO: . . . Well, the manager has seen the proof I presented, which a regular Japanese would not have to have shown. Even then, it resulted in my being refused entry. This is a matter of physical appearance . . . [The Manager] personally says that this is not so, but the fact is that if I am let in, afterwards the customers are going to have problems bathing with a gaijin [*sic*] and will stop coming, right?

MANAGER: Well, I wouldn't say it's all a matter of one person being let in having all this impact. But if this does start happening, in future, gaijin [*sic*] are going to come and [make trouble all over again].

A-SAN: But this is why you ought to tell customers that this person is a Japanese national.

MANAGER: I understand that. . . . We can explain his status. But most customers aren't going to come up and say anything, are they? . . .

DEBITO: The bottom line is that you are refusing me.

MANAGER: Uh-huh . . .

DEBITO: You are giving me lots of apologies, but the fact is that this is a matter of human rights. I am a Japanese, yet the Japanese Only policies are being applied to me. You took my money but you cannot take me like any other Japanese . . .

MANAGER: But we can see you are foreign. (*Mite mo wakarimasu kedo.*)

A-SAN: Okay, well, that's all right then for a Chinese, right? They look similar to a Japanese, and they can sneak in without your knowing it.

MANAGER: Acknowledged. In that case, if we don't talk to them, there's no way we would know otherwise . . .

DEBITO: Still, I showed you my proof [of Japanese citizenship].

MANAGER: I understand and acknowledge that.

DEBITO: And what are we supposed to do? Are we supposed to stamp on our foreheads "I'm a Japanese"? How are we supposed to show that we are Japanese? Look, I can't take off my face. I am a White person, but I am also a Japanese. I wonder if your customers are all that unable to understand that. I don't know for sure, but even though nobody has said that they are going to stop coming if you let me in, based upon your anticipation of such you are refusing me entry. That makes it a problem of human rights, right?

MANAGER: (*demurrer*)

DEBITO: Alright, I understand. Please give me my money back.

This excerpt is included in this chapter because it provides insights into the mindsets and terms involved in this discussion. Japanese citizenship was no longer a factor in the "Japanese Only" businesses' concept of a "Japanese." It was only a factor of visual identification. A person who "looked Japanese" could enter. Japan's Invisible Minorities could "pass." However, Japan's Visible Minorities—the Gaijin—could not, even after naturalization.

Result: After fifteen months of negotiations with city administrators, politicians, and the bathhouses (which resulted in Osupa and Panorama changing their rules to an open-door policy), Yunohana refused to remove their "Japanese Only" signs. On February 1, 2001, three excluded citizen and non-citizen patrons (the author was the Japanese citizen) took Onsen Yunohana to civil court for violations of the Japanese Constitution (Article 14 Clause 1), violations of the CERD, the International Covenant on Civil and Political Rights (ICCPR), and Japan Civil Code Articles 1 and 90. The claims were for racial discrimination, unequal treatment before the laws, and consequent mental duress (*seishin kutsū*). Plaintiffs also took the City of Otaru to court on the same grounds, further claiming that Otaru's negligence regarding the existence of racial discrimination in its jurisdiction from 1993 onward violated the CERD. Plaintiffs maintained that the City of Otaru must take responsibility for being the epicenter of racial discrimination in Hokkaidō, for its negligence provided the template for discriminators nationwide to put up their own "Japanese Only" signs (see Misawa section above).[54]

On November 11, 2002, the Sapporo District Court ruled that Onsen Yunohana was guilty of racial discrimination and would have to pay damages of one million yen to each plaintiff.[55] However, in contrast to the Bortz Case, the ruling held that although Yunohana had acted in a manner tantamount to racial discrimination, racial discrimination *per se* was not the illegal activity. Ruled illegal was, under judges' interpretation of the Civil Code, the act of "unrational discrimination [*sic*]" (*fugōriteki na sabetsu*)—in other words, "discrimination that transcended the boundaries of what is socially acceptable" (*shakaiteki ni kyoyō shiuru gendo o koeru sabetsu*).[56]

The court also ruled that the City of Otaru was not guilty of any violation of the law or international treaty. Plaintiffs argued that, as per the CERD (Article 2 1(d)), that Otaru must, as a local government bound by the treaty, take all measures, including legislation, to eliminate racial discrimination within its jurisdiction. Because the city government did not pass or draft legislation (such as a local ordinance (*jōrei*)) to that end, plaintiffs had argued that the city was culpable. The court disagreed, saying inter alia that drafting ordinances, and so on was "no more than a political duty" (*seijiteki na gimu*), and "the city does not have the specific duty towards each citizen without any other option (*ichigiteki*) but to pass an ordinance to outlaw a concrete case of racial discrimination." In other words, the court interpreted the CERD to say that the city could take other measures (e.g., issuing antidiscrimination pamphlets and holding awareness-raising forums) to eliminate racial discrimination, but it was not bounded to pass a law *in specific* against it, and could not be held accountable in court because it did not. The District Court added that the Japanese Constitution contains no statutes that "clearly oblige without any other option to establish an anti-discrimination ordinance"; matters such as these must be left to the city government's "discretion" (*sairyō*). The court also mentioned that the CERD (Article 6) makes no specific claim to substantive restitution or assistance.

Both Plaintiff Arudou and Defendant Yunohana appealed to Sapporo High Court. Plaintiff appealed against the ruling in favor of Otaru City, claiming the CERD requires all signatories to take all *effective* measures against racial discrimination, and all their measures (pamphlets, forums, etc.)[57] had clearly not been effective against onsens with exclusionary signs up since 1993; therefore, because they had not passed an antidiscrimination ordinance, they had not taken all effective measures. Meanwhile Defendant Yunohana's appeal claimed the ruling was too punitive, insinuating that Plaintiffs were troublemakers who deliberately got refused for personal profit (*atariya*), not intending to be real customers.

On September 16, 2004, the Sapporo High Court upheld both sides of the District Court ruling.[58] Defendant Yunohana was still liable for one million yen to each plaintiff, while the City of Otaru was again not liable. The High Court accepted the lower court's arguments against Defendant Yunohana verbatim, while it amended inter alia the court's arguments regarding the Plaintiff Otaru City side of the ruling to say that a court holding a local government responsible for not passing laws would be a violation of the separation of powers (*sanken bunritsu*) between the legislative and judicial branches.[59] The Sapporo High Court thus countermanded the precedent set in the Bortz Case by interpreting the CERD as a general abstract treatise, not as a concrete law or policy, providing no absolute terms for the establishment or promulgation of concrete antidiscrimination laws. Therefore, the discretionary powers of legislation in the city's hands were now a matter of domestic political duties, not of international treaties.[60]

Defendant Yunohana did not appeal. Plaintiff Arudou appealed the Otaru City decision to the Supreme Court. On April 7, 2005, the Supreme Court dismissed the appeal under Civil Lawsuits Code Article 312 Clauses 1 (regarding misinterpretations of the law and constitutional issues) and 2 (regarding void court judgments), and under Article 318 Clause 1 (regarding misinterpretations of the law and conflicting precedents with other Supreme Court rulings).[61] Judges ruled that this matter was not matériel for the Supreme Court, as it was somehow not a constitutional issue. The CERD was not alluded to in the ruling.

In conclusion, the Otaru Onsens Case further clarified Japanese jurisprudence after the Ana Bortz Case. Although the Bortz Case ruled that the CERD had the force of law in Japan—due to the lack of another law against racial discrimination—judges in the Otaru Case instead ruled that the CERD was not binding, and that civil laws (e.g., "discriminating that went beyond social conventions," implying that there were tolerable levels of discrimination within social convention) were binding instead—to be adjudged case-by-case at the discretion of each case of discrimination brought before Japan's judiciary. It also ruled that for Defendant Otaru City, the CERD was not binding due to its lack of concreteness, and that the lack of a law against racial discrimination was not legally actionable (thereby creating an incentive system for governments to not pass laws at all).[62]

Postscript: The Otaru Onsens Case has been alluded to in US State Department Country Reports on Human Rights (2002–2008), the MOJ's Human Rights Week programs (2009, item seven), and in GOJ reports to the CERD Committee (1999, 2001, and 2008; see chapter 8). Its legal reasoning has been cited as precedent in at least one other civil court case regarding discrimination.[63] It also appears in general discussions on whether or not discrimination by *race* actually exists in Japan because (as mentioned in chapter 2 and further developed in chapter 7) the phenomenon is generally rendered in Japanese not as *racial* discrimination (*jinshu sabetsu*) but as *ethnic* discrimination (*minzoku sabetsu*), or as discrimination against people for physical appearance (*gaiken sabetsu*), national origin (*mimoto sabetsu*), nationality (*gaikokujin sabetsu*), or more general cultural misunderstandings (*gokai*)).

As mentioned earlier (more in chapter 8), the UN has repeatedly noted how racial discrimination in Japan is "deep and profound" and "practiced undisturbed in Japan,"[64] concluding that Japan is not respecting its international treaty obligations. Devoting an entire paragraph in his 2006 report to the Otaru Case, UN Rapporteur Diene recommended that domestic educational practices be modified to encourage racial tolerance, and a comprehensive national law against discrimination be drafted. The UN Committees covering the CERD and the ICCPR have also noted on multiple occasions that the fundamental legal logic grounding the Otaru Case, that of "unrational/irrational discrimination" (or "reasonable discrimination," depending on the translation), is "incompatible with Article 26 of the [ICCPR] Covenant," most notably in 1998 (long before the Otaru Case was taken to court) that "the arguments advanced by the State party in support of this concept are the same as had been advanced during the consideration of the third periodic report, and which the Committee found to be unacceptable."[65] In response, the Japanese government refused to comment on individual cases; and through its interpretation of the definition of "descent" (as in ethnic origin), effectively asserted that the CERD covers nobody in Japan.[66] Thus, the Otaru Case made clear to the world how the debate on racial discrimination is avoided or studiously ignored in Japan.

The McGowan Case, Daitō City, Ōsaka Prefecture (2004–2006)

Background[67]: On September 4, 2004, African American and Kyōto resident Steve McGowan was introducing an eyeglass store named "G.Style," from whom he had purchased glasses before, to a black South African friend. However, the manager of the store, Narita Takashi, seeing two black people standing in front about to enter, rushed outside and said to them, according to McGowan, "I don't like black people (*kokujin ga kirai*)! Don't touch the door! Don't touch the shop window! Go away!" Narita later claimed both in an interview with the author and in court that he had been advised to turn away the two customers by a neighbor who, frightened of black people, had telephoned him shortly beforehand; he also acknowledged that he had refused McGowan entry due to a personal and visceral dislike of black people due to a prior negative experience with one in Germany. McGowan took G.Style to Ōsaka District Court for mental distress and demanded damages of 5.5 million yen.

On January 30, 2006, the Ōsaka District Court rejected McGowan's claim. The legal logic was as follows: (1) McGowan's Japanese language abilities were (in the judge's estimation) low enough that the former might have misunderstood Defendant's Japanese, as Plaintiff was apparently not able to distinguish between the words "foreigner" (*gaikokujin*) and "black person" (*kokujin*); (2) when confirming Defendant's actions, Plaintiff's wife also did not confirm whether the refusal was due to him being specifically black, or just "foreign"; (3) since Plaintiff was suing for discrimination against black people (*kokujin sabetsu*) *in specific* (i.e., not discrimination against "foreigners" in general), the case was dismissed.

Although the decision acknowledges that Defendant Narita's "racial discrimination is clear," he was not adjudged guilty of racial discrimination as an illegal activity, or of any illegal activity.[68] Scholars and journalists investigating the case afterward raised troubling questions about precedents set,[69] for example, (1) Why did the ruling focus less upon G.Style's motivations for refusing McGowan entry, more on debunking McGowan's wife's testimony and reconfirmation of evidence? (2) Why did the judge base his verdict on alleged communication misunderstandings between McGowan and G.Style, especially since there was recorded evidence and court testimony by G.Style's manager admitting, (a) he does not like black people, and (b) he refused McGowan entry because McGowan is black? (3) Why was a semantic differentiation made between "black" and "foreign"—is one not a subset of the other, and is the effect not the same?

Result: The Ōsaka District Court ruling thus set the standard of evidence for proving discrimination impossibly high. By claiming a language barrier, the judge now created precedent for dismissing a "foreigner's" testimony by dint of not being a native speaker. The judge also dismissed testimony on semantics, without dealing with the motives of the Defendant's refusal. Under these judicial litmus tests, the only way to litigate against a discriminator would be for a "foreigner" (a) to be a native speaker, or to have a native speaker accompanying at all times when the discriminating act perchance happens; (b) to have a recording device (audio or video) ready and switched on at all times; (c) to have the alleged discriminator make it clear that the motive is discrimination is due to "race" or "nationality," and then sue for mental duress due to discrimination under those terms verbatim. Even when all these terms would reasonably be satisfied, there is apparently no guarantee—for all these conditions were satisfied in the McGowan Case. Yet the court ruled against the Plaintiff.

Postscript: McGowan appealed. On October 18, 2006, the Ōsaka High Court overturned the District Court ruling, awarding McGowan 350,000 yen, which was, according to McGowan in a 2006 conversation, insufficient to cover incurred legal fees. However, the ruling did not recognize the refusal as a result of disliking black people as an act of racial discrimination (i.e., "not enough to be recognized as racially discriminatory"), rather as an illegal act for being "beyond social norms," that is, "a one-sided and outrageous act beyond common sense."[70] As in the Otaru Onsens Case, this left the interpretation of "discriminating too much" up to the judiciary on a case-by-case basis. The District Court ruling, however, indicated how much discretion Japanese judges have to determine that degree. In the absence of a law against racial discrimination, the legal codification remains vague, and court awards were thus reduced below any punitive or rewarding level—from the around one million yen set by the Otaru Case etc to 350,000 yen. This would neither punish the discriminator sufficiently to deter further discrimination, nor cover the legal costs of any plaintiff who wished to spend the years and substantial court fees on a civil suit in Japan.

The Ibrahim Yener Case, Yodogawa-ku, Ōsaka Prefecture (2016–2017)

Background[71]: In October 2016, Ibrahim Yener, a Turkish national, was refused service by an Ōsaka secondhand car auction dealer named Nihon Autoplaza when he applied to buy a car through their web page contact form.

Nihon Autoplaza replied with an email in Japanese indicating they do not serve foreign customers, also that even if the customer legally holds Japanese citizenship, they only deal with people who can "hold their own" (*sonshoku ga nai*) in a conversation with native speakers of Japanese. After a follow-up phone call where the owner refused to compromise or apologize, Yener, who said he had suffered enough cases of discrimination in his fourteen years of residence, decided to take Nihon Autoplaza to court in March 2017, claiming damages for racial discrimination (*jinshu sabetsu*). Notably, Yener navigated the Japanese judicial system alone, without a lawyer speaking on his behalf.

Result: In August 2017, Yener won in the Ōsaka District Court, ruling that the case was a case of "discriminating against him merely on grounds that he is a foreign national," not of discrimination by race. Yener says the reason for his victory was (a) because the evidence was "100 percent legitimate" and in writing, and (b) because of the Defendant's courtroom antics. In Yener's words:

> Anyway, that sick-minded person shows up at court room with a mask on his face. And the judge asked him to remove that mask, but he replied, "There is a foreigner here. I have to protect my privacy." The judge became so angry and told him that "Here is a court room, there is no privacy in here. Either you take that mask off or leave the court room." So, he replied, "Let me think about it." The judge told him that "I am not asking you to remove that mask off, I am ordering you to take that mask off or leave immediately."

This testimony is included because the case is unclear, given the standards of evidence seen above in the McGowan Case, whether Yener would still have won if the Defendant had not angered the judge. Nihon Autoplaza did not appeal.

The Yener Case shows three important developments: First, it is another affirmed court case where the judge unilaterally ruled that the discrimination was by nationality, not race. Second, it demonstrates the unbroken downward trend of court awards in discrimination cases. As noted above, Bortz was awarded two million yen (about $20,000), and each plaintiff in the Otaru Case one million yen. Despite suing for one million yen in damages, Yener was only awarded 200,000 yen, about half of McGowan's award of 350,000 yen after appeal. Third, Nihon Autoplaza's management refused Yener service despite any visual identification. Their interactions were only online and on the phone, not in person, yet Yener was refused on the grounds of Japanese language ability only (despite their written and phone communication taking place only in Japanese, and Yener's demonstrated ability to navigate a legal system that even native speakers would find challenging). Thus, as online interactions in business increase, the default presumption that "foreigners" cannot communicate in Japanese is being used to deny service.

SUMMARY OF FINDINGS

Patterns of Exclusionism within Exclusionary Businesses

Patterns of exclusionism follow, with the locations in parenthesis afterward:
Types of Exclusionism

1) Exclusion of "all foreigners" (however determined), with no exceptions (e.g., Wakkanai, Monbetsu, Otaru dining bar, Fukushima, Akihabara, Asakusa tempura, Aoyama Dōri, Ōmiya, Azuma-Mura, Okazaki, Hiroshima, Kurashiki, Kōfu, Sapporo, Misawa, Ōkubo, Tōkyō Azabu, Koshigaya, Kurashiki, Isesaki, Gunma Ōta, Saitama Toda, Ishikawa Nonoichi, Tsukiji, Kyōto, Kōbe soul bar, Nagasaki steakhouse, Okinawa billiards, Hamamatsu, Ōsaka realtor, Okinawa diving, Hokkaidō orthopedic, Takadanobaba job search agency, *Japan Times* want ads, online exclusions)
2) Exclusion of "all foreigners" unless they spoke sufficient Japanese (Kōfu, Kyōto, Fukushima, Monbetsu, Ogikubo, Ōkubo, Akita, Kitakyūshū, Wakkanai, Sapporo, Misawa, Okinawa karaoke, Ōsaka Yodogawa, Kyōto hotel, Tōkyō gym chain)
3) Exclusion of "all foreigners" unless they were accompanied by "Japanese" (Fukushima, Monbetsu, Kitakyūshū, Misawa, Hokkaidō golf)
4) Exclusion of "all foreigners" unless they themselves were verifiably "Japanese" despite "foreign" phenotype (Kabukichō, Ogikubo, Kōfu)
5) Targeted exclusion of "certain types of foreigners" (such as black people or specific nationalities) due to excluder's personal dislike of that type (Daitō, Otaru, Wakkanai, Monbetsu, Misawa, Hamamatsu)
6) Separate facilities for "foreigners" only (Wakkanai, Kyōto)
7) "Members only" systems (where all Japanese are automatically "members" but "foreigners" are not) (Sapporo, Nagoya)

Justifications Offered by Excluders for Exclusionism (most frequent first, including duplicate cases)

1) Language barriers/lack of language support/lack of multicultural or multilingual support/lack of appropriate facilities on the part of the excluder: 17 (Wakkanai, Monbetsu, Misawa, Ōkubo, Fukushima, Aoyama Dōri, Tsukiji, Kōfu, Kyōto, Kitakyūshū, Okinawa billiards, Okinawa karaoke, Asakusa tempura, Ōsaka Yodogawa, Hokkaidō orthopedic, Tōkyō gym chain, Kyōto hotel).

2) General fear of "foreigners" by either the excluder or the excluder's alleged customer base: 11 (Otaru, Sapporo, Monbetsu, Wakkanai, Kōfu, Kitakyūshū, Hiroshima, Misawa, Okinawa billiards, Hamamatsu, Asakusa tempura).
3) An allegedly demonstrated (or anticipated) inability of "foreigners" (in general) to follow Japanese rules: 8 (Otaru, Wakkanai, Akita, Kōfu, Azuma-mura, Tsukiji, Hamamatsu, Asakusa tempura).
4) Foreign crime or fear of foreign crime: 8 (Monbetsu, Misawa, Akihabara, Kōfu, Ōkubo, Sapporo, Okinawa billiards, Hamamatsu).
5) Preservation of "Japanese atmosphere" (*fun'iki*) of safety and calm (e.g., *anzen to anshin*): 7 (Otaru, Wakkanai, Monbetsu, Misawa, Akita, Ogikubo, Hiroshima).
6) Organized standardized signposting of exclusionary rules: 6 (Sapporo, Misawa, Monbetsu, Kabukichō, Fukushima, Kyōto).
7) Precedent (set by other excluders, such as exclusionism in neighboring businesses or other cities): 5 (Otaru, Wakkanai, Misawa, Monbetsu, Kōfu).
8) Sanitation and health concerns: 5 (Otaru, Kōfu, Kabukichō, Asakusa tempura, Nagasaki).
9) "Foreigners'" undesirable behavior by specific nationality, such as Russian sailors or American soldiers: 4 (Otaru, Wakkanai, Hiroshima, Misawa).
10) Survival of the excluder's business: 4 (Otaru, Monbetsu, Wakkanai, Kōfu)
11) An alleged basis for exclusion in Japanese law: 3 (Akihabara, Kōfu, Okinawa diving).
12) Claimed psychological inability to handle "foreigners": 2 (Asakusa tempura, Ōsaka Yodogawa).
13) Wartime memories: 1 (Kōfu).
14) Personal dislike of certain races: 1 (Daitō).
15) Excluded "foreigners" deliberately coming to the premises to be excluded and make trouble: 1 (Otaru).
16) Miscommunication: 1 (Tōkyō Minami-Azabu).
17) Reasons unknown (i.e., no justification given) 14+ (Ōmiya, Takadanobaba, Koshigaya, Kurashiki, Ishikawa Nonoichi, Nagoya, Fukushima, Toda, Isesaki, Ōta, Ōsaka realtor, Otaru dining bar, Kōbe soul bar, *Japan Times* want ads, online exclusions).

Discussion: Of the cases discussed in this book, refusals have been most frequently justified by language issues, followed by customer pressure, potential crime and rule-breaking, safety, and peer pressure. Less frequent, at least as vocalized by excluders, were overt hatred of specific races, business survival, health concerns, and legal issues. In other words, the most likely reason for refusing "foreigners" service is the assumption they cannot communicate in Japanese, followed by the fear-based anticipation of either Japanese or foreign customer behavior. None of these factors are based upon the evidenced behavior of the individual foreigners themselves, which is, naturally, the definition of prejudice.

Patterns within Administrative Guidance Regarding Exclusionism

In cases where incidents of exclusionary establishments were brought before (a) local authorities, (b) bureaucratic organs entrusted with enforcing human rights, (c) official law enforcement agencies, and/or (d) media outlets (for exposure of the issue to public debate), these were the outcomes:

1) Officials claimed they were powerless to stop the exclusionary behavior due to a lack of legal enforcement framework: 4 (Otaru Onsens, Wakkanai, Hamamatsu).
2) Officials ignored or refused requests for public action: 10 (Sapporo, Monbetsu, Kitakyūshū, Wakkanai, Ōkubo, Misawa, Otaru Onsens, Otaru dining bar, Ōsaka realtor, *Japan Times* want ads).
3) Officials took action: 12 (Otaru Onsens, Sapporo, Misawa, Kyōto, Kitakyūshū, Kōfu, Monbetsu, Fukushima, Ōsaka Yodogawa, Hokkaidō orthopedic, Kyōto hotel, Nagasaki).
4) Media reported on the exclusionary behavior and official-level actions, if any: 13 (Otaru Onsens, Wakkanai, Monbetsu, Akita, Kōfu, Fukushima, Kabukichō, Azuma-mura, Daitō, Hamamatsu, Hokkaidō golf, Ōsaka Yodogawa, Hokkaidō orthopedic).
5) Media did not report on the exclusionary behavior, despite having it brought to their attention: 4 (Misawa, Ishikawa Nonoichi, Sapporo, Ōsaka realtor).
6) Activists put pressure on the excluder without any appeals to government or media: 16 (Ōmiya, Okinawa billiards, Okinawa karaoke, Okinawa diving, Kabukichō nightlife, Koshigaya nightlife, Aoyama Dōri, Ogikubo, Azabu, Central Japan nightlife, Tsukiji, Nagoya, Kyōto, Kōbe soul bar, Takadanobaba, Tōkyō gym chain).

Discussion: In cases discussed in this book, government officials taking action on discrimination happened less than half the time; more frequently, officials ignored the situation or abdicated their responsibility. Media was more responsive, reporting on discrimination when notified three out of every four times. However, activists in recent years have been more likely to take matters into their own hands, opting to use internet communities to apply pressure on the excluder.

Patterns within Judicial Opinions Regarding Exclusionism

In instances where cases of exclusionary businesses were taken before a court of law with claims of racial discrimination (the Ana Bortz Case, the Otaru Onsens Case, the Steve McGowan Case, and the Ibrahim Yener Case), the following patterns were observed:

Patterns for Punishing or Admonishing Excluders

1) Excluders were told that categorically denying entry to "foreigners" evinces discrimination by nationality (Yener Case). But denial to a naturalized Japanese citizen is discrimination based upon "whether one appears to be foreign, [which is] discrimination by race, skin color, descent, ethnic origin or racial origin" (Otaru Case, Sapporo District Court).[72]
2) Excluders were told that as an institution open to the public and licensed by the authorities, they were "discriminating too much," that is, beyond what is "rational discrimination" under social norms permitted by society (Otaru Case, Sapporo District Court).
3) Excluders were told their actions were illegal as racial discrimination under international treaty, which in the absence of domestic law against racial discrimination instead had the force of law (Bortz Case).
4) Excluders were told that actively disliking a particular "race" was a form of racial discrimination (McGowan Case).

Patterns for not Punishing or Admonishing Excluders

1) Excluders were excluding based upon unclear or unconfirmed grounds (McGowan Case).
2) Excluders were excluding for grounds not specifically claimed in court by the excluded (McGowan Case).
3) Excluders were misunderstood, due to a language barrier on the part of the excluded (McGowan Case).
4) Excluders were misunderstood due to incomplete questions from the excluded (McGowan Case).
5) Excluders were misunderstood due to insufficient evidence of "racially discriminatory remarks" presented by the excluded (McGowan Case).[73]

Patterns for Punishing or Admonishing the Authorities

There was no legal sanction taken or admonishment given against the authorities in the only case where a government body was sued for racial discrimination (Otaru Case).

Patterns for Not Punishing or Admonishing the Authorities (Specifically as Seen in the Otaru Case)

1) The details of the case are not a constitutional or international treaty issue, because the Japanese Constitution and the CERD and ICCPR only govern relations between the state and the individual, not between private persons such as excluded Plaintiffs and Defendant Onsen (Sapporo District Court).[74]
2) No applicable domestic law applies to issues of racial discrimination. Extant laws apply to issues of public hygiene (Sapporo District Court).
3) Punishing the government for the lack of applicable laws punishing racial discrimination would be a violation of the separation of powers on the part of the judiciary (Sapporo High Court).
4) Punishing the government for lack of legislative action to outlaw racial discrimination would be a violation of the separation of powers on the part of the judiciary (Sapporo High Court).
5) Eliminating racial discrimination is a political obligation, not a "clear and uniform obligation to prohibit and bring to an end specific acts of racial discrimination by enacting laws between individual citizens" (Sapporo District Court).[75]
6) The government has a political obligation toward the citizenry as a whole, with "no legal obligation to pass a law relating to the rights of an individual citizen" (Sapporo District Court).[76]
7) The government did take some measures that were effective in raising public awareness and eliminating racial discrimination behavior in some places (Sapporo District Court).
8) It is difficult to see what else the government could have done to eliminate racial discrimination beyond the measures they did take (Sapporo District Court).
9) There is no provision in domestic law or in international treaty to a "substantive requirement to provide compensation or relief" to claimants of racial discrimination (Sapporo District Court).[77]
10) Eliminating racial discrimination and the choice of what measures to take, if any, is at the "discretion" of the government (Sapporo District and High Courts).
11) Application of international treaty banning racial discrimination (such as the CERD) is problematic since there is no clear codification within for application (Sapporo District Court).
12) The details of the case are not a constitutional issue, for reasons unspecified (Supreme Court of Japan).

THEMES OF DISCRIMINATION WITHIN CHAPTER 3'S FINDINGS

These were some of the more abstract themes seen within each category of findings:

Themes within Exclusionary Businesses' Practices

1) "Foreigners" were excluded based upon verifiably "foreign" characteristics, as defined and determined on sight by the staff/manager on duty. If no visible contact was possible (such as Yener's remote interactions), then alleged language barriers and the potential for miscommunication became grounds for refusal.
2) Sometimes mitigating circumstances were taken into account, such as the excluded person's local knowledge, Japanese citizenship, and Japanese language ability.
3) Although some "foreigners" were sometimes excluded based upon fear or hatred of a certain "race"/"type" of "foreigner," the more common justification given was based upon probable language barriers, or behaviors/attributions that excluders' or their Japanese customer base was allegedly making about "foreigners."
4) Most excluders, when asked, offered justifications for their exclusionism, and many were willing to listen to counterarguments from activists and/or the excluded people.
5) Fundamentally, there was a demonstrated confusion on the part of excluders about how to define "foreigner" when excluding—whether it meant all *gaikokujin* (i.e., including Invisible Minorities, which would include Zainichis born and raised in Japan), or whether it meant strictly those they could visually identify as Gaijin (i.e., strictly the Visible Minorities). Further confusion was created when the author and multiracial children were excluded then identified as Japanese citizens.
6) This confusion was haphazardly resolved, sometimes with continued exclusion despite Japanese citizenship, sometimes with admittance to the premises being granted.
7) Few excluders said that they saw their actions as specifically constituting "racial discrimination" (*jinshu sabetsu*), more as managerial prerogative.
8) Even if excluders acknowledged the unfairness of the situation, it was usually justified as a tragic circumstance one could do nothing about (*shikata ga nai*), or as a simple business decision based upon "differentiation" of customer base (*kubetsu*), not active "discrimination" (*sabetsu*).

Themes within the Official/Structural-Level Reactions to Exclusionary Businesses' Practices

Again, defining the "official/structural" level as local authorities, bureaucratic organs entrusted with enforcing human rights, official law enforcement agencies, the judiciary, and/or media outlets, these were the general themes found:

1) Officials were more likely to be inactive when simply notified of the exclusionary practices, citing the lack of legal enforcement framework to stop this kind of exclusionism.
2) Officials were more likely to be active while the media was in the process of reporting on the exclusionary practices.
3) The media and organs of the state, including the judiciary, rarely portrayed the exclusionary practices as grounded in "racial discrimination" (*jinshu sabetsu*), more as issues of misunderstandings and differences in culture (more in chapter 7).
4) Even when these exclusions were deemed "discriminatory" in nature, they were still generally not seen as an illegal activity *due to racial discrimination*, because of a lack of domestic legal framework against racism.
5) Over time, within the scope of the Bortz, Otaru, McGowan, and Yener Cases, less judicial emphasis has been put on the force of international treaty, more on the burden of proof regarding the nature of the discrimination, the constitutionality and the structure of governance, the quality of proof presented by the excluded regarding their own exclusions, and the Japanese language ability of the people being excluded.
6) Over time, court awards to victims of discrimination have steadily diminished, reducing incentives for the discriminated to file cases (i.e., they will probably lose money after court fees, even if they win after many months of litigation), and reducing the effectiveness of the judiciary as a means to deter discriminators through financial penalties.

As this lengthy chapter demonstrates, the rubrics that excluders use to distinguish between a "Japanese" and a "foreigner" is a complicated one. This is what happens when Japanese citizenship/nationality are not determined and enforced through one simple rubric: legal status. When racists are able to resort to phenotype, in comes the gray area: Japanese citizens who by any arbitrary standard do not "look Japanese" get excluded as foreign. This is also what happens when no laws exist to protect people against racial discrimination: bigots and xenophobes can exclude people they visually disapprove of, justified by any reason they can come up with—regardless of the situation, the qualifications and backgrounds of the people involved, or the behavior of the individual excluded. Prejudice and discrimination are thus odious forces, corrupting societies with cognitive dissonances that foster all manner of dehumanizing behavior discussed in the Introduction. That is why all of the other G7 advanced industrialized societies have some form of a law against them, and the UN established an international convention against it.

POSTSCRIPT FOR THE SECOND EDITION

As some of the cases in this chapter are around twenty years old, it is necessary to reflect upon the impact of time on the data set. Most of the places surveyed in the First Edition's data set have taken their signs down and, if still in business, kept them down. Part of this no doubt due to Japan's "Yōkoso Japan" tourism boom, with international arrivals tripling from 2013 to hit a pre-pandemic record of 31 million in 2018.[78] Foreign tourists have been a boon for these service industries (particularly bathhouses!)[79] and created a huge incentive to rescind their exclusionary rules. Other businesses have simply disappeared due to a shrinking market or natural attrition, and their exclusionary rules probably did not help. So does this mean that one can make the case that "discrimination is bad business," that is, that economic forces will resolve the situation, therefore laws against racial discrimination are unnecessary?

That would be a hasty conclusion. Some of the businesses are still in business despite maintaining exclusionary rules (notably, the Hokkaidō Classic Golf Club), and other exclusionary businesses have been added anew since the First Edition; there will no doubt be more in future because the activity remains legal. In fact, this new round of research found the largest proliferation of "no foreigner" rules is in cyberspace, as xenophobic landlords find support in online accommodation sites willing to overlook or abet their exclusionary practices. This is in fact part of a worldwide trend. With the rise of internet ideological extremism (see chapter 11 in this book), xenophobic views and business practices have found succor in communities of online bigotry.

This is why Japan needs codified antidiscrimination laws to stop racists from putting prejudice into practice (for as seen in the Kōfu and Nagasaki cases above, if a local government has an interest or a duty to get exclusionary signs down, this can be accomplished quite rapidly). Without them, it has become increasingly hard to stop this activity. As noted above, activists and protestors of discrimination are increasingly resorting to tactics outside regular channels of appeals to government or media, as there are fewer opportunities to confront discriminators face-to-face, less manageable "hooks" about the problem to provide media, or any specific laws to point to for government agencies to enforce.

In fact, as seen in the case of Plaintiff Yunohana (which became very successful after all the Otaru Onsens lawsuit publicity, opening three new branches and prospering to this day),[80] discrimination can even become a sales point, especially as exclusions proliferate to the point of being "normal": part of, as we saw in the opening of chapter 2, "how Japan does business."

In addition, the argument that "discrimination is bad business," which assumes that the invisible hand of capitalism has karmic powers, ignores the requirement that Japan observe its United Nations treaty promises. When Japan effected the UN CERD in 1996, it promised to eliminate all racial discrimination with legal measures "without delay." As of 2021, more than a quarter century later, that unfulfilled promise is older than almost all of the cases cataloged in this book, strongly indicating this situation cannot be ignored in favor of economic arguments. Anticipating economic solutions to human rights problems is generally untenable, because "Japanese Only" rules, like many socially toxic practices throughout history, will always be advantageous and profitable to someone until a society outlaws them.

SUMMARY AND CONCLUSION

This chapter analyzed fieldwork surveys of exclusionary businesses nationwide in Japan between the early 1990s and 2021. The data was summarized and then categorized by patterns and themes. The conclusive findings from this chapter point to a confusion between who is "Japanese" and "not Japanese" on two levels. One confusion takes place at the Micro level, that is, on the part of individual "Japanese Only" businesses that exclude "foreigners." Their criteria for determining "foreignness" are sometimes based upon legal extranationality (i.e., people without Japanese citizenship, regardless of physical appearance), and sometimes visual identification despite legal nationality (i.e., people with Japanese citizenship who do not "look Japanese"). The other confusion takes place at the structural/official Macro level, where local authorities, bureaucratic organs entrusted with enforcing human rights, official law enforcement agencies, the judiciary, and/or media outlets found it difficult to define "a Japanese" in a non-racialized way. This research argues that this confusion occurs because the dominant discourse in Japan encourages all levels of Japanese society to differentiate between "Japanese" and "foreign" on physical appearance and visual identification. This discourse also encourages people to "other" those who are identified as "not Japanese" and subordinate them in terms of civil rights and equal protection under the law.

The next chapters in part III of this book will explore the elements of this discourse within Japan's laws, law enforcement, policymaking, and media.

NOTES

1. Cited in Majima (2013: 398).

2. The anger that racial discrimination incurs has in Japan's case caused a history of irrationality that influences its identity and self-image to the world to this day. According to Majima (2013: 398–401):

> [T]he Emperor Showa (1901–1989) saw the exclusion Act as "a remote cause of the Pacific War." . . . In fact, opinions against the Japanese Exclusion Act were an immediate reason for public outcry in Japan. The population had become exasperated by the weak-kneed diplomacy that brought national dishonor amidst the emotional bashing from the mass media. This manifested in extremely emotional and near mass-hysteric situation, such as the suicides near the American Embassy on May 31, the follow-up suicides, the events for consoling the spirits of the deceased, and the countless letters sent to the Naval Department calling for war against the United States . . .
>
> American's racial categorization aggravated Japan's anger, which turned to anxiety as a result of Japan's diminishing sense of belonging in the world; "the world being limited to the Western powers," as Tokutomi cited earlier, even if Japan earned a status equal to that of the Western powers, there would still be a great "distance" between them, namely one of racial and religious differences, and the whole difference between the East and West. The sentiment of being a "solitary wanderer" rejected by the West contradicts the manner in which Japan brought about its own isolation. Tokutomi also asserted that the express "Asian" had no other meaning beyond the geographical, and thus Japan's self-perceptions and identity no longer belonged to Asia. The sense of isolation was actually based on the denial of "Asia," and it came from Japan's own identification built upon the idea of "Quit Asia and Join Europe." It could be said that Japan's contradictory identification came to reveal Japan's inability to identify with either the East or the West, a situation that came about through the emergence of a consciousness of the racial distance, especially from 1919 to 1924.

Let's highlight the irrational behavior caused by racial discrimination: Mass hysteria? Suicides? Rumors of war? Feeling rejected by the West after the elites had taken a risk and turned the national narrative away from the East? Thereby laying the groundwork for Postwar Japan's narrative of uniqueness and exceptionalism that contributes to the irrational and hypocritical behavior (especially vis-à-vis racial discrimination toward anyone NOT "Japanese") found in future chapters of this book?

Yet during Prewar Japan (when Japan was colonizing), the GOJ denied that it could even ideologically *practice* racial discrimination, since it was liberating fellow members of the Asian race (Oguma 2002: 332–333). As will be discussed in chapter 8, to this day there are still official denials that it exists in Japan, or that Japanese even understand the concept of racial discrimination because Japanese society allegedly has no races (see chapter 7). However, as this chapter documents, racial discrimination does happen in Japan. When that is pointed out, out comes an irrational torrent of logic denying that it's actually racial (or that it's happening at all), or arguing that it's not the same as the racial discrimination in other countries. This thread is intertwined, as Majima demonstrates, with a historical narrative of racialized victimization.

3. This cognitive dissonance sometimes appears in opinion columns. On February 11, 2015, the mainstream daily newspaper *Sankei Shinbun* ran a column by octogenarian novelist and adviser to the Abe Shinzō government Sono Ayako, who called for racial segregation in Japan, specifically citing South Africa's Apartheid system favorably. "Since learning about the situation in South Africa twenty or thirty years ago, I've come to think that whites, Asians, and blacks should live separately. . . . People can work, research, and socialize together. But only in terms of residence should they be separated." She specifically called the Apartheid system "racial discrimination" (*jinshu sabetsu*) before going on to advocate it. One logical outcome of this cognitive dissonance was that if Japan instituted Apartheid, it would not be racial discrimination—just an obvious means of social ordering for Japan due to the inherently irreconcilable differences between the races. Despite widespread domestic and international criticism, and written protests from a domestic Japan-Africa NPO and the South African Ambassador to Japan, neither the author nor the newspaper retracted the story. *See* "*Tekido na kyori tamochi ukeire o*" [Let them in—but keep a distance]. *Sankei Shinbun*, February 11, 2015; "*Sono Ayako-san 'imin o ukeire, jinshu de wakete kyojū saseru beki' Sankei Shinbun de shuchō*." [Sono Ayako claims in Sankei Shinbun that "immigrants should be accepted, but should have their living places separated by race]." *Huffington Post Japan*, February 11, 2015; "Author Sono calls for racial segregation in op-ed piece." *Japan Times*, February 12, 2015; "Japan PM ex-adviser praises apartheid in embarrassment for Abe." *Reuters*, February 13, 2015; "*Sono shi koramu de minami-A chūnichi taishi ga honshi ni kōgi*" [South African Ambassador protests Sono's column in this paper]. *Sankei Shinbun*, February 14, 2015; "*Sankei Shinbun: Sono Ayako shi ga koramu ni NPO hōjin ga tekkai motome kōgibun*" [Sankei Shinbun: NPO demands Sono Ayako column be retracted in protest letter]. *Mainichi Shinbun* February 14, 2015; "South African ambassador slams Sankei op-ed by Sono praising apartheid." *Japan Times*, February 15, 2015; "Outrage as top author backs racial segregation." *South China Morning Post*, February 15, 2015; and so on.

4. The fact that these "Japanese Only" businesses are open to the public is not insignificant, because if Japan were to observe the CERD, these exclusions should not be happening. CERD Article 5(f) guarantees: "The right of access to any place or service intended for use by the general public, such as transport, hotels, restaurants, cafes, theatres and parks." Thus, these signs and rules are in place in violation of Japan's signatory status to UN treaty.

5. In the context of these cases, I put "foreigners" in inverted quotes throughout this chapter as it reflects the invective used in the original Japanese (usually *gaijin* or *gaikokujin*, but sometimes other epithets, such as *Rosuke* (Russkie), *fūrigan* (hooligan), or *Beigun* (US military serviceman), but applied to mean all "foreign-looking" people on sight). This is to acknowledge flawed terminology with imperfect translation and unproblematized categorization.

6. Online archive with images and fieldwork notes at www.debito.org/roguesgallery.html#Wakkanai. Exclusionary signs found in Wakkanai, Hokkaidō Prefecture. Photographs supplied and notated by the author, taken April 9, 2000, outside Onsen Yuransen, Wakkanai, and Shidō Sports Store (which says "No Russians may enter"

on the sign in Russian). Another image (in green) is a screen capture dated November 13, 2012, of hotel Minshuku Itsuki's online bilingual refusal of all "foreign" reservations.

7. *See Kōshū yokujō hō shikō jōrei* [enforcement ordinance on public bathing facilities], partially archived at www.debito.org/koshuyokujojorei.jpg.

8. Online archive with images and fieldwork notes at www.debito.org/roguesgallery.html#Sapporo. Viewable are exclusionary signs found in Sapporo: Multilingual "Members Only" sign (*sans* Japanese) first found in June 2002 at several bars, nightlife establishments, and restaurants around Sapporo Susukino, created as an "anti-hooligan" measure during World Cup 2002; and pachinko parlor Donkey's garbled exclusionary sign; photo courtesy of the author June 3, 2002.

9. *See* archive of international news articles regarding the Japanese government's anti-hooligan measures at www.debito.org/worldcup2002.html.

10. www.debito.org/sapporocitylobby2004.html.

11. Online archive with more images and fieldwork notes at www.debito.org/roguesgallery.html#Misawa and www.debito.org/misawaexclusions.html. Viewable are template exclusionary sign (a copy of Otaru Onsen Osupa's sign, see Otaru section below) for bar Globe in Misawa, Aomori Prefecture; garbled template exclusionary sign for disco/bar King Mhu; garbled template exclusionary sign for bar San Rose; garbled template exclusionary sign for bar Roje; garbled template exclusionary sign for bar Sarii (*sans* Japanese template text); exclusionary sign for bar Heart Beats from the same template as Globe. All dated March 28, 2002.

12. www.debito.org/deamericanize.html.

13. Online with images and fieldwork notes at www.debito.org/roguesgallery.html#Akita. Viewable are photos of exclusionary sign found in Akita City, Akita Prefecture, at disco Honey Bee, April 2003; author removing exclusionary sign with permission of the manager, November 28, 2003.

14. Primary source information archived at www.debito.org/?p=1941 and www.debito.org/?p=5619.

15. According to an opinion poll, this hotel behavior might be within character: The GOJ reported, in an October 2008 nationwide survey of 7,068 responding hotels, that 27 percent of all Japanese hoteliers did not want "foreign" clients. *See* "Japan: No room at inn for foreigners." AP/CNN, October 9, 2008; "*'Gaikokujin tometakunai' hoteru/ryokan 3-wari: 07-nen koku chōsa.*" ["We don't want foreigners to stay here," says 30 percent of Japanese inns: 2007 nationwide survey] *Asahi Shinbun*, October 9, 2008.

16. In the wake of the 2011 nuclear meltdowns, Fukushima residents seeking refuge elsewhere were being turned away by hotels and shops around Japan due to fears about their radioactivity. *See*, for example, "*'Fukushima Kenmin Okotowari' nyūten, shukuhaku, fūhyō higai aitsugu*" [Fukushima Prefectural Residents Refused at shops and lodgings as damage from misinformation continues]. *Yomiuri Shinbun*, April 9, 2011, archived at www.debito.org/?p=8768. Fortunately for them, the national government took awareness-raising measures to prevent discrimination against them; *see* "*'Fukushima kenmin okotowari' nyūten shukuhaku, fūhyō higai aitsugu*" [Refusing entry and accommodation to Fukushima Prefectural residents:

The damaging rumors continue]. *Yomiuri Shinbun*, April 9, 2011. Unfortunately, that effort has not been extended to "foreigners," for example, regarding scientists and consultants offering to assist the nuclear cleanup, Nishiyama Hidehiko, deputy director at the Environment Ministry, said in 2013, "if we have foreigners roaming around Fukushima, they might scare the old grandmas and granddads there" (*gaikokujin ga fukushima o urouro shitetara, otoshiyori no ojīchan obāchan ga kowagaru deshō*). *See* "In Japan, a painfully slow sweep." *New York Times*, January 7, 2013, and "NYT: Xenophobia in Environmental Ministry re exclusionary Fukushima decontam efforts: 'Japanese soil is different,' 'NJ assistance might scare local grandmas.'" *Debito.org*, January 11, 2013, at www.debito.org/?p=11013.

17. Online with images and fieldwork notes at www.debito.org/roguesgallery.html#Shinjuku. Exclusionary signs found in the Shinjuku area: Hotel Tsubakuro's signs in English and Japanese, dated July 21, 2003, photo courtesy of Declan Murphy; Hotel Sanremo's garbled sign refusing "foreign lady" who are [waiting on the road], date of photo unknown, but sight-confirmed by the author in March 2005; Bar Word Up's sign courtesy of Vince Ting, submitted to *Mainichi Daily News*'s "My Japan Photo Contest," May 22–28, 2006; linguistically sophisticated template signs found at several Kabukichō bars, photo courtesy of the author, March 16, 2008. As of 2021, web searches reveal that these hotels are still in business (Hotel Tsubakuro has now changed its name to Hotel Empire). Word Up is a "men-only underwear cruise bar" on weekdays with no indication of information that they refuse foreigners entry.

18. *See also* Koenig & Kremers (2009) (minute 30: author's interview with the management of a Kabukichō nightlife emporium).

19. www.debito.org/roguesgallery.html#misc.

20. www.debito.org/whattodoif.html#refusedhotel. More in chapter 5.

21. Koenig & Kremers (2009), minute 34.

22. www.debito.org/roguesgallery.html#misc, third sign down.

23. "'Japanese Only' at Tokyo Takadanobaba private-sector job placement agency." *Debito.org*, October 20, 2008, www.debito.org/?p=1949. The agency is named "Workers" (*wa-ka-zu*). They are not alone; I have heard from many non-Japanese that being refused work at job agencies, particularly the government unemployment agency "Hello Work," is commonplace, regardless of what the law says—because technically the law does not protect workers until they get hired. This will be discussed further in chapter 4. What sets agency "Workers" apart is their putting "no foreigners" on their corporate sign, removing all plausible deniability.

24. Online archive with images and fieldwork notes at www.debito.org/roguesgallery.html#Aoyama, Women's esthetic salon Princess Plumeria's "Japanese women only" notice. Courtesy of anonymous contributor in February 2005.

25. "'Japanese Only' exclusionary Tentake tempura restaurant in Asakusa, Tokyo, allegedly due to NJ 'hygiene' issues." *Debito.org*, April 5, 2014, at www.debito.org/?p=12256. Courtesy of Yoshio Tanaka and Iselita Arlen.

26. Online archive with image and fieldwork notes at www.debito.org/roguesgallery.html#Ogikubo. Exclusionary sign at Ogikubo nightlife bar RIZAL, photo courtesy of the author January 2004.

27. Online archive with image and fieldwork notes at www.debito.org/rogues gallery.html#minamiazabu. The ballet school's bilingual website is at www.mg-ballet.org.

28. Online archive with image and fieldwork notes at www.debito.org/roguesgall ery.html#Akihabara.

29. "Seven killed, 10 injured in Akihabara stabbing spree." *Japan Times/Kyodo News*, June 9, 2008.

30. The Akihabara store's final message to customers is at www.akiba-mad.stores .jp. No goods appear to be available for sale.

31. Online archive of images and fieldwork notes at www.debito.org/roguesgallery .html#Kofu. Photo taken June 7, 2004, of a sign outside Kōfu City's family bathhouse Isawa Kenkō Land, with the author pointing to two exclusionary rules: (1) people who cannot understand Japanese, and (2) foreign visa overstayers (unlawfully requiring official proof of personal identification to be displayed before service). *See also* historical newspaper articles, reports, and interviews conducted with Isawa Kenkō Land manager and with the family of Takenoyu bathhouse owner June 7, 2004, archived at www.debito.org/kofuexclusions.html.

32. Ibid., *Reuters*, June 24, 1992.

33. Willis Witter, "Japanese commonly show anti-foreigner biases: US military, Latin American settlers targeted." *Washington Times*, September 18, 1998, archived at www.debito.org/azumamura.html.

34. Online archive with photos and field notes at www.debito.org/roguesgallery.h tml#Koshigaya.

35. Online archive with photos and field notes at www.debito.org/roguesgallery .html#Toda, www.debito.org/roguesgallery.html#Isesaki, www.debito.org/rogues-gallery.html#Ohta, www.debito.org/roguesgallery.html#Kurashiki, and www.debito .org/roguesgallery.html#Hiroshima. Exclusionary signs from Central Japan. Signs from bar Club Sepia, Toda City, Saitama Prefecture, courtesy of Michael Cash, March 4, 2005; Signs in Portuguese and English from bar Abend, Hamamatsu City, Shizuoka Prefecture, courtesy of Ana Bortz, dated 1998; Signs from "esthetic salon" Popo, Isesaki City, Gunma Prefecture, submitted by anonymous contributor May 2004; Signs from Filipina pub Aliw, Ōta City, Gunma Prefecture, submitted by anonymous contributor, undated, circa. 2005.

36. Online archive with photos and field notes at www.debito.org/roguesgallery.h tml#Nonoichi. Redacted newspaper subscription contract dated November 13, 2007, for the *Hokkoku Shinbun*. Reverse of postcard dated November 14, 2007, from the salesman indicating that his contract had been refused.

37. *See* photos and accounts by activists at "Nagasaki Yorozuya-machi Steak House 'Bronco' sign: 'Foreign people are forbidden to enter this restaurant to prevent infection.' Exclusionary racism evolves with Covid." *Debito.org*, April 25, 2021, www.debito.org/?p=16606. Information on MICE is at https://mice.nagasaki-visit.or .jp and www.city.nagasaki.lg.jp/syokai/792000/792100/p034938.html.

38. Online archives and sources: "Mark Austin reports that Otaru, site of the famous onsen lawsuit, still has a 'Japanese Only' establishment, 'Monika.'" *Debito .org*, July 7, 2011; www.debito.org/?p=9187; "'Japanese Only' hospital Keira

Orthopaedic Surgery in Shintoku, Tokachi, Hokkaido. Alleged language barrier supersedes Hippocratic Oath for clinic, despite links to METI medical tourism." *Debito.org,* December 20, 2012, www.debito.org/?p=10915; "Former England striker turned away from golf club in Japan 'because he is foreign.'" *Daily Express*, May 30, 2018, archived at www.debito.org/?p=15013; "'Japanese Only' sign on Izakaya Bar '100' (Momosaku) in Asakusa, Tokyo." *Debito.org*, May 23, 2018, www.debito.org/?p=14981; "NJ company 'J Hewitt' advertises 'Japanese Only' jobs in the Japan Times!" *Debito.org*, March 10, 2009, www.debito.org/?p=2645; "Human rights violations at a J Gym Chain: 'Young, Healthy Japanese Only,' by Jim Dunlop." *Debito.org*, September 5, 2007, www.debito.org/?p=550; "'No Foreigners' (and no women) Capsule Inn Omiya hotel in Saitama." *Debito.org*, www.debito.org/?p=12590; "'Japanese speakers only' Kyoto exclusionary hotel stands by its rules, says it's doing nothing unlawful." *Debito.org*, November 10 and 14, 2009, www.debito.org/?p=4879 and www.debito.org/?p=5114; "Rogues' Gallery: Kansai Kensetsu Inc., a 'No Foreigners' realtor in Osaka—according to its catalog." *Debito.org*, www.debito.org/?p=723; "'Japanese Only' soul bar in Kobe, 'Soul Love,' Nishinomiya Yamanote Doori. Advertises the music of people they would no doubt exclude." *Debito.org*, May 4, 2011, www.debito.org/?p=8897; and "Japanese Only sign in Tsukiji Fish Market." *Debito.org*, www.debito.org/?p=1210; "'Japanese Only' diving and hiking tour company in Tokashikimura, Okinawa: 'Begin Diving Buddies.'" *Debito.org*, www.debito.org/?p=14989. Other germane Debito.org "Rogues' Gallery of Exclusionary Establishments" sections: www.debito.org/roguesgallery.html#Kyoto; www.debito.org/roguesgallery.html#Nagoya; www.debito.org/roguesgallery.html#Okazaki; www.debito.org/roguesgallery.html#Kokura; www.debito.org/roguesgallery.html#Uruma; and www.debito.org/roguesgallery.html#Misc.

The businesses in question: Keira Orthopedic Surgery (*seikei geka iin*), Shintoku, Hokkaidō, courtesy of Hilary; Izakaya Momosaku in Asakusa, photos dated April 20, 2018, courtesy of KD; one archived *Japan Times* want ad is for cosmetics company "J. Hewitt," selling to plastic surgeons, and run by a Jon Knight in Tōkyō Setagaya—who as of 2021 no longer appears to be in business; Disco Abime in Nagoya, photo dated February 12, 2005, courtesy of Ian Brown; Onsen hotel Yamazaki Ryokan in Kyōto City, November 28, 2005, courtesy of David Woods; Kyō no Yado in Fushimi, Kyōto, October 25, 2009, courtesy of the author; Soul bar Soul Love in Sannomiya, Kōbe, photos dated May 4, 2011, courtesy of Sean Maki; Billiards hall B-Ball in Uruma City, Okinawa Prefecture, photos dated May 13, 2006, courtesy of Jeff Norman; Internet café Dragon BOZ in Okazaki City, Aichi Prefecture, photos dated December 10, 2006, courtesy of Jonas Svensson; Unnamed seafood restaurant in Tsukiji fish market, Tōkyō, photo February 2008; Karaoke hall Maimu in Moromizato, Okinawa, photos dated July 14, 2013, courtesy of Justin; Kansai Kensetsu Fukushima Branch in Fukushima-ku, Ōsaka, materials dated November 13, 2007, courtesy of Martin Oickle; Hokkaido Classic Golf Club in Yūfutsu-gun, Hokkaidō, dated May 30, 2018; Begin Diving Buddies in Tokashikimura, Okinawa, screen captures dated May 2, 2018, courtesy of Steve.

39. www.debito.org/?p=5114.
40. http://en.hcgc.jp/contents/access/index.html.

41. As of March 27, 2021. *See* the most recent *Japan Times* want ads at https://job.japantimes.com/jinzai_anken_search.php.

42. www.begin.jp/index.php under "今日の島."

43. Start by googling "外国人お断り" and then browse. Add a job sector or industry to your search term to narrow. It is not really a hidden practice. For example, I plugged in "外国人お断り 職業の募集" [foreigners refused, want ads] and at the top was "The best way to refuse foreigners who respond to your job ad" from Yahoo Japan's *Chiebukuro* crowd-sourced answers forum.

44. www.debito.org/?p=15013#comment-1664256. Note: I declined to visit all 1,150 sites. There is also photographic evidence of scattered exclusionary rental signs and rules up around Japan. *See*, for example, www.debito.org/?p=15852&cpage=1#comment-1765924, www.debito.org/?p=14981&cpage=1#comment-1663710, all courtesy AnonymousOG.

45. www.debito.org/?p=12590&cpage=1#comment-667555. And as noted in the previous section mentioning the Ōmiya capsule hotel discovered via Rakuten, even after being notified by activists of "no foreigner" rules violating the Hotel Management Law, Rakuten has not changed its policy and refused listings to exclusionary hotels; *see* www.debito.org/?p=12590&cpage=1#comment-723651.

46. In addition, some Japanese realtors are categorizing certain types of apartments as "Foreigners OK," creating a niche industry reflecting the default of apartments *not* being OK for foreigners; this can even be seen in foreign brands doing business in Japan, such as Century 21. *See* "'Foreign nationalities OK' apartments bin at Century 21 Saitama realty." *Debito.org*, March 28, 2021, www.debito.org/?p=16541.

47. *See*, for example, "Terumi Club refuses NJ for travel fares and tours, has cheaper fares for Japanese Only. Like H.I.S. and No.1 Travel." *Debito.org*, May 11, 2010, www.debito.org/?p=6430; "Jeff Smith on Yahoo Japan auctioneer denying foreign bidders, and what he did about it." *Debito.org*, February 17, 2012, www.debito.org/?p=9958; "Overseas online info site Traveloco.jp's 'Japanese Only' rules: 'People with foreign-sounding names refused service.'" *Debito.org*, July 5, 2016, www.debito.org/?p=14078; "Bitcoin purchasing and racial profiling by Quoinex and BITPoint Japan: Hurdles for NJ customers only." *Debito.org*, December 3, 2017, www.debito.org/?p=14820; and so on.

48. Primary source archives on the Ana Bortz Case: Bortz 1998, TV Asahi 1999, Webster 2007b. The *Hamamatsu Sengen's* full text is at www.debito.org/hamamatsusengen.html. *See also* the October 12, 1998 TV Asahi broadcast viewable in full at www.debito.org/?p=4460.

49. TV Asahi 1999, Webster 2007b.

50. Webster (2007b: 631).

51. Information gleaned through interviews, conducted over several months between 1999 and 2002, with bathhouse managers, Otaru City officials, and activists (Arudou 2004, 2006a, b).

52. There is anecdotal evidence from Otaru residents (interviews 1999–2001) suggesting that Yunohana's previous sauna had encouraged Russians to come to their baths, and that its location and old facilities were in fact the cause of bankruptcy.

53. Full transcript with original Japanese at www.debito.org/yunohanatranscript10 3100.html.

54. Arudou (2006a): Chapter 4, particularly 277–295.

55. Arudou 2006a: 238–242, 2006b: 407–410, Webster 2007a.

56. Regarding the issues with Japan's legal test of "unrational discrimination," legal scholar Craig Martin writes, "A closer examination of this test . . . informed by the underlying theory of equality rights, suggests that it is not only tautological, and the basis for result-oriented decision making, but that it also creates confusion over what constitutes the essence of discrimination and the substantive content of the rights to equality. The test thus provides the lower courts with no assistance whatsoever in terms of how to analyze issues of discrimination. Its application almost invariably leads to a finding that the discrimination is reasonable." *See* "Glimmers of Hope: The evolution of equality rights doctrine in Japanese courts from a comparative perspective." *Duke Journal of Comparative & International Law*, Vol. 20, p. 170, 2010.

57. *See*, for example, Otaru City International Communications chief Takeuchi Kazuho, Sapporo District Court testimony March 15, 2002, page 20, and Otaru City *Kōhō* (the official city monthly newsletter) April 2000, No. 620, cited in Arudou (2006b: 311–2, 342–51).

58. Arudou 2006a: 263–8, 2006b: 411–3; Webster 2007b.

59. The logic behind the separation of powers argument proceeds like this: If a law exists, claimants may challenge its constitutionality in court. However, if a law does *not* exist, and claimants wish to challenge the constitutionality of its *nonexistence* in court (as plaintiffs were doing against Otaru City), this cannot be done, because a government (as in the Legislative Branch (*rippōfu*)) cannot be forced to pass laws, or be held culpable for not passing laws, by the Judicial Branch (*shihōfu*).

60. The Sapporo High Court also cited a court precedent where a physically handicapped plaintiff sued a local government for unequal access to public facilities, and the suit was rejected by the Supreme Court due again to "separation of powers" *See* Supreme Court of Japan 1985.

61. Arudou 2006a: 415–416, 2006b: 279.

62. Although this case reaffirmed the right for the discriminated in Japan to sue and win, it also removed any incentives for local or national governments to pass any antidiscrimination laws. Here is the logic: If passing a law may get you in trouble with the constitution and treaties, while not passing one is not hereby unconstitutional or against treaties, then why pass a law? You are culpable if you do, but not culpable if you do not.

63. "*Nyūkyo kyohi: 'sabetsu' to nintei; ienushi ni baishō meirei Kōbe chisai Amagasaki*" [Rental refusal: Kobe District Court Amagasaki acknowledges "discrimination," orders landlord to pay compensation], *Mainichi Shinbun*, January 25, 2006. Court called the landlord's refusal to rent a third-generation Zainichi Korean couple an illegal activity, as it "transgresses the boundaries [of discrimination] permitted by society." But the illegal activity was not adjudged racial discrimination in specific. Moreover, the court award was 220,000 yen, much less than the Otaru Case award, and less than a tenth of what plaintiffs sued for.

64. United Nations (2001, 2006: para. 63), archived at www.debito.org/rapporteur.html.

65. Ibid. 1998: sec. 11.

66. Ministry of Foreign Affairs 1999, 2001 and 2008. Archived at www.debito.org/japanvsun.html and discussed further in chapter 8.

67. Case materials archived at www.debito.org/mcgowanhanketsu.html. *See also* Webster (2007b).

68. Webster (2007a: 352).

69. Webster ibid.

70. "African-American wins JPY 350,000 in damages for being denied entry into Osaka shop." *Kyodo News*, October 18, 2006.

71. "Turkish man wins solo battle in fight against discrimination." *Asahi Shinbun*, September 4, 2017. "'Attach the evidence and wait for your day in court,' says Turkish plaintiff after Osaka victory." *Japan Times*, October 12, 2017. Other archived materials at www.debito.org/?p=14739, www.debito.org/?p=14743, and www.debito.org/?p=14773.

72. Webster 2007b: 317.

73. Webster 2007a: 361.

74. Webster 2007b: 317.

75. Webster ibid.: 319.

76. Webster ibid.: 319–320.

77. Webster ibid.: 319.

78. Nguyen, Anh Thi Ngoc, "Japan's inbound tourism boom: Lessons for its post-COVID-19 revival." *International Monetary Fund*, Working Paper WP/20/169, August 2020.

79. It is a delicious irony that the bathhouses that adamantly shut out foreign customers now see them as crucial to their survival. *See*, for example, "Tokyo bathhouses scrub up to lure visitors." *Yomiuri Shinbun*, October 22, 2010; "Japan's public baths hope foreign tourists will help keep the taps running." *Japan Times*, January 5, 2016.

80. www.yunohana.org.

Part III

THE CONSTRUCTION OF JAPAN'S EMBEDDED RACISM

Chapter 4

Legal Constructions of "Japaneseness"

"What's with this passport? You don't look Japanese." This is a typical comment I get from Customs officials worldwide whenever I cross a border on my Japanese passport. It demonstrates how hegemonic the linkage is between Japanese nationality and physical appearance.[1] (In contrast, imagine the public reaction to an American Customs official audaciously claiming aloud that an American passport holder did not "look American.") How did this discourse of "you have to look Japanese in order to be accepted as a Japanese" become so unquestioned—even outside of Japan?

This chapter begins the survey of Japan's "national discourse" governing how people "belong" to Japanese society. As discussed earlier, a Macro-level discourse at the national level is found in all nation-states to promote domestic narratives of community, and it often normalizes a mindset that "foreigners" are unentitled to the same rights as citizens. By examining the structural elements that generate these narratives (i.e., laws, public policy papers, jurisprudence, public notices, media, etc.), we can see how they encourage the concepts of "Us" vs. "Them" and "Self" vs. "Other" that are at the root of all racialization processes, that is, the systemic differentiation, "othering," and subordination of people who do not "belong" within any body politic.

However, in Japan's case, discourses go beyond differentiation based on legal status (citizen vs. noncitizen) and into bloodlines and visual identification (how people must "look Japanese" in order to belong). This creates Visible Minorities that also include citizens, and generates another layer of in-group/out-group structure in Japan that we shall call "Wajin" vs. "Gaijin."

First, some definitions:

THE COMPONENTS OF A "NATIONAL DISCOURSE"

This research analyzes the following structural components of Japan's nation-state narrative:

1. *Laws and administrative regimes*, as they codify the treatment of peoples in Japan, and set up the "Japanese" vs. "foreigner" dichotomy for enforcement by administrative authorities (covered in this chapter).
2. *Government bodies and legislative policymakers*, as they set agendas for the creation of laws and policy, then create, enact, and enforce those laws and policy (e.g., local governments (*jichitai*), the national ministries, the National Police Agency (NPA), the Diet and its members (MPs), and the judiciary) (covered in chapters 5 and 6).
3. *The media* (e.g., print media, broadcast media, online media, government sources of media influence), as it influences the public view of "foreigners" and their role in Japanese society, and controls and underrepresents "minority voices" within Japan (covered in chapter 7).[2]

DEFINING "WAJIN" AND "GAIJIN"

As mentioned in the Introduction, the terminology on "race" and "racism" within a Japanese context is not an exact match with concepts in English. The word "Japanese" itself is confusing, as it can mean both "a Japanese citizen" (a legal status that can include people of different races and ethnic backgrounds), and "a Japanese by blood" (a racialized paradigm that can include people without Japanese citizenship). "Japanese" also overlooks those who are "Japanese" (such as the Burakumin) who have citizenship, physical appearance, and full acculturation as "Japanese," yet suffer from discrimination by descent and social origin. So for the purposes of this research, a new term is necessary to enhance the contours of power relations within Japan's social groupings: "Wajin." For ease of reference, see table 4.1.

A brief discussion grounding the word "Wajin" in a historical and linguistic context may be found in the endnotes.[3]

Now let us turn to the building blocks of national narratives of inclusivity, starting with the most fundamental law of national membership possible—the law governing Japanese citizenship.

Table 4.1 Definitions and Examples of the Terms Wajin, Non-Wajin, Invisible Minorities, and Visible Minorities

Wajin	*Non-Wajin*	
Defined as: Members of Japan's dominant, enfranchised, and privileged majority. This group has been portrayed in the canon as "Pure Japanese" (Fukuoka 1993), "Most Japanese" (Sugimoto 1997), and the "Dominant Japanese" (Aoki 2009).	*Defined as*: People who are not members of Japan's dominant, enfranchised, and privileged majority. These people are often called "Ethnic Minorities" (Aoki 2009), but ethnicity is but one qualifier that forces these minorities into a subordinate status in Japan's social power structure. Non-Wajin are further differentiated through visual identification into an "invisible minority" and a "visible minority," regardless of Japanese blood/"lineage," Japanese citizenship, and fluent/native Japanese ability.	
Examples: Visually identifiable Japanese who have enfranchised claims to Japanese blood/"lineage" and Japanese citizenship, moreover verifiably fluent/native Japanese language ability, and visually identifiable markers that enable them to "look Japanese."	**Invisible Minorities** *Examples*: People with ethnic backgrounds (e.g., Ainu, Okinawans, Zainichi, and other people with origins in other Asian regions), historical origins (Burakumin),[1] or formative experiences (e.g., naturalized citizens, "Returnee Children" (*kikoku shijo*)) that are not within the milieu of "Dominant Japanese," and behaviorally distinguish them from Wajin. However, they have visually identifiable biological markers that enable them to "pass" as Wajin, but once "outed" are treated differently and often subordinately to Wajin.	**Visible Minorities** *Examples*: Foreigners and naturalized Japanese citizens who do not "look Japanese"; Children of Japanese/foreign relationships who do not "look Japanese." Aka Gaijin.

[1]My categorization of the Burakumin as Non-Wajin is contentious, given that many Burakumin themselves naturally wish to be considered "Japanese" like any Wajin. However, (1) this classification is not a self-identification process (or else anyone regardless of how they look, act, or lay claim to their historical or social origins would claim Wajin status; that is unfortunately not how structural power relations work in a society), and (2) the terms within this chart analyze power relations in Japanese society, and Burakumin are a verified subgroup that is verifiably subordinated in Japan's power relations. As Sugimoto (1997: 188) notes when he includes Burakumin as part of Japan's "ethnic and racial diversity," Burakumin representatives self-identify their way out of the dominant majority: "Buraku Liberation movements argue that *their minority status* derives from community prejudice based upon lineage or pedigree, precisely the realm of discrimination which the [CERD] attempts to eliminate" (emphasis added). Takezawa (2011: 1) even calls Burakumin, along with Zainichi Koreans, an "invisible race" in Japan. In short, because Burakumin are a disenfranchised group in Japan, they are by definition not part of the enfranchised group called Wajin.

JAPAN'S NATIONALITY LAW (*KOKUSEKI HŌ*)

As discussed in chapter 2, laws frame and codify how people will be treated in the modern nation-state. If laws themselves are racialized, then due to the "performative" aspect of race and law, people will be similarly codified and singled out for differential treatment due to their racialized characteristics. This is made clear within Japan's Nationality Law (*kokuseki hō*). Let us discuss how this law defines "a Japanese" (in vernacular legal terms, the appropriate word is *kokumin*) in terms of rights, privileges, and immunities with regard to Japanese citizenship.

Jus Sanguinis *Requirements for Japanese Nationality*

Biology and state membership are explicitly linked in Japan's Nationality Law.[4] Article 2 requires that a person have one "Japanese national" (*kokumin*) parent in order to qualify for Japanese nationality. Citizenship is thus officially conferred through *jus sanguinis* (law of blood), which precludes birthplace ties (*jus soli*). This means that Japanese citizenship is not conferred by dint of being born in Japan.

In application, this means a child born in Japan to two nonnationals, even if they were born in Japan, is still a nonnational. Amendments have made this law less restrictive, such as in 1985, when the law permitted Japanese nationality to be recognized through the mother as well as the father (previously it was only through the father).[5] However, the preponderance of the Nationality Law still focuses on blood ties as a condition for most people qualifying for Japanese citizenship, with pernicious racialization effects that will be this chapter's focus.

Jus Sanguinis and Postwar Zainichi Legal Exclusion

One reason why Japan's *jus sanguinis* citizenship is problematic is Japan's history.[6] As discussed in chapter 2, between 1895 and 1945 Japan was a colonial power, where subjects of the Japanese Empire, including Koreans, Chinese, and Taiwanese (aka *Sangokujin*), were considered Japanese subjects with Japanese citizenship. This entailed certain *kokumin* privileges and duties, such as the option to reside and work in Japan indefinitely without a visa (notwithstanding those who came to Japan or its colonies as forced labor) and to serve in the Japanese military. As mentioned above, the postwar decision to strip away nationality and *kokumin* status was due both to endogenous factors and contemporary geopolitics, and by 1950, under the new Nationality Law, the Sangokujin (now the Zainichi) who elected not to leave Japan were required to be registered under the new Foreign Registry

Law (*gaikokujin tōroku-hō*) as "foreigners" (i.e., "Special Permanent Residents" (*tokubetsu eijūsha*)). In practice, this meant that Zainichi would be fingerprinted, be forced to carry officially issued identification at all times, and be legally subject to police questioning at any time without probable cause (more below). As of June 2020, according to the MOJ,[7] nearly 11 percent of all "registered foreigners" in Japan are still Zainichi, meaning that despite four generations of being born in Japan, they remain generational foreigners by dint of blood—without the right to vote, hold administrative jobs in many branches of Japan's civil service (more below), or run for public office.

The conditions of Japan's Zainichi are an appropriate introduction to Japan's perpetual and self-sustaining differentiating and "othering" dynamics. After several generations of living in Japan, the Zainichi, who generally can "pass" as Wajin in every aspect, do have the option through naturalization to become legally *kokumin* (see below). However, many do not elect to naturalize.[8] There are social stigmas both by Wajin (including a domestic media that speculates on which Japanese celebrity or sports figure is "really a Korean," including careful considerations of semi-established "Korean" phenotypes, even after naturalization) and by the Zainichi communities themselves. Many of the older generation of Zainichi consider naturalizing to be an insult given their colonial contributions to the empire. There is also the issue of identity sacrifice, because Japan does not permit dual nationality, and naturalizers would have to relinquish their Korean citizenships, cultural affiliations, and even the expression of their names. Another reason for not naturalizing is inertia: living as a disenfranchised segment of Japanese society has simply become "normalized" for many Zainichi.[9]

Naturalization: The Racialized Process of Becoming a Japanese Citizen

Japan's Nationality Law (Articles 5–9)[10] makes the procedures clear for gaining *kokumin* legal status through naturalization. Characteristic of most naturalization processes, there are significant barriers to entry, including an extensive application process; officially certified documents to retrieve and translate at cost; intrusive information about family history, income, and personal stability; and proof of non-criminality under paradigms set by the nation-state. Japan's specific requirements for qualification are that the candidate (a) currently reside in Japan continuously for five years (with some exceptions made for spouses and children of Japanese nationals who do not hold Japanese citizenship themselves), (b) be an adult (as of 2018, age eighteen) and without criminal record in the country of current citizenship, (c) be of "upright conduct" (*kōdō ga sokō de aru*) however defined, (d) have the wherewithal to support oneself and dependents, (e) renounce other nationalities (with some exceptions made with permission of the Minister of Justice), and (f) uphold Japan's Constitution and not advocate the overthrow of the government. There are other exceptions made for applicants who (a) were born in Japan but are stateless by birth,[11] (b) are former Japanese citizens who "lost" their citizenship but live in Japan, (c) have been adopted as minors by Japanese citizens, (d) have been married to Japanese for three years and living in Japan for one to three years, and (e) have done "meritorious service to Japan."[12] However, it is still possible to become a Japanese citizen (the author has accomplished this), and around 9,000 people per year on average are successful.[13]

However, a closer look at Japan's Nationality Law reveals not only the potential of arbitrary or discriminatory enforcement, but also evidence of how the naturalization process is systematically racialized. When I successfully went through the process between 1998 and 2000, there was an initial interview at the MOJ that functioned as a preliminary screening; potential candidates are told, after about an hour of questions about vital statistics, contributions, and commitments to Japan, immediately whether or not they may proceed to the next step of retrieving substantiating documents. Although the MOJ reports that most candidates who complete the full process receive citizenship, it is unclear how many are rejected at the first screening, due to, say, a lack of "upright conduct" adjudged prima facie. There is, moreover, no right of review or of appeal—only reapplication at a later date. Thus, there is much ministerial latitude for personal bias in pre-selecting candidates.[14]

In my case, I was told during my screening that due to my length of time in Japan, secure job, and fluent Japanese, I qualified for citizenship.[15] In subsequent interviews during the next year of collecting overseas documents, many questions to me (and to other candidates I interviewed about their naturalization experiences) were intrusive. There were questions about what my family and I eat, where and how we sleep, what toys our children play with. We were required in our application to provide the police with photos of and hand-drawn maps to our home and workplace. The application also had a personal survey of our relatives (siblings and parents) asking whether they approved of our naturalization ("for Korean families," I was told); my mother had to sign an affidavit indicating that she approved of my naturalizing. (Incidentally, she did not approve, and refused; my stepfather, also objecting, signed on her behalf because he too is a naturalized American and wished to avoid hypocrisy.) Officials visited our Wajin neighbors to inquire about how "Japanese" they thought I was (meaning other Wajin, who were otherwise unqualified in any way except as fellow Wajin to determine my "Japaneseness," had input into the process). When I asked MOJ representatives what being "sufficiently Japanese" entailed, for example, whether I had to wear *yukata* robes around the house or demonstrably ingest some of

Japan's more challenging delicacies, they answered, "Just don't inspire any 'feeling of incongruity' (*iwakan*) in our officers."

It is also unclear under what premises other people are vetted; some candidates (of both similar and different nationalities and ethnic backgrounds to me) experienced home visits and refrigerator inspections from ministerial officials; two Filipina candidates I interviewed informally in 1999 and 2000 said they were asked about their previous sexual partners. My second-generation Zainichi Korean neighbor was screened, then rejected for citizenship, because, he said he was told, he had a history of parking tickets. The screening process is thus open to racialized differentiation, enabling anonymous bureaucrats the discretion to select for whatever arbitrary qualities, such as car parking skills or non-Korean backgrounds, would in their view suit the Japanese State.

"Gaikokujin Shimin": The GOJ Perpetually "Others" Japan's International Residents and Citizens

Even after one has naturalized, the GOJ performatively appends an asterisk to its "new Japanese" to distinguish them from Wajin Japanese. In the late 2010s, governments nationwide (the excerpt below is from Nagoya) adopted a new term, "*Gaikokujin Shimin*" (literally, "foreigner city denizens"), to classify the following types of people:

> In addition to people with foreign nationalities with an address within the City of Nagoya, this includes people like those who obtained Japanese citizenship, children born from international marriages, people with foreign cultures in their backgrounds, and people who have foreign roots. (*Nagoya-shi Jiki Sōgō Keikaku, Chūkan'an* [Nagoya City Next Term General Plan, Intermediate Draft], August 2018, translated by the author)[16]

This merits parsing. Note how the term not only includes naturalized citizens and people with mixed roots, but also lumps in people with backgrounds of foreign "culture" and "roots" as "*gaikokujin.*" This performatively renders anyone with any international connections into "foreigners," including Japanese citizens both born and naturalized. Notwithstanding the questionable legal standing of this definition under the Nationality Law, official terminology matters in terms of public policy framing and enforcement. As discussed in the context of the postwar "*Konketsuji Mondai*" (Mixed-Blood Children Problem) in chapter 2, asterisking like this has historically led to stigmatizing people with biological connections outside the in-group. It also activates a eugenicist, anti-assimilationist stance, erecting a firewall between Wajin and Gaijin; a person with international connections can never escape being tagged as a "*Gaikokujin Shimin*" in Japan even with Japanese citizenship.[17]

A quick 2021 google search for "*Gaikokujin Shimin*" found it being used by dozens of city, town, and local government websites, as well as several ministries including the Ministry of Foreign Affairs, MOJ, Ministry of Education, Ministry of Internal Affairs and Communications, and the Prime Minister's Office, indicating that it is now an established term within the bureaucracy.[18]

Legal Renunciation/Revocation of Japanese Citizenship and Wajin Privilege

Japan's Nationality Law also allows for renunciation and unilateral revocation of citizenship, which may happen, for example, because dual nationality is not permitted. According to Articles 14–16, if a child has two nationalities, the child must have surrendered one of them with written proof to the MOJ by age twenty-two. If not done promptly and correctly, the Law states that criminal penalties, including revocation of Japanese citizenship, can apply. Also, according to the Law, *kokumin* who take out (or choose) another citizenship must also declare it to the GOJ and renounce Japanese citizenship.[19]

However, people who can claim blood ties to Japan's Wajin majority enjoy significant privilege under the Nationality Law. Notwithstanding the entitlement-by-blood privileges that are the definition of a *jus sanguinis* system, Nikkei persons of Japanese descent get a faster track for obtaining nationality (Article 6), and even former citizens get special Wajin privileges after renunciation (Article 17, neither of which happen, for example, under United States' nationality laws).[20] Moreover, Wajin children of international marriages often keep dual nationality beyond the age of twenty-two due to unenforced regulations.[21]

That said, the GOJ has been given more latitude in recent years to put Japan's international children on legal tenterhooks: In 2015, the Supreme Court creatively interpreted Article 12 to allow the unilateral revocation of Japanese citizenship for clerical errors in cases where Japanese children were born overseas; and in 2021, a lower court ruled that citizens discovered with dual passports beyond the age of twenty-two can be stripped of their Japanese nationality at the GOJ's discretion.[22] Naturally, this incentivizes adults with international backgrounds to suppress their diversity in favor of Japan's pure-blooded monoethnic narrative.[23]

An Example of Wajin Privilege and Politics under the Nationality Law: The Alberto and Aritomi Fujimori Cases

An instructive case of Wajin privilege under the Nationality Law is that of former Peruvian president Alberto Fujimori,[24] born in Peru to two Japan-born émigré Wajin parents. Fujimori was reportedly a dual citizen of Japan and

Peru due to his parents registering him in Kumamoto from within Peru as a child (more on Japan's registry systems below). In 2000, after a decade in office laden with allegations of corruption and human rights abuses,[25] Fujimori infamously resigned his presidency via a Tōkyō hotel room fax and declared himself a Japanese citizen. Despite holding public office overseas, in contravention of Nationality Law Article 16.2, Fujimori received a Japanese passport weeks later (when most applications can take a year or two to process).[26] Then, despite international arrest warrants, Fujimori was not extradited and enjoyed a comfortable lifestyle with his fellow naturalized brother-in-law Aritomi[27] in Tōkyō's high society until 2005.[28] Although the media assigned cause to political connections, for example, "favorit[ism] among conservative politicians . . . enamored with the idea of a man with Japanese ancestry reaching political heights abroad,"[29] Fujimori's case is nevertheless one of privilege.[30] This is in contrast to scenarios under Japan's nationality regime where even half-Wajin children caught in bureaucratic registration dilemmas (such as being born of one North Korean parent)[31] have been rendered *stateless* due to geopolitical conceits, with legal protections of no country.

Supreme Court 2008 Interpretation of the Nationality Law: Human Rights in Japan Predicated upon Having Japanese Citizenship

Other recent developments have made clear that human and civil rights in Japan are connected to having Japanese citizenship. Japan's Supreme Court, in a landmark decision in June 2008, declared unconstitutional a clause in Article 3 requiring acknowledgment of Wajin paternity through marriage. That is to say, enforcement of the Nationality Law could no longer deny Japanese nationality to a child of a noncitizen woman and a Wajin man who had been born out of wedlock (or else had not been properly registered before birth). The Supreme Court's express legal reasoning behind declaring this situation unconstitutional was, inter alia, that *a lack of Japanese nationality is the cause of discrimination*, and that obtaining Japanese nationality is *essential for basic human rights to be guaranteed in Japan*.[32] This systematic linkage between rights and citizenship has also been reaffirmed in pinpoint examples, such as the GOJ's biased Prime Ministerial Cabinet surveys of human rights in Japan;[33] and, famously, a police prosecutor in Saga Prefecture bravely admitted in 2011, "We were taught that . . . foreigners have no human rights" when under police detention and interrogation.[34]

At this juncture, it is important to emphasize the embedded discourse behind the Supreme Court's legal reasoning here: *Human rights in Japan are not linked to being human; they are linked to holding Japanese citizenship*.[35] That is the crux of this research. That means the process of granting, restricting, or denying citizenship to select people is the gatekeeping mechanism any nation-state has over the enforcement of civil and political rights and privileges. However, as will be described below, the systemic granting of special privileges to people with Wajin blood ties also embeds a racialized framework behind equal protection under the law. It is the essential ideology justifying a structurally unequal treatment of non-*kokumin* at all other levels of society.

Japan's Nationality Law from an International Comparative Perspective: Becoming an Outlier

Although the gatekeeping mechanism of naturalization is available to any nation-state through its citizenship laws, Kashiwazaki (2000) offers a comparative perspective of structural inequality in Japan's citizenship rules:

> In the 1980s and 1990s, laws regulating nationality and citizenship were revised in immigrant-receiving countries such as Germany, the Netherlands, Sweden, and Switzerland, where nationality transmission was mainly based on *jus sanguinis* (by parentage). These revisions eased criteria for acquiring nationality by first-generation, long-term resident aliens as well as by the second and subsequent generations. Major types of legal administrative changes include introduction or expansion of the as-of-right acquisition of citizenship [i.e., Japan has no "as-of-right acquisition" system; anyone who was not attributed Japanese citizenship by birth must go through the process of naturalization]; double *jus soli*, by which the third generation obtains citizenship automatically; and toleration for dual nationality. . . . [On the other hand], there is no unified, coherent policy that could be called the Japanese citizenship policy. (436–437)

Kashiwazaki also cites five characteristics of how Japan is distinctive in restricting access to citizenship: (1) *Jus sanguinis* only for nationality transmission, with no concession made for former "Commonwealth"-style colonial historical ties, (2) tight border control, (3) strict naturalization rules that only go through the MOJ, (4) a close relationship between nationality and family registry, and (5) restrictive access to Permanent Residency status (437–447).

Now that we have established the barriers to becoming a *kokumin*, let us proceed to the second hurdle for national membership as a national: how *kokumin* are officially registered as citizens, and, conversely, how noncitizens have been officially excluded as residents of Japan.

JAPAN'S FAMILY REGISTRY SYSTEM (*KOSEKI*)[36]

With the exception of Japan's royal family, all Japanese citizens are required to have a Family Registry (*koseki*) registered with the GOJ in order to be acknowledged as citizens, according to the Family Registration Law (*koseki hō*) Articles 6 and 7. Additionally, only Japanese citizens may be fully registered on *koseki*.[37] Although registry systems exist in other countries (e.g., the *hukou* in China and Taiwan, the *ho khau* in Vietnam, the *hoju* in North Korea,[38] the *familienbuch* in Germany, the *livret de famille* in France, the *libro de familia* in Spain, etc.), Bryant (1991-2) notes that Japan's system is grounded in paradigms not found in other societies.[39]

Many countries effectively compile "dossiers" on their citizens (and noncitizens), but they are dossiers on individuals. However, only Japan (and Taiwan, who received the system under Japanese colonization) has a system predicated upon the notion of *the citizen as a member of a family unit*.[40] This is different from Occidental notions of state power; according to Levin (2012), Anglo-European state/society relations are based on the historical notion of a social contract between an individual serf and his lord; Japan's nation-state, however, is based on the notion of a contract between a familial head of household and their lord, putting potentially more intrusive means of social control at the disposal of lower levels of society.[41] Thus, the Japanese State intrinsically has an interest not only in "upright" individuals but also in "upright" *families*.[42] The further systematic exclusion of noncitizens (already selected by racialized *jus sanguinis* paradigms) from the Japanese family unit in terms of registry therefore creates and further embeds the Wajin/Non-Wajin dichotomy.

A practical example to illustrate: I was married to a Japanese citizen as a noncitizen between 1989 and 2000 (then married as a Japanese citizen after naturalization to the same person between 2000 and 2006). We have two daughters, born in Japan before I naturalized, who have been automatically granted Japanese citizenship through blood ties with their Japanese mother under the Nationality Law. Here is how our family was rendered on a redacted copy of her Family Register, or *koseki tōhon*, dated September 20, 1999 (figure 4.1).

I will translate sections of the *koseki*: On the bottom right-hand column is Ayako's married and maiden names.[43] The top half of the *koseki* (rendered in this form until 2011) describes family history, with the non-redacted sections indicating that Ayako married an American named David Christopher Aldwinckle (my former name) on June 28, 1989; they had two children (in their own separate sections in the left half of the *koseki*); listed below are birthdates and birthplaces and other private details redacted. Thus, the *koseki* duly notes marriage and parentage.

However, the legalized exclusionism of noncitizens is found in the section denoted as "wife" (*tsuma*), as there is no "husband" (*otto*) listed in this family unit. If this were a marriage between two Japanese citizens (as it would become when I naturalized in 2000),[44] there would be an additional column provided with my name rendered in a separate section (as my children are) and denoted as "husband," thus establishing a clear household unit (*setai*),

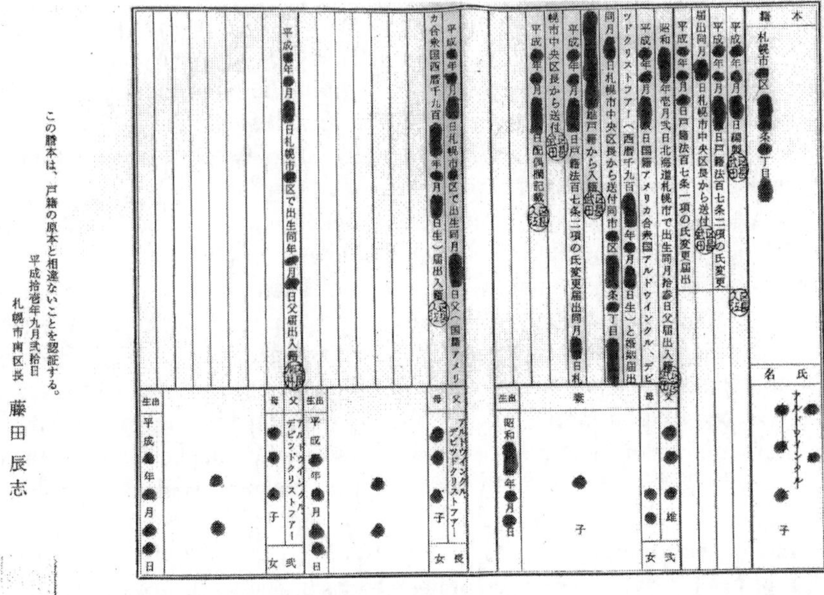

籍本 札幌市 区 条 丁目

名氏 アルドウィンクル

平成 年 月 日編製

平成 年 月 日戸籍法百七条二項の氏変更
届出同月 日札幌市中央区長から送付

平成 年 月 日戸籍法百七条一項の氏変更届出

昭和 年壱月弐日北海道札幌市で出生同月拾参日父届出入籍

平成 年 月 日国籍アメリカ合衆国アルドウィンクル、デビ
ッドクリストファー（西暦千九百 年 月 日生）と婚姻届出
同月 日札幌市中央区長から送付同市 区 条 丁目
戸籍から入籍

平成 年 月 日戸籍法百七条二項の氏変更届出同月 日札
幌市中央区長から送付

平成 年 月 日配偶欄記載

父 母 弐女 妻 生出 昭和 年 月 日

平成 年 月 日札幌市 区で出生同月 日父（国籍アメリ
カ合衆国西暦千九百 年 月 日生）届出入籍

父 アルドウィンクル、デビッドクリストファー 母 子 長女 生出 平成 年 月 日

平成 年 月 日札幌市 区で出生同年 月 日父届出入籍

父 アルドウィンクル、デビッドクリストファー 母 子 弐女 生出 平成 年 月 日

この謄本は、戸籍の原本と相違ないことを認証する。
平成拾壱年九月弐拾日
札幌市南区長 藤田辰志

Figure 4.1 Ex-wife Sugawara Ayako's koseki tōhon, Dated September 20, 1999, Issued by Sapporo Nishi-ku Ward Office. Redacted and annotated by the author. *Source:* Courtesy of author, by permission of Sugawara Ayako.

and the opportunity for either the husband or wife to be Head of Household (*setai nushi*; more below). However, for an international marriage in Japan, the noncitizen is officially not considered part of the vestigial "*ie*" household in the *Ie Seido* (see chapter 2), so to the untrained eye (i.e., readers not looking for an explicit listing within the upper text of a death or divorce) this looks like the *koseki* of a single-parent family.

Bryant (ibid.) describes several ways in which Japan's *koseki* system embeds superior/subordinate hierarchies that disenfranchise minority voices in Japan. For example, the system subordinates adopted and illegitimate children, maintains Burakumin historical inequalities, excludes Zainichi, and enfranchises patriarchal systems that subordinate women's identities. Reflecting the historical values and conceits of upper-class Japanese familial relations, the *koseki* system ultimately normalizes "value-laden hierarch[ical]" relations throughout Japanese society, including "employer-employee, teacher-student, government-governed, male-female, and even greater or lesser economic opportunity based upon historical/familial background." It also fosters an internalization of a meme of "the stability of the family equals the stability of the country," moreover constructs a majoritarian version of reality that categorizes and labels people positively (if they are part of the dominant majority) or negatively (if they are part of the minority or in support of minority views).

Given how constant and systematic these negative labels become through time, repetition, and precedent, Bryant argues that "[many people] have internalized the predominant view that negative labels reflect real distinctions intrinsic to subordinate groups rather than social constructions of reality" (159–160), to the point where many people inured to this system cannot imagine things any other way; moreover, many assume that similar things happen in other societies, entrenching further resistance to change. This system also makes it difficult for the disenfranchised minority to garner public support against the system, or even claim discrimination under it—for there is no intentional discriminator—therefore disenfranchisement must be due to unintended consequences (161).

However, three issues that Bryant's excellent analysis of the *koseki* system overlooks are (1) divorce and child abduction/parental alienation, (2) registration of noncitizens in general, and (3) how the *koseki* system influences other forms of official registry of noncitizens, such as the *jūminhyō* Residency Certificate. Issue 1 is too large an issue to take up within this research,[45] issue 2 was discussed above, so let us now focus on issue 3, the Residency Registration system:

JAPAN'S *JŪMINHYŌ* RESIDENCY REGISTRATION SYSTEM (1947–2012)

Japan's residents (*jūmin*) are formally listed on the Basic Residency Register (*jūmin kihon daichō*) under the Basic Residency Register Law (*jūmin kihon daichō hō*) Article 1. This is separate from the Family Register, under the jurisdiction of the Ministry of Home Affairs (now Ministry of Internal Affairs and Communications (*Jichishō/Sōmushō*)). The contents of the Residency Register are based upon information found in the *koseki*, which is administered by the Regional Legal Affairs Bureau (*Hōmukyoku*) under the jurisdiction of the MOJ. In other words, the *koseki* is an official family lineage record grounded in spatial location (*honseki*), the *jūminhyō* is an individual place of residence record, both maintained by local governments but administered by separate ministries.[46]

According to Basic Residency Register Law Articles 22 and 24, when residents of Japan move and change addresses, they are required to update their previous and current local government offices of their current whereabouts on a public register (they may of course move their *koseki* and *jūmin* registries to the same government office, but that can be a cumbersome process). According to Articles 6, 30, and 34 of the same law, a document called the Residency Certificate (*jūminhyō*) is issued as official certification of individual's whereabouts and household's composition. The *jūminhyō*, along with the *koseki tōhon*, is officially required as personal identification by employers, banks, credit agencies, taxation bureaus, law enforcement agencies, and other government offices as clearance for official matters, meaning access to employment opportunities, bank accounts, lines of credit, welfare, and other social benefits. Thus, registration within and access to these official documents is fundamental to life in Japan.[47]

Noncitizens Officially Rendered as "Invisible Residents"

However, under the Basic Residency Registry Law Article 39, until 2012 only people with Japanese nationality (i.e., people listed on a *koseki*) were allowed to be listed on a *jūminhyō*. Noncitizens were required to be listed on a separate system in local government offices under the Foreign Registry Law (*gaikokujin tōroku hō*) Article 4.3. For identification purposes, noncitizens were issued with a special document called the "Certificate of Completed Foreigner Registration" (*gaikokujin tōroku zumi shōmeisho* or *tōroku genpyō kisai jikō shōmeisho*), issued by the Immigration Bureau under the jurisdiction of the MOJ. The Certificate served the same function as a *jūminhyō*, but listed noncitizens as individuals without ties to their Japanese households. This official invisibility due to extranationality becomes clearer when one looks at an actual *jūminhyō* from an international marriage (figure 4.2).

The top line of this *jūminhyō* issued to my wife at the time denotes that this document is proof of all members of the household. However, tables within (redacted) list members of the household: Sugawara Ayako and two daughters. However, not listed is the noncitizen father of the household. In fact, the father, in order to be listed at all, had to make a special request of the Ward Office that he be listed in the only way possible for noncitizens—as "Actual Head of Household" (*jijitsujō no setai nushi*).

Importantly, in terms of bureaucratic extralegal powers discussed later in this research, this was permitted not because of a law passed through the Diet, but because of an "ordinance" (i.e., *Seirei* 292) issued by bureaucrats at the MOJ in 1967, as a form of official "guidance" (*shidō*) to local governments regarding the enforcement of Article 39. With a copy of this ordinance in hand, I (and many other local activist noncitizens)[48] was able to have my name officially included as part of my household certificate, handwritten by a local bureaucrat as a "remark" (*bikō*) (see arrow in figure 4.2) on my wife's *jūminhyō*.

The point is that noncitizens in Japan, although resident in Japan and paying Residency Tax (*jūminzei*), until July 2012 were officially invisible, that is, not listed as "residents" because Japan's registry systems required citizenship for residency. The unfairness of this system became apparent as

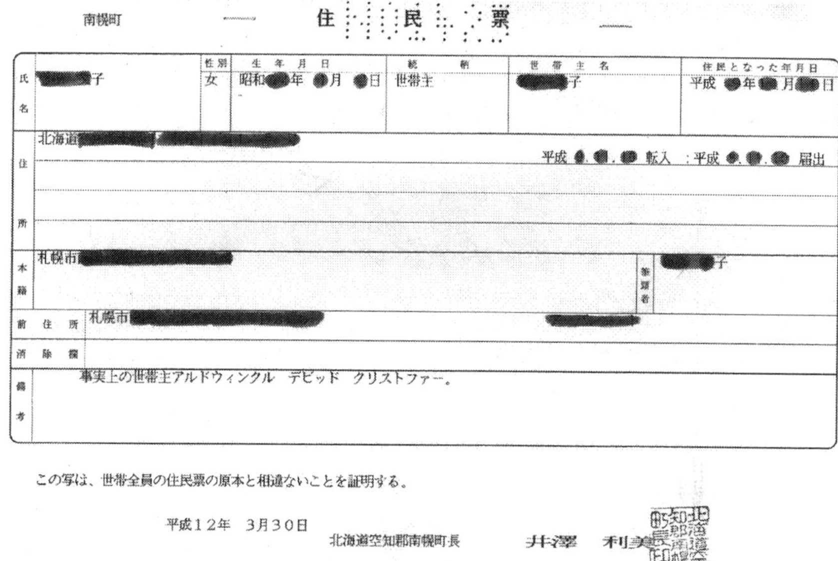

南幌町　住民票

氏名	性別	生年月日	続柄	世帯主名	住民となった年月日
子	女	昭和　年　月　日	世帯主	子	平成　年　月　日

住所: 北海道　　平成 . . 転入 : 平成 . . 届出

本籍: 札幌市　　筆頭者: 子

前住所: 札幌市

消除欄:

備考: 事実上の世帯主アルドウィンクル　デビッド　クリストファー。

この写は、世帯全員の住民票の原本と相違ないことを証明する。

平成12年　3月30日　北海道空知郡南幌町長　井澤　利美

Figure 4.2　Sugawara Ayako's jūminhyō, Dated September 26, 1997, Issued by Sapporo Nishi-ku Ward Office. Redacted by the author. *Source:* Courtesy of author, by permission of Sugawara Ayako.

some municipalities began issuing "honorary residency certificates" to local animals and fictional characters (but not foreigners),[49] but on a practical level, this resulted in noncitizens not being counted by some local governments as part of their population (*jinkō*) (e.g., in Tōkyō Nerima-ku).[50] A further complication of the system arose when some local governments were reported to have counted deceased Wajin as alive.[51]

As of this Second Edition, nearly a decade after opening the *jūminhyō* to foreign residents, this exclusionary process remains standardized and normalized: A 2021 google search using the term "人口総数には、外国人登録数を含んでいません" [registered foreigner numbers are not included in the total population numbers] reveals that many other local governments still will not officially count "noncitizens" as "residents" in terms of households or population. This probably represents the ultimate in Wajin privilege: immorality in the residency registry while Non-Wajin residents are omitted.

The complications of this exclusionary system extend to the national level, where mainstream media also exclude foreigners from their articles on Japan's total population tallies. For example, the *Yomiuri Shinbun* reported that a population rise in Japan in 2008 was solely due to the "rise in the number of repatriates and newly naturalized citizens," glibly noting, "The figure was based on resident registrations at municipal government offices and does not include foreign residents."[52] As of 2020, some media now carefully tailor the wording on population tallies as referring to "the population of Japanese people" (*nihonjin no jinkō*), again removing "foreigners" (rendered as *gaikokujin*, without noting their status as residents) from the total.[53]

Consequences of Official Statistical Invisibility for Noncitizens: Problematic Demographic Science

Rendering noncitizens into "invisible residents" also affects Japan's demographic science. For example, during an international demography symposium I attended on June 2, 2009, a talk given by Takahashi Shigesato, deputy director of Japan's National Institute for Population and Social Security Research (*Kokuritsu Shakai Hoshō Jinkō Mondai Kenkyūjo, fuku shochō*), offered his prediction that "Japanese will be extinct by the year 3000," yet explicitly omitted population inflows, that is, immigration (meaning that people exclusive of naturalized Japanese citizens—Wajin—were the ones being referred to as "extinct").[54] When asked why, Takahashi replied (my translation), "Immigration is not an option for our country. Inflows must be strictly controlled for fear of overpopulation." Thus, despite being a country in demonstrated demographic decline, a sudden theoretical "overpopulation problem" was due to an overabundance of Non-Wajin in Japan. This is to argue, in essence, that "more 'foreigners' means less Japan." This is a political, not scientific, conceit, and a meme that will be seen in future chapters within xenophobic political debates and official discourse on human rights.

Finally, when the GOJ surveys the citizen and noncitizen population, for example, every five years in the form of the National Census (*kokusei chōsa*), demographic science embeds the Wajin/Non-Wajin dichotomy further. The National Census does not survey for ethnicity (*minzoku*), only for nationality (*kokuseki*), meaning that participants can only choose one option to self-identify as their social origin.[55] In practice, this means that the author, who wishes to register himself as a hyphenated American-Japanese, can only indicate "Japanese" (*Nihonjin*) on the form. His children face the same situation, where their Wajin roots officially mask their ethnic American origins. Thus, this officially surveyed invisibility ignores the existence of Wajin from international marriages with "multiethnic" origins. Of course, this multinational situation, as the Nationality Law indicates, must be legally reconciled by the age of twenty-two with the official choice of one nationality (therefore, officially, one ethnicity). Thus, Japan's registry and official population surveying systems not only reify the national narrative of monoethnic Japan, but also officially render the potential multiethnicity and multinationality of Wajin themselves as invisible.

Japan's Registry Systems and the Potential Exclusion of Mixed-Blood Citizens

Registry systems in Japan have also presented a barrier to children being listed on a *koseki*, therefore ineligible for Japanese citizenship. Until 1985, citizenship could only pass through a Japanese-citizen father, not a Japanese-citizen mother, which disqualified all children from relationships between noncitizen men and Japanese-citizen women. After 1985, the Nationality Law was amended to allow any children born to Japanese-citizen mothers to have Japanese citizenship automatically conferred. For Japanese-citizen fathers, however, getting official recognition of paternity continued to be an issue, as illegitimate children (*hichakushutsu-shi*) born out of wedlock to noncitizen mothers either had to have Japanese paternity formally acknowledged by registry at a government office before birth, or within fourteen days of birth,[56] as per Article 49 of the Family Registry Law.[57] If not, the child would not be recognized as a Japanese citizen. Modern methods independent of the state used to establish paternity, such as DNA testing, are still not officially recognized.[58]

Further complicating matters is Article 12 of the Nationality Law, which states that a Japanese national born in a foreign country acquiring foreign nationality by birth shall be denied Japanese nationality, unless properly registered at a GOJ registry office within three months of birth as per Family Registration Law Article 49. Several children with one Japanese parent recently claimed in Tōkyō District Court that Article 12 of the Nationality Law was unconstitutional if their parents had been unaware of this requirement. On March 23, 2012, Tōkyō District Court declared Article 12 constitutional. This put a boundary on the abovementioned 2008 Supreme Court decision ruling the denial of Japanese citizenship was a violation of the human rights of Japanese citizens.

Thus, bureaucratic registry convenience has been given priority over biological fact in Japanese registry laws. This has embedded a special hurdle for mixed-blood Wajin children—for if both parents giving birth overseas were pure-blooded Wajin Japanese citizens, Article 12 would not apply.[59]

Some Positive Amendments to the System for the Second Edition

There have been some positive changes. As noted above, in 2012 the Residency Registration system was changed to allow noncitizens to be issued official *jūminhyō* Registry Certificates. The Foreign Registry Law was also abolished, meaning noncitizens are now registered as "residents" (*jūmin*) in Japan and listed both within their households and as Head of Household with their Japanese families. (They may also be included in total population tallies, at the local government's discretion.)

Other discriminatory policies were amended or withdrawn. The Re-Entry Permit (REP) (see chapter 5) was almost completely abolished, meaning noncitizen residents no longer face a tax to visit outside Japan. The GOJ also lengthened the maximum duration of visas from three years to five (although the actual duration of any visa awarded remains at the discretion of the bureaucrats). For a time, there was also a more transparent "points system" visa regime (that eventually turned out to be too limited and too strict).[60] The GOJ also issued a new form of ARC (a RFID-chipped *Zairyū* Card) that promised more centralized efficiency in registration but raised privacy concerns, and took away discretional power from local municipalities (which had previously issued the cards, including to visa overstayers) in order to combat "illegal foreigners."[61] (Also, as of December 25, 2020, the Zairyū Card was subject to an app that the general public could download from the MOJ website; it could scan anyone's card and read personal information, confirming earlier fears of technologically enhanced invasions of privacy.)[62]

Notwithstanding these changes, the fundamentals remain intact. Because these new cards are still required to be carried by noncitizens only at all times under criminal penalty, this system performatively encourages the racial profiling, official bullying, and systemic subordination of Visible Minorities throughout Japanese society. Let us now turn the focus of the chapter in that direction, and start with how the citizen/noncitizen dichotomy affects employment opportunities and access to social welfare.

"NATIONALITY CLAUSES" AND "*KOKUMIN* CONCEITS"

Within Japan's laws, national policies, and public policy papers the words *wagakuni* (our country), *wareware nipponjin* (we Japanese), and *kokumin* (people of the nation, that is, Japanese nationals) are commonly embedded as part of the discourse. This is unnecessary, since semantically reasonable substitutes are available in the Japanese language, including *shimin* (people of the city, or citizen, as part of the word *shiminken*),[63] *jūmin* (residents), *hitobito* (people in general), and *ningen* (human beings); these words would include all people, if not resident taxpayers, regardless of nationality.[64] Thus, both the choice of *kokumin* and the application of the dichotomous *kokumin/gaikokujin* paradigm in laws and social systems differentiate between citizen and noncitizen taxpayers. This has not only excluded noncitizens from equal access to social benefits, but also, as we shall see below, denied them the right to privacy and freedom from official and public harassment.

Kokumin-Based Exclusions from Social Welfare Benefits

The most famous example of the *kokumin* dichotomy is within the Japanese Constitution itself—in Article 14, the very article that forbids discrimination by race and social origin. The original English version writes, "All of the *people* are equal under the law" (emphasis added), while in the Japanese translation (the version with legal force in Japan) the word "people" is rendered as *kokumin*, that is, Japanese nationals. Although legal precedent has established that human rights protections in civil court will technically apply equally to citizens and noncitizens,[65] differences in application by nationality become apparent through the application of what Dower (1999) unequivocally calls the "blatantly racist . . . linguistic subterfuge" endemic to Japan's postwar constitutional history.[66] Dower labels it the product of "language games" in translations, deliberately chosen by designers of postwar Japanese society to eliminate equal civil rights and protections under the law for resident noncitizens, particularly the abovementioned *Sangokujin* former citizens of empire.

For example, the basic National Health Insurance plan is indicatively titled *Kokumin Kenkō Hoken.* Despite health insurance being mandatory for all workers (*rōdōsha*) in Japan regardless of nationality (under the Labor Standards Law (*rōdō kijun hō*) and Health Insurance Law (*kenkō hoken hō*)),[67] noncitizens were excluded from *Kokumin Kenkō Hoken* entirely until 1982.[68] Even after reforms to remove the requirement of nationality, the Shizuoka Prefectural Government, for one, continued to exclude all foreigners (including its comparatively large and then-growing Nikkei South American workforce) from coverage until the late 1990s.[69]

These exclusions continue to the present day. In 2008, Ōita Prefecture denied minimum welfare benefits (*seikatsu hogo*) under the Public Assistance Law to a seventy-nine-year-old Zainichi Chinese woman born and raised in Japan, claiming that Japanese nationality was required for social welfare. This was affirmed in 2010 by the Ōita District and High Courts, which ruled that welfare (even though paying into social security is mandatory for anyone of a working age residing in Japan)[70] was not a "charity" for noncitizens. These rulings were overturned by the Fukuoka High Court in 2011, citing treaty obligations governing *refugees* (!) that guaranteed public welfare be on par with citizens.[71] Finally, in 2014 the Supreme Court ruled decisively that foreigners, even if they are permanent residents, do not have access to social welfare "as a right" (*kenri de wa nai*), explicitly because they are not *kokumin.* Soon afterward, far-right politicians mean-spiritedly submitted a bill to halt welfare benefits to any poverty-stricken foreigner as "a burden on the Japanese government" (even though most European countries do not have a Nationality Clause for welfare benefits).[72] Thus, Japan's "conceit of *kokumin*," embedded within a postwar history of excluding *Sangokujin* from the benefits of the state, and currently grounded in laws that treat "foreigners" as refugees,[73] purposefully denies noncitizens equal treatment under the law.

The "Nationality Clause": Kokumin-*Based Exclusions from Public-Sector Employment*

Another example of *kokumin* as a requirement for employment involves the dispensation of public authority. Some employment in Japan explicitly requires Japanese nationality. The "Nationality Clause" (*kokuseki jōkō*) is found in public-sector job descriptions, with embedded clauses such as "*Nihon kokumin*" and "*kokuseki o yū suru hito*" (person with (Japanese) citizenship). It was promulgated from 1953 by the Cabinet Legislative Bureau as an "unwritten government decree" to bar resident noncitizens (again, at the time the *Sangokujin*) from having authority "making decisions that affect the [Japanese] public," or "which have a bearing on the formulation of national intention."[74] This mandate has been interpreted broadly: As of this writing, job positions that require Japanese nationality include foreign service bureaucrats, elected politicians and sometimes their staff, Self-Defense Forces, notary publics, judges and jurors, members of boards of education, public safety officials, public election staff, public welfare staff, public prosecutors, Human Rights Bureau staff, tax collectors, and firefighters.[75]

Of course, some public-sector employment is available to noncitizens at the national- and local-government level. However, noncitizens now face a second barrier, that is, being ineligible to take examinations for promotion to higher-level administrative positions (*kanrishoku*). In effect, noncitizens remained full-time workers (generally on a renewable contract basis) unable to rise to positions where they could manage citizens. There were some amendments: By 1993, Kawasaki became the first major city to open up public-sector administrative posts to noncitizens (when Kōchi Prefecture and Ōsaka City attempted to follow suit, the Home Affairs Ministry, according to the *Yomiuri Shinbun*, pressured them to desist).[76] By 1996, the national government relented, stating that local governments may decide for themselves whether they would enforce a Nationality Clause,[77] and subsequently locales both large and small, including Ōsaka City, Kōchi Prefecture, Niigata's Jōetsu City, and Minami Uonuma City,[78] opened up their hiring practices.[79]

Nevertheless, some municipalities, notably Tōkyō-to, have remained closed to equal employment opportunities for noncitizens, illustrated famously by the case of second-generation Zainichi Korean nurse Chong Hyang Gyun. In

1994, Chong sued the Tōkyō Metropolitan Government for being denied the right to take the promotion exam to become a section chief of hygiene (*eisei kachō*) at her health care facility. Chong's precedent-setting case took more than ten years, from 1994 to 2005, where the Tōkyō District Court ruled her exclusion from examination was constitutional in 1996. Tōkyō High Court later that year reversed, as it violated constitutional freedoms to choose one's occupation. Finally after nearly ten years, the Supreme Court in January 2005 ultimately reversed the High Court's decision and confirmed the constitutionality of Chong's exclusion. The reasoning, according to the *Japan Times*, was as follows:

> The majority of the justices said that some local government-level civil servants are entrusted with tasks that involve the exercise of public authority, and that in doing so their actions greatly affect the lives of residents. "Based on the (constitutional) principle of national sovereignty and in view of the fact that the people should in the end be responsible for how the central and local governments govern, (the Constitution) should be viewed as presuming that Japanese nationals [*kokumin*] in principle will assume local civil service positions" that require the exercise of public authority, they stated.[80]

Thus, the highest level of Japan's judiciary had incontrovertibly legalized Japan's embedded employment discrimination by nationality, and performatively separated foreigners, even the Zainichi generational "foreigners," from the concerns of "the lives of residents."

The implications of this decision are wide ranging, beyond being denied a position in Japan's administrative leadership. Japan's procuracy is being denied beneficial know-how. Some areas of Japan have significant numbers of noncitizens as a percentage of the population,[81] thus many important positions that might effectively use minority voices and insights when dealing with minority issues, such as law enforcement, have been denied them. Despite some further movements toward openness,[82] Japanese authorities continue to demonstrate a latent distrust of noncitizens in "sensitive positions of trust involving public power" by enforcing exclusionary clauses embedded within bureaucratic rules. By design, the embedded "conceit of *kokumin*" disenfranchises noncitizens from being better represented in public policy formation and enforcement.[83] It also sets a precedent for other job sectors:

Kokumin-Based Exclusions from Private-Sector Employment

Noncitizens are similarly denied equal employment opportunities in the private sector. For example, one nonsensitive non-policing sector—education—has systematically denied noncitizens non-term-limited contracted employment (i.e., academic tenure) through perpetual *gaikokujin kyōshi*, *gaikokujin kyōin*, and *tokubetsu shokutaku* positions in Japan's National and Public Universities (*kokuritsu* and *kōritsu daigaku*). These precedents set in influential universities were then similarly applied to create contract-only employment of noncitizen educators in Japan's private-sector universities (*shiritsu* or *watakushiritsu daigaku*).[84] There are also cases of employment agencies (such as "Hello Work," Japan's official job-finding unemployment office) and other private-sector job-placement companies permitting employers to specify "no foreigners" in their job advertisements.[85] The practice of explicit Nationality Clauses within the private sector is so embedded and normalized that even the *Japan Times* prints want ads for "Japanese only" jobs.[86]

More important is that this practice explicitly violates Japan's Labor Standards Law (*rōdō kijun hō*), Article 3, which states: "An employer shall not engage in discriminatory treatment with respect to wages, working hours or other working conditions by the reason of the nationality, creed or social status of any worker." However, this is unenforced due to a Catch-22 loophole, that is, the law does not apply until the person is hired—until then, he or she is technically not yet a "worker" protected by labor law.[87]

To sum up this section: Thanks to informal national policy created by the "Nationality Clause" to exclude noncitizens for public-sector work nationwide, discrimination was enabled for the private sector as well. Combined with a lax enforcement of labor standards law banning discrimination by nationality, and a judiciary that further legitimized explicit discrimination by nationality, overt job advertisements for "Japanese only" positions further normalize "Japanese only" practices nationwide. These create unstable,[88] limited-term work for noncitizens in many limited employment sectors, and reinforce a lack of precedent for noncitizen opportunities in untested job markets in Japan.[89]

REGISTRY SYSTEMS AND POLICING

This chapter has so far outlined how Japan's official registry systems distinguish between citizens and noncitizens, showing how public policy not only "others" and excludes noncitizens from equal treatment or benefit under the law, but also renders noncitizens into invisible residents with unstable employment or access to social welfare. Now let's turn to how these embedded differentiations affect the Visual Minorities, by targeting people who "look foreign" for unequal and subordinated treatment.

Portable Personal Identification in Japan: Required for Noncitizens Only

Japan's registry systems issue personal identification (ID) for official business. For people who do not wish to carry their *koseki tōhon* and *jūminhyō* with them at all times, there are other forms of ID, including driver licenses (*unten menkyo shō*), health insurance cards and passbooks (*kenkō hoken shō*), resident registry cards with photo issued under the *Jūki Netto* system (*jūmin kihon daichō kādo*), student ID (*gakusei shō*), pension passbooks (*nenkin techō*), and of course Japanese passports (*ryoken*) (along with additional identification if *inkan* signature seals are necessary on documents).[90] However, except for the new *jūmin kihon daichō kādo* issued under the controversial[91] *Jūki Netto* system, Japan has as of this writing no single, standardized certificate that is required for all citizens as ID (as not everyone drives, travels abroad, is a student or pensioner, etc., or has opted to receive the *Jūki* Card). Moreover, citizens have no legal requirement to carry ID on their person at all times. This is not the same for noncitizens.

The Foreign Registry Law (1947–2012) and Criminal Penalties for Noncitizens Only

As discussed in chapter 2, Japan was setting up its postwar "homogeneous society" narratives by ethnically cleansing itself of empire. From 1947 it began differentiating, othering, and subordinating its noncitizen population by treating them like criminals would be treated in Japan fingerprinting, tracking, and constantly policing them. For example, Japan instituted a tracking system for all noncitizens and former citizens of empire through a special and separate registry system, backed up with criminal penalty within the Foreign Registry Law (*gaikokujin tōroku hō*). To this day, the Immigration Control and Refugee Recognition Act (*shutsunyū koku kanri oyobi nanmin nintei hō*) Article 23 states that noncitizens under the age of sixteen in Japan on short-stay visas (under ninety days) must carry passports at all times and surrender them to policing authorities upon demand.

However, this scrutiny also applies to residents with visas longer than ninety days (i.e., people not in Japan on tourist or temporary visas). They must register with their local Ward Office and receive a special Alien Registration Card (*gaikokujin tōroku shōmeisho*, aka the "Gaijin Card," hereinafter ARC) as official personal ID. Like short-stay tourists, under the Foreign Registry Law noncitizens must carry the ARC at all times in lieu of a passport (Article 13), and also surrender it to authorities on pain of criminal punishment of up to one year in jail or a 200,000 yen fine (Article 18). As mentioned above, after 2012 the ARC was officially changed to the "Residence Card," or *Zairyū*

Kādo, but the enforcement system remains the same under the Immigration Control Act. (Therefore, since they both serve the same function, I will refer to both cards as the ARC.)[92]

This system "othered" not only "Newcomer" noncitizens born abroad, but also "Oldcomer" *Zainichi* noncitizens born and raised in Japan; many suddenly found themselves alienated from age sixteen from their Wajin peers, forced to choose a future of either "passing" as Wajin, or rewiring their self-identification to become a "foreigner" in Japan, moreover required to carry official proof of their foreignness at all times on their person.

"Othering" and Racial Profiling of Visible Minorities under the Immigration Control Act and Foreign Registry Law

ARC holders thus found themselves being permanently policed. The Immigration Control Act Article 23 states that noncitizens must display ID in the form of a passport or the ARC on request at any time to "the authorities" (*kanken*), particularly those representing the MOJ in some capacity.[93] Under Article 70, refusal to do so may incur a penalty of 3 million yen or three years' imprisonment. Technically, however, Article 23 also states that an ARC acts in place of a passport, so if a police officer demands a passport and nothing else, noncitizens are legally under no obligation to display. However, standing on the letter of the law here does not preclude subsequent detention or arrest of the refuser under Articles 95 and 96 of the Penal Code, covering "interference with the duties of a public official" (*kōmu shikkō bōgai*), penalties of up to 5 million yen and three years' imprisonment, not to mention the legal power to detain any criminal suspect for questioning and detention for up to twenty-three days (more in chapter 6).[94]

This degree of policing power enabled racial profiling, normalizing police instant ID checkpoints of anyone who "looked foreign." The Foreign Registry Law Article 13 explicitly empowered police to stop any noncitizen at any time and demand an ARC. There is no requirement of probable cause (*sōtō na riyū*). Citizens, on the other hand, by law are protected against this form of random stoppage, search, and seizure. Article 2 of the "Police Execution of Duties Law" (*keisatsukan shokumu shitsumon shikkō hō*) requires probable cause for suspicion that a crime is about to be committed, or has been committed, before police investigations can be carried out. This law does not explicitly limit coverage to *kokumin*, so technically noncitizens are also covered by it, but in practice the Immigration Control Act and the Foreign Registry Law created precedent that overrides.

The results are clear: normalized are random police stoppages, the asking of personal questions (*shokumu shitsumon*), and searches, seizures, arrests, and detentions for noncitizens, particularly Visible Minorities, simply for not carrying an ARC. This these "instant ID checkpoints" have happened on the street in public, in public transportation systems, at airports and connected train stations, even inside apartment complexes known to have noncitizen residents.[95] Although the author has conducted several interviews (1998–2008) with people visibly identified and sometimes detained by police as "suspicious persons" (*fushinsha*) just for "looking too foreign," there have since been more independently verified cases of Japanese citizens also being stopped, harassed, and detained by police for looking "too foreign" without ID—including an Ainu woman detained for "looking too tall" and not carrying her *passport* (not her ARC—neither of which she possessed).[96]

Sometimes these inspections are carried out repeatedly, with the same person stopped literally more than a hundred times for walking or cycling within a particular area, sometimes repeatedly by the same police officers or by officers in mufti.[97] As the US Embassy's American Citizen Services Newsletter (January 1, 2007) substantiates for the Tōkyō area:

> The Embassy has been advised that Japanese police and immigration officials are currently conducting random identification inspections in several different areas of Tokyo to ensure that all visitors to Japan possess the appropriate immigration documents. Most inspections occur at or near Tokyo metro stations, and the police are both uniformed and in plain clothes. To all of our customers in Tokyo and beyond, be sure to carry your key documentation with you at all times in the event that you are the subject of an inspection.[98]

How these police "random identification inspections" are supposed to distinguish on sight between "foreign visitor" and "foreign resident" (not to mention "foreign-looking Japanese citizen") remains unclear in interviews I have conducted with several police departments. I too been subjected to police spot searches and ID checks on several occasions (both before and after naturalization—finding myself in the Catch-22 situation of being forced to show proof of citizenship to be exempt from showing ID). It was also reported in 2017 that at least one local police agency (Hokkaidō) has launched "arrest quotas" for certain crimes that "foreigners" are seen as more likely to commit (such as gun possession), incentivizing cops on the beat to target anyone who "looks foreign" (to the point of entrapment through "illegal sting operations" and "false statements in investigative documents" that were later overturned in court).[99]

Thus, the law differentiates, "others," and subjects visually identified "foreigners" to unequal due process under the law, in conflict with other laws that restrict police invasions of privacy. Attempts to curtail this activity by appealing to the MOJ's Bureaus of Human Rights (more below),[100] to the mass media, or to the police directly have not produced any revisions or additional protections against noncitizens being racially profiled.[101] As of this Second

Edition, it has since become clear that the Japanese police have the legal prerogative not only to stop, but also frisk *anyone* they consider "suspicious" (*fushin*) on the street,[102] meaning the application of laws to target foreigners can later be used to provide pretense for targeting Japanese as well.

Naturally, it is difficult for the police in any society to be everywhere at once. But in Japan's case this has given license for the GOJ, as we shall see below, to liberally interpret current laws to enlist non-policing organs (and even the general public) to willfully target "illegal foreigners," by launching public campaigns against "international crime," "overstayers," "terrorists," and "infectious diseases."

EXPANDING THE POLICING OF NONCITIZENS BEYOND THE IMMIGRATION CONTROL ACT

On July 9, 2012, the Foreign Registry Law was abolished and the ARCs were reformed, but the policing system has been expanded (ostensibly under the Immigration Control Act) to non-policing agencies. For example, tax offices from 2010 began to require that noncitizens submit their ARCs for processing of household tax returns, as have local Departments of Motor Vehicles (*shikenjō*) when renewing Japanese driver licenses.[103] From that, ID and visa checks have unlawfully expanded into the private sector (e.g., hotels, banks, fitness centers, cellphone companies, Airbnb private accommodations, and even employers), giving rise to people not trained as law enforcement officials unlawfully demanding private information from Visible Minorities as a precondition of service. Each in turn:

Hotels Unlawfully Demand ARCs from "Foreign Guests"

From 2005, hotels nationwide began requiring "foreign guests" display an ARC as a precondition for service. On January 24, 2005, the Ministry of Health, Labor and Welfare (MHLW) issued Ministerial Ordinance (*shōrei*) 4018, reinterpreting Hotel Management Law (*ryokan gyōhō*) Article 4.2 to require hotels ask noncitizen lodgers *without addresses in Japan* (my emphasis) for proof of their nationality and their passport numbers (whereas the display of personal ID remained unrequired for *kokumin*). This has led to racial profiling on several occasions both of the author and of other eyewitnesses,[104] with demands for ID under threat of denial of lodging (in violation of the Hotel Management Law).[105] This even occurs after "foreign-looking" customers have written their addresses in Japan on the hotel's check-in sheet—sufficient proof for Wajin customers. According to interviews conducted by the author with hotel managers and staff nationwide (2005–2011), these hotels had been requested to follow *Shōrei* 4018 directly through visits and written notices from local police authorities.[106]

The MHLW also issued two standardized multilingual forms for all hotels to display at their check-in counters (see figures 4.3 and 4.4)

Let's parse how the notices have different wording and thus different applications. The version in figure 4.3 says explicitly, "Japanese law requires that we ask every foreign guest to present their passport, a photocopy of which we will keep on file during their stay with us" (even though there is nothing within *Shōrei* 4018 or in applicable laws requiring photocopying of passports). The Japanese is the same: "*Gaikokujin no kata no shukuhaku*." However, in the version in figure 4.4, this is clarified as a "non-resident foreign guest," with the Japanese explicitly saying that the noncitizen guest must have no address in Japan in order to require ID.

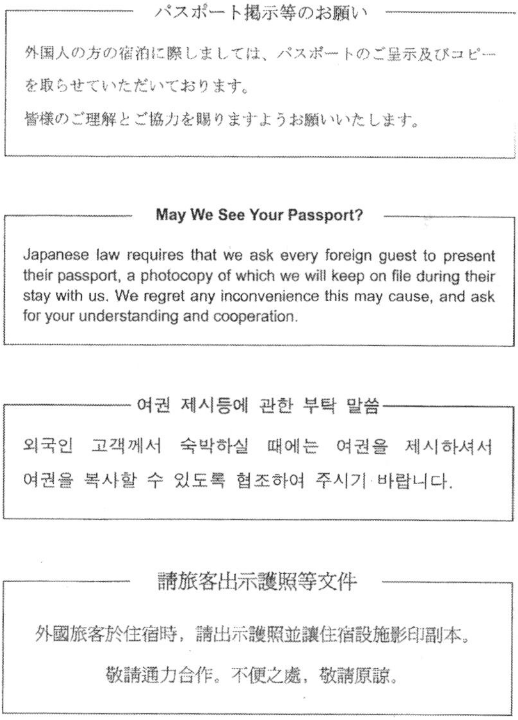

パスポート掲示等のお願い

外国人の方の宿泊に際しましては、パスポートのご呈示及びコピーを取らせていただいております。
皆様のご理解とご協力を賜りますようお願いいたします。

May We See Your Passport?

Japanese law requires that we ask every foreign guest to present their passport, a photocopy of which we will keep on file during their stay with us. We regret any inconvenience this may cause, and ask for your understanding and cooperation.

여권 제시등에 관한 부탁 말씀

외국인 고객께서 숙박하실 때에는 여권을 제시하셔서 여권을 복사할 수 있도록 협조하여 주시기 바랍니다.

請旅客出示護照等文件

外國旅客於住宿時，請出示護照並讓住宿設施影印副本。
敬請通力合作。不便之處，敬請原諒。

Figure 4.3 Notice Shows Official Multilingual Clarification of Check-in Procedure for "foreign guests." On display at public places of lodging nationwide, issued by the MHLW in 2005. *Source:* Courtesy of Tokyū Stay Gotanda, Tōkyō.

<問い合わせ（苦情）対処用>

日本政府は法令により、2005年4月1日から「日本国内に住所を持たない外国人」の方の宿泊に際しては、＊氏名　＊住所　＊職業　等の記載に加えて＊国籍　及び　＊旅券番号　の記載とパスポートの提示及びコピーを義務付けましたので、ご理解、ご協力をお願いいたします。

Effective April 1, 2005, Japanese legislation makes it mandatory that you, as a "non-resident foreign guest," present your passport and have it photocopied as well as having your nationality and passport number, in addition to conventional information such as full name, address, occupation, etc. entered on the registration form. Your understanding and cooperation are appreciated.

일본 정부는 법령에 의거하여, 2005 년 4 월 1 일부터 '일본 국내에 거주하지 않는 외국인' 손님이 숙박하실 때에는 ＊성명 ＊주소 ＊직업등과 함께 ＊국적 및 ＊여권번호를 기록하고, 여권의 제시 및 복사를 의무화하였습니다.
여러분의 많은 이해와 협조를 부탁드립니다.

日本政府依據法令要求自2005年4月1日起
「在日本國內沒有住址的外國人」於住宿時，
除了＊姓名＊住址＊職業等之外，還必須填寫
＊國籍及護照號碼，並出示護照，讓住宿設施影印副本。
敬請通力合作。不便之處，敬請原諒。

Figure 4.4 Notice Shows Clarification "in the Case of Questions or Complaints." On display at public places of lodging nationwide, issued by the MHLW in 2005. Annotations by author. *Source:* Courtesy of Tokyū Stay Gotanda, Tōkyō.

Also, figure 4.3 (the first one generally seen and displayed to the public) unlawfully extends enforcement to "every foreign guest" regardless of address, while figure 4.4 does not. Not only does this encourage policy creep to target all noncitizens (effectively requiring any "foreign guest" resident of Japan to be treated as a tourist), it also "others" Visible Minorities, encouraging unsophisticated profiling by private-sector employees to treat all people who "look foreign" as a monolithic group regardless of their legal status in Japan, and as suspicious. In sum, official directives are encouraging hotels nationwide to engage in systemic racial profiling.

The US Embassy in Tōkyō asked the GOJ for clarification of *Shōrei* 4018, and reported the following in its American Community Update of May 2005:

> After we sought clarification, according to the Environmental Health Division, Health Service Bureau, Ministry of Health, Labor and Welfare, the new

> registration procedure at lodging facilities does not apply to foreigners who are residents of Japan but only to tourists and temporary visitors. If you write a Japanese address on the check-in sheet, hotels are not supposed to ask for your passport. If your passport information is recorded, the Government of Japan has requested hotels to retain the record for three years, though the law itself does not mention how long records should be retained. The authority to decide the period of retention actually resides with the local government. So, some local governments might enact an ordinance to set a specific retention period. If not, the period is three years as advised by the central government.

Thus, this three-year period is at odds with the MHLW notice in figure 4.3, that passport records will only be kept "during their stay" with the hotel.

In sum, this ministerial ordinance (again, not an actual law that passed through the Diet) officially created extralegal powers for the police. These have since been expanded to require passports in specific (not just the ARC) to be photocopied as a precondition for service.[107] With this precedent set, the NPA unlawfully expanded its ID checkpoint powers from street checks into private-sector businesses.

GOJ's Next Campaign: Policing "Foreigners" as Official Agents of Terrorism and Contagion

Embedded within the mandate of *Shōrei* 4018 is the view that noncitizens should be treated as potential terrorists and members of international criminal gangs (*kokusai soshiki hanzai*). It was created, according to MHLW, under the "Action Plan for Pre-empting of Terrorism" (*tero no mizen bōshi ni kansuru kōdō kikaku*), approved by the Prime Minister's Cabinet (*naikaku*) on December 10, 2004.[108] The Ministry of Foreign Affairs clarified the hotel policy on their Embassy of Japan website.[109]

Two things are notable about *Shōrei* 4018. First, the justification for targeting "foreign visitors" is not only prevention of terrorism (i.e., not "foreign crime"), but also prevention of "infectious diseases." Second, (a) despite the unlawful stretches of bureaucratic interpretations of the Hotel Management Law to require in practice photocopied ID from "foreigners" on sight, and (b) despite the later clarifications in the directives made by government agencies and the US Government to distinguish between noncitizen tourist and resident, no official amendments to the erroneous 2005 hotel circular, as verified by the author at Japanese hotels through 2010, have been made by the MHLW.[110]

As of this Second Edition, official policy encouraging racial profiling by the accommodations industry has intensified. Even though the NPA has been cautioned multiple times by local and national authorities about the letter of the law exempting foreign residents, there have been more cases of local police pressuring hotels to target all "foreign guests," some falsifying laws in the name of (and without the knowledge of) the relevant ministries.[111]

Notwithstanding some embarrassing retractions, the tendency is still toward targeting "foreigners" thanks to the explosion of foreign tourism to Japan in the 2010s (see chapter 8). To make up for the shortfall in accommodations, private room rentals (such as Airbnb) have been legalized, governed by the new Minpaku Law of 2018. However, now local authorities have requested (if not required under local ordinances) private citizens renting out rooms to check, photocopy, and report the visa statuses of "foreign" guests to the police. Indicatively, authorities have expressly cited factors such as the dangers of "terrorism" connected to ISIS and the Tōkyō Olympics, and "unsafe strangers" around places where children walk to school.[112]

Other Private-Sector Businesses Targeting "Foreign-looking" Customers

The practice of unlawfully demanding ARCs from "foreign-looking" customers with "foreign-sounding" names has become so normalized that is no longer limited to accommodations and policing institutions. Japanese banks and other financial agencies began requiring noncitizens to provide an ARC before opening a bank account (which affects life profoundly, as bank accounts are required by some employers for payment of salary and by utility companies for direct debit), or again years *after* opening a bank account.[113] And from September 22, 2006, bank scrutiny toward noncitizens became even tougher, as the abovementioned Action Plan against Terrorism took effect, and financial institutions, at the behest of the NPA, began tightening their qualifications against noncitizens under measures against "money laundering." They began profiling bank account transfers by account holder, origin of overseas transfer, or amount of overseas transfer. (As of January 4, 2007, cash transfers of more than 100,000 yen are subject to increased security checks; however, in practice, myself and others have been profiled and subjected to extra scrutiny for transfer amounts as little as 5,000 yen.)[114] Accounts have also been arbitrarily denied to noncitizens based not upon registered legal status, but upon actual physical time in Japan and/or proof of gainful employment in Japan.[115] Some banks have refused to honor or issue travelers' checks to noncitizens "without a permanent address in Japan."[116] Many bank automatic tellers refuse to take cash cards issued in other countries or to permit timely withdrawals from overseas accounts.[117] This paranoia is in fact due to a narrative: As will be described below, noncitizens tend to be portrayed by Japanese authorities as potential international criminals and money launderers merely by dint of their (likely) overseas financial connections.[118]

However, suspicion has not stopped at international money transfers. Other private-sector institutions unlawfully requiring ARCs for service have included video stores, gymnasiums, computer stores, cellphone companies, and even public bathhouses.[119] As mentioned in chapter 3, Isawa Kenkō Land in Kōfu had a sign out front explicitly denying service to, inter alia, "people who cannot understand Japanese" and "foreign illegal visa overstayers (please present your ID)" (which logically requires a passport or ARC).[120] From April 1, 2002, NTT DoCoMo, Japan's largest cellphone company, began requiring ARCs and Permanent Residency from noncitizens before renting out cellphones to noncitizens; further, noncitizens without PR were required to pay a 30,000 yen deposit, publicly claiming (without presenting verifiable evidence) that noncitizens represent a flight risk (e.g., "skipping out on mobile phone bills at six times the rate of Japanese");[121] after public protests, this deposit requirement was amended by September 2002 to all noncitizens without a credit card, but the deposit requirement only for noncitizens still remained.

This expanded across industries. In 2008, outlets of Softbank phone company refused to sell noncitizens new iPhone 3Gs without a verifiable visa longer than ninety days.[122] Noncitizens were denied Smart Loans from Apple Computers Japan in 1999.[123] In 2003 and 2018, fitness centers in Tōkyō and Sendai required ARCs for noncitizen membership to their gymnasium, claiming the Personal Identification Law required ID for financial transactions with the club (and for noncitizens, the ARC—not a driver license, etc.—was only acceptable as ID).[124] There are also reports, as of 2009, of ARC checks and photocopies required for opening an account in the Postal Savings system, and for enrollment in private-sector drivers-education courses (which required for getting a driver license as ID in Japan).[125] The GOJ also proposed in 2018 that hospitals demand ARCs as a precondition for medical treatment.[126] Finally, during the switch from ARCs to the *Zairyū* Card in 2012, the Japan Postal System unilaterally began refusing ARCs (despite outstanding ones remaining valid for up to three years) as ID for noncitizens (presenting an obstacle to noncitizens without any other form of GOJ-issued photo ID who wished to open accounts, pick up packages, or receive registered mail).[127]

Again, there is often a direct National Police Agency connection to noncitizen profiling in the private sector. In addition to the stores and hotels I have interviewed above, who claimed the local police told them to ID "all foreigners" at check-in, the manager of the jewelry store in the Bortz Case (see chapter 3) mentioned that the local police had advised him of the threat of foreign crime, and he offered this as in court justification in court for his exclusionary policies toward noncitizens, specifically the exclusion of Plaintiff Ana Bortz.[128]

Thus, the NPA bears some responsibility for encouraging the general public to see "foreigners" as "suspicious," and, as will be discussed further below, promoting a general fear of noncitizens upon sight-identification.

Employers Required to Engage in ARC and Visa Status Checks

Policing of "foreigners" has even expanded into workplaces. From October 1, 2007, the MHLW issued a directive[129] clarifying the Employment Policy Law (*koyō taisaku hō*), requiring that all employers of part- and full-time noncitizens (excepting the Zainichi Special Permanent Residents and diplomats) check visa status, photocopy ARCs and passports, and file a report at "Hello Work" (the GOJ's employment agency) for later reporting to the MOJ. Criminal penalties were established of up to 300,000 yen for noncompliance.[130] Not all of these requirements were lawful, as they were not stipulated in the text of the law, and legal experts have claimed that they violate the Personal Information Protection Law (*kojin jōhō hokan hō*) Articles 16 and 26. Further, these requirements have caused confusion within employers regarding enforcement (allegedly deterring some from hiring "foreigners"), sometimes occasioning harassment of noncitizen employees by office staff not properly trained in Immigration guidelines for what constitutes a legal visa status.[131]

THE GENERAL PUBLIC OFFICIALLY ENCOURAGED TO SPY ON "FOREIGNERS" AS AGENTS OF CRIME

Japan's policing authorities have a long history of asking the general public for information about their neighbors, including Neighborhood Associations (*chōnaikai* or the archaic *tonarigumi*) that were historically used for spying on neighbors, rationing, disseminating propaganda, mobilizing for civil defense, and enforcing public order.[132] Although Japan's nearly 300,000 Neighborhood Associations nationwide are not in themselves necessarily exclusionary[133] nor run by policing authorities, they are sometimes asked by authorities for assistance in surveillance of neighborhoods known as "areas where many foreigners reside"[134] (such as Tōkyō Ikebukuro, Roppongi, and Kabukichō), and during times of "increased security" (such as international summits) when there allegedly may be actions by "foreign terrorists" (more below).

For example, on February 27, 2002, Kabukichō became the first neighborhood in Japan to install full police camera surveillance in order to combat "foreign crime."[135] By January 2010, this surveillance system was expanded to fifteen residential areas in fourteen prefectures "to prevent crime and protect children."[136] However, for the first time this system was not manned by official representatives of Japan's police forces, but by "volunteer groups of residents" to "ensure safety by themselves." How this will be used to prevent "crime in general" is unclear, as the precedent-setting justification for the neighborhood cameras has been "foreign crime."

Further, in April 2008, months before the G8 Summit in Tōyako, Hokkaidō, the Tōkyō Metropolitan Police asked 3,000 amateur "local people" (*kinjo no hito*) in Neighborhood Associations to watch for "suspicious people" (*fushinsha*), and maintain security around "stations and important facilities" more than 800 kilometers away from the summit site.[137] Since then, there have been other reports of local police encouraging vigilantism against "illegal foreign workers" and "overstayers" (e.g., through online notices distributed by the Fukushima Prefectural Police in 2017).[138] Thus, with the tools of surveillance being outsourced to the general public, not trained police officers, it remains unclear what safeguards are in place to prevent abuses of privacy and potential racial profiling when clear official attributions are being made between "foreigners" and "crime."

Anonymous Official Online "Snitch Sites" and Codified Suspicions about "Foreigners"

Moreover, despite the potential for abuse and unaccountability, there have been cases where the general public has been asked to help with policing noncitizens anonymously. On February 16, 2004, the MOJ's Immigration Bureau announced an online website[139] where anyone could notify authorities of the whereabouts (name, address of home and/or employer, etc.) of potential "foreign illegal overstays" (*gaikokujin no fuhō taizai*). Derided as "snitch sites,"[140] the original version of the informant site offered no clear criteria of what verifiably constituted an "illegal" noncitizen on sight. It also offered preset "reasons" for reporting noncitizen's names and address to the police (translations by the author): 1. "can't let violators escape justice" (*ihansha ga yurusenai*), 2. "neighborhood disturbances" (*kinjo meiwaku*), 3. "repugnance/anxiety" (*ken'o fuan*), 4. "personal stake in the matter" (*rigai kankei*), 5. "the police haven't dealt with it" (*keisatsu futai-ō*), 6. "have suffered damages" (*higai o uketa*), 7. "sympathy or compassion" (*dōjō*) [*sic*], 8. "can't let the employer or business escape justice" (*koyō nushi kigyō ga yurusenai*), 9. "can't let a job broker[141] escape justice" (*burōkā ga yurusenai*), 10. "was fired due to violator" (*ihansha no tame ni kaikō sareta*), 11. "couldn't get work due to violator" (*ihansha no tame ni kyūshoku sarenakatta*), 12. "something else" (*sono ta*), and 13. unclear (*fumei*).

These preset options created by the authorities are indicative of official mindsets toward noncitizens as potential criminals. Justifications for public "snitching" thus had low standards of evidence, as they could include personal hatred and xenophobia (items 2–4), scapegoating (items 6, 10, and 11), or no explicit reason whatsoever (items 12 and 13). Not all of these criteria involved specifically illegal activities (e.g., item 7), and most options targeted the individual visa overstayer, not the institution employing them. Further, the privacy of the informant was protected more than the suspect, since the website does not require from the informant a verifiable address, phone number, or a name (i.e., pseudonyms were permitted).

After more than a dozen human rights groups (including Amnesty International, some municipal governments, and thousands of individuals) decried this website as "racist," "xenophobic," "defamatory," and "discriminatory,"[142] amendments were made by March 2004. First, the website explicitly offered a disclaimer that "this website is not to be used for harassment of lawful foreigners" (*tekihō ni taizai shite iru gaikokujin ni tai-suru hibō chūshō wa kataku okotowari shimasu*) but left penalties for false leads unclear. Then the preset submission reasons were removed entirely and left open-ended. However, the Immigration Bureau in May 2004 refused to abolish the anonymous online informant system completely, arguing, "such tips lead annually to the apprehension of tens of thousands of illegals."[143] In 2015, after more than a decade of anonymous snitching that predictably led to xenophobes targeting and harassing Korean residents, the "snitch sites" were finally suspended.[144]

"EMBEDDED RACISM" MINDSETS BEHIND OFFICIAL RACIAL PROFILING: THE NATIONAL RESEARCH INSTITUTE OF POLICE SCIENCE'S "FOREIGN DNA INDEX"

The clearest example of an officially sanctioned paradigm for the sorting for people under racialized biological constructions was created by the National Research Institute of Police Science (*kagaku keisatsu kenkyūjo*), or NRIPS. It received taxpayer funding for a program called "The Development of an Index Using Biological Materials for Use in Investigating Foreign Crime" (*gaikokujin hanzai o kyūmei suru tame no seitai shiryō o mochiita shihyō no kaihatsu*).[145]

This program warrants a careful reading for this research, as it is primary source material for insights into (a) the racialized science behind Japan's policing, and (b) the embedded political justifications offered for official taxpayer funding of policies for public order (according to the proposal document, more than 21 million yen was earmarked for this policy for 2002). The outline of this policy (*shisaku no gaiyō*) reads (my translation):

> In our country (*wagakuni*), with the advent of economic and social internationalization, there has been a rapid rise (*kyūzō*) in heinous crimes (*kyōaku hanzai*) connected to foreigners coming to Japan. There has likewise been a huge increase in social insecurity (*shakai fuan*) in citizen (*shimin*) lifestyles both in Tōkyō and across the nation. With a criminal environment like this, the development of an index giving us a lead on whether or not a crime has been committed by a foreigner is being demanded (*motomerarete iru*). Foreigners (*gaikokujin*) have a wide variety of characteristic melanin proteins that are different than Japanese (*Nihonjin*), which can be found in bloodstains and bodily fluids left at the scene of the crime. This is why we will develop an index which reveals, even in minute traces of organic material, the special characteristics of foreigners, in order to make heads or tails of things (*suitei*) in ways we never could before.

As part of uncovering embedded narratives, let us consider this policy's justifications: Social insecurity in Japan has allegedly decreased, as measured by the lifestyles not of all people in Japan, but of *citizens*—rhetorically differentiating, "othering," and subordinating the subject and object of this policy into citizen and noncitizen. It also rhetorically links "internationalization" to "foreign crime," connecting the influence of outsiders in Japan to something implicitly negative, a social problem. To deal with this problem, an abstract and unsourced demand for a solution specifically dealing with "foreigners" is cited as the trigger for this policy, since foreign crime is allegedly rising rapidly.

However, the official crime rise claim warrants closer scrutiny, as it is erroneous. A closer examination of the statistics that were contemporaneous to this policy for January–July 2003 reveals that the crime rate (when weighted for the rising registered noncitizen population vs. the static citizen population)[146] has been static, and in many crime categories lower than the citizen crime rate. Further, for crimes classified as "heinous" (*kyōaku*), such as mugging (*gōtō*, down 5.4 percent) and breaking-and-entering (*shin'nyū gōtō*, down 24.1 percent), it is dropping. Thus, depending on how one chooses to calculate the crime rate, between 96 percent and 99 percent of all non-visa-related crimes[147] in Japan are committed by Japanese citizens. Since the population of registered noncitizens at the time was around 1.5 percent of the total population, this can mean crime, both in terms of raw numbers and the comparative rate, is lower for noncitizens than for citizens—contradicting the assertions within the policy of a "rapid rise." Recent statistics for this Second Edition have not reversed this trend.[148]

Next, let us consider the science behind the NRIPS policy. It clearly claims that "foreigners" are biologically different than "Japanese," and extranationality can be determined empirically through biological analysis of DNA. This officially conflates nationality and biology. As discussed in chapter 2, asserting an empirical basis for this method of measurement is highly problematic. I do not wish to belabor the point, except to emphasize that this Embedded Racism does not stand up to rigorous examination: (a) there is a long history of mixing of different peoples (e.g., Koreans, Chinese, Ainu, and Ryūkyūans) within the Japanese archipelago; (b) there are noncitizens in Japan with genotypically "Japanese melanin proteins" (e.g., the Nikkei South Americans); and (c) there are citizens in Japan with "foreign melanin proteins" (e.g., children of international families and naturalized citizens). Thus if a Nikkei Brazilian noncitizen and I (as a citizen) were to commit a crime in Japan and leave biological evidence, this Index would reveal him as "Japanese" and me as "foreign," meaning the results are empirically unsound.

Now let us consider the narrative behind the stated purpose of this policy (in archived document: *shisaku no ito, mokuteki*) and its purported results (*kōka tō*) (my translation):

> *Purpose*: In our country (*wagakuni*), crimes by foreigners coming to Japan (*rainichi gaikokujin*) are rising in recent years. This policy aims to swiftly clear heinous crimes which foreigners (*gaikokujin*) are thought to have had a hand in. Because it will greatly contribute to securing public safety as well as safety in the livelihoods of Japanese citizens (*kokumin*), development of this research will come under the "Restoration of Livelihoods Program" (*seikatsu ishin puroguramu*) in the "Seven Reforms Program" (*nanatsu no kaikaku puroguramu*), raised within our "Basic Aims" (*kihon hōshin*). It will fall under the goal of "securing public peace and safety for Japanese citizens (*kokumin*), and securing a society where they can be reassured of making a living" (*anshin shite kuraseru shakai*).
>
> *Results*: Thanks to the development of an index that will reveal the varied organic materials different from Japanese (*Nihonjin*), we expect that this policy will contribute to making the investigation and clearance of crimes committed by foreigners (*rainichi gaikokujin*) much easier and shorter, and be useful in securing peaceful and safe livelihoods for Japanese citizens (*kokumin*).

This is the political application of Embedded Racism: to prioritize between peoples and subordinate. The conceptual dichotomy between "*Nihonjin*" and "*Gaikokujin*" is clearest as this policy is explicitly directed to protect "Japanese" (*Nihonjin*; not just "Japanese citizens" (as *kokumin*), when it could possibly be interpreted as legally based construct including naturalized citizens) against "foreigners." This is particularly underscored by the repeated use of the rhetorical construction of "our country" (*wagakuni*).

The policy's fundamental assumption of a biological basis behind nationality is thus so normalized, embedded, and unquestioned in the national discourse that it has repeatedly received public funding—despite incorrect statistical information and racialized analytical paradigms ungrounded in a rigorous scientific method. In sum, this policy is a classic and irrefutable example of officially sanctioned racial profiling. It has also performatively created the two biologically based categories used in this research: Wajin vs. Non-Wajin.[149]

THE PERNICIOUS CONSEQUENCES OF LINKING BIOLOGY TO NATIONALITY: UNSCIENTIFIC, INHUMANE, AND NONSENSICAL BORDER POLICIES DURING THE COVID-19 PANDEMIC

In 2020, COVID-19 became a global pandemic, and countries worldwide enforced border policies to contain the spread of the disease. In April, Japan decided to effectively close its borders to all "foreigners," including Non-Japanese resident reentrants.[150] However, Japanese nationals traveling under the same conditions were permitted reentry, and at first were subjected to lax honor-system self-quarantines.[151] This made Japan the only G7 developed country to ban reentry to all foreign residents with legal visas,[152] leading to thousands of Non-Japanese residents stranded overseas for many months, separated from their families, jobs, schools, and lives in Japan—and thousands of Non-Japanese residents stranded in Japan, unable to venture overseas to attend to ailing loved ones during a deadly pandemic.[153]

After much international and domestic criticism,[154] border restrictions were loosened later in 2020 and in 2021 to allow noncitizens with long-term visas and Japanese spouses to reenter. Nevertheless, the GOJ still instituted harsher penalties for foreign residents than Japanese for quarantine violations (i.e., summary cancellation of visas), moreover proposed new border controls that prioritized "business travelers" and "foreign tourists" over foreign taxpayers.[155] Meanwhile, MHLW released infection statistics that separated foreign and Japanese patients,[156] and some MPs (one an American-Japanese named Onoda Kimi) began calling for the denial of welfare benefits to foreign residents; another, Sugita Mio, argued aloud that financial support of foreigners should be the responsibility of their home countries, not Japan.[157]

Leaving aside the increasing mean-spiritedness of these developments, Japan's unscientific enforcement of a "Japanese Only" border policy had many odd presumptions. One was that a Japanese passport made the bearer less susceptible to COVID. Another was that somehow "foreigners" (not

Japanese) were more likely to be importers and "cluster" transmitters of COVID (as was specifically argued by one influential Japanese virologist advising the GOJ)[158] than Japanese travelers not subjected to quarantine. Then in 2021, when "overseas spectators" were unprecedentedly banned from the postponed Tōkyō Olympics, the argument became that people from overseas (not including Japanese overseas) would bring in COVID variants.[159] This logic stood despite (a) the lax quarantine system for Japanese reentrants eventually bringing in COVID mutations anyway;[160] (b) the GOJ not testing asymptomatic people within Japan, resulting in potentially underreported national case numbers and overlooked domestic clusters;[161] (c) overseas vaccinations happening at much higher rates than Japan;[162] (d) quarantine exemptions being made for Olympics VIPs;[163] and (e) Japan nevertheless possibly incubating its own COVID variant.[164] The culmination of this cognitive dissonance was when the ban on "overseas spectators" did not include Japanese citizens living overseas, including Wajin who were no longer Japanese citizens because they had renounced their citizenship.[165]

The takeaways of this event are stark for Japan's minorities: The Supreme Court had ruled in 1992 that Japan's foreign residents have no "right of sojourn" (meaning, as the *Japan Times* put it, a "reverse Hotel California," i.e., a situation where "you can leave but you can never check back into").[166] This meant that legal Non-Japanese residents who have given their lives to Japanese society basically have the same status at the border as tourists (if not subordinate to "foreign tourists" and "business travelers"), whereas overseas people with Japanese blood (including people without Japanese citizenship) could be grandfathered in. Thus, Wajin privilege, institutionalized under the law in ways outlined in this chapter, became crystal clear during the COVID pandemic, as blood ties were repeatedly prioritized over both legal status and scientific evidence.

SUMMARY AND CONCLUSIONS

The legal distinction between citizen and noncitizen in Japan has in application been applied through a mindset of Embedded Racism in Japan's law enforcement. Not only have GOJ policies targeting and policing "foreigners" been applied mainly through visual identification to people who "look foreign," but also the policing mechanisms have expanded beyond their legally sanctioned mandates through extralegal enforcement directives and clarifications. Not only are certified police officers engaging in racial profiling, but other public- and private-sector institutions (including hotels, banks, stores, neighborhood associations, and even anonymous private individuals) are being officially encouraged in the name of "crime prevention," and so on to single out Visible Minorities as "suspicious."

The implicit justifications for these normalizing and systemic policy drives, including prevention of disease, crime, terrorism, and even internationalization itself (see chapter 5), have further "othered" and subordinated Visible Minorities in Japan by officially connecting them to negative social trends and societal problems. Over time, these sustained policies have shown how Japan can activate the enforcement powers of a police state, with cops and local policing agencies unaccountably resorting to extralegal means to accomplish policing goals, targeting people who "look foreign" and are therefore presumed to have weaker civil rights. Thus, racial profiling by Japan's authorities is demonstrably a standardized operating procedure. By extension, when society is in crisis (such as during a pandemic), noncitizen residents can be legally subordinated to tourist status, have their visas cancelled, and be separated from their lives in Japan without sufficient recourse or equal treatment under the Constitution. In order to avoid this systemic bullying, the onus is on Visible Minorities to performatively validate themselves as Wajin, as we shall see in the next chapter.

Having established how the normalized dynamic of alienation and subordination by "nationality" in Japan is supported by Japan's laws and law enforcement, let us now turn to how legislative policies and procedures build on those laws to further generate and embed racialized alienation, going beyond "citizen vs. noncitizen" and into "Wajin vs. Non-Wajin" conceits.

NOTES

1. The oddest reaction I have had to my Japanese passport is where Jamaican Customs took it back to the main office and showed it around for a laugh. US Customs, however, consistently has the most severe reaction: More than once I have been taken into custody for further questioning, once for several hours, missing my flights. A 2011 request to the Department of Homeland Security for improvements was answered with a request for me to comply with their security measures: "We rely on the patience, cooperation, and understanding of travelers to ensure the effective protection of our borders," with no promises for improved procedures.

2. In addition to referencing sources discussed in chapter 3, I cite below other published academic works, as well as an archive I created and manage since 1996 (www.debito.org), housing as of April 2021 more than 8,000 files, academic journal articles, newspaper articles, primary source testimonies, reports, and essays relating to the human rights of "foreigners" living in Japan.

3. According to Robert Huey (University of Hawai'i at Mānoa, personal correspondence, April 23, 2012), "Wajin" is an old word phonetically (albeit once rendered in different kanji) found in China's Wei Chronicles written in the third

century, which labeled peoples settled in present-day Japan territory as "*wajin*" (倭人, "midget people"), living in *wa no kuni* (the land of *wa*). Other writings from the Han Dynasty (206 BCE–220 CE) also used the term, enabling it to gain currency in Japan as Japanese scholars increasingly studied and adopted Chinese scholarship (cf. *Jidaibetsu Kokugo Jiten*). During Japan's Heian Period (794–1185), *wa* as a prefix (with the current 和 kanji in use, with the historically appropriate reading 和人 as *yamato no hito* (Wetherall in Willis ed. 2008: 272)) became appended to "Japanese things" (such as paper, poetry, and musical instruments) to differentiate them from "Chinese and Korean things," including people. However, Alexander Vovin (Interview, May 1, 2012, University of Hawai'i at Mānoa) disagrees; his preliminary research could not find *wajin* in Japanese books until the Tokugawa Era (cf. *Nihon Gaishi*), and even then *wajin* was used by "outsiders" only (i.e., Chinese and Ainu) to refer contrastingly to Japanese people. According to Vovin, Wajin became a self-referent around the end of the nineteenth century, when it was found in the *Kokugo Daijiten*.

Furthermore, according to Huey (ibid.), it is also unclear if *wajin* ever was used by Japanese to imply superiority over other peoples. Nevertheless, *wajin* is used in contemporary scholarship on Hokkaidō's Ainu to differentiate Ainu from Japanese colonizers and present-day Japanese (Kramer ed. 1993, Sjöberg 1993, Siddle 1996, Hardacre & Kern 1997, Kayano, Iijima, & Suzuki 2003, Irish 2009, Weiner 2009). Although many native speakers of Japanese outside of Hokkaidō I have consulted with do not use *wajin* in regular conversation (I nevertheless heard it frequently during my two decades living in Hokkaidō), *wajin* has been used by the Japanese government (cf. Ministry of Foreign Affairs 1999) as a self-identifier, a racialized term to divide "the entire population of 'Japanese' into two putative races, 'Ainu' and 'Wajin,'" even though Okinawans and "most naturalized Japanese . . . would probably not choose to classify themselves as 'Wajin'" (Wetherall 2008: 281). It is a word based upon birth, not legal status.

This research will use the term Wajin as defined in table 4.1 for two reasons: (1) it is a legitimate, non-pejorative word in modern Japanese language long used to describe Japanese people, particularly before Japan as a nation-state (or proto-state) began colonizing others; (2) it enables the author to define its meaning under new and flexible paradigms. Just as "White" can be made useful as both an indicator of social status and a visual identifier/enforcer of those who have that social status (and allow for flexibility of "shades of White" as people attempt to "pass" as "White," in order to gain power or privilege in White-majority societies), Wajin will also (a) allow for visual differentiation between people who "look Japanese" and "do not look Japanese"; and (b) similarly allow for "shades" as people "pass" and "don't pass" as "Japanese," finding their status, privileges, and immunities affected when they are suddenly revealed as "Non-Wajin."

4. Official English translation of the Nationality Law of Japan is on the Ministry of Justice website at www.moj.go.jp/ENGLISH/information/tnl-01.html.

5. Another important amendment to the Nationality Law took place in 2008, when the Supreme Court ruled that nationality could be conferred even when the paternity of a child of an international marriage was not recognized by a Wajin father before birth, or when paternity was not properly registered after birth. Children born

to Wajin mothers, on the other hand, have since 1985 been automatically granted Japanese citizenship, regardless of the nationality of the father or their marital status. There have, however, been some recent caveats; more below. *See* "Top court says marriage requirement for nationality unconstitutional." *Kyodo News*, June 4, 2008.

6. For Prewar histories of Japan's nationality laws and regulations, and how the equation of nationality became intertwined with ethnonational identity, *see* Kashiwazaki (2009: 16–30) and Asakawa (2007).

7. In 2013 during the First Edition of this book, the Zainichi were nearly 18 percent of the total Non-Japanese resident population. Part of the reason for the swift decrease is deaths outpacing births within the Zainichi community, intermarriage with Japanese, and naturalization. Another factor is that the Non-Japanese resident population in general has increased. *See* www.e-stat.go.jp/stat-search/files?page=1&layout=datalist&toukei=00250012&tstat=000001018034&cycle=1&year=20200&month=12040606&tclass1=000001060399 (accessed March 31, 2021).

8. Morris-Suzuki (2010): 233–235; interviews by the author with Zainichi 2000–2008.

9. A tangentially related but illuminating discussion of how ethnicities in general are self-policing communities that not only "other" and racialize themselves, but also do so under incentive systems created by the hegemonic majority in a society, can be found in Balibar & Wallerstein (1998), chapter 4.

10. A version of the following sections was published as Arudou, Debito, "Embedded racism in Japanese Law: Towards a Japanese critical race theory." *Pacific Asia Inquiry* 4(1) Fall 2013. Reprinted with permission.

11. *See*, for example, "Voiceless minority: People lacking family registry live on the outside, buried in red tape." *Japan Times*, February 17, 2015.

12. *See also* www.moj.go.jp/MINJI/kokuseki.html (accessed April 4, 2021). These odd loopholes allow for fast-track exceptions, such as for Nobel Prize winners and imported athletes representing Japan in the Olympics, in the name of recognizing Wajin roots and allowing for the political externalities of national pride. More below.

13. *See* Ministry of Justice, *Kika hyōka shinseisha sū tō no sui'i*, at www.moj.go.jp/MINJI/toukei_t_minj03.html (accessed March 31, 2021). According to www.moj.go.jp/content/001343141.pdf, the majority of successful applicants are former Korean and Chinese citizens.

14. Asakawa (2007, particularly 48–73) describes the historical process of how Japan's laws regarding naturalization arose from arbitrary extralegal measures (*chōhōkiteki na sochi*) and bureaucratic fiat connected to the annexation of the Ogasawaras, the development of Hokkaidō, the Sino-Japanese War, and other case-by-case decisions regarding how individual noncitizen denizens would benefit the state. Asakawa argues that a legacy of extralegal ministerial latitude continues to the present day.

15. Ministry of Justice naturalization interview, August 7, 1998.

16. Archived at www.debito.org/?p=15820. For the record, the original Japanese for this definition is 名古屋市内に住所を有する外国籍の人のほか、日本国籍を取得した人や国際結婚によって生まれた子どもなど外国の文化を背景に持つ人など、外国にルーツを持つ人.

17. For more development of the issues connected to this problematic term, *see* Debito Arudou, "Local Governments classifying Japanese Citizens as foreigners." *Shingetsu News Agency*, December 16, 2019; www.debito.org/?p=15883; "Nagoya City officially classifies 'Foreigner City Denizens' to include 'naturalized persons, children of international marriages, people with foreign cultures or roots in their backgrounds'. Viva Eugenics." *Debito.org*, www.debito.org/?p=15820. When local governments were asked by activists about this term, Kawasaki City mayor Okunoki Nobuo responded inter alia, "It has that definition because even if someone has naturalized and taken Japanese citizenship, it is assumed (*sōtei*) that they might still require some assistance in regards to multicultural coexistence. Please understand that this does not mean our city has any intention of forcefully framing (*gōin ni minasu*) people who have taken Japanese citizenship as foreigners." *See* "'*Gaikokujin Shimin*': Kawaguchi City Mayor Okunoki answers a query about the racialized application of this term that officially makes Japanese into 'foreigners.'" *Debito.org*, February 1, 2020, www.debito.org/?p=15921.

18. Google search as of April 7, 2021. Incidentally, another racialized term being used by the GOJ to permanently offset "real Japanese" from "naturalized Japanese" is *honpōgai shusshinsha* (本邦外出身者), or "people originating from outside our homeland state." Ironically found on a MOJ, BOHR website, the term creates another, this time very nationalistic, definitional line a Non-Wajin cannot cross. *See* "*Kokusai jinshu sabetsu teppai dei ni muketa jinken yōgo kyoku kara no messeiji*" [a message from the Bureau of Human Rights on the International Day for Eliminating Racial Discrimination], Ministry of Justice, undated, www.moj.go.jp/JINKEN/jinken02_00025.html, archived at www.debito.org/?p=16573.

19. Independent researcher and translator William Wetherall disputes this research's interpretation of "renunciation" on his website (www.wetherall.sakura.ne.jp/yoshabunko///nationality/Dual_nationality.html), writing as of 2017 that the converse, dual nationality, is "not forbidden, unpreventable, and tacitly permitted," because the GOJ works under a "pragmatic recognition of its inability to force Japanese nationals to renounce other nationalities." He disputes the GOJ's power of revocation under the Nationality Law between the semantics of "abandoning" (*hōki*) vs. "revoking" (*ridatsu*) vs. "choosing" (*sentaku*) Japanese nationality. In other words, in Wetherall's reading, as far as the GOJ is concerned, the only issue is the "choice" or "revocation" of Japanese nationality, not the "revocation" or "abandonment" of foreign nationalities, so the GOJ has no power to force dual nationals to "abandon" foreign and "choose" Japanese.

That said, the Nationality Law nevertheless officially demands the "choice" of Japanese nationality only, and does not allow citizens to "choose" other nationalities without (in principle) "losing" (*sōshitsu*) Japanese nationality. Parts of this law are backed up by criminal penalties for noncompliance (Article 20), direct permissions and punishment by the Minister of Justice (e.g., Article 16), and recent court decisions mentioned in this chapter further empowering the GOJ's ability to punish dual citizenship holders. My read is that whether or not the GOJ chooses to enforce the Nationality Law remains at their discretion; as we shall see below in this chapter, Japan's administrative branch has great extralegal power to "clarify" laws through ministerial directive (*see also* Asakawa ibid.). This enables bureaucrats, acting on behalf of the Minister of Justice, to activate or strengthen formerly dormant sections of the law given the exigencies of current political policy.

20. US Department of State, personal communications, January and March 2011.

21. Furthermore, under Nationality Law Article 2.3, babies born in Japan whose nationality is unknown, or whose parents are unknown, are by default Japanese nationals (which leads to a conundrum when Non-Wajin babies are left in hospital "baby hatches" for abandoned children; incidentally, this loophole is the only way Japanese citizenship may be acquired by *jus soli*). *See* "Foreign baby left at 'baby hatch.'" *Kyodo News*, September 8, 2008; "*Akachan pōsto ni gaikokujin no kodomo: Kumamoto-shi no Jikei Byōin*." [Foreign baby left in "baby hatch" at Kumamoto clinic], *47News.jp*, September 8, 2008. Vaguely, the media determined the "foreignness" of the baby as due to the unknown parents reportedly being Zainichi. More at www.debito.org/?p=1900.

22. "Top court backs repeal of Japanese nationality due to parents' lapse abroad." *Asahi Shinbun*, March 11, 2015, at www.debito.org/?p=13144; "Court rules in favor of Japan's ban on dual nationality." *Mainichi Shinbun*, January 21, 2021, at www.debito.org/?p=16393.

23. "Dual citizenship in Japan: A 'don't ask, don't tell' policy leaves many in the dark." *Japan Times*, feature undated, mid-2018.

24. Sources for this section include: "Ex-President Fujimori should face Justice." *Japan Today*, July 16, 2001; "Fujimori dismisses Interpol notice." *Japan Times/Associated Press*, March 30, 2003; "Fujimori gets Peru passport, eyes return." *Japan Times*, September 15, 2005; "Japan 'uncooperative' in Fujimori probe." *Kyodo News*, November 19, 2005; "Fujimori tied to $300,000 in 'hidden' bank account." *Kyodo News*, November 30, 2005; "Ending Impunity: Pinochet's involuntary legacy." *The Economist*, December 13, 2006; "Ex-Peruvian President Fujimori asked to run in Japan elections." *Mainichi Daily News*, June 19, 2007; "Editorial: Fujimori's Candidacy." *Asahi Shinbun*, July 12, 2007; "Diet seat eludes absentee Fujimori." *Kyodo News*, July 31, 2007; "Fujimori returns to Peru to face trial." *Associated Press*, September 23, 2007; "Fujimori convicted." *Associated Press*, December 11, 2007; "Peru's Fujimori gets 25 years for death squad." *Associated Press*, April 8, 2009; Debito Arudou, "Fujimori gets his; Japan left shamed." *Japan Times*, May 5, 2009.

25. *See*, for example, "Mass sterilisation scandal shocks Peru." *BBC News*, July 24, 2002; and so on.

26. The GOJ expedited the process by claiming the "Master Nationality Rule," an interpretation of Article 4 of 1930's League of Nations Convention on Certain Questions Relating to the Conflict of Nationality Laws, where a state has the option to recognize a dual national as a sole national if it so chooses, as long as the person in question has the nationality of that state. The Japanese government chose to recognize only Fujimori's "Japanese nationality," based upon childhood family registration in Kumamoto from abroad, which is also in contravention of Japan's Nationality Law. The GOJ also claimed that under the 1985 revision of the Nationality Law, which permitted citizenship to pass through the Japanese mother's blood as well as the father's, that children with multiple nationalities had until the end of 1986 to declare or forfeit

Japanese nationality; those who declared nothing would be assumed to have retained Japanese nationality and forfeited all others. Since Fujimori had not declared either way, he was reportedly grandfathered in. *See* "The many faces of citizenship." *Japan Times*, January 1, 2009. *See also* Anderson & Okuda (2003: 334–289). They conclude that Fujimori's Japanese citizenship was legally binding, as he had never notified the Japanese government of his intent to give it up, and the Japanese government had declined to notify him that he had lost it.

27. Anderson & Okuda (2003: 310–318); *see also* "Fugitive Fujimori relative is shielded by Japan." *New York Times*, July 19, 2001, regarding the case of Fujimori's brother-in-law, and former Peruvian ambassador to Japan, Victor Aritomi Shinto's expedited naturalization into Japan. Although Anderson & Okuda conclude that Fujimori's Japanese citizenship was not necessarily a politically motivated move (albeit one of government "discretion" not to a priori notify Fujimori of his lost citizenship), since he legally retained it by not giving it up, the authors also conclude that Aritomi's example was of dubious legal standing, since it was a naturalization procedure (not a latent holding of Japanese citizenship). Moreover, (a) it took only six months, much less time than average, and (b) it was awarded despite an outstanding international arrest warrant, in violation of the Nationality Law's abovementioned requirement for "upright conduct."

28. *See*, for example, "Author Sono calls for racial segregation in op-ed piece." *Japan Times*, February 12, 2015, which mentions Sono opening her home to Fujimori. There is an even more curious epilogue to the Fujimori Case. Reportedly bored with his Tōkyō lifestyle (Sims, ibid.), Fujimori renewed his Peruvian passport and flew to Chile in 2005 to stand for election in absentia in Peru, whereupon he was immediately put under arrest pending extradition. He lost the Peruvian election, but was able to *run for election in Japan* in absentia in 2007 (where he lost again). Then Chile extradited Fujimori to Peru, where he was ultimately sentenced to prison in 2009 for twenty-nine years for human rights violations, including abuses of power, murder, and kidnapping. After being pardoned by the President of Peru in 2017, Peru's Supreme Court reversed the pardon and put Fujimori back in prison in 2019.

29. Ibid., *Associated Press*, March 30, 2003.

30. This is not the only case of an alleged criminal facing extradition for criminal charges overseas taking refuge in Japan's naturalization processes. Delfo Zorzi, aka Hagen Roi, despite accusations of neo-fascist terrorism and mass murder by the Italian judiciary for allegedly taking part in a massacre in Milan in 1969, was also granted Japanese citizenship even though government officials had been aware for years that he was a convicted criminal under extradition proceedings. The GOJ refused extradition, and Zorzi currently directs an import-export business in Aoyama, Tōkyō. *See* "Zorzi got citizenship despite criminal past." *Mainichi Daily News*, June 2, 2000.

31. "24 defectors from DPRK still stateless: Prejudice rife in Catch-22 situation." *Yomiuri Shinbun*, June 13, 2007.

32. "Top court says marriage requirement for nationality unconstitutional." *Kyodo News*, June 4, 2008. *See also* Iwasawa (1998: 303), and Bryant (1991–1992). Bryant's discussion of how the very definition of "Japanese citizenship" (official

koseki family registration) creates discrimination toward children born out of wedlock or insufficiently registered is particularly informative.

33. More on this below, but the abovementioned BOHR survey asked leading questions casting doubt on foreigners' grounds to have human rights, and consequently got responses indicating that a majority of the Japanese public "does not believe that foreigners should have the same human-rights protections as Japanese." *See* "Human rights survey stinks: Government effort riddled with bias, bad science." *Japan Times*, October 23, 2007.

34. Debito Arudou, "For the sake of Japan's future, foreigners deserve a fair shake," *Japan Times*, December 6, 2011; Colin P. A. Jones, "Schizophrenic Constitution leaves foreigners' rights mired in confusion." *Japan Times*, November 1, 2011; "*'Yakuza to gaikokujin ni jinken wa nai to oshierareta', moto kenji ga bakuro shita odoroku beki 'shinjin kyōiku' no jittai*" ["We were taught that foreigners have no rights": A former prosecutor confesses how new entrants are educated in surprising ways], *Niconico News*, May 23, 2011.

35. Dōshisha Law School Professor Colin P.A. Jones (ibid.) concurs: "[T]he Japanese Constitution speaks of defining equality and 'fundamental human rights' as being conditioned on nationality rather than being human."

36. A version of this section was published as Debito Arudou, "Embedded racism in Japanese official registry systems: Towards a Japanese critical race theory." *International Journal of Asia Pacific Studies* 10(1), Spring 2014. Reprinted with permission.

37. Sources for this section include: Interview with Jeremy D. Morley JD, *Canadian Broadcasting Corporation*, March 31, 2006; "New law takes on patriarchal family system." Korean Women's Development Institute, June 7, 2007; Jones (ibid.).

38. South Korea abolished their *hoju* system in 2008.

39. Bryant ibid.

40. As further evidence of Japan's outlier status in this regard: "Japan and Israel surely stand out as the 'odd couple' of the comparative citizenship project, each of them being an outlier in which one element of citizenship policy has been extrapolated into a dominant feature. In short, Japan comes closer than any other economically advanced constitutional democracy to retaining a fundamentalist version of *jus sanguinis*, and the 'blood' involved is the immediate and concrete one of family or lineage, rather than merely the usual 'imagined' national community" (Zolberg 2000: 385).

41. Lecture, University of Hawai'i at Mānoa, April 11, 2012.

42. Kashiwazaki (2000: 445). *See also* Miyamoto Yūki, Ninomiya Shūhei & Shin Ki-young, "The Family, Koseki, and the Individual: Japanese and Korean experiences." 9 *Asia-Pacific Journal* 36 (1), Sept. 5, 2011.

43. When we married, my wife took my pre-naturalization last name, Aldwinckle (アルドウィンクル), but reverted back to Sugawara due to the practical unwieldiness of "Arudouinkuru" in Japanese; this is why it is stricken from the record in the bottom right-hand corner.

44. As a further complication, when I naturalized, I wished to render my name from *Arudouinkuru Debitto* in katakana to Debito Arudou in kanji (有道　出人).

Since Japan does not recognize separate last names for Japanese married couples (since the GOJ says the whole family must be on the *koseki* in order to be a married household unit, or *setai*), we were faced with a choice of either rendering myself as Sugawara Debito or the rest of my family as Arudou Ayako, and so on. However, my children disliked the last name "Arudou," so I officially rendered myself as Sugawara as a last name, and Arudoudebito as my official first name, which I split into a pseudonymous surname and first name for professional and interpersonal purposes. When we divorced in 2006, I received my own, single household *koseki* but not a name change, until I went to civil court in November 2006 and directly petitioned the government to allow me to have "Sugawara" stricken from my name. A court ruled that I was permitted to officially render "Arudou Debito" as my official surname and given name because of the large number of professional and academic publications under my pen name.

Further, nomenclature for Non-Japanese names becomes complicated when Japan's registry systems only permit Chinese characters found in Ministry of Education-certified *jōyō kanji* or kanji name registers. These systems also do not permit middle names or non-Hepburn spellings on Japanese passports (sometimes refusing to allow citizens to respell their names in more approximate English transliterations, for example, surnames ほんま and もんま must be rendered as the mispronounceable "Homma" and "Momma." Twice I have had to handwrite formal petitions (*mōshitate-sho*) to the Ministry of Foreign Affairs just to allow my Japanese passport to be Romanized as "Arudou" as I preferred—with a U on the end, not as the Hepburn-transliterated Arudo or Arudoh). The inflexibility of Japan's registry systems, as Bryant (ibid.) mentions passim, thus enforces conformity and suppression of individual will or ethnic custom for little more than the bureaucratic convenience of the state, further alienating and "denormalizing" those with ethnic backgrounds. *See* more at Higuchi & Arudou (2008: 248–251), and Debito Arudou, "MOFA gets E for effort in 'with or without U' farce." *Japan Times*, December 7, 2010.

45. In brief: Divorce in Japan means, as Bryant (ibid.) mentions, the family unit dissolves into two households, and each parent is put on separate *koseki*. This means that that they have legally become not only two separate individuals, but also two separate families, no longer legally connected as far as family ties are concerned. However, the children as dependents can only go on one parent's *koseki*, so legally one parent (usually the mother) retains full custody and title to the children. Consequently, thanks in large part to the *koseki* system, after divorce in Japan there is no joint custody and no guaranteed visitation rights of one parent to his or her children. Although this degree of separation systematically happens to everyone connected with this system regardless of nationality, noncitizen spouses are at a particular disadvantage. They have no *koseki* for their children to be rendered on as "belonging" to them (Morley ibid.)—meaning the Japanese citizen retains custody in Japan, or the Japanese-citizen children go on their own *koseki* with a minor as Head of Household (while the noncitizen parent remains legally unlisted within the household). This also presents a major legal disadvantage for noncitizens in child custody battles, particularly when Japanese Family Courts strongly link "interests of the child" to "family stability." Sources for this footnote include inter alia Regis Arnaud, "A killing

separation." *No. 1 Shimbun*, December 20, 2010; Colin P. A. Jones, "Judges fill the gaps in Japan's family law" and "Children's rights, judicial wrongs." *Japan Times*, January 26, 2010, and February 2, 2010, respectively.

On a personal note: After my divorce from my Japanese wife, I, even as a Japanese citizen, was denied all access to my children, including visits, letters, phone calls, photographs, and so on. I was even denied school visits with their teachers and access to their school records because, in the words of one of the local educational representatives, "[My daughters] are not listed on my *koseki*, therefore I had no more ties to them as a parent." (Phone conversations, November 2009 and February 2010, with Hokkaidō Sorachi-gun Nanporo-chō junior high school representatives.) *See* more cases and primary source information on the child abductions and parental alienation issues at the Japan Children's Rights Network archive, www.crnjapan.net.

46. Correspondence with Saga City Hall, February 2003. Thanks to Edward Crandall, reporter, *Saga Shinbun*, for helping to untangle this complicated system of jurisdictions.

47. *See* inter alia "Living off the record." *Japan Times*, January 20, 2002.

48. *See* archive regarding *jūminhyō* activism at www.debito.org/activistspage.html#juuminhyou. Then the loophole within the loophole became whether or not the bureaucrat in charge accepted that *women noncitizens* could financially be "actual heads of households." There have been instances reported to the author of administrators exercising discretion and refusing to render females, further dividing the issue of enforcement by gender as well as by nationality.

49. In contrast to how noncitizens are registered, there have been cases of local governments "honoring" nonhumans with "Honorary Residency Certificates" (*kari jūminhyō*) as publicity stunts. The most famous case was "Tama-chan," a bearded seal found upriver at Yokohama's Tamagawa River, which was granted "honorary residency" in 2003 by the Nishi-ku Ward Office reportedly for his inspiration of hope to Yokohama residents. This occasioned protest by noncitizens, some of whom dressed up as seals and asked for their own *jūminhyō* in a public demonstration (their request was denied; Nishi-ku officials stated that the register was a national-level system and they could not themselves amend it to allow in noncitizens). Other municipalities also granted not only animals but also fictional characters "honorary residency," including Saitama's Nīza City (2003) to anime character "Astro Boy" (*tetsuwan atomu*); Saitama's Kusakabe City (2004) to anime character "Crayon Shin-chan"; Aichi's Seiyo City (2008) to three local blue-eyed dolls; Hokkaidō's Kushiro City (2009) to sea otter "Kū-chan" (2009); Tōkyō's Itabashi-ku (2010) to local household dogs; and Aichi's Handa City (2011) to fictional character "Gonkichi-kun." *See* "*Jūminhyō to gaikokujin*" [Foreigners and Residency Certificates], *Saga Shinbun*, February 12, 2003; "*Watashitachi ni mo jūminhyō o*" [Give us [foreigners] Residency Certificates too], *Asahi Shinbun*, February 22, 2003; "*Zainichi Gaikokujin wa Tamachan ika?*" [Are foreign residents of Japan lower than Tamachan?], *Newsweek Japan*, March 5, 2003; Debito Arudou, "Sealing the deal on public meetings." *Japan Times*, March 4, 2003; "*Tetsuwan Atomu wa jūminhyō o.*" [Astro Boy gets a Residency Certificate], *Kyodo News*, March 19, 2003; "*Tamachan yūjinkai no minasama*" [To everyone in the Tamachan friendship group], *Yokohama Nishi-ku Ward Office*, March 31, 2003;

Debito Arudou, "*Jūminhyō anime ni kōfu, gaikokujin ni wa?*" [Animated characters issued Residency Certificates, so what about foreigners?], *Asahi Shinbun Watashi no Shiten* column, November 8, 2003; Debito Arudou, "If cartoon kids have it, why not foreigners?" *Asahi Shinbun* "Point of View" column, December 29, 2003; "*Aoi me no ningyō' ni 'shiminken'*" [Blue-eyed dolls get "city citizenship"], *Sankei Shinbun* March 17, 2008; "Popular sea otter receives special residency status." *Mainichi Daily News*, May 3, 2009; "*Itabashi-ku ga inu no tōroku-ritsu appu mezashi, jūminhyō hakkō e.*" [Aiming to get dog registrations up in Itabashi Ward, government issues them Residency Certificates], *Sankei Shinbun*, January 20, 2010; "*Inu no Jūminhyō.*" [Dog Residency Certificates], Itabashi-ku's official rabies awareness-raising website, dated January 20, 2010; "*Himago 'Gonkichi-kun' uke toru.*" [Great Grandson Gonkichi-kun gets [a Residency Certificate]], *Yomiuri Shinbun*, October 3, 2011.

50. *See* online archive with analysis at www.debito.org/?p=1972. This is Nerima-ku's official tally of "Households and Population, as per the Basic Resident Register," as of October 1, 2008. As a clear indication of how normalized this process is, the sentence above Nerima-ku's chart explicitly states noncitizens are not included in the tally.

51. The shortcomings of a system making a section of Japan's population invisible became clearer during a scandal in 2010, when it came to light that long-dead citizens were still being counted as alive, due to bureaucratic errors and lack of registry notification by the next of kin. There are also cases of people being registered as deceased for nefarious purposes. *See* inter alia, "Tokyo's oldest listed person, age 113, is missing." *Associated Press*, August 3, 2010; "Man, 63, declared dead by kin in 1995 arrested in burglary." *Kyodo News*, August 6, 2010.

52. "Population rises 1st time in 3 years." *Yomiuri Shinbun*, August 1, 2008. On a related note, Dr. John Morris of Miyagi Gakuin Women's University posted on the H-Japan discussion website, July 15, 2012, that Japan's birthrate was likewise being measured by Yoshida Hiroshi, Graduate School of Economics, Tōhoku University, to exclude "foreign births" in Japan. Yoshida justified this omission during an NHK interview by saying that excluding all foreign residents from official population tallies would help Japan formulate more appropriate public policy. *See* "H-Japan on 'Apartheid or Academic Accuracy: Japan's Birth Rate,' Tohoku U. Prof. Yoshida's demographic research methodologically excludes 'foreigner births.'" *Debito.org*, July 18, 2012, www.debito.org/?p=10441.

53. "Population drops for fifth year as migration to cities continues." *Yomiuri Shinbun*, June 25, 2014; "Japan's population declines for 5th straight year." *Mainichi Shinbun*, June 26, 2014; "*Nihon no jinkō, 5-nen renzoku gen, rōdōryoku no toshibu chūshin tsuyomaru*" [Japan's population falls for fifth consecutive year, labor force concentrates in the cities]. *Nihon Keizai Shinbun*, June 25, 2014, all archived at www.debito.org/?p=12482. For more recent examples of how foreign resident numbers are elided, *see* "*Nihonjin no jinkō, 50 manningen, Tōkyō, Kanagawa, Okinawa nomi zōka*" [Population of Japanese people drops by 500,000, rises only in Tōkyō, Kanagawa, and Okinawa]. *Asahi Shinbun*, August 5, 2020; "*Jinkōgen saidai, 50 mannin, 11 nen renzoku gen, gaikokujin saita 286 mannin*" [Population drops by a record 500,000 for eleventh consecutive year; foreign population at its highest yet at 2,860,000 people]. *Nihon Keizai Shinbun*, August 5, 2020.

54. Speech, "Demographic Changes in Japan: Economic Globalization and Changes in Family Formation," given at international symposium entitled, "Imploding populations: Global and local challenges of demographic change," June 2–4, 2009, sponsored by the German Institute of Japanese Studies, Tōkyō. Interestingly, all Wajin scientists presenting at this symposium omitted immigration as a factor from their presentations, eliminating a fundamental scientific phenomenon from their demographic science (i.e., births, deaths, outflows, and inflows). *See* Debito Arudou. "Demography vs. demagoguery: When politics, science collide." *Japan Times*, November 3, 2009.

55. *See* inter alia "Census blind to Japan's true diversity." *Japan Times*, October 5, 2010. The official multilingual 2010 National Census website may be found at www.stat.go.jp/data/kokusei/2010/special/index.htm.

56. Acknowledgment of Japanese paternity after birth is a relatively new development, for until 2008, Japanese fathers of illegitimate children with noncitizen mothers could only register their children as their own if they acknowledged paternity before birth. As mentioned above, a Supreme Court judgment on June 4, 2008, declared that this was an unconstitutional violation of their human rights. The Nationality Law was amended accordingly later that year. That said, the window was extended to only fourteen days after birth, with further disqualifications placed upon children with Non-Japanese citizenships added through a 2012 court decision, ostensibly due to a "false paternity" media scare in policy circles during 2008. *See* "Citizenship for kids still tall order." *Japan Times*, November 5, 2008; "Steps mulled for preventing false paternity." *Yomiuri Shinbun*, November 26, 2008; and "Nationality Law tweak lacks DNA test: Critics." *Japan Times*, November 27, 2008.

57. The procedures involve the Japanese-citizen father taking a signed and translated acknowledgment of paternity from the noncitizen mother to a Ward Office before birth and submitting a form for "Recognition of an Unborn Child" (*taiji ninchi*). The Ward Office will issue a "Certificate of Acceptance of the Recognition of an Unborn Child" (*ninchi todoke juri shōmeisho*). Once the baby is born, the father must take the birth certificate (translated if from overseas) and get an official registered Japanese birth certificate (*shussei todoke*). *See* Higuchi & Arudou (2008: 270–3).

58. Japan's Civil Code Article 772 establishes that any child born within 300 days of a legal divorce is still legally considered as fathered by the ex-husband (regardless of nationality), without regard to actual paternity, meaning mothers must settle the often-complicated process of divorce before starting families anew. *See* "New divorcees push for DNA testing to be allowed to prove paternity of newborn children." *Mainichi Daily News*, January 8, 2007; also ibid., *Japan Times*, November 27, 2008. For more information on divorce proceedings in Japan, *see* Higuchi & Arudou (256–71), and Fuess (2004).

59. *See* "Court rules nationality law on foreign country-born children legal." *Asahi Shinbun*, March 25, 2012. As mentioned above, this differentiation between pure-blooded and mixed-blooded Wajin was reaffirmed as constitutional by the Supreme Court in 2015.

60. "Few foreigners tempted by points system." *Yomiuri Shinbun*, August 7, 2013; "Initiative fails to lure high-skilled workers." *Japan Times*, December 24, 2013.

61. "Immigration reforms spell Big Brother, Japan Federation of Bar Associations warns." *Japan Times*, March 26, 2009; "Drawing a bead on illegal residents: New law would tighten up oversight of foreigners." *Japan Times*, June 27, 2009. *See also* Higuchi & Arudou (2nd Edition 2013: chapters 1 and 2).

62. "Justice Ministry's new 'Gaijin Card Reader App' now unlawfully enables the general public to scan you. So much for GOJ promises of privacy." *Debito.org*, June 8, 2021, www.debito.org/?p=16688.

63. *Shiminken* is used in the context of civil and human rights, particularly political rights overseas (giving it the flavor of an exotic imported ideological construct). *See Hyakka Jiten* online, at http://100.yahoo.co.jp/detail/市民権/. *See also* related word *kōminken*, "civil rights," commonly used in reference to the American Civil Rights movement under Martin Luther King Jr.

64. That said, Japan lacks a semantic distinction between foreigners fresh off the airplane and foreign residents living in Japan for years. They are all simply categorized as *Gaikokujin* (or *Gaijin*). There are some words in the bureaucratic community to distinguish between legal statuses (such as *eijūsha*, Permanent Resident), but these are not found in popular discourse. Also, even though there is a word for "immigration" (*imin*) meaning relocation, there is no popularized word as yet for "immigrants" (as people) to Japan (as Japan has no official immigration policy). For the record, I suggest *imin jūmin* (immigrant resident). For a discussion of what a lack of terminology does to long-term foreign residents, *see* Debito Arudou, "The World's First 'Japanese Only' Olympics?" *Shingetsu News Agency*, March 15, 2021. As for a lack of immigration policy, *see* "Mr. Abe's Missing Arrow: The absence of immigration reform from Abenomics bespeaks a deeper problem." *WSJ Business Asia*, June 26, 2013.

65. Interviews, Itoh Hideko, lawyer for plaintiffs in Otaru Onsen Case, 2001–2002.

66. Dower 1999: 393–394.

67. All full-time (*jōkin*) workers (i.e., working more than 30 hours per week) in Japan must be enrolled in some form of health insurance by their employer. People working part-time (*hijōkin*) are required by law to enroll in the National Health Insurance program and pay full premium costs by themselves. However, every worker in Japan must be in some form of health insurance regardless of nationality. *See* Higuchi & Arudou (2008: 90–95).

68. This was legalized at the time under Public Pension Law Article 7. *See* Iwasawa 1998: 301.

69. Bortz 1998: Note 2, Item 4.

70. www.jetro.go.jp/en/invest/setting_up/section4/page9.html.

71. "Court rules noncitizens eligible for welfare." *Yomiuri Shinbun*, November 17, 2011; and Debito Arudou. "Kim to 'flyjin,' a top 10 for 2012." *Japan Times*, January 3, 2012, No. 6: "What caused the confusion was that in 1981, the Diet decided that revising the public welfare law to eliminate nationality requirements was unnecessary, since practical application already provided Non-Japanese with benefits. Three decades later, Oita Prefecture still hadn't gotten the memo."

72. "*Saikōsai ga shohandan 'gaikokujin wa seikatsu hogohō no taishōgai'*" [Supreme Court's first decision: Foreigners are not subject to the Public Assistance Law]. *NHK News*, July 18, 2014; "Foreign residents can't claim welfare benefits:

Supreme Court." *Japan Times*, July 18, 2014; and so on. Although there have been disputes as to whether the court ruled noncitizens as ineligible or just not automatically eligible (local governments and the Health, Labor, and Welfare Ministry have said that this ruling will not change their policies toward deciding noncitizen eligibility), this has resulted in gains in political capital for Japan's right-wing parties, and further attempts to disenfranchise noncitizen taxpayers (more in chapter 7). *See* "Welfare ruling stuns foreigners." *Japan Times*, July 19, 2014; "A closer look at the Supreme Court's welfare benefits ruling: Officially, things will stay as they are, but some are not so sure." *Japan Times*, July 25, 2014; "Safety net is for all taxpayers." *Japan Times*, July 26, 2014; "Ruling denying welfare for foreign residents finds homegrown, biased support." *Japan Times*, October 17, 2014; "Conservative party to submit bill halting welfare for needy foreigners." *Japan Times*, August 26, 2014; "Louis Carlet et al. on the misunderstood July 2014 Supreme Court Ruling: 'No rights' does not mean automatic NJ denials." *Debito.org*, November 11, 2014; "Hate, muzzle and poll: A Top 10 of issues for 2014." *Japan Times*, January 1, 2015; "Conservative party to submit bill halting welfare for needy foreigners." *Japan Times*, August 26, 2014; "Ruling denying welfare for foreign residents finds homegrown, biased support." *Japan Times*, October 17, 2014, which also notes,

> Most European countries do not have a nationality clause for welfare benefits, but do list a residency period as a condition for eligibility, said Shinichi Oka, a professor of social security at Meiji Gakuin University in Tokyo. At the same time, in Europe there is little distinction among different visa statuses, Oka said, noting that whether people have permanent resident status doesn't affect their chances of qualifying for welfare. "I'm not aware of any major European countries that (enforce) a nationality clause for public assistance eligibility," Oka said. "The only requirement they have is that the applicants have lived in the country for a certain period of time."

Some mathematical insights on just how much of a burden noncitizen welfare recipients are (they amount to 0.03 percent of Japan's GDP) are at www.debito.org/?p=12769.

73. In an insightful article for the *Japan Times* ("Think you've got rights as a foreigner in Japan? Well, it's complicated," August 6, 2014), legal scholar Colin P.A. Jones gives granular context for Japan's foreign residents being treated as "refugees":

> This newspaper's well-intentioned July 27 editorial declaring that the social safety net should be for all taxpayers is perfectly understandable—particularly given that the petitioner was an elderly Chinese who was born and spent her whole life here. Unfortunately, it is a mistake to equate feeding the maw of whatever tax-fueled Leviathan nation state you happen to live in with being entitled to anything from it in return. This is particularly true in Japan, where by law it is generally more important that one of your parents be Japanese than where you were born, raised or paid taxes. After all, being a dutiful taxpayer alone won't get your visa renewed or keep you from getting kicked out of the country; why should it get you a welfare payment either?
>
> Thus, if you live here on a foreign passport, you might want to . . . read through the Immigration Control and Refugee Recognition Act, since for most purposes, that is your

constitution. Having its roots in an Occupation-era decree modeled after U.S. immigration laws then in effect . . . , the ICRRA did not become a "law" until 1982, when it was amended in connection with Japan's accession to the U.N. Convention Relating to the Status of Refugees. I say it is your constitution because in 1978, the Supreme Court acknowledged that most constitutional protections did extend to foreigners, but only within the framework of the immigration laws and regulations, including the broad administrative discretion granted by these to Ministry of Justice officials.

So, you can pay your taxes . . . but at the end of the day your ability to live in Japan may ultimately be at the discretion of a bureaucrat's view of some of the very subjective standards set forth in the immigration laws and regulations, such as whether you have been "good" or "engaged in the activities related to your residence status." . . . [In] any dispute with the government, it is probably safe to expect that you will lose, and nothing in the Constitution will likely affect that outcome.

74. "Government permits hiring of foreigners." *Yomiuri Shinbun*, November 23, 1996; "Kochi defies Tokyo and will hire foreigners." *Asahi Evening News*, February 21, 1996; "Supreme Court scraps Japanese nationality requirement for legal training." *Asahi Shinbun*, October 29, 2009.

75. Although I am loath to cite Wikipedia under any circumstances, its substantiating section of footnotes under *kokuseki jōkō*, containing the exact text chapter and verse of certain public-sector job descriptions, is excellent. So I do not have to list dozens of sources, for brevity's sake, *see* https://ja.wikipedia.org/wiki/国籍条項#脚注 (accessed April 4, 2021).

76. *See* "Government permits hiring of foreigners." *Yomiuri Shinbun*, November 23, 1996. However, Komai (1995: 238, citing data published in 1993) notes that Amagasaki City was the first to abolish their Nationality Clause in 1974, whereas by his press time in 1995 all cities, towns, and villages in Hyōgo and Ōsaka Prefectures, Yokohama City, and all twenty-seven cities in Tōkyō had not. Some of Komai's data appears to be out of date, and the claim that "foreigners gained access to employment at state and other public universities in 1982" (239) is inaccurate. It does not take into account the lack of enforcement of ministerial directive by the universities themselves, who generally continued to hire noncitizen academics on term-limited nontenured contract work regardless, in what Hall (1998) calls "Academic Apartheid." More below.

77. This turnaround was front-page news because of the bureaucratic resistance this decision had overcome. *Yomiuri* (ibid.) notes:

Kochi Prefecture and Osaka city also planned to hire foreigners for government positions in the current fiscal year, but later dropped these plans, apparently in the face of pressure from the Home Affairs Ministry and prefectural and municipal assemblies. . . . The Cabinet Legislative Bureau announced the policy in 1953 on grounds that foreigners should not hold positions involving the formulation of policies. The Home Affairs Ministry confirmed that stance in 1993 by telling local governments it did not approve of hiring Non-Japanese for administrative positions.

The Nationality Clause is thus enforced by the central government as an instrument of public policy to actively keep "foreigners" out of secure GOJ jobs.

78. Ibid. *See also "Jōetsu-shi ga kokuseki jōkō kanzen haishi* e" [The City of Jōetsu moves towards complete abolition of the Nationality Clause]. *Niigata Nippō*, March 28, 2007.

79. "According to a survey by the All Japan Prefectural and Municipal Workers' Union, 354 small cities, towns and villages—about 30% of the 1,195 around the nation—had either done away with that requirement or never had one. Despite this, and in the absence of any legal stipulation, the Home Affairs Ministry continues to insist on rigidly apply the nationality requirement to all prefectural governments and municipal governments of major cities." *Asahi Shinbun*, February 21, 1996, ibid.

80. "Tokyo court rejects ethnic Korean's promotion bid." *Asahi Evening News*, May 17, 1996; "I just want to make Japan a better place to live." Chong interview on *Japan Focus*, February 4, 2005; "Promotion just for Japanese: Supreme Court." *Japan Times*, January 27, 2005; "Korean worker who sued Tokyo government retires." *Yomiuri Shinbun*, April 3, 2012; an essay written by Chong herself for Debito .org in Japanese on her experience is available at www.debito.org/chongsanessay .html (dated May 9, 2005).

81. https://stats-japan.com/t/kiji/11639.

82. "Supreme Court scraps Japanese nationality requirement for legal training." *Asahi Shinbun*, October 29, 2009, where the highest court determined that non-citizens may also receive legal training for careers as lawyers in Japan. However, since many openings have been based upon specific challenges to the procuracy, the system remains a patchwork of regulations. *See* Colin P.A. Jones, "Schizophrenic Constitution leaves foreigners' rights mired in confusion," *Japan Times*, November 1, 2011. As Jones reports on the arbitrary enforcement of the Nationality Clause:

> Foreigners are not helped by the mishmash of other rules and rulings on the subject of their constitutional privileges. . . . Which of the following vocations are open to Non-Japanese? (1) National university professor (yes); (2) family court mediator (no); (3) non-managerial local government bureaucrat (yes); (4) managerial local government bureaucrat (no); (5) member of a national government panel advising on national policy (yes); (6) trainee at the Supreme Court's legal research and training institute (until 2009, officially no, but actually maybe; since 2009, yes); (7) MP's secretary (yes). Though the official line is that only Japanese nationals may participate in the exercise of state power, it is hard to find any real logic in the answers.

83. For example, a Nikkei Brazilian was denied employment as a probation officer in Shizuoka in 2007. According to the *Yomiuri Shinbun* of July 8, 2007:

> [W]hen the probation office contacted the Justice Ministry's Rehabilitation Bureau to get approval for Kodama's appointment, the [Justice] ministry rejected the idea, saying it would be problematic to offer the post of probation officer to a foreigner because the exercising of public authority would be involved in cases such as when a probation officer informs the chief of the probation office if a youth breaks a promise with a probation

officer, which could result in the chief applying for parole to be canceled. According to the ministry's Rehabilitation Bureau, it provided the opinion based on the opinion of the Cabinet Legislation Bureau in which Japanese citizenship is required for public servants who exercise public authority and make decisions that affect the public. In January 2005, the Supreme Court gave a similar viewpoint in a lawsuit filed over the Tokyo metropolitan government's refusal to let a foreigner take management position tests.

84. A full discussion of the term-limited-contract (*ninkisei*) employment issue is too complicated to do justice to within this research, given that "optional" (*sentaku*) *ninkisei* as of 1997 (cf. *Dai 4-ki Daigaku Shingikai Tōshin Hōkoku Shū*, November, 1997, page 9, item 6) has also been instituted for Japanese-citizen educators (although in practice not on the same scale as it has been implemented for noncitizens). In the interests of brevity, *see* an online archive of referential materials, academic publications, and primary sources at www.debito.org/activistspage.html#ninkisei. *See also* Hall (1998), Ch. 3.

85. Interview, Zeus Enterprise Inc., found through Hello Work, October 2010. Archive and "Japanese only" screen capture at www.debito.org/?p=7661. Interview, job placement agency Workers KK Takadanobaba, Tōkyō, October 20, 2008. Archive and "Japanese only" sign at www.debito.org/?p=1949. Both archives contain comments from readers corroborating their experiences with Hello Work turning a blind eye to "Japanese only" job restrictions.

86. *See* three "Japanese only" advertisements within the *Japan Times* Classified Ads of March 9, 2009, for example. *Japan Times*' explicit policy regarding Classified Ads is, "We will not accept ads that solicit companionship, etc., or that are, or may easily be construed as illegal, misleading, fraudulent, indecent, suggestive or offensive." Although "discriminatory" is not listed as a disqualifier, "illegal" under Labor Standards Law Article 3 should technically apply. When one of Japan's premier English-language newspapers permits ads of this nature, it is indicative of how standard and normalized these exclusionary practices are in Japan. Archive at www.debito.org/?p=2645.

87. Interview, Sapporo Labor Standards Bureau, July 1992. I was experiencing unlawful rules and practices within my then-workplace (a Japanese trading company) and found out about this enforcement loophole in passing. This lack of a priori enforcement mechanism would have to be tested in civil court with a noncitizen plaintiff, who would probably be unwilling to work at defendant's workplace anyway after winning against them in court.

88. Regarding noncitizen lack of job stability through contract work: As Terrie's Take, an economic newsletter notes regarding Japan's economic downturn from 2007:

> So, given that there are at least 755,000 foreigners (as of 2006) working here in Japan, and probably another 350,000 or so working illegally, you can bet that this group will be another at-risk segment to lose their jobs. The AP article says that the government Hello Work centers used to get about 700 foreigners looking for jobs each month, but in August due to the massive layoffs by auto manufacturers, the numbers of foreign newly jobless people doubled to 1,500 a month. Local officials note that the number of Japanese

applicants has not changed appreciably (yet)—so clearly Toyota, Honda, and Yamaha are dumping on their Brazilian-Japanese and Chinese workers first.

See Terrie's Take No. 492, November 2, 2008; and "Foreigners laid off in Japanese downturn." *Associated Press*, October 22, 2008.

89. On a historical note, *Tōkyō Shinbun* ran a feature in their January 8, 1988, morning edition outlining the types of jobs by visa that were being assigned to "foreigners" in terms of the top seven working visas in Japan as of end 1984. Of the 15,832 noncitizens listed, nearly half (7,436) were listed as "entertainers and pro sports players," then (in descending order) corporate workers (3,004), foreign language instructors (1,799), cooks (1,366), artists and artisans (1,207), educators in higher education (1,007), and technical specialists (13). All the noncitizens were illustrated in the feature as Caucasians (archived at www.debito.org/?p=930), and no mention was made of the other noncitizens (the Zainichi, for example). The point is these are the jobs that Non-Wajin, particularly the caricaturable Visible Minorities, have been assigned by the media; with the exception of the Nikkei South American and Chinese factory workers imported in the millions from 1990 under special visa regimes, these stereotypical job sectors have not significantly changed. Thus, Japan's visa regimes, as will be discussed in chapter 5, constrain the employment opportunities of noncitizens.

90. These are the requirements for identification for doing business at, for example, the Bank of Tokyo-Mitsubishi UFJ. *See* www.bk.mufg.jp/ippan/law/kakunin.html (accessed April 4, 2021).

91. Ironically, when a universal ID system was promulgated under the *Jūki-Netto* system in 2002, there was great controversy over privacy issues for Japanese citizens, occasioning civil disobedience: By 2010, according to the *Asahi Shinbun*, January 20, 2010, only 3 percent of residents nationwide had applied for the card, with public protests, lawsuits, and even entire municipalities (including Nagoya, Tōkyō Kunitachi, and Fukushima Yamatsuri-chō) opting out of the system. *Jūki-Netto* was for a short time even declared unconstitutional by the Ōsaka High Court (until the presiding judge committed suicide; the Supreme Court later reversed his decision), despite the fact that a harsher system of ID for noncitizens had been in place for half a century. However, Article 13 of the Constitution only infers a right to privacy, defined in application as (a) the right to not have your personal lifestyle (*shi seikatsu*) disclosed, and (b) the right to control public disclosure of one's own information.

As discussed above the Constitution limits the application of human rights to *kokumin* only; further, noncitizens are technically not in Japan as a right, but as a privilege under the GOJ's discretion, meaning rights to presence and privacy can be denied and regulated. Nevertheless, the *Jūki Netto* controversy demonstrated that in Japan's dominant public discourse, the concept of a right to privacy is predicated upon having Japanese nationality. For more on the *Jūki-Netto* controversy, *see* inter alia "Glitches, protest greet launch of resident registry network." *Japan Times*, August 6, 2002; "Court, citing privacy, orders data cut from Juki Net." *Asahi Shinbun*, December 1, 2006; "Juki Net judge in apparent suicide." *Kyodo News*,

December 4, 2006; "Gaijin as guinea pig; Non-Japanese, with fewer rights, are public policy test dummies"; *Japan Times*, July 8, 2008; "Top court: Juki Net not against the Constitution." *Kyodo News*, March 7, 2008. "Nagoya to withdraw from Juki Net." *Asahi Shinbun*, January 20, 2010. *See also Japan Times* online advanced search engine, search term "Juki Net."

92. *See also* Chapman (2012).

93. Letter of the law and MOJ interpretation at https://hourei.net/law/326CO0000000319 and www.moj.go.jp/isa/applications/guide/ryoken.html.

94. *See* the Ministry of Justice website outlining crimes and punishments of noncooperation with the police in Japan (regardless of nationality) at www.moj.go.jp/content/000073753.htm.

95. *See* inter alia MOJ (2013b); "A decade of harassment by Tokyo police." *Japan Times*, July 20, 2010. *See also* primary source testimonials of racial profiling and noncitizen public targeting at: "Gaijin Card Checks and racial profiling at Sakura House." *Debito.org*, November 25, 2006, www.debito.org/?p=86; "Instant Checkpoints in Japan; Extranationality as sufficient grounds for criminal suspicion." *Debito.org*, December 16, 1998, www.debito.org/instantcheckpoints.html; "Two *Cries du coeur* from ethnic residents of Japan being shaken down by the Japanese police." *Debito.org*, November 17, 2007, www.debito.org/?p=714; "Japan Today: Shinjuku cops rough up Singaporean women during 'passport check.'" *Debito.org*, April 25, 2008, www.debito.org/?p=1643; "Hokkaido Police at Chitose Airport only stop non-Asian passengers for G8 Summit anti-terrorist ID Checks, ask me for ID three times. Voice recording as proof." *Debito.org*, June 21, 2008, www.debito.org/?p=1752; "Naturalized Japanese citizen Jiei stopped by Osaka cops for Gaijin Card Check." *Debito.org*, July 25, 2009, www.debito.org/?p=3925; "Narita cops allegedly stopping newly-arrived 'foreigners' for passport checks before boarding Narita Express trains." *Debito.org*, September 16, 2009, www.debito.org/?p=4411; "Ariel updates experience with not-random Gaijin Card and Passport Checks by Narita cops." *Debito.org*, February 5, 2010, www.debito.org/?p=5901; "Sendaiben digs deeper on those Narita Airport racially-profiling Instant NPA Checkpoints." *Debito.org*, September 5, 2010, www.debito.org/?p=7461; "Eyewitness report on how NPA is targeting NJ in Gotanda as security risk for APEC Summit in Yokohama." *Debito.org*, November 9, 2010, www.debito.org/?p=7747; "Gaijin card checkpoint at apartment: Immigration doing door-to-door checks, using physical force." *Debito.org*, January 27, 2012, www.debito.org/?p=9900; and so on.

96. "Too tall for Japan?" *New York Times*, July 8, 2010; and "Police erroneously arrest 'Asian-looking' Japanese woman on immigration law breach." / "*Ryoken fukeitai de taiho no josei, jitsu wa nihonjin: Saitama*." *Mainichi Shinbun*, February 28, 2006, where the detainee was arrested overnight for not carrying her *passport*, even though that is not required by law. In terms of other Visible Minorities unable to "pass" as Wajin: "Former panel member says state responsible for hardship facing Ainu." *Kyodo News*, December 6, 2009, which reports: "Tomoko Yahata said she was stopped and searched in Tokyo nine times over the six months through October.

'Responding to my question as to why they had stopped me, the police officers said it is because there are many overstaying foreigners,' she said."

A more recent case occurred in 2014 where a Japanese citizen of Japanese Filipino ethnicities was arrested and questioned for several hours for "looking suspicious" while standing outside a JR station in Ibaraki, and on suspicion he was not carrying foreigner ID. *See* "*Gaikokujin to omoikomi, ryoken fukeitai yogi de gonin taihō: Ibaraki-ken kei*" [Presuming he was a foreigner, Ibaraki Prefectural Police mistakenly arrest someone on suspicion of not carrying his passport]. *Asahi Shinbun*, August 14, 2014; "*Nihon kokuseki kizukazu gonin taiho: Ibaraki, ryoken fukeitai to handan*" [Mistakenly arrested for not noticing he had Japanese citizenship: Decided he was not carrying a passport]. *Nihon Keizai Shinbun*, August 14, 2014; "Visible Minorities are being caught in the dragnet." *Japan Times*, September 4, 2014.

Furthermore, Japanese police can be so eager to arrest "foreigners" that they will ignore the law that says children under sixteen are not required to carry ID; *see* "*Saitama kenkei ga gaikokujin shōnen gonin gaiho*" [Saitama Prefectural Police mistakenly arrest foreign youth]. *NHK News*, March 6, 2016, archived at www.debito.org/?p=13854. *See also* "XY on being racially profiled—by a designated police task force looking for 'bad foreigners'—for a traffic fender bender caused by someone else!" *Debito.org*, August 28, 2019, www.debito.org/?p=15730.

97. Police frequently stop people riding bicycles on suspicion of them being stolen property, and while in the process of asking for proof of ownership ask for personal ID, specifically the ARC from visibly Non-Wajin people. *See* Debito Arudou, "Pedal pushers cop a load on Yasukuni Dori." *Japan Times*, June 20, 2002; "Good cop, bored cop." *Fukuoka Now Magazine*, February 2007. *See also* a primary source testimony from Tōkyō resident "Mark in Yayoi," a college student who also worked at the night markets near the Tōkyō Stock Exchange, and his count (as of March 20, 2009) of being stopped by police (often the same officers) while cycling home in the early morning *123 times* over the past decade, archived at www.debito.org/?p=2806.

98. There have also been cases of people masquerading as cops demanding street ID checks from people they target as "foreign." *See* "Knowing your rights can protect against fake cops." *Japan Times*, April 2, 2014.

99. "Russian's conviction for handgun possession thrown out." *Japan Times/Kyodo News*, March 7, 2017, archived at www.debito.org/?p=14514. This is not a new policy; according to the *Japan Times*, pressure is being placed upon police officers to seek out people who fit police profiles of potential criminals: "Hiromasa Saikawa, an authority on the police, states that officers are being browbeaten to come up with results, or else. 'Officers are under pressure to meet quotas for nabbing suspects who can be prosecuted,' he says. 'Low achievers might be passed over for promotion or denied leave time.'" *See* "Police shakedowns on the rise." *Japan Times*, October 8, 2006. If you would like to see a comparative example of police treatment of foreigners vs. Japanese, consider these two videos: "YouTube video of Tokyo Police using excessive force to subdue a Non-Japanese in public." *Debito.org*, May 5, 2016, www.debito.org/?p=13981; and videos found on google using "警察官職務質問" as a search term, such as the ones viewed millions of times at www.youtube.com/watch

?v=_CHPPYtjmio, or www.youtube.com/watch?v=sSdEW5gCiDQ (accessed April 22, 2021).

100. A clear example of "foreign" profiling of the author for spot police ARC checks in 1998 and 2003 (before and after naturalization), and the MOJ BOHR's response, is at www.debito.org/policeapology.html.

101. More below, but *see* inter alia "July forecast: Rough, with ID checks mainly in the north." *Japan Times*, July 1, 2008, with primary source evidence grounding the article at www.debito.org/?p=1767.

102. This is according to Ishizuka Akira, an attorney with the Foreigners and International Service Section at Tōkyō Public Law Office, clarifying the law for the *Japan Times*. *See* "Legal hurdles are high when it comes to seeking redress. Limits on 'stop and frisk' open to interpretation by Japan's police and courts." *Japan Times*, July 20, 2014. For what can be done when targeted, *see* "Remain calm when stopped by the police in Japan." *Japan Times*, January 20, 2020.

103. Scanned tax form from Tokorozawa Tax Office, dated April 12, 2010, requiring the submission of an ARC for income tax form processing (item 2), is at www.debito.org/?p=6506. Word has also reached me of at least one prefectural tax department devoting resources to audit foreigners in specific for their potential international holdings; *see* "'Tired Panda' on how rural tax authorities specialize in targeting foreign taxpayers for audit." *Debito.org*, January 10, 2021, www.debito.org/?p=16373. As for DMVs, *see* "Japan Driver License renewals and questionable legality of residency/Gaijin Card checks to ferret out 'illegal overstayers.'" *Debito.org*, July 13, 2014, at www.debito.org/?p=12515.

104. "Creating laws out of thin air: Revisions to hotel laws stretched by police to target foreigners." *Japan Times*, March 8, 2005; "Ministry missive wrecks reception: MHLW asks hotels to enforce nonexistent law." *Japan Times*, October 18, 2005. Regarding racial profiling and refusals of service for noncooperation at hotels, moreover directives from local police to target all "foreign guests," *see* primary source testimonials at the Debito.org archive: "Olaf Karthaus on Hotel gaijin card checks." *Debito.org*, January 19, 2005, www.debito.org/olafongaijincarding.html; "Report: Racial Profiling at Toyoko Inns; suggest boycott (letter of complaint unanswered)." *Debito.org*, December 2, 2007, www.debito.org/?p=797; "Updates on Toyoko Inn's discriminatory treatment of NJ clients." *Debito.org*, January 13, 2010, www.debito.org/?p=5716; "Comfort Hotel Nagoya unlawfully tries Gaijin Card check on NJ resident, admits being confused by GOJ directives." *Debito.org*, February 26, 2010, www.debito.org/?p=5733; "Chand Bakshi fights back against 'NJ ID Checkpoint' hotel, gets apology." *Debito.org*, October 8, 2010, www.debito.org/?p=7580; and so on.

105. Hotel Management Law Article 5 explicitly states that an establishment cannot turn away lodgers unless there is (1) a health issue involving contagious disease, (2) a clear and present endangerment of public morals, or (3) because all rooms are full. There is no provision for turning away lodgers for not showing ID. For example, police prosecutors cited a violation of the Hotel Management Law when Japanese lodgers were turned away from a Prince Hotel in Tōkyō, because the latter revoked a contract for a Japan Teacher's Union conference. *See* "Police move Prince Hotels/teachers union case to next level." *Asahi Shinbun*, March 17, 2009.

106. This is not an isolated instance of mandate expansion through ministerial notification of hotels. During 2008's G8 Summit in Hokkaidō, the Health Ministry's Environmental Health Division (*kenkō seikatsu eisei ka*) sent all local governments and hotels nationwide a directive (*Eisei hatsu dai*-06004001, dated June 4, 2008), reminding them to check and photocopy the passports of all noncitizen guests without an address in Japan as part of a national policing action for summit security. The text of the directive is archived at www.debito.org/?p=1764, courtesy of Kamesei Ryokan, Nagano, June 26, 2008.

107. "Hotel calls cops on NJ Resident at check-in for not showing passport. And cops misinterpret laws. Unlawful official harassment is escalating." *Debito.org*, April 12, 2019, www.debito.org/?p=15590; "Last word on NJ hotel passport checks (thanks to a lawyer): It's as Debito.org has said for more than a decade: NJ Residents are exempt from showing any ID." *Debito.org*, October 15, 2019, www.debito.org/?p=15785.

108. *See* the Health Ministry's justification for the ministerial ordinance as prevention of terrorism and international crime at www.mhlw.go.jp/topics/2005/03/tp0317-1.html. *See* the Action Plan for the Pre-empting of Terrorism at www.kantei.go.jp/jp/singi/sosikihanzai/kettei/041210kettei.pdf (both accessed April 3, 2021).

109. Online archive with analysis at www.debito.org/japantimes030805.html#Update and www.debito.org/japantimes101805.html. Embassy of Japan, Washington, D.C. website title: "Registration Procedure at lodging facilities in Japan to be changed as of April 1, 2005, clarifying registration procedures for "foreign nationals who visit Japan," dated March 2005; screen capture dated January 30, 2008.

110. It is important to note that these directives were enforced with some resistance from the hotels themselves. *Asahi Shinbun* ("Survey: 1 in 4 hotels fails to record foreign guests," January 5, 2008) reports: "One in four hotels and ryokan inns across Japan is not complying with government anti-terror initiatives that require them to record nationalities and passport numbers of foreign guests [*sic*—not foreign *tourists*], according to a survey. Many hoteliers and inn owners say they are reluctant to do so for fear of treading on customers' privacy." The NPA reportedly reiterated their need for fuller cooperation from hoteliers.

111. "Onur on Fukuoka hotel check-ins in: Police creating unlawful 'foreign passport check' signs in the name of (and without the knowledge of) local government authorities." *Debito.org*, November 20, 2016, www.debito.org/?p=14305; "Onur update: Ibaraki Pref. Police lying on posters requiring hotels to inspect and photocopy all foreign passports; gets police to change their posters." *Debito.org*, April 13, 2016, www.debito.org/?p=13930; "Onur on continued racial profiling at Japanese hotel check-ins: Discrimination is even coin-operated!" *Debito.org*, March 12, 2016, www.debito.org/?p=13852; "Police still unfettered by the law, or the truth: Repeat-offender Ibaraki force called to account for backsliding on the issue of hotel snooping." *Japan Times*, June 6, 2016, with sources at www.debito.org/?p=14036; Debito Arudou, "Racial Profiling at Japanese Hotel Check-Ins." *Shingetsu News Agency*, October 23, 2019; "'Every Foreign Guest must present passport for photocopying' at Hotel Crown Hills Kokura; Japanese Police up to same old unlawful tricks in Fukuoka Prefecture." *Debito.org*, December 11, 2019, www.debito.org/?p=15863.

112. For general background on the Minpaku Law, *see* "New minpaku law will alter Japan's rental and hospitality landscape." *Japan Times*, April 1, 2018. For commentary about the racialized enforcement, *see* mainstream news articles archived with commentary at: "Shibuya Police asking local 'minpaku' Airbnb renters to report their foreign lodgers 'to avoid Olympic terrorism.' Comes with racialized illustrations." *Debito.org*, June 27, 2016, www.debito.org/?p=14071; "Reuters/Asahi: New 'minpaku' law stifles homesharing with tourists, on grounds insinuating foreigners are 'unsafe' for children walking to school! (or ISIS terrorists)." *Debito.org*, June 30, 2018, www.debito.org/?p=15051; "New Minpaku Law and NJ check-ins: Government telling Airbnb hostels that 'foreign guests' must have passports photocopied etc. Yet not in actual text of the Minpaku Law. Or any law." *Debito.org*, February 23, 2019, www.debito.org/?p=15559; Debito Arudou, "Know your rights when checking in at an Airbnb." *Japan Times*, April 17, 2019.

113. The Financial Services Agency, as a crime prevention measure under the Personal Identification Law (*hon'nin kakunin hō*) of 2008, requires personal identification from all account holders, regardless of nationality. Satisfactory for ID are the abovementioned driver license, passport, pension passbook, *Jūki* Card, and ARC. There is nothing, however, within those regulations requiring the ARC *in specific* from noncitizens if the latter produces any of these other forms of ID, but many banks unlawfully list the submission and photocopying of the ARC as a precondition for service for noncitizens only. *See* the Financial Services Agency's official rules on ID at www.fsa.go.jp/access/18/200610b.html. *See also* Higuchi & Arudou (2008: 142–7); "Fox on getting interrogated at Sumitomo Prestia Bank in Kobe. Thanks to new FSA regulations that encourage even more racial profiling." *Debito.org*, March 18, 2019, www.debito.org/?p=15584; "DF on Chugoku bank unlawfully demanding to check NJ customers' visa stay durations and photocopy their Gaijin Cards or face discontinuation of service." *Debito.org*, March 8, 2020, www.debito.org/?p=15881.

114. *See* inter alia primary source testimonies: "Olaf Karthaus on problems for Non-Japanese cashing even small amounts of money at Hokkaido Bank." *Debito.org*, April 5, 2001, www.debito.org/TheCommunity/karthausondogin.html; Hokkaido Bank's letter of apology for overuse of scrutiny towards Karthaus, dated April 18, 2001, www.debito.org/doginshimatsusho041801.jpg; "Getting better service from a Japanese bank." *Debito.org*, March 11, 2003; Hokkaido Bank's letter of apology for overuse of scrutiny towards the author, dated February 17, 2003, www.debito.org/doginsapapology.jpg; "Third Degree given Non-Japanese who wanted Post Office money order." *Debito.org*, August 18, 2008, www.debito.org/?p=1874; "Jerry Halvorsen on suspicious bank treatment for receiving money from overseas while Non-Japanese" (Halvorsen was required to appear in person at the bank and present ID to receive an overseas bank transfer), *Debito.org*, October 11, 2008, www.debito.org/?p=1939; "Fun and Games at Hokuyo Bank: Extra questions for the gaijin account holder." *Debito.org*, February 10, 2009, at www.debito.org/?p=2293 (I received no apology this time). This is happening despite Foreign Exchange Order (*gaikoku kawase rei*), Cabinet Order (*seirei*) No. 260 of October 11, 1980, Article 7.2, which exempts small payments of less than two million yen (amended to 100,000 yen

in 2007) from the obligation to identify customers (*hon'nin kakunin gimu no taishō ni naranai*). The point is that there is no legal reason to profile noncitizen customers, except for the probable reason that Japanese financial institutions have been encouraged by police and public anticrime campaigns to noncitizens as suspicious and warranting extra scrutiny.

115. Banks (Interview, Hokuyo Bank, February 10, 2009, ibid.) cite the Bank of Japan's directive regarding the Foreign Exchange and Foreign Trade Act (*gaikoku kawase oyobi gaikoku bōeki hō*, aka *gaitame hō*, *see* www.boj.or.jp/about/services/tame/faq/data/t_sihon.pdf), Articles 17 and 55, along with sections of the Personal Identification Law. These have been interpreted as guidelines by Japan's financial system to mean that noncitizens without (a) clear employment and (b) a prior six-month duration in Japan cannot receive bank accounts (even though neither law specifically lists these conditions as requirements). Primary source testimonies on the application of this interpretation for the sake of money laundering at "No bank accounts allowed at Mitsui Sumitomo for NJ without minimum six-month stays." *Debito.org*, April 2, 2008, www.debito.org/?p=1400 (*see also* comments); and so on.

116. "Anti-money laundering measures snag tourists with travellers' checks." *Debito.org*, July 12, 2007, www.debito.org/?p=482.

117. "7-Eleven ATMs will finally accept foreign cards." *Japan Probe*, July 12, 2007.

118. *See also* National Police Agency 2009, "*Heisei 20 nen no soshiki hanzai no jōsei*" [The status of organized crime for 2008], which focuses primarily on "foreign criminals" and downplays the extent of crimes committed by Japan's already well-established organized-crime syndicates.

119. *See* primary source testimonial, "Ben on credit card problems with Isetan Credit Company and Mitsubishi Bank." *Debito.org*, January 29, 2001, www.debito.org/wesoncreditcards.html. Isetan's credit card companies have different standards for customers based upon nationality. Citizens can use their cards for cashing, have their credit limits reviewed every six months, and have card validity for five years with automatic renewal. Noncitizens cannot use their cards for cashing, never have their credit limits reviewed, and have card validity for one year with mandatory use of once every six months or they will face cancellation (due to the express assumption that noncitizens have left Japan if the card is unused). Further, Mitsubishi Bank's DC Card has refused applications to noncitizens on the (unconfirmed) assumption that they cannot understand Japanese.

120. www.debito.org/kofuexclusions.html.

121. "Docomo's 'foreign tariff.'" *Asahi Evening News*, April 12, 2002; and Debito Arudou, "Questions over foreigners' phone deposit." *Japan Times*, August 29, 2002.

122. "Softbank's policy towards NJ customers re new iPhone." *Debito.org*, July 20, 2008.

123. www.debito.org/jacksononcreditproblems.html.

124. Primary source testimonials at www.debito.org/julianonoasisintro.html and www.debito.org/julianonoasisfinal.html. *See also* "SendaiBen on Anytime Fitness sports gym Gaijin Carding him, and how he got them to stop it." *Debito.org*, December 13, 2018, www.debito.org/?p=15222.

125. "Driver License schools now doing Immigration's job too, checking NJ visas? Also at Postal Savings." *Debito.org*, October 8, 2009, at www.debito.org/?p=4679.

126. "Yomiuri: GOJ now requiring hospitals (unlawfully) demand Gaijin Cards from NJ as a precondition for medical treatment." *Debito.org*, May 12, 2019, www.debito.org/?p=15214.

127. "Gaijin cards valid until 2015—but not at the post office." *Japan Times*, September 25, 2012. Primary source information at www.post.japanpost.jp/service/fuka_service/honnin/ (accessed April 4, 2021). Although the MOJ was notified of this poor coordination between Japan's ministries, there were no reports of official attempts to rectify this situation, indicating that contradictory policies affecting foreign residents are a low priority.

128. "In mid-May 1996, three policemen visited [Defendant] S store, and posted a sign saying, 'Beware of burglaries.' They also orally warned defendants to 'be careful of foreigners.' Afterwards, defendants put a sign on their wall in Japanese to the effect that 'No foreigners allowed.'" Webster (2007b: 644). *See also* "ICI Hotel Kanda unlawfully requires ID from all 'foreign guests,' including NJ residents of Japan, as a precondition for stay; claims it's demanded by Tokyo Metropolitan Police." *Debito.org*, September 23, 2019, www.debito.org/?p=15750.

129. *See* www.mhlw.go.jp/stf/seisakunitsuite/bunya/koyou_roudou/koyou/gaikokujin/todokede/index.html (accessed April 4, 2021).

130. "*Gaikokujin rōdōsha hōkoku gimuzuke: shūchi susumazu, sabetsu no osore mo.*" *Kobe Shinbun*, October 1, 2007; "Gaijin Card checks spread as police deputize the nation." *Japan Times*, November 13, 2007. The article alludes to the growing public perception of noncitizen as potential criminal, covered in more detail below: "The manager realizes illegal Vietnamese laborers in the area will be exposed but worries that, 'foreigners who lose their jobs will unnecessarily turn to crime.' Furthermore, data gathered by the MHLW plans to be shared with the MOJ. The Japan Federation of Bar Associations and others criticize this scheme because it 'violates foreigner's rights to privacy.'" They point out, "there is a possibility that discriminatory treatment based on race, skin color or ethnic origin might arise."

131. For example, Kansai University assumed a Permanent-Resident noncitizen employee was an overstayer simply because he no longer had a valid REP (*sainyūkoku kyoka*: Necessary only if temporary leaving the country and coming back in on the same visa status). *See* "Kandai PR Harassment: Why you don't let non-Immigration people make Immigration decisions." *Debito.org*, January 28, 2008, at www.debito.org/?p=1015.

132. *See*, for example, Pekkanen 2006: 2, 107.

133. "A life less complex as foreigners join local board." *Asahi Shinbun*, August 19, 2008. I was the vice-chair of my Neighborhood Association in Sorachi-gun Nanporo-chō, Hokkaidō, from 1999 to 2000, both before and after I naturalized.

134. "Police to take measures for safety in foreign communities in Japan." *Kyodo News*, March 5, 2009. The article notes:

> The police will also join hands with local government organizations, business corporations and citizen groups in implementing crime prevention measures, the NPA said,

adding that they will monitor employment conditions in foreign communities as factors that may induce crime. The guidelines are based on an action program the government's anticrime council worked out last December to help build a crime-free society and make Japan the world's safest country again. The latest measures are designed to enable foreigners in Japan to live a better life, as well as to prevent organized crime groups and terrorists from sneaking into certain foreign communities to plot crimes, an NPA official said.

135. "Generating the foreigner crime wave." *Japan Times*, October 4, 2002.

136. "The 15 locations include the prefectural capitals of Otsu, Okayama, Hiroshima, Tokushima and Fukuoka. The 10 other areas are in Higashi-Matsushima, Miyagi Prefecture; Oyama, Tochigi Prefecture; Toda, Saitama Prefecture; Higashi-Yamato and Musashi-Murayama, both suburban Tokyo; Fujieda, Shizuoka Prefecture; Neyagawa, Osaka Prefecture; Himeji, Hyogo Prefecture; Iwade, Wakayama Prefecture; and Amami, Kagoshima Prefecture." Under what criteria these places were chosen is unclear. *See* "Residential streets to get cop cameras—Neighborhood groups to be in charge: NPA." *Kyodo News*, June 26, 2009.

137. *Yomiuri Shinbun* Podcast, April 14, 2008, from minute 13.

138. "Fukushima Prefectural Police HQ online poster asking for public vigilantism against 'illegal foreign workers, overstayers.'" *Debito.org*, April 23, 2017, www.debito.org/?p=14559. For reasons unknown, this was categorized under a general alert about "black market financiers" (*yami kenkin gyōsha*).

139. *Nyūkoku kanrikyoku—jōhō uketsuke* at www.immi-moj.go.jp/zyouhou/index.html, accessed April 4, 2021. Starting from October 6, 2007, this online vector was later expanded to a phone-in service by the Tokyo's Immigration Bureau, available 9 a.m.–5 p.m. daily (excepting weekends and holidays) (ibid.). From April 1, 2004, the Fukuoka Prefectural Police (*Fukuoka-ken keisatsu honbu keiji sōmuka kokusai sōsa shitsu*) also created their own "snitch site" (http://police.pref.fukuoka.jp/onegai/keiji/gaikokujin.html), but this went offline at a later date, later to surface at an unknown date as a submission site for information about "international group crime" (*kokusai soshiki hanzai*), with only a phone number contact (www.police.pref.fukuoka.jp/i/boutai/sotai/001.html). It also clearly stated, "this site is not discriminatory towards foreigners."

140. "Downloadable discrimination: The Immigration Bureau's new snitching web site is both short-sighted and wide open to all manner of abuses." *Japan Times*, March 30, 2004.

141. "Brokers" are middlemen acting as headhunters and liaisons between hired noncitizen and employer, often exploiting or assisting in the exploitation of migrant workers in Japan. *See* inter alia Roth (2002: Introduction).

142. "Groups demand end to cyber-informing on foreigners via email." *Kyodo News*, March 18, 2004; "Human Rights Groups protest Immigration site as 'cyber xenophobia.'" *Reuters*, March 19, 2004; "Suspicious minds: Japan is hoping to boost foreign investment and tourism by promoting the country as a land of hospitality. However, institutional racism and the media's tendency to blame foreigners for rising crime means many visitors find themselves less than welcome." *Guardian*, March 10, 2004; "Rights activists rap tougher immigration measures." *Inter Press Service*,

March 10, 2004; "Ministry of Justice plugs gaps in 'racist' telltale site." *Mainichi Shinbun*, April 1, 2004; "Amnesty International also renews calls for site's abolition." *Japan Today*, April 14, 2004; "Kobe protests e-snitching on immigrants." *Yomiuri Shinbun*, April 15, 2004; "Scrap rat-on-foreigners Web site: Hyogo." *Japan Times*, April 18, 2004; "Japanese immigration web site fuels anger among foreigners, rights groups." *Voice of America*, May 5, 2004.

143. Voice of America ibid., which continues: "The web site reportedly generated more than a thousand e-mailed tips in its first 45 days online, but the authorities are not saying if it has actually resulted in any arrests." Immigration Bureau's assistant director Maruyama Hideharu defended the system by saying, "allowing Japanese to alert authorities anonymously about suspect foreigners is no different than what has been done traditionally by telephone or fax." He argued that "cutting the number of illegal aliens will help to increase the proportion of legal foreigners, improve the image of foreigners among Japanese, and thus eventually lead to a liberalization of regulations on immigration." However, to some protesters, "the idea of spying and informing on foreigners harkens back to the early Twentieth Century special agents of the 'Tokkō'—the Japanese thought police—which used citizen cooperation to keep tabs on everyone in the country."

144. "Xenophobic wave of tips target 'illegal' Korean residents; immigration bureaus overwhelmed." *Japan Times*, July 21, 2015; "Immigration Bureau inundated with e-mails 'snitching on' Korean nationals, suspends program." *Asahi Shinbun*, December 24, 2015, archived at www.debito.org/?p=13722.

145. Online Archive of scanned NRIPS proposal document archived at www.debito.org/NRIPSprofilingpolicy.jpg. Analysis at www.debito.org/NPAracialprofiling.html and www.debito.org/japantimes011304.html.

146. Archived at *Debito.org* at www.debito.org/crimestats.html, with a detailed analysis of NPA statistics and the statistical problems with analyzing "foreign crime" in Japan. *See also* Herbert (1996) for a historical perspective on this process.

147. Since citizens cannot commit "visa-related crimes" because they do not have visas, these crimes arguably should not be included in crime rate comparisons. They are not, in any case, officially classified as "heinous crimes," the target of this policy.

148. *See*, for example, "Crime at New Low in Japan, But Seniors Commit 22 Percent of Offenses." *Nippon.com*, January 12, 2021, which says, "The figure for reported crimes in Japan fell to its lowest point on record in 2019" (the most recent statistics available at this writing). That said, it is difficult to find an article that includes and compares foreign and Japanese crime rates, since (as will be discussed in chapter 7) the NPA reports them separately and analyzes them differently. The most recent NPA report covering years 2009–2018 can be found in Japanese at www.npa.go.jp/hakusyo/r01/data.html, item 4–7, depicting a leveling-off in already-low foreign crime numbers (despite an increase in the registered Non-Japanese population).

149. *See* Debito Arudou, "Forensic science fiction: Bad science and racism underpin police policy." *Japan Times*, January 13, 2004. In response, the NRIPS had a Letter to the Editor published in *Japan Times* on February 8, 2004, entitled "Forensic tools no cause for bias." It shifted the focus of the research from nationality to "geographic area" (i.e., "where someone was born," again assuming extranationals are not born in Japan):

We believe the writer incorrectly assumes that our efforts are aimed at "gaijin-bashing" or "loosening public purse strings" for an overlapping program by instilling fear of foreigners. With the globalization and diversification of crimes, a study to swiftly narrow down possible identities of unidentified victims and/or offenders is a very important method in criminal investigations. Besides screening persons connected with the crime by conventional methods, we are aiming to develop new analytical tools using human biological specimens. Even if DNA typing of an unidentified victim or offender has been performed using a bloodstain at the crime scene, it will remain impossible to promptly determine the DNA type without candidates to check it against. So, if it is possible to estimate the geographic area where an unidentified victim or offender was born, an identity will be narrowed down; as a result, a more rapid solution of the case can be expected. This study is not about carrying out racial discrimination. Signed: T. TSUDA, National Research Institute of Police Science, Tokyo.

An unidentified representative at NRIPS issued a similar denial during a telephone call on January 27, 2004, when I called the NRIPS to talk about this policy further. "This policy has nothing to do with foreigners," the representative claimed. I then read aloud the policy (which includes the word *gaikokujin* in the very title) to him over the phone, indicating that I was not misreading the Japanese. He offered no rebuttal.

150. "Japan's Locked Borders Shake the Trust of Its Foreign Workers." *New York Times*, August 5, 2020; "A despotic bridge too far." *Shingetsu News Agency*, July 20, 2020, www.debito.org/?p=16172; "New Covid foreign resident re-entry rules still racist." *Shingetsu News Agency*, October 19, 2020, www.debito.org/?p=16284.

151. "Japan to halt new entry from around world amid new virus variant." *Kyodo News*, December 27, 2020; "Japan confirms first case of new COVID-19 strain that slipped through net." *Japan Times/Jiji*, December 28, 2020; "Tokyo girl believed to be first local case of U.K. coronavirus variant." *Japan Times/Jiji*, December 28, 2020.

152. "Foreign residents stranded abroad by Japan's coronavirus controls: Japan is the only Group of Seven member denying entry to long-term and permanent residents." *Japan Times*, May 19, 2020. "What prompted some of the most intense criticism of the [border] policy was its failure to distinguish between short-term visitors and long-term residents—a decision that made it the only member of the Group of Seven that refused to allow residents with foreign passports to return to their homes in Japan from overseas." *See* "Tokyo's pandemic border policy highlights insecure status of foreign residents." *Japan Times*, December 30, 2020.

153. *New York Times,* ibid.; "Japan's entry policies increase alienation and deepen division." *Japan Times*, August 27, 2020; "Tokyo's pandemic border policy highlights insecure status of foreign residents." *Japan Times*, December 30, 2020.

154. "The American Chamber of Commerce in Japan calls on Government of Japan for equal treatment of all residents." *Statement*, July 13, 2020, archived at www.debito.org/?p=16166; "*Shingata korona uirusu kansenshō no eikyō ni tomonau gaikokujin ryūgakusei, kenkūsha tou ni kansuru yōbō*" [Request regarding the effects of coronavirus transmission pertaining to foreign exchange students and researchers]. Japan Association of National Universities, July 13, 2020, archived at www.debito.org/?p=16162.

155. "Latest visa rules could purge any foreigner." *Shingetsu News Agency*, January 18, 2021, www.debito.org/?p=16382; "Japan considering ways to lift entry ban for foreign tourists: The government is considering ways to lift its entry ban on foreign tourists with the coming of the Tokyo Olympic and Paralympic Games, postponed to the summer of 2021." *Japan Times/Jiji Press*, October 5, 2020; "Japan to exempt business travelers and returnees from 14-day quarantine: Business travelers and returnees will be exempt from Japan's 14-day quarantine policy, government sources say." *Japan Times/Kyodo News/Jiji Press*, October 8, 2020.

156. *See* www.mhlw.go.jp/stf/newpage_10636.html, archived at www.debito.org/?p=16010. Incidentally, the GOJ also required all returnees carry cellphones with location tracking software installed. *See* "Japan developing tracking system for travelers from overseas as anti-virus measure." *Kyodo News/Japan Today*, December 27, 2020; "Glitches and design flaws limit value of Japan's COVID-19 tracing app." *Japan Times*, February 1, 2021; "Travelers entering Japan have to install location confirmation app, Skype on smartphones." *Japan Today*, March 20, 2021.

157. "COVID-inspired racism as NJ Residents are separated and 'othered' from fellow Japan taxpayers by Dietmembers and bureaucrats." *Debito.org*, April 8, 2020, www.debito.org/?p=16010.

158. "Interview with Dr. Oshitani Hitoshi, Department of Virology at Tōhoku University Graduate School of Medicine." *Japan Foreign Policy Forum*, June 5, 2020, archived at www.debito.org/?p=16130; Felix Lill, "*Vorbild oder Sorgenkind? Japan testet wenig auf das Virus, die Infektionszahlen sind niedrig. Doch die Angst wächst, dass die offiziellen Angaben nicht der Realität entsprechen.*" [Role Model or Problem Child? Japan does little virus testing; the number of infections is low. However, the fear that the official numbers do not match reality is growing stronger.] *Die Zeit*, June 9, 2020, translated at www.debito.org/?p=16130. Presumptions of differences in contagion were further borne out in September 2020, when the GOJ relaxed restrictions to allow some Non-Japanese residents to reenter, but then required them to undergo pre-entry tests at testing sites overseas before boarding (Japanese citizens were again exempt); conditions were so strict that they amounted to a de facto entry ban. *See* "As Japan partially lifts re-entry ban on foreign residents, concerns grow over strict procedures." *Japan Times*, August 31, 2020; "Japan's Kafkaesque and faulty re-entry procedures (even after October revisions to 'open borders to Re-entry Visa foreign residents'): More elaborate racist barriers now." *Debito.org*, October 16, 2020, www.debito.org/?p=16271.

159. "Japan to keep foreign spectators away from Tokyo Olympics, Kyodo says." *Reuters*, March 9, 2021, archived at www.debito.org/?p=16480; "'Unavoidable': Overseas fans barred from Tokyo Olympics over virus." *Japan Times*, March 21, 2021, which notes, "'It has never happened that foreign spectators were banned from entering the host country at the time of the Games, even during the Spanish flu at the time of the Antwerp 1920 Olympic Games,' said Jean-Loup Chappelet, a Lausanne-based professor who specializes in the Olympics."

160. "Japan bars entry for new arrivals and business travelers due to new COVID-19 strains." *Japan Times*, January 14, 2021.

161. "Debate over Japan's virus testing resurfaces amid nationwide outbreak." *Japan Times*, July 21, 2020.

162. "Why Japan took so long to start Covid-19 vaccinations, even with the Olympics looming." *CNN*, February 27, 2021; "Japan's slow COVID vaccine rollout turns hope into frustration." *Nikkei Asia*, March 23, 2021.

163. "Japan bars entry for new arrivals and business travelers due to new COVID-19 strains." *Japan Times*, January 14, 2021; "*Quarantäne wie im Knast: Die Regierung in Japan scheint wenige Monate vor den Olympischen Spielen nervōs: Viele Einreisende mūssen in ein Quarantänehotel—und das hat es in sich: Keine Frischluft, Morgenappell, kaltes Essen*" [Jail-like quarantine: The government of Japan gets seemingly nervous a couple of months to the Olympic Games: Many travelers from abroad have to go to a quarantine hotel—and that is a ripsnorter: No fresh air, roll call in the morning, cold food]. *Tagesschau* (German TV), April 1, 2021, translated at www.debito.org/?p=16570.

164. "Japan Discovers New Coronavirus Variant." *US News and World Report*, February 19, 2021. Note how Japan is trying to portray the variant as exogenous. "New coronavirus variant 'Eek' found in Japan, lowers vaccine protection." *Hindustan Times*, April 5, 2021; "Troubling 'Eek' variant found in most Tokyo hospital COVID cases—NHK." *Reuters*, April 3, 2021, which noted, "For the two months through March, 12 of 36 COVID patients carried the mutation, with none of them having recently travelled abroad or reporting contact with people who had, [NHK] said."

165. "It's official: Tokyo 2020 is a 'Japanese Only' Olympics: Japanese living abroad still allowed to attend, not foreigners. (This probably includes Japanese who have given up their Japanese citizenship.)" *Debito.org*, March 23, 2021, www.debito.org/?p=16523.

166. Colin P. A. Jones, "Citizen or not? A conditional love story." *Japan Times*, August 12, 2020.

Chapter 5

How "Japaneseness" Is Enforced through Laws

So far we have surveyed of Japan's national discourse by analyzing how existing laws regarding the determination of citizenship reinforce the differentiation, "othering," and subordination of peoples in Japan. This is carried out, of course, under a rubric of citizen vs. noncitizen, but also in Japan's case under racialized paradigms of Wajin vs. Gaijin. This chapter will focus on how (a) existing laws unrelated to the determination of citizenship, and (b) the legislative process behind those laws, also create racialized public policies and further normalize racial discrimination.

Let us open with how the Japanese government (GOJ) "catches them young" by embedding racialized memes of "citizen vs. noncitizen" in compulsory education (*gimu kyōiku*).

THE BASIC ACT ON EDUCATION: OVERT AND EMBEDDED EXCLUSIONISM

First, consider the legal codification of differentiation by nationality within Japan's Basic Act on Education. Japan's current version (*kyōiku kihon hō*) has a built-in "Nationality Clause" (see chapter 4). From its Preamble:

> We, the citizens of Japan (*wareware Nihon kokumin*), desire to further develop the democratic and cultural state we have built through our untiring efforts, and contribute to the peace of the world and the improvement of the welfare of humanity (*jinrui*). To realize these ideals, we shall esteem individual (*kojin*) dignity, and endeavor to bring up people who long for truth and justice, honor the public spirit (*kōkyō no seishin*), and are rich in humanity (*ningensei*) and creativity, while promoting an education that transmits tradition and aims at the

> creation of a new culture. We (*wareware*) hereby enact this Act, in accordance with the spirit of the Constitution of Japan, in order to establish the foundations of education and promote an education that opens the way to our country's (*wagakuni*) future.[1]

Note that the invective seen in chapter 4 embedding fundamental essences of "Self," as in "we Japanese" and "our country," is present even after Japan's postwar democratization and liberalization.

Nevertheless, in recent decades Japan's basic approach to education and democracy has become a perpetual hot issue in public debates. Repeta (2013) reports that revisionist conservatives have been trying to revise Japan's Constitution, removing "foreign" embedded concepts considered to be "Western" in heritage. Revisions include (a) prioritizing duty to the state and maintenance of public order over the rights, freedoms, and constitutional protections of the individual; (b) rejecting the universality of human rights as a "Western theory of natural rights"; and overall, in Repeta's view, (c) putting "Japan's democracy at risk" by reverting the concept of "citizen" closer to "subject" under the Emperor, as per "the history, tradition, and culture of Japan."[2]

Moving closer toward these ideals, in December 2006 the first PM Abe Shinzō administration revised the Basic Act on Education to reflect greater "nurturing of patriotic attitudes" and "an attitude that loves the nation" over inculcating individual rights and autonomy.[3] Lebowitz and McNeill (2007) ponder this potential change from citizens to subjects:

> Much criticism of the amended education law has focused on statements clearly privileging the state over the individual; that is, statements affirming civil liberties still appear, often unchanged, from the original version, but are often undercut and diluted by new language. Perhaps more importantly, however, what makes the amended version of the law appear less a legal document than an expression of authoritarian will is not so much what is said, but how it is said. That is, the language of mystique and belief makes the very notion of individual rights seem anachronistic at best. For this reason the amended version is not a reflection of a democratic and constitutionally law-driven society but resembles in content and in intent the Edict, a product of a wartime regime.

This development is important because it is again firming up the "Self" side—"Japaneseness." But in terms of this research, overlooked in Lebowitz and McNeill's analysis is the converse treatment of the "Other," especially of people with multiple identities. For example, what happens to the noncitizen children in Japan's education system? Or worse, to the multinational/multiethnic *kokumin* of international relationships who may not wish to "love" one nation over another, and who are forced in the same vein as the Nationality Law to suppress or overwrite their ethnic identities?

With that comes the subordination and exclusion of the "Other." Similar to the Postwar "language games" that inserted a Nationality Clause into the Constitution (see chapter 4), the Basic Act on Education also embeds *kokumin* conceits by *reserving compulsory education for citizens only* (Article 5). In practice this has resulted in noncitizen children being legally refused an education by Japanese schools. Justifications have included "a lack of facilities," "too much work for teachers," or alleged language barriers or acculturation problems.[4]

For example, in 2019 "foreign" children were reportedly being put into "special education" (*tokubetsu shien gakkyū*) schools (headlined as "prison camps for Brazilians" in the *Mainichi Shinbun*) against their wishes, and at rates more than twice that of Wajin. Assigned manual labor during school time (e.g., digging potatoes instead of learning math), these "foreign" children were assumed to be low IQ because they were not proficient in Japanese. This policy was further justified by Wajin Privilege, with a school vice principal claiming, "When foreigners increase in number, the learning process of Japanese students is delayed."[5] Consequently, the Embedded Racism within the Act has fostered an uneducated underclass of noncitizen or ethnic minority children where, according to the *Yomiuri Shinbun* in 2007, 20,000 noncitizen children lacked sufficient Japanese ability to follow classroom instruction, and the *Asahi Shinbun* estimated 20–40 percent of all Brazilian children never attended or were not attending school in Japan.[6]

Further, the Act's focus on the cultivation of a monolithic monoethnic "Japaneseness" has encouraged the racialization of school rules. Many schools enforce extra hurdles or draconian rules specially targeting Non-Wajin or Visible Minority children for unwanted attention: famously the school "hair police" that force diverse children to dye and straighten their natural hair color,[7] and bullying (*ijime*) by Wajin children and even teachers.[8] Despite much press attention, public shaming, and even lawsuits, these phenomena have not abated, resulting in high dropout numbers, even suicides, for ethnic children unable to "pass" as Wajin.[9]

Educational alternatives for multiethnic children are available in Japan, such as ethnic schools with foreign curricula, such as from North/South Korea, Brazil, Great Britain, Germany, India, and the United States. However, there are still structural barriers for children who opt out of the official Japanese education system. Only schools certified by the Ministry of Education as an official educational institution may receive GOJ funding, issue graduation diplomas that will be valid for all Japanese universities, or even qualify for Student IDs (*gakuseishō*) that will enable student discounts for public transportation and other institutions.[10] Ethnic schools that refuse to adopt a

Japanese curriculum are generally not certified, so with few exceptions most ethnic schools face an economic disadvantage: a nonsubsidized cost of operation and a greater cost of attendance for students and their families.

To sum up: This systemic differentiation, "othering," and subordination of Non-Wajin children is grounded in the Basic Act on Education's permitted right to refuse noncitizen children, that is, foreign children are not legally guaranteed a compulsory education in Japan.[11] Further, school rules enforce Wajin standards of conformity on Visible Minorities, including blackened hair and suppressed expressions of multiethnicity, thus further splintering the "citizen/noncitizen" dichotomy into a racialized "Wajin/Non-Wajin" subset. This process that sanctions the alienation and denial of opportunities to a segment of Japan's population—at an impressionable age when Wajin are most likely to be socialized toward Non-Wajin as peers—has created a forced suppression of latent diversity within Japan, with lifelong and sometimes fatal consequences.

OTHER EMBEDDED EXCLUSIONARY PRACTICES IN THE JAPANESE EDUCATION SYSTEM

Other school activities embed exclusionary tendencies based upon blood and nationality conceits. Three examples of officially sanctioned activities excluding Non-Wajin and Visible Minority students enrolled in Japanese educational institutions are the National Sports Festival, the *Ekiden* Sports Races, and the Takamado English Contests.

The Kokutai National Sports Festival

Japan's largest amateur athletic sports meet,[12] the National Sports Festival (*Kokumin Tai'iku Taikai*, or *Kokutai*), holds three seasonal nationwide sports events per year for forty-two different sports (most famously high school baseball, but there are also adult leagues). Sponsored by the Ministry of Education under the Basic Sports Law (*supōtsu kihon hō*), and organized by the Japan Sports Association (*Nippon Tai'iku Kyōkai*, or JASA) and the annual hosting prefecture, the Kokutai is funded by national and local taxes and had as its slogan (in English): "Sports for all." However, despite the taxpayer status of noncitizen residents, only citizens (*kokumin*) are allowed to participate, enforcing an implicit Nationality Clause (the exception being Zainichi born and raised in Japan, but this was permitted only from 1981). With this precedent, other local amateur sports leagues also bar noncitizens from participation, as they cannot advance to national tournaments organized under the Kokutai.

This has been challenged in Japan's judiciary. When a Sendai hockey league refused to let university educator Douglas Shukert play expressly because he was not a Japanese citizen, he sued Miyagi Prefecture for racial discrimination, citing a 1993 court case in Fukushima that ruled that the Kokutai was also for "prefectural residents" (*kenmin*)—which, unlike the word *kokumin*, could include noncitizens. However, on July 25, 2003, the Sendai High Court ruled against Shukert, citing the same logic cited in the Otaru Onsens Case (see chapter 3), that the Constitution's equal-protection clause in Article 14 allows for "rational discrimination" (*gōriteki na sabetsu*) such as banning "foreigners": "The purpose of the Kokutai is for raising the awareness of sportsmanship and health, and contributing to the development of culture and sports amongst Japanese . . . the Kokutai effectively uncovers representative athletes for international competitions." As Shukert commented for the *Japan Times*, "There is a belief in Japan that sports should be divided into 'serious sports' and 'sports for fun.' Serious sports are for winning gold medals and glorifying Japan, so resources should be devoted to developing Japanese athletes, not wasted on foreigners." However, JASA has been unaffiliated with the Japan Olympic Committee since 1993, making it problematic to treat local competitions as potential Olympic trials. Nevertheless, other sports leagues follow the precedent set by JASA and the Kokutai. For example, the Fukushima Prefectural Sumō League refused an application from a local educator named Marshel Copple to compete in a prefectural tournament in December 2002. The grounds given were because he is not a Japanese citizen (*kokumin*).

Further, when noncitizen students, some of whom have played beside their peers since grade school, suddenly realize that they are not permitted to compete due to their extranationality (as Oh Sadaharu, as a Zainichi Taiwanese schoolboy, experienced despite being the "best player on the team," before he later went on to become a baseball legend in Japan),[13] it becomes normalized for young Wajin athletes to believe (a) that the lack of a level playing field for Non-Wajin is normal and permissible, and (b) that people who lack Japanese citizenship cannot represent their local team because they cannot represent all of Japan.[14]

The Ekiden Sports Races

Further reinforcing a nominal separation between Non-Wajin and Wajin on the athletic field is the *Ekiden* Road Relay (*ekiden kyōso*), an extremely popular series of races across the country sponsored by various governments, educational institutions, and corporations, with a history dating back to 1917.[15] Although noncitizen students (including exchange students) are allowed to compete in events, there are some restrictions. Consider the widely publicized All-Japan High School *Ekiden* Championship (*zenkoku kōtō gakkō ekiden kyōso taikai*), a relay marathon that runs for 42 kilometers for men and 21 kilometers for women. Divided into five legs (the first leg being 6 kilometers long), the All-Japan High School Athletic Association decided in 2007 that "foreign exchange students" (*gaikokujin ryūgakusei*) may not run the first leg of the marathon. The reason officially justifying this was making the race "more interesting for fans."[16] Cited were previous race results where noncitizens (from Kenya, Ethiopia, etc.), who had allegedly been imported to bring greater athletic prowess to their school, were overwhelmingly winning the first leg. This set the pace for the rest of the race, with Wajin athletes lagging far behind (cf. teams with "foreign students" competing had won the race five times between 1996 and 2006), thus "spoiling" (*kyōzame*) the race. So "foreign" athletes were capped at two per team, where only one could run at a time in each leg in a group race. This complemented the 1994 rule that said "foreign students" attending any competition within the *Ekiden* mandate must be 20 percent or less of all participating students.

These rules have been extended in one form or another beyond the classic *Ekiden*: down through other prefectural qualifying races, to corporate national *Ekiden* championships, and to other sports such as basketball, volleyball, soccer, and table tennis. Thus, there is an embedded presumption not only of difference but also superiority/inferiority, where students of African descent (or of Chinese descent in table tennis) purportedly have an innately unfair physical advantage in strength and endurance sports over Wajin bodies.[17] As expressed, this is a complicated admixture of (a) a physical inferiority complex toward Non-Wajin with (b) a nationalistic domestic society and media culture allegedly unable to "root for" (or find "interesting") athletes who are Non-Wajin. Thus, Japanese must not only win, they must *visibly* win, putting Visible Minorities on unlevel playing fields.

The Takamado English Contests

This inferiority complex extends beyond physical contests to intellectual competitions, where not only Non-Wajin children, but also multiethnic Wajin children, are singled out for disqualification. Consider the Takamadonomiya All-Japan Junior High School English Speech Contest (since renamed the All-Japan Inter-Middle School English Oratorical Contest).[18] It is a prestigious event, organized by the private-sector Japan National Student Association Fund (JNSA, *Nihon Gakusei Kyōkai Kikin*) and the *Yomiuri Shinbun*, supported by NHK, the Ministry of Foreign Affairs, the Ministry of Education, Prefectural Boards of Education, and Prefectural Associations of English Education, sponsored by Coca Cola Japan, and named after a member of Japan's royal family. First held in 1949, the HRH Prince Takamado

Trophy has become Japan's largest English-language competition, with its official goal, "To create an internationally rich youth culture, both proficient in English and widely popular [*sic*], which aims to develop Japanese culture and contribute to international relations."

However, its rules have used "foreign ancestry" to disqualify students with an alleged advantage in the English language. In 2004, Takamado's Rule 3 stated you may not enter the contest if (*English original*): "any of your parents or grandparents are foreigners (including naturalized Japanese)"; Rule 2a: "you are born in a foreign country and have stayed abroad past your 5th birthday"; and 2b: "after your 5th birthday you have lived in a foreign country for over a total of one year, or if you have lived in a foreign country over a continuous six-month period." This is problematic because it assumes that anyone with "foreign" roots, including those from a non-English-speaking country, has an innate advantage in learning the English language.

This resulted in several regional winners, even winners of English-language speech contests not directly affiliated with the Takamado Trophy, being disqualified by local Boards of Education because they had, for example, Chinese or Mongolian relatives dating back three generations. Not only does this provide a strong disincentive for Non-Wajin or mixed-blood Wajin to become proficient in English, but it also subjected children at impressionable ages to differentiation, "othering," and subordination through extra hurdles or the public shame of disqualification. It also encourages children to keep their "foreign" roots secret, and, ironically for an international language contest, puts "multicultural Japan" and "internationalization" in a negative light.

Responding to protests from international families in Japan, the JNSA, in a letter dated October 29, 2002, refused to amend any of the conditions, citing (in the official English version) a "traditional and historical regulation" that could not be contravened. Deputy Executive Secretary Kotani Hiroyuki did acknowledge an "unwritten regulation [*sic*]" for the Zainichi, where "those students whose parents or grandparents came from Korea or Taiwan (the former Japanese oversea prefectures) during or before the WWII and lived continually in Japan and who go to Korean or Chinese schools in Japan (not an international or any foreign school) could take part in the Contest." However, Kotani continued, "In future we may further modify the terms and conditions of the Contest as time goes. However, we want to maintain the present regulations for the time being as all the persons on the sponsor side made a decision a few years ago based on the original terms."

The Takamado Trophy did amend its rules for its fifty-eighth event in 2006.[19] Rule 2 states: "Students who fall into any of the following categories are not eligible to participate in the contest: a) Those who were born and raised in English speaking countries/regions* beyond the age of five; b) Those who lived in English speaking countries/regions or studied in

International and American Schools beyond the age of five for a total of one year or six months continuously; c) Those whose parent or grandparent with nationalities of English Speaking countries or naturalized Japanese, having lived in Japan for less than 30 years; d) Those who won 1st to 3rd places in any previous contests." As of 2021, the latest rules in Japanese have adjusted rule c) further to narrow elimination down to children whose parent/guardian or domiciled relatives are native speakers of English, or who originate from an English-speaking country. Designated as "English speaking countries/regions" are seventy nation-states with English as an official language or with a history of being part of the British Empire (including Somalia, whose official languages are Somali and Arabic with English as a designated second language).[20] This ameliorated one blanket hurdle against people with generic "foreign" roots or connections, but instead directed it specifically toward people with "English" roots or connections. This new set of qualifications may become more problematic as Japan further increases its overseas experiences and international connections, or has more Non-Wajin or mixed-blood Wajin children in its education system.

Thus, the Takamado Trophy, in the interests of "fairness," is still putting up hurdles to favor Wajin, advantaging those children who have restricted themselves to "book study" within the officially sanctioned Japanese education system, and subordinating those children who have certain international roots or have otherwise garnered international experience.

Other Sports in Japan: Baseball, Rugby, and Sumō

With these precedents set at a secondary- and tertiary-school level, it becomes easier to understand why other professional sports in Japan, including sumō, rugby, and baseball, have strict, embedded, and unproblematized restrictions on "foreign players" on their teams. For example, professional baseball only allows three "foreigners" on any Japanese team, only two of whom may play in a game at any time,[21] while professional sumō allows for only one "foreign wrestler" (*gaikokujin rikishi*) per stable (*heya*). (NB: There are only fifty-two stables, meaning a maximum of only fifty-two noncitizens may compete professionally.) Further, on February 23, 2010, the Sumō Association (*sumō kyōkai*) ruled that their "foreign wrestler" slot was a loophole (*nukemichi*) and would now count naturalized *rikishi* (labeled as *gaikoku shusshin*, or "of foreign origin") as "foreigners," in direct contravention of Japan's Nationality Law.[22] Similarly, in September 2020 the Japan Rugby Football Union announced that they would also deny Japanese-citizen eligibility to its foreign-born naturalized players;[23] the *Asahi Shinbun* reports that similar exclusionary rules have spread to other sports such as basketball and table tennis.[24] Sumō, however, is apparently a special case, as it is officially recognized as Japan's "national sport" (*kokugi*), and the Sumō Association is under the direct supervision of the Ministry of Education and Sports. So the fact that this rule could be approved by a government-associated organization to discriminate against other Japanese citizens indicates how normalized and embedded the racialized Wajin conceit is for determining "Japaneseness": Even legally becoming a *kokumin* is not enough to be "Japanese," and this is normalized in Japan from a young age in the education system.

Coda: Japan's Sports and Exclusionary Patriotism

This strong division between citizen and noncitizen is symptomatic of a strong linkage between patriotism and sports in Japan. Although an undercurrent of nationalistic representationalism in sport is prevalent worldwide (especially in international competitions such as the Olympics), in Japan's case the visual identification of "Japaneseness" (as seen in the *Ekiden* races) reinforces a phenotypical qualification for competition, where competitors who do not "look Japanese" are assumed not to represent or hold interest for Japan. Moreover, competitions held under Japan's sporting and competition regimes are still considered to be "fair" even when there are overt hurdles and barriers toward participation for Non-Wajin (not to mention Wajin related to Non-Wajin)—in order to ensure that Wajin can "win." Thus, the Embedded Racism in competitive educational regimes in Japan calls into question how the concepts of "sportsmanship," "fair play," and "level playing fields" are envisioned in Japan.

More significantly, there is a strong reinforcement of the Japanese "blood" meme first underscored by the Nationality Law in chapter 4: This meme within the hegemonic discourse toward sports in Japan not only unscientifically links "blood" to individual qualification and ability but also strongly correlates physical and mental attributes (in terms of strength or weakness, be it in the sumō ring or the language contest) with nationality or national origin.[25] Consequently, Japan's competitive regimes have clear instances where, in practice, naturalized Japanese citizens and even mixed-blooded Wajin are considered different from one-blooded Wajin.

For the Second Edition, we should note some significant developments: Visible Minorities have since risen to prominence and represented Japan on the world stage in international competitions. In 2015, African American/Japanese Miyamoto Ariana became the first mixed-background Miss Japan sent to the Miss Universe beauty pageant. In 2016, Subcontinental Indian Japanese Yoshikawa Priyanka represented Japan in the Miss World beauty competition. During their tenure as representatives, both made attempts to push for the rights of their fellow Visible Minorities in Japan, but were basically ignored by Japanese media if not overtly criticized by internet denizens as "not real Japanese," and so on.[26] Other Visible Minority Japanese athletes have also risen to prominence in their fields, including the spectacular play by the multiethnic "Brave Blossoms" rugby team in the 2015 Rugby World Cup,[27] and while they were winning they were "claimed" as Japanese (a phenomenon known in racism studies circles as "They'll claim us if you're famous").[28] However, their impact on Japanese identity narratives was also arguably limited (particularly for the beauty queens) by the fact they did not win a world championship.

This brings us to the best test case—a Visible Minority who did become world champion: tennis star Ōsaka Naomi, an American Japanese with Haitian ancestry. After her breakthrough victory against Serena Williams in 2018, she is as of this writing the top women's tennis player in the world, and thanks to major Japanese sponsors now the highest-earning female athlete of all time. She has used her position as champion to visibly and vocally advocate against racial discrimination. However, she has essentially opted to limit herself to the Black Lives Matter movement in the United States, thus far declining to advocate on behalf of fellow Visible Minorities in Japan, moreover notably discounting racism in Japan as an issue of "a few bad apples."[29] (This is despite, for example, being "whitewashed" by her own sponsor's advertising and racialized by Japan's comedians.[30])

These developments for Visible Minorities have caused some media speculation that Japan may finally be "embracing diversity,"[31] but I would argue that the fundamentals of Japan's Embedded Racism remain intact.[32] As defined in this research (and discussed in chapters 2 and 9), even though these people are "Japanese" in terms of citizenship and in some cases assimilation, they are still not Wajin because they are only conditionally included within the narratives embedded in the power structure. They are still being offset as "*Haafu*" or "not fully Japanese" by appearance and/or behavior,[33] and it is unclear that this situation will change for them or others if they do not continue winning (see next section) or when their abilities as athletes inevitably fade. Consequently, even though these prominent Visible Minorities are being held up as challenges to the status quo, for now they remain incapable of fundamentally changing the narrative of Japan as a monoethnic society, which would involve them being portrayed as "Japanese" without any asterisks or qualifiers.

DUAL NATIONALITY AND "JAPAN CLAIMING"

Chapter 4 discussed the GOJ's racialized concept and enforcement of dual nationality (viz. the Fujimori Case). Now let us consider how multiple citizenships are affected by racially politicized public policy.

First, Japan's official lack of dual nationality (*nijū kokuseki*) goes against international trends, according to Kashiwazaki (2000):

> The current international trend in coordinating nationalities is to have a greater degree of tolerance for the incidence of multiple nationality than for statelessness. The principle of "one nationality for everyone" is therefore increasingly understood to mean at least one nationality, rather than "only one," for each person. Furthermore, migrant-sending countries have tended to support dual nationality, which would allow their nationals to retain close relationships with their country of origin while enjoying full rights and protection in the host country. Outside Europe, Mexico's recent move to allow dual nationality for those who became naturalized U.S citizens is another example. Insisting on the desirability of "only one" nationality, the official stance of the Japanese government, therefore deviates from the current international norm.[34]

However, Japan's lack of dual nationality becomes inconvenient in times of enhanced national pride, which brings forth odd cases of "Japan Claiming" (i.e., claiming people as "Japanese" regardless of legal status). Consider the case of the "three Japanese Nobel Prize winners" in 2008.[35] On October 7, the Japanese media reported that "three Japanese" (*Nihonjin 3-shi*), Masukawa Toshihide, Kobayashi Makoto, and Yoichiro Nambu, had won the Nobel Prize in Physics, bringing the historic total of "Japanese" Nobel Laureates to fifteen. But Nambu had taken American citizenship in 1970 and was living permanently in the United States. In the English-language headlines the laureates were "two Japanese and one Japan-born American," while in the Japanese media the discourse of "three Japanese" was maintained. The argument thus became that Nambu should still be counted as "Japanese," regardless of his citizenship, because his ethnicity included him within the Wajin group. Within a week, however, the Ministry of Education decided that Nambu was American only.[36] However, the same issue came up when Japan-born Briton Kazuo Ishiguro won the Nobel Prize for Literature in 2017.[37]

By November 2008, the issue occasioned a debate, led by MP Kōno Taro of the conservative Liberal Democratic Party (LDP), about amending the Nationality Law to allow dual nationality. Kōno argued that by not forcing people to choose one nationality, Japan could claim more notable international people as its own, as well as increase its population as demographic numbers declined. Further, Kōno argued for the law to reflect reality, since lax enforcement of the single-nationality requirements under the Nationality Law was allowing dual nationality in children of international marriages anyway.[38]

Kōno had a point. Even though he was essentially advocating that Japan should have the option to "claim" people in case they became famous, this debate nevertheless exposed how putative international competitive advantages/

disadvantages (in regard to, for example, strength and intelligence) were poking loopholes in the Nationality Law. Examples surfaced of Non-Wajin athletes receiving expedited Japanese naturalization procedures to increase Japan's sports competitiveness,[39] and examples of Wajin quietly using dual nationalities to expand their options in international sporting competitions.[40] Conversely, cases emerged of Wajin taking out other citizenships because they did not make it onto Team Japan, occasioning criticism in Japan's media. Such was the case with Yūko Kawaguchi, a Wajin naturalized Russian pairs skater, who was "branded a traitor in her native Japan when she changed nationality" in order to compete internationally outside Team Japan.[41] On the other hand, when mixed-blood Wajin athletes competing for Team Japan do not win, their Non-Wajin roots have been made an issue of; for example, during the 2014 Sochi Olympics, Japan Team figure skaters Chris and Cathy Reed (with a Wajin mother and Non-Wajin father) were erroneously criticized by Tokyo 2020 Olympics Chair Mori Yoshiro inter alia specifically for being "naturalized" losers.[42]

In the end, Kōno's 2008 debate died down with no changes to the Nationality Law, a lost opportunity to break down the oversimplified and inflexible Wajin/Non-Wajin dichotomy within Japan's citizenship laws. The status quo remains, where the self-deterministic interests of the individual have been subordinated to the interests of the state in order to maintain the embedded racialized binary. Wajin are either officially citizens or they are not, and by age twenty-two they are legally forced to declare their choice. If they do not choose to be Japanese citizens, they would also be choosing the subordinated legal status of a Non-Wajin in Japan. If they do choose to be Japanese citizens, they are to "abandon" (*hōki*) (or else hide) their foreign citizenship and suppress their Non-Wajin roots. That is, if they are fortunate enough phenotypically to "pass" as Wajin in the first place and not face differentiated status as a Visible Minority.

As discussed in chapter 4, the embedded "bloodline"-based racism advantaging the Wajin majority is embedded in the laws establishing Japanese citizenship. And also as discussed in chapter 4, civil, constitutional, and human rights in Japan are predicated not on being human but upon having Japanese citizenship. In essence, as a noncitizen in Japan, you only have as many rights as your visa grants you. So now let's turn to Japan's visa regimes, and see how people with Japanese blood are favored in terms of work and residence status for imported foreign labor, and how the visa regimes themselves become the source of unequal protection under the law.

"STATUS OF RESIDENCE" (VISA) REGIMES[43]

All nation-states grant official permission to noncitizens to stay within their borders as guests or temporary/conditional residents, in the form of visas (officially called "Status of Residence" (*zairyū shikaku*) in Japan). However, under Japan's visa regimes, advantages are given to those who have "Japanese ancestry" in the form of Wajin bloodlines.[44]

Visa Regimes and Human Rights Protections in General

Chapter 4 discussed the structural disadvantaging of noncitizens in regard to *kokumin* reservations of civil and political rights. However, there is another layer of systematic disadvantage added through visa regimes. As Doshisha University law professor Colin P. A. Jones writes:

> So what rights do foreign residents have under the Constitution? Well, according to the Supreme Court, they are entitled to all the same rights as Japanese people, except for those which by their nature are only to be enjoyed by Japanese people. Does that help? This Delphic guidance comes from a very important 1978 Supreme Court ruling in what is known as the McLean Case. Ronald McLean came to Japan as an English teacher in 1969 but quickly got involved in the local anti-Vietnam War protest movement. When he sought to renew his visa, the Ministry of Justice refused. He challenged the denial in court, asserting that he was being punished for engaging in lawful political activity, exercising his rights to free speech, assembly and so forth. He lost . . .
>
> Rooted in principles of customary international law holding that countries are free to deny entry to non-nationals, this reasoning potentially renders all rights enjoyed by non-Japanese in Japan subject to legislative restraints imposed through their visa status (constitutional rights, of course, are supposed to trump legislation). Not only that, but since the immigration statute at issue in the McLean case granted broad leeway to the Minister of Justice in deciding whether to renew visas, whatever constitutional rights he did enjoy were limited by that administrative discretion, a discretion the court found not to have been abused. In summary, therefore, the McLean case says that non-Japanese have constitutional rights that may be subject to both statutory limitations and administrative discretion. Or as some might be inclined to put it, they have constitutional rights that are not actually constitutional.[45]

This illustrates the arbitrary amount of power the administrative branch of government has over fundamental constitutional rights (including freedom of speech and assembly) that are in practice being expressly reserved to *kokumin*, since *kokumin* do not have an extra hurdle of requiring visa permission from the state to reside in Japan.

Now let us look at specific visa statuses and see how blood conceits are layered upon the implicit Nationality Clauses required for civil and political rights in Japan.

Permanent Residency vs. "Returnee" Permanent Residency: Embedded Wajin Blood Conceits

Permanent Residency (*eijūken*) in Japan (similar to other countries' regimes, such as the "Green Card" in the United States) allows recipients to stay in Japan indefinitely without any restrictions on employment. This is generally awarded (at the discretion of the Immigration Bureau) within three to five years if the recipient is married to a Japanese citizen, or after about ten years if the recipient is not married to a Japanese citizen.[46] That said, anecdotal evidence suggests there is a degree of discretion for arbitrary decision-making,[47] with no right of appeal if fulfilled qualifications appear to be ignored by officials.[48]

Moreover, for the purposes of this research, a racialized paradigm may be seen in the Long-Term Resident Visa regime (*teijū*, or "Returnee Visa" in the vernacular), where a form of Permanent Residency is given immediately to Nikkei "returnees" (descendants of Wajin who emigrated from Japan a century ago) applying from countries such as Brazil or Peru. This special visa status enabled Nikkei to reside in Japan indefinitely (subject to renewal) without job restrictions, a five- to ten-year wait to qualify, or marriage to a citizen. It was thus technically a Permanent Resident visa specifically for Wajin blood, and successfully selected and brought in millions of Wajin-blooded South Americans; during the 2000s (peaking in 2007 at around 370,000 people) they were the third-largest noncitizen group residing in Japan.[49] The logic behind this preferential treatment, according to Nippon Keidanren policy designer Inoue Hiroshi, was explicitly blood-based: an express assumption that "foreigners" with Wajin blood would be more easily assimilated into Japanese society than Non-Wajin.[50] This sentiment was also borne out in a 2013 Cabinet survey, where more than 80 percent of the surveyed (Wajin) public favored living alongside "foreigners" if they were of "Japanese ancestry."[51]

Actual Permanent Residency (*eijūken*) requires overcoming several hurdles, including a prior record of stable visas (which in themselves may or may not entitle you to work and support your family, or may require you to work only within certain job sectors with lower incomes),[52] a record of obeying laws and bureaucratic guidelines,[53] and further intrusive inspections by the state (such as the stability of your marriage or the state of your household, including personal home visits) into the applicant's private life.[54] Thus for Nikkei, merely by dint of bloodline, these requirements and hurdles can be officially bypassed, once again selecting for Wajin in terms of stable, permanent lives and livelihoods in Japan.

VISA REGIMES AND UNSTABLE EMPLOYMENT: JAPAN'S "REVOLVING DOOR" WORK MARKET FOR NON-WAJIN

Let us now turn to visas that are not specifically Permanent Resident, that is, those with limitations on work status. As mentioned above, while Nikkei "returnees" receive de facto Permanent Residency due to their special visa granted through Wajin blood ties, Non-Wajin face visa regimes with significant barriers to staying in Japan permanently.

First, I have argued elsewhere[55] that the number of immigrants to Japan has been held artificially low under GOJ visa regimes. Not only does the GOJ have an official policy stance stating no imports of "unskilled labor" (*tanjun rōdō*), it also has no official policy for immigration (*imin seisaku*) to help people settle in Japan.[56] As Kashiwazaki argues, "The system of naturalization is not designed to transform foreign nationals promptly into Japanese nationals. Restriction on naturalization corresponds to the government's stance on border control, namely that Japan does not admit immigration for the purpose of permanent settlement."[57] Instead, Japan's visa regimes favor importing people as migrant labor during their most productive ages, then offering clear incentives for them to "go home" instead of making Japan their new home. This has affected the Non-Wajin disproportionately badly, as we will see in outcomes for specific visa regimes:

The "Trainee" Visa Regimes

This set of visas have been covered in great detail in other research,[58] but a brief recap is necessary: During Japan's "Bubble Era" of high economic prosperity (approximately 1986–1991), there was a labor shortage. Despite the official policy of not accepting unskilled labor, in 1989 according to the Ministry of Labor, 46 percent of all domestic manufacturers were "labor deficient" (*rōdō fusoku* or *jinzai fusoku*); by 1990, this figure had risen to 56 percent. The shortage was acute in the blue-collar "3K" industries (standing for *kitanai*, *kitsui*, and *kiken*, or dirty, difficult, and dangerous), which were jobs many Wajin did not want to do. Moreover, due to rising wages coupled with the high yen (*endaka*), Japan's domestically manufactured goods were being priced out of export markets. Japan's industry faced a major restructuring due to a phenomenon called "hollowing out" (*kūdōka*), where they could (a) go bankrupt, (b) move production overseas for cheaper labor costs but a decreased tax base for the GOJ, or (c) make labor costs cheaper domestically by importing cheaper foreign workers. The influential Japan Business Federation (*Nippon Keidanren*) among others lobbied for importing labor,[59] and from 1990, a "backdoor" labor market was created through new visa regimes to bring in unskilled and lesser-skilled labor.

This regime of import labor immediately differentiated between Wajin and Non-Wajin. As mentioned above, the "Long-Term Resident" (*teijūsha*) Visa was created for overseas Nikkei, and the "Trainee" (*jisshūsei*) and the "Researcher/Intern" (*kenshūsei*) visas were assigned to Non-Wajin. The *teijū* visa was ostensibly designed to allow Nikkei to reconnect with their heritage, while the latter two were to provide an "on the job training system" in Japanese technical skills, technology, and knowledge. "Trainees" were managed by the GOJ under the Japan International Training Cooperation Organization (JITCO) under two programs: the Industrial Training Program and the Technical Internship Program,[60] collectively grouped together as "Trainees" under an umbrella system (*kenshū-ginō jisshū seido*).[61] *Jisshūsei* were, by the nature of their job description of people being "trained" in a job skill, therefore not legally defined as "workers" (*rōdōsha*).[62]

Significantly, "Trainees" on this visa status were *the only people in Japan officially made exempt from Japanese labor laws*, meaning they were not covered by legislation, guidelines, or protections in terms of full- and part-time hours; social safety net benefits (including health and unemployment insurance that employers were otherwise required to pay into the system);[63] or the minimum wage (*saitei chingin*—which varies by prefecture and industry, but as of 2020 is between 792 and 1,013 yen per hour).[64] Technically, "Trainees" were not receiving an actual wage (*chingin*), rather a "training allowance" (*kenshū teate*). Consequently, the vulnerability of these "quasi-workers" and the potential for abuse (such as perpetually hiring cheap labor as "Trainees") were soon apparent: Originally the GOJ placed a one-year limitation on *jisshūsei* status (meaning that after one year, veterans were to graduate up to *kenshūsei* status, thereby becoming classified and protected as "workers"). However, in 1993, the advantages of cheap labor pressured the GOJ to remove this safety catch by creating a new visa status, the twice-renewable "Practical Trainees" visa (*kenkyū jisshūsei*)—essentially extending the *jisshūsei* status for two more years, creating a three-year revolving door work force also not covered by labor laws.[65]

Naturally, these exemptions left foreign workers open to widespread abuse, and over the past three decades they have faced exploitative and deadly job conditions sponsored by the GOJ. According to media outlets, NGOs, advocacy groups, and labor unions, many "Trainees" got paid far less than minimum wage (figures of 300 yen per hour have been reported, but there have also been reports of unpaid servitude due to unanticipated deductions by employers ostensibly for living expenses, and room and board),[66] were working long hours (one newsmagazine reported 22-hour days),[67] and suffering mental, physical, and sexual abuse.[68] There have also been reports of excessive and uncompensated overtime; illegal activities such as confiscation of passports and prison-like living/working conditions, and clauses in employment contracts unconstitutionally forbidding dating, marriage, or any "conduct that could result in pregnancy"; there were also numerous deaths due to overwork and other undetermined circumstances.[69] There have been instances of child labor, uncompensated job injuries and health concerns, forced deportations by the employer, and murder.[70] People who dropped out of these programs and returned home early faced debt collection and indentured servitude from local "brokers" who had initially funded their costs to come to Japan.[71] NGOs, labor unions, pundits, and politicians have severely criticized these programs as a "swindle" (*ikasama*), "a racket," and "sweatshops in disguise," noting that the lack of official regulation and oversight has encouraged the systematic abuse.[72] The United States State Department's Trafficking in Persons Report has for years criticized the program for its "deceptive recruitment practices," and others have called it "forced labor" "human trafficking," and "slave labor."[73] Court cases sponsored by domestic activist groups have resulted in some rulings substantiating these claims and awarding compensation to the employees.[74]

As Jorge Bustamante, UN special rapporteur on the Human Rights of Migrants, reported in March 2010:

> The Industrial Trainees and Technical Interns program often fuels demand for exploitative cheap labor under conditions that constitute violations of the right to physical and mental health, physical integrity, freedom of expression and movement of foreign trainees and interns, and that in some cases *may well amount to slavery*. This program should be discontinued and replaced by an employment program.[75] (Emphasis added)

Meanwhile, this unofficial "unskilled job market" has become less attractive to certain nationalities—as Japan's economy continues to stagnate, domestic wages drop while comparative wages within neighboring economies grow; Japan's programs, peaking in 2007 at around 88,000 "Trainees" per year,[76] plunged to around 40,000 by 2010 (with the 68,860 Chinese "Trainees" dropping by nearly 60 percent to 28,964).[77]

As of this Second Edition, despite all the problems with the "Trainee" program, the GOJ announced in April 2014 that it would be *expanded* to help with, among other things, the construction of the 2020 Tōkyō Olympics, and to bring in more nursing caregivers for Japan's expanding elderly population.[78] It announced changes, enacting a law in 2016 improving the supervision of participating companies, and lengthening visas from three to five years. However, PM Abe was on record reassuring supporters that this was not an "immigration policy," as these reforms did not allow "Trainees" to bring in their families, or allow any of the years to be counted toward Permanent Residency—meaning that foreigners would still contribute many of their productive working years keeping Japanese industry competitive and receive no long-term rewards.[79] The new special supervising agency also remained under the MOJ, not the Ministry of Labor, meaning the focus would remain on policing foreign workers rather than safeguarding their labor rights.[80]

A similar plan introduced in 2018 announced new visa categories for foreign workers, with PM Abe again cautioning that foreign workers would not become immigrants; they would only would be here "for a limited time" without their families, and working only in "designated sectors" with labor shortages for a maximum of ten years (which again, did not count toward Permanent Residency).[81] The "Trainee" program had thus become a template for other "revolving door" import labor visas.

It is unclear that the "Trainee" program has improved despite its expansion. The MOJ has reported that "Trainees" have increased dramatically, from 167,641 people in 2014, to 192,655 in 2015, to 228,589 in 2016.[82] The Organization for Technical Intern Training's most recent statistics (2019) reported 366,167 people, over half now coming from Vietnam.[83] However, OTIT also reported that "major violation cases" by implementing and supervising organizations for 2019 alone totaled 10,078 cases—an 18 percent rise from the previous year's total of 8,513, or mathematically well over one major violation per hour.[84] Further, media in 2018 still reported that "Trainees" were dying on the job at more than twice the rate of Japanese, even after accounting for workplace accidents and violence involving foreign workers being underreported.[85] In 2019, shortly after the abovementioned expansion of "Trainee"-styled working visas, Tōkyō Electric Power Co. (TEPCO) announced that it would take advantage of the new system to hire thousands of foreign workers to decommission the Fukushima nuclear power plant; this was after previously exploiting the poor, itinerant, and homeless, and even "tricking" foreign asylum seekers into working under dangerous levels of radiation.[86] Thus, after more than a quarter century of the program's existence, it is safe to conclude that these abuses are a design feature, not a flaw.

In contrast, the Nikkei "Returnees," although their working conditions and wages were not equal to those of Wajin (the former often working 10–15 hours a day, six days a week), their jobs had been nonetheless comparatively more stable and protected by labor laws. Many managed to get jobs in Japan's blue-chip export factories making substantially more than the minimum wage[87] and have resided in Japan in the hundreds of thousands for up to two decades. They were not similarly exposed to the "revolving door" labor market until 2009 (more below).

The "Student" and "Entertainer" Visa Regimes

Other visa regimes have imported cheap foreign labor into other sectors of Japan's job markets. "College Student" (*ryūgaku*) and "Pre-College Student" (*shūgaku*) visas have brought in other Non-Wajin youth from countries including China, Thailand, The Philippines, and Indonesia, ostensibly to "study" in Japanese universities, technical colleges, and tertiary educational institutions (which are suffering from diminished student enrollments due to Japan's population decline, and facing Ministry of Education (MEXT) cuts in subsidies).[88] However, many "students" became absentees working in low-wage jobs like restaurants and convenience stores in violation of their visas, leading to crackdowns on fake "schools" laundering visa statuses for migrant labor, and the abolition of the "Pre-College Student" visa entirely in 2010.[89] Entrants on the "College Student" visa increased significantly from 131,789 in 2006 to more than 201,511 in 2010. This is due not only to Japan's declining domestic student population due to the low birthrate, but also because of MEXT's Global 30 Project to increase Japan's global university ranking, funding major Japanese universities to internationalize and accept more foreign students.[90]

However, foreign students remain deprived of equal opportunities compared to Wajin students—justified by MEXT's express rationale that many foreign students leave and thus do not contribute to Japan's future.[91] MEXT has not addressed the possible lack of job opportunities in Japan for Japanese university graduates, the lack of any fast-tracking visa policy to assist against structural inequalities in Japan's labor force, or the lack of protections from workplace and other systemic harassment.[92] Nevertheless, as of May 1, 2020, one month after the pandemic closed Japan's borders to foreigners, the number of exchange students stood at 279,597.[93]

A second visa regime, the "Entertainer" (*kōgyō*) visa, offered an underground labor market to employ Non-Wajin in the "water trades" (*mizu shōbai*) sex industry.[94] Although officially for actors, musical performers, thespians, or other show business people, this visa regime has brought in many women ostensibly to work as "dancers" and "entertainers," who then found themselves trapped working in Japan's sex industry connected to organized crime. Conditions have been reported as horrendous, including physical and sexual abuse, no freedom of movement, unpaid wages and debt bondage, little punishment of offenders, little protection of victims due to their status as visa overstayer (often because their passports had been confiscated by employers), and arrests and deportations of victims if they report their abuses to the police. In 2004, Japan was declared a "Tier-Two Human Trafficker" by the United States State Department. Afterward the GOJ officially reformed its laws on trafficking to some degree, but abuses and problematic enforcement of the laws continue.[95] Entrants on the "Entertainer" visa dwindled sharply from 21,062 in 2006 to 9,247 in 2010.[96] However, as of 2019, numbers have rebounded to 46,674 entrants, and as of 2021, despite what Hepburn and Simon (2013) have called "ethnocentric policies" that have "created opportunities for exploitation and human trafficking," Japan is no longer on the State Department's human trafficking lists.[97]

The Bilateral Health Care Worker Program and "Foreign Nurses"

Japan's aging society has also increased the number of elderly needing health care, with the Health Ministry estimating that the majority of Japan's population (57 percent) will by 2050 be *kōreisha*, or elderly people above the age of sixty-five, that is, beyond a prime working age.[98] Coupled with a perpetual shortage of health care workers,[99] Japan launched bilateral work programs (called the Japan-Philippines and Japan-Indonesia Economic Partnership Agreements)[100] from July 1 and December 11, 2008, bringing in nurses and caregivers from Indonesia and The Philippines, respectively. Although they had already received their nursing licenses abroad, they were to be "trained" for health care in Japan. As an extension of the "Trainee" programs, foreign health care workers were also not legally protected as "workers" in Japan, receiving a "training allowance" instead of a salary. Moreover, in order to keep their visa, they were required within three years to pass the same national nurse licensure examination (*kangoshi kokka shiken*)[101] as Japanese native speakers do, but after only receiving six months of Japanese language instruction while working full-time in low-skilled hospital labor. Consequently, as of 2012, few nurses managed to pass the exam, with most (including a handful who did pass) returning to their countries of origin after a few years.[102] So by 2018, the GOJ changed tack, setting targets to import 10,000 "caregivers" from Vietnam, saying that by 2025 at least half a million would be needed.[103]

Critics have decried the program as having "unfair hurdles" and lax oversight leading to workplace abuses.[104] However, I would argue that this visa regime was designed as a revolving door program, discouraging foreign nurses to stay in Japan permanently while exploiting them temporarily as young, cheap, eager workers. After all, if applicants were already qualified overseas as nurses, and a kanji test was the main hurdle to a more stable visa, why did the GOJ not invite nurses from already kanji-literate countries, such as China, Taiwan, Macao, Hong Kong, or Singapore? Instead, when the number of applications dropped from Indonesia and The Philippines,[105] the GOJ indicatively invited nurses from Vietnam[106] next—another non-kanji society. Although in 2012 the health care worker program was reportedly to be discontinued, it was instead incorporated into the abovementioned "Trainee" program, again with official warnings against opening a "Pandora's Box" of allowing imported labor to become immigration.[107]

Japan's Economic Downturn of 2008 and the "Nikkei Repatriation Project": Favoritism for Wajin Bloodlines

Another bellwether of Japan's "revolving door" work market was also seen during the 2007 Asian economic crisis, affecting Japan's economy in 2008.[108] As companies began to rationalize and cut labor costs, noncitizens, including the Nikkei, were among the first to go.[109] From April 1, 2009, the GOJ launched the "Project to support repatriation [*sic*] of *Nikkeijin* with employment difficulties" (author's translation) (*Nikkeijin nanshokusha ni tai-suru kikoku shien jigyō*). Administered through the GOJ's unemployment office (Hello Work), the program offered 300,000 yen for Nikkei South American beneficiaries and 200,000 yen for each dependent to purchase plane tickets "back home," thereby forfeiting their Long-Term Resident status.[110] Thousands of Nikkei took the stipend[111] (sometimes under compulsion from authorities denying them welfare benefits),[112] and Japan's Brazilian population nearly halved, from 312,582 in 2008 to 177,953 in 2013 (falling below the Filipino population tally).[113]

In terms of this research, this project is demonstrative in regard to Japan's racialization processes: Although Wajin-blooded foreign workers suddenly became as disposable as Non-Wajin foreigners, the GOJ repatriation stipend was only offered to Nikkei[114]—not to the other noncitizens (such as the Chinese "Trainees" and "Interns"), who were now on their own if they got laid off or had their visas cancelled.[115] Once again, blood ties were given preferential treatment; Non-Wajin were unassisted as Japan's revolving door work regimes rotated them out of national unemployment statistics in times of economic duress.[116]

As of 2020, the Brazilian population has bounced back to 211,178; this may be due to a change of heart by the GOJ in 2013 and 2017 to re-invite South American Nikkei (rendered as "fourth-generation Japanese"). This time, however, visa conditions did not provide de facto Permanent Residency, but did allow for minors to work full-time (something expressly illegal for Wajin minors).[117]

Other Visa Regimes and Miscellaneous Hurdles Encouraging "Revolving Door" Work

This research does not have the space to discuss in detail each of Japan's visa categories. Like all visa regimes allowing migrant work within any nation-state, permission is contingent upon public policy needs and political whim. But Japan's visa system has been not only exclusionary but also arbitrary and increasingly xenophobic in enforcement. For example, until 2012, there was neither a standardized "points system" for objectively granting visas to skilled international migrant laborers, nor a valid visa period longer than three years. (When a "Points System" visa was introduced after 2012, it was soon phased out due to lack of applicants for being too strict.[118])

Noncitizens have seen their civil and political rights abrogated due both to legal fiat and administrative "discretion." Specialists corroborate anecdotal evidence that even one-year visas for skilled labor, such as the "Specialist in Humanities/International Services" (*jinbun chishiki/kokusai gyōmu*) that is the mainstay of language teachers in Japan, is sometimes only granted for one year at a time (despite Japan's hitherto three-year maximum duration for long-term visas);[119] there have been cases where longer-term residents have found their visa *reduced upon renewal* from three years to one at whim (with no explanation or possibility of appeal).[120] Moreover, strict punishments have been meted out for administrative infractions, such as overlooked visa expiries and expired Re-Entry Permits (REPs) (*sainyūkoku kyoka*), that have resulted in cases of automatic invalidation of all accrued time under the visa regime, or in cancelled visas with high fines, deportation, and expulsion from Japan for up to a decade.[121]

Furthermore, procedurally, noncitizens are not issued verifiable evidence by Immigration when their applications are being processed (in contrast, the Ministry of Transportation issues temporary licenses during processing); so if an unlucky noncitizen gets racially profiled and stopped for an instant ID check on the street by police (see chapter 4), then arrest and incarceration is likely for appearing to be an overstayer. Although people in Japan are routinely sent reminders of other important expiries (such as driver licenses), noncitizens in contrast are issued no reminders about something as essential to life in a foreign country as a valid visa. In sum, my quarter century of life in Japan (as well as anecdotal evidence and interviews from dozens of sources) attests to a general attitude of the MOJ's Immigration Bureau procedurally looking for ways to "trip foreigners up," so to speak, and "reset their visa clock."

REPs, which were in common currency until 2012, were a contentious issue that deserve a short mention: Decried by activists as a "gaijin tax"[122] on resident noncitizens who wish to leave Japan for short periods, REPs cost 3,000 yen for a single reentry or 6,000 yen for multiple reentries for up to three years. REPs have also been criticized as another excuse for Immigration to void valid visas. In email correspondence (dated May 31, 2012), a concerned Debito.org reader notified me:

> I had a permanent resident visa that took me 12 years to get. They took it away in 5 minutes. . . . I got on the plane [back to Japan] and realized halfway there that my re-entry permit had expired 2 weeks prior. . . . They pulled me out of line, took me to a windowless room, . . . left me there. Then came back and handed me my passport. My permanent resident visa was stamped "VOID." They never even asked me any questions! I'd never even had a parking ticket in Japan, was a responsible college professor, etc. . . . I was told that I could start over again with a spouse visa: 6 months, 6 months, 6 months; 1 year, 1 year, 1 year; 3 years, 3 years, 3 years . . . and then try for the permanent resident visa again. But by that point I had lost any desire to live in Japan at all, much less permanently. So when I need to go to Japan for conferences or to visit in-laws, I have a tourist visa.

Although the REP was phased out after 2012, it remains symptomatic of how the often-unforgiving nature of Japan's Immigration Bureau and visa regimes make it clear to noncitizens that their status in Japanese society is tenuous, revocable even for minor administrative infractions, and applicable even to Permanent Residents.[123]

Interim Conclusions

Japan's visa regimes for granting temporary permission to stay and work have shown not only large hurdles regarding visa longevity and job stability but also implemented racialized degrees of privilege. Noncitizens in general have faced visa regimes strict in standard and unforgiving in punishment for even minor bureaucratic infractions, as part of a "revolving door" labor market, with short-term young workers being imported as cheap temporary migrant labor and discouraged from making Japan "home" as immigrants. However, noncitizens with Wajin blood ties (as Nikkei) have enjoyed Wajin Privilege, including the visa equivalent of Permanent Residency, while Non-Wajin noncitizens have had to wait for up to a decade for the same conditions. Other Non-Wajin workers have also been excluded from labor law protections, leading to three decades of exploitative and deadly work regimes that have been decried as human trafficking. Japan remains as of this writing a country without an official immigration policy, disinclined to show significant flexibility toward new potential immigrants unless they have Wajin blood.

Let's move on. From the 1990s, Japan's visa regimes brought in millions of foreigners and subjected them to abusive work conditions, but from the 2000s onward, the abuse changed tack from official disenfranchisement to official defamation. The MOJ and other government bodies began launching coordinated media campaigns targeting "bad foreigners" (*furyō gaikokujin*) and "illegal overstayers" (*fuhō taizaisha*) (more in chapter 7), resulting in draconian and racialized law enforcement. Let us now consider how the GOJ's systemic criminalization of Japan's "foreign" population is also governed by racialized paradigms and narratives.

NONCITIZENS AS A PUBLIC SECURITY ISSUE: TARGETING VISIBLE MINORITIES

Chapter 4 outlined how noncitizens are tracked and policed via public registry systems that, through formal and informal administrative enforcement mechanisms, encourage racial profiling. However, there are other public policies that in application elect to target noncitizens, specifically Japan's Visible Minorities, as a threat to Japan's body politic, leading to an Embedded Racism that has public policy ramifications.

Security Policing in General, and Its Selective Enforcement against "Foreigners"

Every nation-state has at its core the means to preserve internal order as a means of survival. However, in Japan's case, public policies have connected threats to public order with "foreigners," resulting in extraordinary and racialized measures taken by Japan's police forces to preserve public safety. Consider two excerpts from Edward Seidensticker's *Tokyo Rising* (1991):

> One powerful force in the workings of [Tōkyō's] city and the prefecture is not entirely under the control of the prefectural government: the police. The chief of the Tokyo prefectural police is appointed by a national police agency with the approval of the prime minister and upon the advice of a prefectural police commission. . . . None of these agencies is under the control of governor and council. *Tokyo becomes a police city when it is thought necessary to guard against the embarrassment of having someone shoot at a president or a queen or a pope.*[124] It has more than twice as many policemen as Osaka, though it is less than twice as large in population. The problem of police excesses is by no means limited to Tokyo . . . but it is most conspicuous in the prefecture in which national embarrassments are most likely to occur (169).[125] (Emphasis and endnotes added)

The point of this excerpt is to show, historically and structurally, how Japan's capital police force has the power to lock down Japanese society when deemed necessary from a public policy point of view. However, historical enforcement of public order has specifically targeted foreigners (in an era before Japan had many Visible Minorities). Japan's public security forces have prioritized targeting them instead of Wajin criminals. Seidensticker continues (emphases mine):

> There was in those days [during the Occupation] the problem of the "third nationals" [*Sangokujin*]. It was conspicuous in the underworld and in gang squabbling. Third nationals were for practical purposes Chinese and Koreans resident in Japan [i.e. the Zainichis]. The expression . . . distinguish[ed] them both from Japanese and from the Occupation, which favored them, treating Chinese as allies and Koreans as quasi allies (enemies of the enemy) . . .
>
> If the police could not intercede on behalf of Japanese gangs . . . , there is much evidence that they managed to aid them surreptitiously. In the "Shinbashi Incident" of 1946, American military police and Japanese police intervened to prevent an armed battle between Chinese and Japanese gangs for control of the market. The non-battle was in effect a victory for the Japanese. It showed the Chinese, who were progressively weaker, that they could not have everything their way even in that day of confusion and demoralization. . . . [I]n Chiba, later in 1946, the police seem to have actually encouraged a showdown between Japanese and third-national gangs. . . . *The Japanese police told the Japanese gangs what was to happen and invited their cooperation.* The Americans do not seem to have accorded the same favor to the third nationals . . . *in the end only third nationals were rounded up.* (154–55) (Emphases added)

In sum, police forces in Postwar Japan have been granted sufficient power, precedent and practice to enforce strong security during international events of great national pride and prestige. And if Japan's police see "foreigners" (particularly the Visible Minorities) as a threat to that security, they have great structural leeway (in addition to the laws and extralegal practices described in chapter 4) to engage in racial profiling and target "foreigners" on sight.[126] Let us illustrate this with the GOJ's security policies during the last two G8 Summits and the 2002 Korea-Japan World Cup.

Security Policing during the Okinawa and Hokkaidō G8 Summits

The Group of Eight (G8, which since has become the G7) Summit is an annual meeting of the governments of eight of the world's largest economies, with the host location of the summit rotating every year between member economies. Officially, world leaders under this forum umbrella meet to coordinate fiscal and monetary policy, as well as discuss outstanding agendas such as globalization and terrorism. It also has a history, as do all international summits, of attracting critics and protesters, some of whom hold public demonstrations and cause property damage. Japan held the G8 Presidency in 2000 and 2008, and it hosted G8 Summits in Nago, Okinawa and Tōyako, Hokkaidō, respectively. This is where the GOJ's extraordinary latitude for security and policing measures became most apparent.

In terms of costs, security alone for the 2008 Summit was projected in 2007 to cost 14 billion yen out of the total 18.5 billion yen (at the time, about 180 million US dollars); total costs later ballooned to an estimated 60 billion yen, far more than previous G8 Summits outside of Japan.[127] Costs were partially due to police security and logistics on the ground. Hokkaidō's domestic police force of 5,000 officers was supplemented by 16,000 NPA police and their vehicles brought in from other prefectures; another 20,000 police and hundreds of deputized members of neighborhood associations went on alert in Tōkyō more than 800 kilometers away to watch for "suspicious persons" (*fushinsha*). From the lead-up to the aftermath of the Summit, festivals and all "gatherings" (*shūkai*) in public places and parks (including the Flower Festival, the Pacific Music Festival, the Nakajima *Kōen* Flea Market, and the Sapporo Summer Festival, all about 100 kilometers away from the Summit site) were cancelled by the local government at the behest of the Hokkaidō Police.[128] Police forces were present at all major thoroughfares, public spaces, and intersections with road barricades at all times.[129]

Germane to this research were instances of racial profiling, where plain-clothes police were stationed at New Chitose and (faraway) Memanbetsu Airports before and during the Summit, targeting potential "terrorists" by phenotype. I confirmed with a police officer that he had received specific orders to stop and demand identification from all people who looked like "foreigners" (*gaikokujin*).[130] Protests to authorities by the author, other activists, and overseas journalists[131] were answered with NPA denials of any standard procedure involving racialized treatment of "suspicious persons," and with renewed requests for public cooperation.[132] There was no explanation of the criteria for spotting "terrorists."

This was not an isolated incident. The Kōbe G8 Environmental Ministers Summit, which took place two months beforehand, occasioned similar excessive and unaccountable security measures.[133] Moreover, the Okinawa G8 Summit in 2000 reportedly cost even more than the Tōyako Summit:

> Of the 81 billion yen Japan spent on hosting the summit—ten times more than any country ever spent before—about half went for security. Some 22,000 policemen specially flown in from across Japan, backed up by twenty aircraft and one hundred naval vessels (including destroyers), patrolled the land, sea, and sky of Okinawa. Swimmers and divers were flushed from surrounding seas, the cavernous insides of ancient tombs were carefully inspected, and elaborate

> security precautions around all major roads used by the G8 motorcades made it virtually impossible for local Okinawans to leave their homes, let alone get near the precincts of the summit conference. If anyone tried, police were quick to take down name and license number, and secret service officials in black suits stealthily recorded on camera the faces of local demonstrators conducting an innocuous "Nago peace walk.". . . As the correspondent of the English newspaper Guardian noted, holding the G-8 meeting in a remote island setting "briefly converted into a deluxe version of Alcatraz, did the trick." "By the end of the meeting," wrote the Sydney Morning Herald's correspondent, Michael Millet, on July 24, "the cost of the whole exercise and the tight Japanese grip on its proceedings had become as much of an issue as the agenda itself."[134]

While there were fewer reported issues of racial profiling during the 2000 Okinawa Summit (probably because this summit was held before Japan's antiterrorism policies starting from 2005; see below), the point is that when Japan hosts a high-profile international event, the "international" aspect brings in heightened policing concerns and racial profiling of Visible Minorities. One more case study of an international event before 2005 will illustrate this:

Security Policing during the 2002 Korea-Japan World Cup

As previously discussed, it became overt GOJ policy during the 2000s to publicly portray "foreigners" as potential "criminals," "terrorists," and carriers of "infectious diseases." In 2001, foreign soccer "hooligans" (*fūrigan*) were added to the list during the lead-up to the World Cup 2002 in Sapporo. From 2000 onward, domestic media both on TV and newspapers focused on how "foreign" hooligans coming to Japan would disrupt society (as they had done during the 1998 World Cup in France), and what measures the NPA (in consultation with European police agencies) would take to maintain public order.

Then public discussion and policy measures expanded beyond tracking individual soccer fans with a history of violence, and into tracking "foreigners" in general. For example, the Immigration Control and Refugee Recognition Act (*shutsunyūkoku kanri oyobi nanmin nintei hō*), the guiding law for administering noncitizens in Japan (see chapter 4), was amended to allow government agencies at the national and local level to take countermeasures against "hooligans," specifically in cases of "international competitions etc." (*kokusai kyōgikai tō*), implying that hooliganism is solely an exogenous force. Legislators normalized the trepidation in public debate: Miyagi Prefectural Assemblyman Konno Takayoshi remarked in an official meeting regarding upcoming soccer matches in Sendai: "Wrapped up in this abnormal atmosphere, there will be problems up to babies born against one's will (*fuhon'i*) due to foreign-Japanese (*naigaijin*) rapes";[135] Konno also warned of "foreigners selling cocaine and heroin, burning parked cars and paralyzing traffic systems."[136]

The atmosphere surrounding the World Cup occasioned heavy-handed security measures on par with the G8 Summits. Particularly in Sapporo, the site of the England-Argentina match, fears were high that old geopolitical grudges over the 1982 Falkland Islands War would erupt into violence, and thousands of extra police were brought in from nationwide.[137] As a Sapporo resident then for more than a decade, I witnessed and personally experienced public attitudes of suspicion and scorn toward Visible Minorities as potential "hooligans" in ways I had never experienced before in Sapporo. The official police response remained: "There is no such thing as being too careful."[138]

This argument of "if we hadn't taken these measures, there would have been an undesirable outcome" is frequently used after the fact to justify extreme public policy measures. However, this method of self-justification is based upon hypothesis and speculation, and rarely addresses the counterhypothesis—that "there *might be* such a thing as being too careful," that is, whether less extreme measures could have been taken and still achieved the same outcome.[139] However, as will be discussed in chapter 7, Japan's minorities are so disenfranchised in Japan's domestic media that counterarguments on behalf of minorities are rarely expressed, especially when it comes to domestic security issues involving "foreigners." In the end, only the negative image of "foreigners" was broadcast through the media; and even when practically no foreigners committed any crime during the event,[140] there was no public retraction or positive images broadcast in the media afterward to provide a sense of balance. Thus, minority interests, as in the ill effects of Japan's foreign residents being lumped in with visiting foreign "hooligans," "drug dealers," and "rapists," remained invisible in Japan's public debate.

For this Second Edition, other international sports meets have triggered similar overreactions in Japan. During the Brazil 2014 World Cup, Tōkyō police flooded Shibuya to "control crowds" and "reduce possible vandalism," for a match against the Ivory Coast in a stadium more than 10,000 miles away.[141] Japan's 2019 Rugby World Cup prompted the Nuclear Regulation Authority to adopt "antitheft measures" for the sake of Japan's "nuclear security," expressly to prevent Japan's radioactive materials from falling into the hands of "terrorists" and "intruders" who were apparently not in Japan before these games.[142] Now with Tōkyō being awarded the 2020 Olympics, these dynamics have helped make it the most expensive Summer Olympics in history, costing as of February 2021 close to five times more than its original budget.[143]

Through these case studies of official "overcarefulness," we can begin to see the emergence of a domestic discourse that, through policing actions in the name of "public security" and "order" for the sake of the *kokumin*, embeds innate fears of "foreign" behavior and criminality in the general public—to the point where public fear of "foreigners" supersedes common sense and moderation in policy measures. Let us now consider other policy measures against "foreigners" that have been adopted and normalized in the name of "security."

Miscellaneous Treatment of "Foreigners" as a Public Security Threat

The GOJ has justified other public security policies in the name of dealing with "foreigners." We discussed in chapter 4 how the Nationality Clause was explicitly designed to exclude noncitizens from positions with public authority over citizens, and how precedents normalized similar subordinated treatment in the private sector. Likewise, an institutionalized fear of "foreigners" as a security issue has developed into overall national security threats.

For example, the Transport Ministry has worried aloud about Japanese freight ships being staffed by too many noncitizens,[144] the NPA and the Japanese Self-Defense Forces have expressed concern about their ranks being married or related to noncitizens,[145] and government offices in general were warned by the Cabinet Secretariat in 2014 that civil servants who have studied abroad or worked for foreign companies "have a higher risk of leaking secrets."[146] Various governments at the local and national level have also debated the consequences of noncitizens purchasing land (particularly land controlling an aquifer).[147] Other issues, such as spying on, infiltrating, and arresting members of Muslim communities in Japan for suspected links to al-Qaeda terrorism, have been reported in the press,[148] resulting in ruined public reputations and court cases for libel and invasions of privacy; this was capped by a 2016 Supreme Court ruling that police surveillance targeting Muslim residents for their religion was "unavoidable" to uncover terrorism.[149] Finally, in 2015, the Abe administration proposed new immigration controls to crack down on "fraudulent visa holders" (*gizō taizaisha*), in order to fine and imprison people not working under the correct visa status, or living in "sham marriages" (which raised concerns that people might wind up incarcerated for registry errors, such as after changing jobs, moving house, getting divorced, or being widowed).[150]

These pinpoint issues are part of a larger trend to officially depict and target "foreigners" as a destabilizing force in Japan. Let us now to turn to how the GOJ has gone beyond the enforcement of exclusionary laws and utilized the media to disseminate and normalize the image of "foreigner" as a terrorist and criminal.

"Foreigner" as Terrorist and Criminal

Antiforeign crime and antiterrorism policies in Japan are rich topics for discussion for this research. However, as they involved a great deal of media publicity, they are better discussed in relation to media campaigns embedded within the national discourse. To avoid repetition, I will cover the media in chapter 7. So first, let us consider the philosophy behind official policy targeting "foreigners"—as mentioned earlier, one of "more foreigners means less Japan": How public policies were developed with the aim of combating the effects of "internationalization" itself.

National Police Agency Countermeasures against "Internationalization": The Kokusaika Taisaku Iinkai

As a public security measure, in May 1999 the NPA launched the "Committee for Policy against Internationalization" (*kokusaika taisaku iinkai*), specifically to "undertake suitable policies and laws against foreign crime for provincial police agencies, and strengthen their investigative organs" against "bad foreigner groups" (*furyō gaikokujin shūdan*), "foreign crime groups" (*gaikokujin hanzai soshiki*), and "illegal overstayers" (*fuhō taizaisha*) in "our country" (*wagakuni*).[151]

The rhetoric behind this committee provides a window into embedded NPA mindsets toward noncitizens. The committee's title does not use the more neutral word "policy" (*seisaku*). It uses "policy countermeasure" (*taisaku*), semantically meaning the specific targeting of an issue or counteracting a problem; that "problem," however, is not "foreign crime" (*gaikokujin hanzai*), but "internationalization" (*kokusaika*) itself. In terms of setting the tone of a national-level discourse, the existence of this committee problematizes not what illegal acts individual people (albeit noncitizens) might commit, but *the process of domestic change due to Japan's interaction with the outside world*. The *iinkai* was thus created to counteract foreign influence in specific, providing a line item in the public purse to fund government activities specifically targeting noncitizens and their ideas. Products of this state-sponsored xenophobia, for example, NPA notices regarding "bad foreigners," "visa overstayers," and "foreign crime," will be discussed in chapter 7.

NPA Bunker Mentalities toward "Foreign Crime" and the Outside World

One question that frequently arises in political science is, "What are actors thinking when they create public policy?" Fortunately, we have evidence of that: NPA policy directives, which have long displayed a clear "bunker mentality" toward "foreigners."

Consider this undated statement (circa 2010) from the MOJ, entitled "Recovery of Public Safety," issued as a joint statement by several policing bodies,[152] which offers insights into official policy mindsets toward international terrorism, cybercrime, and the presence of noncitizens in Japan, as well as logical justifications for policy drives on "foreigners" (Excerpted from English original; emphases added in italics by the author):

> *In the past Japan was proud of its image in the world of being an exceptionally safe country, but in recent years, the number of criminal cases that have been identified by the authorities has increased remarkably*, while the clearance rate has dropped drastically and remains at a very low level, which makes the deterioration of public safety an issue of grave concern to the nation. *In particular, exceptionally violent crimes attracting public attention and the occurrence close at hand of many offences committed by youngsters or by foreign nationals coming to Japan are making people uneasy about the maintenance of public order*. . . . Further, effective measures against international terrorism such as the multiple terrorist attacks on the United States, and efforts toward solving problems concerning the abduction of Japanese nationals by North Korea, are needed.
>
> Under such circumstances, the Government, *aiming at restoration of Japan as "the safest country in the world,"* inaugurated the Ministerial Meeting Concerning Measures against Crime, which formulated in December 2003 "The Action Plan for the Realization of a Society Resistant to Crime," and the Conference is actively promoting comprehensive measures such as *various countermeasures against crime including shoreline countermeasures*, the consolidation of a social environment under which it would be difficult to commit crimes, and the strengthening of the structure of agencies and organs responsible for public safety . . . thus trying to *secure the safety of the public and ease the fears and the anxiety of the Japanese people*. (Signed: Criminal Affairs Bureau, Correction Bureau, Rehabilitation Bureau, Immigration Bureau, Public Security Intelligence Agency, and Public Security Examination Commission)

The subtext of this official statement is that Japan's former "safe" past has been interrupted by exogenous influences, for example, international terrorists, international (not domestic) organized crime syndicates, and Chinese; and that public order must be restored for the sake of "the Japanese people" (as opposed to "residents of Japan," including noncitizens), starting from the shoreline. In sum, crime flows into an otherwise peaceful Japan.

This is not a new policy stance. Kashiwazaki cites the following government statement from 1959 (Kashiwazaki's translation)[153]:

> Since Japan is one of the most densely populated countries in the world, policies of controlling both population growth and immigration are strongly called for. It should therefore be a government policy to severely restrict the entry of foreigners into Japan. This is all the more so because there are undesirable foreigners who would threaten the lives of Japanese nationals by criminal activity and immoral conduct. (Ministry of Justice, *Shutsunyūkoku Kanri* (Administration of National Entrants and Leavers) 1959: 3)

In other words, as far back as early Postwar Japan, the government saw any new influx of foreigners as a destabilizing force—not only in terms of simple population control (Japan's major urban areas were indeed inhumanely crowded back then in terms of housing),[154] but also in terms of safety, criminality, and public morals. That generational policy impulse to "control" (*kanri*, i.e., to police) noncitizens, as opposed to provide them equal service and protection as residents, has continued to the present day.

CONCLUSIONS

Social stability is a concern for the maintenance of integrity and sovereignty of any nation-state. However, the GOJ and law enforcement have a history of targeting noncitizens, both as residents (i.e., foreigners here as part of Japan's "internationalizing" society) and nonresidents (i.e., foreigners here for international events) as a public security threat. This has justified extreme policing measures overtly othering "foreigners" and racial-profiling Visible Minorities. This is not by accident: the NPA has inter alia created a committee specifically devoted to combating the effects not only of foreign crime, but also of *internationalization itself*, enabling police and policymakers to portray "foreigners" as terrorists, criminals, and security threats. More on this in chapter 7, where we discuss how these policies percolate through the media. But as this chapter has demonstrated, a steady stream of anti-internationalizationism has percolated through public policy.

The GOJ has steadfastly resisted anything that might be construed as an immigration policy. Instead, over the past three decades, while millions of foreigners have come to Japan as workers, students, caregivers, and entertainers, they have been subjected to visa regimes that deliberately make it difficult to settle in Japan. Their visas have expressly (a) exempted foreign workers only from legal protections guaranteed all "laborers" in Japan; (b) promoted "revolving door" labor conditions that exploited their best working years and set up hurdles to qualify for Permanent Residency; and (c) allowed widespread labor abuses to become a design feature of the system, not a flaw. For those foreigners who toughed it out and stayed long enough to start families and set down roots in Japan, their children were often denied or hindered from getting a compulsory education, or were left unprotected from systemic bullying, relegating many of them to an uneducated underclass.

These "revolving door" visa regimes were so successful at getting Japan cheap labor without actually having to deal with the needs of laborers that they were later expanded to award more job sectors, more people, and finally even Nikkei foreigners of Wajin descent (who were hitherto granted de facto Permanent Residency by dint of bloodline) with insecure and abusive jobs. New conditions hindered foreigners from associating with Wajin or starting lives and families in Japan. As for the higher-skilled jobs, visa durations were lengthened on paper but in practice often shortened to one year upon renewal, with minor clerical issues used to void progress toward Permanent Residency. Thus, Japan's mandate to quietly cap the foreign population at around 2 percent of total population has been successful, even as Japan's Wajin population continues to fall.

As for the international people in Japan not living under a visa, that is, the Visible Minorities, they have had some successes, but still face systemic measures to suppress their diversity and limit their influence on the "monoethnic Japan" narrative. These include draconian school rules ("hair police," etc.) to enforce an artificial conformity to uniformity, barriers in public competitions to make sure children with international exposure do not have an "unfair" advantage over pure-blooded Wajin, a culture of fear behind retaining dual nationality, official terminology to "other" and asterisk anyone "international" (including citizens) as "foreign" (*gaikokujin shimin, honpōgai shusshinsha,* etc.), and a dynamic where minorities can be "claimed" as "real Japanese" *iff* they are "winners" and world class in their field. Otherwise they face a perpetual treadmill of "proving oneself worthy" to Japanese society, which is psychologically draining and zero sum toward their minority status. In short, the system encourages Japan's Visible Minorities to racially profile themselves.

Up to now, this research has covered two components of the construction of Japan's "Macro-level" national discourse outlined at the beginning of chapter 4: (1) Laws and Administrative Regimes codifying in law the "Self" and "Other" of "Japanese" vs. "Foreigner"; and (2) Government Bodies Creating Laws and Policy, procedurally separating people in Japan into "Wajin" vs. "Gaijin." Let us now turn to another segment of Japan's government bodies—the judiciary—which (if working properly) offers any society a sense of justice through jurisprudential redress and equal enforcement of the law. Unfortunately, it is not working properly. As chapter 6 will discuss, Japan's laws are in fact enforced in a racialized manner in Japan's Criminal and Civil Courts, where the prosecution of "Japanese vs. foreigner" crimes, or the settlement of disputes through civil lawsuits, gives systemic advantages to Wajin both as plaintiff or defendant.

NOTES

1. Courtesy Ministry of Education website, provisional translation by the Ministry, at www.mext.go.jp/english/lawandplan/1303462.htm.

2. *See also* "Japan's Dangerous Anachronism." *New York Times* Editorial, December 16, 2013, which notes,

> The [state secrecy] law is an integral part of Mr. Abe's crusade to remake Japan into a "beautiful country," which envisions expanded government power over the people and reduced protection for individual rights—a strong state supported by a patriotic people. His stated goal is to rewrite the nation's Constitution, which was imposed by the United States Army during occupation seven decades ago. . . . Mr. Abe's aim is to "cast off the postwar regime." Critics in Japan warn that he is seeking to resurrect the pre-1945 state. It is a vision both anachronistic and dangerous.

3. "Fundamental flaw remains in education law." *Asahi Shinbun* "Point of View" column, February 12, 2007. As for the 2006 reforms to the Education Law under PM Abe, *see*, for example, Tawara Yoshifumi, "Japan's Education and Society in Crisis." Lecture at the University of Chicago, May 17, 2007; Lebowitz & McNeill (2007). A very concise comparison between the old and new text of the Education Law is at www.japanfocus.org/data/ed.law.file.pdf. For a discussion of the GOJ's reintroduction of a mystical patriotism in Japan, *see also* "Reviving Shinto: Prime Minister Abe tends special place in Japan's soul; Conservatives seek to expand the role of Japan's indigenous faith in public life. But critics warn that could feed a simmering nationalism." *Christian Science Monitor*, October 5, 2015.

4. Interview, John and Ruth Anna Mather, missionaries, *Baputesto Seisho Kyōkai*, Wakkanai, Hokkaidō, April 9, 2000, at www.debito.org/onsennyuuyokutimes041300.html. *See also* Arudou (2006b: 228–229); "Foreign schoolgirl's admittance delayed due to teachers' opposition." *Kyodo News*, July 28, 2009.

5. "'Prison camps for Brazilians': Foreign kids in Japan being ushered into special education." *Mainichi Shinbun*, September 4, 2019, archived with commentary at www.debito.org/?p=15734, noting, "One day, when the girl was in her fourth year of elementary school, it emerged that she couldn't do multiplication. When the girl was asked, 'Don't you learn that in school?' she replied, 'We dig for potatoes at school.'" Also archived at that link is "High ratio of foreign students put in special education after sitting IQ tests in Japanese." *Mainichi Shinbun*, September 3, 2019, noting:

> 5.37 percent (584 children out of 10,876) of foreign students were enrolled in special education classes, which was over twice the 2.54 percent (8,725 children out of 343,808) of students who were enrolled in special education classes out of the entire student population in those cities. In all 25 cities and towns [surveyed by the Ministry of Education], the ratio of foreign children in special education classes was higher than the ratio of all students in special education classes, with foreign students comprising nearly 20 percent of special education classes.

Surveys conducted on this situation in 2016 and 2019 were never made public by the Ministry of Education until the *Mainichi Shinbun* exposés. *See also* "Educating the Non-Japanese underclass." *Shingetsu News Agency*, September 17, 2019.

6. "Deliberative Council for Instituting a Society Coexisting with Foreigners" (*gaikokujin to kyōsei shakai jitsugen kentō kaigi*) Cabinet meetings May–July 2012, with ministries and experts deliberating in particular on the under-education of Nikkei children. The briefs from the Health Ministry, Hamamatsu Mayor Suzuki Yasutomo, NPO Aidensha chief Sakamoto Kumiko, and the Cabinet itself lament their lack of language ability and unemployability, thus confusing cause and effect. *See also Asahi Shinbun* ibid.; "20,000 in language pickle: Foreign students in need of specialized Japanese teachers." *Yomiuri Shinbun*, May 22, 2007; "School forced girl to change hair color." *Japan Times Weekly*, April 16, 2005; and so on.

7. By "hair police," I am referring to the concern expressed by activists and concerned parents at how some schools assume that any hair that is not black and straight must have been permed and colored, and after regular public inspections force multiethnic children to dye and straighten it. In interviews of school officials by the author, the justification was that "students understand the importance of rules" (*kihan ishiki*) and have an "awareness of society" (*shakai ishiki*), as per their "student handbook" (*seito techō*). Less discussed are the toxic effects of hair dyes, particularly on developing children. *See* "School forced girl to change hair color." *Japan Times Weekly*, April 16, 2005; "Schools single out foreign roots: International kids suffering under archaic rules." *Japan Times*, July 17, 2007. For a primary source investigation and interviews with officials at Ikeshinden High School, Ōmaezaki City in Shizuoka Prefecture, regarding their alleged enforcement of "hair policing," *see also* "Report: Immigrant children and Japan's hair police." *Debito.org*, May 24, 2007, www.debito.org/?p=412 (*see also* comments section for more testimonials). My younger daughter, who attended a Japanese junior and senior high school, was also visible in school photographs with her naturally brown wavy hair dyed and straightened black.

A lawsuit against this practice awarded modest damages to student plaintiffs in 2021, but still ruled that hair policing has a "reasonable and legitimate educational purpose"; *see* "School 'Hair Police' lose case in Osaka: Court awards the victim a pittance, but rules that enforced hair coloring has 'reasonable and legitimate educational purpose.' Another setback for Visible Minorities." *Debito.org*, February 20, 2021, www.debito.org/?p=16430. For a sense of the scope of this problem, *see* "Survey: 57 percent of Tokyo high schools demand hair-color proof." *Asahi Shinbun*, May 1, 2017, archived at www.debito.org/?p=14592.

8. *See*, for example, the U Hoden Case (2000–2006) regarding the bullying of a Chinese Japanese grade schooler, which resulted in a successful lawsuit for post-traumatic stress disorder, archived at www.debito.org/kawasakiminzokusabetsu.htm. There was also a case in 2003 of a child with a mixed racial background being bullied by his teacher in a Fukuoka grade school; his ears were pulled in class while being called "Mickey Mouse," his nose was pulled until it bled while being called "Pinocchio"; he was also accused of having "dirtied blood" (*chi ga kegareta*) and told by the teacher to "die immediately." On July 28, 2006, the boy won damages in Fukuoka District Court for PTSD and was awarded 2.2 million yen. The teacher, however, only received a suspension from duties for six months. *See* "City told to pay for teachers' bullying." *Asahi Shinbun*, July 29, 2006.

Also, there is the pseudonymous "Senaiho" Case, where a child with a mixed racial background dropped out of school in 2018 after being bullied by classmates and having her hair forcibly cut in public by teachers. A 2021 civil case against the parents of the bully children rejected damages for Senaiho because the Yamanashi District Court found that junior high school students are immature, and since this is an educational environment where their characters are molded, "one cannot readily apply illegal activity to behaviors that make one feel uncomfortable" (16), thereby voiding the option for bullied people in school to seek legal recourse as long as the abuse is only mental. *See* anchor site for the Senaiho Case at www.debito.org/?p=16636.

In terms of nonmental abuse, *see also* "*Cinco alumnas japonesas denunciadas por ultrajar sexualmente a una compañera peruana en Shizuoka*" [Five Japanese students reported for sexual offense against a Peruvian partner in Shizuoka]. *IPC International Press*, April 18, 2014, google translated at www.debito.org/?p=12313.

9. *See*, for example, one pertinent case of Wajin bullying of multiethnic children leading to suicide: The Uemura Akiko Case. "Suicide prompts major bullying study." *Kyodo News*, November 11, 2010; "Picture of classroom out of control emerges in wake of bullied 6th grader's suicide." *Mainichi Shinbun*, November 5, 2010; "Father of schoolgirl suicide victim says daughter was teased about mom's nationality." *Mainichi Shinbun*, October 27, 2010; "Cause of a girl's suicide." *Japan Times* Editorial, November 11, 2010, which notes:

> On Oct. 23, Ms. Akiko Uemura, a sixth-grade girl in Kiryū, Gunma Prefecture, died after hanging herself. On Nov. 8, Kiryū's board of education made public a report saying she had been psychologically bullied. It denied a cause-and-effect relationship between the bullying and her suicide. But on Oct. 25, Mr. Yoichi Kishi, principal of the municipal Niisato Higashi Primary School, said school authorities had known that the girl "was not in good condition as indicated by her isolation at lunch time." We wonder why the school could not act soon enough to prevent her suicide. . . . Why does the board of education deny a cause-and-effect relationship between the bullying and her suicide? It appears as if the board and school authorities refused to squarely deal with the tragedy and their responsibility in the case.

NHK similarly downplayed the racialized aspect of the bullying, when both its 7 p.m. and 9 p.m. national news broadcasts on November 8, 2010, reported Uemura's suicide without mentioning her multiethnic status. There are of course other cases worthy of mention, but this research lacks further space.

10. Personal communications and interviews, Mr. Yoko-o Akichika, Chair, NGO *Gaikokujin no Kodomo no Kyōiku to Jinken* [Foreign Children's Education and Human Rights] Network, Nagoya, November 2003 to March 2004. *See also* "Hiroshi Tanaka: Japan must open its arms to foreign workers." *Asahi Shinbun*, "Point of View" column. July 3, 2007.

11. "Currently, the most important law on education in Japan, as well as the very Constitution, does not guarantee the right to education for children with foreign nationalities. . . . 'If the child is a Japanese who had reasons to be enrolled in a grade lower than the appropriate one, obviously he or she needs extra year(s) to finish his or her "obligatory education" and will be granted an exception. However, obligatory education does not apply to you,' [a public junior high school in Setagaya Ward, Tōkyō] said." *Asahi Shinbun*, February 12, 2007, ibid.

12. References for this section include "A level playing field? National Sports Festival bars gaijin, and amateur leagues follow suit." *Japan Times*, September 30, 2003; "Sumo shutout in Fukushima." *Japan Times*, September 30, 2003; "Top court upholds foreigner ban." *Japan Times*, June 12, 2004. *See also* Douglas Shukert's testimonial about his case at www.debito.org/TheCommunity/kokutaiproject.html. Also, JASA's information on the *Kokutai* is at www.japan-sports.or.jp/kokutai/, in English at www.japan-sports.or.jp/english (which makes no mention of nationality requirements for participants).

13. Robert Whiting, "Devoted to the game: Looking back at Oh's career," and "Equaling Oh's HR record proved difficult." *Japan Times*, October 29 and 31, 2008, respectively. In a three-part series, Whiting argues that no matter how highly praised Oh's record became, he could never escape being in the shadow of his rival, Nagashima Shigeo, because Nagashima was a Japanese and Oh was not. *See also* Whiting (1990) passim.

14. In 2011, the Basic Sports Law was amended to restructure how the games were organized, but left intact was the embedded *kokumin* conceit of sports for "citizens' healthy minds and bodies" (*kokumin no shinshin no kenzen*) and "citizens' bright and plentiful livelihoods" (*akaruku yutaka na kokumin seikatsu*) (Article 1), not to mention participation reserved for citizens only (Article 7). Ministry of Education notice to this effect, dated August 11, 2011, at www.mext.go.jp/a_menu/sports/kihonhou/attach/1309800.htm.

15. Sources for this section include "Foreign students can't start *ekiden*." *Asahi Shinbun*, May 24, 2007; "Let's be fair, let Japanese win." *Deutsche Press-Agentur*, October 4, 2007. The official site for the High School *Ekiden* is at www.koukouekiden.jp. Restrictions on "foreign exchange students" are at www.koukouekiden.jp/summary/point.html, and prior race results are at www39.atwiki.jp/highschoolekiden.

16. There is also the issue of the pressure put upon Japanese athletes not to bring "shame" to Japan as a nation by losing as an individual in competition to other nationalities. Although a complex psychological profiling of sportspeople in Japanese society is not within the bounds of this research, consider the case of Hakone *Ekiden* founder and "father of the Japanese marathon" Kanakuri Shiso, one of Japan's first Olympic runners. Unable to finish his event in the Stockholm Games in 1912, Kanakuri went "missing" in order to avoid bringing "shame to his countrymen." Since he never notified officials, he never officially finished the race, and as a lifetime achievement award was technically allowed to "finish" his race in Stockholm in 1967, more than fifty-four years later. The point is, conceits of "fair play" in Japan do not seem only to be influenced by Wajin winning but also by avoiding the shame of losing allegedly unfairly, in this case due to attributes that correlate to nationality. *See* "Better late than never for Japan's first, 'slowest' Olympian." *Japan Times*, July 15, 2012. For an insight on what toll this nationalistic pressure takes on Japanese athletes (e.g., early deaths and suicides), *see* Mark Schreiber, "Star-studded sportsmen speed swim the Styx." *Flash*, October 31, 2000, archived at www.debito.org/olympics2004.html.

17. "From the standpoints of 'internationalization' and school education, it would be ideal not to have any restrictions," [Sawaki Keisuke, a director of the Japan

Association of Athletics Federations] said. "In reality, however, the differences in physical capabilities between Japanese and foreign students are far beyond imagination" (*Asahi Shinbun* ibid.). "The decision came after the [All Japan High School Athletic Federation] received mounting complaints from fans that 'African runners lead the race so much that the Japanese athletes can't narrow the difference or catch up throughout the race'" (*Deutsche Press Agentur* ibid.).

18. "Freedom of Speech: 'Tainted blood' sees 'foreign' students barred from English contests." *Japan Times*, January 6, 2004. The current official site of the Takamado speech contests may be found at www.jnsafund.org (accessed April 9, 2021, English site with entry qualifications under construction). An archive of the protest correspondence with the JNSA and their official responses is at www.debito.org/takamadoproject.html.

19. The rules of entry as of 2021 are in Japanese only at https://jnsafund.org/info/shikaku/. Year 2006's amended rules were at www.jnsafund.org/en/ptt58th/yoko.pdf, while 2005's rules were at www.jnsafund.org/en/ptt57th/yoko.pdf.

20. www.britannica.com/EBchecked/topic/553877/Somalia/37721/Languages#ref419600.

21. Compare this to the United States, where 1,141 players, that is, more than 28 percent of the 4,025 pro ball players who were active between 2009 and 2021, were foreign born. Source: Baseball-reference.com at www.baseball-reference.com/friv/placeofbirth.cgi?TYPE=active&from=2009&to=0&DIV=countries (accessed April 9, 2021). In Japan, there is some rule relaxation for the rare noncitizen who has played for a decade on Japanese teams, such as Tuffy Rhodes, who is no longer included in the "foreigner" quota. *See* "Tuffy Rhodes likely to play 13th season in Japan." *Japan Times*, November 23, 2008.

22. *See* "*Gaikokujin rikishi hitoheya hitori o saikakunin*" [Reconfirmed: Foreign sumō wrestlers are to be one to a stable]. *Asahi Shinbun*, February 23, 2010; "*Kika de mo dame, gaikokujin rikishi 'hitoheya hitori tettei tsūtatsu*'" [even naturalization is out: Full notification that foreign wrestlers are one to a stable]. *Yomiuri Shinbun*, February 23, 2010; "JSA to change rule on foreign sumo wrestlers." *Kyodo News*, February 24, 2010; "Sumo body deserves *mawashi* wedgie for racist wrestler ruling." *Japan Times*, March 2, 2010. As justification, since four Mongolians and two Chinese wrestlers had taken Japanese citizenship in 2009, a stablemaster was quoted, "You get the impression it is a severe measure but if the brakes are not applied somewhere, there will be more and more stables overrun with foreign wrestlers, so it can't be helped" (*Asahi Shinbun* ibid.). Given that in 2007, one-third of *Banzuke* top-ranked sumō wrestlers were foreign born (*see* www.debito.org/?p=464), this overreaction to view naturalization as a "loophole" may be logical but remains problematic from a "fair play" sporting point of view, not to mention in terms of legal precedent under the Nationality Law. *See also* "Sumo star charges racism in Japan." *New York Times*, April 22, 1992, on the Konishiki Case.

23. "JRFU rules certain Japan passport holders will be regarded as non-Japanese." *Japan Today*, September 26, 2020.

24. "Groups try to level playing field by limiting foreign players." *Asahi Shinbun*, June 29, 2007, archived at www.debito.org/?p=466. As an aside, it merits mention

that the sport of *jūkendō* (bayonet practice) was formally revived in Japanese schools as a "martial art" for physical education classes in 2017, despite its history of being a weapon of oppression and massacre in Imperial Japan's colonies. If voices of diversity had any influence on Japan's curriculum changes, it is hard to see any students of, for example, Chinese descent favoring this revision. *See*, for example, "Prewar bayonetting martial art makes return to schools." *Japan Times*, April 24, 2017; "World War II practice bayonets discovered, evoking memories of Japan's wartime student military training." *Japan Times/Chūnichi Shinbun*, June 26, 2017. In "War Museum Resists Japan's Historical Amnesia." *Chronicle of Higher Education*, April 27, 2007, David McNeill notes, "[Archivist and war veteran] Ebato says he himself trained recruits to use captured Chinese for bayonet practice. 'Terrible things like this happened all the time. Now people are saying that they never happened. Japan wants to keep a lid on a stinking pot.'"

25. The converse of the "Japanese are weaker than foreigners" meme is also true. Consider the case of John Kirwan, former coach of the Japan national rugby team (2007–2011), who was fired in 2011 for an unsatisfactory showing in the 2011 Rugby World Cup. He was criticized inter alia for having "too *many* foreigners" (emphasis mine) on the team (i.e., ten). These ten also included five naturalized Japanese citizens, categorizing them as still "foreign" in direct contravention of the Nationality Law. Consequently, the Japan national rugby team's new lineup, announced March 19, 2012, had only one Non-Wajin name within its ranks, with five other Non-Wajin (and only Non-Wajin) listed as not selected for the team due to "injuries." Thus, under Japan's sporting regimes, in the likely event that Japan (like every national team; there can only be one winner) does not win, the Non-Wajin tend to become the scapegoats for that loss.

In sum, "fairness" in Japanese sports only works one way: in favor of the Wajin. If "foreigners" are on the other team as opponents, they are accused of an unfair size or strength advantage; if they are on the same team (and the team loses), they are accused of a number of *Nihonjinron*-based shortcomings (such as a lack of "Japanese spirit" (*yamato damashii*) allegedly inherent to Wajin athletes). *See* "Kirwan under fire for using too many foreign-born players." *Japan Today.com*, October 30, 2011; on *yamato damashii*, *see* inter alia "Renewed national pride will shape Japan's future." *Japan Times*, April 3, 2011. The 2012 Japan rugby team lineup and staff was at http://sakura.rugby-japan.jp/japan/2012/id13531.html (accessed August 7, 2012; dead link, but visible on the online Wayback Machine).

26. Much social media in Japan has questioned whether a *Hāfu* can represent Japan, and Miyamoto herself has noted how the domestic media, in contrast to the international media, has basically ignored her and her attempts to raise awareness of racial discrimination in Japan. *See* "The beauty queen criticized for not being Japanese enough." *CNN*, March 25, 2015; "Miss Universe Japan facing backlash at home from those who object to biracial beauty queen taking the crown." *E!*, March 27, 2015; "Japan in Focus: Japan's Miss Universe race debate." *ABC (Australia) NewsRadio*, March 30, 2015; "Beauty queen wants Japan to open minds and borders." *Bloomberg*, April 6, 2015; "Miss Japan: First mixed-race winner provokes debate." *BBC News*, June 5, 2015; "Mainichi: 'Not Japanese Enough?' Bog-standard

article about Miss Japan Miyamoto Ariana's fight against racial discrimination in Japan, not in Japanese for J-audience." *Debito.org*, July 26, 2015, www.debito.org/?p=13425; "Mainichi Shinbun: Miss Universe Japan Ariana Miyamoto spurns 'half Japanese' label, seeks end to prejudice. Good, but article in English only, not for Japanese-reading audience." *Debito.org*, November 17, 2015, www.debito.org/?p=13657; "ABC NewsRadio Australia, Japan in Focus: The winner of Miss World Japan, Yoshikawa Priyanka, prompts another racial debate." *Debito.org*, September 12, 2016, www.debito.org/?p=14203; "The politics of identity in Japan: The conversation on race and ethnicity widens in the island nation" (interviews Yoshikawa). *"The Stream"* program, *Al-Jazeera.com*, September 14, 2016; "Tennis queen Osaka a role model, says 'Indian' Miss Japan: Mixed-race beauty queen believes tennis ace can break down racial barriers in homogenous Japan." *South China Morning Post*, September 24, 2018.

27. "Imagining a Japan that thinks beyond blood and binary distinctions." *Japan Times*, October 28, 2015; "Multiracial athletes sparking debate in Japan ahead of 2020 Games." *Kyodo News*, August 7, 2019; "Nike Japan ads featuring Japan's Minorities and Visible Minorities taking solace and courage from doing sports." *Debito.org*, December 2, 2020, www.debito.org/?p=16328; "Nike Japan ad does some good." *Shingetsu News Agency*, December 21, 2020.

28. *See*, for example, "Claim us if you're famous." *Code Switch, NPR*, November 10, 2020.

29. www.debito.org/?p=16230.

30. *See*, for example, "Naomi Osaka's Breakthrough Game: The 20-year-old is poised to burst into the top tier of women's tennis. Can she also burst Japan's expectations of what it means to be Japanese?" *New York Times Magazine*, August 23, 2018; Debito Arudou, "Warning to Naomi Osaka: Playing for Japan can seriously shorten your career." *Japan Times*, September 19, 2018; "'Nippon Claimed' multiethnic tennis star Osaka Naomi gets 'whitewashed' by her sponsor. Without consulting her. Compare with singer Crystal Kay." *Debito.org*, January 25, 2019, www.debito.org/?p=15506; John G. Russell, "Whitewashing racial bias: The ball's in Japan's court." *Japan Times*, February 17, 2019; "Japanese comedians apologize for saying Naomi Osaka 'needed some bleach.'" *Reuters* and *Yahoo! Sports*, September 25, 2019; "Naomi Osaka Returns After Protest Prompts Tournament's Pause: Osaka won her semifinal match on Friday, walking to the court with a T-shirt bearing the Black Lives Matter slogan." *New York Times*, August 28, 2020; "Japanese sponsors of tennis star Naomi Osaka not 100 percent on board with anti-racism actions." *Mainichi Shinbun*, September 11, 2020; "Reuters: Tennis star Osaka Naomi 'a Jesse Owens of Japan.' I don't think the comparison is apt, yet. She should also speak out for Japan's Visible Minorities." *Debito.org*, September 12, 2020, www.debito.org/?p=16230.

31. *See*, for example, "In Japan, Will Hafu Ever Be Considered Whole? Mixed-race individuals and their families seek acceptance in a homogeneous Japan." *The Diplomat.com*, October 3, 2013; "AFP: 'Tarento Rola changing DNA of Japanese pop culture.' I wish her well, but the hyperbolic hype is not warranted." *Debito.org*, July 16, 2014, www.debito.org/?p=12520; *South China Morning Post* ibid.;

"Celebrating Japan's multicultural Olympians: Meet the athletes flying the flag and challenging traditional views of what it is to be Japanese." *Japan Times*, August 17, 2016; "Is Japan embracing diversity?" *BBC*, February 24, 2020, with a critique at Debito.org at www.debito.org/?p=15953.

32. *See*, for example, some anecdotal evidence of official treatment at "J bureaucrat exclusionary attitudes when registering his newborn multicultural child at Shibuya Kuyakusho." *Debito.org*, July 9, 2011, www.debito.org/?p=9201; Glenn Newman, "Japan loses, rest of the world gains from 'one citizenship fits all' policy." *Japan Times*, December 7, 2010; and so on.

33. *See*, for example, Miyake Kunihiko, "How Japanese is Naomi Osaka?" *Japan Times*, January 28, 2019, in which he opines, "Japan's mainstream media reported the breaking news referring to Naomi Osaka as the first Japanese female tennis player to win two consecutive Grand Slam titles and to be ranked World No. 1. Yes, she is. But not quite so, is she? I felt something odd, if not wrong, about those media stories," before going on to judge how "Japanese" he thinks she is. My analysis of Miyake's piece is at www.debito.org/?p=15541.

34. Kashiwazaki (2000: 451).

35. *See* "The Nobel Prize in Physics 2008," at www.nobelprize.org/nobel_prizes/physics/laureates/2008 (which lists Nambu only as a US citizen); "Japanese trio wins Nobel Prize for physics." *Mainichi Shinbun*, October 7, 2008.

36. Despite the 2008 Kōno debates, the same media confusion over citizenship happened again when "three Japanese scientists" won the Nobel Prize in Physics in 2014: Akasaki Isamu, Amano Hiroshi, and Shūji Nakamura—even though Nakamura had become a naturalized American citizen and relinquished his Japanese citizenship. Although many outlets were careful to say "Japan-born," some media for example did not: "Three Japanese scientists shine brightly with Nobel Prize in Physics for blue LED." *Asahi Shinbun*, October 7, 2014; "Three Japanese collect Nobel Prize in Physics." *NTV News*, December 11, 2014; and so on.

37. "'Who's Kazuo Ishiguro?' Japan asks, but celebrates Nobel author as its own." *Reuters*, October 5, 2017, archived with commentary at www.debito.org/?p=14769.

38. Kōno claimed that there are 600,000–700,000 citizens past the age of twenty-two with dual nationality, meaning that around 90 percent of Wajin duals have tacitly chosen to maintain both. Naturally, enforcing a single nationality would be diplomatically difficult for the GOJ since it has no jurisdiction over other nationalities.

39. *See*, for example, "Former UCLA player gets Japanese citizenship, spot on national hoops team." *Japan Times*, July 17, 2007, on J. R. Sakuragi, formerly J. R. Henderson, who received his Japanese citizenship in time for his participation on the Japan National Basketball Team at the FIBA Asia Championship. *See also* a discussion of "citizenship nationalism" for Tongan players in Japan's rugby leagues in Besnier (2012: 501).

40. For example, the Reed siblings, Cathy and Chris, children of a Wajin mother and an American father, were allowed to skate for Team Japan in the 2010 Vancouver Olympics due to their dual nationality. However, Cathy was at the time older than twenty-two, meaning she was in apparent violation of the Nationality Law by not

choosing Japanese only. This issue was not raised in the domestic media, and they did not win any Olympic medals. *See* "Three siblings carry two different flags." *New York Times*, February 19, 2010.

41. "Kawaguchi braves taunts to skate for Russia." *Reuters*, October 14, 2009. A more curious case was that of comedian Neko Hiroshi, who renounced his Japanese citizenship in order to compete as an Olympic runner representing Cambodia. When Neko was disqualified from the Cambodian team for not having Cambodian citizenship for more than one year, he asked for his Japanese citizenship back. *See*, for example, "Many angles to acquiring Japanese citizenship." *Japan Times*, December 27, 2011.

42. Mori's comment about the Reed siblings was reportedly, "They live in America. Although they are not good enough for the U.S. team in the Olympics, we included these naturalized citizens on the team," further complicating the issue by insinuating that the Reeds were inferior leftovers. *See* "Tokyo 2020 chairman Mori critical of Asada, ice dancing brother and sister." *AP*, February 21, 2014, and other articles on the event in English and Japanese archived at www.debito.org/?p=12130.

43. A version of this section was published as Arudou, Debito, "Embedded Racism in Japanese Migration Policies: Analyzing Japan's 'revolving door' work visa regimes under Critical Race Theory." *Journal of Pacific Asia Studies* 3(1) May 2013: 155–185. Reprinted with permission.

44. This section heavily references the Ministry of Justice Immigration Bureau website at www.immi-moj.go.jp. There have been some changes to Japan's visa regimes as of July 9, 2012, and these are listed at www.moj.go.jp/nyuukokukanri/kouhou/nyukan_nyukan65.html (accessed April 15, 2021); however, how these new rules will be applied is yet unclear (i.e., even though the maximum validity of the Status of Residence has been extended from three years to five, it is unclear how many people will actually receive the five-year SOR in practice), especially since there is no process of appeal permitted in Immigration SOR decisions (cf. www.immi-moj.go.jp/english/tetuduki/kanri/shyorui/05.html).

45. "Schizophrenic Constitution leaves foreigners' rights mired in confusion." *Japan Times*, November 1, 2011.

46. Higuchi & Arudou (2008: 20–33, 56–61), and so on.

47. One case of discretionary decision-making that is not anecdotal is Charles Jenkins, an American defector to North Korea in 1965, who married a Japanese national who had been abducted to North Korea in 1978. He was allowed to leave North Korea with his family in 2004 and live permanently in Japan. He received Permanent Residency from the GOJ in 2008 within weeks of application. *See* "Jenkins granted permanent residency status." *Kyodo News*, July 11, 2008.

48. *See* inter alia "Arbitrary rulings equal bad PR." *Japan Times*, May 27, 2008. More primary source testimonials at "People clearly qualifying for Permanent Residency are being rejected by Immigration." *Debito.org*, May 19, 2008, www.debito.org/?p=1664. Questions are raised therein with how "permanent" PR actually is if, for example, lapsed REPs (*sainyūkoku kyoka*) and overseas visits have resulted in immediate revocation of PR status or the applicant's "visa clock" (i.e., the tabulation of one's continuous period of residency being counted toward PR) being reset

to zero. *See* current official qualifications for PR at www.immi-moj.go.jp/english/tetuduki/kanri/shyorui/05.html.

49. www.moj.go.jp/content/000081971.pdf.

50. Interview, Inoue Hiroshi, Nippon Keidanren, in documentary "Sour Strawberries" (2008).

51. "Poll: 81 percent welcome foreigners of Japanese descent." *Japan Times/ Kyodo News*, March 2, 2013, archived at www.debito.org/?p=11213. Why the GOJ specifically phrased the question to focus upon "foreigners with Japanese ancestry" (as opposed to foreigners in general) is unclear.

52. Higuchi & Arudou (2008: 20–33).

53. *See* primary source testimonials on how laws influencing Immigration decisions can be altered through new bureaucratic guidelines and arbitrary enforcement: "How Japan's Immigration Bureau uses unlegislated bureaucratic guidelines to trump the letter of the law, in this case re obtaining Permanent Residency." *Debito.org*, December 18, 2011, www.debito.org/?p=9650; "Arbitrary bureaucratic hurdles for registering international marriages in Tokyo Edogawa-ku Ward office." *Debito.org*, December 15, 2011, www.debito.org/?p=9731; and so on.

54. *See* marriage screening procedures (down to what language the couple speaks together, how many people attended their wedding, and how many times the couple crossed the border both before and after marriage) using an official questionnaire (*shitsumonsho*) for Spouse Visas (*haigūsha biza*) at "Immigration Bureau violates privacy of marriage, in questioning Japanese spouses for longer-term visas." *Debito .org*, January 11, 2007, at www.debito.org/?p=158; Interview, January 19, 2007, with Sapporo Immigration Bureau's Mr. Yamamoto, regarding the purpose of this Spouse-Visa Questionnaire (which he had never seen before) at www.debito.org/?p =176. Regarding house visits, see primary source account at "Gaijinwife blog on her house check—is having authorities visit Permanent Residency applicant's home and thoroughly photograph its interior now standard operating procedure?" *Debito.org*, December 21, 2011, at www.debito.org/?p=9623.

55. "Japan's revolving-door immigration policy hard-wired to fail." *Japan Times*, March 6, 2012.

56. *See* inter alia "Competing foreign-worker plans face off." *Japan Times*, June 7, 2007; "Keidanren: Immigrant worker influx to halt labor shortage." *Japan Times*, October 15, 2008; and so on.

57. Kashiwazaki (2000: 443).

58. *See* inter alia Linger (2001), Roth (2002), Lesser, ed. (2003), Tsuda (2003), and so on.

59. Interview, Inoue Hiroshi, Nippon Keidanren, in documentary "Sour Strawberries" (2008).

60. www.jitco.or.jp/english/overview/index.html.

61. Example of discussions about said system at MHLW website at www.mhlw .go.jp/houdou/2008/06/h0613-6.html.

62. "*Ippō zenshin mo tarinu seifuron: Gaikokujin rōdōsha no taigū kaizen no yukue wa?*" [Arguments by the government lack even one step in the right direction. What is the direction for the better treatment of foreign laborers?] *Tōkyō Shinbun*,

December 3, 2006, page 24, section demanding the creation of an actual "*Rōdōsha Biza*" [Worker Visa] for the "Trainees." Full article translated by the author at www.debito.org/?p=105.

63. Higuchi & Arudou (2008: 72–77).

64. Japanese Trade Union Confederation (*Rengō*) minimum wages mapped out by prefecture at www.jtuc-rengo.or.jp/activity/roudou/chingin/, dated October 1, 2020.

65. Given the economic incentives behind employing cheaper workers with no labor law protections, one would assume far more workers have been hired as non-laborer Trainees than as laborer Researchers; official statistics, however, have been unclear and difficult to obtain. The Ministry of Justice Immigration Bureau reports that the *kenshūsei* in 1999 were 47,985 and the *ginō jisshūsei* were 11,032. By 2006, they were 92,846 and 41,000, respectively. *See* "*Kenshūsei oyobi ginō jisshūsei no nyūkoku, zairyū kanri ni kan-suru shishin*" [Aims in regard to administration of entry and status of Trainees and Practical Trainees], page one (www.moj.go.jp/PRESS/nyukan67-2.pdf). Managing agency JITCO says that the total number of "Trainees" hired between 1992 and 2005 was 416,009 (www.jitco.or.jp/english/overview/staticstics1.html). However, the same site notes the number of Technical Internship Program (as in *ginō jisshūsei*) *applicants* (i.e., people not necessarily accepted into this status) has only been 210,863 between 1993 and 2005 (www.jitco.or.jp/english/overview/staticstics2.html). Since neither of these sources separate *jisshūsei* from *kenshūsei*, it is difficult to ascertain how many "Trainees" graduated into the workforce as laborers protected by law.

66. *Tōkyō Shinbun*, December 3, 2006, ibid.

67. *Shūkan Diamondo*, June 5, 2004, cover. Archived at www.debito.org/shuukandiamondo060504.html.

68. *See Tōkyō Shinbun*, December 3, 2006, ibid., and more cases too numerous to include in their entirety here. Sample cases of abuse: (1) Chinese males and female assaulted, denied wages, and attempted forced repatriation; two different cases in "Foreign trainees injured in row with dry-cleaning firm over measly pay." *Mainichi Shinbun*, August 27, 2008; and "Wage row erupts between strawberry farms, sacked Chinese apprentices." *Mainichi Shinbun*, January 29, 2008. The latter resulted in a successful lawsuit for back pay; *see* "Employees win suit against Tochigi farms for unpaid wages, unfair dismissals." *Mainichi Shinbun*, February 11, 2008; "Foreigners win ¥17 million for trainee abuses." *Japan Times*, January 30, 2010. (2) Abuses inciting murder, "Slain farm association official took fees from both Chinese trainees, farmers." *Asahi Shinbun*, May 28, 2007. (3) Denial of basic rights, such as praying, religious fasting, cellphone use, writing letters, wiring money home, riding in a car, or staying out past 9 p.m., "Factory denies Muslim basic human rights." *Yomiuri Shinbun*, December 5, 2006. And (4) Child labor of boys and girls aged 13–15, "Gifu firms warned on Brazilian child labor." *Japan Times*, December 30, 2006. (4) Overwork and deaths, *see* "Dying to work: Japan Inc.'s foreign trainees." *Japan Times*, August 3, 2010. (5) Insights into how widespread and systematic these practices are: "Foreign trainees facing chronic abuses." *Kyodo News*, January 3, 2007;

"Foreign trainee abuse found at 452 entities." *Yomiuri Shinbun*, April 11, 2009, which writes:

> The Justice Ministry says it has found irregularities at a 452 companies and organizations that hosted foreign trainees last year. . . . Officials of the ministry said it had confirmed that the companies and organizations violated labor laws, such as by paying lower-than-minimum wages to foreign trainees. Of the total, 169 cases of entities making trainees work unpaid overtime were found and 155 cases concerned other labor law violations such as payment of illegally low wages.

See also "Foreign trainee program 'like human trafficking.'" *Yomiuri Shinbun*, June 29, 2011.

69. *See*, for example, "27 foreign trainees died in Japan in FY 2009." *Kyodo News*, July 6, 2010. Two facts of note were that eight "Trainees" had died from "unknown causes" (the others had died of "brain or heart diseases," bicycle accidents, and suicides); and that this was at that time reportedly the *second*-worst number of fatalities per annum. As for bans on dating, marriage, and sex, *see* "Left in limbo: Japan's haphazard immigration policies, disrespect for human rights." *Mainichi Shinbun*, April 19, 2019, archived at www.debito.org/?p=15634.

70. *See*, for example, "Slain farm association official took fees from both Chinese trainees, farmers." *Asahi Shinbun*, May 28, 2007; "Gifu firms warned on Brazilian child labor." *Japan Times*, December 30, 2006.

71. *See*, for example, "Sour Strawberries," 2008.

72. *See*, for example, Interview, labor union leader Torii Ippei, in "Sour Strawberries" ibid., who notes that places employing "Trainees" without labor abuses are "very rare" (*goku mare*). *See also* "Special Report: Foreign interns pay the price for Japan's labor shortage." *Reuters*, June 12, 2014.

73. "Japan sanctioning mass 'slave labor' by duping foreign trainees, observers say." *Japan Times*, November 23, 2014; U.S. State Department Country Reports on Human Rights Practices, Japan (2018) on the "Trainee" Program archived at www.debito.org/?p=15599.

74. *See*, for example, "Wage row erupts between strawberry farms, sacked Chinese apprentices." *Mainichi Shinbun*, January 29, 2008; "Dry-cleaning company boss reported to prosecutors over treatment of Chinese trainees." *Mainichi Shinbun*, April 9, 2009; "Chinese trainees file complaint with labor bureau over 350 yen per hour overtime." *Mainichi Shinbun*, October 27, 2009; "Employees win suit against Tochigi farms for unpaid wages, unfair dismissals." *Mainichi Shinbun*, February 11, 2008.

75. www.unic.or.jp/news_press/features_backgrounders/2805/?lang=en.

76. The Mainichi reports higher figures: "Japan received a total of 102,018 foreign trainees in 2007, according to the Immigration Bureau." *See* "1,000 foreign trainees forced to return home as firms feel pinch." *Mainichi Shinbun*, April 7, 2009.

77. "Japan enacts law to prevent abuse of foreign trainees." *Japan Times/Kyodo News*, November 18, 2016; "Japan looks to offer longer stays for technical interns, with caveats it hopes will limit immigration debate." *Japan Times*, April 12, 2018.

78. www.moj.go.jp/content/000081971.pdf.

79. "Japan moves to expand controversial foreign worker scheme." *Reuters*, April 2, 2014.

80. "Government to tighten controls on foreign trainee program." *Japan Today*, January 31, 2015.

81. "Japan's Cabinet approves bill to introduce new visa categories for foreign workers, to address shrinking workforce." *Japan Times*, November 2, 2018.

82. "Foreign trainee fatality data highlight safety and exploitation issues in Japan." *Japan Times/Kyodo News*, January 15, 2018.

83. www.otit.go.jp/files/user/statistics/e201002-1-5.pdf.

84. *See* 2019 statistics at www.otit.go.jp/files/user/statistics/e201002-6-2.pdf and www.otit.go.jp/files/user/statistics/e201002-6-3.pdf. 2018 statistics at www.otit.go.jp/files/user/statistics/e191001-18-6-2.pdf and www.otit.go.jp/files/user/statistics/e191001-18-6-3.pdf. More at www.otit.go.jp/fy2019statistic/.

85. "Japan Times & Kyodo: Foreign 'trainees' dying at rate of two to three a month, takes two years for one to be declared 'from overwork' (*karoushi*), more than a quarter from 'unknown causes.'" *Debito.org*, July 6, 2010, www.debito.org/?p=7111; "Mainichi Shinbun: NJ medical intern death from overwork finally officially recognized as *karoushi* after 2 years." *Debito.org*, February 14, 2013, www.debito.org/?p=10959; "Probe reveals 759 cases of suspected abuse and 171 deaths of foreign trainees in Japan." *Japan Times*, March 29, 2019. *See also Japan Times/Kyodo News*, January 15, 2018, ibid. This article notes:

> Akira Hatate, director of the Japan Civil Liberties Union and an expert on the trainee system, points out that there could be more cases involving foreign trainees due to the government's lax reporting standards. He said work-related accidents are more frequent among non-Japanese because they are "unfamiliar with Japanese workplaces (and) as they are usually working for small and midsize companies that give little consideration to safety and health in the workplace. Trainees (also) cannot communicate fluently in Japanese. There are also cases where trainees, who cannot work due to an injury, are forced to return home. Concealment of work-related accidents is rampant."

In terms of workplace violence, *see*, for example, "Kyodo: Foreign trainee slain, colleague wounded in rural Ibaraki attack, in oddly terse article (updated with news of another underreported NJ death)." *Debito.org*, February 26, 2015, www.debito.org/?p=13096.

86. "Japanese Workers Braved Radiation for a Temp Job." *New York Times*, April 9, 2011; "Japan's 'throwaway' nuclear workers." *Reuters*, June 24, 2011, archived at www.debito.org/?p=9162; "Special Report: Japan's homeless recruited for murky Fukushima clean-up." *Reuters*, December 29, 2013; "Bangladeshi asylum seekers tricked into radiation clean-up: Media." *Reuters India*, March 8, 2017; "Japan needs thousands of foreign workers to decommission Fukushima plant, prompting backlash from anti-nuke campaigners and rights activists." *South China Morning Post*, April 26, 2019, which subtitled, "Activists are not convinced working at the site is safe for anyone and they fear foreign workers will feel 'pressured' to ignore risks

if jobs are at risk. Towns and villages around the plant are still out of bounds because radiation levels are dangerously high."

87. Higuchi & Tanno (2003: 36).

88. "The scramble for foreign students." *Yomiuri Shinbun*, May 31, 2008.

89. Herbert (1996: 107–116).

90. "Global 30 Project Establishing University Network for Internationalization." Ministry of Education, undated, accessed April 13, 2021 at www.mext.go.jp/en/policy/education/highered/title02/detail02/sdetail02/1373894.htm.

91. *See*, for example, "Only top 30 percent of foreign students to be eligible for government handouts." *Kyodo News*, May 21, 2020, commentary at www.debito.org/?p=16086. In explaining this policy, MEXT commented, "With many foreign students eventually returning to their home countries, we have set a condition to limit the handout to promising talent most likely to contribute to Japan in the future."

92. *See*, for example, "Times Higher Education on MEXT: 'Japan's entrenched ideas hinder the push to attract more foreign students and staff.'" *Debito.org*, November 20, 2010, www.debito.org/?p=7616, quoting Dr. Paul Snowden, dean of the School of International Liberal Studies at Waseda University: "recruitment ads are often posted only in Japanese and on obscure government websites. There is also a general reluctance to hire foreigners, as Japanese universities either prefer very long-term commitments or offer only 'guest-style' short contracts. 'Attitudes have long been against foreign recruitment, and that needs to change.' He said it is common to encounter the view: 'We'll only take foreigners of Nobel prize standard—otherwise why should we deprive Japanese people of jobs?'"

For other systemic harassment that scholars are not protected from, *see also* "Cautionary tale: Bern on how a lack of protections against harassment in Japan's universities targets NJ regardless of Japan savviness and skill level." *Debito.org*, April 11, 2017, www.debito.org/?p=14552; "New discriminatory policy by Rakuten Mobile Inc., now 'stricter with foreigners,' refusing even Tokyo University MEXT Scholarship Students cellphones." *Debito.org*, May 4, 2019, www.debito.org/?p=15641; "Anonymous on Ethical Issues/Discriminatory practices being carried out by Tokyo and Kyoto Universities against MEXT scholars." *Debito.org*, June 14, 2019, www.debito.org/?p=15680; "Former student reports on how Tokyo International University segregates and exploits its foreign students." *Debito.org*, August 21, 2020, www.debito.org/?p=16212. For a perspective on how students were unprotected from official and administrative negligence during the 2020 COVID Pandemic, *see* "International Students Given Short Shrift by Japan Government." *Shingetsu News Agency*, March 31, 2021.

93. www.moj.go.jp/content/000081971.pdf; www.mext.go.jp/a_menu/koutou/ryugaku/1412692.htm

94. "Japan installs caution signal for sex traffic." *WomensENews.org*, July 18, 2005; "Law bends over backward to allow '*fuzoku*.'" *Japan Times*, May 27, 2008, noting, "There were approximately 1,200 soaplands in Japan and 17,500 sex-related businesses, including massage parlors and strip clubs, in 2006, according to statistics

released by the NPA"; "UN expert calls on Japan to boost action in combating human trafficking." *UN News*, July 17, 2009. *See also* interview with Jake Adelstein, *National Public Radio* "Fresh Air," November 19, 2009, transcribed at www.debito.org/?p=5148; the Japan Network Against Trafficking in Persons: http://jnatip.blogspot.com; and Patricia Aliperti's informative powerpoint, "Human Trafficking: Modern-day slavery for commercial sexual exploitation," delivered at Peace as a Global Language Conference, October 27, 2007, archived at www.debito.org/HumanTraffickingShortPresentation.ppt

95. "U.S. State Department blasts Japan in human trafficking report." *Asahi Shinbun*, June 30, 2011, quoting the report saying Japan is a destination, source, and transit country for men, women, and children subjected to forced labor and sex trafficking. The text of the 2011 State Department report is available at www.state.gov/g/tip/rls/tiprpt/2011/164232.htm.

96. www.moj.go.jp/content/000081971.pdf.

97. www.e-stat.go.jp/stat-search/files?page=1&layout=datalist&toukei=00300500&tstat=000001142246&cycle=0&stat_infid=000031964056&result_page=1&tclass1val=0 (accessed April 11, 2021); www.state.gov/report-to-congress-on-2021-trafficking-in-persons-interim-assessment-pursuant-to-the-trafficking-victims-protection-act/. Hepburn & Simon (2013) note:

> Among the nations examined is Japan, which has not elaborated a comprehensive anti-trafficking law. Although the government took a strong step forward in its 2009 Action Plan to Combat Trafficking in Persons by acknowledging that sex trafficking is not the only form of human trafficking, forced-labor victims continue to be marginalized. As a result of ethnocentric policies, the government prohibits foreign unskilled laborers from working in Japan. But the disparity between the nation's immigration posture and its labor needs has created a quandary. With a demand for inexpensive labor but without an adequate low wage labor force, Japan uses the government-run Industrial Training Program and Technical Internship Program to create a temporary and low-cost migrant workforce for employers. The stated purpose of the program is to transfer skill, technology, and knowledge to persons of other nations and thereby play a central role in the economic growth of developing nations, specifically those in East Asia. Instead, it has created opportunities for exploitation and human trafficking.

98. *Ekonomisuto*, January 15, 2008, page 16. The original policy trial balloon, as it appeared in the Western press, was to robotize Japanese health care. *See* "Japan's humanoid robots, better than people." *Economist* (London), December 20, 2005.

99. *See* inter alia "80 percent of hospitals interested in employing foreign nurses." *Yomiuri Shinbun*, March 12, 2008; "Language sets high hurdle for caregiver candidates." *Japan Times*, May 11, 2010; "Strict immigration rules may threaten Japan's future." *Washington Post*, July 28, 2010.

100. These agreements were accused of political subterfuge due to links with bilateral trade and investments. *See* "JPEPA lowers labor standards for Pinoy nurses, caregivers." *ABS-CBN News* (Philippines), October 11, 2008, which reports:

> [Dr. Gene Nisperos, vice chairperson of the Health Alliance for Democracy, or HEAD] said that under JPEPA, nurses' labor standards, job security, migrant and labor rights, benefits and wages, and other protection for Filipino nurses and caregivers will be compromised "in exchange for so-called trade and investments." Because of this, the HEAD is calling on all nurses, doctors, caregivers and health professionals to denounce all the 16 senators who voted in favor of what they described to be as "onerous trade agreement. . . ." "This is labor export policy at its worst. Senators are conniving with the Arroyo government in allowing the unbridled exploitation of Filipino health workers and professionals," [HEAD Secretary General Dr. Geneve Rivera] said.

101. More information on the nursing examination at the MHLW website: www.mhlw.go.jp/kouseiroudoushou/shikaku_shiken/kangoshi/index.html.

102. "First foreign nurses pass national exam." *Yomiuri Shinbun*, March 27, 2010; "Strict immigration rules may threaten Japan's future." *Washington Post*, July 28, 2010; "High language barrier for nurses." *Yomiuri Shinbun*, April 13, 2010; "Nurse trainees leave Japan despite 1-year extension." *Asahi Shinbun*, June 15, 2012.

103. "Government sets target for 10,000 Vietnamese caregivers, needs additional 550,000 by 2025." *Japan Times/Kyodo News*, July 25, 2018. Cambodia and Indonesia were also on the shortlist for invites.

104. "Foreign nursing trainees face unfair hurdles." *Asahi Shinbun*, Point of View Column, May 13, 2009; "EPA foreign nurses and caregivers working in Japan urgently need help." "Language hurdle trips up Indonesian nurses." *Yomiuri Shinbun*, January 5, 2012. An example of the language hurdle in the nurses' exam cited in the media was the word *jokusō* 褥瘡 (bedsore), which is so obscure that an English translation was not available on the Yahoo Japan Dictionary. However, when calls for amendments to examinations for these "Trainees" came forth in the media, the official response was as follows: "An official at the Ministry of Health, Labor and Welfare dismissed suggestions that special considerations be made for language barriers, saying that both Japan and Indonesia agreed that the trainees would 'attain the required qualifications in line with Japanese law under the (economic partnership) agreement.'"

105. "Job offers for Indonesian nurses drop by 60 percent in Japan." *Antara News* (Indonesia), February 18, 2010.

106. "Language hurdle trips up Indonesian nurses." *Yomiuri Shinbun*, January 5, 2012.

107. "Foreign caregiver exits put program in doubt," and "Foreign caregiver program faces tightening." *Kyodo News*, June 2, 2012, and August 4, 2012, respectively. For the incorporation of nursing and care-giving visa programs into "Trainees," *see*, for example, "Government to tighten controls on foreign trainee program." *Japan Today*, January 31, 2015.

108. MHLW's project outline at www.mhlw.go.jp/houdou/2009/03/dl/h0331-10a.pdf (accessed April 13, 2021). The *New York Times* reports a broader goal of this project—housecleaning:

> Japan has been keen to help foreign workers go home, thus easing pressure on domestic labor markets and getting thousands off unemployment rolls. "Japan's economy has hit

> a rainstorm. There won't be good employment opportunities for a while, so that's why we're suggesting that the Nikkei Brazilians go home," said Jiro Kawasaki, a former health minister and senior lawmaker of the ruling Liberal Democratic Party. "Naturally, we don't want those same people back in Japan after a couple of months," Mr. Kawasaki said, who led the ruling party task force that devised the repatriation plan, part of a wider emergency strategy to combat rising unemployment in Japan. "Then Japanese taxpayers would ask, 'What kind of ridiculous policy is this? . . .'"
>
> Mr. Kawasaki, the former health minister, said the economic slump was a good opportunity to overhaul Japan's immigration policy as a whole. "We should stop letting unskilled laborers into Japan. We should make sure that even the three-K jobs are paid well, and that they are filled by Japanese," he said. "I do not think that Japan should ever become a multi-ethnic society" like the United States, which "has been a failure on the immigration front," Mr. Kawasaki added. That failure, he said, was demonstrated by extreme income inequalities between rich Americans and poor immigrants.

See "Japan Pays Foreign Workers to Go Home." *New York Times*, April 22, 2009.

Similarly, Arimura Haruko, minister for the empowerment of women in the Abe administration, said:

> Many developed countries have experienced immigration. The world has been shaken by immigrants who come into contact with extremist thinking like that of ISIL, bundle themselves in explosives and kill people indiscriminately in the country where they were brought up. If we want to preserve the character of the country and pass it on to our children and grandchildren in better shape, there are reforms we need to carry out now to protect those values.

See "Japan Cabinet minister wary of opening 'Pandora's box' of immigration." *Bloomberg*, May 12, 2015, commentary at www.debito.org/?p=13314.

See also "Japan: Now open to foreign workers, but still just as racist?" Subtitle: "Japan is opening its doors to blue-collar workers from overseas to fill the gaps left by an ageing population, Resident 'gaijin' warn that the new recruits—whom the government refuses to call 'immigrants'—might not feel so welcome in Japan." *South China Morning Post*, May 11, 2019.

109. *Terrie's Take* No. 492, November 2, 2008, ibid.

110. From an accounting point of view, this up-front subsidy probably meant long-term savings for Japan, because leaving Japan would mean the Nikkei would forfeit their *nenkin* pension, since Japan's *nenkin* system currently requires ten years of minimum investment for any payout upon retirement (www.nenkin.go.jp/international/japanese-system/nationalpension/nationalpension.html; *see also* Higuchi & Arudou (2008: 280–289); there is no totalization agreement in place between Japan and Brazil/Peru so that employment on either side of the Pacific would count toward their pension). Thus, the terms of the subsidy also meant Nikkei not collecting their paid-in unemployment benefit. In fact, the program offered financial incentives for those already collecting unemployment benefit to leave Japan quickly, where those with more than thirty days left on their collection would receive a bonus of 100,000 yen, and with more than sixty days left would receive 200,000 yen.

111. The Health Ministry reported that it had received about 16,000 Nikkei applicants for the stipend between April and November 2009, while 40,000–50,000 were reported to have returned to South America at their own expense. *See* "Number of immigrants applying for repatriation aid hit 16,000 by mid-November." *Kyodo News*, November 24, 2009.

112. "Local government makes foreign welfare applicant sign up for cash to return to Brazil." *Mainichi Shinbun*, September 14, 2009.

113. www.e-stat.go.jp/SG1/estat/List.do?lid=000001089591 (accessed August 12, 2012); Ministry of Justice sites www.moj.go.jp/content/000105779.pdf, www.moj.go.jp/content/000108878.pdf (accessed April 28, 2014), and www.e-stat.go.jp/SG1/estat/List.do?lid=000001127507 (accessed February 13, 2015).

114. As the AP reports, Wajin blood conceits were fundamental to these visa regimes:

> In the early 1990s, Tokyo relaxed its relatively tight immigration laws to allow special entry permits for foreigners of Japanese ancestry in South America to make up for a labor shortage at this nation's then-booming factories. They took the so-called "three-K" jobs [which] Japanese had previously shunned. Before their arrival, many such jobs had gone to Iranians and Chinese. But the government . . . was eager to find a labor pool it felt would more easily adapt to Japanese society, said [Nishiyama Iwao, of the Association of Nikkei & Japanese Abroad, a government-backed organization that connects people of Japanese ancestry]. So by virtue of their background, these foreigners of Japanese descent . . . were offered special visa status. "They may speak some Japanese, and have a Japanese way of thinking," Nishiyama said. "They have Japanese blood, and they work hard."

See "Japan government gives cash for jobless foreigners of Japanese ancestry to go home." *Associated Press*, April 1, 2009.

115. The GOJ offered a retraining program for 5,000 *Nikkei* unemployed (*see* www.mhlw.go.jp/houdou/2009/03/dl/h0331-10a.pdf). However, this amounted to only about 1 percent of all Nikkei workers. Also, the retraining program was only offered to Nikkei, meaning preference was again given to Wajin blood ties.

116. "Golden parachutes' mark failure of race-based policy." *Japan Times*, April 7, 2009; "Japan to Immigrants: Thanks, but you can go home now." *TIME Magazine*, April 20, 2009. Regarding the "revolving door" labor market, *TIME* notes:

> And if Nikkei Brazilians, Peruvians and others who have lost their jobs go home, what will Japan do? Last week, Prime Minister Taro Aso unveiled a long-term growth strategy to create millions of jobs and add $1.2 trillion to GDP by 2020. But the discussion of immigration reform is notoriously absent in Japan, and reaching a sensible policy for foreign workers has hardly got under way. Encouraging those foreigners who would actually like to stay in Japan to leave seems a funny place to start.

Four years later, following its successful bid for the 2020 Olympics and fearing a labor shortage for infrastructure construction, Japan lifted its three-year visa ban on the Nikkei who accepted the airfare deal. The GOJ has also announced a similar relaxation of visa policy for other foreign workers. *See*, for example, "Ban lifted on Nikkei who got axed, airfare." *Japan Times*, October 15, 2013; "Foreign trainee program given OK for expansion; extra labor urgently needed for 2020 Games, Tohoku rebuilding." *Japan Times*, April 4, 2014.

117. *See*, for example, "Ban lifted on 'nikkei' who got axed, airfare. But Japanese-Brazilians must have work contract before coming back." *Japan Times*, October 15, 2013, commentary at www.debito.org/?p=11916; "Yomiuri: 4th generation Nikkei to get new visa status. Come back, all is forgiven! Just don't read the fine print." *Debito.org*, August 9, 2017, www.debito.org/?p=14702. However, Nikkei could qualify for the visa as long as they (a) passed a Japanese language test, (b) were young enough to devote their best working years here, (c) came alone, and (d) only stayed three years. That did not attract many applicants. *See* "Japanese-Brazilians snub Tokyo's diaspora residency program. Effort to bring over young workers attracts zero applications in 3 months." *Nikkei News*, October 25, 2018, commentary at www.debito.org/?p=15191.

This initial snubbing was even after the GOJ loosened the law enough to allow child labor; *see* "Japan Times: Preferential visa system extended to foreign 4th-generation Japanese [*sic*]: Allowing even NJ minors to build Olympic facilities!" *Debito.org*, June 11, 2018, www.debito.org/?p=14970, where it was reported, "At present, fourth-generation ethnic Japanese are required to meet certain conditions to get a visa, such as being single minors who live with their parents, but can't work full-time. Under the new system, minors will be able to work." However, under the law, Wajin under the age of eighteen can only work part-time (*arubaito*), not full-time, starting from age fifteen. *See* https://workin.jp/work/mc-parttime-jobage. On a related note, NHK reported in 2012 that even Burmese refugees turned down GOJ invitations to work in Japan, electing instead to remain in a Thai refugee camp! *See* archive and discussion at www.debito.org/?p=10943.

118. *Japan Times*, March 6, 2012, ibid. As of July 9, 2012, the nominal maximum visa period is five years, although administrative "discretion" does not necessarily guarantee that it will be awarded frequently. *See* Immigration's official website on the changes in the Immigration laws at www.immi-moj.go.jp/english/newimmiact/newimmiact_english.html. Further, the "Points System" itself became problematic for being too strict and not giving many "points" for people who might be well assimilated by having, for example, high Japanese language ability. The policy was deemed a failure by 2013, with only 700 people applying for the 2,000 slots six months after its launch. *See* "GOJ's new 'Points System' to attract 'higher-skilled' NJ being reviewed due to dearth of applications, impossibly high hurdles." *Debito.org*, March 24, 2013, www.debito.org/?p=11300; "Initiative fails to lure high-skilled foreigners." *Japan Times*, December 24, 2013; "Yomiuri on 'Points System' visa: 'Too strict,' few takers, under review by Justice Ministry." *Debito.org*, August 7, 2013, www.debito.org/?p=11817; Debito Arudou, "Hate, muzzle and poll: A top ten of issues for 2014." *Japan Times*, January 1, 2015.

Indicatively, the Immigration Bureau also issued a website in English (offline as of 2021) advertising for "highly skilled foreign professionals," complete with racialized images, mostly non-Asian in appearance, belying an apparent presumption that "highly skilled" meant Western. *See* "Immigration Bureau: Points System visa and visual images of who might be qualified to apply." *Debito.org*, March 7, 2014, www.debito.org/?p=12142.

119. According to Administrative Solicitor Akira Higuchi (interviews, 2007–2008).

120. Even the largest government employer of language teachers in Japan, the Japan Exchange and Teaching (JET) Programme, had until recently for almost all of its foreign employees only one-year contracts with the possibility of two extensions. This has since been extended to five years maximum, but almost no noncitizen JET can find a permanent career within the JET Programme. It is, by design, a temporary work program. *See* the official JET website at www.jetprogramme.org.

121. "Japan gets tough on visa violators: One-day overstay can bring time in cell, 5-year banishment." *San Francisco Chronicle*, May 10, 2004, which cited cases of people being strip-searched, incarcerated (at their own expense of around $600 per day) as hardened criminals, and banned for five years for renewal oversights. From May 27, 2004, fines for visa expiries increased tenfold from 300,000 yen to 3 million, and maximum expulsion from Japan after deportation doubled from five to ten years. *See also* Debito Arudou, "Visa villains: Immigration law overdoes enforcement, penalties," and Eric Johnston and Debito Arudou, "Visa crackdown: Don't get burned." *Japan Times*, June 29, 2004, and June 28, 2005, respectively.

122. Regarding the "gaijin tax" criticism, the comparison of REPs to a tax is appropriate. When reforms to the Immigration law that were promulgated in 2009 revealed the abolition of the REPs, Eurobiz Magazine ("Your new alien registration card," August 2010) reported, "Without re-entry permit income, currently ¥6,000 for multiple re-entry, the changes are likely to lighten the government's coffers. 'This is a huge reduction in our revenue,' said [Matsuno Hiroaki, a deputy director at the Ministry of Justice]. 'The Ministry of Finance is angry.'"

123. There is also the issue of Japan's admittance of refugees, which is one of the lowest of refugee-admitting countries worldwide and a source of international criticism; the "Temporary Refuge" visa, for example, is capped at only thirty people per year (www.moj.go.jp/content/000081971.pdf), and has only granted, out of 3,118 applicants between 1982 and 2003, refugee status to 315 people (*Kyodo News*, May 27, 2004). More in Kashiwazaki (2000: 450). That said, refugee status is not an issue of Japan's labor import labor markets and is not easily reduced to a racialized issue within the scope of this research, so let us have this footnote suffice as acknowledgment of the issue. *See also* "Mainichi Shinbun on emerging GOJ policies towards refugees and immigration, still not allowing them to stay in Japan: 'tourists yes, refugees and immigrants no.'" *Debito.org*, October 1, 2015, www.debito.org/?p=13567.

124. Or a Beatle. A 1966 Beatles concert given at the Budōkan was reportedly the first one done by a foreign pop group in an arena allegedly reserved for Japanese events, such as sumō, so it occasioned loud protests from conservative elements in Japan. They were considered a "bad influence on Japanese society," after John Lennon was quoted at a press conference as saying, "We're more interesting than wrestling, anyway." Security measures restricted them to their hotel rooms meeting business sponsors (Paul and Linda McCartney managed to briefly escape and go shopping, but they were soon apprehended by police), while 3,000 police were seated

in the Budōkan with telephoto lenses to stop the 10,000 spectators waving fan banners or even standing up during the concert. George Harrison likened their stay in Japan to "a military manoeuver," while Ringo Starr remarked that people had simply gone "barmy." The Beatles never returned to Japan as a group to perform. *See The Beatles Anthology* DVD (2003) Disc 5, Section 14.

125. This may be one reason why the Tokyo Metropolitan Police (*keishichō*) seem to be much more assiduous in random ARC ID checks and racial profiling, as I have heard more reports of stoppages in the Kantō Area than anywhere else in Japan.

126. Also at issue is a matter of linguistics when searching for suspects. As I wrote in "Police, media must consider plight of those caught in linguistic dragnet: Racialized terms thrown about by cops and parroted by news outlets have consequences." *Japan Times*, May 14, 2013:

> If there is a crime where the perpetrator might be a non-Japanese (NJ), the National Police Agency (and by extension the media, which often parrots police reports without analysis) tends to use racialized typology in its search for suspects. The NPA's labels include *hakujin* for Caucasians (often with Hispanics lumped in), *kokujin* for Africans or the African diaspora, *burajirujin-kei* for all South Americans, and *ajia-kei* for garden-variety "Asians" (who must somehow not look sufficiently "Japanese," although it's unclear clear how that limits the search: Aren't Japanese technically "Asian" too?). . . . But when the suspect is of uncertain ethnic origin but somehow clearly "not Japanese," the media's default term is *gaikokujin-fū* (foreign-looking). Lumping suspects into a "Japanese" or "not Japanese" binary is in fact extremely unhelpful during a search for a suspected criminal, because it puts any NJ, or visible minority in Japan (including many Japanese citizens), under the dragnet.

127. An eyewitness account, as I was living in Sapporo; I even saw footage on NHK of lines of policemen systematically searching grassy highway hillsides as a clear example of busywork overkill. *See also* "G8 Summit: Breathtaking venue with no protesters to spoil the view." *Guardian*, July 4, 2008; Debito Arudou, "Summit wicked this way comes." *Japan Times*, April 22, 2008; Debito Arudou, "July forecast: Rough, with ID checks mainly in the north." *Japan Times*, July 1, 2008.

128. *See* "*Samitto kaisai ni awaseta kōen shiyō no jisshuku yōsei ni tsuite*" [About our demand for you to refrain from using the park during the Summit]. Author: *Kankyō-kyoku midori no suishinbu midori no kanri ka* [Environmental Bureau, Administrative Section for the Promotion of Greenery, Sapporo City), fax dated January 17, 2008, archived at www.debito.org/wp-content/uploads/2008/04/sapporoshi011708.jpg.

129. Hokkaidō was not the only place on alert. Primary source testimonials on the level of security measures may be found on Debito.org from www.debito.org/?p=1770#comment-164272.

130. Interview, police officer Ōtomo, Hokkaido Police badge #522874, at the Japan Air Lines Arrivals Lounge, New Chitose Airport, June 19, 2008. Transcript at www.debito.org/?p=1752.

131. "Reports of reporter detentions upon entry at Tokyo Immigration." Kimura Kayoko, *Nikkan Berita*, June 28, 2008.

132. For example, I was racially profiled for an ID check and personal questions at New Chitose Airport on June 19, 2008. I hand-delivered a public letter of protest (*kōgibun*) to the Hokkaidō Police Headquarters and held a press conference on June 25, 2008 (archived at www.debito.org/?p=1761). The police representatives refused to accept the "letter of protest" as is, because it was not entitled "letter of request" (*yōseibun*). They also refused to go on the record regarding any of my questions ("What are your criteria being used to stop people for ID checks?" and "How will you improve this system so that there is no racial profiling?"), refused to be quoted for a newspaper column, refused to allow a recording of our meeting, and refused to allow any reporters to be present at our meeting. The representative in charge, *Dōkei Sōdan Madoguchi's* Mr. Kawabe, refused to give me his namecard (*meishi*), and said, in defense of police operations targeting "foreigners" (in paraphrase), that "foreigners" might be illegal workers or visa overstayers, so checking their identities on a regular basis is necessary.

When I asked him about more sophistication toward Japan's international residents, multiethnic children, naturalized citizens, and other Non-Wajin who would not fall into these categories, he avoided answering and instead asked for continued cooperation with their enforcement of public safety. Afterward, the Hokkaidō Police sent me no written response about this issue. Archive of this event and Japanese media reactions at www.debito.org/?p=1763.

133. "Big Brother comes to Kobe." Reporter Eric Johnston, writing for Debito .org, June 4, 2008 (www.debito.org/?p=1710), who notes, "Among those of us in the foreign press who have an inkling as to how Japan works, the consensus was the prominent display of force [by the police presence at the environment summit] was less about beefing up security for visiting dignitaries and more about beefing up the police and security budget." *See also* "G8 security steps hit as dangerous precedent." *Japan Times*, June 28, 2008.

134. McCormack & Yonetani (2000: 2).

135. *"Ijō na fun'iki ni tsutsumarete naigaijin reipu ni yoru fuhon'i na akachan shussan made ga mondai ni natte orimasu."* *Miyagi Kengikai Teireikai* 283, June 27, 2000. When I interviewed Konno by phone on July 5, 2002, after the World Cup had finished without instances of rape or property damage, I asked him if he would retract his public statement. He said he would not, as he personally has nothing against "foreigners" and he has many "foreign" friends. He also argued that if these measures and caution had not been taken, perhaps there would have been more of the incidents he had anticipated. *See* Konno's initial remarks in context at www.2002rifu.net/problem/prb-hooligan2.html.

136. "Beware the soccer hooligans." *Los Angeles Times*, May 22, 2002.

137. These security measures were also implemented nationwide; *see* "Hooligan phobia triggers siege mentality." *Japan Times*, May 31, 2002.

138. Complete archive of World Cup 2002 articles, eyewitness reports, and opinion pieces at www.debito.org/worldcup2002.html.

139. Compare this with the lax enforcement of measures regarding drunk and disruptive twenty-year-old Wajin "hooligans" at local government *Seijinshiki* Coming of

Age Ceremonies nationwide. Of course, these miscreants are not called "hooligans" in the Japanese media. *See* my archive of *Seijinshiki* disruptions and lax enforcement reported in the media in January 2004 at www.debito.org/seijinshikihooligans.html.

140. www.debito.org/worldcupkonnofollowup.html.

141. "Police to flood Shibuya as Japan kicks off World Cup campaign." *Japan Times*, June 11, 2014.

142. "Japan to beef up nuclear security before Rugby World Cup, Olympics." *Mainichi Shinbun*, July 11, 2018.

143. "Triumph of Tokyo Olympic bid sends wrong signal to Japan's resurgent right." *Japan Times*, October 1, 2013; "Over budget and fraught with problems, Tokyo Games spark calls for Olympic reforms." *VOA News*, February 04, 2021.

144. "Move eyed to raise Japanese crew numbers." *Asahi Shinbun*, May 22, 2007, which notes:

> The Ministry of Land, Infrastructure and Transport aims to increase the number of Japanese crew members by about 50 percent in 10 years to secure stable maritime transportation, an integral part of the nation's trading infrastructure. Foreign nationals account for more than 90 percent of crews of ocean-going vessels operated by Japanese companies. . . . The transport ministry's move was prompted by concern there would be too few people to operate ships if natural disasters, political turmoil or other emergencies flared in the home nations of non-Japanese crew members.

145. Regarding the NPA, there is no public guideline saying police officers cannot marry noncitizens, but anecdotal evidence from several sources suggests that it will affect their advancement potential. *See* "Japanese police cannot marry non-Japanese?" *Debito.org*, November 11, 2006, www.debito.org/?p=71. Regarding the Self-Defense Forces, *see* "MSDF officers with foreign spouses to be moved from sensitive posts." *Kyodo News*, June 28, 2007, which reports, hilariously:

> The Maritime Self-Defense Force plans to move officers with foreign spouses away from posts with access to military secrets after sensitive data was leaked through an officer with a Chinese wife, the *Sankei Shinbun* reported. . . . A thirty-three-year-old petty officer allegedly obtained confidential data on the [US-developed Aegis combat system] without authorization. The leak came to light after the officer's Chinese wife was arrested in January for a visa violation. However, an unconfirmed newspaper report later said the leak may have occurred by accident when the officer was swapping pornography over the Internet.

More serious was the feedback Debito.org received regarding this article:

> My current spouse is in the SDF and the other day I learned a very disturbing fact about the nature of our relationship—when he is on base and when he talks to his military associates I am Japanese. The reason for this he says is a very old rule in the SDF that members are not allowed to fraternize with foreigners. Period. And that while the penalty for him is negligible . . . his violation of this rule could bring the military police to my doorstep for interrogation and a search and seizure of my electronic equipment. He believes it's more doubtful as I'm non-Asian but says this has happened recently with the Chinese wives of SDF personnel. . . . I'm a national security risk because I'm not Japanese? My spouse

> couldn't cite the wording of the law but I'm curious—how are second and third generation citizens perceived? It's the grey "gaijin" box again.

Full text archived at www.debito.org/?p=460.

146. "Overseas work, study seen as negative point for anyone handling state secrets." *Japan Times/Kyodo News*, December 8, 2014, which notes, "The documents presented by the intelligence and research office at a meeting with other government bodies in November 2011 state that the experience of attending schools overseas or foreign schools in Japan as well as working abroad or working for foreign companies 'could be an opportunity to nurture a special feeling about foreign countries.' The papers said such people 'tend to be influenced by' approaches from foreign countries and there is a 'risk' that they 'prioritize the benefits of foreign countries and voluntarily leak secrets.'" How this will affect Japan's international citizens and Visible Minorities trying to get civil service jobs despite the Nationality Clause is unclear. *See also* Julian Ryall, "Firms' conservative hiring holds back Japan." *DW.com*, May 31, 2013, which notes:

> Many young Japanese students go abroad to study with high hopes. They return home with foreign degrees and even higher hopes, only to be shot down by conservative company ideals. . . . Tanaka, who does not want her real name or the name of her company used in this article because it could affect her career, began work in April of this year and had high hopes that the years she spent studying overseas would make her a popular candidate with Japanese employers. Instead, it seems, the effort and money that went into perfecting her English skills in the UK may have been wasted as Japanese firms do not always welcome potential recruits who have been exposed to foreign ways of thinking and behaving. . . . A survey conducted in March 2012 by Disco, a Tokyo-based recruitment company, determined that less than one in four firms planned to hire Japanese applicants who had studied abroad. Even among major, blue-chip companies, less than 40 percent said they would employ Japanese who had attended a foreign university.

147. "Fears growing over land grabs: Foreigners buying here; Japan may be tardy overseas," and "Debate starts on restricting foreign purchases of land." *Japan Times*, December 18, 2010, and January 21, 2011, respectively. Ironically, the first article inadvertently refers to a hypocritical lack of comity: "With water and food security becoming a hot topic in recent years, aggressive land purchases by foreign interests are also taking place worldwide. Many emerging economies, including China, South Korea and the United Arab Emirates, have reportedly snapped up farmland in Africa with the aim of producing crops there. Perhaps belatedly, Japan has also started investing in overseas farmland." *See also* "Foreign buyers snap up land: Survey shows many people use Japanese names to hide acquisitions." *Yomiuri Shinbun*, April 28, 2012; "Local governments swallow scare stories over 'foreigners' buying strategic land." *Asahi Shinbun*, December 25, 2012.

148. This spying and infiltration activity targeting Muslims and people connected to the Muslim communities was discovered thanks to a leak through file-sharing software within the Tōkyō Metropolitan Police Department counterterrorism database. *See* "Muslims in shock over police 'terror' leak." *Japan Times*, November 9, 2010.

Japan Times notes the detail of the investigations and data, including "vast amounts of personal information, including birthplaces, home and work addresses, names and birthdays of spouses, children and associates, personal histories and immigration records. Even the names of local mosques visited by the 'suspects' are included." Within a month, this data had hit bookshelves: "Published by Tokyo publishing house Dai-San Shokan, the 469-page book is titled '*Ryūshutsu "Kōan Tero Jōhō" Zen Dēta*' (Leaked police terrorism info: All data) [and] carries the names, photos and addresses of foreign residents who have apparently been subject to MPD investigations, as well as those of MPD bureau investigators in charge of international terrorism." *See* "'MPD data' book wreaks havoc: Foreign residents who had private info exposed express fear, anger." *Yomiuri Shinbun*, November 29, 2010. *See also* "Japan Center for Michigan Universities: Report and video interview of Muslim Lawyer Hayashi Junko on issues faced by Muslims in Japan (surveillance by police, including of Japanese kith and kin)." *Debito.org*, August 12, 2016, www.debito.org/?p=14151.

149. On January 15, 2014, the Tōkyō District Court ordered the Tōkyō Metropolitan Government (Tōkyō-to) to compensate seventeen Muslims, who had been "forced to leave their jobs and live apart from their families," and sued for 90.2 million yen for invasion of privacy. However, the Court ruling punished only the leaking of the information, not the collection of it. Judge Shiseki Masumitsu acknowledged the need for surveillance of the Muslims as "an unavoidable measure to prevent international terrorism," meaning that NPA racially profiling and spying on Japan's Muslims is neither discriminatory nor illegal. This was upheld by the Supreme Court in 2016. *See* "Muslims file suit over anti-terror investigations." *Yomiuri Shinbun*, May 18, 2011; "Tokyo ordered to pay police leak compensation." *NHK World*, January 15, 2014; "Tokyo ordered to pay Muslims." *Japan Times*, January 16, 2014; "Plaintiffs win damages for privacy violation: Tokyo ordered to pay Muslims." *Kyodo News*, January 16, 2014; "It's OK to snoop on Muslims on basis of religion, rules top court." *Asahi Shinbun*, August 2, 2016, commentary at www.debito.org/?p=14145.

See also details of the Islam Mohamed Himu Case, whose forty-three days of detention and erroneous publicizing of alleged al-Qaeda links resulted in a court victory against media, at "High-profile arrest, low-key release spells disaster for Bangladeshi businessman and his compatriots living in Japan." *Japan Times*, August 31, 2004; "Alleged al-Qaeda link sinks vindication: Bangladeshi wants apology, claims he was falsely accused by police, press." *Japan Times*, April 2, 2005; "Sankei newspaper ordered to compensate foreigner over Al Qaeda slur." *Mainichi Shinbun*, December 11, 2007.

150. "Immigration crackdown seen as paving the way for state to expel valid visa-holders." *Japan Times*, August 19, 2015, commentary at www.debito.org/?p=13491.

151. *See* Arudou (2006a: 139–140; 2006b: 206–207). Primary source material is "*Rainichi gaikokujin hanzai no genjō*" [current situation of crimes committed by foreigners coming to Japan], Chapter 2, "*Rainichi gaikokujin hanzai taisaku*" [policy against crimes committed by foreigners coming to Japan], Section 1.1, National Police Agency White Paper, 2000. Courtesy of www.npa.go.jp/kokusai2/h12/contents.htm [dead link as of October 2010].

152. *See* www.moj.go.jp/ENGLISH/issues/issues04.html (earliest download November 2010, link now dead but available on Wayback Machine).

153. Kashiwazaki (2000: 441).

154. The average height of buildings in Tōkyō in 1965 was only 1.7 stories, meaning people living in the increasingly overpopulated capital were sleeping several to a room. From then, GOJ policy focused on increasing vertical living space, creating the cheap, hastily constructed *danchi* "rabbit hutch" system that is still a hallmark of life in Japan. *See* "Japan: $18 million an acre." *TIME Magazine*, January 8, 1965, archived with analysis at www.debito.org/?p=333.

Chapter 6

A "Chinaman's Chance" in Japanese Court

As discussed in the previous two chapters, the components of any national discourse include laws on the books, the creation of those laws in the public policymaking arena, and the interpretation and enforcement of those laws. This chapter will focus on the interpretation.

The role of any judicial branch is to interpret the law on a case-by-case basis. When managers and administrators create policies and directives counter to the spirit of the law, an impartial judiciary should offer safeguards. However, Japan's judiciary has not fulfilled this: noncitizens and Visible Minorities have been overtly denied equal protection under the law in numerous criminal or civil cases. Let us now consider the differentiated judicial standards in bellwether cases, with the caveat that this shorter chapter is a seminal attempt to launch a debate on racialized jurisprudence in Japan.

CIVIL CASES: LAX STANDARDS OF JURISPRUDENCE IF CLAIMANT IS A NONCITIZEN

Chapter 3 has already mentioned a few cases of civil court decisions regarding racial discrimination in Japan (i.e., the Bortz Case, the Otaru Onsens Case, the McGowan Case, and the Yener Case). The first two initially found for the noncitizen plaintiff due to international treaty obligations, but the latter two eroded the scope of those precedents (to the point where a self-admitted racist defendant was found not guilty due to alleged language barriers and semantic technicalities). Also, punitive damages were reduced to the point where they neither compensate the victim nor deter the discriminator. This chapter will argue how other cases demonstrate clear discriminatory patterns emerging within the jurisprudence itself. Let's open with the Valentine Case:

The Valentine Case: Racialized Conceits Delegitimize Eyewitness Testimony

U. C. Valentine,[1] a black man of Nigerian nationality, was apprehended by police on December 9, 2003, during a NPA policy campaign against touts handing billets to passersby in Roppongi. Pinned to the ground by several police, Valentine claimed that (a) during the scuffle he was kicked by a police officer below the knee several times until his leg broke; and (b) while in detention and under interrogation for ten days, he was denied access to medical attention and hospitalization until he signed a confession, which permanently damaged his leg and leaves him in constant pain.[2] The police claimed in court that there was no specific violence directed toward him during restraining, and that he had run into a bar sign when trying to flee from police. Valentine sued the Tōkyō Municipal Government (*Tōkyō-to*) in civil court for damages (including medical bills for several surgeries to his leg and mental trauma), but on March 29, 2007, the Tōkyō District Court ruled against Valentine.

While there were several irregularities in the jurisprudence (including an implausible explanation for how the leg got injured, evidence lost and unsubmitted, and medical testimony from qualified doctors dismissed which indicated that police denying Valentine medical treatment had made his leg worse),[3] the important precedent set for the purposes of this research was the judges' dismissal of testimony (stating that the police had injured Valentine) by an eyewitness named "Francis." In the judges' words (19): "*As Francis is closely acquainted with the plaintiff, visiting him in hospital and associating with him in Kabukichō's black community*, under no circumstances (*tōtei*) can we accept his eyewitness testimony as having any objectivity or credibility"[4] (my translation and emphasis). This clear attribution of doubt to an eyewitness due not only to community proximity but also to being part of the "black community" was not similarly applied to the community of police officers, indicating a different standard of evidence based upon nationality/racialized grounds. Upon appeal, more doctors testified that police claims about the causes of injuries were implausible, but the Tōkyō High Court upheld the District Court verdict on June 29, 2010.[5]

CRIMINAL CASES: LAX STANDARDS OF JURISPRUDENCE IF CRIME VICTIM IS A NONCITIZEN

While it is difficult to offer a comprehensive report on Japanese jurisprudence in a book this expansive, let us now consider a few cases where racialized paradigms influenced how crimes involving noncitizens are treated by Japan's law enforcement. For example, there have been at least three high-profile murders of noncitizen women in Japan in recent years by Japanese men, and four murders/unexplained deaths of noncitizen men. For the sake of brevity, I will devote one paragraph describing each case and relate them to the scope of this research.

The Lucie Blackman Case

The Lucie Blackman Case involves the drugging, rape, and murder by sexual predator and serial killer Obara Jōji of several women who worked in Japan's "water trades" (*mizu shōbai*) over three decades.[6] Lucie Blackman, a Caucasian former British Airways stewardess who switched to Tōkyō's lucrative nightclub hostess scene, disappeared on July 1, 2000. Her dismembered body parts were found encased in cement in a Kanagawa cave near Obara's seaside dacha in February 2001. After seven months of bungled police searches, Obara was later arrested, but only after investigations by overseas private detectives paid for by the Blackman family, ignored leads involving other women who had escaped Obara's clutches, videotaped sexual assaults on drugged and unconscious women, botched police searches of Obara's premises despite strong motive and circumstantial evidence, and at least nine other rapes (including another Non-Wajin, an Australian named Carita Ridgway in 1992, which resulted in her death by an overuse of chloroform) that Obara was ultimately convicted of in April 2007.

What made this case curious in terms of jurisprudence was that Obara was never charged with murder, but rather of "rape leading to death," and in Blackman's case, he was acquitted of her homicide and dismemberment due to a lack of "evidence to link the suspect directly." In December 2008, this was overturned on appeal by the Tōkyō High Court, adding Blackman's "abduction and mutilation of a corpse" (but not murder, as "there was no video recording of her rape"). Obara is currently serving a life sentence.

The Lindsay Ann Hawker Case

The Lindsay Ann Hawker Case involves the stalking, rape, and strangulation of a Caucasian British language teacher in Chiba Prefecture by Ichihashi Tatsuya in March 2007.[7] After befriending and convincing Hawker to enter his apartment reportedly for a private English lesson, Ichihashi raped, mutilated, and buried Hawker's nude corpse in a tub of sand on his balcony. He managed to evade investigating police who came to his apartment on March 26 by absconding barefoot, remaining on the run for more than thirty-one months. After at least five trips to Japan by the Hawker family to keep pressure on the case, Ichihashi was apprehended on November 10, 2009, after he had undergone plastic surgery to disguise his features (the surgeon, suspecting something was odd when Ichihashi asked to be made more ugly, notified the police).

What made the case curious in terms of jurisprudence was that the initial charge was the "abandonment of a corpse" (*shitai iki*),[8] not murder, and this was upgraded to murder (*satsujin*) only after his arrest.[9] Although Ichihashi was convicted of murder and sentenced to life imprisonment on July 21, 2011 (upheld in Tōkyō High Court on April 11, 2012), within six months there was a book published and a movie biopic optioned about his fugitive days[10] (earning Ichihashi royalties of at least 9.12 million yen, which he unsuccessfully offered to the Hawker family), as well as a fan club for him established on Mixi social media.

The Kamiosawa Honiefaith Ratila Case

The Kamiosawa Honiefaith Ratila Case involves the murder and dismemberment of a Filipina bar hostess in Tōkyō around April 3, 2008.[11] The crime was discovered when a colleague checked Honiefaith's apartment in Ōdaiba, Tōkyō, after she did not appear at work, and found suspect Nozaki Hiroshi (a roommate) absconding with some of her body parts. Nozaki stowed the remaining parts in a locker in the World Trade Center Building in Hamamatsuchō, Tōkyō, and then unsuccessfully attempted suicide in Saitama. After he called an ambulance for himself, he notified the crew of the location of Honiefaith's body parts and was arrested for "mutilating a corpse."

What made the case curious in terms of jurisprudence is that Nozaki had previously been caught in a similar act: In January 2000, he was arrested for flushing an unreported Filipina roommate's body parts down a Yokohama public toilet several months earlier, in Spring 1999. Since he reportedly never confessed during interrogation any intent to kill her (*satsu-i*, see footnote to previous section), he was sentenced to 3.5 years for "mutilating and abandoning a corpse" (*shitai songai, iki*). He was released after three years' incarceration. In 2008, he admitted to the charge of strangling Honiefaith and was given a life sentence that year; upon appeal, on October 8, 2010, the Tōkyō High Court sentenced him to the death penalty. Honiefaith's story has been adapted into an eponymous play with two runs at the Tokyo International Players theater in 2009.[12]

Let us now consider high-profile cases of jurisprudence when the homicide victim is a noncitizen male.

The Scott Tucker Case

The Scott Tucker Case involves a Caucasian male, a well-off building owner in Tōkyō, who on February 29, 2008, reportedly went into a neighboring nightclub irate at its noise level.[13] Reports vary, but court testimony and police reports to the media maintained that he had been drinking and was aggressive and belligerent. Bar employee Watanabe Atsushi then reportedly kicked Tucker in the groin and put him a chokehold until he was asphyxiated. Media correctly forecasted that Watanabe (who claimed that he felt his life was in danger; they were both of the same height, although Tucker was nearly 90 pounds heavier) would get off leniently: Due to claims of lack of intent to kill, moreover the mitigating motive of attempting to halt the disturbance, Tōkyō District Court handed Watanabe a suspended sentence of five years. Unusually, public prosecutors decided not to appeal. Also unusually, given cases of "excessive use of force" (*kajō bōei*) resulting in death (cf. the highly publicized Steven Bellamy Case of 1984),[14] precedent indicates that the assailants in those cases are usually punished for "assault resulting in death," making the court's leniency toward Watanabe exceptional.

The Matthew Lacey Case

The Matthew Lacey Case involves a Caucasian male found dead in his Fukuoka apartment on August 17, 2004, on a blood-soaked futon.[15] Although Lacey's family overseas suspected foul play, Fukuoka Police initially ruled that his death was due to "dehydration" and "diarrhea" but did not perform an autopsy. When Lacey's family demanded one, it revealed that Matthew had a twenty-centimeter crack in his skull, so police revised the cause of death to "cerebral hemorrhage." Despite reporting that "it is suspected the subject was hit on the head," police ruled out foul play, claiming that Lacey had died after accidentally falling down in the kitchen. Further research revealed an unthorough police investigation and an unlikely accident scenario, but the Fukuoka Police initially refused to release a copy of their autopsy report for independent analysis.[16] When they did, after constant pressure from the family for years, three independent medical examiners ruled that accidental death was implausible. But by then, according to Lacey's family, the case had gone cold and Fukuoka Police were unwilling to reopen the investigation.

The Hoon "Scott" Kang Case

In a similar vein, the Hoon "Scott" Kang Case involves the death of a Korean American male tourist, whose unconscious body was found in the stairwell of a Kabukichō hostess-club high rise on August 26, 2010.[17] Dying five days later, the MPA ruled his death from severe head trauma was due to an accidental fall after too much drinking. After family demands to investigate further, the Tōkyō Metropolitan Police Agency officially closed his case in February 2011, despite crime prevention video footage indicating a probable assault by unknown assailants in an elevator, differing testimonies from possible crime suspects, and other implausible evidence regarding where the alleged fall took place. The Shinjuku Police have also reportedly refused to release the crime camera video footage or their autopsy report to the family for independent investigation.

The Abubakar Awudu Suraj Case

Finally, let's consider the Abubakar Awudu Suraj Case, which involves a Ghanaian visa overstayer dying in police custody while being deported on March 22, 2010.[18] First coming to Japan on a tourist visa in 1988 (which he overstayed), he was living with a Wajin for sixteen years (they were married in 2006, the year he was arrested). Although the Tōkyō Suginami Ward Office had officially certified their marriage, a new visa status was not approved (reportedly due to a contemporary crackdown on "visa overstayers" at the time; more in chapter 7); although Suraj's deportation order was initially quashed in February 2008 by Tōkyō District Court, the High Court reversed it in March 2009.

On March 22, 2010, after twenty months of detention, Immigration made a second attempt to deport Suraj (the first attempt was aborted due to Suraj reportedly struggling), where he was restrained face down with handcuffs, a rope, four plastic restraints, ankle cuffs, and a rolled towel gag stuffed tightly into his mouth (the last two being prohibited practices)—so tightly that he had reportedly bitten through it. Then he was forcibly boarded upon an airplane by ten Immigration officers at Narita International Airport. The videotaping of the proceedings was halted "when things got hot," and Suraj was unconscious before takeoff; he was deplaned and pronounced dead in Japan.

Two official autopsies (one noting "abrasions to his face, internal bleeding of muscles on the neck, back, abdomen, and upper arm, along with leakage of blood around the eyes, blood congestion in some organs, and dark red blood in the heart") determined the cause of death as "unknown," then a third one called it "heart disease" and "illness" (although these reports were not made public for more than a year after his death, and only after the widow won a disclosure lawsuit against the Justice Ministry). Further, Suraj's body was not returned to the family for three months. There was no official apology to the next of kin, and the case was not automatically sent to the Chiba Prefectural Police Headquarters and the Chiba District Public Prosecutor's Office for prosecution (Suraj's family and support groups claimed they had to notify them). Then the case went quiet for nearly a year.

On November 2, 2011, the Chiba District Public Prosecutor's Office announced there would be no indictment of any officers, and on July 3, 2012, the case was formally dropped, with public prosecutors stating for the record:

"There is no causal relationship between the action (by the immigration officers) and the death (of the Ghanaian man), and the action was legitimate." On August 4, 2011, Suraj's widow and mother filed a civil suit against the GOJ for 136 million yen for wrongful death, which found in her favor on March 19, 2014, awarding her a significantly reduced award of 5 million yen due to Suraj's behavior during the first deportation attempt. Although the judges ruled that the restraints were "dangerous" and "illegal," it noted that Suraj was "gravely at fault" for causing the officials to restrain him. Suraj's widow filed a criminal complaint against ten Immigration officials for an official apology, but on January 18, 2016, nearly six years after Suraj's death, the Tōkyō High Court ruled the government was not responsible (claiming Suraj had died of a preexisting heart condition), reversing the 2014 ruling.[19]

Analysis of These Cases

It is of course difficult to talk about trends within an entire judiciary by triangulating from only seven cases. However, in these cases, police investigations tended to be on the slow and incomplete side when a noncitizen is a victim, until the media (and in the Kang, Suraj, Blackman, and Hawker Cases, the family) makes them into higher-profile cases. Further, in all of the cases of manslaughter/wrongful death described above, police seriously bungled if not interfered with the investigation, enabling killers to escape prosecution or sentencing for homicide for years (if not entirely).

Finding a racialized pattern to jurisprudence in general in Japan is inconclusive at this juncture and necessitates further research. However, there is utility in comparing these cases of violence against Non-Wajin women with other high-profile cases of murder and mutilation of female corpses where both the male perpetrator and the female victim were Wajin (cf. Kodaira Yoshio, Ōkubo Kiyoshi, Kurita Genzō, Hidaka Hiroshi, Miyazaki Tsutomu, etc.)[20]: The Wajin men killing Wajin women were charged with murder, not corpse mutilation, and received the death penalty, not a life sentence. Further, consider the case of Sagawa Issei, who killed, raped, and ate a Dutch woman named Renee Hartevelt in Paris in 1981. After being charged with murder and cannibalism in France, he was eventually extradited to Japan and released from incarceration entirely in 1986. He currently lives in Tōkyō as a minor celebrity with books, TV and film appearances, freelance articles, and even restaurant reviews in his name.[21] It is difficult for this author to imagine the same reception in Japan being given to a Wajin who mutilates and cannibalizes Wajin in Japan (as Miyazaki Tsutomu did).

Further, in terms of the Non-Wajin male victims, police not only chose milder charges (with no appeal by prosecutors) toward defendants when there were clear assailants, but also portrayed otherwise clear evidence of foul play as "accidents," not to mention interfering with third-party investigations of evidence that would undermine the police's conclusions. Moreover, a different standard of evidence by nationality becomes clearer when one considers criminal jurisprudence when the Wajin suspect and Non-Wajin victim are reversed:

CRIMINAL CASES: HARSH STANDARDS OF JURISPRUDENCE IF THE CRIME SUSPECT IS A NONCITIZEN

The Govinda Prasad Mainali Case

The Govinda Prasad Mainali Case involves a Nepalese man who had sexual relations with a TEPCO economist named Watanabe Yasuko, who moonlighted as a prostitute with several clients a night (including, according to media, TEPCO officials), she having kept their contact details in a notebook found at the scene.[22] When she was found strangled in her Tōkyō apartment on March 19, 1997, Mainali was arrested four days later initially for overstaying his visa (but acknowledged during questioning that he had a physical relationship with the deceased, as police had discovered his key to her apartment, and his semen was found in a condom in the apartment's toilet). He was charged on May 20 with murder and robbery (*gōtō chishi shōzai*). On April 14, 2000, the Tōkyō District Court acquitted Mainali due to lack of conclusive evidence, but the prosecution appealed, and on December 22, 2000, the Tōkyō High Court overturned the acquittal and sentenced Mainali to life imprisonment. The Supreme Court affirmed the conviction on October 10, 2003.

What makes this case germane to this research was a large domestic support group for Mainali pushed for a retrial, getting a DNA test on the evidence in July 2011. This established that (a) the hair, semen, saliva, and blood stains present in the room and on the victim's body that were not Mainali's, and (b) Tōkyō prosecutors had withheld this vital evidence from the court. Nearly a year after the DNA test, on June 7, 2012, the Tōkyō High Court overturned Mainali's conviction and ordered a retrial. He was released after fifteen years of incarceration (and soon deported to Nepal), and on November 7, 2012, the Tōkyō High Court officially exonerated him with no appeal from public prosecutors.

There are of course wrongful arrests and incarcerations in judicial systems worldwide. Wajin have also been victims, such as Sugaya Toshikazu (who was released for retrial in 2009 after more than seventeen years in custody by being acquitted of a murder through a DNA test),[23] Sakurai Shōji and Sugayama Takao (who, after nearly thirty years in custody, were exonerated fifteen years after being released on parole),[24] and Hakamada Iwao (incarcerated for forty-eight years, including a record thirty years on death row, despite exonerating DNA tests; he was released on March 26, 2014).[25] They indicate that Wajin status does not exculpate—Mainali was only the eighth case of exoneration in Japan after a retrial under a life sentence or the death penalty.[26] However, in Mainali's case, because he was a noncitizen, instead of receiving a retrial and a formal apology, Mainali was immediately incarcerated by the Immigration Bureau and deported for overstaying his visa (which he could not renew because he was incarcerated).

Also, despite an acquittal in lower court, Mainali was never allowed release on bail (*hoshaku*), serving not only time for a crime but also time for being a suspect of a crime. The effects of a general lack of bail for noncitizens in Japan are clearer in the next case:

The Claudia Zaberl Case

In October 2006, Claudia Zaberl, a Swiss national, was caught in Narita Airport with over 2 kilograms of amphetamines in her suitcase.[27] She claimed innocence, and Chiba District Court acquitted her of drug smuggling in August 2007. However, prosecutors appealed, and under the Criminal Procedure Law and the Immigration Control and Refugee Law she was kept in an Immigration detention facility during her trial in Tōkyō High Court. In April 2008, she was acquitted again, but was then deported to Switzerland only after prosecutors dropped the case; she was then, despite her reaffirmed innocence, barred from reentering Japan for five years.

Compared to other cases of citizens, who were released on bail despite criminal court *convictions* (including high-profile businessman Horie Takafumi, and corrupt Hokkaidō politician Suzuki Muneo—who was not only convicted twice and bailed twice, but also *reelected to the Diet* while out on bail), bail in Japan is generally not granted to noncitizens. The reasoning, according to lawyers I have interviewed, is that for noncitizens only there is an alleged risk of flight from the country and possible destruction of evidence (actions that citizens could also engage in).[28] The double standards for jurisprudence in Japan systematically give advantages to suspects who have Japanese citizenship.

OTHER JURIDICAL DISADVANTAGES FOR NONCITIZENS IN THE JAPANESE CRIMINAL JUSTICE SYSTEM

Japan's criminal investigation system is draconian, and its extremely high conviction rates (over 99 percent) come from the police's enhanced power to extract a confession from the suspect to build a criminal case.[29] As there is no Writ of Habeas Corpus in Japan, there are "voluntary investigations" (*nin'i no tori shirabe*) without charge in "substitute prisons" (*daiyō kangoku*, police holding cells, not actual prisons) for up to twenty-three days, as well as interrogations of up to twenty-three days on each charge before indictment. Also, there are few to no recordings of interrogation proceedings, and limited access to the outside world and to lawyers during questioning. Consequently, there have been cases of coerced confessions under conditions of stress, physical and mental abuse, and torture, not to mention cases of deaths in custody.

This system has been called "hostage justice" (*hitojichi shihō*) by experts in the field, where detainees must prove their innocence to the prosecution, face further incrimination if they invoke their constitutionally guaranteed right to remain silent (*mokuhiken*), and are held in detention for extended periods until they crack and confess under the stress. In other words, suspects are held "hostage" to the system, detained unless they pay their release "ransom" by confessing, even if that requires detention and interrogations for weeks, months, or in some cases more than a year. Japan's Federation of Bar Associations and the UN Committee Against Torture have, respectively, called this system "a breeding ground for false charges" and "tantamount to torture."[30]

This system affects all criminal suspects regardless of nationality, but noncitizen suspects, particularly nonnative speakers of Japanese, face systematic disadvantages that are germane to this research. First, as discussed above (chapter 5) and below (chapter 7), noncitizens, particularly Visible Minorities, are more likely to be subjected to racial profiling for investigations of crimes such as visa violations (due to the enforcement of policing laws, and the raising of public consciousness due to NPA "crime prevention" campaigns). This will make Non-Wajin more likely than Wajin to be targeted and detained by Japan's harsh criminal justice system. Second, during jurisprudence, there is "no professional title or public qualification" for interpreters involved in court translation or police interrogation, putting them at a distinct linguistic disadvantage; there have been cases of noncitizens who were not fluent in Japanese signing confessions they could not read, and being tried while not fully comprehending the court proceedings.[31] Third, as mentioned above, noncitizens when detained or incarcerated are far less likely to be released on bail, even if exonerated in criminal court.

There is also an extra layer of incarceration that only noncitizens must deal with: the Immigration Bureau. Because noncitizen detainees cannot renew their visas while in detention, any incarceration by police increases the probability of detention later in separate Immigration detention facilities (specifically reserved for noncitizen visa overstayers and refugees/asylum seekers). Detainees in these Immigration facilities (*nyūkoku kanri sentā*) face a different system both in terms of criminal procedure and living conditions. In terms of procedure, inmates convicted of a specific crime and sentenced to a Japanese prison have a legally defined release date, often with the possibility of parole; visa overstayers being detained in an Immigration detention center, however, have no specific limit to their detention period, resulting in people detained for several years (and for some, still counting).

In terms of living conditions, rights of detainees to adequate food, exercise, and living space in Immigration Bureau detention centers are less regulated than in Japanese prisons (which are subject to international oversight regarding standards of favorable treatment). Consequently, inhospitable, unsanitary, and generally unmonitored conditions in these detention centers have occasioned protests both from human rights organizations and from the detainees, in the form of hunger strikes and suicides. Immigration detainees have also suffered and died from their medical conditions being neglected by detention officials, and from the overprescription of sedatives and painkillers.[32]

In 2021, the senseless death of a Sri Lankan named Ratnayake Liyanage Wishma Sandamali, due to medical negligence in a detention center, brought national attention and protest against the GOJ's treatment of visa overstayers and asylum applicants—and the withdrawal of a bill before the Diet that would have only strengthened the ability for bureaucrats "to keep any foreign national in custody without the approval of a judge," thus violating constitutional guarantees of due process.[33]

Japan's "Hostage Justice" Personified: The Carlos Ghosn Case

For this Second Edition, the Ghosn Case warrants a detailed section at the end, as it is an excellent example that substantiates this entire chapter.

Carlos Ghosn is the former CEO of the Renault-Nissan-Mitsubishi strategic alliance, brought in from 1999 to streamline operations in Japan's automotive industry.[34] After nearly two decades of widespread successes turning around the fortunes of nearly bankrupt Mitsubishi Motors, and making Nissan the industry leader in electric vehicle production, Ghosn and his top aide Greg Kelly were arrested on November 19, 2018, on suspicion of false accounting of their income, for example, "using company funds for personal investments and misusing corporate assets." While the case against Ghosn for financial wrongdoing has been decried as "thin soup" by at least one legal analyst (especially since other Japanese corporate executives, including those at Nissan, admitted to accounting misdeeds similar to Ghosn's yet were not arrested),[35] the issue in terms of this research is how Ghosn was treated while in police custody, bringing to light the issues of "hostage justice" described above.

Ghosn was not only treated like any suspect under interrogation in Japan—he was treated like a foreign suspect. In addition to enduring more than a year of arrests, rearrests, and near-daily tag-team interrogations (with 129 days in solitary confinement) to wear him down until he confessed,[36] he was denied visitation rights with family members (including his wife) for months, and, after being granted bail under strict conditions and house arrest,[37] he was suddenly rearrested hours after announcing a press conference to talk to international media.[38] Most indicative of separate and unequal treatment of Ghosn as a foreign suspect is that some of the charges, which normally would fall under a statute of limitations of seven years under the Companies Act, were still being considered applicable after seven years. Prosecutors argued that these statutes did not apply to Ghosn because he spent time overseas; meaning even the passage of time is different for foreigners—because the clock stops if they ever leave Japan.[39]

On December 29, 2019, Ghosn, again out on bail, escaped from custody and was spirited off to Lebanon (where he has citizenship), finding sanctuary when the Lebanese judiciary refused Japan's extradition order. As I wrote for the Shingetsu News Agency shortly after:

> I understand why [Ghosn] decided to do a runner. It wasn't just because he was denied access to his wife for months as a means to break him down psychologically. It wasn't just because prosecutors have decisive power over the evidence (even exculpatory evidence) submitted to court. It wasn't just because they decided to have separate trials for each charge, and the first trial would probably begin in 2021 and then take years. And it wasn't just because there is a separate and unequal jurisprudential track for foreigners than for Japanese. . . . It was that given this level of legalized bullying over the accused in Japan, Ghosn knew he wouldn't get a fair trial with the presumption of innocence—neither in the courtroom nor in the court of public opinion. And he was exactly right.
>
> Even Japan's Justice Minister demanded Ghosn return and "prove his innocence" [which contravenes human rights principles of presumption of innocence].[40] That was not a gaffe. That's exactly the system in Japan. And he would never be able to prove it when the courts and media follow the same presumption: you got arrested, so you must have done something wrong to bring The System down upon yourself. You'll never get a fair hearing because your side will not be heard. Not within Japan, anyway. Especially as a foreigner.[41]

This interpretation was shared by the United Nations, where a panel of human rights experts on the Working Group on Arbitrary Detention found in November 2020 that Ghosn's arrest was "arbitrary" under international norms of justice, ruled that he had been "wrongly detained," and urged that he be accorded an "enforceable right to compensation and other reparations."[42] Ghosn currently remains in Beirut as an international fugitive wanted by Interpol.[43] His associate, Greg Kelly, as of this writing remains ensnared in the Japanese criminal justice system.[44]

SUMMARY AND CONCLUSIONS

Japan's national discourse as created by judicial interpretation of laws indicates a double standard of justice based upon nationality, race, and social origin. Although Japan's criminal justice system can be harsh toward all criminal suspects and detainees, there have been incidents that strongly suggest that jurisprudence tends to more harsh if the criminal suspect is a noncitizen, but more lenient if a citizen commits a crime against a noncitizen. Statistics on Japan's prison population in 2008 would suggest the same conclusion, as the proportion of incarcerated noncitizens is about four times higher than incarcerated citizens.[45] Although more research is needed for an exhaustive study, the several cases of homicides cited above have repeatedly indicated that investigations proceed slower and sentences are lighter (or nonexistent) if the victim is a noncitizen, particularly when compared to Wajin-Wajin murder cases.[46]

More systemic and overt, however, is the treatment of noncitizens detained for investigation. Unlike citizens, noncitizens find themselves under a separate standard of detention, where they are generally denied bail, face unresolved language barriers, and endure a secondary incarceration system (which does not apply to citizens, as they are not subject to the Immigration Control and Refugee Recognition Act) that receives its intake from the primary criminal justice detention system (except with less official oversight and more potential for abuse). The treatment of a high-profile, well-connected person like Carlos Ghosn in particular demonstrates the weaker position that noncitizens are in due to their enhanced lack of civil rights.

This chapter described how an officially sanctioned separate track of human rights treatment for minorities in Japan validates and reinforces a national discourse of differentiated and subordinated treatment not only by nationality but also by physical appearance: Non-Wajin are more likely to be racially profiled by Japanese society and put through this judicial system. This is due in part to media campaigns that promote and normalize national-level policies that specifically criminalize Japan's Visible Minorities by phenotype. These media campaigns will be discussed in chapter seven.

NOTES

1. "Abuse, racism, lost evidence deny justice in Valentine case: Nigerian's ordeal shows that different standards apply for foreigners in court." *Japan Times*, August 14, 2007. The Tōkyō District Court decision, *Heisei* 17 (Wa) *Dai* 17658, handed down March 29, 2007, and analysis is archived at www.debito.org/valentinelawsuit.html.

2. Although not an issue of nationality, the issue of harsh treatment of detainees in Japanese detention and incarceration facilities has been criticized by the UN Committee Against Torture. In a report (CAT/C/JPN/CO/1) dated May 18, 2007, the UN body expresses concerns about, inter alia, "the lack of authority of the Board of Visitors for Inspection of Penal Institutions to investigate cases or allegations of acts of torture or ill treatment" (Section 20b); "the unsuitability of the use of police cells for prolonged detention, and the lack of appropriate and prompt medical care for individuals in police custody" (Section 15c); "allegations of undue delays in the provision of medical assistance to inmates as well as the lack of independent medical staff within the prison system" (Section 17); "restrictions on the right to compensation, such as statutory limitations and reciprocity rules for immigrants; the Committee regrets the lack of information on compensation requested and awarded to victims of torture or ill treatment" (Section 22). However, what is an issue of nationality are conditions for nonnationals incarcerated in Immigration detention facilities, which are also heavily criticized in this report; we shall discuss this in more detail below. *See also* "UN body attacks Japan's justice system." *Financial Times*, May 23, 2007.

3. This includes the medical record (*karute*) from the Police Hospital (*keisatsu byōin*), representatives of which were present at Valentine's ten-day interrogation; the NPA claimed that it was lost. A more curious piece of evidence not submitted by Defendants (despite demands from the Plaintiffs) was footage of the event from the anticrime surveillance cameras installed throughout Kabukichō by the police in 2002 specifically because it is a "foreign crime" neighborhood (see chapter 4); it is logical to assume that if footage had supported the Tōkyō Metropolitan Police claims of nonviolent restraint, it would have been submitted.

4. "*Shōnin wa, jūzen kara genkoku to menshiki ga ari, honken kossetsu go mo genkoku o byōin wo mimatteiru nado kanari shitashī koto ga ukagatteiru yūjin de ari, kabukichō no kokujin no komyunitei no nakama de atta koto tō o terasu to, shōnin Furanshisu no kyōjutsu wa, mokugeki shōgen to shite kyakkansei o yūsuru mono to wa iezu, kono mama shinyō suru tōtei dekinai.*"

5. Support Network for State Redress Lawsuits in Japan (*kokubai nettowāku*) report on the Valentine High Court Decision at http://kokubai.net/knet2nd/?p=322.

6. More on the Blackman Case in Parry (2011). Other reports used in this section are "Serial rapist Obara gets life term: Developer acquitted in Blackman slaying but sent up over Ridgway's murder," and "Approach to Blackman slaying hit, likened to Keystone Cops: Faulty police procedures seen foiling quick action, prevention." *Japan Times*, both April 24, 2007; "Guilty verdict ends Blackman family's fight for justice." *Independent* (London), December 17, 2008; "Serial rapist's life term is upheld; abduction added to convictions." *Japan Times*, December 17, 2008.

7. *See* inter alia "Police mum about escape of Hawker murder suspect." *Japan Times*, April 6, 2007; *Japan Times*, April 24, 2007 (ibid.); "Hawker's friends try new appeal." *Japan Times*, December 11, 2007; "Lack of progress in search for Hawker's killer frustrates family." *Japan Times*, March 25, 2009; "Police charge Ichihashi with murdering British teacher Hawker." *Mainichi Shinbun*, December 2, 2009; "Ichihashi gets warrant for Hawker rape-murder." *Japan Times*, December 3, 2009.

8. Under Criminal Code 190, "A person who damages, abandons or unlawfully possesses a corpse, the ashes or hair of a dead person, or an object placed in a coffin shall be punished by imprisonment with work for not more than 3 years."

9. NPA "Wanted" posters (*jūyō shimei tehai*), photographed by the author March 10, 2009 outside Sapporo Ōdori Police Box, archived at www.debito.org/?p=2748. When I contacted the Chiba Police on March 17, 2009, to ask why Ichihashi was, of all the fugitives on that poster (at least one of whom had committed a crime similar to Ichihashi), the only one not accused of murder, the investigator, a Mr. Shibusa, said he could not comment in specific on the case. When I asked how one distinguishes between charges of murder vs. corpse abandonment, he said that it depended on the details of each case, but generally if the suspect admits homicidal intent (*satsu-i*), it becomes a charge of murder. When I asked how the other suspects on the poster were so cooperative as to let the police know their will to kill before escaping, I received a demurrer and a claim that his department was too busy to field any more questions. I suspect that the NPA may have charged Ichihashi with a lesser charge so that they can rearrest him later on a greater charge, as this is eventually what happened (even though the NPA had DNA evidence, not to mention Hawker's body found in his apartment with his teeth marks on it, linking Ichihashi to the deed for more than two years).

10. Ichihashi (2011); Movie: "I am Ichihashi: Journal of a Murderer" (2013); "*Ichihashi genkoku tōbōki o eiga ka: Sho kantoku & shuen ni Dean Fujioka daibatteki*" [Suspect Ichihashi's escape journal to become movie; with surprising choice of freshman director and lead actor Dean Fujioka]. *Yahoo News Sports Hōchi*, November 23, 2011. Archive of the movie on the Internet Movie Database at www.imdb.com/title/tt2120075/, movie preview reel at www.youtube.com/watch?v=QlCIHYYmIlc).

11. References for this section include "Man arrested for mutilation of Filipina hostess." *Mainichi Shinbun*, April 7, 2008; "Murder suspect hid body parts in locker." *Kyodo News*, April 8, 2008. "Clumsy cops make the link between mutilated Filipina, slain stalker victim." *Nikkan Gendai/Mainichi Waiwai*, April 10, 2008; "Serial mutilator Hiroshi Nozaki also a serial killer." *Trans-Pacific Radio*, April 19, 2008; "Fresh warrant over hostess slaying." *Japan Times*, April 30, 2005; "*Nishin wa shikei, muki chōeki o haki: Hi josei satsugai de Tōkyō kōsai hanketsu.*" [Appeal rules death penalty, throws out life imprisonment: Tōkyō High Court rules on Filipina murder]. *Asahi Shinbun*, October 8, 2010. *See also* some translations and analysis of media tone of reportage on this case archived at www.debito.org/?p=1633.

12. https://japantoday.com/category/entertainment/tokyo-international-players-to-stage-2nd-production-of-honiefaith, written by Monty DiPietro (accessed April 25, 2021).

13. "Death of American in bar fight likely to draw leniency." *Japan Times*, March 13, 2008; "Tokyo killing of Charleston native 'seeded in past events.'" *Charleston Gazette*, March 7, 2008; "No appeal in Japan murder of state man." *Charleston Gazette*, September 20, 2008; "Anonymous re Scott Tucker, killed in a Tokyo bar by a man who got a suspended sentence." *Debito.org*, June 16, 2009, at www.debito.org/?p=3534.

14. Untitled article, *Kyodo News*, November 22, 1984, which reported on Steve Bellamy, who in 1981 reportedly intervened in a physical quarrel between a Wajin man and woman in public, and, when threatened with assault by the man, used a karate technique and knocked him to the ground, where he died from a head concussion to the curb. The Chiba District Court judged Bellamy innocent of any wrongdoing due to self-defense, but on appeal, the Chiba High Court said that his high level of karate training (he was a British All-Styles Karate Team Member) ruled out self-defense, then sentenced him to eighteen months in prison (suspended to three years' probation). This was overturned in the Supreme Court and became the substance of a mock lay-judge trial in Ōsaka in 2006. *See* "Mock trial under lay judge system held in Osaka." *Kyodo News*, November 23, 2006, and "Odd mock trial of foreigner to test new jury system." *Debito.org*, November 24, 2006, archived at www.debito.org/?p=83.

Contrast the Bellamy Case with a 2015 court ruling about a Filipino Japanese man, who was charged with "assault" after defending himself from two drunk Wajin men and fined 300,000 yen. After the former filed a complaint in Summary Court, two years later the fine was quashed because police investigators had not supplied an interpreter or charged the Wajin drunks. *See* "Filipino-Japanese exempt from fine after Osaka police botch assault probe." *Kyodo News/Japan Times*, April 24, 2015, archived at www.debito.org/?p=13269.

15. "Bungled police probe; uncooperative prosecutors: U.S. man on quest to find cause of brothers." *Japan Times*, February 6, 2007; "Family queries cause of U.S. man's death." *Yomiuri Shinbun*, January 30, 2008; "Kang family take fight for justice to Tokyo." *Japan Times*, September 6, 2011.

16. According to the *Japan Times*, ibid., September 6, 2011:

> Maiko Tagusari, a lawyer and secretary general of the Japan Federation of Bar Associations, says that in cases where an autopsy is conducted for "administrative reasons"—namely cases where the cause of death is unclear but foul play is not suspected—autopsy results are made available to family members. But in cases when it is suspected that the death was caused by a crime, the autopsy results become part of the records of a criminal investigation and are not available to any party outside the justice system. In such cases, family members have to make a request to get access, and this is only possible after an indictment, she adds. "For me, this seems like a failure of the system," says Tagusari. "At the very least autopsy reports should be disclosed to family members, because it is just objective evidence which does not harm the privacy of anyone other than the victim themselves."

17. "Buford man dies in Japan; family wants answers." *Atlanta Journal-Constitution*, September 7, 2010; TV Show "*America's Most Wanted*," aired

November 6, 2010, archived at www.amw.com/fugitives/case.cfm?id=75251 and www.debito.org/?p=7771; "Dead American's kin seek justice: Answers elude in student's shady death in Kabukicho." *Japan Times*, December 7, 2010; "Family slams stalled probe into Kabukicho death." *Japan Times*, May 31, 2011; ibid., *Japan Times*, September 6, 2011. The family and other members of the Korean American community have made accusations of latent anti-Korean bias in Japan, while the family also reportedly believes the US Embassy in Tōkyō has been lax in their follow-up, having taken five months to notify the family that the case was closed in February 2011.

18. "50 rally for investigation of deportee's death." *Japan Times*, April 13, 2010; "Formal Letter of Grievance to Keiko Chiba, the Minister of Justice." Asian People's Friendship Society, April 10, 2010, archived at http://apfs.jp/report20100410_571.php; "Another illegal immigrant in Japan, another death: The fatal journey of Mr. Suraj." Press Conference by Tatara Yūko, Kodama Kōichi, and Yoshida Mayumi, Foreign Correspondents' *Club of Japan*, April 20, 2010; "A nation's bouncers: A suspicious death in police custody." *Economist* (London), May 13, 2010; "Prosecutors get case of deportee's death." *Japan Times*, December 29, 2010; "Japan's immigration policy: Gone but not forgotten." *Economist*, August 5, 2011; "Justice stalled in brutal death of deportee: Autopsy suggests immigration officers used excessive force in restraining Ghanaian." *Japan Times*, November 1, 2011; "No plans to charge officers in death of Ghanaian man." *Yomiuri Shinbun*, November 3, 2011; "Justice in Japan: An ugly decision." *Economist*, November 4, 2011.

19. "Officials faulted in death of Ghanaian." *Japan Times*, March 19, 2014; "Widow challenges no charges for Ghanaian husband's deportation." *Kyodo News*, April 18, 2014; "In reversal, Tokyo High Court rules government not responsible for Ghanaian deportee's death." *Japan Times*, January 18, 2016.

20. *See* inter alia Schreiber (1996).

21. *See* inter alia Morris (2007); Kushner (2007).

22. *See* inter alia Hayes (2005: 50–2), "*Tōden OL jiken, saishin no kanōsei . . . betsujin DNA kenshutsu*" [Tōkyō Electric Power Co. Case: DNA test reveals different person, probability of retrial]. *Yomiuri Shinbun*, June 21, 2011; "Mainali granted retrial, is let out of prison." *Japan Times*, June 8, 2012; "Order issued to deport Nepalese man granted retrial over 1997 Tokyo murder." *Kyodo News*, June 11, 2012; "Govinda Mainali: Justice 15 years too late." *Terrie's Take*, June 11, 2012; "Don't delay justice any longer." *Japan Times* Editorial, June 12, 2012; "Mainali to be deported soon." *NHK World*, June 12, 2012; "Prosecutors in Nepali's case are 'sore losers.'" *Japan Today*, June 14, 2012. "Mainali case exposes flaws, bias in judicial system: Prosecutors withheld evidence, detained Nepalese after acquittal." *Japan Times*, June 14, 2012; "Japan held innocent foreigner 15 years." *Washington Times*, June 25, 2012; "Tokyo High Court finally exonerates Mainali." *Japan Times*, November 8, 2012.

23. *See* inter alia "New DNA evidence wins release for man after 17 years of life term for murder." *Mainichi Shinbun*, June 4, 2009; "Man falsely convicted of child murder: 'I want my own life back.'" *Mainichi Shinbun*, June 5, 2009. Sugaya was eventually found innocent upon retrial and issued a formal apology; *see* "*Ashikaga jiken: Sugaya-san muzai; saibanchō ga shazai: Utsunomiya chisai*" [Ushinomiya

District Court: Ashikaga Case: Mr. Sugaya innocent; judge apologizes]. *Mainichi Shinbun*, March 26, 2010.

24. "Two men acquitted in retrial after serving nearly 30 years in prison." *Kyodo News*, May 24, 2011.

25. "Hakamada Iwao" *Amnesty International*, March 31, 2015, www.amnesty.org .uk/hakamada-iwao-death-penalty-row-japan; *see also* www.amnesty.org.uk/search /Hakamada; "Criminal justice in Japan: Japan's Supreme Court misses a chance to right a 42-year-old wrong." *Economist*, March 27, 2008; "Hakamada released after 48 years." *Kyodo News*, March 27, 2014.

26. Ibid., *Japan Times*, November 8, 2012.

27. This is according to interviews with lawyers Mizunuma Isao, Shiba-ike Toshiteru, and Tsurusaki Motoyuki in June 2009, January 2006, and August 2007, respectively. *See also* "Swiss woman acquitted of drug smuggling again; questions raised about her detention." *Asahi Shinbun*, April 10, 2008; "Held despite acquittal, now barred from re-entry, woman slams legal system." *Kyodo News*, October 10, 2008. *See also* "Horie handed 2 ½ years." *Japan Times*, March 17, 2007; "High court finds Suzuki took bribes, rejects appeal." *Japan Times*, February 27, 2008.

28. *See* inter alia "Ex-immigration boss: detentions too long." *Japan Times*, July 14, 2010.

29. Sources for this section include: "Japan crime: Why do innocent people confess?" *BBC World Service*, January 2, 2013; "Prison conditions in Japan under scrutiny." *GLOCOM Europe Report* #32, November 22, 2002; "68 prison deaths warranted autopsy in decade." *Japan Times*, March 27, 2003; "Ministry plans new law to stop prison abuse." *Japan Times*, March 21, 2003; note that the prison guards involved in the deaths of Wajin inmates were all indicted, unlike the Immigration staff involved in the death of Abubakar Awudu Suraj; "Justice ministry report: 'Structural' woes behind prison deaths." *Japan Times*, April 1, 2003; "Human rights abuses behind bars." *Japan Times* Editorial, March 17, 2003; firsthand experiences of police detention at "12 Days of Detention." *Debito.org*, December 19, 2003, archived at www.debito.org/policeinterrogations.html; Sakanaka 2005; "Justice system flawed by presumed guilt: Rights advocates slam interrogation without counsel, long detentions." *Kyodo News/Japan Times*, October 13, 2005; "Confess and be done with it." *Economist*, February 8, 2007; "Pressed by police, even innocent confess in Japan." *New York Times*, May 11, 2007; "Japan thwarts abusive police." *TIME Magazine*, January 25, 2008; ibid., *Economist*, March 27, 2008; Higuchi & Arudou (2008: 180–6); "Just plead guilty and die." *Economist*, March 13, 2008. "Criminal justice in Japan: Throw away the key." *Economist*, March 27, 2008; "Carlos Ghosn and Japan's 'hostage justice' system." *BBC News*, December 31, 2019; "Japanese justice: Innocent until proven guilty or innocent until detained? A closer look at the 'hostage justice' debate sparked by Ghosn's escape." *Japan Times*, February 2, 2020; and so on.

30. "Japan's 'Substitute Prison' Shocks the World." Japan Federation of Bar Associations, September 2008, at www.nichibenren.or.jp/library/en/document/data/ daiyo_kangoku.pdf.

31. *See* inter alia "Ichihashi trial bares translation woes: Courts refuse to admit interpreters often lack the necessary skills." *Japan Times*, July 21, 2011. I have also

sat in on a number of civil and criminal court cases in Japan where proceedings broke down due to mistranslations (corrected sometimes by members of the courtroom audience, who sometimes apparently understood the testimonies better than the official court interpreters). However, skilled interpreters of course do exist in Japan: I have seen them hired on a similar pay scale for media events, business gatherings, academic conferences, and international summits doing excellent work; the conclusion I draw is that the Japanese judiciary does not seem to put as high a priority on selecting and screening of interpreter candidates as organizers of other public events do.

32. *See*, for example, CCPR/C/79/Add.102, which notes, "[T]he Committee is concerned that there is no independent authority to which complaints of ill-treatment by the police and immigration officials can be addressed for investigation and redress. The Committee recommends that such an independent body or authority be set up by the State party without delay." *United Nations*, November 19, 1998; "Welcome to Japan?" *Amnesty International*, 2002, alleging extortion and physical abuse at the Narita Airport detention center, excerpt archived at www.debito.org/?p=9846; "Detention centers lack doctors: Two facilities holding visa violators not offering proper medical care." *Daily Yomiuri*, December 22, 2006 (the Japanese version of this article, dated December 21, has the more revealing headline, "*Ōmura nyūkan sentā de jōkin-i fuzai 2 nen ni, kakuho no medo tatazu*" [The Ōmura Detention Center has had no full-time doctor on call for two years now, and no idea when they will secure one]; Interviews, Michael. H. Fox, Director, Japan Innocence and Death Penalty Research Center, 2004–2008; "Caterpillars and cockroaches: Foreigners lead hunger strike in immigration detention center." *Asahi Shinbun*, October 18, 2007; "Detainees allege abuse at Kansai holding center." *Japan Times*, March 9, 2010; "Immigration detainees end hunger strike." *Japan Times*, March 22, 2010; "Inmates on hunger strike in Japan immigration center." *AFP*, May 20, 2010; "Running to nowhere." *Kansai Time Out*, June 2010; "Deportee center hunger strike abates, detentions drag on." *Japan Times*, September 1, 2012; "Nigerian dies after hunger strike in Japan detention center." *Reuters/Asahi Shinbun Asia-Japan Watch*, June 27, 2019; "Death in Detention: Grim toll mounts in Japanese detention centers as foreigners seek asylum." *Reuters*, March 8, 2016, archived at www.debito.org/?p=13885, noting: "The watchdog report drew attention to what it said was the heavy prescription of drugs to detainees. At the time he died, Ghadimi had been prescribed 15 different drugs, including four painkillers, five sedatives—one a Japanese version of the tranquilizer Xanax—and two kinds of sleeping pills, the report said. At one point during his incarceration, he was on a cocktail of 25 different pills."

In ibid., *Japan Times*, July 14, 2010, former Immigration Bureau chief Sakanaka Hidenori proposed that detentions in Immigration facilities not exceed *one year*; however, once oversight mechanisms were activated in August 2011, the number of detainees awaiting deportation or asylum permission for more than six months dropped dramatically (indicating how lax oversight had hitherto been). *See* "Foreigners held by immigration sharply down after reviewing rules." *Mainichi Shinbun*, February 4, 2012. Nevertheless, abuses, some resulting in fatalities, continue to the present. *See*, for example, "Asylum-seeker dies after collapsing at detention center while doctor at lunch." *AFP/Japan Today* and *Japan Times*, October 25, 2013; "Immigration detention centers under scrutiny in Japan after fourth death." *Reuters*, December 3, 2014; "Immigration detention centers like prisons, U.K. inspectors say." *Japan Times*, February 6, 2015—and I make the case that they are worse than prisons at www.debito.org/?p=13056; "Progressive News Service: Deaths of unknown persons in the custody of the Tokyo Metropolitan Police: At least 5 in past year." *Debito.org*, March 9, 2015, www.debito.org/?p=13136. "Sri Lankan woman dies in detention, wrote about her hunger." *Asahi Shinbun*, March 15, 2021; "A Sri Lankan's tragic death in Japan casts a harsh spotlight on controversial refugee system." *Straits Times*, April 24, 2021, which notes, "Ms. Wishma was vomiting blood in her final days, and was so weak that she had no control of her arms and legs. The immigration authorities allegedly turned a blind eye to medical expert advice to put her on an intravenous drip or to grant her provisional release to ease her stress. A report by public broadcaster NHK suggested that officials tend to suspect malingering for minor illnesses in their reluctance to grant provisional release."

Finally, "Left in limbo: Japan's haphazard immigration policies, disrespect for human rights." *Mainichi Shinbun*, April 19, 2019, notes,

> As of the end of July 2018, of the 1,309 detainees nationwide, 54 percent had been detained for six months or longer. According to attorneys and others who provide assistance to foreign workers in Japan, 13 foreign nationals died by suicide or from illness while in detention between 2007 and 2018. Many detainees complain of appalling health conditions at detention centers, saying they are hardly permitted to see physicians. A damages lawsuit brought against the central government at the Mito District Court for the 2014 death of a then 43-year-old Cameroonian man while he was detained at Higashi Nihon Immigration Center in the Ibaraki Prefecture city of Ushiku is ongoing. His mother, who resides in Cameroon, filed the suit.
>
> According to the legal complaint that was filed, the man had been confirmed as diabetic after a medical consultation at the immigration center. He began to complain of pain in February 2014, and died at the end of March that year. Security cameras at the center captured him saying in English that he felt like he was dying starting the night before his death, and the footage has been saved as evidence. Even after the man fell from his bed, he was left unattended, and a staff member found him in cardiopulmonary arrest the following morning. He was transported to a hospital where he was confirmed dead. "Immigration officials have a duty to provide emergency medical care," says the plaintiff's attorney, Koichi Kodama. "The government should be accountable for revealing who was watching the footage of the man rolling around on the floor, screaming in pain, and whether anyone went directly to his room to check on his condition."

33. "Sri Lankan's death in spotlight as Japan debates immigration bill." *Japan Times/Kyodo News*, May 12, 2021; "Immigration reform fails to resolve asylum contradictions." *Japan Times*, March 13, 2021; "Withdrawal of immigration bill underscores Suga's precarious standing." *Japan Times/Kyodo News*, May 19, 2021.

34. Sources for this section: "Nissan's Ghosn Arrested in Japan, Threatening Three-Way Alliance." *Bloomberg*, November 19, 2018; "Ghosn charges are thin

soup—case for ex-Nissan boss: Prosecutors fail to make a strong case against car maker's former chief." *Nikkei Asian Review*, January 29, 2019; "Carlos Ghosn's 'Great Escape' Writes a Hollywood Ending to Japanese Imprisonment." *Daily Beast*, December 31, 2019. *See also* commentary: "Seven questions about Ghosn and Nissan: The case of Carlos Ghosn raises the question of whether a non-Japanese can be successful running a Japanese firm." *Japan Times*, December 20, 2018; "Debito.org's stance on the Carlos Ghosn Case, at last: A boardroom coup making 'thin legal soup' that might shame Japan's 'hostage justice' judicial system into reform." *Debito.org*, December 31, 2019, www.debito.org/?p=15548; "From new visas to a tourism backlash, the Top 10 issues that affected us in 2018 may forecast our future treatment." *Japan Times*, January 27, 2019, with Ghosn at #2, archived with commentary and sources at www.debito.org/?p=15535.

35. According to Reuters, Kobe Steel underreported income in 2008, 2011, and 2013, and committed data fraud for "nearly five decades." According to Bloomberg, much the same happened with Toray and Ube Industries, Olympus, Takata, Mitsubishi Materials, Nissan, and Subaru. *See* "Kobe Steel admits data fraud went on nearly five decades, CEO to quit." *Reuters*, March 5, 2018; "A backlash is coming to Carlos Ghosn's Arrest." *Bloomberg*, December 6, 2018; "Nissan CEO Saikawa admits receiving too much pay under executive equity plan." *Kyodo News/Japan Times*, September 5, 2019.

36. How many hours was revealed by Ghosn's lawyer to total 482 hours between November 11, 2018, and March 21, 2019. This went on seventy near-continuous days, eighteen of them with interrogations lasting 8 hours or more, without a lawyer present, and with solitary confinement before and after. Archived at www.debito.org/?p=15907#comment-1771681.

37. "Strict conditions attached to Ghosn's bail." *NHK World*, March 5, 2019.

38. "Carlos Ghosn's lawyer slams rare rearrest on bail in Tokyo as 'act of aggression.'" *Japan Times*, April 4, 2019.

39. "Ghosn rearrested for alleged aggravated breach of trust: Nissan chairman faces up to 10 further days in custody." *Nikkei Asia*, December 21, 2018.

40. "Ghosn's lawyer slams minister's gaffe on proving innocence." *Associated Press*, January 10, 2020. Ghosn's lawyer Francois Zimeray also agreed that this sentiment reflected Japanese justice, and the prosecution must prove guilt, not the other way around. "The presumption of innocence, respect of dignity and rights of defense have been essential components of what constitute a fair trial. Japan is an admirable, modern, otherwise advanced country. It deserves better than an archaic system that holds innocent people hostage. The onus is on you to abolish it."

41. "Carlos Ghosn's Escape from Japan Was the Right Move." *Shingetsu News Agency*, January 20, 2020.

42. "Human rights panel: Japan was wrong to detain Carlos Ghosn; owes him compensation." *Associated Press/Japan Today*, November 24, 2020.

43. "Interpol issues wanted notice for Ghosn after his escape from Japan." *CNBC/Associated Press*, January 2, 2020. You can read Ghosn's take on his case at https://carlosghosn.info/hostage-justice/.

44. The people who spirited Ghosn out of Japan are also currently incarcerated in Japan's "hostage justice" system, having been extradited by American authorities in March 2021. *See* "Carlos Ghosn: US father and son extradited to Japan." *BBC News*, March 2, 2021.

Also worthy of a mention in this footnote are similar fates suffered by high-profile foreign executives: Michael Woodford, former CEO of Olympus Corporation, and Mark Karpeles, former CEO of bitcoin exchange Mt. Gox.

Woodford was fired in 2011 for whistleblowing on corrupt practices in his company, but fortunately for him his corporate associates were unable to make any accusations of corporate malfeasance on his part stick in the Japanese media; so unlike Ghosn, he was not subjected to Japanese criminal procedures. *See*, for example, "Woodford and Ghosn: Foreign executives not in charge." *Shingetsu News Agency*, April 21, 2021.

Similar to Ghosn, Karpeles was arrested multiple times in 2015 on charges of embezzlement and data manipulation, and, despite claiming his innocence due to a computer hack, was subjected to almost a year of "nightmare" detentions and interrogations before being released on bail in 2016. In 2019, he beat the 99 percent conviction rate by being found not guilty of embezzlement, but was handed a four-year suspended sentence for data falsification. *See*, for example, "The Carlos Ghosn case is putting Japan's system of 'hostage justice' under scrutiny." *CNN*, January 20, 2019; "Former Mt. Gox chief Mark Karpeles acquitted of most charges in major bitcoin case." *CNN Business*, March 14, 2019. As of April 2021, according to their LinkedIn profiles, Karpeles remains in Japan while Woodford is based in London.

45. "Where foreigners fill prisons." *Economist.com*, August 5, 2009, citing the US State Department. Unclear, however, is if this is specifically noncitizens in Japan's prison system or also noncitizens in Immigration Detention Centers.

46. "Punishing foreigners, exonerating Japanese: Growing evidence that Japan's judiciary has double standards by nationality." *Japan Times*, March 24, 2009. As David T. Johnson (2002: 137, 157–159, 181) notes, public prosecutors consider "crimes committed by foreigners" as "one of the three main challenges facing the procuracy." Although Johnson acknowledges that "[c]ompared with America, Japan has few studies that systematically searches for bias in the criminal process" (158) regardless of nationality, he references Tōkyō University law professor Daniel H. Foote's prediction (1992: 374–377) that a multiethnic Japan will have "a separate track" for criminal prosecution of "foreigners": Criminal justice officials "have stepped up their surveillance and prosecution of [foreign workers]," and the influx of foreigners poses "the greatest external challenge" to Japan's "benevolent paternalism" in criminal justice. "Because of differences in language and values, prosecutors are unlikely to devote significant resources to the rehabilitation and reintegration of foreigners, instead concentrating simply on processing such cases efficiently." Thus, Foote predicts, the criminal justice process is likely to follow "a separate track" for foreigners, "Some degree of bias—on regional, class, or other grounds—seems inevitable [and] . . . there are numerous points at which such bias—conscious or not—could and at least in some cases clearly does affect outcomes" (156–157).

Although Johnson goes on to say, "Though more research is needed, it appears that compared to their American counterparts, Japanese prosecutors discriminate less, and less severely, against racial and ethnic minorities" (ibid.), I respectfully disagree, especially when Ichikawa Hiroshi, the chief public prosecutor in a major frame-up (*enzai*) case in Saga City, Kyūshū, revealed at a May 23, 2011, symposium, "We were taught that yakuza and foreigners have no human rights." Ichikawa also disclosed that "public prosecutors were taught to make up confessions and then have suspects sign them . . . after being trained in that way, I began to almost believe that this was natural." *See* "*Yakuza to gaikokujin ni jinken wa nai to oshierareta. Moto kenji ga bakuro shita odoroku beki shinjin kyouiku no jittai*" [We were taught that yakuza and foreigners have no human rights. A former prosecutor reveals the actual situation of educating new entrants that should surprise]. *Nikoniko News*, May 23, 2011, archived at www.debito.org/?p=8997. Ichikawa has also written a book on this issue, *Kenji Shikkaku* (A Prosecutor Disbarred: Shinbusha 2012), with chapter 2 translated by the Japan Innocence and Death Penalty Information Center and archived at www.debito.org/?p=15854.

Moreover, I hope the above examples in this book, almost all of which occurred after Johnson's book was published, will add to some of that needed research.

Chapter 7

Fetishization and Fear of Foreigners in the Japanese Media

As discussed in the previous three chapters, the construction of any national discourse involves laws, the creation, interpretation, and enforcement of those laws, and media messaging that disseminate the narratives behind those laws, generating a national identity and a concept of "Us" and "Them" that is essential to the survival of any nation-state. This chapter will conclude the construction by focusing on Japan's media narratives.

The Japanese media (e.g., print, broadcast, and online, combined with government avenues of influence over the media) shapes the contours and direction of Japan's national discourse on any issue. For this research, this affects mindsets not only toward what constitutes "a Japanese" but also what constitutes a "non-Japanese," with strong tendencies toward racialized concepts on both sides.

A BRIEF OVERVIEW OF JAPAN'S MEDIA MILIEU AND MINORITY VOICES WITHIN

Japan's media is a powerhouse for communication and social organization, tied for the highest penetration and concentration of daily newspapers in the world, and the sixth largest number of television sets (99 percent of all households, watching on average 30.6 hours per week as of 2018) in the world.[1] Media campaigns, both in terms of popular culture and public policy, are very effective in disseminating information and influencing Japanese public opinion; the knock-on effects of the Japanese *kisha kurabu* (Press Club) system (often closed to foreign correspondents) have been discussed thoroughly elsewhere in the literature.[2]

However, minority voices are underrepresented in Japan's media. There are a few ethnic newspapers/magazines published in Japan in Japanese and foreign languages (including Chinese, Korean, Portuguese, Spanish, and English, not to mention the Burakumin Liberation League press in Japanese), with a few regional "free papers" (e.g., Metropolis, Japanzine, the defunct Sapporo Source, etc.), but they generally offer less "hard news," more "news and events" bulletin-board-style information funded by advertising. As for minority voices in Japanese media, broadcasting in foreign languages is strictly regulated by the Japanese government,[3] while national-level newspapers in English (*Japan Times*, *Daily Yomiuri/Japan News*, *International Herald-Tribune/Asahi Shinbun*, plus online *Mainichi Daily News*, *Japan Today*, and *Kyodo News/Jiji Press* wire-based services, etc.) are entirely controlled by Japanese publishers. (Now that *Japan Today* and *Japan Times* have been bought up by Japan media companies in 2015 and 2017, respectively,[4] the only daily news media outlet independent of Wajin control is the *Shingetsu News Agency*.)

With the exception of *Japan Times* and *Japan Today*, these venues started off as English-language vanity projects of the four major Japanese newspapers to have a voice in worldwide media conversation. (After all, Japan's English-language resident community was never large enough to sustain four daily English-language newspapers!) Consequently, these outlets have few in-house foreign-language reporters, or staff beyond translators and proofreaders, and they fill space by republishing translated in-house articles from their Wajin writers, domestic wire-service articles, or outsourced overseas articles.

Thus, almost no national-level professional journalism in Japan, even in foreign languages, is independent of Wajin editorial control, generating less content to serve minorities and foreign residents of Japan. Moreover, in recent years there has been a distinct "Wajinizing" of news content. For example, in 2017 the *Japan Times* announced it would adopt language conforming to GOJ boilerplate for controversial topics, such as the "Comfort Women" wartime sexual slavery issue.[5]

Effect of Minority Underrepresentation in Japan's Media: Misrepresentation

Consequently, the voices of the noncitizen and ethnic minority communities in Japan are often muted, if not at times ignored. For example, a special Cabinet Survey on Nikkei Long-Term Residents (*Nikkei teijū gaikokujin*) inter alia asked Wajin (only, as *kokumin*) if they were aware of Nikkei foreigners currently living in Japan under a special visa status.[6] Despite Japan at the time having visa regimes that for nearly a quarter century imported South American laborers of Japanese descent, *nearly half of respondents* (46.4 percent) answered that they were not aware. This quantifiably underscores the invisibility of minority representation in Japan's dominant media discourse, and their exclusion from Japan's "public sphere" of influence[7] on Japan's social consensus on both the micro- and macro-levels.

Further, the author, a columnist for *Japan Times* since 2002 and *Shingetsu News Agency* since 2019, and a spokesperson for several minority causes, has extensive personal experience addressing domestic media campaigns that were disparaging or unfavorable to noncitizens and minorities.[8] I have also participated in domestic media debates that have (inadvertently or deliberately) misrepresented minority issues (both when translated into Japanese, and even when originally presented in Japanese). This was due to media filtering through Japanese editorial constraints or anticipated Wajin readership biases (as seen when I faced editorial pressure to conform to an editorial line while writing for *Japan Times* under its new ownership).[9] In terms of how this affects public discussions of discrimination against Non-Wajin in Japan, here is an example:

"Racial Discrimination" Becomes a Taboo Word under Editorial Constraints

Let us consider how "racial discrimination" has been reported on in the Japanese media. In a 5½ year survey of 114 Japanese-language articles[10] dealing with the Otaru Onsens Case (1999–2005, discussed in chapter 3), the word "racial discrimination" (*jinshu sabetsu*) was clearly and specifically referred to as the cause of discrimination in *only one article* in Japan's mainstream Japanese-language daily print media: an editorial by the *Hokkaidō Shinbun* on September 17, 2004 (five years into the Otaru Case), which was drawing conclusions from a Sapporo High Court decision that had just ruled in favor of plaintiffs accusing a public bathhouse of racial discrimination.[11] In all other articles before or since, the word "racial discrimination" was used only in the context of a claim by the plaintiffs (or the rulings of the Sapporo District and High Courts) and was never rendered objectively as a specific cause of this issue.

Instead, milder and misleading terms were used, such as generic "discrimination" (*sabetsu*), "discrimination by nationality" (*kokuseki sabetsu*), "discrimination by physical appearance" (*gaiken sabetsu*), "discrimination by ethnicity" (*minzoku sabetsu*), "discrimination against foreigners" (*gaikokujin-* or even *gaijin* [*sic*] *sabetsu*), even when it was clear within the article that one of the plaintiffs involved was not a "foreigner" but a naturalized Japanese citizen. However, this terminology was used if the articles referred to racism or discrimination at all; many articles instead attributed the issue to manners (*manā*), cultural differences and misunderstandings (*bunka no chigai, gokai*, etc.), the allegedly preternatural shyness of Japanese toward foreigners (sometimes referred to in print as an "allergy" (*arerugii*)), or to other tangential causes, such as the excluders allegedly protecting their businesses from foreign crime or from customers' alleged fear of foreigners (*gaikokujin hanzai mizen bōshi, kyaku banare bōshi*, etc.).

In other words, even after being adjudged as *jinshu sabetsu* by two Japanese courts of law, not to mention depicted as such in Defendant Otaru City's official publications and court testimony,[12] *jinshu sabetsu* in the Japanese media was treated as merely the opinion of parties involved, not an objective fact of the case. This editorial slant in Wajin-controlled media would appear to be part of official policy: The UN CERD Committee (76th Session, 2010) in official reviews with the GOJ clearly noted, "It seems that [racial discrimination] is something that the state in question prefers to avoid as a term."[13] (More in chapter 8.)

This had a profound effect on how public discourse in Japan was constructed on this issue. The Otaru Onsens Case became couched as two camps with voices equal in merit: the "maligned foreigner" vs. the "troubled bathhouse business" (i.e., not "the discriminated against" vs. "the discriminator/racist"). The effect of this was that, for the sake of "balance," media editorial policies could not report on allegedly discriminatory practices without also interviewing discriminators for "their side of the story." This encouraged an apologist tone in the reportage. It also disseminated bigoted views on "foreigners" for other discriminators nationwide to justify their own exclusionary actions (see chapter 3). On the other hand, the domestic and international English-language media showed little reservation in calling the issue one of "racism" from nearly the start of the issue, eventually isolating the apologist discourse within Wajin-controlled media as part of "inscrutable" Japanese culture.[14]

Thus, within Japan's media, enfranchised dominant majority actors are not only able to dull debate on discriminatory discourse involving disenfranchised minorities, but also say negative things about those disenfranchised actors; meanwhile, the disenfranchised lack a "right of reply" to defend themselves or shape domestic discourse.[15] As discussed below, this lack of "checks and balances" leads to excessive stereotyping of minorities in Japan's media, including, in extreme examples, hate speech and propaganda.

GOJ DEPICTIONS OF "FOREIGNERS" AS CRIMINALS IN THE MEDIA

Let us now take a closer look at how official propaganda (see definition in endnote)[16] targeting "foreigners" has been disseminated to the general public.

NPA Public Notices Warning about "Bad Foreigner Crimes" with Racialized Illustrations

The end of chapter 5 mentioned the NPA's new "Committee for Policy Against Internationalization" in their 2000 White Paper. Within a year, NPA funding materialized for nationwide police notices, banners, and pamphlets specifically warning the Japanese public to be wary of "bad foreigners" (*furyō gaikokujin*) and "foreign crime," even though the crimes mentioned were also being committed by Japanese nationals, and in far larger numbers (more below).

It is important to pause here and underscore something significant about these official police flyers. Not only did they often exaggerate or outright fabricate claims and statistics about local "foreign crime," but they also used racialized depictions of "foreign" perps. Police illustrations included large noses and distorted facial features, slitted eyes (for Non-Wajin Asians), darkened skin, and accented speech. Reproducing all of these flyers would increase this book's printing costs significantly, so please go to the endnote for this section (and other places in this chapter) to see summaries and access an online visual archive.[17]

In sum, while using tax monies to specifically combat "internationalization" in the form of "foreign crime," the NPA was explicitly linking "criminals" to "people who do not *look* Japanese," meaning "foreigners" (particularly "illegal foreigners") were identifiable on sight. Thus, the Wajin public was being enlisted in official racial profiling.

Other Official Notices and Campaigns Targeting "Foreign Crime"

To keep the Japanese public apprised of foreign crime (*gaikokujin hanzai*) in specific, the NPA began semiannual (around March and September) reports, accompanied with widespread press releases targeting "foreign crime." In addition to periodical media saturation campaigns focusing on "foreign crime" in particular, there are also annual campaigns such as the monthlong "Campaign for Policies against Illegal Foreign Labor" every June since 2004, focusing on "illegal foreign workers." For greater exposure, there is a huge banner displayed in Shinagawa, one of Tōkyō's most prominent JR stations, every year[18]—even though the official number of visa overstayers peaked in 1993 and decreased every year during that time period in question.[19] (In recent years, it has risen with a rise in the foreign population and since plateaued.)[20]

Further, NPA campaigns enlisted Wajin celebrities and other public notables to draw attention to "foreigners" as potential criminals (later terrorists; see below), asking the public's cooperation in finding, reporting, and combating the effects of Japan's internationalization.[21] Even Emperor Akihito underscored this alienating narrative in a speech marking the fiftieth anniversary of the NPA on July 26, 2004: "In recent years, with the rise in crime, and the threat of international terrorism, the importance of your duties is increasing. I ask you, in accordance with the ideals of the laws, to redouble your efforts to realize a society where citizens (*kokumin*) can live peacefully and securely (*anshin*)."[22] Eventually, this created a perpetual "foreign crime wave" campaign that became illogical and unstoppable.

Differentiated Crime Statistics in Japan for Wajin and "Foreigners"

The NPA's annual White Papers on crime illustrate how crime reportage in Japan is differentiated into "*kokumin* vs. *gaikokujin*," with no comparison between them in scope or scale (as you read, please view the online archive of a past example).[23] Note the difference in scale. Comparing a base year of 2009 (H.21), there were a total of 30,569 total cleared cases of crime committed by all foreign nationals (the total of the dark and light bars). For *kokumin*, corresponding thefts and regular penal offenses not including traffic violations (the total of the bottom dark and middle light bars, on a scale of 10,000 cases per interval) total to over *1.5 million cases*, or a difference of about a factor of 49. If put on the same chart with the same scale, foreign crime numbers would thus be practically invisible compared to *kokumin* crime numbers.[24] However, the NPA has chosen to avoid this comparison, focusing instead on the rise and fall—mostly the purported rise—of foreign crime.

The Effects and Externalities of Propagandizing "Foreign Crime"

This propagandizing is an established practice by Japan's policing forces. Herbert (1995) traces the arc of NPA White Papers after they introduced a new term into Japanese crime reportage from 1987: *rainichi gaikokujin* (visiting foreign nationals) indicating a new breed of "foreignness" in Japan (separate from Zainichi, American military and dependents within US bases in Japan, etc.) as a byproduct of Japan's "internationalization" and foreign labor influx.[25] Herbert notes that the tone, particularly in the NPA's 1990 White Paper, focuses on the "rapid increase in foreign workers and the reaction of the police," and "functions to suggest that 'illegal' migrant laborers were involved" (197). This led to a "prompt media echo" and a "moral panic"[26] of a purported foreign crime wave that, in Herbert's assessment, was "rash and thoughtless" (197). In his thorough recounting and analysis of media reaction, Herbert concludes that police reportage and media reaction successfully aroused suspicion and criminalization of noncitizens, where Japan as a nation was portrayed as "defenseless against international crime" (198). Even Herbert argues that this set a template for future NPA campaigns against "foreign crime" that played dirty pool, by manipulating statistics, incurring periodic moral panics in the media, and justifying budgetary outlay for bureaucratic line-item projects (179).

By the 2000s, the NPA had normalized statistical manipulation to create perpetual "foreign crime rises." For example: On May 1, 2000, the *Sankei Shinbun* cribbed from the NPA's April periodic foreign crime report to produce the front-page headline: "Foreign Crime Rises Again, Six-Fold in Ten Years";[27] overlooked was that this rise was in only one sector of crime, which had a comparatively small numbers of cases compared to cases committed by citizens. Another example is where the NPA announced in their September 2002 periodic foreign crime report that the number of crimes committed by foreigners on temporary visas had jumped by 25.8 percent over the previous year, and serious crimes like murder, robbery, and arson likewise were up 18.2 percent. However, this was not the whole story: there were also rises in crime numbers committed by *kokumin* in the same time period (see statistics above, H.10). But the mass media headlined not only that foreign crime had increased, but also that foreigners are *three times more likely than Japanese* to commit crimes in groups.[28]

This argument of how "foreigners" were more likely to be criminals became a meme, even when the statistics did not support it. For example, the NPA made the following argument within a 2010 *Kyodo News* article: "The number of foreigners rounded up last year on suspicion of being involved in criminal activities was about 13,200, down roughly 40 percent from 2004 when the number peaked. 'The extent of how much crime has become globalized cannot be grasped through statistics,' the [NPA White Paper of 2010] says, attributing part of the reason to difficulties in solving crimes committed by foreigners—which are more likely to be carried out by multiple culprits than those committed by Japanese."[29] So even when the statistics showed a dramatic drop in foreign crime, the NPA started to claim that "foreign crime" was now unquantifiable, mooting the need for numerical analysis of actual evidence. Worse, *Kyodo News* quoted it at face value without analysis (more on this below).

Efforts to discount or discredit any "foreign crime" drop continue to the present day. From 2009, NPA coined the word *hanzai infura* (crime infrastructure) to refer to "things and organizations that are that are the basic foundation of crime" (my translation), such as cellphones under fake names, fake websites, false marriages, false adoptions, and fake IDs. Although this "crime infrastructure" technically assists thieves of any nationality, the NPA's online explanations focus on noncitizens, with the majority of their examples depicting crimes involving "foreigners."[30] In other words, even if "foreign crime" numbers are smaller than "Japanese crime" numbers, the NPA claims there must be a statistical understatement, because the latent "groupism" of "foreign crime" causes discrepancies when compared to "Japanese crime" (ironically countering the stereotype of "Japanese groupism" seen in *Nihonjinron*, etc.).

Moreover, as seen in police notices above, the NPA was claiming "rapid rises" (*kyūzō*) in foreign crime when foreign crime rates and numbers were concurrently *decreasing*. Even after "foreign crime" numbers eventually dropped below any reasonable NPA excuse of statistical discrepancies or pinpoint rises in types of crime, the NPA widened the scope of its sample to make it appear as though noncitizen crime had still risen (refer to online archive).[31] For example, compare the scale of its 2001 statistics (issued April 1, 2002), when noncitizen crime had plateaued, with 2012's statistics, when it had significantly dropped. Year 2011's numbers have thus dropped below 1993's numbers. So from 2007's semiannual crime report, the NPA moved the goalposts, shifting the scale back behind 1993 to show a rise compared to the past (similar to how *Sankei Shinbun* above depicted a sixfold rise in 2000, by comparing numbers to a decade earlier). However, there is no deflator to account for the fact that the noncitizen population before 1990 was less than half that of 2011.

As of this Second Edition, the NPA's obfuscating tactics have since become normalized. For example, when the MOJ announced in 2016 the overall good news that a new record high number of foreign residents were not in Japan (after a downward trend following economic downturns of the late 2000s and the Fukushima nuclear disaster), the *Japan Times* buried the lede by headlining "Japan sees record high number of foreign residents," then devoted more than half of the article's space to parroting NPA arguments on how this has brought in more foreign crime (in the form of visa overstayers and deportations; without any caveats or analysis of how these are victimless or, as we shall see below, incomparable crimes).[32]

This brings us to the next issue to consider: how the Japanese media enables NPA propaganda to construct a foreigner-targeting and criminalizing narrative:

Overlooked Statistical Foreign Crime Deflators by the Media

The domestic media has been complicit in NPA propagandizing not only in terms of disseminating the information to the public, but also their lack of scrutiny over the data. Despite an extensive search during each semiannual "foreign crime rise media campaign," I could find no NPA media report or mainstream domestic media article on "foreign crime" comparing "foreign crime" to "Japanese crime," or to total crimes committed in Japan (more below). If it had been, several logical and statistical discrepancies would have come to light. As a case study, consider these basic sources of statistical inaccuracy within past reportage[33]:

1) Crime committed by noncitizens accounted for 1–3 percent or less of all crime in Japan, and in many cases, crime rates were lower for noncitizens than citizens as a proportion of the population.

2) There are inherent difficulties in counting "perpetrators" (*jin'in*), "cases" (*kyokensū*, i.e., one perpetrator can commit more than one case of crime, and sometimes within gangs of Japanese), and "cleared cases" (*tekihatsu sha*, i.e., people actually caught for a specific crime). Because the NPA also counts suspected (yet-uncaught) noncitizens (as well as noncitizens arrested but later released without indictment) as bona fide "crime cases,"[34] crime data inputs were complex enough for manipulation to accentuate rises and downplay falls.

3) Foreign crime over the interim had in fact plateaued and would go down continuously after 2005, but this trend would not be reflected in the media.

4) The claims of a rise of "visa overstayers" (*fuhō taizaisha*), rendered in NPA publications more colorfully as "bad" or "illegal foreigners" (*furyō/fuhō gaikokujin*) were in fact a complete fabrication—they had at the time fallen without pause since 1993.[35]

5) The NPA counted "visa overstays" (*fuhō taizai*, subsumed under a more ominous-sounding category of *tokubetsu hōhan kensū*, or "special penal offenses") as part of total "foreign crimes." However, visa violations are not quite the same breed of crime, as (a) they are "victimless crimes," unlike heinous crimes (*kyōaku hanzai*) like rape or murder, and (b) they are crimes that Japanese citizens, by definition, cannot commit, as citizens have no visa to overstay. However, by lumping in these incomparable crimes, gross "foreign crime" statistics were inflated *by as much as a third.* Again, these figures were reported as such in the media without differentiation, comparison, or caveat. Thus, if one removed incomparable visa violations from the tally, this would generally lower the "foreign crime" rate significantly below the proportion of registered noncitizen population, meaning the "foreign crime" rate was actually substantially below the (then also-rising) "Japanese crime" rate.

6) Finally, the NPA generally reported "foreign crime" rate changes in terms of percentages more than raw numbers, which mathematically exaggerated the crime rates further. That is to say, for example, if one case last year becomes two cases this year, this is a rise of a small number (one), but mathematically a 100 percent increase. Thus, an increase in already small numbers in noncitizen crime became markedly more sensationalized in the media than the much larger numbers (but smaller proportional rises) in citizen crime. That is assuming, of course, that citizen and noncitizen crimes were compared. They were not.

Thus, constant official differentiation between *kokumin* and *gaikokujin* in the dominant discourse had created a normalized firewall. Activists have repeatedly pointed out (in Japanese) the need for all of these mitigators and deflators to domestic media, but no mainstream domestic daily media body (as of 2000–2020) has offered analysis to this degree of the inherent biases in the data. Other potential mitigators (which are standard practice in other societies analyzing crime)[36] have been likewise ignored or underreported, such as the following:

1) Noncitizen migrant workers tend to be younger, male, in less-lucrative, less-stable, and lower-status jobs, and thus statistically are disproportionately more likely to commit crime than average.

2) Racial profiling by Japanese police (see chapters 4 and 5) could comparatively inflate noncitizen numbers of suspects and detentions, thus biasing the sample.[37]

3) The noncitizen population has more than doubled since 1990 (from around one million to over two million), while the citizen population plateaued, and now has continuously fallen since 2006. More noncitizens means more potential criminals, yet *kokumin* crime numbers have also risen at times despite the population fall.[38]

4) There have been cases of Wajin criminals taking advantage of this "foreign crime wave" discourse, posing as "foreigners" at crime scenes (e.g., adopting what sounded to victims and police like Chinese or Portuguese accents). Or, when caught, Wajin have blamed "foreign criminals" for their misdeeds to throw police investigations off the scent.[39] This may have further inflated estimates of "foreign crime" statistics.

"Foreign Crime" Campaigns Become Illogical

Campaigns against "foreign crime" have been taken to a logical extreme, where rates or numbers can never fall far enough to permit a more relaxed attitude toward policing noncitizens.

In 2008, foreign crime statistics had fallen again from 2007, and by double-digit percentages. Yet during the NPA's annual spring "foreign crime" media update, *Kyodo News* parroted the official announcement calling this crime drop a *rise* (putting the word "high plateauing" (*takadomari*) in the Japanese headline), while portraying it as a *fall* in the English translation headline. Let us cite the English version of the article to view the NPA's propagandizing techniques:

> *Number of crimes committed by visiting foreigners down*
>
> TOKYO, February 28, 2008 (AP)—(*Kyodo News*):
>
> The number of crimes committed by foreigners visiting Japan dropped for the second straight year to 35,800 last year, down 10.8 percent from the previous year, after hitting a peak in 2005, the National Police Agency said Thursday.

> However, the number of crimes detected by police during the five-year period from 2003 to 2007 increased some 70 percent from the period of with an NPA official stressing the need for further crackdown on them. [*sic*]

This sloppy translation of the second paragraph is better understood by looking at the Japanese original (literal translation mine):

> On the other hand, when looking at the number of cases committed within five-year periods, comparing the number of crimes committed between 2003–2007 and 1993–1997, there has been a 70 percent rise. The NPA says, "Although there have been some rises and falls, in recent years it's 'been stopped at a high point'. From now on it will be necessary to for us to strengthen our crackdown even more."[40]

Let us parse this method of manipulating the statistics into a "foreign crime" rise: The NPA has arbitrarily chosen a five-year time frame from the past (even though the noncitizen population was smaller), noted that the crime rate was lower than the current five-year time frame, and called the current time frame a comparative rise. This is bad science, yet it was reported as is by *Kyodo News* with no analysis (or a professionally proofread translation). Furthermore, by logical extension of this argument, one can never reach any other conclusion but the justification of a further crackdown against "foreigners." For *even if foreign crime fell to zero*, the NPA could argue that the fall is due to their strict policies; therefore the crackdown must be maintained under all circumstances.

Thus, the discourse of "foreigners as criminals" became dominant thanks to the Japanese media's high tolerance for officials' statistical games and unquestioned narratives. Even when evidence was inconclusive that noncitizens were involved, the media nevertheless reported NPA claims that certain crimes were "possibly committed by foreigners" based upon circumstantial evidence or just plain prejudice: such as an alleged modus operandi (*teguchi*), a crime having a "violent nature," or having perpetrators who were allegedly "daring" (*daitan*) (Japanese criminals are apparently more subtle in their approach).[41] Media also reported largely unsourced claims that certain business sectors were more likely to be "breeding grounds for crime,"[42] and that international gangs were generally infiltrating Japan through the domestic criminal gang infrastructure thanks to "globalization" (*gurōbaruka*).[43] Some just explicitly assumed that foreigners would be the prototypical criminals in anticrime proposals, as NHK did in 2017 when reporting on new facial recognition measures (zeroing in on the only foreign face in a crowd).[44]

Moreover, the prejudice of "foreign crime" being more heinous (*goku'aku*) than *kokumin* crime is deeply rooted, for example, in Japanese cop movie

"Heavenly Sins" (*Tengoku no Taizai*: 1992), where in one scene a victim's face was boiled off in a kitchen; the detectives theorized aloud that this crime was so heinous that a "foreigner" must have done it; the movie later revealed their hunch was correct. The attitude also appeared in Tōkyō Governor Ishihara Shintarō's *Nihon Yo* column in the *Sankei Shinbun*, where he wrote about being convinced by Tōkyō Metropolitan Police reports that certain crimes (Ishihara cites a real case of a victim's face being peeled off) must be committed by Chinese due to their degree of heinousness (for, Ishihara alleges, a Japanese could never conceive of doing that). Ishihara later attributed this breed of criminality to Chinese "Ethnic DNA" (*minzokuteki* DNA; more on this below).[45]

There is one more phenomenon within this discourse that will emerge as this chapter continues: "piling on," that is, the official linkage of unrelated issues to "foreigners," even when noncitizens were uninvolved. For example, in July 2003, there was a shocking crime involving a twelve-year-old Wajin sexually assaulting, then murdering, a four-year-old Wajin in Nagasaki (cutting off his penis with scissors, then throwing him from a multistory parking garage). In response, Tanigaki Sadakazu, public safety commissioner in the first PM Koizumi Cabinet, said (translation by the author): "Representative of the decline in public safety, one can raise the issue of foreign crime and youth crime. For example, there has been a marked increase in crimes committed by Brazilian youths."[46]

In sum, with this degree of access to domestic media, an official body such as the NPA could dramatically alter Japan's domestic discourse, convincing public policymakers and the public to fear an already differentiated and disenfranchised "Other." Accordingly, Japan's politicians took advantage of the NPA-generated public shock to demand tougher "foreign crime" policies for their own political gain.

THE EFFECT OF NPA PROPAGANDA: MEDIA "BLAME GAMES" ENTER THE POLITICAL SPHERE

As per the function of propaganda mentioned above, the more people read media and official reports about "foreign crime rises" in Japan, the less people knew about the subject, and the more people surveyed would support GOJ policies, including those depriving noncitizens of equal rights and protections under the law (more below).

The themes behind these NPA anticrime campaigns focus less on the crime (which, aside from visa violations, citizens can and do commit in higher numbers and generally higher rates), more on the nationality of the criminal. In fact, due to the racialized images being used to depict potential miscreants, the NPA has encouraged racial profiling in the public, asking them to be on the lookout not just for noncitizens, but also for people who looked "different" and "suspicious" (*fushin*) (see chapter 4).

This matters to our discourse of constant differentiation, since, as noted above, Wajin were being officially reminded by police flyers that a foreign criminal *looked* foreign. Further, the frequency and saturation of media campaigns influenced public discourse to the point where noncitizens were seen less as a social benefit (e.g., cheap labor keeping Japan's factories competitive in the export market, not to mention as people contributing to Japan's tax coffers and national pension plans), more as a social bane and threat to public security.

The Particular Vulnerability of "Foreigners" to Racialized Crime Narratives

An important question to raise is, why is "foreign crime" so easy and unquestioned a target? One reason is, as mentioned above, Japan's media is loath to say that "racial discrimination," and so on is a cause or effect of domestic behavior. Naturally, most people do not want to be labeled or dismissed as a "racist," but there was little chance of that happening, because the people being targeted and racialized were so disenfranchised from the public sphere that they could not fight back. For no matter how racially or illogically the Wajin-dominated power structure denigrated "foreigners," there were, and still are, no national-level minority media outlets powerful enough to offer corrections and counter-defamatory arguments to the dominant majority discourse.

The second reason is a fundamental issue of the sociology of crime: It just so happened that prior to these "foreign crime" campaigns, there was a shift in how crimes themselves were being recorded and reported, boosting Japan's overall crime numbers regardless of nationality.[47] This played into a sense of urgency to restore Japan's "safe" society. However, public attitudes differ by nationality. If crimes committed by "Japanese" go up, then the public will be critical of the NPA for not doing their job of crime prevention. However, if crimes committed by "foreigners" go up, the criticism tends to go the other way. Politicians and pundits can (and did) argue, "Why should foreigners be allowed into our country at all if they're going to commit crime?"

Noncitizens silenced in Japan's public sphere are a soft target, and it gave the NPA a clear incentive structure: Portray them as a threat (as they often are in nation-states worldwide), and get even more policy latitude and budgetary outlay. And the NPA did this with policies targeting "foreigners" phenotypically. And then Japan's politicians began to pile on.

Legislators Targeting and Denigrating "Foreigners" for Political Gain

On April 9, 2000, newly elected Tōkyō governor Ishihara Shintarō gave his infamous "Sangokujin Speech" before the Ground Self-Defense Forces (SDF) in Nerima, Tōkyō. He worried aloud about *Sangokujin* (third-country nationals, which is, as mentioned in chapters 2 and 4, a derogatory Postwar word used to refer to people from the former Japanese colonies of Korea and Taiwan), as well as "bad foreigners" (*furyō gaikokujin*), who were allegedly repeat offenders of "heinous crimes" (*goku'aku hanzai*).[48] He claimed they might (unprecedentedly) riot in the case of a national emergency. Ishihara then called for the use of the SDF to maintain public order.

This caused some controversy, since this sentiment of "lawless foreigners unleashed by natural disasters" is redolent of the false and deadly rumors of ethnic Korean residents poisoning Wajin water supplies during the 1923 Great Kantō Earthquake. However, domestic media missed the mark, debating less about whether Ishihara's claims were accurate or exaggerated, more about whether the use of the epithet Sangokujin was offensive or discriminatory. Public debate also overlooked the more serious problem: enforceability. How was the SDF to decide who was "foreign" in the event of a "foreigner" roundup? This left Visible Minorities vulnerable to racial profiling. Although Ishihara later offered some clarifications, he refused to retract the essence of his statements. (This became especially ironic after the multiple disasters in Fukushima on March 11, 2011, when, despite his fears, there were no "foreigner" riots.)

Further, amid several disparaging statements about noncitizens that Ishihara would make in subsequent years, Ishihara wrote in his *Nihon Yo* [Listen up, Japan] regular *Sankei Shinbun* column (May 8, 2001)[49] metaphorically about Chinese "ethnic DNA" innately predisposing Chinese to criminal activity, and warned of the dangers of Chinese crimes spreading throughout Japanese society. He also refused to retract these claims. Then, under his mandate as Tōkyō Governor, Ishihara took high-profile steps against "foreign crime," including appointing former chief of the NPA Department of Public Safety "Safe Livelihoods Bureau" (*seikatsu anzen kyokuchō*) Takehana Yutaka as his Vice Governor. He placed police surveillance cameras in parts of Tōkyō with high noncitizen populations and had the Tōkyō Metropolitan Police launch several highly publicized raids of purported "hotbeds" (*anshō*) of "foreign crime" (such as Shinjuku, Ikebukuro, or Roppongi, which he alleged were places no longer like Japan at night, where even the yakuza "feared to tread" (*habakaru*)).[50] He also promised to find and "boot out" any illegals.[51]

Other politicians followed Ishihara's lead. For example, during an election stump speech for a local candidate on November 2, 2003, Kanagawa Governor Matsuzawa Shigefumi stated that "foreigners" were "all sneaky thieves" (*kosodoro*), and that because Ishihara had cracked down on "foreigners" in his jurisdiction, they, along with juveniles and other gangs, had migrated to neighboring Kanagawa Prefecture. Under press scrutiny, Matsuzawa then "clarified" his remark to "some" instead of "all," and added, "There is a marked rise in the number of cases in which some foreigners who enter Japan on working and other visas remain (in Japan) illegally and commit heinous crimes. My view is that such crimes need to be stamped out." He retracted his remarks entirely the next day but was not forced to resign his position.[52]

Targeting "Foreigners" Becomes Policy at the Highest Levels of Government

On September 22, 2003, the first day of the second PM Koizumi Cabinet, no fewer than three Cabinet ministers focused on "foreign crime" as a political issue du jour. Justice Minister Nozawa Daizō explicitly stated that one of his policy goals would be to "make Japan the world's safest country again."[53] In the same Cabinet announcement, the *Yomiuri Shinbun* reported on National Public Safety Commission chairman Ono Kiyoko stating she wanted to devote her total energies (*zenryoku*) to "strengthening policy against foreign and youth crime." "Foreign crime" was also mentioned that day by Public Management Minister (and future Prime Minister) Aso Tarō on NHK News.

These sentiments soon became formal legislative policies targeting noncitizens. In December 2003, the Tōkyō Metropolitan Government, in conjunction with the Immigration Bureau and NPA, announced a campaign to "reduc[e] the number of illegal foreign residents by half in the next five years to ensure public security."[54] By December 2004, an "Action Plan for Preempting Terrorism" was passed by this Cabinet, with explicit provisions made "to prevent terrorists from entering Japan," specifically targeting "foreigners." In practice, as seen in chapters 3 and 4, these policies encouraged racial profiling of Visible Minorities at hotels and other private-sector businesses.

Once again, Japanese media abdicated their responsibility to question authority. Timely counterarguments did not appear in any major Japanese media querying whether or not this official targeting of "foreigners" was based upon any historical evidence. There had never been what could be construed as a terrorist attack by "foreigners" on Japanese soil (as opposed to, for example, homegrown terrorism such as the Japanese Red Army, radical leftist groups Chūkakuha or Kakumaruha, or the Aum Shinrikyō sarin gas attacks of 1995). In terms of infectious diseases, another of the GOJ's policy planks, there had only been one case of SARS influenza from a noncitizen tourist in 2003 (which did not spread to the general public, but nevertheless panicked many hotels into closing their doors to "foreigners"—including refusing service to this author, despite his Japanese citizenship).[55] Hence the facts did not support the claims, but Wajin media did not hold officials accountable.

This is how racial profiling was being embedded within these new public-security laws against exogenous "foreign terrorists." It would not stop there. Soon foreign scares would target not only resident noncitizens but also Japanese citizens with foreign contacts and roots.

Enforcing Disenfranchisement: Targeting "Foreigners" and "Foreign Influences" within the GOJ

As discussed in chapter 2, definitions of a "foreigner" in Japan can be blurry, for it depends not only on citizenship, but also on blood-based origins and phenotype ("looking like" a Japanese), acculturation ("acting like" a Japanese), and even ideology ("thinking like" a Japanese). However, even after all these conditions have been met, in Japan's political circles a person's "foreign" roots have been tied to disloyalty to Japan as a nation. These controversies have benefited xenophobic political camps, and stymied efforts at progressive public policies that could have benefited Non-Wajin and Visible Minorities.

For example, conservative politicians piggybacking off the "illegal overstayer foreign crime and terrorism" narratives of the 2000s claimed that several progressive proposals were influenced by unpatriotic "foreign" infiltration. This caused resignations, political exiles, and muted voices of open-minded and sympathetic Wajin. Examples follow:

Scandalizing Reformer Renhō for Her Non-Wajin Roots

In September 2009, the long-ruling conservative LDP fell out of power, and the liberal opposition Democratic Party of Japan (DPJ) established one of Japan's few leftist political administrations in its Postwar history. On January 17, 2010, former LDP Trade Minister Hiranuma Takeo made obnoxious remarks about the ethnic origins of DPJ politician Murata Renhō (aka Renhō), a former TV star and model who was widely seen as a political reformer. Renhō, in the course of her duties demanding budget justifications during the PM Hatoyama administration's early austerity drives, asked bureaucrats in a public hearing why so much money was being earmarked for developing the world's fastest supercomputer, saying, "What's wrong with being the world's number two?" Hiranuma not only called her remarks "imprudent" (*fukinshin*), but also claimed they were because "she is not originally Japanese" (*motomoto Nihonjin ja nai*): "She was naturalized, became a Diet member, and that's why she said something like that."

Renhō, born in Tōkyō in 1967 to a Taiwanese father and a Wajin mother, had taken Japanese citizenship in 1985. Under press scrutiny, Hiranuma denied that he had said anything discriminatory (arguing that he could not be saying anything *racist* because Renhō is a Japanese citizen), refused to retract his remarks, and accused her instead of trying to "sensationalize" politics for more media attention. Renhō refused to comment and did not publicly question why her loyalties and judgment were being questioned because her father is not Wajin. Fortunately, due to her performance under criticism, she further developed a reputation as a tough reformer and was later awarded three DPJ Cabinet posts.[56] (Unfortunately, as we shall see shortly below, this goodwill would not last.)

Foreign Minister Maehara's Resignation Due to a "Foreign" Donor

On March 6, 2011, DPJ foreign minister Maehara Seiji was forced to resign his Cabinet post for taking political donations from "a foreigner"—a seventy-two-year-old Zainichi Korean Special Permanent Resident restaurant owner in Kyōto. Having known Maehara from junior high school, she had contributed a modest total of 250,000 yen (US $3,000) to his campaign over five years. The Political Funds Control Law (*seiji shikin kisei hō*) stipulates that Japanese politicians cannot accept donations from noncitizens.[57] However, given the modest amount of donation (and the fact that Maehara reportedly never knew she was "foreign"), it is clear that Maehara's resignation was less due to the amount of money received, more to the fact that it came from a "foreigner"—even if the "foreign" contributor had been born and lived her entire life in Japan as a Zainichi.

Problematizing Liberal DPJ Policy Proposals by Generating a Stigma toward "Naturalized" Japanese

On April 17, 2010, Tōkyō Governor Ishihara Shintarō stated to a national gathering of 450 LDP MPs that, in a current debate about the ruling DPJ granting local suffrage rights to noncitizen Permanent Residents (see below), that many of the supporters of the proposal were naturalized or had relatives that were naturalized. He called into question their loyalties due to "foreign" roots:

> I don't know if they're doing it out of obligation (*giri-date*) to their ancestors, but they're trying to ram through (*mawari tōsou*) laws that will decide the fate of Japan. . . . Are there people who have been naturalized or are the children of fathers or mothers who have been naturalized here? The heads of more than one party in the ruling camp and many veteran senior officials in the camp are.

This was a veiled reference to a ruling coalition leader, Fukushima Mizuho of the Social Democratic Party, who was currently a Cabinet member.

Fukushima rebuked Ishihara immediately, saying, "Naturalized people are Japanese, and have totally equal rights and obligations with Japanese. It must be racial discrimination to make an issue of them." She also demanded Ishihara retract his remarks, which he refused to do. However, Fukushima also emphatically denied that she or anyone in her family had been naturalized, which did not counteract the social stigma that Ishihara was generating toward Japanese citizens of diversity.[58]

Normalization of the Non-Wajin's Permanent "Foreigner" Status: The Self-Identified Naturalized "Foreigner" MP Tsurunen Marutei

In 2010, an actual naturalized citizen lawmaker undermined Japan's naturalization regime by stigmatizing *himself*. Tsurunen Marutei, Japan's first European-born Caucasian MP, assumed office in Japan's Upper House in 2002 promising to "speak up for the outsiders," "promote intercultural tolerance and laws banning discrimination in housing and employment" while cultivating support from the Zainichi Korean minority.[59] However, after distancing himself from "foreigner issues" in a 2002 interview with the author and in a 2006 interview with *Metropolis* magazine,[60] he was conspicuously absent from a Diet meeting with UN special rapporteur Doudou Diene in 2006 (see chapter 8) regarding the latter's preliminary report on racial discrimination in Japan.[61]

Then, in an interview with the *Japan Times* conducted in English, Tsurunen was quoted as follows:

> We are foreigners and we can't change the fact. But still Japanese accept us into this society as foreigners. . . . I don't need to try to be Japanese or assimilate too much. I want to be accepted as a foreigner and still contribute to this society. It's no problem for me to be a foreigner—it's a fact. . . . I always say I am Finn-born Japanese.[62]

There were many critiques of this statement, with some questioning the legal validity of the statement "Japanese foreigner" from a national representative in the Diet sworn to uphold Japan's laws, including those connected to naturalization. But as racialized concepts of "Japaneseness" were being established beyond legal parameters by xenophobic Wajin public officials, Tsurunen, the most prominent Non-Wajin naturalized citizen of Japan, was hereby playing into their hands: normalizing and justifying the racialization of Japanese citizenship—by calling himself a "foreigner" and enforcing his Non-Wajin status upon himself.

Tsurunen responded to the criticism:

> I wish to thank everyone for their comments. As people have pointed out, my use of the English word "foreigner" was inappropriate. I was trying to express

> that I am not a "Japan-born Japanese" and used "foreigner," but strictly speaking I should have said "foreign-born person," or, as I said in the article, "Finn-born Japanese." I regret using expressions that gave rise to misunderstandings, and would like to offer my apologies.[63]

Notwithstanding this gaffe, Tsurunen, facing reelection in 2013, published a pamphlet, which is reproduced in the online archive in this endnote.[64] The slogan on the right third of his pamphlet read, "*'Me' no iro kaete, ganbarimasu.*" (I will change the color of my "eyes" [i.e., change my outlook] and do my best). Further rendering the kanji for "eye" in blue to match his eyes, Tsurunen thus highlighted his physical attributes as a Visible Minority as part of his public appeal, further "othering" himself to maintain his Diet seat. It was unsuccessful; he resoundingly lost his seat in July 2013.[65] Thus, not only had Tsurunen remained silent during the debates on hyphenated identities affecting other politicians mentioned above, he had also relinquished control over his own public identity by pandering to Wajin narratives, and lost his popular appeal.

Further Developments for the Second Edition

Since the First Edition of this book, Japan's politics and rhetoric have become more brazenly xenophobic. This is due in part to the LDP's return to power in 2012 (and the subsequent collapse of the leftist opposition), the rise of the ultraconservative interest group Nippon Kaigi,[66] and the revisionist[67] Abe Administration becoming Japan's longest in history, ruling with a parliamentary supermajority for most of the 2010s. It became so pronounced that even the *New York Times* in 2010 noted that "new dissent in Japan is loudly anti-foreign," and when those dissenters returned to office, the *New York Times* Editorial Board in 2013 openly criticized Abe and the LDP for its "counterproductive" and "unnecessary nationalism" inflaming regional tensions.[68] With this far-rightward swing of the political pendulum offering little hope of public policy benefiting Japan's foreign residents, overt foreigner-bashing became an established tool for attracting attention and consolidating power.

For example, in 2017, when Renhō led a new assemblage of the DPJ (the DP), her mixed-blood status was again made an issue of. Questions were raised for months about whether she had actually given up her Taiwanese citizenship, and Renhō ended up publicly releasing a portion of her Family Registry to prove it.[69] The implication was that she could only represent Wajin and be loyal to Japan if she was a "real" Japanese, that is, *only* Japanese. Shaken by "scandals" like these, the DP lost big in a 2017 local election, Renhō resigned her leadership to take responsibility, and then the DP disappeared entirely in 2018. Thus, not only did a "foreigner" issue sound the death knell of an entire viable leftist opposition party, it also became another setback for dual nationals (see chapter 4) and Visible Minorities, who will no doubt face similar scrutiny if they ever seek political office in Japan.

Further, during the 2010s even crass foreigner-bashing became acceptable. For example, Tōkyō Governor Ishihara, in addition to trolling the media by calling old women "useless" and "toxic" to civilization, gay people "gadding about" as "pitiable," French as unqualified to be an international language because of its counting system, and the 2011 Fukushima multiple disasters as "divine retribution" for Japan's sins and "egoism," he insinuated that Japan's African residents were unintelligent, stated in an official press conference regarding Tōkyō's Olympic bid that commentators on Japan "don't matter" if they're foreign,[70] and opined to reporters that Westerners performing judō at the 2012 London Olympics was like "watching beasts fight," and that it had "lost its exquisite charm" by becoming an internationalized sport.[71]

More malevolently, Ishihara in 2012 deliberately worsened Sino-Japanese relations by entangling the Tōkyō Metropolitan Government in the purchase of some of the disputed Senkaku/Diaoyu Islands in an attempt, as he would admit in 2014, to start a war with China.[72] There was little discernable blowback to Ishihara's bigotry and brinkmanship. Tōkyō was still awarded the 2020 Olympics,[73] Ishihara never lost an election as governor, and he only left the post in 2012 to head a new further-right political party in the Diet's Lower House (where he was again elected), only leaving office in 2014 at age eighty-two when his energies were spent. Yet establishment media worldwide pulled its punches throughout Ishihara's tenure, normalizing his racist and warmongering rhetoric as merely "hawkish," "firebrand," "nationalist," "populist," "outspoken," and "controversial to the end."

Ishihara was not acting in isolation. Other high-profile politicians became emboldened by the rising historical revisionism of the Abe Era and by the increasing mobilized impact of supportive online far-right communities (*Netto Uyoku*). In 2012, Nagoya Mayor Kawamura Takashi repeatedly denied that the 1937 Nanking Massacre of Chinese by the occupying Japanese military ever happened (which led to the suspension of the Nagoya-Nanjing Sister City Relationship).[74] In 2013, Ōsaka Mayor Hashimoto Tōru used dismissive language about the "Comfort Women" GOJ wartime sexual slavery issue (which also enslaved foreign women in conquered lands), calling it "necessary for Japanese soldiers to rest" and for maintaining discipline. (He later backpedaled with whataboutism regarding sexual services for the military worldwide, and a vehement denial that the GOJ was ever involved.)[75] In July 2013, Deputy PM and Finance Minister Aso Tarō expressed admiration for how Nazi Germany had clandestinely transformed the Weimar Republic, and suggested that leaders study their techniques to similarly amend Japan's Constitution.[76] Meanwhile,

Ishihara's successor as Tōkyō Governor, Inose Naoki, publicly denigrated fellow Olympic candidate city Istanbul as less safe than Japan, that is, one of those "Islamic countries always fighting with each other" (thereby getting away with violating Article 14 of the Olympic Rules of Conduct that strictly forbids bidders tarnishing each other's bid).[77]

Xenophobia percolated further downballot. For example, regional governments in 2012 were being advised to deny social services to foreign residents, due to an allegedly rising number of "illegal foreigners" being "scammers" and "social parasites."[78] An LDP Assemblyman in Saitama's Kawaguchi City, in the course of asking about potential foreign tax dodgers at a 2015 public meeting, mused that the city's registered foreign population had somehow become larger than its registered dogs.[79] And in 2017, Tōkyō Governor Koike Yuriko's "Party of Hope" (*Kibō no Tō*) required other politicians fleeing from Renhō's disintegrating DP to sign a pledge explicitly denying all foreign residents (including Regular Permanent Residents and Zainichi) the right to vote or run for office in any Japanese elections.[80] (More on this issue below.)

Campaigns for political hopefuls also shifted tone. In the 2011 Tōkyō Governor Elections, every constituent received a government-funded mailing with statements from each candidate. One proclaimed, "Protect the capital. Protect Japan. Japan is for Japanese people," using prewar language calling for the "expulsion of the barbarians" (*jōi*), namely "Chinks" (*shinajin*) and Koreans.[81] Another campaign by Diet Upper House candidate Suzuki Nobuyuki, running under the "Restoration Political Party—New Wind" (*Ishin Seitō Shimpū*), created a poster headlining, "I'm Banned from Entering South Korea," with a platform advocating cutting all ties with Korea, closing Japan to immigration, arming Japan with nuclear weapons, weeding out "masochistic" (*jigyaku*) history from Japan's education curriculum, and making Japan the "world's safest country" again.[82] In 2013, another "Restoration Political Party—New Wind" candidate ran for a Tōkyō Katsushika Ward seat with the slogan "Japanese First Over Foreigners!" (*Gaikokujin yori Nihonjin ga dai'ichi!*)[83] In 2014, the new far-right "Party for Future Generations" (*Jisedai no Tō*), headed by abovementioned former LDP MP Hiranuma Takeo (who enjoyed a safe seat in Okayama despite decades of xenophobia), released a campaign video insinuating that that his freedom was being violated, because somehow leftists had made any discussion about foreigners claiming social welfare into a "taboo" topic. The video illustrated the need to cut through apparent self-censorship, with an anime showing a dancing "taboo pig" (*tabū buta*, a clever palindrome) being grotesquely sliced in half.[84] In 2020, Suzuki Nobuyuki, now an elected Katsushika Ward Assemblyman chairing the "National Party of Japan" (*Nippon Kokumintō*), publicly argued that any foreigner who engages in a street protest or public demonstration (such as a labor union march or BLM demo, both legal activities) should be summarily expelled from Japan.[85]

By 2016, xenophobia was mainstream enough for Sakurai Makoto, the former leader of Zaitokukai (Association of Citizens against the Special Privileges of the Zainichi), which had become a "hate group" on police watchlists by publicly advocating the killing of Koreans,[86] to run as an individual for the Tōkyō Governorship. He offered an explicitly antiforeign platform, including eliminating all social welfare for foreigners, cutting "illegal foreign overstayers" in half, passing a law protecting Japanese against "hate speech" from foreigners, and suspending the building of Zainichi Korean schools. Sakurai came in fifth, garnering 114,171 votes (2 percent of the total).[87]

Nevertheless, political parties with overtly anti-immigration and ultranationalistic platforms have proliferated since the First Edition, including the Japan Restoration Party (*Nippon Ishin no Kai*), the Party for Future Generations (*Jisedai no Tō*), the Japan First Party (*Nippon Daittō*; Sakurai Makoto's latest political organization), the National Party of Japan (*Nippon Kokumintō*), the Restoration Political Party—New Wind (*Ishin Seitō Shimpū*), and a reconstituted Party of Hope (*Kibō no Tō*, independent of Governor Koike), in addition to the abovementioned Nippon Kaigi.

As the fortunes of the Wajin far-right were rising, proposals from Wajin who supported liberalization, immigration, diversity, and equal protections under the law (not to mention "human rights," which was being dismissed by revisionists as a foreign concept grounded in Western individualism)[88] were being steadily defeated in the political sphere. Examples follow.

UNSUCCESSFUL ATTEMPTS TO ESTABLISH LEGISLATION AGAINST RACIAL DISCRIMINATION IN JAPAN[89]

The Protection of Human Rights Bill Debates of the Mid-2000s

One proposal to protect disenfranchised noncitizens was the Protection of Human Rights Bill (*jinken yōgo hōan*), an amalgamation of several proposals (such as the Foreign Residents' Basic Law (*gaikokujin jūmin kihon hō*)) that would have defended the rights of residents regardless of their nationality, ethnic status, or social origin. A comprehensive Human Rights Bill (which did not focus specifically on noncitizen protections against discrimination, and established clear oversight committees and a criminal-penalty structure) was submitted in 2002 by the first PM Koizumi Cabinet, but died in committee in October 2003 with the dissolution of the Upper House. When talk was raised of resubmission afterward, it was shouted down by online arguments against giving Zainichi North Koreans any political power in Japan. This re-proposal had been ill-timed, given the degree of the political capital gained by rightists during a 2002–2006 debate concerning geopolitical stances toward the *rachi mondai* (i.e., North Korean kidnappings of Wajin that had officially occurred between 1977 and 1983). The Bill remains in limbo, with a different incarnation (the Human Rights Relief Bill, *jinken kyūsai hōan*) that was wending its way through committees until the DPJ's defeat in the December 2012 election.[90]

However, arguments to defeat the Protection of Human Rights Bill took latent elements of Japan's foreigner-phobic domestic discourse and crystallized them into a xenophobic social movement—one that went beyond political circles and appealed to the general public. Let us focus on one notable publication and parse the narratives within:

Danger! The Protection of Human Rights Bill: The Imminent Threat of the Totalitarianism (zentai-shugi) of the Developed Countries (Tentensha Inc. 2006)[91] was a far-right publication available in bookstores nationwide. It galvanized Japan's right wing by linking several side issues with the Human Rights Bill: gender equality, the rights of children, the North Korean kidnappings, the treatment of history in educational textbooks, and patriotic visits to war-celebrating Yasukuni Shrine—all divisive issues of the day between rightists and leftists in Japanese politics.

An excellent short manga within the *Danger!* book makes the opposition's arguments clearly. (I recommend readers look at it as I describe their narratives below, as it has been translated into English and available in the online archive in the endnotes.)[92] Pages 37–39 make a number of racialized claims about human behavior and abuses of power, for example, that darker-skinned or narrower-eyed "foreigners," if granted any civil or political rights in Japan, would become lazy, delinquent, or disobedient toward social contracts. Moreover, the human rights law would lead to abuses between Japanese in terms of personal revenge or crime-syndicate blackmail. The manga assumed that members of a newly created Human Rights Committee (as opposed to the existing system of Human Rights Protection Officers footnoted on page 37 of the *Danger!* book) would not sufficiently investigate the validity of claims and would always find in favor of the minorities.

Danger! pages 143–5 focus on the potential official abuses of enforcement, where a person in a position of power is being victimized. For example, one Wajin landlord is taken advantage of by "Asian foreigners"; another Wajin barkeep is caught in the pugilistic crossfire of a violent racist "Western foreigner"; another shows a teacher being bullied by a vindictive student, and another depicts a private individual being singled out in a crowd while exercising his right of public protest against a cult (which the cult claims violates its "human rights").[93] *Danger!* page 40 expands the meme of victimization into the political sphere, where Japan's politicians have been muzzled from debate and criticism of geopolitical issues, and freedom of the press has been abrogated. Thus, any tempering or control of one's dislike of people for their ethnicity/race/social origin (○○*jin ga kirai* in the Japanese) necessarily leads to political correctness (*kotoba gari*), thought police (*shisō keisatsu*), arrest, and the North Koreanization of Japanese society. (Kim Jong-Il even appears on a computer screen in an apparent coup d'etat.)

In sum, *Danger!* argued that "foreigners" (particularly the Visible Minorities, rendered as darker-skinned or narrower-eyed in the manga) would victimize Wajin if granted any rights. In other words, if somebody does something that somebody else personally does not like, under this Bill the activity will automatically become a violation of human rights, and a chance for disenfranchised minorities to exact revenge. Unproblematized within *Danger!*, however, were narratives grounded in normalized and unchecked abuses of majoritarian power—for example example, the underlying prejudices against women, and the racialized stereotyping of Non-Wajin. Thus, the Human Rights Bill was challenging Wajin power, and Wajin were making fear-based arguments to defeat it.

It is unclear how many copies *Danger!* sold, or how much impact the book itself had. Nevertheless, this genre of alarmist and xenophobic arguments had been made forcefully in a well-organized media campaign, and successfully killed the Human Rights Bill during the DPJ's liberal leadership window of 2009–2012. Thus, politically organized xenophobia is one reason why Japan cannot pass legislation against racial discrimination in Japan. Here is another:

The Tottori Prefecture Human Rights Ordinance That Was Passed and Then Unpassed

On October 12, 2005, after nearly a year of deliberations and amendments, the Tottori Prefectural Assembly approved a comprehensive human rights ordinance (*Tottori-ken jinken shingai kyūsai suishin oyobi tetsuzuki ni kansuru jōrei*). Sponsored by Tottori Governor Katayama Yoshihiro, it was to be a trial measure—taking effect on June 1, 2006, and expiring on March 31, 2010. The ordinance had been carefully planned and shepherded through the process, created by a committee of twenty-six people over the course of two years, with input from a lawyer, several academics and human rights activists, and three noncitizen residents. It passed the Tottori Prefectural Assembly by a wide margin: 35–3.

The ordinance was like none ever seen before. It would not only financially penalize eight types of human rights violations (including physical abuse, sexual harassment, slander, and discrimination by "race"—including "blood race, ethnicity, creed, gender, social standing, family status, disability, illness, and sexual orientation"), but also set up an investigative panel for deliberations and provide for public exposure of offenders.[94] Going further than the already-existing MOJ Bureau of Human Rights (*jinken yōgobu*, or BOHR, which has no policing or punitive powers; more below), the panel could launch investigations, require hearings and written explanations, issue private warnings (making them public if they went ignored), demand compensation for victims, remand cases to the courts, and even recommend cases to prosecutors if they thought there was a crime involved. It also had punitive powers, including fines up to 50,000 yen.

However, the blowback was immediate.[95] The major local newspaper in the neighboring prefecture, the *Chūgoku Shinbun* (Hiroshima), claimed in its October 14 editorial entitled, "We must monitor this ordinance in practice," that the ordinance would "in fact shackle (*sokubaku*) human rights." Online accusations flew that assemblypersons had not read the bill properly or had supported abstract ideals without thinking them through. Others said the governor had not explained to the people properly what he was binding them to. Internet petitions blossomed to rescind it. Some sample complaints made (with my counterarguments in parenthesis, for brevity):

1) The ordinance had only been deliberated upon in the Assembly for a week (though it was first brought up in 2003 and discussed in committees throughout 2005).

2) The ordinance's definitions of human rights violations were too vague and could hinder the media in, for example, investigating politicians for corruption (even though the ordinance's Clause 31 clearly states that freedom of the press must be respected).

3) Since the investigative committee was not an independent body, reporting only to the governor, this could encourage arbitrary decisions and cover-ups (similar to the BOHR, which reports only to the secretive MOJ; see below).

4) This invests judicial and policing powers in an administrative organ, a violation of the separation of powers (which means that no oversight committee in Japan is allowed to have enforcement power—but this calls into question many other ordinances in Japan, such as those governing garbage disposal, that include criminal penalties such as fines and incarceration).

The Japan Federation of Bar Associations (Nichibenren) sounded the ordinance's death knell in an official statement of November 2, 2005: Too much power had been given to the governor, constricting the people and media under arbitrary guidelines, under a committee chief who could investigate by diktat, overseeing a bureaucracy that could refuse to be investigated. This called into question the policymaking discretion of the committees that had originally drafted it, and the common sense of the 35 Assembly members who overwhelmingly passed it.

The Tottori Prefectural Government issued an official Q&A to allay public concern, and the governor said problems would be dealt with as they arose; but the original supporters of the ordinance, feeling the media-sponsored and online pressure, did not stand up to defend it. On March 24, 2006, less than six months after passing the ordinance, the Tottori Prefectural Assembly voted unanimously to suspend it indefinitely. "We should have brought up cases to illustrate specific human rights violations. The public did not seem to understand what we were trying to prevent," said a Mr. Ishiba, a representative of the Tottori Governor's office.[96] The ordinance was later resubmitted to committees in 2007, where Japan's first legislation explicitly penalizing racial discrimination was voted down for the last time.[97]

Widening the Scope: The Gaikokujin Sanseiken Debates of 2009–2011

When the DPJ took power from the LDP in 2009, one of their liberalizing party platforms was granting noncitizen Permanent Residents (both the Regular *ippan eijūsha* and Zainichi *tokubetsu eijūsha*) the right to vote in local elections (Foreigner Suffrage, *gaikokujin sanseiken*). This was in part because long-term noncitizens, particularly the Zainichi, had historically spent their lives born in, living in, and contributing to Japan; moreover, they already had the vote on local referendums in some municipalities.[98] The proposal seemed politically advantageous when first proposed in 2008 (when the DPJ was the opposition party), as it threatened to split the contemporary ruling coalition by tempting away LDP partner Kōmeitō (a religious-based party founded by the Sōka Gakkai, which initially supported the proposal due to the group's international following).[99] Expanding suffrage would also stem some of the rising antiforeign tide by forcing politicians to seek votes from the Non-Wajin community.

At first, the more reasoned counterargument to Foreigner Suffrage was, "If non-citizens want to vote, they should naturalize." However, Wajin LDP representatives (including some within the DPJ) and the Netto Uyoku far-right netizens found the proposal a convenient means to decry any putative external and internal "foreign" influences over Japanese society. They promoted the fear-based argument that sharing electoral power with noncitizens, particularly ethnic North Koreans, was a security threat under any circumstances. When Ishihara made the abovementioned claim that even naturalized citizens and people with overseas ancestry were suspicious, the option for Non-Wajin to assimilate into Japanese society through any legal means was effectively mooted.

Public fears were further stoked by frequent public meetings, demonstrations, and leaflets that argued granting any more rights to noncitizens would be "the end of Japan." Alarmist invective depicted North Korean or Chinese-controlled representatives being elected to Japanese office, secessions of parts of Japan to China and South Korea, and even alien invasion.[100] (Note how the invective coasted on narratives covered earlier in this chapter: from the official imagery and rhetoric of invasions of Japan by "foreign criminals" to the imagery of invasion and subversion of Japan through the electoral process. There was even formal linkage made to it within the Foreigner Suffrage debate.)[101]

Foreigner Suffrage became a wedge issue hobbling the fledgling DPJ Hatoyama Administration, as he faced mounting opposition even within his own party. Rightists and xenophobes then connected it to other DPJ proposals that would have protected the rights of noncitizens, such as the aforementioned Foreign Residents Human Rights Bill (which became moribund). Even though proponents took a stand (including the *Asahi Shinbun* of July 6, 2010, citing an opinion poll of 49 percent of respondents in favor of Foreigner Suffrage and 43 percent against), the lack of a unified and nationwide voice in the media for minorities (and tautologically their inability to elect sympathetic political representatives) enabled it to be shouted down. The DPJ formally "postponed" the Foreigner Suffrage Bill by February 2010, eliminating it from the DPJ Manifesto entirely by the July 11, 2011, Upper House Elections.

But even with Foreigner Suffrage no longer on the table, rightist social movements continued to leverage it: Protests against any "foreign rights" then shouted down even DPJ liberalizing proposals that would have also benefited Wajin, such as separate surnames for married couples (*fūfu bessei*) (which LDP head Tanigaki Sadakazu claimed, in now-normalized apocalyptic invective, "would destroy the country").[102] An anti-suffrage rally on April 17, 2010, in the Budōkan reported 10,257 attendees.[103] Rightist grassroots activists also successfully pushed several local and prefectural assemblies nationwide to pass formal resolutions against any future attempts to enfranchise.[104] Meanwhile, the Netto Uyoku created a self-sustaining online media presence,[105] legitimized by prominent politicians/pundits (such as erstwhile and future PM Abe Shinzō, MP Hiranuma Takeo, MP Kamei Shizuka, former Air Self-Defense Forces Chief of Staff General Tamogami Toshio, etc.) participating in their forums and basking in the attention.

By the end of the 2000s, Japan's Non-Wajin and Visible Minorities had become a political football within a whirlwind of money, organization, and energy devoted to nationalistic, xenophobic, and exclusionary causes.[106] Hate speech by the general public both online and on the street became more overt and frequent. Wajin hate rallies in 2013 and 2014 increased to an average of around one per day, often in Japan's ethnic neighborhoods.[107] Placards appeared during this time calling foreign residents "cockroaches," advocating genocide by saying, for example, "Good or Bad, Kill all Koreans." A Wajin junior high school girl at a hate rally called for a "massacre like the Nanking Massacre" of ethnic Koreans in Tsuruhashi, Ōsaka.[108] Wajin Neo-Nazis marched in Tōkyō Edogawa Ward bearing swastika flags, and other demo messages included "Kill people," "Die Korea," "Throw them into the ocean," "Destroy Korean schools," "You smell like kimchi," and "This [Kyōto Zainichi Korean School] is nurturing North Korean spies."[109] There were also instances of hate-related violence toward foreigners and foreign-owned property, some lethal.[110]

Up to now, this chapter has discussed how Japan's police, politicians, and civil society have shaped xenophobic and exclusionary national narratives toward noncitizens and Visible Minorities in Japan. In passing, we have touched upon how the mass media bears responsibility for not questioning authority or reporting with a critical eye. Let us now turn to how the media has also been complicit in propagandizing xenophobia and foreigner-bashing.

THE COMPLICITY OF JAPAN'S MEDIA IN GENERATING, NOT JUST DISSEMINATING, RACIALIZED XENOPHOBIC PROPAGANDA

As this research segues into issues of how Japanese media has its own influence over generating domestic discourses, let us begin with another instructive case study of media complicity in drumming up public support behind GOJ policy (i.e., propaganda). A brief recap is necessary to give a concise timeline of how measures against the "foreign crime wave of the 2000s" became a self-sustaining media phenomenon beyond GOJ policy drives:

Japan's Media Sensationalizes from GOJ Policy Platforms

If one could ever catch a policy drive in its larval stage, in this case it would be May 1999, with the NPA's new "Committee for Policy against Internationalization." We first mentioned this group at the end of chapter 5, but let us now contextualize its effects. This Committee was designed to "undertake suitable policies and laws for provincial police agencies, and strengthen their investigative organs."[111] As covered earlier in this chapter, this not only included public dispersal of biased and factually erroneous posters and announcements to the general public, but also high-profile "foreign crime" reports to the press twice a year, parroted by media outlets with little analysis (i.e., little grounding in scope or scale regarding crime numbers or frequencies, no comparison to crimes committed by citizens, and far fewer counterbalancing articles on how noncitizen residents were also serving Japan as workers and taxpayers).

To be fair, reporters (according to interviews I have done with several, usually cub reporters first assigned to the police beat) have indicated they had little time to analyze the crime statistics. They stated that the NPA gives out the information shortly before press deadline, meaning they could do little more during the news cycle than quote the NPA accurately.

That said, there have been cases of the Japanese media egregiously parroting the NPA's bias. The clearest example is the *Mainichi Shinbun*'s articles of February 8 and 9, 2007, where the Japanese original headlined a thirty-five-fold increase in regional foreign crimes, while the next day's English translation of the same article headlined an overall *decrease* in foreign crime.[112] An interview I carried out shortly after the articles appeared with a *Mainichi* editor revealed the reason: The headline was adjusted as per the "preferences of their readership," as the "impact would be different" (*inpakuto ga chigau kara*).

In a similar "impact" dynamic, on February 23, 2012, the *Mainichi Daily News* via Kyodo English wire services reported foreign crime had fallen in 2011, but only in English; other mainstream Japanese-language outlets (*Yomiuri*, *Sankei*, *Asahi*, and the *Mainichi itself*) *did not report the fall at all* to Japanese readers. Meanwhile, other contemporaneous new media (such as Zakzak), regardless of any factual news, concurrently portrayed Japan as becoming even more dangerous due to foreign crime.[113]

This is part of a historical pattern. In a survey of news articles in the *Asahi Shinbun* between January and July 1998, Nara University Associate Professor of Sociology Mabuchi Ryōgo noted that foreign crime was 4.87 times more likely to be covered than crimes by Japanese.[114] This was, however, before the NPA's "Committee for Policy against Internationalization" had created a regular semiannual media cycle on "foreign crime." This not only instilled fear in the public toward "foreigners" as phenotypes, but also whetted the public's appetite and curiosity about "foreigners and their underground activities." This further incentivized media compliance through economic demand. Future articles would headline specific foreign crimes going up even when the overall trend was downward,[115] would engage in "whataboutism" to excuse or provide "false balance" for antiforeign behavior by Wajin,[116] would squeeze in information about foreign crime even when the news story was unrelated to crime (e.g., a rise in the registered foreign population),[117] or would just openly speculate without conclusive evidence that foreigners may be behind certain crimes (such as a story about an apparent increase in human excrement on Mt. Fuji).[118]

Both media and advertisers profiteered from foreign fear.[119] For example, the *Shūkan Asahi* weekly tabloid (February 25, 2000) published a Miwa

Locks advertisement that promoted new "foreigner-proof locks." It read, "Are your anti-theft measures okay? Now damages from foreign robber gangs are increasing very rapidly. This is an era when investments in safety must also be made at Western levels." On a separate page, camouflaged as a regular full-length article, was a locksmithing advertisement with the headline: "Behind the scenes of foreign robber gangs, which can open your front door's lock in five seconds."[120]

This media-generated xenophobia had a quantifiable impact on the general public. Many "Japanese Only" establishments I interviewed in chapter 3 suddenly began claiming from early 2000 that the prospect of "foreign crime" was a new reason for refusing "foreigners" entry. Trade paperbacks found audiences for "foreign crime," foreign victims of crime, and the seedier side of alleged "underground foreign lifestyles" (including prostitution, fake marriages, fake citizenships, and other unlawful profiteering).[121] Television specials on crime (modeled on the Fox Network's hit reality show "COPS") showed Wajin miscreants mixed in with citizens going about their daily lives, while foreigners (with their nationalities prominently noted) were only showed if they were being apprehended, further "othering" them from society. Nippon Terebi's two-hour show on crime, which aired on September 16, 2003, devoted more than 25 percent of its airtime to foreign crime (which, mathematically, was more proportional attention by at least a factor of ten than the actual amount of noncitizen crime in Japan). To hammer the point home, Tōkyō Governor Ishihara came on after every foreign-specific segment to remark on the cruelty of Chinese crooks and the need for more police.[122] A similar prime-time Fuji Terebi show, which aired on October 6, 2018, made reality TV into a sporty Gaijin hunt: *Taikyo no Shunkan* ("The very instant of deportation") portrayed "Immigration G-Men" [*sic*] heroically chasing down Chinese and Vietnamese "illegal overstayers" and "foreign squatters" on camera (while the Wajin employers responsible for these "illegal aliens" were not made into an issue).[123]

Established media commentary also began to vilify foreigners as foreign agents. For example, Mitsuhashi Takaaki, a self-styled Wajin "economist," failed LDP candidate, and frequent TV commentator publicly claimed in various venues in 2016 that importing foreign workers will "destroy Japanese culture," and "80 percent of Chinese in Japan are spies."[124] *Sankei Shinbun* ran a column in 2015 saying that foreign correspondents should have their visas contingent upon passing a Japanese language test, in order to weed out their "anti-Japan slants" and ensure a "correct understanding of Japan" being reported to the world.[125] Reporters from the Foreign Correspondents' Club of Japan faced similar pressure regarding the content of their articles, except this time coming directly from the GOJ.[126] Pundit Sakurai Yoshiko, representing the far-right "Japan Institute for National Fundamentals" (*kokka kihon mondai kenkyūjo*), ran an opinion ad in the September 16, 2014, *Yomiuri Shinbun* entitled, "Time to hit back at international aspersions over 'comfort women'"; she called for a "task force charged with protecting Japan's reputation . . . directly controlled by the prime minister."[127] GOJ pressure then expanded beyond Japan's borders in attempts to censor overseas publishers writing about Japan.[128]

Foreign Media Internalize Wajin Narratives

Ironically, even without GOJ pressure, foreign media has sometimes offered lazy and biased reportage on Japan that internalizes established Wajin narratives. Journalist colleagues at the Foreign Correspondents' Club of Japan (where I was an Associate Member as a columnist for the *Japan Times*) have joked that overseas interest in Japan boils down to the "Three Es": Economics, Exotica, and Erotica, with the genre of "weird Japan" stories (such as vending machines selling used women's underwear)[129] being the most effective at garnering the widest audience without requiring deep research.

But even clusters of well-researched pieces have shown foreign correspondents exhibiting group "buy-in" to a racialized Japan narrative. A good example is January 2017's reportage on sumō, where, after years of domination by foreign and naturalized Japanese sumō wrestlers, a Wajin named Kisenosato finally ascended to the champion rank of Yokozuna. Reputable outlets published misleading and problematic headlines about the event. BBC: "Japan gets its first sumo champion in 19 years"; *Washington Post*: "After 19 long years, Japan has a grand champion of sumo once again"; *New York Times*: "For the first time in years, Japan boasts a sumo grand champion"—all of which exclude foreign Yokozuna as real "Japan grand champions" or imply that Japan had no champions unless they are Wajin. The *Guardian* and *Japan Times* used weasel words like "homegrown champion" and "Japanese-born" to launder implicit racialization, since some Yokozuna during that time period were in fact naturalized Japanese citizens yet somehow didn't count. Further, the *Washington Post* claimed that sumō has been "in decline" partly because of the "increasing dominance of foreigners," and the BBC called Kisenosato's ascension "a boost to the traditional sport," echoing the above-mentioned sentiments of Ishihara that a "Japanese sport" (like judō) has been despoiled by internationalization.

None of these articles mentioned the issues of unfair play in Japanese sport covered in chapter 5, for example, how much harder it is for Non-Wajin to become Yokozuna after the Sumō Association put strict limits on how many foreign wrestlers may join a stable in 2010; or how racially restrictive Japan's sports leagues are in general. Instead, foreign correspondents gave Japan a free pass for its Embedded Racism, appropriating Wajin arguments that Sumō is an ethnosport.[130]

But one case of news stories bashing foreigners that was generated by both the foreign and domestic media is exemplary: the "Flyjin" phenomenon.

"Foreigner as Deserter": The Fictitious Fukushima "Flyjin" Media Myth

The so-called Flyjin media phenomenon occurred after the Tōhoku tsunami and Fukushima nuclear disasters of 2011. As Fukushima's nuclear reactors melted down in real time, potentially threatening northern and eastern Honshū with dangerous levels of radioactive fallout, people regardless of nationality fled afflicted areas, as well as from Tōkyō and Japan proper. However, media both domestic and foreign zeroed in on the flight of foreigners, with media wags coming up with the term "Flyjin" (a portmanteau of Gaijin in flight; or as Japanese media put it even more pejoratively, *Nihon saru Gaikokujin*—"Japan defecting foreigners"), insinuating that noncitizens were craven deserters of their posts while "stoic" Wajin braved the danger.[131] This epithet led to much journalistic and online trollery that foreign residents were not really a part of Japan after all, while wild rumors proliferated online and in print that foreigners were forming criminal gangs, looting, and otherwise actively sabotaging Japan (which the GOJ, in a rare show of solidarity with foreign residents, actually spoke out against).[132]

Indicatively, world-famous Japan scholar and researcher Donald Keene, leveraging the Flyjin narrative, announced to the Japanese media in March 2012 that he was taking Japanese citizenship to "show solidarity" and "endure the hardships with the Japanese," and to "encourage the Japanese people"—contrasting himself with, the *Asahi Shinbun* reported, "the large numbers of foreigners who distanced themselves after the Great East Japan Earthquake."[133] As a joking aside at a press conference, Keene pandered aloud, "As a Japanese, I swear not to commit any crimes" (*Nihonjin to shite hanzai o okosanai koto o chikaimasu*).[134] Thus, the discourse of foreigner as criminal and deserter had become so hegemonic that it had entered the realm of humor.

The Flyjin myth was eventually debunked, as statistics published in *Japan Times* showed that Wajin and Non-Wajin had fled Japan in proportionally similar numbers.[135] Further, Japan's judiciary agreed that fleeing Japan at the time was not disloyalty or desertion, but a reasonable fear, with one lawsuit ruling against NHK for firing a French anchorwoman because she had temporarily left Japan, awarding her back pay. The ruling noted, "Given the circumstances under which the Great East Japan Earthquake and Fukushima No. 1 plant's nuclear accident took place, it is absolutely impossible to criticize as irresponsible her decision to evacuate abroad to protect her life."[136]

Nevertheless, the generational discourse of "foreigners will take advantage of a natural disaster to do bad things" still persists, emerging with alarming regularity during chaotic events of earthquakes, typhoons, or as we saw in chapter 5, global pandemics.[137] This is quantifiable social damage generated, and rarely later counteracted, by Japan's media; one academic study indicated that *80 percent* of Wajin believed, for example, the fake rumors of crimes by foreigners during the 2011 Tōhoku disasters.[138] This is also due to a Japan-related intelligentsia and media milieu that remains careless about fact-checking and sensationalizing, and insufficiently considers how news information "in the public interest" will impact a public that includes noncitizen residents and Visible Minorities.

Biased Media Reportage to Conceal GOJ Policy

However, some Japanese media coverage is not careless. Some make a conscious editorial effort to support the "home team," tailoring announcements of GOJ policy to avoid potential criticism or international attention.

For example, as mentioned above, when the second PM Koizumi Cabinet was launched on September 22, 2003, no fewer than three Cabinet members prioritized "foreign crime" within their policy statements. The media, however, filtered the contents to bury the lede about potentially unpalatable policies targeting foreigners. For example, on September 23, the *Yomiuri Shinbun* gave its regular feature to acquaint readers with the new Cabinet members. The Japanese headline for National Public Safety Chair Ono Kiyoko read, "A former Olympian, [Ono] wishes for policy against foreign crime," making that her foremost priority. Below that, her policy goals were "to devote my full energies to things including the strengthening of policy against foreign crime, food safety, and policy towards the falling birthrate."

However, in the English translation of that feature, the *Daily Yomiuri* removed any mention of "foreign crime" from the headline, and shifted the focus of her policy goals to her political experience; her Olympics gymnastics background; her knowledge about culture, education, and welfare issues; and her college background; it eventually mentioned that her goal was to "make Japan the world's safest mention again, by fighting various crimes—particularly those committed by juveniles and foreign residents."[139] Thus, the translation was deliberately changed for English- and Japanese-reading audiences, significantly altering the substance.

The irony of this 2003 Koizumi Cabinet "foreign crime" policy push is that, if citizen and noncitizen crimes were actually compared in the media,[140] more attention would have been drawn to Japan's "worst [postwar crime figures] in the postwar period"—crimes that were in fact being committed by Wajin; as *Japan Times* noted, "crimes allegedly committed by foreigners accounted for a scant 1.39 percent of cases."[141] Once again, they were not compared. In any case, the actual low foreign crime rates were not the news "impact" that Wajin media decided the public needed to hear. Moreover, these questionable journalistic ethics are not limited to the *Yomiuri*; they concertedly happen across media outlets, as the next case study will attest:

Media Coverage of the 2007 Reinstitution of Foreigner Fingerprinting

In 2000, the mandatory inclusion of a fingerprint on all Gaijin Cards (with the exception of the Zainichi) was abolished, having been decried as a "violation of human rights" by the presiding Justice Minister two years earlier.[142] However, from November 20, 2007, Japan reinstituted mass fingerprinting with facial photography at the border for all non-Zainichi entrants and reentrants.[143] Initially proposed as a measure to prevent infectious diseases and terrorism, one week before the program was launched the media included "fighting foreign crime" and "international terrorism."[144] While this policy U-turn is instructive in terms of Non-Wajin political disenfranchisement, let us consider how Wajin media dynamics gave the public a lopsided view while stifling public dissent:

On November 19, 2007, a *Yomiuri Shinbun* editorial parroted the following GOJ justifications for the program focusing on foreigners as terrorists (English original):

> The main objective of the revised law is to block terrorists and foreign criminals from entering the country. If it is proven to be effective, Japan's reputation as a safe country will be bolstered. . . . Japan will host the Group of Eight summit meeting at the Lake Toya hot spring resort in Toyakocho, Hokkaido, next year. Together with strengthening immigration checks, we hope the government will take all possible means to ensure coastal security and prevent terrorism in this country.[145]

On the day of reintroduction, networks and newspapers carried news in real time about concerns for human rights, the malfunctioning fingerprint machines, and angry tourists. However, not one network interviewed a Non-Wajin resident or immigrant, or showed video of the large demonstrations against fingerprinting outside the MOJ.[146] This included NHK, whose 7 p.m. News only devoted three minutes to it, strictly adhered to the government's line of protecting "citizens" (*kokumin*) [*sic*] from the outside world. NHK's 9 p.m. News devoted 6 minutes to positive feedback from a couple of visiting foreign tourists, but no word from any foreign residents of Japan whatsoever. NHK's BS News at 10:50 p.m. did not even carry the story.

On November 21, the *Nikkei*, *Sankei*, and *Yomiuri* morning editions all had the same article headlines: "Five Foreigners Caught." However, *Sankei* admitted within the text that they were snagged for odd passports, not fingerprints, which happened every day on average anyway before the fingerprinting system was reintroduced. In subsequent days, new GOJ justifications for reintroduction were disseminated through the Wajin-dominated media with blanket coverage. Some were in a form simple enough for the next generation of impressionable Wajin to understand: For example, *Yomiuri Shinbun* ran an article on foreign fingerprinting (with a racialized illustration) for its weekly "children's news" page less than two weeks later.[147]

Thus, Japan's media made the national discourse on the need to keep "foreigners" fingerprinted irresistible: In order to keep Japan safe, all noncitizens (including, as the *Yomiuri* depicted, Visible Minorities) must be policed. Insufficient concern was ever raised by politicians or Wajin media about protecting their civil, political, or human rights from abuses, excesses, or discriminatory language.

As the fearful 2000s became the hateful 2010s, the effects of this discourse would be seen in insensitive/denigrating language toward Visual Minorities in Japanese media, including examples of stereotyping, "othering," and even hate speech for profit.

GAIJIN AS "EVIL": EXAMPLES OF RACIALIZED HATE SPEECH IN JAPAN'S MEDIA

"Gaijin Hanzai" Mook: Profiteering through Xenophobia

One famous case of hate speech[148] and profiteering from lurid public interest was the publication of magazine-book (*mook*) *Gaijin Hanzai Ura Fairu 2007* ("The Underground Files of Gaijin Crime 2007"; see figure 7.1) by Eichi Shuppan, Inc.[149]

This mook, with its racialized cover of "Gaijin" [*sic*] in attack mode, was available at bookstores and convenience stores (such as Family Mart) nationwide from January 31, 2007. Its cover denoted police cooperation (citing interviews and documentation of noncitizen suspects that appear to have been supplied from police surveillance cameras and files)[150] to save Japan from "devastation" (*jūrin*) due to the "foreign" element.

Inside contents of the magazine were as racialized and accusatory as the cover, with "evil gaijin" (*goku'aku gaijin*), such as Chinese, South Koreans, Iranians, Brazilians, Filipinas, and Africans/African Americans (whose faces, unlike the Wajin in the photographs, were not pixelated out for privacy) creating "lawless zones" (*fuhō chitai*) within Tōkyō ("We cannot allow this

Figure 7.1 Cover of *Gaijin Hanzai Ura Fairu 2007 mook*. Note caricatures of not only Korean leaders, but also frenzied faces of various ethnicities, including Chinese, Africans, Caucasians, and Middle Easterners. Note also subtitles: "Interview with NPA: We will thoroughly hunt down *gaijin* crime"; "Former police detective Kitashiba Ken confesses: 2007 will be a year when anyone will become a target of *gaijin* crime"; and at the bottom, "Are we going to let the *gaijin* lay waste *(jūrin)* to Japan?" *Source:* Originally published in *Gaijin Hanzai* magazine.

to happen!" screamed page one). Page 64 offered a screed on how Wajin criminals may be taking refuge in the cruelty of "foreign crime," and illustrations showed white-skinned Wajin being victimized by "foreigners" rendered in racialized and colorized caricature. Moreover, some claims of "foreign" misdeeds (such as having consensual public displays of affection with Wajin girlfriends) were in fact not crimes under Japan's Criminal Code (figure 7.2).

Other topics within the mook included a guide on how to avoid being shot on the street by a black man, a manga about particularly horrible ways Chinese commit crimes against Wajin *because* they are Chinese, an essay on the lives of Korean women in the sex industry (*deriheru*), and speculation on whether Korean female genitalia smell like kimchi. The overall theme was

Figure 7.2 Examples of Noncrimes Included in *Gaijin Hanzai* Magazine (page 102–3): Caption in Photo at Bottom Left Reads: "Shibuya: Hey nigger (*nigāa*)!! Take your goddamn hand off that Japanese lady's ass!!" Photo at right's horizontal caption reads (smaller text): "If left this way, gaijin will pull up the Traditional Japanese Woman (yamato nadeshiko) by the roots and make off with her/drive her crazy." Larger text: "You bitches! Are gaijin THAT good? Well, Japanese are small, but we've got swell and we're hard and grumble grumble grumble." Vertical caption reads at right reads: "Roppongi: Aw crap, he's goddamn good at kissing." At left: "Shibuya: Hey hey hey hey! This is a public space!!" It would appear that this magazine on "gaijin crime" reflected the editors' frustrations regarding their relations with the opposite sex. N.B.: "Yellow Cab" at very top is slang for Japanese women who will give a (sexual) ride to any (non-"yellow") man who flags her. *Source:* Originally published in *Gaijin Hanzai* magazine.

that crime is a function of nationality (with danger ratings of fourteen different countries "targeting Japan") (*Nihon o nerau*; back cover), not a function of individual behavior. Although statistics on "foreign crime" were included, there was yet again no comparison with statistics of crime committed by Wajin.

It is unclear how many sales or much of an impact this mook would have had if it had remained on sale. Significant coverage in the overseas media thanks to domestic activists quickly condemned *Gaijin Hanzai* as "hate speech" (the mainstream Japanese media, despite repeated press releases by activists in Japanese, offered no coverage for reasons unconfirmed by the author).[151] Publisher Eichi Shuppan made claims in the English-language media that this mook was defying a "taboo" on debating "foreign crime,"[152] but the

English-language blogosphere began a boycott of convenience stores that sold the mook (particularly Family Mart). This caused all copies to be pulled from shelves and returned to the publisher within a week of going on sale. Eichi Shuppan took an enormous loss on the publication, and by April 2007 was bankrupt.[153]

The conclusion I draw from this case is that Eichi Shuppan took a risk with a scandalous publication—one of many that comes out in Japan's tabloid media every day—but the extremely racialized and hateful invective of the contents made it an easy target for shame and potential international embarrassment. (An activist just had to show the convenience store manager the abovementioned page saying *nigaa*, and the magazine was summarily removed from the shelves.) Nevertheless, *Gaijin Hanzai* mook remains available for purchase in Japan as a collector's item through secondhand outlets (such as Amazon Japan, as of May 13, 2021), because "hate speech" (*ken'o hatsugen*), like racial discrimination, is not until recently an activity governed or penalized by criminal laws in Japan (more in chapter 8).

Similar but generalized media claims that denigrate "foreigners" without much evidence and scientific rigor cite "cultural differences" (*bunka no chigai*), "linguistic barriers" (*gengo no shōheki*), "unruliness" (*ōabare*), or even "invasive propagation" (*zōshoku*). Some claims were surreal, including stinginess from foreign tourists,[154] foreign takeovers of Japanese businesses,[155] and even periods where foreigners were "on the rampage."[156] Other claims were more concrete and template-setting for entire industries, such as the sacking of whistleblowing CEO Michael Woodford from a corrupt Olympus Corporation in 2011 for reportedly having a "style of management incompatible with traditional Japanese practices,"[157] and of course the biased Japanese media treatment of CEO Carlos Ghosn covered in chapter 6. Even children's schoolbooks were not exempt from careless or deliberate "othering": A 2020 Ministry of Education-approved "morals" (*dōtoku*) textbook for first graders in primary schools nationwide depicted a Japanese Australian Visible Minority classmate as a racialized "*Gaikoku no hito*" (person from a foreign land), not a *Nihonjin*, therefore full of differences to study like a specimen.[158] Also, *Chagurin*, a magazine aimed at sixth graders sponsored by the Japan Agriculture lobby and the PTA, in 2012 published an article entitled "Children of America, the Poverty Superpower" (*Hikon taikoku Amerika no kodomotachi*), portraying the United States as a country in peril. It exaggerated and falsified statistics about American crime, diet, obesity, health care, homelessness, and education, concluding, "What can we do so that we do not wind up like America?"[159]

This list of examples is by no means exhaustive, but as examples of touchstones within the national discourse, it provides grounding and context for many of the themes, memes, and tropes fomenting fear of foreign lands and peoples, narratives easily found within the justifications for businesses excluding "foreigners" on sight in chapter 3.

GAIJIN AS COMMODITY: RACIALIZED DIFFERENCES AS A MARKETING TOOL

Of course, all societies use stereotypes of people in varying degrees for the purposes of social patterning, satire, humor, marketing, and so on. However, again, minorities' lack of access to Japanese media makes it difficult to offer checks and balances toward excessive/abusive behavior, or enable them to remold their image within the dominant domestic discourse. Consider the following cases of racialized media and their outcomes:

McDonald's Japan's "Mr. James"

Between August and October 2009, McDonald's Japan used a nerdy Caucasian male mascot named "Mr. James" as part of a campaign to advertise exotic hamburgers. Marketed to both children and adults, McDonald's presented "Mr. James" in TV advertisements, billboards, and a daily blog (written by his character on a tour of McDonald's restaurants nationwide) as speaking in broken Japanese (rendered only in the *katakana* loanword syllabary when written).[160] (This is a stark contrast to the multiethnic image that McDonald's in North America portrays itself and its staff.)[161]

Complaints from a domestic interest group (comparing the pandering of "Mr. James" with Negro caricature "Stepin Fetchit") occasioned mixed media commentary overseas, but no Japanese newspaper articles.[162] An explanatory letter from McDonald's Japan director of Corporate Relations Kawaminami Jun'ichi (written in English only, despite being contacted in Japanese, which kept the debate out of the Wajin media) stated that "no offence was meant." But he did not apologize for, or promise to suspend, the campaign (which continued for two more months). Although the "Mr. James" mascot itself was quietly retired weeks before the "Nippon All Stars" campaign officially concluded, the issue occasioned no Wajin media attention or protest.

Zui'unsha's Little Black Sambo and the Commodification of Race

In 2005, the Japanese version of *Little Black Sambo* (*chibi kuro sanbo*, or LBS) was republished by Tōkyō publisher Zui'unsha Inc.[163] Originally published by Helen Bannerman in 1899 with a brown-skinned character (reportedly based upon the Indian children where Bannerman was based), LBS was first published in Japanese in 1953 by Iwanami Shoten Inc. The Japanese version elected to use a jet-black gollywog version of Sambo that had been published in the United States in 1927. Over the next thirty-five years, various versions of LBS sold over a million copies in Japan. Meanwhile, Sambo became a problematic character overseas (thanks to media criticisms by prominent minority authors such as Langston Hughes), occasioning the appearance of less-racialized versions of the LBS story as substitutes (such as *Sam and the Tigers* and *The Story of Little Babaji*, which themselves were published in Japan by 1997). After a pressure group accused Iwanami and other LBS publishers of racism, LBS was withdrawn from the Japanese market in January 1989. Sixteen years later, Zui'unsha republished LBS with no historical context within about its controversial history, resuscitating the 1927 gollywog version. It again became a bestseller, selling over 100,000 copies within the first two months on the market and spawning two sequels.[164]

Defending the book, Zui'unsha's president Inoue Tomio stated, "Times have changed since the book was removed. Black people are more prominent in politics and entertainment, so I don't think this book can be blamed for supporting racial stereotypes. We certainly had no intention of insulting black people."[165] Mori Kazuo, a psychologist at Shinshu University, concurred, stating for the record in his professional opinion that racism without racist intent cannot be racism: "The Japanese people can be racist when it comes to Koreans living here. But racist against blacks? We have no experience in dealing with black people. Where would we get it from?"[166]

However, within five years of republication, this media-validated expression of racialized treatment became self-generating, with Midori Hoikuen nursery school in Tokorozawa, Saitama Prefecture, creating a song for its preschool children to sing in a school play:

Little Black Sambo, Sambo, Sambo
His face and hands are completely black
Even his butt is completely black
ちびくろ・さんぼがサンボサンボ
顔もお手ても真っ黒け
ついでにおしりも真っ黒け[167]

Protests to the school and the local authorities by parents of a biracial child in the school (and by other concerned international residents nationwide) neither resulted in a less-racialized version of this play being adopted, nor in the school play being cancelled. Racialization in primary education was thus performatively being normalized for the next generation of schoolchildren. After the success of LBS, Zui'unsha resuscitated other racialized books from a different era of media awareness about minorities. These in turn have created and legitimized more racialized merchandise.[168]

However, the commodification of the "Sambo-style" phenotype has precedent, as Japan has a long history of selling racialized "black" dolls to the public. Consider *Dakko-chan*:[169] Marketed by toymaker Tsukudaya Inc. in 1960 and later by Takara Inc., this plastic toy had racialized and stereotyped characteristics, such as jet-black skin, thick red lips, pierced large ears, and a "primitive" grass skirt. It was at first called "Tree-climbing Winkie" (*ki nobori winkii*) and "Little Blackie Swinger" (*kuronbo burachan*) before becoming what is best translated as "Little Hugger" (*dakko-chan*). Made of inflatable plastic and relatively cheap when it first went on sale in the early 1960s, *Dakko-chan* got its name through arms that could clamp on to surfaces, such as people's arms or curtains, and it became a fast-seller at over 2.4 million dolls within its first six months on the market. The doll later went out of style, and, after media criticism of discrimination against black people, by December 2001 Takara TOMY Inc. had changed it into a figure without a recognizably human flesh tone (such as green, red, or blue) or into other comic characters (e.g., Peko-chan, Hello Kitty, or Hanshin Tigers sportsmen). However, at the start, as can be seen by the "blackie" (*kuronbo*) name it was first marketed under, it was sold in ways that gollywogs have been marketed in the West—as cute representations of a minority group which eventually objected to the representation (in Japan's case, a more worldwide audience for its products).

Thus, the successful and sustained reintroduction of Sambo as both an image and a plush toy could be due to Zui'unsha's appeal to "nostalgic" (*natsukashii*) or "retro" (*retoro*) markets. The reason why protests were unsuccessful at removing it from the market could be a backlash against perceived "foreign" pressure on Japan (*gaiatsu*), seen as perceptions of "oversensitivity," "political correctness," or "cultural imperialism" based on values found in other societies.[170] (Russell (2015) notes, "Many Japanese view racism as *Amerika byō*, a uniquely 'American disease' from which their putatively monoracial state has been spared.")[171] Or it could also be evidence of how a product racialized from childhood has the additional tendency to be seen as "normal" when consumers reach adulthood, thus making marketing across generations more powerful and sustainable.

Mandom's "Gatsby" Male Cosmetics Marketing Associates "Black People" with Monkeys

Distributed by cosmetic company Mandom Corporation from March 28, 2005, the "*Mogeha*" mentholated face towels were marketed with an image of black Jamaican Rastafarians (with a bewigged dreadlocked Japanese model) refreshing their faces with the product in a hot room overseas, with swiveling-pan camerawork and a backbeat of Reggae music.[172] A chimpanzee in clothing akin to the black models was also using the product similarly. It was a visual linkage of cool, relaxed, "Jamaican/African," and animalistic with a male-oriented product. After public protests and domestic media coverage, on June 9, 2005, the advertising campaign (although not the product) was pulled from media with apologies from Mandom Corporation. By the end of 2005, unlike the Sambo books concurrently being protested, the Mogeha product went off the market entirely.[173]

"Blackface" Resurges in Japanese Entertainment

Apposite to the Nissin "white-washing" of Japanese-Haitian-American tennis champ Ōsaka Naomi in their 2019 advertising (see chapter 5), there have also been high-profile cases of Japanese entertainers blackening their faces as an apparent "homage" to overseas celebrities and performers of African descent, such as *tarento* entertainer Hamada Masatoshi mimicking Eddie Murphy during prime-time New Year's Eve broadcasts in 2017.[174] Before that, in 2015 do-wop band Rats & Star again darkened up (as they had done for many years without international attention) to clown around backstage with popular girl group Momoiro Clover Z. There has also been a strong background culture of black cultural appropriation and fetishization in Japan,[175] including an apparent deracination of blackened faces in the *Ganguro* ("face black") subculture fashions from the mid-1990s, and a Wajin anime character named "Afro Tanaka" being used by Mini-Stop convenience stores to sell black bread in 2010 (encasing it within a transparent package that made the product look like Tanaka's Afro hairstyle.)[176]

While defenders of this practice claim a lack of racist intent because Wajin "have nothing but respect and adoration for black people and music, and that this minstrel show of theirs is their way—the Japanese way—of paying homage to black music history" (McNeil 2015), others (such as Mori above) overtly claim that it cannot be racism because Wajin have "no experience in dealing with black people." Historian Russell (2015) notes, however, that blackface has been performed in Japan for more than 150 years, starting with an American minstrel show for Japan's delegates during Commodore Matthew Perry's 1854 trade-opening mission to Japan. Blackface has been popular for generations since then in places such as Tōkyō's Takarazuka and Asakusa Districts, jazz revues, and soul bars. It enjoyed a revival in the 2010s thanks to döppelgangers of President Obama (Russell calls it "Barackface") appearing worldwide.

As of this Second Edition, the practice now causes some circumspection in Japanese media, leading to, for example, the cancellation of the Rats & Star/ Momoiro Clover Z collaboration airing on Fuji TV, but a change of course usually requires international attention. As Russell (2015) notes, "[F]or many blacks . . . there is an unpleasant sense of déja vu that belies any suggestion that much has changed. And it is doubtful they will until the issue of Japanese racism in all its forms is honestly and unflinchingly confronted."

Treatment of Haafu Visible Minorities in Japanese Media

Japanese citizens with "foreign" ethnic roots of course exist in Japan. How many people exactly is unclear, due to the difficulties discussed in chapter 4 with a National Census that does not measure by ethnicity.[177] But the people labeled as Haafu (or Kuwataa, etc. for generational extractions) face differentiated treatment in the Wajin media depending on how phenotypically "visible" their foreign roots are, with their putative ethnic characteristics being thrust upon them. This section alone could fill a book, but let us touch upon a few instructive examples:

According to Edward Y. Sumoto, the founder and director of support group Mixed Roots Japan, the Postwar children of international roots became differentiated into Konketsuji (see chapters 2 and 4) and Haafu. "Konketsuji referred to the common mixed-race child as well as those who were orphaned or reported on media for committing a crime, while Haafu was used for pin-ups, with a Caucasian-centric idealization in terms of standards of beauty." This image became so normalized that a contemporary dictionary entry refers to "Haafu" as "mixed-race female." However, more recently, according to Sumoto, "While mainstream media still covers more topics about the non-idealized reality such as *ijime*, racism, language education and nationality, the voices of mixed-race individuals and celebrities have been amplified through social media, contributing to a slow change of public perception of what it means to be Haafu. Afro-Japanese mixed individuals are also making regular appearances as emcees on TV, and even Asian mixed-race individuals are using the term Haafu casually to refer to themselves."[178]

Nevertheless, there are still Wajin media portrayals of Visible Minorities that revert to type. For example, Okoye Rui, a high school baseball player with Japanese Nigerian roots, made some stellar plays in the 2015 Summer National High School Baseball Championship. This brought forth reactions from the Japanese sports press that portrayed him as a "beast" (*yajū*) with his "wild instincts on full display" (*yaseimi zenkai*), "exhibiting instincts" (*honnō mukidashi*) like a "hungry" (*ueta*) "panther" (*hyō*) looking for "prey" (*emono*) on the "savannah," and so on.[179] Other media have portrayed Haafu as not quite belonging to either the Wajin or Gaijin worlds, using discourses that "other" them by focusing on putative differences, and minimizing their situations of being treated like Gaijin as merely "chuckleworthy" (*tohoho na*).[180] These anecdotes published with this tone serve as a vernacular confirmation that treating people as "different" because they *look* "different" is a natural, if not inevitable, part of life in Japan.

In terms of social media, there have also been confirmed issues of racialized abuse and Wajin taunts of diverse Japanese. This research has already covered their structural harassment in chapter 5, for example, the general background of *ijime* bullying of Haafu by Wajin classmates and Japan school rules; the official exclusionism and racial cleansing of Japanese sports leagues; and the identity policing of high-profile representatives of Japan such as the Reed ice skaters, beauty queens Yoshikawa Priyanka and Miyamoto Ariana, and tennis champ Ōsaka Naomi. In addition, other athletes, such as Japanese Beninese Hachimura Rui and his brother Aren (who currently play basketball for the Washington Wizards and Tōkai University, respectively), reportedly receive targeted and threatening messages (e.g., "Die, you darkie (*kuronbo*) whose birth was a mistake") from Wajin outlets "almost every day"; Aren notes on Twitter, "Some people say racial discrimination doesn't exist in Japan . . . but I would like everyone to be concerned about this."[181]

Whitening the Image of "Foreign" in Marketing: "Gaijin" as Caucasian

Then there is the more general issue of caricaturing "foreigners" into a racialized generic "other." In Wajin marketing campaigns, there is concrete evidence that a "foreigner" (*gaikokujin*) in Japan is not only legally a noncitizen, but also *visibly* a noncitizen, that is, a person who cannot "pass" as a Wajin. However, this does not necessarily mean a person of Asian, Subcontinental Indian, African, Hispanic, and so on descent. As evidenced by the marketing in Japan by these "*dokkiri*" party-joke products below (figure 7.3), the default image for *gaikokujin*, especially the racialized epithet *gaijin*, is "white" (*hakujin*), as in "white European" (*ōbeijin*) stock.

Note the stereotypical racialized characteristics (as advertised in both images) include a large nose, blue eyes, cleft chin, blond hair, "Hollywood smile," and grand gesticulations. The default language (as seen by the *harō* and *ha-i!*) is English (if not *katakana* Japanese for the *desu* copula in the image on the right). The company selling these products, JiG Paradise KK, currently has other types of Gaijin Masks on sale (see archive in Endnotes),[182] with Sakata (2012) noting that the appeal of the genre of this product was "to help the user transform" (*henshin*) into a differentiated, "foreign" character, in this case for humorous purposes.[183] A similar "transformative" marketing strategy

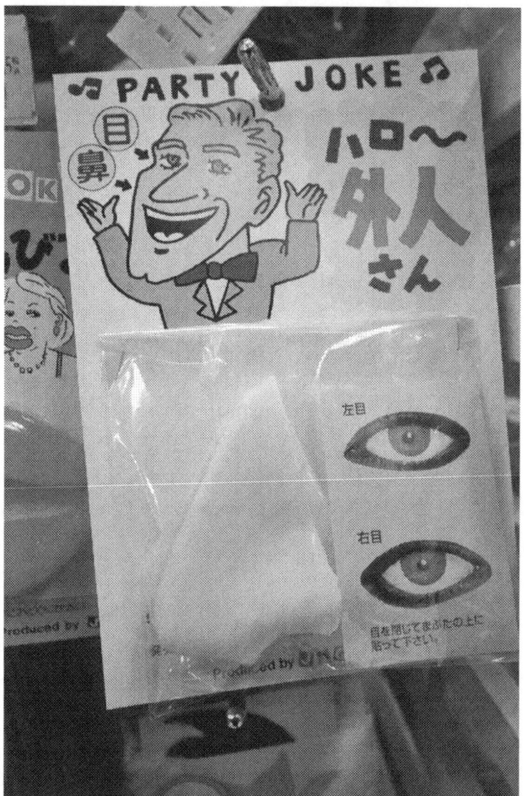

Figure 7.3 Racialized Commodification of Gaijin as Caucasian. Note large plastic nose and eyes that are colored sky blue. With softer wording (cf. gaikokujin) for "foreigner" and slightly altered illustration, an updated version of the product went on sale August 21, 2012, and is listed as "currently unavailable" to buyers with addresses outside of Japan. *Source:* Courtesy of an anonymous contributor, taken at Tokyu Hands Shinjuku, November 17, 2008.

was used by Nagasakitabi.net (www.nagasaki-tabinet.com), an online travel guide for tourists, in July 2010. Sponsored in part by the Nagasaki Prefecture Convention and Visitors Bureau, Nagasakitabi's sales pitch for Nagasaki was "like a trip to a foreign land" (due to its long history of outside influences on culture and architecture). In a TV spot,[184] this "trip to a foreign land" made the traveler feel "foreign," which for this advertisement visually meant racializing the featured Wajin tourists with stereotypical Caucasian phenotypes (blond hair and big noses) and heavily accented spoken Japanese.[185]

Racialized transformation is in fact a surprisingly frequent theme in Japan's product advertising. "Let's change the image of Japanese people" was exactly the slogan used by Japanese major airline All Nippon Air (ANA) in 2014, to celebrate the opening of new direct international air routes from Tōkyō Haneda Airport. Two famous comedians were hired to speak English with Japanese subtitles, with one appearing "Caucasian" with a blond wig and large prosthetic nose (even though most of their overseas routes, including one of the new ones, flew to non-Caucasian-majority countries). The internet and some mass media had discussions that proceeded down the path of "the foreigners are being oversensitive" in Japanese, but in English more criticism was directed at the airline. Gerry Nacpil, supervisor of ANA Sky Web, apologized and said the ad's intent was "to encourage Japanese to travel abroad more and become global citizens" (raising a new question whether "global citizen" equals "Caucasian") before the ad finally got pulled.[186]

Less attention was paid to other products where Wajin characters used props like blond wigs and big noses (please see online archives in corresponding endnotes), such as Toshiba's 2013 SuiPanDa bread maker (because Caucasians are apparently specialists in eating bread, not rice),[187] 2013's "Kobito-Zukan" racialized collectable figurines,[188] Choya's 2008 plum saké (also featuring stick-on paper blue eyes),[189] or Japan Proctor & Gamble's 2014 racialized laundry detergent ad, "Cinderella and the Nose Ballroom Dance" (where the charm point was not glass slippers, but White people with elongated noses twitching at clean clothes).[190] Nor did many notice how Japan celebrity singer Crystal Kay, a Zainichi-African-American Visible Minority, became progressively lighter in skin tone with each successive album.[191] Other examples are available in endnote,[192] but the sheer number of incidents indicates how normalized the visual differentiation and identification of "foreignness" is in Japanese media.[193]

"Difference" Normalized to the Point Where "Lack of Difference" in "Foreigners" Becomes Abnormal

Sometimes even when differences are verifiably nonexistent between Wajin and Gaijin, the desire for them to exist is reiterated and reinforced in the dominant discourse. For example, during an October 14, 1996, broadcast of popular news program "News Station," a "foreign" interviewee (a Subcontinental Indian who lives in Japan) commented for a segment in Japanese "too fluently," whereupon famous TV anchor Kume Hiroshi jokingly quipped on air, "It's better if gaijin [*sic*] speak broken Japanese" (*shikashi, gaijin wa nihongo ga katakoto no hō ga ii yo ne*).[194] Despite protests and media coverage,[195] Kume's comment was not retracted. Fourteen years later, long after his retirement from News Station, Kume apologized for his comment in a direct communication with the author.[196] However, the normalized need for "foreign" to be "different," in this case "a different language ability" from Wajin, fostered more than a decade of cognitive dissonance in this otherwise conscientious, educated, and well-informed public commentator. There is plenty of similar media depicting foreigners as permanent "guests," not residents,[197] so Kume is not alone in being blindsided by Japan's latent diversity:

CONSEQUENCES OF A RACIALIZED MEDIA: "WALLING IN THE WAJIN"

Japan's racialized media also has deleterious effects on the dominant majority insiders. I call it a "walling in of the Wajin." The Wajin-created social milieu tautologically expects "foreign" to be "not Japanese" (axiomatically expecting and requiring "difference" in order for a person to be "foreign"), and conversely it tends to *expect and require an enforced "similarity"* between Wajin in order for a person to be classified as "Japanese." Consequently, this dynamic makes it extremely difficult for a person who does not perceptibly "think," "act," or "look" "foreign" to traverse the walls and become a Wajin (especially if that person is a Visible Minority, no matter how hard the person acculturates and attempts to "pass" within Japanese society). It also becomes extremely difficult for Wajin to go outside the wall as well—because denying the hegemonic Wajin collective "similarities" would be tantamount to a fundamental denial of one's individual identity as a "Japanese" (often engendering criticism and identity policing from fellow Wajin as well).

Moreover, the "walling in" makes it difficult for Wajin to empathize with the Non-Wajin "outsider." If a person never experiences life as part of a social "Other" in a society, then that person will find it difficult to understand the process and effects of "othering." As long as Wajin stay comfortably within the boundaries of Japan's dominant discourse, communicating in Japanese with Wajin under a normalized racialized context of identity, they will perpetually enjoy or endure the "similarities" that ground their "Japaneseness" without the experience of ever becoming the "Other" in a *racialized* sense. Thus, even when outside of Japanese society, Wajin, in order not to be policed back inside the walls, must generally be completely removed from other Wajin—in other words, leave most social aspects of Japan behind at the border (including the language). Given the comparative lack of currency of Japanese as a second language overseas, this process can be extremely daunting and isolating; self-removal is a path chosen by startlingly few.[198]

How does the shoe fit on the other foot, where Non-Wajin attempt to remove themselves from "Other" status and try to become more "Japanese"? They still have extreme difficulty becoming Wajin because of Japan's

Embedded Racism. As described in chapter 4, "Wajin" is a blood-based social status of majoritarian dominance, regardless of knowledge, acculturation, or even legal status of the hopeful minority. The more acculturated a "foreigner" becomes (such as, for example, by learning the Japanese language or even taking Japanese citizenship), the more likely there will be questions about the person's "authenticity" as either a Wajin *or* a Gaijin. These questions come in the form of microaggressive behavior, such as comments such as *hen na gaijin* (a "strange foreigner," that is, for being "less foreign than expected"), in the form of "feelings of incongruity" (*iwakan*, as seen in Kume Hiroshi's quip preferring "foreigners" be less fluent in Japanese), or even in the form of losing one's qualifications as a professional (as seen in Kitakyūshū University professor of English Noriguchi Shin'icho's *Asahi Shinbun* columns in 2006, where he accused "foreign" educators of unprofessionalism for becoming "too Japanese").[199] Non-Wajin are thus policed back outside the walls.

The Wajin/Non-Wajin paradigm thus presents an ideological worldview that perpetually erects barriers between peoples due to their bloodlines. It is a caste system[200] that not only subordinates Non-Wajin but also blinds the subordinator, meaning that most Wajin, no matter how sympathetic or well intentioned, will lack fundamental sympathy or empathy for minorities. (This may explain the relative indifference most Wajin surveyed have toward defending equal rights for "foreigners": see chapter 8.) The Wajin/Non-Wajin paradigm also calls into question the promise of the oft-touted "next generation of Japanese"—allegedly more traveled, more "acculturated to foreigners" from a young age through things like the JET Programme, and thus more experienced with the outside world—ever becoming more open-minded to outsiders.[201]

The copious findings of Critical Race Theory (CRT) and the lessons of Whiteness Studies (see appendix 2) would substantiate these "walling-in" dynamics, asserting that "racial transparency"[202] will make most Wajin unable to empathize with, comprehend, or even entertain the notion that Japan has a racialized society with ethnic minorities. Further, Wajin will become concerned when Non-Wajin, particularly Visible Minorities, seek to become the dominant group in any interaction. The claim then becomes that "more foreigners means less Japan" (cf. even written as such in a 2010 "Doomsday for Japan" book),[203] and this justifies the racially motivated laws and measures to maintain Wajin Privilege covered in this chapter.

Thus, to return to our original research question, this "walling-in" dynamic makes the creation of antidiscrimination legislation in Japan extremely difficult to achieve—not only due to the insiders' lack of empathy with the outsider, but because the insider often sees any compromise with (or potential enfranchisement of) the outsider as an act of surrendering hierarchical power and structural dominance. The fear of unknown outcomes due to a change in the status quo will give pause to anyone truly unfamiliar with people of differences.

THE LONG-TERM SOCIAL DAMAGE CAUSED BY SUSTAINED RACIALIZED PROPAGANDA: DEHUMANIZATION

Years of NPA and GOJ propaganda have caused quantifiable social damage toward noncitizens regarding their constitutional rights. A GOJ Cabinet "Public Survey on the Defense of Human Rights"[204] (*jinken yōgo ni kansuru yoron chōsa*), carried out every four to five years, asked 3,000 respondents (again, *kokumin* only) aged twenty and up whether they agreed with the following statement: "Foreigners should have the same protection of human rights as Japanese" (*Nihon kokuseki o motanai hito demo, Nihonjin to onaji yō ni jinken wa mamorubeki da*). The 2003 Cabinet Survey reported that *only about half* (54 percent) of all respondents agreed. This was a dramatic decline from 65.5 percent in 1997, 68.3 percent in 1993, and 61.8 percent in 1988.[205]

The reason for this downward trend, according to the Justice Ministry's BOHR, was due to "a sudden rise in foreign crime."[206]

By the 2007 Survey, the figure supporting equal rights for noncitizens had rebounded to 59.3 percent, but the percent of people agreeing with the opposite option, "It can't be helped if people who do not have Japanese citizenship to not have equal rights with Japanese" (*Nihon kokuseki o motanai hito wa Nihonjin to onaji yō na kenri o motte inakute mo shikata ga nai*) also rose to its highest level ever: 25.1 percent.

Therefore, when a quarter (and growing) of the surveyed (Wajin) public indicate that *noncitizens do not deserve the same human rights as their fellow humans*, by definition this depicts the dehumanization of noncitizens. It is also quantifiable social damage, directly attributed by GOJ officials to a social trend (foreign crime) that itself had been generated, propagandized, and normalized in the dominant discourse by officialdom and media.

This is the outcome of the processes of Embedded Racism.

Another important consequence of Japan's Embedded Racism, as discussed in chapter 2, is the methodological "blind spots" that arise in scholarship and policymaking inputs on racism. The Cabinet Public Survey had numerous methodological problems.[207] First, of course, is their surveying attitudes about domestic minorities without asking at least one group of minorities at least one group of minorities or noncitizens. Second, the Survey once again did not include the category of "racial discrimination" (*jinshu sabetsu*): It is rendered as "foreigner discrimination" (*gaikokujin sabetsu*). Further, the Survey does not include the possibility that people who look "foreign" might actually be Japanese citizens.

Third, the public is asked about their awareness of other types of discrimination (including by gender, physical and mental disability, age, ethnicity/social origin, etc.). But when a question asked about "foreigner discrimination," options for answers offered possible justifications for their "disadvantageous treatment" *not found in other questions about disadvantaged groups*. Out of six preset options, half say "nothing can be done" to improve things because (a) "foreigners have trouble getting used to Japanese situations," (b) "differences in customs, culture, and economic standing" (which got the most votes, 33.7 percent), and the tautological (c) "because they are foreigners, there's no other option but that they get disadvantageous treatment" (*gaikokujin da kara furieki na tori atsukai o ukete mo shikata ga nai*).

When a GOJ human rights survey allows for the possibility of *human rights being optional* (or offers embedded questions that essentially justify unequal rights based on nationality), there is a profound conceptual problem in Japan's approach to human rights.[208] From this comes poor social science at the highest levels of government, where noncitizens are relegated to a specially differentiated, "othered," and subordinated category in Japanese society, whose human rights are optional, while Visible Minorities are ignored completely.

The UN has expressed disagreement with this survey's methodology. In 1998, the Committee of Civil and Political Rights wrote: "The Committee stresses that protection of human rights and human rights standards are not determined by popularity polls. It is concerned by the repeated use of popularity statistics to justify attitudes of [Japan] that may violate its obligations under the Covenant."[209] Regardless, as seen above, the GOJ used this survey and its problematic questions two more times.[210]

MOJ's Landmark 2017 Survey of Foreign Residents: Better Methodology

For this Second Edition, a positive development should be noted in the GOJ's social science practices—the act of researching domestic discrimination by surveying the people being discriminated against.[211] In March 2017, the MOJ's Center for Human Rights Education and Training issued the GOJ's first nationwide survey of discrimination against "foreign residents" [*sic*] in Japan's history.

The Survey's introduction self-justified the effort by acknowledging the need to "coexist" (*kyōsei*) with foreigners due to internationalization, globalization, and the upcoming 2020 Tōkyō Olympics. Along with the boilerplate of bringing up problems with intercultural differences due to language and customs, the Survey circumvented the entrenched Abe-Era political debate about the un-Wajin "Western concepts" of individual rights and freedoms, and instead specifically cited "numerous human rights problems" facing foreigners who "come to live in Japan" (*ijū*) or "stay in place for the time being" (*zairyū*). The Center also did not allow Japan's police forces to set the Survey agenda, instead convoking a board of academics from prominent universities—experts in the fields of sociology, statistics, international human rights law, and anthropology. They met six times over the course of a year to discuss goals, consider how to word questions and interpret results, and come up strategies for reporting the findings to the public.

Complementing this concern for better social science methods, the Center sent surveys to 18,500 registered non-Japanese residents (500 surveys × all 37 municipal areas) in fourteen languages, receiving a 23 percent response rate. The responses were interesting: 39.3 percent said they had been refused housing for being foreign, and more than a quarter (26.8 percent) said they saw properties with "no foreigners" rules. Another quarter (25 percent) said they had been refused jobs specifically because they were not Japanese, and another third said they were given a lower salary or other disadvantages in work conditions or promotion (19.6 percent and 17.1 percent, respectively) for the same reason. Although the overwhelming majority (92.2 percent) said they had never been refused entry by a "Japanese only" establishment, a significant number instead experienced "hate speech" in the form of public displays of xenophobia through the broadcast media (42.9 percent) and/or the internet (33.3 percent). More analysis and commentary in the endnotes link above.

The biggest flaw of the 2017 Survey was the approach of seeing this activity as "foreigner discrimination," not racial discrimination, meaning once again Visible Minorities were left out. It also ignored discrimination being caused by GOJ policies.[212] Nevertheless, it was a good first step, as it finally gave policymakers concrete statistics from the government to point to as a social problem to address.

The 2017 Survey also demonstrated that there are people in Japan who do not accept the Wajin-Gaijin system as unimpeachable or inevitable, and are willing to take into account the human rights of noncitizens and Visible Minorities. We will discuss their works in chapter 8.

CODA: EXCLUSIONARY EXTREMES OF DIFFERENTIATION, "OTHERING," AND SUBORDINATION: A FEW OUTSTANDING EXAMPLES REDUX

Let us begin to wrap up this lengthy chapter by bringing together themes covered over part III of this book: Differentiation of peoples by citizenship and phenotype in Japan has reached a degree of normalization where not only do the *actions* of a "foreigner" come under suspicion and scrutiny, but also the *very presence* of "foreigners" is problematized as a possible security or integrity risk to Japan. An embedded and constantly enforced binary of Self and Other, Insider and Outsider, Nihonjin/Wajin and Gaikokujin/Gaijin offers little neutral ground. Many people feel compelled to "have awareness of" or "have an opinion" about "foreigners"—including, as we saw above, the often overly self-conscious "foreigners" themselves! Non-Wajin, especially the Visible Minorities, thus cannot easily be accepted as "normal" as an assimilated part of Japanese society. The consequence of this dynamic is a zero-sum paradigm—again, "more foreigners means less Japan"—meaning that to the dominant majority, "foreigners" in Japan ultimately threaten Japan's very existence.

Media has reinforced this by devoting more time to discussing the "problems" (*mondai*) than the benefits of "foreigners" coming to live, work, and cohabit in neighborhoods in Japan. Before the hateful politics of the 2010s, articles during the fearful 2000s regularly cite alleged "cultural issues" resulting in inevitable differences and therefore conflicts. These "problems" became a "blame game," including "proper sorting of garbage" (*gomi bunbetsu*) on trash collection days, disruptions of the peace due to noise levels of "foreigner" parties and gatherings, unpleasant smells (such as from kimchi or Chinese spices) or messes in apartment complexes, even tooth decay in local children![213] And of course the fear of foreign crime was reinforced by biannual NPA media campaigns, which gave license to exclusion and eventually hatred. This oversensitivity and anxiety encouraged by a normalized fear of difference has the effect of legitimizing illogical and egregious acts of unfairness and inequality, and it went beyond the "Japanese Only" exclusionary establishments covered in chapter 3.

The following cases were mentioned in chapter 1, but they warrant reiterating at this juncture, since now they might seem less confounding given what we have covered so far in this research (sources endnoted in chapter 1):

In December 2006, the Setaka Town Assembly in Fukuoka Prefecture, under pressure from fearful local residents, passed a resolution (*seigan*) without debate granting building permission for a new university in town only if it had no exchange students (*ryūgakusei*). The reported reason given was a fear of "foreign crime" that foreign students might cause.

In June 2009, parents from a "Southeast Asian nation" tried twice to enroll their twelve-year-old daughter in a public junior high school in Ōsaka, but teachers at faculty meetings tried to block her enrollment due to worries about their "lack of preparations" and her "insufficient Japanese language ability." Faculty demands that the girl attend language school elsewhere were eventually rejected by the Ōsaka municipal board of education, where the school was told the student could enroll with outside lessons at a Japanese language school or an interpreter. Due to this imbroglio, the student was forced to miss the first six weeks of school.

In September 2007, it was reported that a pregnant "foreign woman" who had given birth at home was refused postnatal medical care seven times by five hospitals in Tsu, Mie Prefecture. This was reportedly due to hospital claims of a "lack of proper facilities" and because "her Japanese wasn't good enough." The hospital only admitted her after she had "begged to be treated over two hours," and only after being rejected by two of the hospitals twice.

In June 2007, local residents unlawfully blocked a realtor from selling a plot of land for housebuilding to a Nikkei Brazilian factory worker in Nakamizo, Fukuroi, Shizuoka Prefecture, quoting residents' fears of "Brazilians being prone to committing crimes." "The head of the Nagamizo community association stated bluntly that non-Japanese were not welcome in the neighborhood. 'Honestly speaking, we don't want (Brazilians) to move into the neighborhood if possible.'"

In May 2014, media reported that a confectionary vocational school (*senmon gakkō*) named Konshō Gakuen in Kumagaya, Saitama Prefecture, had a formal school regulation (*hōshin*) refusing admission to all "foreign" students since it opened in 1976. Although a Peruvian student had lodged a complaint with Saitama Prefecture in November 2012, educational authorities found it had no mandate to force the school to repeal it. Although justified as necessary to avoid being vocationally responsible for "illegal foreign students," and with excuses including, "other schools are doing the same," "it's no big deal," and "we didn't know it was wrong," on May 23, due to media pressure, the school formally withdrew its restriction, although as of this writing it is still unclear if foreigners have been admitted in practice.

On February 23, 2010, Japan's Sumō Association (*sumō kyōkai*) announced that it would further narrow opportunities for "foreign" wrestlers in the sport (already fixed at only one foreign wrestler per stable). It would now count any wrestler with foreign roots (*gaikoku shusshin*) as "foreign," even if he had obtained Japanese citizenship through naturalization, in direct contravention of Japan's Nationality Law regarding the legal status of naturalized citizens. Similarly, in September 2020, the Japan Rugby Football Union announced that they would also deny Japanese-citizen eligibility to its foreign-born naturalized players.

On February 11, 2015, a column in the prominent daily newspaper *Sankei Shinbun* by Sono Ayako, a famous novelist and former advisor to PM Abe Shinzō on education reform, cited the alleged behaviors of "black people" (*kokujin*) in South Africa after the fall of Apartheid, and advocated racial segregation in Japan: "Since learning about the situation in South Africa twenty or thirty years ago, I've come to think that whites, Asians and blacks should live separately." Despite widespread domestic and international criticism, including a formal letter of protest from the South African Ambassador to Japan, neither the author nor the newspaper retracted the article.

From 2018, local governments began using the term *gaikokujin shimin* (foreign city citizens) to classify people in their jurisdictions as "foreign" not only if they had foreign nationalities, but also if they were "people like those who obtained Japanese citizenship, children born from international marriages, people with foreign cultures in their backgrounds, and people who have foreign roots." This effectively not only re-classified naturalized citizens as "foreign," but also essentially categorized as "foreign" anyone with foreign connections, including Wajin Japanese.

In 2019, it was reported that non-Japanese children were being put into "special education" schools (headlined as "prison camps for Brazilians" in the Mainichi Shinbun) for years against their wishes, at rates more than twice the rate for Japanese schoolchildren. Given manual labor such as digging potatoes instead of learning math, these non-Japanese children were assumed to be low IQ because they were not proficient in Japanese. This policy was justified by a school vice principal claiming, "When foreigners increase in number, the learning process of Japanese students is delayed."

From March 2020, due to the COVID-19 pandemic, Japan instituted a ban on all noncitizens (including Permanent Residents) reentering Japan, effectively treating all foreigners regardless of visa status in Japan the same as tourists. However, Japanese citizens traveling under the same conditions were exempted from this ban. This led to hundreds of thousands of non-Japanese residents being stranded abroad for months, unable to work their jobs, pay their bills, continue their studies, or be with their Japanese families in Japan; conversely, non-Japanese residents in Japan found themselves stranded within Japan, unable to leave the country to take care of family matters and tend to ailing or deceased relatives overseas. *Japan Times* noted that no other G7 developed country instituted this kind of "Japanese Only" border control policy, banning all foreign residents with legal visas but letting in all citizens.

These are but a few pinpoint examples, but the roots of their underlying premises, assumptions, and prejudices have all been covered in some form or another in the course of this book. To anyone who has not lived under them for an extended period, they are often written off as "inscrutable" Japanese behavior.[214] To anyone who has, and studied GOJ and Wajin social dynamics in depth, they take on the form of a normalized dynamic that actually makes sense under its own internal logics: "This is Japan. *Shikata ga nai*."

Thus, the differentiation, "othering," and subordination (if not outright exclusion) of peoples deemed to be outsiders—Gaijin—is extreme in Japan. So extreme that minority voices and views are not only widely underrepresented, but also the *very existence of any minorities in Japan whatsoever has been repeatedly denied by the GOJ*. This is thanks to the dominant national discourse stating that Japan is a monocultural, monoethnic society. We will cover that in chapter 8.

CONCLUSIONS

This chapter completes part III of this book, which outlined how Japan's Embedded Racism is constructed through national narratives. It focused upon how racism from official bodies is disseminated, normalized, and embedded in Japanese society through the media. Although national narratives worldwide naturally create "Self" and "Other" as a necessary element for a nation-state's self-existence, this chapter found that Japan's exclusionary narratives transmitted by the media can be so extreme that they (a) wind up dehumanizing Japan's "foreign" outsiders, and (b) "wall off" the Wajin dominant majority from empathizing with them. There are, of course, many exceptions. Chapter 8 will now discuss how this system is criticized both within and outside Japan's polity, and how the status quo is defended and ultimately sustained by the GOJ.

NOTES

1. Highest newspaper penetration and concentration: Gamble & Watanabe (2004: 33–4). Television and viewership: *Economist* (2005: 90, 92, 94). Updated for this Second Edition: According to Nationmaster.com, Japan is tied with Norway in daily newspapers produced per capita and has risen from tenth to sixth in terms of televisions per 1,000 people. According to World Atlas, Japanese households spent 262 minutes per day, or 30.6 hours a week, watching TV in 2018, up from 17.9 hours a week in 2004; this ranks third in the world behind Poland and the United States. More sophisticated figures based upon viewing platforms (where Japan is more of a laggard) are in "How people watch: A global Nielsen consumer report." *Nielsen.com*, August 2010.

2. Media influence over public opinion: Gamble & Watanabe ibid. Press Clubs and other sources: cf. Freeman 1996, Gamble & Watanabe ibid.: Ch. 2, particularly 53–60, 360–361; Hall (1998): Ch. 2.

3. Broadcasting in foreign languages strictly regulated by the GOJ: Gamble & Watanabe: 43; Krauss (2000: 196–198).

4. As I wrote in "Media redraw battle lines in bid for global reach." *Japan Times*, July 6, 2015:

> GPlus Media Co., which operates English-language websites Japan Today and GaijinPot, was sold to Fuji TV-Lab, a subsidiary of Fuji Media Holdings Inc. The Fuji Media

group has the Fuji Television Network under its wing, as well as the conservative daily Sankei Shinbun as an affiliate. This matters to Japan's resident non-Japanese communities. Fuji TV was recently caught fabricating subtitles falsely quoting South Korean commenters as "hating Japan" ("Fuji TV apologizes for subtitles inaccurately quoting South Koreans." *Japan Times*, June 29, 2015). That's an incredibly dishonest thing for a nationwide broadcaster to do, especially when it may have a nasty impact on Japan's Korean minorities.

However, the Sankei Shinbun as a newspaper I believe is no less nasty. Over the past 15 years, for example, they have run articles grossly exaggerating foreign crime ("Generating the foreigner crime wave." *Japan Times*, October 4, 2002), a column claiming that Chinese had criminal "ethnic DNA" (May 8, 2001, written by regular columnist and former Tokyo Governor Shintaro "let's fight a war with China" Ishihara) and an opinion piece by Ayako Sono on February 11 that praised the racial segregation of South African apartheid as a model for Japanese immigration policy. The Fuji-Sankei group offers pretty much unwavering support to the country's right-wing causes and talking points. They are further right than the Yomiuri—and that's saying something.

More articles on this issue and commentary at "Online media outlet Japan Today acquired by right-wing Fuji Media Holdings, meaning Japan Times is last E-media news organization independent of J-media conglomerates." *Debito.org*, May 10, 2015, www.debito.org/?p=13286.

Echoing this trend, the Nihon Keizai Shinbun group bought into U.K. media group Monocle in 2014 in order to, according to its CEO, "further boost its global reach." In June, *Monocle* magazine declared Tokyo "the world's most livable city," as it would for the next two years. Japan's understanding of how media control of narratives influence societies thus strengthened its mission of micromanaging criticism of Japan not only domestically but also abroad.

5. As I wrote in "The Japan Times becomes servant to the elite." *Shingetsu News Agency*, February 2, 2019:

The Japan Times came under new ownership in June 2017 by the media group News2u Holdings, a PR company. In an unexpected editorial shift, last November the Japan Times announced that it would henceforth be rewording the "potentially misleading" (and internationally-recognized) terms "Comfort Women"—which is already a direct translation of the official euphemism of *ianfu*—as "women who worked in wartime brothels, including those who did so against their will, to provide sex to Japanese soldiers." Likewise, the term "forced laborers" would now be rendered merely as "wartime laborers," following the new government policy.

Aside from journalistic concerns about cramming a wordy term into concise articles, it wasn't hard for media observers to understand this as a response to government pressure, already manifest in Japanese media and world history textbooks, to portray Japan's past in a more exculpatory light. Reuters has since reported that the executive editor of the Japan Times, Hiroyasu Mizuno, was recorded at a meeting with staff as saying, "I want to get rid of criticism that Japan Times is anti-Japanese." Another executive added that this would increase advertising revenues from Japanese companies and institutions. Reuters added that the Japan Times "had already increased government ad sales and scored an exclusive interview with [Prime Minister Shinzo] Abe after dropping a column by Jeff

> Kingston, director of Asia studies at Temple University Japan, who had been writing weekly on what he saw as the Abe administration's historical revisionism." Symbolizing this shift, Shingetsu News Agency last December drew attention to a photo of News2u Publisher and Chair Minako Kambara Suematsu literally cozying up to Prime Minister Abe at a public event.
>
> Reuters concluded by pointing out a remarkable coincidence: Late last year, the ultraconservative think tank Japan Institute for National Fundamentals zeroed in on the Japan Times, demanding they refer to plaintiffs in a controversial Korean court ruling on the Comfort Women as "wartime Korean workers," thereby leaving out the nuance of forced labor or sexual slavery. Two weeks later, the Japan Times changed its wording.

See also "'Comfort women': Anger as Japan paper alters description of WWII terms": "Change prompts concern that country's media is trying to rewrite wartime history under rightwing pressure." *Guardian*, November 30, 2018; "'Fear' and 'favor' chill newsroom at storied Japanese paper." *Reuters*, January 24, 2019; McNeill & McCurry (2019).

Incidentally, the *Japan Times* is not alone in bowing to GOJ pressure. On February 5, 2015, the chair of Japan's government sponsored broadcast network NHK, Momii Katsuto, stated publicly that his network would not report on contentious subjects until the government has "an official stance" on them—meaning that NHK is willfully acting as a government mouthpiece. *See* "Effort by Japan to stifle news media is working." *New York Times*, April 26, 2015. Consequently, Reporters Without Borders reports that Japan has dropped precipitously in the World Press Freedom Index, from eleventh in 2010 to sixty-seventh in 2021 (behind Romania, Bhutan, and Ivory Coast) out of 180 countries ranked.

6. Cabinet of Japan 2013.

7. Habermas (1962).

8. Cf. Arudou 2005a, b, 2006a, b, Arudou *Japan Times* columns 2002–present, Arudou *Shingetsu News Agency* columns 2019–present, and so on.

9. "Japan Times officially sanitizes WWII 'comfort women' and 'forced laborers'. Pressure on my Japan Times Just Be Cause column too." *Debito.org*, November 30, 2018, www.debito.org/?p=15227. Accordingly, the scaling down of my human rights columns from monthly to about one a year, the toning down of the *Japan Times*' "Community Page" to milquetoast topics, and the removal of many harder-hitting columnists in favor of Wajin spokespeople with GOJ connections, also reflect this trend of media Wajinization.

10. Arudou (2005a, b, 2006a, b). An exhaustive vault of all collectable non-tabloid (and some tabloid) media regarding the Otaru Onsens Case from its inception on September 19, 1999, to its end on April 8, 2005, is available for reading in chronological order at www.debito.org/nihongotimeline.html#keii.

11. "Mainstream daily print media" in this research refers to newspapers *Asahi*, *Mainichi*, *Yomiuri*, *Sankei*, and *Nikkei*, regional paper *Hokkaidō Shinbun*, and other regional daily newspapers using wire services from *Kyodo*, *Jiji*, or other sources.

These are the influential, non-tabloid media that are seen as more trustworthy, and all have disseminated information about media campaigns in which the author was involved. The same trends were observed by the author in broadcast radio and television media, but these are harder to substantiate since records were difficult to collect and reproduce in print or online, as the time period is pre-YouTube. However, a select number of television reports on cases germane to this research have been archived starting from www.debito.org/?p=4462.

12. Otaru City International Communications Chief Takeuchi Kazuho, Sapporo District Court testimony March 15, 2002, page 20, and Otaru City *Kōhō* (the official city monthly newsletter) page, both cited in Arudou (2006a).

13. Transcription of the Japanese Government CERD Review (76th Session), February 24, 2010, comment from CERD Committee Member Pastor Elias Murillo Martinez (Colombia): "I listened attentively to the head of [Japan] delegation's speech, and I can't remember whether he actually used the concept of racism or racial discrimination as such in his speech. [NB: He does not.] It seems that this is something that the state in question prefers to avoid as a term." Full transcript of the proceedings archived at www.debito.org/?p=6145. Even a prominent book regarding discrimination in Japan, published by prominent human rights publisher Akashi Shoten, blunted its title to convert "racial" (*jinshu*) into "ethnic" (*minzoku*) discrimination, and I had to push against editorial constraints to include "*jinshu sabetsu*" as part of the title of my chapter within the book. *See* Okamoto (2005): *Nihon no Minzoku Sabetsu: Jinshu Sabetsu Teppai Jōyaku kara Mita Kadai* [Japan's ethnic discrimination: Issues in regard to the CERD], with chapter by Arudou (2005): "*'Gaikokujin' nyūten kinshi to iu jinshu sabetsu*" [Banning "Foreigners" Entry is Racial Discrimination]. *See also* Kawai (2015: 2, 5–8).

14. Archived starting from www.debito.org/lawsuitbackground.html.

15. This phenomenon of "unbalanced coverage if a foreigner is involved" was also seen in the Japanese media's treatment of CEOs Woodford of Olympus and Ghosn of Nissan/Mitsubishi. *See*, for example, "Carlos Ghosn's escape from Japan was the right move." *Shingetsu News Agency*, January 20, 2020; "Woodford and Ghosn: Foreign executives not in charge." *Shingetsu News Agency*, April 21, 2021.

16. Webster's Dictionary's definition of the term "propaganda" for the purposes of this research is "doctrines, ideas, arguments, facts, or allegations spread by deliberate effort through any medium of communication in order to further one's cause or to damage an opposing cause." However, this author is also fond of *The Problem of the Media* (2004) author Robert W. McChesney's succinct interpretation: "The more people consume your media, the less they will know about the subject, and the more they will support government policy" (Greenwald 2004, minute 50). *See also* Arudou (2010b).

17. Archived at www.debito.org/TheCommunity/nakanohittakuri.html with images and analysis: Banner from the Tōkyō Nakano-ku police says, "BEWARE: Bagsnatchings by bad foreigners coming to Japan happen frequently." Photo taken by the author September 29, 2002, by automatic teller machines (ATMs) at Nakano-ku Chūō Mitsui Shintaku Bank and others. An investgative phone call to Nakano Police Headquarters on October 1, 2002, revealed that there had been *zero* recent

bagsnatchings by "foreigners" in Nakano-ku, despite official claims of "frequent." Another poster was issued by the Nakano Police, found on September 29, 2002, in Nakano Sakaue Subway Station and other banks in the Nakano-ku area. It warns in ways germane to this research the public to be wary of "suspicious foreigners" (*fushin na gaikokujin*), and for readers to clutch their money or bags tighter if one of them is lurking around banks. What constitutes "suspiciousness" (other than "foreign" linguistic or possibly phenotypical differences) is unclear.

Archived at www.debito.org/mitakapolice0702.html is a public flyer issued by the Tōkyō Mitaka police warning against "bad foreigners" and their frequent bagsnatchings, and "foreign" criminal activity around cash-carrying bank customers. Note the illustrations depicting a "foreigner" being subdued by police (having been disarmed of his knife, visible in the background), and the grateful granny saying "I can rely on you" while being saluted by four police officers. Dated July 2002, found September 18, 2002, by ATMs at Asahi Bank by the author.

Archived at www.debito.org/?p=473 with analysis is a public flyer issued by Ōsaka Ikuno-ku police (specifically, a local division of the Committee for Policy Against Internationalization), found on car windshields in the Ikuno-ku area, May 2007. Warning against visa overstayers and illegal workers (who also allegedly forge passports and enter into fake marriages) in this time "when foreign crime is on a rapid rise" (even though, according to contemporary NPA crime statistics, it was falling; see above), this flyer encourages racial profiling through caricature of potential criminals as blond-haired Westerners with exaggerated half-moon profiles (plus one token dark-skinned "foreigner"). Note how in these and all posters below, the target audience of Wajin are racially portrayed as light-skinned or White.

Archived at www.debito.org/?p=11177 with analysis and companions is a flyer issued by Tōkyō Ueno police, dated August 9, 2002, found at the Asakusa Dōri UFJ Bank ATMs, October 2002. Note the story played out: Panel 1 establishes two darker-skinned *katakana*-speaking (as a form of accented Japanese) people (presumably "foreigners") spying an emerging light-skinned woman exiting a bank bearing cash. The thought balloon reads, "A mark, a mark!" Panel 2 shows one of the darker-skinned people dropping money behind the light-skinned woman and advising her to that effect. Panel 3 shows the distracted woman thanking him for the advice, and while distracted, having her bag snatched by Panel 4. Although the word "foreigner" is not used, the accented speech and the racialized visuals compensate.

Archived at www.debito.org/?p=3996 with analysis are three flyers issued by the Ibaraki Prefectural Police, specifically the Coast Guard Cooperative Union, found in train stations in Mito City and environs June 10, 2007, and October 24, 2008, and July 18, 2009. Warning against overstayers and illegal entrants (in a prefecture next to Tōkyō facing the Pacific Ocean), the flyer has the subtitle, "Stop them at the shores, protect [our country]," with visuals of a crowd of police subduing the lone "foreigner" on the scale of a military maneuver, warranting automatic weapons and beachhead landings.

Archived at www.debito.org/shizuokakeisatsuhandbook.html with analysis is the entire 26-page manual issued in February 2000 by the Shizuoka Prefectural

Police. Entitled "Characteristics of Crimes Committed by Foreigners Coming to Japan" (*rainichi gaikokujin hanzai no tokuchō*), it portrays "foreigners" (particularly Nikkei) as indolent, violent, conspiring in groups to shoplift, and so on. Note on pages 20–1 the NPA's advice to shopkeepers who witness a "foreign group" (defined as two or more "foreign" shoppers) entering their store: "write down their car license plate number and report it to police." According to local resident and contributor Ana Bortz, it was distributed to shopkeepers and the general public throughout Shizuoka Prefecture.

Archived at www.debito.org/?p=11177 with analysis is a flyer from the Ōsaka Prefectural Government Minami Police Station Safe Livelihoods Section, reported February 2013, warning of "foreign crime gangs" with dark-skinned thick-lipped "foreigners" shouldering a music box and distracting a Japanese in preparation for, the text notes, bag-snatching. This is a development from the Nishi Yodogawa Police poster dated June 2009 that merely asked employers to cooperate in campaigns against "suspicous illegal foreign workers," archived at www.debito.org/?p=3740. Similarly, archived at www.debito.org/?p=7296 is a 2010 Kanagawa Prefecture Yamate Police notice about "illegal foreigners," including exaggerated noses and "Western" facial features and demeanors, warning employers to check their visa statuses. The Shibuya Police offered their own racialized take on "foreign faces" in a 2016 notice to minpaku Airbnb hostelers, portraying eight people of assorted ethnicities (but no apparent Asians) as potential agents of terrorism and crime—who should be reported by hostelers to the police; archived at www.debito.org/?p=14174.

Archived at www.debito.org/?p=14559 is a 2017 Fukushima Prefectural Police poster asking the public to cooperate in investigations of crime by "foreigners coming to Japan," particularly those engaged in burglaries and auto break-ins, by reporting to the police any "illegal foreign workers" skulking around vending machines, searching for antitheft cameras, or snooping around cars. This has in fact encouraged extralegal vigilantism, such as anonymous neighborhood posters put up in 2016 by unaccredited persons in Nagoya warning of "break-ins by robbers who might be foreigners," archived at www.debito.org/?p=13827.

Finally, after a serious traffic accident involving a rental car driven by "foreign travelers," the Fukuoka Prefectural Police anticipated that future car rentals might involve foreigners, so they put up a multilingual poster in 2016 at Fukuoka Airport telling drivers how to drive more safely, archived at www.debito.org/?p=14174. This was despite no statistics uncovering a clear connection between more foreigners on the road and an increased likelihood of accidents. Hence police posters were now in the business of forecasting foreign fender benders. Similar attitudes were later found in "foreign driver" stickers ("*Gaikoku no kata ga unten shite imasu*") issued to rental cars by Okinawa and Hokkaidō Prefectural Governments, archived at www.debito.org/?p=13942.

18. Archived at www.debito.org/shinagawasigns061106.html are banners spanning the major thoroughfare of Shinagawa Station, Yamanote Line, Tōkyō. Created by the MOJ, Tōkyō Immigration Bureau, obverse and reverse, respectively, designating every June as "Campaign for Policies against Illegal Foreign Labor," and calling

for "Internationalization while Obeying the Rules." Displayed in Shinagawa every year since June 2004, these photos are courtesy of Miki Kaoru, June 11, 2006, used with permission.

19. "*Shutsunyūkoku Kanri: Rūru o Mamotte Kokusaika*" [Immigration Controls: Internationalization that follows the rules]. MOJ pamphlet (2003: 10). Also archived at www.debito.org/?p=9156 is a Tōkyō Metro poster found in all Tōkyō subways in 2011, issued by MOJ Immigration Bureau, advising all employers to check the validity of visas on ARCs (see chapter 4) when hiring noncitizens. Note (a) the phenotypical racialization of "foreigners," and (b) the implicit assumption that "foreigners" are happy to unlawfully display their ARCs to people who are not legal representatives of the MOJ. In effect, the media message disseminated to the general public (not just employers) has a possible interpretation of "illegal foreigners walk among us and they should be investigated."

20. More recent statistics on overstayers, showing a rise and plateauing with the rising foreign population in recent years, can be found at the MOJ website at www.moj.go.jp/isa/publications/press/nyuukokukanri04_00019.html (accessed April 27, 2021).

21. "*Fuhō taizai, shūrō bōshi: Ichijitsu shōchō ga uttae: Minami de Kano Reiko san*" ["Prevent illegal overstay and labor": Kano Reiko's appeal during her one day as chief cop at Minami Police Station] *Yomiuri Shinbun*, June 3, 2006; "Celebrity uses fingerprint photo-op to call for cut in foreign crime." *Mainichi Shinbun*, November 14, 2007; "AKB48's Atsuko Maeda mans police call center." *Kyodo News*, January 12, 2011; after protests *Kyodo* "corrected" its English and Japanese versions from "What nationality was the culprit?" to "How many suspects were there?" during a mock emergency call from a witness to a robbery. As Maeda was reading from an NPA-prepared 110-*ban* call-center script, it would appear that standard operating procedure for the NPA is to assume prima facie that thieves may be "foreign." *See* archive at www.debito.org/?p=8369.

22. "*Keisatsu 50 nen: Ryōheika mukae kinen shiten: Shushō ra ga yaku 300-nin shusseki*" [Fifty years of the NPA: The Imperial Couple's Anniversary visit, with the PM and about 300 people attending]. *Mainichi Shinbun*, July 26, 2004.

23. Online Archive with analysis at www.debito.org/?p=11647 with NPA *kokumin* crime statistics, 1946–2011, courtesy MOJ at http://hakusyo1.moj.go.jp/jp/59/nfm/n_59_2_1_1_0.html (accessed April 27, 2021). In the enclosed chart, the left axis is the rate of incidents of crime, the right axis the number of people involved in cleared crimes. The top layer of vertical bars is all cleared cases of penal crimes including fatal or injurious traffic accidents. The center layer of lighter vertical bars is the cleared cases of penal crimes including theft. The bottom layer of vertical bars is regular violations of the penal code excluding theft or traffic accidents. The top line is the rate of all penal code violation incidents including traffic incidents. The second line below it is the rate of regular penal code violation incidents not including traffic incidents. The three bottom dotted lines are, from top layer to bottom, numbers of perpetrators for all penal code violations, numbers of perpetrators for penal code violations not including traffic accidents, and numbers of perpetrators for penal code violations not including traffic or theft.

Archived with analysis at www.debito.org/?p=11557 are NPA statistics for crimes by foreign nationals, 1980–2009, English original, courtesy MOJ at http://hakusyo1.moj.go.jp/en/59/nfm/n_59_2_3_1_2_1.html#fig_3_1_2_1 (accessed May 18, 2021). The terminology, according to the MOJ (http://hakusyo1.moj.go.jp/jp/59/nfm/n_59_1_2_0_0_0.html): "Visiting foreign nationals" is a direct translation of *rainichi gaikokujin* and refers to foreigners who are not "Other Foreign Nationals" (*sono ta no gaikokujin*), that is, Permanent Residents, Zainichis, or American military on bases in Japan. NB: After comparison with NPA charts below dated April 1, 2002, it is clear that this chart does not include visa violations.

24. *See* www.debito.org/?p=11647 for a chart comparing Japanese and foreign crime on the same scale, with foreign crime the darker shade at the bottom of the x-axis. Courtesy of the *Japan Times*. "Police 'foreign crime wave' falsehoods fuel racism." *Japan Times*, July 8, 2013. *See also* a comparison of foreign crime to Japanese crime rates, 1993–2003, citing NPA and media reports, at www.debito.org/crimestats.html.

25. Herbert (1995: 196–228).

26. Both terms Gibson (2002).

27. "*Gaikokujin hanzai futatabi zōka: 10 nen de 6-bai ni*" [Foreign crime goes up again: Six-fold in ten years]. *Sankei Shinbun*, May 1, 2000.

28. *See* inter alia Debito Arudou, "Generating the foreigner crime wave." *Japan Times*, October 4, 2002; Debito Arudou, "Time to come clean on foreign crime: Rising crime rate is a problem for Japan, but pinning blame on foreigners not the solution." *Japan Times*, October 7, 2003.

29. "NPA says foreign crime groups increasingly targeting Japan." *Kyodo News*, July 23, 2010.

30. Ibid., *Japan Times*, July 8, 2013. The examples of "fake names, fake websites, false marriages, false adoptions and fake IDs" are courtesy of the Kanagawa Police at www.police.pref.kanagawa.jp/images/h0/h0001_04.gif. The Ibaraki Police offer five out of eight examples of "crime infrastructure" specifically depicting "foreigner" misdeeds (with racist caricatures), at www.pref.ibaraki.jp/kenkei/a01_safety/security/infra.html). In case of broken links, this information is archived at www.debito.org/?p=11647. *See also* "NPA 'Crime Infrastructure Countermeasures' campaign also targets 'foreign crime' anew. Justifies more anonymous anti-NJ signs." *Debito.org*, June 20, 2013, www.debito.org/?p=11568.

31. *See* archive at www.debito.org/?p=11557, specifically the crime statistics for "foreign crime" 1991–2001. A chart archived at www.debito.org/wordpress/wp-content/uploads/2013/06/crimestats2001.jpg shows April 2002's NPA semiannual report on "foreign crime." The black portion of the bar chart is the number of visa violations, the gray portion the number of criminal violations, and the black line the total number of noncitizen perpetrators. Compare with www.debito.org/wordpress/wp-content/uploads/2013/06/NPAprelimcrimestats2011barchart.jpg again at www.debito.org/?p=11557, where statistics for "foreign crime" extend from 1982 to 2011, courtesy April 2012's NPA semiannual report on "foreign crime" at www.npa.go.jp/sosikihanzai/kokusaisousa/kokusai/H23_rainichi.pdf. The top darker portion of the bar chart is the number of visa violations, the lower lighter portion

the number of criminal violations, and the line the total number of noncitizen perpetrators.

32. "Japan sees record high number of foreign residents: Justice Ministry." *Japan Times*, March 11, 2016, with commentary at www.debito.org/?p=13887.

33. For a more thorough debunking of crime statistics even when "foreign crime" was allegedly at its peak, *see* "Foreign crime statistics for Japan compared to Japanese crime statistics." *See also* my letter to the National Archive of Criminal Justice Data, University of Michigan, *Debito.org*, January 5, 2003, archived at www.debito.org/crimestats.html.

34. Chris Flynn, "Crime not as simple as ABC." *Japan Times*, Readers in Council, April 21, 2004.

35. MOJ (2003a).

36. *See*, for example, "Study finds immigrants commit less California crime." *Reuters*, February 26, 2008; "Rising immigration not linked to crime rates: Study." *Reuters*, March 19, 2008; and so on.

37. *See also* "Dealing with Racial Profiling." *Japan Today*, October 3, 2001; Debito Arudou, "Pedal pushers cop a load on Yasukuni Dori." *Japan Times*, October 4, 2002; Debito Arudou, "Gaijin Card checks spread as police deputize the nation." *Japan Times*, November 13, 2007; Debito Arudou, "Forecast: Rough with ID checks mainly to the north." *Japan Times*, July 1, 2008.

38. NPA (2020) Wajin crime statistics at www.npa.go.jp/publications/statistics/crime/situation/R02hanzaijousei.pdf (accessed April 27, 2021). On a humorous aside, one crime spree that reached all-time highs was shoplifting by Wajin elderly, reportedly because they are "lonely" and see "no reason to live." *See* "Police combat crime by 'lonely' elderly." *Reuters*, August 27, 2009; "Japanese pensioners' shoplifting hits record high." *BBC News*, January 27, 2011, which notes the NPA taking a softer stance toward these criminals: "A police official told the Mainichi newspaper that pensioners were shoplifting not just for financial reasons 'but also out of a sense of isolation peculiar to the age.'" Nevertheless, at least one shop, Genky drugstores in Gifu, put up multilingual antishoplifting signs in 2013 warning foreign customers, "If we find any kinds of criminal acts of foreigners, we SURELY report not only to the police but also to your workplace and your agency." Archived at www.debito.org/?p=11201.

39. *See*, for example, "Gang eluded cops by using fake accents: Thieves 'acted like foreigners' in 210 million yen crime spree." *Mainichi Shinbun*, July 19, 2000; "Teens lie about fatal bashing, blame foreigners not bikers." *Mainichi Shinbun*, May 3, 2004; "Racist teen biker mob collared over boy's lethal bashing." *Mainichi Shinbun*, May 5, 2004; "Truck driver screams 'foreigners abducted me' after he slept in." *Mainichi Shinbun*, December 21, 2004; "Police arrest murdered hospital worker's son, friend." *Mainichi Daily News*, August 29, 2006; "*Sakai Noriko kakuseizai: 'Gaikokujin kara katta' otto ga kyōjutsu*" [Star Sakai Noriko and stimulants: Her husband attests that "she bought them from foreigners"]. *Sankei Shinbun*, August 10, 2009; "*Tabun Nihonjin, manē manē to odoshi nagutte keitai ubau.*" ["Give me money, money" threats, physical violence, and cellphone snatching was perhaps a Japanese suspect]. *Yomiuri Shinbun*, July 7, 2010; "Police nab man for allegedly

claiming theft of non-existent luggage [by foreigners, for insurance fraud purposes]." *Mainichi Daily News*, April 5, 2012. All are archived at www.debito.org/aichibiker-gangpatsy.html.

40. "*Gaikokujin hanzai, 2 nen keizoku de gen. Keisatsuchō 'takadomari no jōkyō.'*" [Foreign crime: Two continuous years of drop. NPA: "It's plateaued at a high level." *Kyodo News/San'yō Shinbun*, February 28, 2008.

41. For example, "The violent nature of the crime led police to suspect someone with a history of drug abuse, someone connected to organized crime or a foreign criminal was the culprit." "Fingerprints from tape used in 1995 murder linked to man who died 10 years ago," from *Mainichi Shinbun*, February 18, 2015. *See also* "*Ude tokei nado 9300 man en sōtō tōnan, Sapporo*" [Sapporo: Watches etc. valued at about 93,000,000 yen stolen]. *TBS News*, June 25, 2010.

This attitude of "foreigners are naturally violent" even made it into GOJ publications, such as a 2014 Foreign Ministry propaganda pamphlet explaining the Hague Treaty on Child Abductions to the Japanese public, where foreign (Caucasian) fathers are seen beating children and victimizing docile Japanese women. *See* "'Racist' cartoon issued by Japanese ministry angers rights activists: Pamphlet issued by Tokyo to Japan's embassies in response to Hague convention is criticised for depicting a foreign man beating his child." *South China Morning Post*, September 16, 2014; Debito Arudou, "Biased pamphlet bodes ill for left-behind foreign parents outside Japan: Pamphlet on Hague Treaty on Child Abductions displays slanted mindsets favoring the Japanese side of disputes." *Japan Times*, October 8, 2014, www.debito.org/?p=12725, with the full publication archived at www.debito.org/?p=12631.

42. *See*, for example, "Scriveners aid illegal marriages, work." *Yomiuri Shinbun*, October 12, 2009; "Police launch nationwide raids of car scrap yards." *Kyodo News*, June 23, 2010; "*'Tetsuban no yōsai' yādo: Keisatsu tōkyoku ga issai sōsa, tachi iri chōsa shita nerai wa . . .*" ["Fortresses of sheet metal": Local police do a thorough search, and try to figure out what the occupants were up to]. *Sankei Shinbun*, July 11, 2010 (note that of the 426 crime "fortresses" (*yōsai*) raided, only fourteen were reportedly done under search warrants, a practice of questionable legality). *See also* "Ads promoting criminal acts found in free papers for foreigners." *Mainichi Shinbun*, September 15, 2011; "*Gaikokujin muke no furī peipā: Fusei kōku, 58 shi de 736 ken.*" [Free newspapers for foreigners: Disreputable ads, 736 cases in 58 papers]. *Nikkei .com*, September 15, 2011; "Over 730 ads for overstayers, fake marriages uncovered [in free newspapers]." *Yomiuri Shinbun*, September 16, 2011, and so on. Note how these anticrime campaigns (*see also* following footnote) are parroted throughout newspapers and other media the same day as a cluster for public saturation.

43. *See*, for example, "NPA says foreign crime groups increasingly targeting Japan." *Kyodo News*, July 23, 2010; "Foreign criminals building up Japanese operations, threatening public order: NPA." *Mainichi Shinbun*, July 23, 2010, and so on. For more information, see the NPA's report, "*Rainichi Gaikokujin Hanzai no Kenkyo Jōkyō*" [Situation of crime cases for visiting foreign nationals] for 2008, dated April 2009, at www.npa.go.jp/sosikihanzai/kokusaisousa/kokusai6/rainichi.pdf (accessed September 8, 2012, currently dead link; please plug this URL into the Wayback

Machine). Note how the role of Japanese Yakuza (*bōryokudan*) is downplayed throughout the report (particularly on page 22). Also note that despite this reportage of "foreign crime groups" "increasingly" targeting Japan, "crime by foreign visitors" had in fact been concurrently going down for the past three years. *See* ibid., *Associated Press*, February 26, 2009.

44. "NHK repeatedly racially profiles prototypical criminal (the only NJ person in a crowd) on TV program Close-Up Gendai." April 5, 2017, *Debito.org*, April 7, 2017, www.debito.org/?p=14539. This also popped up in a Tōkyō Metropolitan Police anticrime demonstration for the media, where armed jewel thieves were for some reason portrayed as foreign. *See* "Asahi TV: Police public training drill in Tokyo on how to deal with jewelry thieves brandishing knives. Oh, and they're depicted as 'foreign' thieves." *Debito.org*, October 23, 2015, with video at www.debito.org/?p=13598.

45. Ishihara (2002: 98).

46. *See "Shōnen hanzai ni sōgōteki taisho, shushō ga shiji"* [PM signals comprehensive measures against youth crime]. Yomiuri Shinbun, July 11, 2003.

47. Hamai & Ellis (2006) state in their abstract:

> Although Japan continues to be one of the most crime-free economically advanced countries, crime was a crucial issue in the 2003 general election (for the first time since WWII) and a 2004 survey showed that the proportion of the public that thought crime was getting worse had doubled since 1998. Here, we have examined recorded crime and victim surveys in relation to violent offences, to assess the extent to which the public's view of increasing crime is based on sound evidence. We found that in the late 1990s, a specific series of police scandals in Japan fundamentally changed the way the press reported policing issues. These changes provoked policy reactions that ensured that *more "trivial" offences were reported, boosting overall crime figures*. The resulting "myth of the collapse of secure society" appears, in turn, to have contributed to increasingly punitive public views about offenders and sentencing in Japan. (Emphasis added)

48. Cf. Chung (2000), McVeigh (2001), and so on.

49. Ishihara Shintarō, "*Nihon yo: Uchinaru bōei o*" [Listen up, Japan: Guard your inner flank]. *Sankei Shinbun*, May 8, 2001.

50. Ishihara (2000: 100).

51. "Ishihara vows to 'boot out' illegally residing foreigners." *Mainichi Shinbun*, July 29, 2003; ibid., *Kyodo News*, March 5, 2009.

52. "Foreigners are 'sneaky thieves,' governor says." *Kyodo News*, November 4, 2003; "Foreigners not 'sneaky thieves' after all: governor." *Kyodo News*, November 7, 2003.

53. *See* ibid., *Japan Times*, October 7, 2003; "2003 Prime Minister Koizumi Cabinet listings and policy goals." *Yomiuri Shinbun*, September 22, 2003.

54. MOJ, "Basic plan for immigration control" (3rd Edition, English original), *see* www.moj.go.jp/ENGLISH/information/bpic3rd-03.html (last accessed May 18, 2021).

55. Debito Arudou, "*Gaikokujin okotowari: Jinshu sabetsu teppai e hō seibi o*" [Foreigners Refused Service: Towards a law against racial discrimination], *Asahi Shinbun Watashi no Shiten* column, June 2, 2003.

56. *See* inter alia "Ex-minister Hiranuma says lawmaker Renho is 'not originally Japanese.'" *Kyodo News*, January 18, 2010; "Taiwanese-Japanese Dietmember Renho becomes first multiethnic Cabinet member; racist Dietmember Hiranuma continues ranting about it." *Debito.org*, June 9, 2010, www.debito.org/?p=6873.

57. "Maehara quits Cabinet over donations." *Japan Times*, March 7, 2011; "Korean apologizes to Maehara for 'causing trouble.'" *Asahi Shinbun*, March 8, 2011.

58. "*Gaikokujin sanseiken 'Senzo e giridate ka;' Ishihara chiji ga yotō hihan.*" [Gov. Ishihara criticizes the DPJ for foreigner suffrage bill: "Are they doing out of obligation to their [foreign] ancestors?"] *Asahi Shinbun*, April 18, 2010; "Tokyo governor calls ruling party veterans 'naturalized.'" *Associated Press*, April 19, 2010; "*Fukushima Shamintō-shu ga Ishihara tochiji no hatsugen no tekkai motomeru*" [Fukushima [Mizuho], Head of Social Democratic Party, demands Tōkyō Governor withdraw his statement]. *Sankei Shinbun*, April 19, 2010; "Natural born voters?" *The Diplomat*, April 20, 2010; "Ishihara snubs SDP retraction request." *Japan Times*, April 24, 2010.

59. "Yugawaramachi journal: Japan's new insider speaks up for the outsiders." *New York Times*, March 8, 2002. *See also* Debito Arudou, "Last gasps of Japan's dying demagogues." *Japan Times*, May 4, 2010, archived with sources at www.debito.org/?p=6634.

60. Interview, March 4, 2002, archived at www.debito.org/tsuruneninterview.html; "Foreign-born lawmaker puts Japan's acceptance of outsiders to the test." *Metropolis*, August 9, 2006.

61. On May 18, 2006, 2–3 p.m., at the Shūgi'in Dai-ichi Kaikan, Diene gave a preliminary presentation of his findings to MPs and the general public. I was present, as were several MPs, but Tsurunen was not. In cases where the MP is absent due to schedule conflicts, it is protocol to send a secretary to the event to leave the MP's business card (*meishi*) as a show of support. Tsurunen's office sent no representative and left no card.

62. "Mind the gap, get over it: Japan hands." *Japan Times*, December 28, 2010.

63. Debito Arudou, "Naturalized Japanese: Foreigners no more." *Japan Times*, February 1, 2011.

64. Archived at www.debito.org/?p=11633 with analysis is MP Tsurunen's 2013 support pamphlet with bio and basic policy stances.

65. Debito Arudou, "Ol' blue eyes isn't back." *Japan Times*, August 6, 2013. Although he received a reaffirming mandate in his 2007 reelection with 242,740 votes (sixth in his party), in 2013 he only garnered 82,858, coming in twelfth and well under the threshold for Diet Members on Japan's Proportional Representation ticket. *See also* "Assessing outgoing MP Tsurunen Marutei's tenure in the Diet: Disappointing." *Debito.org*, July 15, 2013, www.debito.org/?p=11633.

66. This research does not have the space to go into detail about the revisionist Nippon Kaigi ("Japan Conference") as a dominant political force, which counted as members the majority of the Abe Administration's 2014 Cabinet, including PM Abe himself. *See*, for example, McNeill 2015, Sasagase et al. 2015, Mizohata 2016. For a 7-minute video brief, *see* "Lifting the lid on one of the most influential, and secretive,

political organisations in Japan." *ABC News Australia Lateline*, December 3, 2015, www.abc.net.au/lateline/lifting-the-lid-on-one-of-the-most-influential,/6996204.

67. Japanese "revisionism" for the purposes of this research refers to a rightist ideology that seeks to overwrite Japan's historical wrongs and wartime responsibility in favor of narratives that encourage Wajin unwavering national pride and patriotism. This has since been stretched to include "Japanese" ideologies that by their binary nature preclude "foreign influences," such as the concept of human rights and the "American-imposed" current Japanese Constitution. Naturally, this leads to ethnostatist ideologies, such as seeing Japan as a nation-state both future and past being reserved for Japanese only, and hostility toward sharing equal power with, or offering equal protection under the law to Non-Wajin. *See*, for example, Repeta 2013, Takenaka 2016, Yamaguchi 2017.

68. "New dissent in Japan is loudly anti-foreign." *New York Times*, August 28, 2010; "Japan's Unnecessary Nationalism." *New York Times* Editorial Board, April 23, 2013. *See also* "A rebuke to Japanese Nationalism." Editors, *Bloomberg News*, February 16, 2014.

69. "Renho to disclose family registry in bid to quell furor over dual nationality: Bid to quell furor over dual nationality criticized by some as succumbing to xenophobic pressure." *Japan Times*, July 13, 2017. An insightful analysis of the complicit media coverage around this issue comes from Philip Brasor, "Renho and the 'pure blood' mythos." *Japan Times*, September 17, 2016.

70. Debito Arudou, "If bully Ishihara wants one last stand, bring it on." *Japan Times*, November 6, 2012, archived with sources at www.debito.org/?p=10733.

71. "*Ishihara Tochiji: 'Seiyōjin no judō wa kedamono no kenka'*" [Governor Ishihara: Westerners' judo is a fight between beasts]. *Yomiuri Shinbun*, August 4, 2012, archived at www.debito.org/?p=10511.

72. Drifte (2014); "Controversial to the end, Shintaro Ishihara bows out of politics: Former Tokyo governor welcomes war with China, compares Hashimoto's oratory skills to young Hitler's." *Japan Times*, December 16, 2014.

73. For my opinion on the political ramifications of the IOC awarding Tōkyō the 2020 Olympics, *see* Debito Arudou, "Triumph of Tokyo Olympic bid sends wrong signal to Japan's resurgent right." *Japan Times*, October 1, 2013.

74. "Nagoya mayor repeatedly denies Nanjing massacre." *Mainichi Shinbun*, February 23, 2012; "Nagoya mayor won't budge on Nanjing remark." *Japan Times*, February 23, 2012.

75. "Japan WWII 'comfort women' were 'necessary'—Hashimoto." *BBC News*, May 14, 2013; "Statement by Toru Hashimoto." *Asahi Shinbun*, May 27, 2013; "Japanese mayor apologises for saying US troops should use sex industry: But Toru Hashimoto defends Japan's role in recruitment of 'comfort women' to work in brothels during second world war." *Guardian*, May 27, 2013.

76. "Aso retracts remark citing Nazis as example for constitution change." *Mainichi Shinbun*, August 1, 2013.

77. "In promoting his city for 2020 games, Tokyo's Bid Chairman Tweaks Others." *New York Times*, April 26, 2013. This happened again shortly before the Rio

de Janeiro Games in 2016, when the CEO of the 2020 Tōkyō Olympics, Mutō Toshio, compared street protests against the Games in Rio to "terrorism" and "cyberterrorism," and expressed confidence in Japan's ability to ensure proper security. *See* "2020 Tokyo Olympics CEO weighs in on security, differences with Rio." *Japan Times*, April 4, 2016.

78. "Some municipalities set to deny services to illegal foreign residents: poll." *Kyodo News*, April 24, 2012; "Tabloid blasts growing numbers of foreign welfare chiselers." *Japan Today*, May 29, 2012.

79. "Saitama assemblyman apologizes for remark about number of registered dogs, foreigners." *Japan Times*, December 13, 2015.

80. "Tokyo Governor Yuriko Koike defends her party's policy of not granting foreign residents in Japan the right to vote." *Japan Times*, October 6, 2017. *See also* Debito Arudou, "Non-Japanese suffrage and the racist element." *Japan Times*, February 2, 2010.

81. "Tōkyō Governor Election April 10 posts 'expel the barbarians, Japan for the Japanese' openly xenophobic candidate." *Debito.org*, April 8, 2011, www.debito.org/?p=8726.

82. "Anti-Korean Upper House candidate Suzuki Nobuyuki wants Japan closed to immigrants and rearmed with nukes." *Debito.org*, July 17, 2013, www.debito.org/?p=11664.

83. "Restoration Party Shinpuu's xenophobic candidate in Tokyo Katsushika-ku elections: 'Putting Japanese first before foreigners.'" *Debito.org*, November 10, 2013, www.debito.org/?p=11970.

84. "Japan Election 2014: 'Why taboo?' Grotesque foreigner-bashing cartoon by Hiranuma's Jisedai Party, features 'Taboo Pig' sliced in half over NJ welfare recipients 'issue.'" *Debito.org*, December 11, 2014, www.debito.org/?p=12904.

85. "Info on Black Lives Matter demos in Japan in response to excessive police force towards a Kurdish Resident; also the backlash of right-wing Tokyo Katsushika-ku Assemblyman Suzuki Nobuyuki: 'expel any foreign demonstrators.'" *Debito.org*, June 7, 2020, www.debito.org/?p=16105.

86. "Police in Japan place anti-Korean extremist group Zaitokukai on watchlist: Ultra-nationalist group, which claims to have 15,000 members, deemed a threat to law and order." *Guardian*, December 4, 2014; "Justice Minister Tanigaki 'filled with concern' over hate speech." *Asahi Shinbun*, May 9, 2013, archived at www.debito.org/?p=11443.

87. Sakurai in fact fared much worse in 2016 than the featured far-right candidate in the 2014 Gubernatorial Election, Tamogami Toshio, who got 610,865 votes, or 12 percent of the total. Nevertheless, the victor of that election, Koike Yuriko, has some relationship with Zaitokukai; according to them Koike spoke at one of their meetings in 2010. *See* "Zaitokukai xenophobic hate group's Sakurai Makoto runs for Tokyo Governorship; his electoral platform analyzed here." *Debito.org*, July 26, 2016, www.debito.org/?p=14116; "Meanwhile back in Tokyo: Gov candidate Koike Yuriko allegedly spoke at anti-foreign hate group Zaitokukai in 2010." *Debito.org*, July 19, 2016, www.debito.org/?p=14099.

88. Repeta (2013).

89. A version of these sections was published as Arudou (2013a). Reprinted with permission.

90. "*Minshu bumon kaigi, jinken kyūsai hōan o ryōshō; hantaiha no iken oshikiri.*" [DPJ meetings pass Protection of Human Rights Bill, suppress internal opposition]. *Sankei Shinbun*, August 29, 2012.

91. Pertinent sections of the *Danger!* book, featuring prominent rightist spokespeople MP Hiranuma Takeo and pundit Sakurai Yoshiko on the back cover, are archived and translated at www.debito.org/abunaijinkenyougohouan.html.

92. Ibid., www.debito.org/abunaijinkenyougohouan.html.

93. Of course, the alarmism camouflaged by this manga's absurdist humor neglects to mention that (a) no particular charge has been made clear against the victimized person; if this manga showed NPA officers potentially singling anyone out, it would become an argument against any policing agency—clearly a reductio ad absurdum; and (b) that if anyone does something unlawful (such as violate a residential contract or cause a public disturbance), it would be more prudent for the person being victimized to report it to the police (as a fail-safe against any perpetrator cloaking his illegal activities as his "human rights").

94. "Tottori rights law a first but irks critics." *Japan Times*, October 13, 2005. *See* the text of the ordinance (from a dead-link archive) at web.archive.org/web/20080329214102/http://www.pref.tottori.jp/jinken/jorei-kyusai.html.

95. Debito Arudou, "How to kill a bill: Tottori's Human Rights Ordinance is a case study in alarmism." *Japan Times*, May 2, 2006.

96. Phone interview, Tottori Prefecture Governor's Office, April 25, 2006.

97. www.pref.tottori.lg.jp/89097.htm (last accessed May 18, 2021).

98. A thoughtful overview of this debate may be found in "Disenfranchised: Japan weighs up whether to give foreign residents the vote." *Metropolis*, June 17, 2010.

99. *See* inter alia "Komeito leader welcomes Ozawa's proposal to give foreigners voting rights." *Mainichi Shinbun*, January 24, 2008; "DPJ to push foreign suffrage." *Asahi Shinbun*, January 25, 2008; "DPJ holds opposing meetings on foreigners voting in local elections." *Kyodo News*, January 31, 2008. *See also* www.debito.org/?p=6209 for a list of twenty-five other developed countries that allow PR noncitizens to vote under certain circumstances, showing Japan as the absolutist outlier.

100. Archived with commentary at www.debito.org/?p=6182: (1) Magazine-book (*mook*) purchased by the author at Kinokuniya Book Store, Tōkyō, March 7, 2010, entitled "Urgent Publication: Doomsday for Japan due to Foreign Suffrage." The subtitles read, "China will come to invade [Japan] legally," and "Policies [to bring in] 10,000,000 immigrants will make Japan into a foreign country." Bessetsu Takarajima, 2010. (2) Flyer received February 23, 2010, from an anonymous donor who found it in his postal mailbox in Narita, Chiba Prefecture. Headline reads, "DANGER!! Foreign Suffrage," depicting the alleged results of giving "foreigners" more rights in other countries (such as Canada and Holland): Foreigners commit crimes in higher numbers where they have the vote, elect unqualified ethnic politicians who cannot even speak the local language, and outproduce the local population in terms of births. Note the racialized depictions of slit-eyed midget Chinese hordes

in Mao suits getting elected in small districts, taking over the management of internal natural resources, and ultimately overrunning the Japanese archipelago. Created and distributed by unknown groups.

Archived with commentary at www.debito.org/?p=6017: Flyer received February 19, 2010, from an anonymous donor in Narita, Chiba Prefecture who found this in his postal mailbox. Headline reads, "Something as dangerous as Foreigner Suffrage: We LDP members of Edogawa-ku [Tōkyō] think this way," listing their manifesto, including: "Paying taxes does not equal the right to vote," "There are doubts about the constitutionality of foreigner suffrage," "Governors of the major metropolitan areas are one by one expressing their opposition," and so on. Note how the invective of "alien invasion" has been rendered literally, with a UFO shining a spotlight on the archipelago. Caption below the UFO: "Let's protect Japan."

101. Archived with commentary at www.debito.org/?p=6182: Flyer received February 28, 2010 from an anonymous donor in Nagoya who found this in his postal mailbox. Headline reads, "Be careful of foreign crime," claiming with unsourced (and by then erroneous) statistics that "foreign crime" is on the rise (with breakdowns by crime and nationality). Note the blackened boxes toward the bottom, where in the first box readers are encouraged to do internet searches under terms "Foreign Suffrage" and "Danger," thus formally linking "foreign crime" with "foreign voting rights." *See* archive of other rightist protest flyers from this time period archived at www.debito.org/?p=5353.

102. "Foreigner suffrage, separate surnames stir passions in poll run-up." *Japan Times*, July 3, 2010.

103. Archive of further protests and flyers at www.debito.org/?p=6509.

104. Archive at www.debito.org/?p=8459, courtesy of Tsukuba City Councilor Jon Heese.

105. *See*, for example, the very active far-right internet channel *Nihon Bunka Channeru Sakura*, at www.ch-sakura.jp, where Abe Shinzō has in the past made frequent appearances.

106. *See*, for example, Cabinet member Kamei Shizuka's xenophobic comments as Financial Services Minister in "Foreigner suffrage can fuel nationalism: Kamei." *Japan Times*, February 4, 2010; "New dissent in Japan is loudly anti-foreign." *New York Times*, August 28, 2010; "A black sun rises in a declining Japan." *Globe and Mail* (Canada), October 5, 2010; "Japan: The land of the rising nationalism." *Independent* (London), November 5, 2010.

107. "Diet passes Japan's first law to curb hate speech." *Japan Times*, May 24, 2016, which notes, "A total of 347 such rallies took place in 2013, while 378 were held in 2014 and 190 from January through September last year, the Justice Ministry said."

108. *See*, for example, "In polite Japan, vulgarities rise as hate speech spreads." *Asahi Shinbun*, June 12, 2013; "*Shin-Ōkubo no hankan demo, hatsu no taiho, tairitsu grūpu ni bōkō yōgi*" [Anti-Korea Demo in Shin-Ohkubo results in first arrest: Suspected of violence against opposition protestor], *Asahi Shinbun*, May 20, 2013; "Nationalists converge on Shin-Okubo's Koreatown." *Japan Today*, September 17, 2012; "Feb 9 2013 Tokyo Shin-Ohkubo Anti-Korean demonstrator slogans: 'Good or Bad, Kill All Koreans' etc." *Debito.org*, March 4, 2013, signs archived at www

.debito.org/?p=11234; Tsuruhashi Massacre: "Osaka's move on hate speech should be just the first step." *Japan Times*, January 31, 2016. The *Japan Today* article in particular substantiates concrete threats of violence toward Zainichi minority shopkeepers, citing *Shūkan Kin'yōbi* magazine in saying: "Journalist Koichi Yasuda, who authored a book titled '*Pursuing the Darkness of Internet Patriots, the Zaitokukai*' (Kodansha Inc.), says, 'As far as they are concerned, discriminating against the zainichi (Koreans in Japan) [*sic*] is everything, and they aren't terribly concerned about what will become of the disputed [Takeshima and Senkaku islets] in the future. But they can use the timing of the dispute as a pretext for pushing their own agenda.'"

109. "Anti-Korean voices grow in Japan: Small but venomous rallies become more frequent, prompt soul-searching over hate speech." *Wall Street Journal*, May 16, 2013; "Neo-Nazis march in Tokyo Edogawa-ku March 23, 2014, bearing swastika flags!" *Debito.org*, March 24, 2014, www.debito.org/?p=12218. *See also* substantiation passim within "Anti-Korean activists ordered to pay 12 million yen over hate speech demonstrations." *Mainichi Shinbun*, October 7, 2013; "Editorial: Ruling that hate speech constitutes racial discrimination is rational." *Mainichi Shinbun*, October 8, 2013; *Japan Times*, February 1, 2016 ibid.; "A year after enactment of hate speech law, xenophobic rallies down by nearly half." *Japan Times/Kyodo News*, May 22, 2017; "In wake of Charlottesville, U.S. should follow Japan and outlaw hate speech." *Japan Times*, August 24, 2017.

110. "[Nepalese] Man beaten to death on Osaka street." *Japan Times/Kyodo News*, January 18, 2012, archived with more Japanese sources at www.debito.org/?p=9892; "YouTube: right-wing xenophobia: How the rightists will resort to intimidation and even violence to shut people up." *Debito.org*, October 7, 2009; *Mainichi Shinbun*, October 7, 2013 ibid.; "Rightists arrested over harassment of schoolchildren." *Asahi Shinbun*, August 11, 2010; "Zaitokukai Neo Nazis march in Tokyo Shibuya July 9, 2011, with ugly invective." *Debito.org*, July 16, 2011, www.debito.org/?p=9224; and of course, revisit the hate-related 1997 murder of Herculano Reiko Lukocevicius in Komaki, Aichi, from the previous link.

111. Arudou (2006a: 206–207).

112. "Number of crime cases involving foreign suspects down in 2006," and "*Gaikokujin hanzai: chihō de zōka—chūbu wa 15-nen mae no 35-bai ni*" [Foreign crime: Goes up in the provinces; in the Nagoya area up 35-fold over fifteen years]. English translation of Japanese original with different headlines. *Mainichi Daily News / Mainichi Shinbun*, respectively, February 9 and 8, 2007.

113. The article in question is "Number of crimes by foreigners in Japan drops 12.7 percent in 2011." *Mainichi Daily News/Kyodo News*, February 23, 2012. *See* the comparison with Japanese article from the same day archived with analysis at "Mainichi/Kyodo: NJ crime down again, but once again only reported in English and apparently not in J Mainichi, Asahi, Yomiuri, or Sankei." *Debito.org*, February 29, 2012, www.debito.org/?p=9979.

114. "'Don't stick 'em up!' foreigners cry: The walls of Tokyo banks are plastered with posters depicting non-Japanese as devious thieves," and "Beware: Crime statistics paint misleading picture." Both *International Herald Tribune/Asahi Shinbun*, December 14–15, 2002. *See also* Mabuchi 2003, Moro'oka 2006: 140–141.

115. "Number of white-collar crimes by foreigners up by 31.2 percent in 2009." *Kyodo News*, February 25, 2010, archived with contemporary articles from other Japanese media highlighting the selective crime rise and burying the lede of the overall fall at www.debito.org/?p=6040.

116. *See*, for example, "Nationalists converge on Shin-Okubo's Koreatown." *Japan Today*, September 18, 2012; "Tabloids return fire, urge China business pull-out." *Japan Times*, October 7, 2012, both archived with analysis at www.debito.org/?p=10659; "Shuukan Kin'youbi: Protests against NJ businesses in Tokyo turn ugly, yet J media compares Chinese protests against J businesses to Kristallnacht." *Debito.org*, October 13, 2012, www.debito.org/?p=10659.

117. "Japan sees record high number of foreign residents: Justice Ministry." *Japan Times*, March 11, 2016, which soon digressed and devoted more than half the article to "foreign nationals overstaying their visas," "foreign trainees fleeing workplaces," and so on; it concluded by directly quoting the GOJ: "The [Justice] ministry also said 3,063 illegal immigrants have been served deportation orders." The same thing happened exactly three years later with the next GOJ release of registered population numbers—a concurrent release of crime stats that take up half the articles. *See* "Record 2.73 mil. foreign residents living in Japan in 2018." *Mainichi Shinbun*, March 22, 2019; "Foreign residents increase to record 2.73 mil." *Jiji Press/Yomiuri Shinbun*, March 23, 2019, both archived at www.debito.org/?p=15597. This is what happens when a policing force is in solely in charge of immigration issues—a constant viewing of people under their mandate in terms of crime.

118. "*Fujisan wa tozansha no 'unko' ga takusan: Gaikokujin kankōkyaku ga gen'in na no ka*" [There's lots of 'poop' from Mt. Fuji hikers: Could foreign tourists be the problem?]. *J-Cast.com*, September 18, 2014, archived at www.debito.org/?p=12688. *See also* "TBS: Daring heist of expensive watches in Sapporo. So daring it might have been foreigners! says Hokkaido Police." *Debito.org*, June 26, 2010, www.debito.org/?p=7051; for more linguistic games that fuel antiforeigner speculation, *see*, for example, "Nikkei reports on the effect of '*Nihon saru gaikokujin*', aka Flyjin, with some pretty shaky journalistic practices." *Debito.org*, April 25, 2011, www.debito.org/?p=8806. For a more general overview of how Japanese media coverage of foreigners in Japan has changed little over a quarter century, *see* Debito Arudou, "Nothing has changed: After 25 years, little change for the better seen in the media's coverage of foreigners." Foreign Correspondents' Club of Japan *No.1 Shimbun*, September 2011.

119. Arudou (2006a: 195–209).

120. *Shūkan Asahi*, February 25, 2000, pages 76 and 142–3.

121. Ichihashi ibid. Also, an Amazon Japan search in September 2012 and May 2021 using search term "*gaikokujin hanzai*" alone revealed 340 and 56 titles, respectively. *See*, for example, Ishii (2012); as cited in "Writer talks of 'underground reality' of Japan's foreigners in new book." *Mainichi Shinbun*, February 1, 2012, archived at www.debito.org/?p=9938.

122. Moro'oka ibid.; Debito Arudou, "Time to come clean on foreign crime wave." *Japan Times*, October 7, 2003. *See also*, for example, an undated excerpt

of one of these "COPS"-style TV shows archived at the Wayback Machine at web.archive.org/web/20140417072851/http://www.japanprobe.com/2009/03/19/video-japanese-police-chase-down-illegal-immigrant/. Transcript of the show in English archived at www.debito.org/?p=2806.

123. "Fuji TV's 'Taikyo no Shunkan': Reality TV targeting NJ as sport. Again." *Debito.org*, October 12, 2018, archived with commentary at www.debito.org/?p=15176. A similar lack of media focus on employers employing illegally has been seen in, for example, "Kyodo: Foreign laborers illegally working on farms in Japan increases sharply [*sic*]. How about the J employers who employ illegally?" *Debito.org*, June 12, 2016, www.debito.org/?p=14052.

124. "TV 'Economist' Mitsuhashi Takaaki on foreign labor in Japan: '80% of Chinese in Japan are spies': 'foreigners will destroy Japanese culture.'" *Debito.org*, June 22, 2016, www.debito.org/?p=14057.

125. "Sankei column by Okabe Noburu suggesting Japanese language tests for foreign correspondent visas, to weed out their 'anti-Japan' biases." *Debito.org*, February 29, 2016, www.debito.org/?p=13713. This complemented a *Sankei* column of March 29, 2014, by writer Harakawa Takao, who accused foreign correspondents of "harboring 'blind belief' in the anti-Japanese propaganda being generated by China and South Korea," basing his claim on an earlier press conference at the Foreign Correspondents Club that he says descended into a "blame-Japan" fest. *See* "Foreign correspondents 'blindly swallowing' anti-Japanese propaganda, writer alleges." *Japan Today*, April 10, 2014.

126. Carsten Germis, "Confessions of a foreign correspondent after a half-decade of reporting from Tokyo to his German readers." Foreign Correspondents' Club of Japan *No. 1 Shimbun*, April 2, 2015, which noted:

> What is new, and what seems unthinkable compared to five years ago, is being subjected to attacks from the Ministry of Foreign Affairs—not only direct ones, but ones directed at the paper's editorial staff in Germany. After the appearance of an article I had written that was critical of the Abe administration's historical revisionism, the paper's senior foreign policy editor was visited by the Japanese consul general of Frankfurt, who passed on objections from "Tokyo." The Chinese, he complained, had used it for anti-Japanese propaganda.
>
> It got worse. Later on in the frosty, 90-minute meeting, the editor asked the consul general for information that would prove the facts in the article wrong, but to no avail. "I am forced to begin to suspect that money is involved," said the diplomat, insulting me, the editor and the entire paper. Pulling out a folder of my clippings, he extended condolences for my need to write pro-China propaganda, since he understood that it was probably necessary for me to get my visa application approved.

127. Archived with commentary at www.debito.org/?p=12720. The Japan Institute for National Fundamentals' website is at https://en.jinf.jp.

128. In November 2014, McGraw-Hill, publisher of a world history textbook, *Traditions and Encounters: A Global Perspective on the Past* Volume Two, by history professors Herbert Ziegler and Jerry Bentley, was contacted by Japan's New York Consulate General. The request: that two paragraphs (i.e., the entire entry) on

the "Comfort Women" be deleted. On January 15, McGraw-Hill met with Japanese diplomats and refused to comply with the request, stating that the scholars had properly established the historical facts. Later that month, PM Abe directly targeted the textbook in a parliamentary session, stating that he was "shocked" to learn that his government had "failed to correct the things it should have." This was subsequently condemned by historians worldwide. *See*, for example, Alexis Dudden, "Standing with historians of Japan." *Perspectives on History*, Letter to the Editor, March 1, 2015; "US author recounts 'lecture' he got about 'comfort women' from uninvited Japanese guests." *Japan Times*, March 5, 2015, archived with sources at www.debito.org/?p=13103; Arudou (2015). GOJ denials at "Japan didn't meddle with U.S. 'comfort women' textbook, [Japan Ambassador to the US Sasae Ken'ichiro] claims." *Kyodo News/Japan Times*, February 14, 2015; "LDP panel explores ways to convey Japan's views on sex slave issue." *Japan Times*, March 12, 2015. For an assessment of how the Netto Uyoku have also been involved in putting pressure on reportage on Japan, *see* David McNeill, "Into the Valley of the Trolls: Is growing online harassment just part of the job or should it be confronted? And when does it cross the line?" Foreign Correspondents' Club of Japan *No. 1 Shimbun*, December 27, 2015.

129. www.snopes.com/fact-check/the-love-machine/.

130. Sources for this section: "Media outside Japan must stop normalizing sumo as an ethno-sport." *Japan Times*, February 19, 2017, with further sourcing at www.debito.org/?p=14492 and www.debito.org/?p=14468. Speaking of free passes for Japan, foreign media has had a habit of looking at China's treatment of its minorities (before the incomparable oppression of its Uighur minority became world news) and overlooking parallels with Japan's policies. *See* example articles and commentary at "Newsweek column on 'rising ugly nationalism towards foreign residents' in China. Hm, how about an eye on Japan?" *Debito.org*, August 1, 2012, www.debito.org/?p=10481; "China's crackdown on foreigners called 'xenophobic' by CNN columnist. Yet Japan's been overtly doing the same to its NJ for generations without similar criticism." *Debito.org*, June 16, 2012, www.debito.org/?p=10269; "How 'religious' treatment of things Japanese allows for Japan to be kid-gloved through international public debate." *Debito.org*, December 24, 2011, www.debito.org/?p=9728; Debito Arudou, "Japan makes more sense though a religious lens." *Japan Times*, April 6, 2015.

131. The first mainstream media appearance of the term "Flyjin" appeared in "Expatriates Tiptoe Back to the Office." *Wall Street Journal*, March 23, 2011, in both English and Japanese versions. Japanese media then used this newly legitimized term along with *Nihon saru gaikokujin*; *see also* "Nikkei reports on the effect of '*Nihon saru gaikokujin*', aka Flyjin, with some pretty shaky journalistic practices." *Debito.org*, April 25, 2011, www.debito.org/?p=8806; "Flyjin rather few." *Japan Times* Editorial, May 6, 2012, which noted, "the vast majority of foreigners in Tokyo stayed right where they were—in Tokyo"; "JT Editorial: Tokyo Metro Govt fuels 'Flyjin' myth with flawed survey; yet other NJ who should know better buy into it." *Debito.org*, May 7, 2012, www.debito.org/?p=10181; "Better to be branded a 'flyjin' than a man of the 'sheeple.'" *Japan Times*, May 3, 2011 (archived with sources at www.debito.org/?p=8870), where I wrote:

> [S]uddenly it was open season for denigrating [Non-Japanese]. For example, the Wall Street Journal (March 23) announced in English and Japanese articles an apparent "fly-jin exodus," portraying NJ as fleeing, then sheepishly crawling back to their Japanese workplaces to face hazing. Tokyo Sports Shinbun (April 14) ran the headline "Tokyo Disneyland's biggest reason for closing: repatriating NJ dancers" (oddly, Disneyland reopened days later). Tabloids reported that "all foreigners have fled Japan" (Nikkan Gendai, April 11), or that a wave of migrating "bad foreigners" would render Tokyo's Ueno a lawless zone (SPA!, April 12). The NJ-bashing got so bad that the government—unusually—intervened, quashing Internet rumors that foreign gangs were roaming the rubble, raping and pillaging, or that foreign terrorists had caused the earthquakes,
>
> More moderate media still reported that escaping NJ labor was hurting Japan's economy, citing farms and factories employing NJ "trainees," fast food outlets, convenience stores, the IT sector and language education. Mainichi Shinbun (April 25) shed crocodile tears over the possible death of Japan's textile industry due to the lack of cheap Chinese workers. I saw no articles putting things into perspective, comparing numbers of AWOL NJ with AWOL Japanese. Cowardice and desertion were linked with extranationality.

As for the meme of inherent Wajin stoicism, *see*, for example, Peter Tasker, "The Island Nation: Japan will rebuild, but not how you think. And twenty years of misread history holds the clues." *Foreign Policy*, March 24, 2011. Future Tōkyō governor Koike Yuriko would make the same argument, saying "we Japanese have a deeply ingrained stoicism" to the World Economic Forum in 2015, archived at www.debito.org/?p=13134.

132. Numerous articles archived in context at "More J media regarding NJ within earthquake-stricken Japan: Rumors of 'Foreign Crime Gangs'; rapes and muggings, while tabloids headline 'all NJ have flown Japan' etc." *Debito.org*, April 13, 2011. *See also* the *Debito.org Newsletter*, April 15, 2011, at www.debito.org/?p=8796, which collates reports demonstrating how assistance to Wajin from foreign residents was also being overlooked by media both foreign and domestic.

133. "*Donarudo Kiin-san, Nihon kokuseki shutoku: Shinsaigo eijū o ketsui*" [Donald Keene receives Japanese citizenship: Decided to live here permanently following the disasters]. *Asahi Shinbun*, March 8, 2012.

134. "Congratulations Donald Keene on getting Japanese citizenship. Now stop making yourself out to be somehow morally superior to Non-Japanese." *Debito.org*, March 9, 2012, www.debito.org/?p=10017; Press conference broadcast on *ANN News*, March 7, 2012. More on Donald Keene's sunset behaviors as a naturalized Japanese and his consistent denigration of foreign residents at www.debito.org/?s=Keene. He died in 2019 without recanting those statements.

135. *See also* "Powerpoint presentation on the J media-manufactured Myth of 'Flyjin'; stats are in, lies are exposed." *Debito.org*, March 24, 2012, www.debito.org/?p=10055. As I wrote in "Keene should engage brain before fueling 'flyjin,' foreign crime myths." *Japan Times*, April 3, 2012:

> According to the Ministry of Justice, the NJ population registered with the government (so as to leave out NJ tourists, who must depart within three months anyway) dropped for the third straight year in 2011, by 55,671 souls, or 2.6 percent. This is little different than

2010's drop of 51,970, or 2.4 percent—meaning this is an ongoing trend little changed by the disasters. Moreover, look at the largest drop in terms of nationality: Brazilians, falling by nearly 9 percent, for more than a third of the total. Where are Brazilians clustered? Around Nagoya, nowhere near the disaster areas.

The point is, NJ migration (in a science riddled with caveats and complications) was happening anyway for two reasons unrelated to Tohoku: (1) because NJ are the first downsized whenever our labor market goes sour, and (2) because it is standard operating practice within Japan's visa regimes to boot out unwanted NJ workers. Moreover, if this column does what the Japanese media steadfastly refuses to do (that is, compare Japanese with NJ numbers), we can see that according to the government Statistics Bureau, the numbers of "Japanese flyjin" last year (that is, those who actually left the country, as opposed to the indubitably higher numbers who moved away from the danger zones domestically) also increased: A net 24,889 Japanese left Japan in March and April 2011 alone.

And, as a brief but indicative tangent, consider the comparative migration patterns of "Japanese flyjin" during Thailand's disastrous floods last October. Not only did Japanese not remain in Thailand "in solidarity," they also took Thai workers with them (on one-time temporary six-month visas, of course) so as not to disrupt Japanese factory production schedules. The hypocrisy is palpable. And from what I have seen, the Thai media did not bash either the Japanese fleers or the Thai temps as deserters.

136. "Anchorwoman who fled Japan during Fukushima crisis to get lost salary from NHK." *Japan Times*, November 16, 2015.

137. *See*, for example, "Japanese Government targets 'harmful rumors.'" *Shingetsu News Agency*, April 4, 2011; "Police say rumors of foreign looters in Hiroshima unfounded." *Japan Times*, August 27, 2014; "Social media aids rehashing of historical hate." *Japan Times*, September 13, 2014; "Hate speech in Japan: Spin and substance. A troubling rise in xenophobic vitriol." *Economist* (London), September 27, 2014; "Post-quake social media rife with fake news." *NHK World*, Tuesday, June 18, 2018, archived with commentary at www.debito.org/?p=15037.

138. "80 percent believed fake rumors of crime by foreigners in Japan after quake: poll." *Mainichi Shinbun*, March 13, 2017, archived in English and Japanese at www.debito.org/?p=14521.

139. Archived with commentary at www.debito.org/foreigncrimeputsch.html.

140. This comparison was made almost exclusively in the *Japan Times*, which as noted above was once a media source independent from the Japanese media outlets that govern the editorial content of *Daily Yomiuri* (now the *Japan News*), *Asahi Evening News* (now the *IHT/Asahi*), or the *Mainichi Daily News*.

141. "More police, immigration officers sought." *Japan Times*, September 23, 2003.

142. "Ministry aims to end fingerprint law." *Asahi Evening News*, October 7, 1998.

143. Debito Arudou, "Bad Impressions: Japan's new policy of fingerprinting foreigners is cack-handed and callous." *Metropolis*, October 26, 2007; Debito Arudou, "The Myopic State we're in: Fingerprint scheme exposes xenophobic, short-sighted trend in government." *Japan Times*, December 18, 2007.

144. "Celebrity uses finger photo-op to call for cut in foreign crime." *Mainichi Shinbun*, November 14, 2007.

145. "Use fingerprints, photos to boost security." *Yomiuri Shinbun*, November 19, 2007.

146. *See* photo of demonstrations outside MOJ on the cover of Chung (2010).

147. Archive with illustration and commentary at www.debito.org/?p=863 (English) and www.debito.org/?p=865 (Japanese): *Yomiuri Shinbun "Kodomo no nyūsu uīkurī"* [Children's News Weekly], December 1, 2007, explaining the process and reasoning for fingerprinting all "foreigners" at the border. Girl character #1 says, "This is how foreigners who come to Japan register their fingerprints at places like airports." Boy character says, "The aim is to protect against criminals and terrorists coming to Japan." Girl character #2. says, "But you have to properly manage the registered face photo and fingerprint information."

148. I define for the purposes of this research "hate speech" under the standard dictionary definitions (e.g., Random House, American Heritage) as "speech that attacks a person or group on the basis of race, religion, gender, or sexual orientation."

149. Full contents of book scanned at www.flickr.com/photos/ultraneo/sets/72157594531953574/, and a full synopsis at Arudou (2007).

150. Arudou (2007); Debito Arudou, "Demise of crime magazine historic." *Japan Times*, March 20, 2007.

151. www.debito.org/?p=205.

152. Saka, Shigeki, "Why I published 'foreigner underground crime file:' Editor makes his case and responds to critics." *Japan Today*, February 16, 2007; "Gaijin Hanzai editor Saka responds on Japan Today, with my rebuttal." *Debito.org*, February 6, 2007; both archived at www.debito.org/?p=224. A later publication would also claim, despite the semiannual press releases from the NPA, that the discussion of "foreign crime" and "foreigners" is a "taboo topic" in the publishing world, and that a public reaction to "foreigner discrimination" (*gaikokujin sabetsu*) had victimized Eichi Shuppan Inc. *See "Nihon Tabū Jikenshi 2."* [Magazine of Japan Taboo Events Vol. 2] *Bessetsu Takarajima* 44, September 2007.

153. Teikoku Databank, April 5, 2007.

154. "China tourists stingy in some areas." *Asahi Shinbun*, June 16, 2010, which argued that Chinese spend too much time and money shopping and repatriating their funds through Chinese tour groups, instead of going through Japan's tour groups (even though industries such as JTB and Japanese hotel chains engage in the same practice for Japanese tourists in, e.g., Hawai'i). The Korean media ("Japanese tourists stingy in shopping." *Korea Times*, January 13, 2009) made similar claims about Japanese tourists, indicating that media grumbling about tourist spending habits is not limited to Japan.

155. *See* the cover of *Nikkei Business Magazine*, June 21, 2010, which headlined, "*Atarashii jōshi wa chūgokujin: zōshoku suru 'chapan' keizaiken*" ["Your new boss is Chinese. The propagation of the economic bloc of 'Chapan'" [a portmanteau of China/Japan]). It also notes that Japan's Rakuten Inc.'s "enemy" (*teki*) is Amazon US and China's Alibaba Inc. The image provided on the cover is a photoshopped image of a Chinese market gateway placed in the middle of Tōkyō Ginza beside Mitsukoshi Department Store.

156. "*Monga* [monster *gaikokujin*] in our midst." *Japan Today*, February 11, 2009, citing a Weekly SPA! tabloid article, "Damage Report: *Monsutā gaikokujin ōabare*." February 17, 2009, that offers a four-page report on "rampaging monster foreigners" and ascribes aberrant behavior to nationality.

157. *See* inter alia "Olympus case a black mark for Japan." *Japan Times*, October 24, 2011; "Japan, slowly, waking up to the mess at Olympus." *Reuters*, October 26, 2011; "Ex-Olympus president Shinoyama says hiring foreign CEO regrettable." *Tokyo Reporter*, November 25, 2011.

158. "Problematically racialized Education Ministry-approved primary-school 'Morals' textbook: '*Shōgaku Dōtoku: Yutaka na Kokoro 1-Nen*' (*Kōbun Shoin*, 2020)." *Debito.org*, May 5, 2021, www.debito.org/?p=16621.

159. "PTA-recommended 'Chagurin' mag puts propaganda article 'Children within the Poverty Country of America' in Japan's 6th-Grader classrooms." *Debito .org*, November 29, 2012, www.debito.org/?p=10806; "Update: JA and PTA's Chagurin Magazine responds to protests re Tsutsumi Mika's 'Children within the Poverty Country of America' article for 6th-Grade kids." *Debito.org*, January 23, 2013, www.debito.org/?p=11086; "Child's quibble with U.S. 'poverty superpower' propaganda unravels a sobering story about insular Japan." *Japan Times*, March 5, 2013, archived with commentary and links at www.debito.org/?p=11245.

Interestingly, the author of this piece, Tsutsumi Mika, has a history of muckraking America (without comparison to Japan's problems), directed at Wajin audiences for profit and awards. Her many bestsellers include "America's Revolution of the Weak," "Freedom Disappears from America," and the award-winning "America, the Poverty Superpower" (with a sequel and a manga version). Incidentally, this anti-Semitic manga depicted a profiteering Jew named "Goldberg" selling an exploitative house loan to a Mexican immigrant family during America's 2007 Subprime Mortgage Crisis; ironically, Tsutsumi herself was married to a Jewish American and is currently married to an Upper House MP named Kawada Ryūhei, a former member of the defunct center-right Your Party (*Minna no Tō*). *See* "Tangent: Tsutsumi Mika's crooked Jewish character 'Goldberg' in her 'USA Poverty Superpower' manga." *Debito.org*, March 9, 2013, www.debito.org/?p=11252.

As for the editors of *Chagurin* magazine, they responded (my translation):

> "Chagurin was created as a magazine to convey the importance of farming, food, nature and life, and cultivate the spirit of helping one another. The goal of the article . . . was not to criticize America; it was to think along with the children about the social stratifications (*kakusa shakai*) caused by market fundamentalism (*shijō genri shugi*) that has gone too far. . . . There are many things in this world that we want children to learn. . . . not limited to poverty and social inequality, but also food supply, war, etc. . . . We would like to positively take up these issues and include Japan's problems as well."

They indicated that they would run corrections to Tsutsumi's claims but not retract the article.

160. Archived with images, commentary and debate at www.debito.org/?p=4153 are advertisements featuring McDonald's Japan's "Mr. James" racialized mascot,

used between August and October 2009 to sell exotic hamburgers. Note the broken and accented Japanese dialog rendered in *katakana* only.

161. *See* an example of a multiethnic McDonalds advertisement from 1971 at www.youtube.com/watch?v=XKR1ScQUpcA.

162. *See* "Foreigners fail to see joke over McDonald's dorky-white-guy ad." *South China Morning Post*, August 21, 2009; "Not everyone is lovin' Japan's new McDonald's mascot." *TIME Magazine*, August 24, 2009; Letter from Kawaminami Jun'ichi, Director, Corporate Relations, McDonald's Company (Japan) Ltd., August 25, 2009; ibid., *Japan Times*, September 1, 2009; "McRacism in Japan?" *San Francisco Chronicle*, September 2, 2009; "In McDonald's new Japanese ad campaign, the wacky foreigner joke's on Americans." *Huffington Post*, August 20, 2009. There was one article in weekly magazine *Shūkan Kin'yōbi* more than a month after the media cycle had concluded. *See* "*'Hakujin' e no henken o jochō: Makku CM ni kōgi no koe*" [This promotes prejudice toward white people, say protest voices against the McDonald's commercial]. *Shūkan Kin'yōbi*, October 2, 2009.

163. Background information courtesy inter alia Mori (2005: 455–466).

164. "Japanese publisher defies Little Black Sambo protest." *Guardian*, June 15, 2005.

165. Ibid. *See also* www.debito.org/chibikurosanbo.html for more archived images and debate.

166. "Sambo returns to bookracks in Japan." *Chicago Tribune*, June 13, 2005.

167. Mark Thompson, "Day Care Center in Tokorozawa, Saitama, teaches toddlers 'Little Black Sambo' complete with the epithets." *Debito.org*, February 18, 2010; "Sambo racism row reignites over kids' play." *Japan Times*, April 13, 2010.

168. Archived within www.debito.org/chibikurosanbo.html with commentary is the Japanese translation and republication in 1995 by Zui'unsha Inc. of *The Five Chinese Brothers* by Claire Huchet Bishop, originally published in 1938. Note the racialized and stereotyped characteristics of the Chinese, and the use of *Shina* for China in the title—an older word used by Wajin conservatives such as Ishihara Shintarō as a derogatory epithet. Purchased by the author through Amazon Japan in 2005. Archived at www.debito.org/?p=808 is an example of the racialized commodification of Sambo; note the marketed tie-in with Zui'unsha's book. Photo of gollywog dolls taken at Rainforest Café in Ikspiari Shopping Center (next to Tōkyō Disneyland) Maihama, Chiba Prefecture, by John Clammer, December 3, 2007. Sambo dolls were advertised on Amazon Japan (as of September 21, 2012) as originally on sale from August 9, 2006 (less than a year after the release of the book) and are "currently unavailable" to buyers outside of Japan.

169. Background for this section includes inter alia Sakata (2012: 4–5); and Takara TOMY Inc. Character license information on Dakko-chan website, www.takaratomy.co.jp/tscope/license/dakkochan.html (dead link, accessed via Wayback Machine September 23, 2012). For a picture, do a Google Image search for "dakko-chan."

170. Mori (2005) ibid., might agree, as he makes the unsourced claim that, "Most Japanese people, especially those who had loved LBS in their childhood, were unconvinced by the racism accusation and mourned the sudden disappearance of

LBS." He also insinuates that protests in Japan about LBS's racism were too small to be significant, noting that the protest group consisted only of "a couple with a ten-year-old son" (465). His paper, published in the *Social Behavior and Responsibility* journal, was purportedly an attempt to add to the empirical data on racism in Japan in connection to LBS, but it consists of reactions to a survey he performed, on a sample size of only fifty-four children and forty-three elderly people, regarding racialized and non-racialized versions of LBS for how "amusing" they were. Offering no definition of "amusing," Mori finds that respondents find all versions have "equal levels of amusingness." How this passed peer review remains a mystery.

171. John G. Russell, "Historically, Japan is no stranger to blacks, nor to blackface." *Japan Times*, April 19, 2015.

172. Archived at www.debito.org/mandomproject.html with images and are Gatsby "Mogeha" mentholated face towels. Courtesy of Mandom Inc. website June 7, 2005.

173. "*Mandomu no chinpanjī CM, 'kokujin sabetsu' shiteki de chūshi*" [Mandom's chimpanzee commercial: withdraws after notice of "discrimination against black people"]. *Asahi Shinbun*, June 14, 2005; *see* the commercial archived at www.debito.org/TheCommunity/mandomproject.html.

174. Sources for this section: Baye McNeil, "Time to shut down this modern-day minstrel show: Doo-what?: An image that went viral on the Internet shows members of male doo-wop group Rats & Star and idol group Momoiro Clover Z blacked up backstage during the filming of a show for Fuji TV scheduled for broadcast on March 7." *Japan Times*, February 18, 2015; Baye McNeil, "From a minstrel no-show to a black beauty queen, in a week." *Japan Times*, March 18, 2015; Russell, *Japan Times*, April 19, 2015, ibid.; Patrick St. Michel, "Blackface, suicide and celebrity abuse: Welcome to 2018!" *Japan Times*, January 6, 2018; John G. Russell, Baye McNeil, and Aoki Yūta, "Live panel discussion about blackface in Japan." *Japan Times*, January 8, 2018, www.youtube.com/watch?v=_Pf8M9F-IAw&t=3s. More referential links at www.debito.org/?p=14854.

175. *See*, for example, Sterling (2010).

176. "'Black Melon Pan' Afros as food: Insensitive marketing by Mini-Stop Konbini." *Debito.org*, December 13, 2010, www.debito.org/?p=8045.

177. To give you an idea how difficult it is to calculate Japan's ethnic diversity, consider Michael Hassett, "How many Japanese are a bit of something else? Even taking 1965 as a false racially pure 'year zero,' mathematics muddies the homogeneity myth." *Japan Times*, April 5, 2017, who writes, "[W]e should expect around 7.64 percent of Japan to have at least one foreign parent by 2039, almost 9.21 percent to have one foreign parent or grandparent, and about 9.66 percent to have one foreign parent, grandparent, or great grandparent."

178. Personal communication, June 17, 2021.

179. "*Okoe Rui senshu o 'yaseimi zenkai,' 'honnō mukidashi,' supōtsu hōchi no kiji ni hihan*" [criticism leveled at Sports Hōchi articles for saying "wild instincts on full display," "exhibiting instincts" about player Okoe Rui]. *Huffington Post Japan*, August 14, 2015, archived at www.debito.org/?p=14639. Contrast this with what happened to bigoted language from former *Denver Post* columnist Terry Frei, who

was fired after tweeting that he was "very uncomfortable with a Japanese driver [Satō Takuma] winning the Indianapolis 500 during Memorial Day weekend" in 2017. *See* "Denver Post columnist fired after 'disrespectful' tweet about Japanese driver's Indianapolis 500 victory." *Washington Post*, May 30, 2017.

180. "*'Ippanjin Haafu' no tohohona taikendan o shoukai! Gaiken, kotoba, bunka* . . ." [Introducing the experiences of of "regular-folk Haafu"! Physical appearance, language, cultural [differences]]. *ZAK X SPA!*, October 9, 2012, archived with commentary at www.debito.org/?p=10674.

181. "Rui Hachimura and younger brother Aren receiving racist abuse online." *Japan Times/Kyodo News*, May 6, 2021. Contrast this with how current Japanese Iranian San Diego Padres pitcher Darvish Yū has spoken out against a racist gesture against him during the 2017 World Series, and against COVID-era hate speech and crimes against Asians in the United States. *See* "Racism in US World Series against baseball pitcher Yu Darvish: Immediately punished and turned into learning opportunity." *Debito.org*, October 29, 2017, www.debito.org/?p=14789; "Yu Darvish speaks out against anti-Asian racism in the U.S." *Japan Times*, March 21, 2021. Mixed conditions for other multiethnic Japanese elite athletes are discussed in detail in "Biracial athletes making strides in changing Japanese society." *Japan Times*, October 4, 2015. *See also* John G. Russell, "Online harassment is all a part of Japan's 'post' racism: The racialized bullying of public figures exposes lingering toxic attitudes in society." *Japan Times*, May 24, 2021.

182. *See* the "*Kurohige Gaijin-san*" at www.kk-jig.com/products/orderno_6156/, and the "*Hana Megane Gaijin-san*" at www.kk-jig.com/products/orderno_6084/1/. Accessed September 23, 2012 and archived at www.debito.org/?p=10591.

183. Sakata (2012: 2). Archived within www.debito.org/?p=10591 are images demonstrating the racialized commodification of "gaijin" is not only Caucasian, but also hirsute. At left is the sweaty "Nose Glasses Gaijin-san" with blond hair and eyebrows, blue eyes, and expressions "What's up?" and "Whoop!!" Note the title, "*Henshin* [transformative] Goods"). At right is the more swarthy "Black Beard Gaijin-sama with an image of what appears to be a mullah. Both noses are from the same mold and skin tone. Photo taken at Tokyū Hands Shibuya, September 23, 2012, courtesy of Dave Gutteridge.

184. *See* the commercial archived on YouTube at www.youtube.com/watch?v=DUmazv7UTXI, last accessed June 1, 2015.

185. Archive at www.debito.org/?p=7523 shows the racialized commodification of "foreign" as Caucasian in a TV commercial. First screen capture shows the girlfriend speaking in accented Japanese, saying, "Tomorrow I'd like a hot bath." Second screen capture indicates that both members of the couple have been "foreignized," with exaggerated noses and light blond wigs. Broadcast on Fukuoka TV station FBS September 19, 2010.

186. "ANA ad on Haneda Airport as emerging international Asian hub, talks about changing 'the image of Japan'—into White Caucasian!" *Debito.org*, January 18, 2014, www.debito.org/?p=12077; "Don't let ANA off the hook for that offensive ad." *Japan Times*, January 24, 2014, archived with sources at www.debito.org/?p=12101.

187. "Racist 2013 Toshiba commercial for product APB-R100X, SuiPanDa combination ricecooker/breadmaker." *Debito.org*, June 27, 2013, www.debito.org/?p=11590.

188. "Discussion: Cute 'Kobito-zukan' comic characters for kids and NJ control fantasies?" *Debito.org*, April 15, 2013, www.debito.org/?p=11003.

189. "Choya Pulls Giant Gaijin Nose Commercial After Receiving Complaints." *Japan Probe*, undated, 2011, dead link archived at https://web.archive.org/web/20150217015155/http://www.japanprobe.com/2011/07/22/choya-pulls-giant-gaijin-nose-commercial-after-receiving-complaints/.

190. "Japan Procter & Gamble's racialized laundry detergent ad: 'Cinderella and the Nose Ballroom Dance.'" *Debito.org*, November 19, 2014, www.debito.org/?p=12821.

191. Arudou (2013b). Images archived at www.debito.org/?p=15506.

192. *See* Prieler (2006: 239–266, particularly 257–264 on increasing product appeal and memorability through association with "foreign" images). I personally have seen this theme of racialized characteristics consistently being associated with contexts of "foreign" on Japanese network television broadcasts for decades (especially within the context of foreign language education). There is evidence that it is an established editorial decision. For example, I received a request on December 13, 2004, for a local TV comedy spot as follows (English original):

> HTB [Hokkaidō] television is looking for 3 foreigners to appear on a late night TV programme. They want 3 people who can communicate in Japanese well enough to do the programme: 1 white male (preferably macho), 1 black male (preferably macho), 1 white female (preferably beautiful with blond hair). The programme will involve calling people and speaking only English. They want to see how people deal with a wrong number call from a foreigner who doesn't speak Japanese.

I raised a complaint through online media, and HTB abandoned the idea. Proceedings archived at www.debito.org/HTBstepinfetchit.html. *See also* "*Motomu: Kinpatsu hakujin: aoru jinshu henken. HTB eizō hihan uke kikaku chūshi.*" [Wanted: Blond Whites; brings forth racial prejudice. HTB receives criticism and cancels planned program]. *Hokkaidō Shinbun*, December 18, 2004.

193. Note that turnabout is not in fair play. When racialized images of or problematic language about Japanese appear in overseas media, the Wajin media and the Netto Uyoku pounce, and the GOJ quickly lodges formal and informal claims and protests about "racial discrimination," often engendering apologies and retractions. *See*, for example, "*Kaigai riigu shozoku no nihonjin sakkaa senshu, genchi de no 'jinshu sabetsu' o kokuhaku . . . 'Seikatsu dekinakunatta'*" [Japanese soccer player belonging to an overseas league reveals local "racial discrimination" . . . "I can't make a life there anymore"]. *RBB Today*, January 30, 2013; "*Nihonjin FW, kibishii jinshu sabetsu o riyū ni taidan*" [Japanese Soccer Forward, quits club due to severe racial discrimination]. *Sankei Sports*, January 31, 2013; "Japanese soccer player Yuki Nakamura quits Slovakian club due to racial abuse." *Japan Daily Press*, January 31, 2013; "Nakamura quits Slovakian club over racism." *Japan Today*, January 31, 2013; and so on, all archived at www.debito.org/?p=11120. *See also* "Japan protests to BBC

over treatment of 'double A-bomb survivor.'" *Mainichi Shinbun*, January 21, 2011, archived with commentary at www.debito.org/?p=8427.

194. Archive of this issue starting from www.debito.org/kumegaffeone.html.

195. *See* inter alia "When in Tokyo, don't speak as the Japanese do." *Chicago Tribune*, October 27, 1996.

196. Email from Kume Hiroshi, dated December 1, 2006, archived at www.debito.org/?p=106. *See also* "*'Gaijin no nihongo wa katakoto no hō ga;' Kume Hiroshi san 10 nen go no shazai.*" [Kume Hiroshi's apology ten years later] *Asahi Shinbun*, December 21, 2006.

197. Consider some essays on phraseology, media, and social dynamics perpetuating the narrative of "foreigner as guest in Japan."

Media: *See*, for example, "NHK's 'Cool Japan' TV show keeps their guest NJ commentators naive and ignorant." *Debito.org*, June 25, 2009, www.debito.org/?p=3633, which discusses how NHK shuts out any foreigner with deeper knowledge of Japan by restricting participation to people who have lived in Japan for *less than one year*; "TV Tokyo bangumi: 'Why did you come to Japan?' interviews NJ arrivals at Narita Airport, reifies mainstream media discourse of NJ as tourists, not residents." *Debito.org*, April 12, 2013, www.debito.org/?p=11353.

Phraseology: Debito Arudou, "Tweak the immigration debate and demand an upgrade to denizen class." *Japan Times*, April 2, 2013, where I wrote: "In terms of strict legal status, if you're not a citizen you're a 'foreigner' (gaikokujin), right? But not all gaikokujin are the same in terms of acculturation or length of stay in Japan. A tourist 'fresh off the boat' has little in common with a noncitizen with a Japanese family, property and permanent residency. Yet into the gaikokujin box they all go. The lack of terms that properly differentiate or allow for upgrades has negative consequences. A long-termer frequently gets depicted in public discourse as a sojourner, not 'at home' in Japan."

Social dynamics: There are pushes both official and informal that require foreigners to "like" Japan, since as a matter of general politeness "guests" do not criticize their "hosts." For example, consider the relentless pressure to "like" Japan because critics soon get labeled as "anti-Japan." *See* Debito Arudou, "Do Japan a favor: Don't stop being a critic." *Japan Times*, December 11, 2012. Officially, the GOJ has been pushing for foreigners to shill for a GOJ policy called "Cool Japan," a campaign to make Japan more attractive worldwide in terms of soft power. *See* "A Growing Love for 'Cool Japan' by Gaijin Handler Akira Yamada (of MOFA)." *Debito.org*, July 11, 2010, www.debito.org/?p=7170. It should be noted how this "love" is being enforced through visa incentives: *see* "Yomiuri on 'Sharp decline in tourist spending,' with GOJ measures to certify NJ in 'Cool Japan' for preferential visas." *Debito.org*, April 16, 2017, www.debito.org/?p=14473. Wajin media has even fretted how Japan is losing out to regional rivals in terms of "coolness"; *see* "Editorial: Cultivating 'Japan fans' key to attracting repeat foreign visitors." *Mainichi Shinbun*, November 1, 2016, archived with commentary at www.debito.org/?p=14282; "Asahi: South Korea, China overtaking Japan in 'cool' culture battle, whatever that means." *Debito.org*, July 30, 2010, www.debito.org/?p=7326.

198. That number is becoming fewer as less Japanese study abroad. *See* "Japan's new educational isolation." *Mainichi Shinbun*, December 2010; "Fewer and fewer Japanese want to see the world. Only 24 percent of them even have a passport—the lowest proportion among rich countries." *Economist* (London), February 27, 2020, which notes, "The number of Japanese studying abroad has also fallen, from 82,945 at its peak in 2004 to 55,969 in 2016. . . . A survey in 2019 found that 53 percent of Japanese students are not interested in studying abroad, the highest ratio among the seven countries covered." *See also* Debito Arudou, "Tackling Japan's 'empathy deficit' towards outsiders." *Japan Times*, May 1, 2014.

On a related note, Wajin who have managed to extricate themselves from the system and go outside have publicly extolled the virtues of doing so, saying that if they had not left Japan, they would never have been as successful in their lives. *See*, for example, "Nobel Prize-winner Shūji [Slave] Nakamura to Japan's young people: 'Get out of Japan.'" *RocketNews*, January 23, 2015; "Susumu Tonegawa." *Encyclopedia of World Biography*, 2005, courtesy of www.encyclopedia.com. Tonegawa (as did Leo Esaki in 1973, mentioned ibid. *passim*) also won a Nobel Prize in 1987, but said clearly that he would never have become a Nobel Laureate if he had remained in Japan. This, incidentally, caused the so-called Tonegawa Shock, spurring the Ministry of Education to embark on reforms to "enliven" (*kasseika*) Japan's education system. Ironically, however, this resulted in the firing of almost all noncitizen educators (who were on nontenured permanent contract work, unlike Wajin educators tenured from hire) over the age of thirty-five in Japan's National and Public Universities between 1992 and 1994. *See* chapter 5 and Hall (1998).

199. *See* "Point of View: English education leaves much to be desired." *Asahi Shinbun*, September 15, 2006, and "Point of View: Why the focus on English as a language skill?" *Asahi Shinbun*, November 4, 2006.

200. I use Webster's Dictionary definition of caste: "a division of society based on differences of wealth, inherited rank or privilege, profession, occupation, or race; a system of rigid social stratification characterized by hereditary status, endogamy, and social barriers sanctioned by custom, law, or religion." This term has been applied to Japan in the literature; *see*, for example, Amos (2011, 2019).

201. For an example of the insularity of Japan's "worldly and open-minded" next generation of Wajin, see *Japan Times*, March 5, 2014, ibid., where I argue that even Japan's well-traveled and bilingual Left will resort to xenophobic propaganda to maintain the Wajin-serving discourse.

202. This is a phenomenon discussed in Whiteness Studies where people embedded within the dominant ethnoracial group within white society become less aware of one's race and place within the social array of racial ascriptions (Twine & Warren 2000).

203. "*Gaikokujin Sanseiken de Nihon ga nakunaru hi*" [Foreigner Suffrage Spells Doomsday for Japan]. Bessetsu Takarajima, March 7, 2010, archived at www.debito.org/?p=6182.

204. *See* the text of the survey and its results in Japanese at www8.cao.go.jp/survey/h19/h19-jinken, last accessed September 23, 2012.

205. www8.cao.go.jp/survey/h19/h19-jinken/images/z14.gif.

206. Debito Arudou, "Human rights survey stinks: Government effort riddled with bias, bad science." *Japan Times*, October 23, 2007; *also Mainichi Shinbun*, April 12, 2003 regarding MOJ officials making the connection with "foreign crime."

207. www8.cao.go.jp/survey/h19/h19-jinken/3.html.

208. As further evidence of how ill-defined the concept of "human rights" (*jinken*) is in Japan, there have been publicized cases that bureaucrats with facial hair or advertisements with chest hair amount to violations of human rights! *See*, for example, "JR East links naked festival posters to sexual harassment." *Mainichi Shinbun*, January 8, 2008; "Gunma city does battle with beards: Local government's hairy-chin ban sets example for nation." *Japan Times*, June 1, 2010; "Workplace bans on beards raise hairy questions." *Kyodo News*, June 22, 2010. *See also* "One reason why human rights are not taken seriously in Japan: Childish essays like these in the Mainichi." *Debito.org*, June 18, 2016, www.debito.org/?p=14054. This unsophisticated level of public discussion gives leverage to opponents to dismiss human rights proponents as cranks (more below). Finally, human rights as a discipline is held in such low regard within Japan's ruling elite that Japan's only human rights museum, "Liberty Ōsaka," was in 2012 ordered to be defunded by Ōsaka governor Hashimoto Tōru because the museum's displays are "limited to discrimination and human rights," thereby failing to present Wajin children with an image of the future full of "hopes and dreams." *See* Morris-Suzuki (2012).

209. CCPR/C/79/Add.102 Item C (7).

210. The Cabinet reran this survey in 2012. Perhaps in response to criticisms raised in *Japan Times*, the problematic question about foreigners was revised to be the same as other discriminated parties: "What human rights problems (*jinken mondai*) do you think happen now to foreigners (*gaikokujin*) living in (*kyojū*) Japan?" Eleven multiple-select options included apartment refusals, exclusions at hotels and stores, employment disadvantages, school and workplace bullying, being stared at and socially avoided, and having (foreigners') different customs unaccepted (the highest selected, at 34.8 percent). For the purposes of this research, this is an enormous improvement. Nevertheless, 20.7 percent of respondents said that foreigners faced no problems in particular (*toku ni nai*). *See* www8.cao.go.jp/survey/h24/h24-jinken/ , www8.cao.go.jp/survey/h24/h24-jinken/3.html, and www8.cao.go.jp/survey/h24 /h24-jinken/zh/h14san1.csv (accessed December 16, 2012). This is what happens when you survey discrimination without asking those being discriminated against: respondents tend to see "no problems."

211. Sources for this section include "Government of Japan, survey thyself." *Japan Times*, March 5, 2017; "Time to act on insights from landmark survey of Japan's foreign residents." *Japan Times*, April 26, 2017. A preliminary analysis of the survey as it was released to respondents can be found at "MOJ Bureau of Human Rights Survey of NJ Residents and discrimination (J&E full text)." *Debito .org*, November 24, 2016, www.debito.org/?p=14298. A revised final version of the survey results (June 2017) can be found at www.moj.go.jp/content/001249011.pdf, and the Center for Human Rights Education and Training website is at www.jinken .or.jp.

212. Wajin media also tried to discount the results of this survey. For example, *Nikkei Asian Review*'s "'No foreigners allowed': Survey shows heavy discrimination in Japan" of April 6, 2017, made arguments within their article equivocating or discounting the findings, for example, "Nearly 27 percent of the 2,044 foreign respondents who had sought new housing within the past five years reported giving up on a potential residence after discovering a notice saying 'no foreigners allowed. . . .' These rejections, however, are not necessarily motivated by racism. Many landlords fear they may not be able to communicate easily with foreign tenants. Other reasons for refusal to rent include worries that foreign tenants will not follow Japanese customs, such as taking off their shoes inside the house." However, "racism" wasn't the claim of the survey ("foreigner discrimination" was), and the reporter inserting pedantic presumptions to justify treating "foreign tenants" differently is distinctly defensive editorializing. Further commentary at www.debito.org/?p=14573.

213. "*Sansaiji no mushiba gekigen: Tonai, hamigaki shukan teichaku*" [Cavities in three-year-olds fall dramatically: Firmly establishing toothbrushing habits in the capital region]. *Tōkyō Shinbun*, April 21, 2010, archived with commentary at www.debito.org/?p=6579. The article quotes a city official as saying, "Comparatively we have a lot of foreign residents, so maybe the fact that they drink juice etc. on a daily basis as part of their dietary habits is an influence." More about these media "blame games" at www.debito.org/?p=477 and www.debito.org/?s=blame+game.

214. *See*, for example, Kagawa Hiroshi, *The Inscrutable Japanese* (Kodansha, 1999).

Part IV

CHALLENGES TO JAPAN'S EXCLUSIONARY NARRATIVES

Chapter 8

Maintaining the Binary despite Domestic and International Pressure

"As a world power in an era of globalization, Japan has to expand to the outside world. But its society is still closed, spiritually and intellectually centered. . . . Racial discrimination in Japan is deep and profound . . . and practiced undisturbed in Japan. . . . It can hardly be argued that Japan is respecting its international obligations."[1] This collated quote is from Dr. Doudou Diene of Senegal, UN Special Rapporteur of the Commission on Human Rights on Contemporary Forms of Racism, Racial Discrimination, Xenophobia, and Related Intolerance, during his investigatory visits to Japan in 2005 and 2006. It demonstrates how experts worldwide know that how Japan is not following universal standards of human rights.

Dr. Diene was invited to survey Japan's human rights situation by several human rights groups working in Japan. That's why, for the sake of balance, this research should also note how Japan is a pluralistic society with diverse opinions. People of course visibly and vocally object to government (GOJ) policies, propagandistic media narratives, and intolerant social trends. There are many examples where people, both Wajin and Non-Wajin, have publicly challenged the status quo and suggested alternatives to the racialized treatment of "foreigners" in Japanese society. Further, as per the theory of how racialized narratives become embedded, we should discuss how the Wajin power structure deals with these challenges, as part of the maintenance of the dominant discourse. This chapter will focus on the ideological tugs-of-war between liberal and conservative factions in Japanese society, and conclude that the status quo generally wins out.

DOMESTIC CHALLENGES TO THE STATUS QUO

At the Grassroots and Local Level

First, let us consider instances of popular support for diversity expressed through grassroots network. For example, Japan's labor unions (such as NUGW, Zentōitsu Union, General Union, Tōzen, Fukuoka General Union, EWA Ōsaka, etc.) have noncitizen members, and have held frequent demonstrations outside individual businesses with problematic employment standards toward noncitizen workers (cf. NOVA and Berlitz Cases), as well as the regular "March in March"; they have utilized the media to disseminate clear statements that "foreign" workers are "living in Japan," "working for Japan," and standing up for themselves in both collective bargaining and public demonstrations.[2]

In the same vein, local NGOs and legal service networks have helped migrant workers assimilate, learn Japanese, receive free legal consultations, and find their way around Japan's social safety net.[3] Student groups, most famously SEALDs (Students Emergency Action for Liberal Democracy),[4] began to normalize college-age youth movements that protested GOJ policy without being tarred with the brush of being "violent extremists" (as happened to ultraleftist fringe groups Chūkakuha and Kakumaruha). In 2020, a multiethnic demonstration against police for using excessive force on a Kurdish resident during a traffic stop developed into a summer of awareness-raising about Black Lives Matter as well as minorities in Japan.[5] And as mentioned in chapter 6, protests over the senseless death of a Sri Lankan detainee Ratnayake Liyanage Wishma Sandamali in 2021 brought national attention and protest against the treatment of noncitizens in draconian Immigration custody.

Many of these interest groups have received a positive audience from local governments and some elected representatives. MPs have, for example, publicly pointed out the legal ambiguity of "Trainee" Visas, and so on, and the systematic abuses of imported labor such as virtual slavery and child labor; Lower House member and PM contender Kōno Tarō in 2006 called the entire work visa regime "a swindle" and opened ministerial debate on revising it.[6] Some reforms have arguably taken place, with a separate bureaucratic organ (OTIT) keeping closer track of foreign transplant labor rights abuses—even if, as mentioned in chapter 5, those abuses have not abated. Local governments with high populations of registered noncitizens have likewise provided multilingual services and other benefits for foreigners; Shizuoka Prefecture, like all other prefectures over the past thirty years, eventually abolished their practice of denying *Kokumin Hoken* health insurance to non-*kokumin*. Local governments have also held regular meetings on how to improve life for their noncitizen residents, issuing formal petitions (e.g., *Hamamatsu Sengen* of 2001)[7] to the national government, recommending they improve education, social insurance, and registration procedures for noncitizens. Some pushes for (temporary) municipal grants from the national government for helping foreign residents "settle in their communities" have been successful.[8]

Other NGOs (such as SMJ and IMADR), interest groups (such as the Burakumin Liberation League and Mindan), and concerned citizens have also petitioned the outside world, including the UN, to put outside pressure (*gaiatsu*) on the GOJ to improve conditions in Japan for noncitizens. The abovementioned Special Rapporteur Doudou Diene has thrice visited Japan on their invitation, reporting that racial discrimination in Japan is "deep and profound" and demanding inter alia that Japan pass laws against it.[9] Although the GOJ did not immediately comment on Diene's findings (and then-Tōkyō Governor Ishihara refused to meet with Diene despite Diene's request), the UN Human Rights Council frequently referenced Diene's reports when questioning Japan's commitment to human rights in May 2008.[10]

Follow-up missions, questions, and investigations[11] have arguably tarnished Japan's reputation as a human rights leader, as seen in an exchange where the GOJ human rights envoy at a 2013 meeting of the UN Committee Against Torture was claiming that Japan "is not in the Middle Age [*sic*]. We are one of the most advanced country [*sic*] in this field" of human rights. This elicited ironic giggles from the audience (to which he responded, "Don't laugh! Why you are laughing?! Shut up! Shut up!").[12]

At the Media Level

For more than a decade there have been sustained media campaigns against "Japanese Only" establishments. In many cases, exclusionary signs and rules have been withdrawn due to public pressure.[13] In addition to Ana Bortz's 1999 court victory against a Hamamatsu jewelry store, the Otaru Onsens Case has become, according to Japanese academia and legal professionals I have interviewed, a landmark lawsuit that shifted the domestic narrative on racism in Japan.[14] The Wajin media has even started to break taboos mentioned in chapter 7, explicitly calling "Japanese Only" signs and rules "racial discrimination" (*jinshu sabetsu*) in Japanese, not merely passing it off as "cultural misunderstandings," and so on in their articles.

This started in earnest in 2014 with the Urawa Reds Case, where a "Japanese Only" banner prominently appeared at a team Urawa Reds soccer game in Saitama Stadium, excluding all "foreigners" from an allegedly "sacred ground" section of the bleachers reserved for diehard fans. After initial dithering from Wajin media, J.League Chair Murai Mitsuru and the

Urawa Reds management came out with official statements condemning the practice specifically as *jinshu sabetsu*, indefinitely banned the culprits from future games, and meted out an unprecedented punishment of one home game played to an empty stadium. After that, more Wajin media started using *jinshu sabetsu* as an undisputed fact of the case, without caveat or weasel-wording it as a quote from management or activists.[15]

This has created a positive feedback loop in the narrative. Subsequent discriminatory cases and protests in Japan have cited the Urawa Case,[16] and clubs and teammates have gotten into the practice of calling out the discrimination themselves when management does not act.[17] Although it is still unclear if Urawa is a watershed case (i.e., establishing a standardized threshold for labeling something "racial discrimination" in media discourses),[18] scattered Wajin media and public debates have become emboldened enough to counteract discriminatory narratives—portraying foreigners and Visible Minorities positively as residents, taxpayers, and contributors to society with a place in Japan's future.[19] Moreover, there was great media fanfare for the successes of the multiethnic Brave Blossoms Japan rugby team in 2015 (see chapter 5).

Even the GOJ-generated dominant discourse of "foreigner" as "criminal," "visa overstayer," "terrorist," and "carrier of infectious diseases" (see part III of this book) has faced some criticism. For example, Kubo Hiroshi, former vice-head of the Tōkyō Metropolitan Government's Emergency Public Safety Task Force (*Tōkyō-to kinkyū chian taisaku fuku honbuchō*), was quoted in the Sunday Mainichi tabloid as far back as 2006 saying (translation by *Mainichi Daily News*):

> Put simply, the Tokyo Metropolitan Government's public safety policy involves telling people that public safety standards [related to crime rates among foreigners and juveniles] have worsened and police groups need strengthening to protect the capital's residents. But I've realized there's something unnatural about this "worsening." . . . There's an underlying current of anxiety throughout society. People have no idea what's going to happen in the future, they're worried about employment and pay and declining living standards and somebody who's going to openly talk about the reason for their anxieties is going to attract their interest. Say somebody comes out and says "foreigners' violent crimes are all to blame" then anxious people are going to go along with that. And the national government, prefectural governments, police and the media all jump on the bandwagon and believe what's being said.[20]

The fact that this dynamic has been brought up in Wajin media inspires hope for future critical self-reflection and improvement.

At the GOJ Level

To its credit, the GOJ has carried out some reforms. First, in terms of acknowledging diversity: On June 6, 2008, Japan's Diet formally acknowledged the Ainu as an indigenous people (*senjūmin*) under UN definitions; in May 2019, the Diet legally recognized the need for GOJ policy to support Ainu culture and eradicate Ainu discrimination.[21] This officially nullified Japan's monocultural, monoethnic, homogeneous society Postwar discourse and was even publicly enforced on September 25, 2008, during the first days of the PM Aso Cabinet, when Transport Minister Nakayama Nariaki called Japan "ethnically homogeneous" (*tan'itsu minzoku*). Due to the immediate backlash, Nakayama retracted his comments, apologized, and resigned his Cabinet post after only four days (he lost his Diet seat entirely in 2009).[22] That said, Japan's monoethnic narrative remains strong enough that Aso, this time as finance minister and deputy PM, felt he could reiterate in 2020 that Japan is the only nation where "a single race has spoken a single language at a single location and maintained a single dynasty with a single emperor for over 2000 years." He then apologized if his remark had been "misunderstood," the Abe Cabinet clarified that Aso had "no intention of denying GOJ policy concerning the Ainu people,"[23] and Aso once again retained his post. One month later, Japan's Olympic Committee announced that it had dropped a performance by the Ainu from the 2020 Tōkyō Olympics Opening Ceremonies due to "logistical constraints."[24]

Second, in terms of foreign labor: In 2012, the Cabinet opened official meetings with twelve ministries and several experts to hear policy on how to attract and keep more "high quality" (*kōdo jinzai*) imported labor in Japan. The proceedings offered clear statements from ministries and the Cabinet supporting more measures for supporting Nikkei workers resident in Japan.[25] Liberalizing proposals from local government heads and activists included GOJ-subsidized Japanese language courses, social acceptance (*uke'ire*) policies systematizing social welfare, employment, education, children's upbringing, and lifestyles for noncitizens, coordinated under a national-level "foreigner bureau" (*gaikokujin kyoku*). It also brought up issues such as a "foreign employment law" (*gaikokujin koyō hō*) and training and assistance centers to assist with finding and keeping jobs in Japan. "Hello Work," the GOJ unemployment agency, created an "Employment Service Center for Foreigners" in thirty-one prefectures.[26]

That said, much work needs to be done by the GOJ to compel employers to improve their hiring practices, as anecdotal evidence suggests that official employment agencies do little to promote the labor rights of noncitizen workers.[27] The 2017 GOJ survey of "foreigner discrimination" mentioned in chapter 7 noted that 25 percent of respondents had been refused jobs specifically because they were not Japanese, and another third said they were given a lower salary (19.6 percent) or other disadvantages in work conditions or promotion (17.1 percent) for the same reason.

The chances of this situation improving decrease when top Cabinet officials, such as Arimura Haruko, minister for the Empowerment of Women (and herself married to a Malaysian), continue to denigrate foreign workers, even blame them for their own plight. In 2015, Arimura called allowing immigration to Japan a "Pandora's box," and if opened would bring in foreigners with "extremist thinking like that of ISIL." Her logic ran that foreign workers would be radicalized after building up a "dissatisfaction with society" due to being mistreated by current Wajin labor practices.[28] Similar intellectual defeatism was expressed on the Left by Japan's most famous academic feminist, Tōkyō University's Ueno Chizuko, who argued in a 2017 *Chūnichi Shinbun* column that Japan will never be able to reverse its economic decline from the low birthrate (see chapter 10) or be capable of intercultural understanding. Therefore, instead of an immigration policy she argued, "Let's all become equally poor together."[29]

Finally, in terms of a formal immigration policy that allows for assimilation: The Immigration Bureau was upgraded to an Immigration Agency in 2019,[30] foreshadowing the possible creation of an Immigration Ministry separate from the Justice Ministry. This matters because a ministry dedicated to immigration may have different administrative priorities toward serving (as opposed to policing) foreign residents.

Most significantly, as mentioned in chapter 4, in July 2012 the Foreign Registry Law was abolished; noncitizens are now registered as "residents" (*jūmin*) in Japan with their Japanese families on *jūminhyō* Registry Certificates. The GOJ also officially lengthened the maximum duration of visas from three years to five and for a time created a more transparent "Points System" visa regime. Unfortunately, the GOJ also issued a new form of ARC (in the form of RFID *Zairyū* Cards) that raised privacy concerns, as well as centralized control away from more liberal local municipalities (who had previously issued the cards, including to visa overstayers) to combat "illegal foreigners."[31] The new ARCs are still required to be carried by noncitizens only at all times under criminal penalty, and as of 2020 there is an "Residence Card Checker App" downloadable from the MOJ unlawfully allowing anyone with a smartphone to check the validity of ARCs.[32] This means that the standard operating procedures encouraging police racial profiling (see chapter 5) of Japan's Visible Minorities remain in place. In sum, under an express mandate for the prevention of crime, terrorism, contagious diseases, hooliganism, and other subversive activities, "foreigners" in Japan are (thanks to technological advances as well as new security policies) more carefully scrutinized as a potential threat to society than ever before.

UPDATES FOR THE SECOND EDITION

Seven years between editions is a long time for coverage of any society, and several positive developments deserve a subsection.

"Hate Speech" Becomes Codified in Law

Chapter 7 discussed the antiforeigner hate-speech rallies that became a daily occurrence in the 2010s. However, over the decade Wajin counterdemonstrators started joining the fray, telling Wajin "racists" (*reishisuto*) to "go home" (*kaere*) and desist from their "*heito supiichi*" and "racial discrimination" (*jinshu sabetsu*).[33] Officials followed suit: In 2014, shortly before a UN report demanding that Japan adopt laws against racial discrimination and hate speech, the Ōsaka High Court upheld a ruling that xenophobic demonstrations outside a local Zainichi North Korean primary school were "discriminatory" and did not "serve the public interest," ordering the hate group, Zaitokukai, to pay damages.[34] In 2014, Zaitokukai received a public dressing down by Ōsaka mayor Hashimoto Tōru, who denounced its members as racist and told them they were not welcome in his city.[35] Even PM Abe publicly called hate speech "dishonorable" and counter to "the Japanese way of thinking" in 2013.[36]

The crowning achievement of this debate was the enactment of laws against hate speech (*ken'o hatsugen*), first by local governments such as Kawasaki and Ōsaka, and finally at the national level with the National Act to Curb Hate Speech in Japan on June 3, 2016.[37] "Hate Speech" was clearly defined as "openly announcing to the effect of harming the life, body, freedom, reputation or property of, or to significantly insult, persons originating from outside Japan with the objective of encouraging or inducing discriminatory feelings against such persons."[38] Within a year, hate rallies were estimated to have dropped by about half, and former hate-group members began publicly recanting their stances.[39]

However, due to fears about curtailing freedom of speech, Japan's hate speech laws included no criminal or punitive provisions,[40] meaning that outside of a civil court there are few means to punish people who spread hate against minorities.[41] What the law did do was enable the GOJ to take action, including granting injunctions to minorities to stop hate rallies,[42] further empowering the NPA's "watch lists" of hate groups as a threat to law and order (Zaitokukai was added to one in 2014),[43] and denying those groups permission to use public places and facilities (standard practice before convening outdoor demonstrations in Japan).[44] Critics rightfully pointed out that the Hate Speech Act only applied to "legal" foreigners and their descendants in Japan (therefore not to Wajin or visa overstayers being slandered), and that it did little to deter online hate speech from the Netto Uyoku.[45] It is also no substitute for a criminal law explicitly against racial discrimination. Nevertheless, the existence of the Hate Speech Act is a positive step forward, as it clearly defines "hate speech," frames it as a social ill, and officially stigmatizes people who engage in it.

Once-Normalized Public Slurs Now Face Domestic Boycotts for "Racial Discrimination"

In November 2020, Yoshida Yoshiaki, in his capacity as CEO of DHC (a Tōkyō-based international company selling beauty and health supplements), issued a statement on the corporate website castigating beverage maker Suntory (nicknaming it "Chon-tori," using *chon*, Japan's epithet for Koreans) for allegedly using Japanese models of Korean ethnicity: "From the celebrities we have hired, down to our very roots, we are a pure Japanese company."[46]

This was in addition to Yoshida's statements of February 2016, where he complained again as CEO that the Zainichi were "fake Japanese" (*ese Nihonjin*), and that Japanese society itself was becoming less "pure": "There are quite a few people who are not pure Japanese. We cannot escape the issue of who is genuine, false, or counterfeit when talking about the people living in Japan. . . . The problem is those types who naturalize as Japanese and then say bad things about Japan. . . . These can be called fake Japanese or pseudo-Japanese people." He pointed out that these counterfeit people can be found in Japan's opposition political parties, Left-leaning mass media, graduates of Tōkyō University working in the judiciary and bureaucracy, and entertainers and sportspeople. In April 2021, he called NHK "the enemy of Japan" (*Nihon no teki*) for broadcasting a segment on corporations' connections with enforcing human rights, and tried to purchase advertisements claiming that ethnic Koreans are "extremely dangerous to the Japanese nation" because they allegedly hold key government administrative posts.

This case is instructive because Yoshida's memes of anti-Korean hatred, foreign invasion, ideological impurity and patriotism, and paranoia about Wajin losing power are familiar from part III of this book, and well used by acolytes of former Tōkyō Governor Ishihara. When expressed in the 2000s and 2010s, these slurs rarely occasioned sustained backlash or the end of a political career. However, as of this Second Edition times have changed: Yoshida's statements reportedly caused firestorms on Twitter and other social media for being "discriminatory" (*sabetsuteki*), "hate speech," and "hateful towards Koreans" (*kenkanteki*) each time; and in May 2021, they sparked a boycott. Some advertising agencies refused to run Yoshida's advertisements, and local and prefectural governments announced they would be suspending or severing ties with DHC.

Significantly, officials this time explicitly framed the issue as "racial discrimination" (*jinshu sabetsu*), not anything milder; the city of Kōshi in Kumamoto Prefecture also clearly stated, "We should take action to avoid giving the wrong impression that we are approve of those messages. . . . As a municipality promoting human rights, we can never tolerate such comments." In sum, after a narrative of denialism up through the 1990s that Japanese society was incapable of engaging in "racial discrimination," followed by *jinshu sabetsu* creeping into debates about discrimination against visibly identifiable "Gaikokujin" in the 2000s, by the 2020s the term had expanded to cover prejudice against even fellow Asian residents.

Foreign Tourism Boom Offers Economic Incentives against Xenophobia

International tourism to Japan exploded in the 2010s. In the late 2000s, the GOJ decided to revitalize Japan's regional economies by encouraging foreign tourism, particularly from its Asian neighbors with growing economies such as China and South Korea.[47] Its original goal was 20 million foreign tourists by 2020, which was soon exceeded thanks to GOJ publicity campaigns such as Yōkoso Japan,[48] Cool Japan,[49] and the many major international sports events and summits mentioned above. According to the Japan National Tourist Organization and the World Tourism Organization, overseas tourists to Japan grew nearly fourfold from 8.6 million in 2010 to 28.7 million in 2017, 31.2 million in 2018, and 31.9 million in 2019 before the pandemic closed down the world. During this time the contribution of tourism to Japan's total GDP expanded from 1.7 to 2 percent.[50] Many if not most regional and local governments now accept tourism as a potential part of their growth strategy, with multilingual websites and facilities blossoming nationwide. As a grassroots boost, the passage of the Minpaku Law in 2018 (see chapter 4) enabled Wajin who are not professional hoteliers to Airbnb their rooms to travelers. Foreign tourism has even opened the doors of the "Japanese Only" public bathhouses (see chapter 3) that were once so steadfastly xenophobic, now seeing foreign customers as crucial to their survival.[51]

Accordingly, Japan has been rebranding itself as open to outsiders. Its "international face" was famously shown to the world through a Visible Minority, French Japanese Takigawa Christel, who was appointed as Tōkyō's Bid Ambassador for the 2020 Olympics. Her flawless multilingual presentation before the IOC in 2013, touting Japan's "unique welcome" of "spirit of selfless hospitality" (using the hitherto relatively obscure word *omotenashi*), is widely credited for clinching Tōkyō's bid.[52] Japan even portrayed itself in English as a "land of harmonious diversity" (!) at the Expo Milano 2015, complemented by a series of English-language "We are

Tomodachi" internet newsletters from the Prime Minister's Office of Global Communications, that purposefully advertise Japan as a "friend" (*tomodachi*) to the world.[53]

That said, old habits and narratives die hard. Policies of segregation (e.g., separate facilities) have been seen in "Foreigners Only" information booths and taxi stands (some reportedly refusing service to Japanese-speaking Visible Minorities), "Foreigners Only" hotels and hotel floors, and "Japanese Only" establishments continuing their policies excluding "foreigners" on sight (some included as updates to chapter 3).[54] Local governments have sometimes taken it upon themselves to decide what constitutes "omotenashi," often misinterpreting it, according to one cultural services expert, "to force predetermined services on foreign visitors."[55] And municipalities have also reverted to stereotyping and prejudicial language in their official publications for and about foreign tourists.[56]

MAINTENANCE OF THE STATUS QUO

However, even with all this dissent and progress, the fundamental issue of this research has not changed. Japan still does not have a law against racial discrimination. Why?

One reason may be the disorganization or disagreement among its proponents: For example, the Japan Federation of Bar Associations (*Nichibenren*) and the Japan Civil Liberties Union, despite decades of meetings and discussion sessions,[57] have been unable to agree upon a concrete law drafted by lawyers educated and experienced in human rights matters to outlaw racism.[58] Moreover, on the grassroots level, disorganization has been a problem: I have attended dozens of "coexistence with foreigners" meetings and forums that have arrived at no real conclusions, except that the problem is "difficult" (*muzukashii*) or "complicated" (*fukuzatsu*), and that even more deliberation is necessary.[59]

There is also the issue of conflicting messages from high-profile Non-Wajin, immigrants, and Visible Minorities themselves. This book has already mentioned people who dismiss Wajin racism as merely "a few bad apples" (such as Ōsaka Naomi), portray foreigners as "disloyal criminals" (such as Donald Keene), or decline to push for the rights of fellow Visible Minorities (such as former MP Tsurunen Marutei). There are others who in their twilight of their careers begin collaborating with Wajin narratives, including parroting historical revisionism,[60] offering uninformed opinions about Non-Wajin activism,[61] or denying that Wajin racism even exists.[62] As seen in decades of discordant political efforts by Japan's Left in general (e.g., as of this writing, they have only held the PM post for six of the seventy-six years since the end of World War II), these activities fracture social movements and enable maintenance of the status quo through "divide-and-conquer" tactics.[63]

Another reason may be the public perception that, although there are many other officially recognized types of discrimination in Japan, "racial discrimination" does not affect Wajin—because "race" in Japan's allegedly monoethnic, homogeneous society is moot, and there are no Visible Minorities who need protection as citizens. There is not only a lack of "sense of urgency" among Wajin to fix the "problem," but also a lack of sense in the dominant discourse that there is "a problem" for *kokumin* (the express focus of most GOJ policies) at all. This is best substantiated in the GOJ's official arguments to the UN that explicitly say that racial discrimination is not an issue in Japan.

OFFICIAL ARGUMENTS DEFENDING THE STATUS QUO, AS EXPRESSED TO THE UN

Having ratified the UN CERD in 1996, and the ICCPR in 1979, the GOJ is required as a State Party to submit reports periodically to the respective UN committees on what measures Japan has taken to guarantee civil rights for minorities and to eliminate racial discrimination.[64] Although the CERD requires regular reports every two years, the GOJ missed its first deadline in 1998. After submitting a combined first and second report in June 1999, the GOJ submitted no more reports for nearly a decade, when it released a combined third, fourth, fifth, and sixth report in 2008.[65] In February 2010, Japan came under review by the newly formed Human Rights Council, and the GOJ restated its arguments that discrimination was "not rampant" in Japan.[66] Significantly, the GOJ has continuously stated that a racial discrimination law would have deleterious effects on Japanese society, including infringement on Japan's freedom of speech (the same argument later used to defang the Hate Speech Act; more below).

The debates that ensued between the CERD Committee's 2001 reply to Japan's 1999 report, and the GOJ's response to that, are indicative of past and future patterns of GOJ arguments justifying the status quo. The first section of this chapter will focus on this first series of exchanges. The second section will discuss the combined third, fourth, fifth, and sixth GOJ report submitted in 2008, offering commentary on subtext and assumptions grounding status quo arguments despite UN scrutiny. The third section will demonstrate how negotiations between the UN and the GOJ in February 2010 reached an impasse. Then I will outline the latent "blind spots" on both sides regarding the treatment of noncitizens in Japan as "temporary migrant workers," not immigrants. Comments and analysis will conclude this chapter.

For ease of reading and understanding of the flow of each side's arguments, excerpts of official text from the GOJ and the UN follow in bordered boxes, interspliced as if in a conversation, with sections that warrant attention highlighted by the author in italics.

THE UN-GOJ DEBATES 1999–2001

JAPAN'S FIRST AND SECOND PERIODICAL REPORT ON HUMAN RIGHTS, SUBMITTED [BY THE GOJ] TO THE INTERNATIONAL CONVENTION ON RACIAL DISCRIMINATION, GENEVA, SWITZERLAND, JUNE 1999[67]

GOJ: Respect for Fundamental Human Rights in the Constitution of Japan

3. . . . Foreign residents in Japan are also guaranteed fundamental human rights under the Constitution *except the rights which, owing to their nature, are interpreted to be applicable only to Japanese nationals (*1).*

4. . . . Furthermore, in cases where the rights of the people are infringed, the Court can offer them redress. (Article 32 of the Constitution provides that "no person shall be denied the right of access to the courts.")

(*1 [GOJ Footnote]) In this report, the fact that the treatment of foreigners in Japan has been focused on *does not mean that Japan considers distinction based on nationality as the subject of the Convention.*

Comment: This opening summarizes the GOJ's essential argument that will be further developed below: The GOJ does not interpret the CERD as covering discrimination by nationality, and if there is a human rights problem, Japan's judiciary will offer sufficient redress.

The UN's response to Japan's argument above:

UNITED NATIONS CERD A/56/18 (2001) Report on JAPAN

UN: 159. The Committee considered the initial and second periodic reports of Japan, due on 14 January 1997 and 1999, respectively, at its 1443rd and 1444th meetings (CERD/C/SR.1443 and 1444), on 8 and 9 March 2001. At its 1459th meeting (CERD/C/SR.1459), on 20 March 2001, it adopted the following concluding observations . . .

166. With regard to the interpretation of the definition of racial discrimination contained in article 1 of the Convention, the Committee, contrary to the State

> *party, considers that the term "descent" has its own meaning and is not to be confused with race or ethnic or national origin.* The Committee therefore recommends that the State party ensure the protection against discrimination and the full enjoyment of the civil, political, economic, social and cultural rights contained in article 5 of the Convention of all groups, including the Burakumin community.

Comment: The UN in its response is bringing in the issue of "descent" (in other words, issues of discrimination due to one's ancestry, which includes social/national/historical origin, which the UN argues is also covered by the CERD). This is because Japan's First and Second Report do not mention the Burakumin as part of the people in Japan being protected by the CERD (which was undoubtedly pointed out by Burakumin activists before the UN drafted this response). Thus, the debate is suffering from differences in definition between the UN and the GOJ, which the GOJ exploits in the debate:

Japan's response to the UN's argument above:

> COMMENTS OF THE JAPANESE GOVERNMENT ON THE CONCLUDING OBSERVATIONS ADOPTED BY THE COMMITTEE ON THE ELIMINATION OF RACIAL DISCRIMINATION ON MARCH 20, 2001, REGARDING INITIAL AND SECOND PERIODIC REPORT OF THE JAPANESE GOVERNMENT
>
> GOJ: (2) . . . we consider the scope of application of the Convention as follows.
>
> a. In the first place, Article 1(1) of the Convention provides "racial discrimination" subject to the Convention as "all distinctions based on race, color, descent, or national or ethnic origin. . . ." Therefore, the Convention is considered to cover *discrimination against groups of people who are generally considered to share biological characteristics*, groups of people who are generally considered to share cultural characteristics and individuals belonging to these groups based on the reason of having these characteristics. *Those who live in Okinawa prefecture or natives of Okinawa are of the Japanese race, and generally, in the same way as natives of other prefectures, they are not considered to be a group of people who share biological or cultural characteristics under social convention, and therefore, we do not consider them to be covered by the Convention.*
>
> b. Furthermore, concerning "descent" provided in Article 1(1) of this Convention, in the process of deliberation on the Convention, *there was the problem that the words "national origin" may lead to the misunderstanding that the words include the concept of "nationality" which is a concept based on legal status.* In order to solve the problem, "descent" was proposed together with "place

of origin" as a replacement for "national origin." However, we know that the wording was not sufficiently arranged after that, and "descent" remained in this provision.

Based on such deliberation process, in application of the Convention, *"descent" indicates a concept focusing on the race or skin color of a past generation, or the national or ethnic origins of a past generation, and it is not understood as indicating a concept focusing on social origin.*

At the same time, with regard to the Dowa issue *(discrimination against the Burakumin), the Japanese government believes that "Dowa people are not a different race or a different ethnic group, and they belong to the Japanese race and are Japanese nationals without question."*

Comment: The GOJ is using the term "descent" and invalidating it for coverage under the CERD due to a definitional spur covering "national origin" (an ancestral status), saying this could be interpreted to mean "nationality" (a current legal status)—something the GOJ argues is not covered in a treaty covering biologically based distinctions. By focusing on these biological distinctions, the GOJ asserts that Okinawans and Ainu are not covered by the CERD because (a) they are not biologically different (regardless of their historical or social origin), and (b) they are Japanese citizens. Thus, to the GOJ they are Wajin, undifferentiated from any Japanese citizen due to their legal status.

As for noncitizens, they are not covered by the CERD because the GOJ does not consider "distinction based on nationality" to be covered by the CERD. So that leaves out the Zainichi Koreans, Chinese, and everyone else without Japanese citizenship.

Nowhere else in this exchange above or below does the GOJ or the UN bring up the issue of Visible Minorities who are citizens (such as naturalized citizens and Wajin children of international marriages), who might need the protection of the CERD. The presumption is that there is no Japanese citizen in Japan who is racially different in a biological sense. Essentially, the GOJ is arguing that the CERD covers nobody in Japan.

The GOJ continues in the same vein regarding issues of historical/social origin, particularly in regard to the Burakumin:

GOJ: 3.(1) With regard to the meaning of "descent" in Article 1(1) of the Convention mentioned in paragraph 8, the Japanese government's understanding is as described in the above 1(2)(b), and therefore, *the government does not share the interpretation of "descent" with the Committee.* (2) At any rate, on the basis of the spirit declared in the preamble of the Convention, we take it for granted that no discrimination should be conducted including discrimination such as the Dowa issue (discrimination against the Burakumin). For those related to the Burakumin, *the Constitution of Japan stipulates not only guarantee of being equal as Japanese nationals under the law but also guarantee of equality of all rights as Japanese nationals. Therefore, there is no discrimination at all for civil, political, economic and cultural rights under the legal system.*

Comment: Therefore: "The Japanese Constitution guarantees equal rights for Japanese citizens, so rights must in practice be equal for all Japanese and there are no disenfranchised minorities within the Japanese citizenry. If there is any civil, political, economic, or cultural problem, there is equal access to Japanese courts."

However, as the Otaru Onsens Case in chapter 3 demonstrated, discrimination based upon a biologically based visual identification of a Japanese citizen as a "foreigner" did not avail equal protection of the laws under the Constitution of Japan or in Japan's judiciary. (This is before one addresses this official denial by the GOJ of any discrimination toward Burakumin, which is outside the focus of this research.)

The UN addresses the issue of the efficacy of Japan's judiciary toward racial discrimination in a later section: The UN (2001) continues:

UN: 167. The Committee notes with concern that although article 98 of the Constitution provides that treaties ratified by the State party are part of domestic law, *the provisions of the International Convention on the Elimination of All Forms of Racial Discrimination have rarely been referred to by national courts.* In light of the information from the State party that the direct application of treaty provisions is judged in each specific case, taking into consideration the purpose, meaning and wording of the provisions concerned, the Committee seeks clarifying information from the State party on the status of the Convention and its provisions in domestic law.

168. The Committee is concerned that the only provision in the legislation of the State party relevant to the Convention is article 14 of the Constitution. *Taking into account the fact that the Convention is not self-executing, the Committee believes it necessary to adopt specific legislation to outlaw racial discrimination*, in particular in conformity with the provisions of articles 4 and 5 of the Convention.

JAPAN (2001) replies:

GOJ: 4. (1) The government is not in position to make comments on the ideal way of application of provision of the Convention related to individual cases at the courts. When generalizing, *it is not concluded that the courts are reluctant to apply the Convention immediately because there are few cases referring to provision of the Convention in opinions* in consideration of the following: 1) There is a constraint that applying law by the court premises a fact authorized by the court based on facts claimed or evidence submitted by the parties concerned: 2) *Since the purport of the Convention has already been reflected in the provision of domestic law, there are considerable cases in which the conclusion would be the same even if the provision of the Convention itself is not applied.*

Comment: In other words, few decisions handed down by the national courts refer to the CERD because (1) there are few cases brought before the courts requiring a CERD reference, (2) there is not enough evidence brought before them to back up claims of racial discrimination, and (3) the essence of the CERD is already enshrined in domestic law, so the outcome of these cases would be the same even if the CERD would have been referred to. It is unclear what "domestic laws reflect the purport of the CERD" as Japan has no anti-*racial* discrimination laws. Moreover, the outcome of the McGowan Case in chapter 3 calls that claim into question. The GOJ continues:

GOJ: (2) With regard to status of both the Convention and provisions thereof in domestic law, Article 98, Paragraph 2 of the Constitution of Japan provides that "The treaties concluded by Japan and established laws of nations shall be faithfully observed." Therefore, *treaties, etc. which Japan concluded and published have effect as domestic law.* There is no express provision concerning relation between treaties concluded by Japan and laws in the Constitution of Japan, however *treaties are considered to be superior to laws.* However, since the substantive provision of the Convention (Article 2 to 7) provides "the States Parties undertake . . . ," *the Convention shall be considered not originally to establish individual rights and obligations but to place an obligation of elimination of racial discrimination on the States Parties.* Japan has been fulfilling the obligations which the Convention places on the States Parties as reported in the initial and second periodic report of the Japanese Government.

Comment: This is a contradiction. As noted in the Bortz Case, in Japan treaties have the same force of domestic law in the absence of a specific law in Japan; this is how the judge was able to apply the CERD to protect Ana Bortz's individual right to be protected against racial discrimination. However, according to the GOJ above, due to the alleged wording of the CERD, the CERD is not to be interpreted as a law protecting individuals against racial discrimination, rather as a series of goals for Japan to undertake (i.e., "an obligation of elimination," with no binding timeline for eliminating, despite the UN's exhortations to "adopt specific legislation"). The GOJ claims that even without adopting a specific law, it has been fulfilling its goals, in its own way, in its (late and sporadic) periodic reports to the UN. The UN (2001) continues:

> UN: 169. The Committee notes the reservation maintained by the State party with respect to article 4 (a) and (b) of the Convention, stating that "Japan fulfils the obligations under those provisions to the extent that fulfilment . . . is compatible with the guarantee of the rights to freedom of assembly, association and expression and other rights under the Constitution of Japan." The Committee expresses concern that such an interpretation is in conflict with the State party's obligations under article 4 of the Convention. The Committee draws the attention of the State party to its general recommendations VII and XV, according to which article 4 is of mandatory nature, *given the non-self-executing character of all its provisions, and the prohibition of the dissemination of all ideas based upon racial superiority or hatred is compatible with the rights to freedom of opinion and expression.*

JAPAN replies:

> GOJ: 5. Paragraph 10 of the concluding observations
>
> (1) Article 4 (a) and (b) put the States Parties under an obligation of penalization, however, as mentioned in 6 below, Japan puts reservation stating that the country fulfils obligations of Article 4 as long as it does not conflict with the Constitution. Since Article 4(c) does not provide any concrete measures which the States Parties should take, it is understood to be left to the rational discretion of each States Party.
>
> Also, the preamble of Article 5 states, "In compliance with the fundamental obligations laid down in Article 2 of this Convention . . . ," therefore, it is understood as not exceeding the scope of obligations provided in Article 2. However, on the other hand, as *it is obvious from the provision "by all appropriate means" in Article 2 (1), legislative measures are required by circumstances and are requested to be taken when the States Parties consider legislation appropriate. We do not recognize that the present situation of Japan is one in which discriminative acts cannot be effectively restrained by the existing legal system and in which explicit racial discriminative acts, which cannot be restrained by measures other than legislation, are conducted. Therefore, penalization of these acts is not considered necessary.*

Comment: In other words, "It is up to the GOJ to determine whether legislation is appropriate. We do not consider it appropriate. We have a judicial system. If there is an alleged issue of racial discrimination, then it should be taken before a court. Therefore Japan does not need a law penalizing racial discrimination." Especially, as per the following line of GOJ arguments, existing antidefamation laws can allegedly accomplish the same task: The UN continues:

> UN: 170. Regarding the prohibition of racial discrimination in general, *the Committee is further concerned that racial discrimination as such is not explicitly and adequately penalized in criminal law.* The Committee recommends the State party to consider giving full effect to the provisions of the Convention in its domestic legal order and to ensure the penalization of racial discrimination as well as the access to effective protection and remedies through the competent national tribunals and other State institutions against any acts of racial discrimination.

JAPAN replies:

> GOJ: 6. Expression of concern by the Committee about reservation of Article 4 (a) and (b) in paragraph 11: We are sufficiently aware of General Recommendations VII and XV of the Committee on the Elimination of Racial Discrimination. *However, the concept provided by Article 4 may include extremely wide-ranging acts both in various scenes and of various modes. Therefore, to regulate all of them by penal statute exceeding the existing legislation is liable to conflict with guarantees provided by the Constitution of Japan such as freedom of expression,* which severely requires both necessity and rationality of the constraint, and the principle of the legality of crimes and punishment, which requests both concreteness and definiteness of the scope of punishment. For this reason, Japan decided to put reservation on Article 4 (a) and (b).
>
> Also, *the government does not think that Japan is currently in a situation where dissemination of racial discriminatory ideas or incitement of racial discrimination are conducted to the extent that the government must consider taking legislative measures for punishment against dissemination of racial discriminatory idea, etc. at the risk of unjustly atrophying lawful speech by withdrawing the above reservation.*

Comment: By "putting a reservation" on a clause of the CERD, the GOJ is indicating that they signed the CERD in 1995 with a caveat that they would not observe the treaty in this regard.[68] As argued above by the GOJ, discriminatory speech of a racial nature will not be outlawed in Japan because it was seen in 1995 as infringing upon freedom of speech. If said speech winds up being intentionally hurtful or defamatory, then other domestic laws in Japan, unrelated to racial discrimination, would take effect. In sum, the GOJ is arguing its way out of passing a specific anti-racial discrimination law, which is required by the sections of the treaty, even though Japan agreed to those clauses without "putting a reservation" on them.

Nevertheless, as outlined in this chapter, there are cases of "dissemination of racial discriminatory ideas or incitement of racial discrimination" (including hate speech) in Japan's administrative enforcement of laws, political debate, and media messages. I would argue that this degree of guaranteed "freedom of expression" and "lawful speech" that targets Japan's minorities is in contravention of the CERD.

THE UN-GOJ DEBATES OF 2008

The next overdue report the GOJ submitted to the CERD Committee nearly a decade later made much the same arguments as in 2000. Excerpts (emphases by the author) and commentary follow:

> THE THIRD, FOURTH, FIFTH, AND SIXTH COMBINED PERIODIC REPORT TO THE UNITED NATIONS HUMAN RIGHTS COUNCIL ON THE PROMOTION OF HUMAN RIGHTS IN JAPAN, MARCH 2008.[69]
>
> I. Introduction
>
> *2. Japan has taken every conceivable measure to fight against racial discrimination.*

Comment: One conceivable measure is a law against racial discrimination. This has not been taken.

> *34 . . . The Human Rights Protection Bill, which was repealed in October 2003* and is under further elaboration by the Ministry of Justice, *expressly prohibits any unfair treatment or discriminatory acts based on race, ethnicity and other criteria.* It provides that the independent human rights committee take redress measures in a simple, quick and flexible manner against these human rights abuses, thereby creating a human rights redress system that is more effective than the existing system.

Comment: The GOJ cites the closest thing to a law against racial discrimination, a human rights protection bill, as evidence of a measure against racial discrimination, even though it no longer exists, as it has been repealed. It is unclear how this hypothetical "human rights redress system" can be officially cited as an improvement.

38. The concept laid down in Article 4 may cover an extremely wide range of acts carried out in various situations and in various manners. *Restricting all these acts with punitive laws that go beyond the existing legal system in Japan may conflict with what the Constitution guarantees, including the freedom of expression* that strictly demands the necessity and rationale for its restrictions, and with the principle of legality of crime and punishment that requires concreteness and clarity in determining the punishable acts and penalties. It is on the basis of this judgment that the Japanese Government made its reservations about Article 4 (a) and (b) of the Convention.

In addition, *the Government of Japan does not believe that in present-day Japan racist thoughts are disseminated and racial discrimination are fanned to the extent that would warrant consideration of enactment of laws to administer punishment by retracting the above reservation even at the risk of unduly stifling legitimate speech.*

Japan was advised to retract the reservation it made about Article 4 (a) and (b) in the concluding observations of the Committee on the Elimination of Racial Discrimination in consideration of the Initial and Second Periodic Report. *However, for the reasons given above, Japan does not intend to retract the said reservation.*

Comment: The same "reservations" against creating a racial discrimination law (that of contravening constitutionally guaranteed ideas of freedom of speech) are repeated in this conversation, despite past CERD Committee advisements, and the refusal to retract them is reiterated. Given the situations written above in this chapter, including not only "Japanese Only" signs, but also hate speech disseminated through the published Japanese media, it is unclear how the GOJ can repeat the same argument that the present situation does not warrant improvement.

Thus, the GOJ confuses principle and praxis: It is like saying that few murders are committed in Japan, therefore Japan does not need a law against murder. There is an implicit assumption by the GOJ that racial discrimination simply does not happen in Japan, coupled with a fundamental failure to understand what laws and treaties are for.

Right to utilize Places or Services Intended for Use by the General Public

56. In terms of *equal treatment in using the services at hotels, restaurants, cafes, and theaters, the Law Concerning Proper Management and Promotion of Businesses related to Environment and Hygiene provides that measures should*

be taken to safeguard the benefit for users and consumers at such services. For instance, Centers for Environment and Sanitation Management Guidance ensure proper response to complaints from the consumers.

In particular, *the Hotel Business Law prohibits hotels from refusing a customer merely on the basis of race or ethnicity. Likewise, the Regulations for the Enforcement of the Law for Improvement of International Tourist Hotel Facilities prohibit discriminatory treatment* according to the nationality of guests, such as charging different rates depending on guests' nationality for services such as accommodation and meals provided by registered inns and hotels.

Comment: The citation of the Hotel Business Law as a measure against discrimination is odd given the presence of the "Japanese Only" signs and rules at hundreds of Japanese hotels (see chapter 4). Regarding environment and hygiene issues, as was shown in the Otaru Onsens Case,[70] administrative organs such as the Department of Public Health (*hokensho*) explicitly view their mandate as not enforcing issues of racial discrimination. GOJ assertions are at variance with common practice.

66. Below are examples of civil cases which are recognized as "racial discrimination" cases.

(a) Sapporo District Court Decision on November 11, 2002

A community bathhouse proprietor refused to allow foreign nationals or naturalized citizens to bathe in his bathhouse because they were "foreigners." The proprietor's act was judged as constituting an illegal act of racial discrimination that violated Paragraph 1, Article 14 of the Constitution of Japan, Article 26 of the International Covenant on Civil and Political Rights, and *the spirit of the International Convention on the Elimination of All Forms of Racial \ Discrimination.* Recognizing the tort liability of the defendant, the court granted the plaintiffs right to claim compensation for damages from mental suffering etc.

Comment: This is again at variance with the facts of the case. As outlined in chapter 3, the verdict in the Otaru Onsens Case was not that racial discrimination was the illegal activity, but that the proprietors were "discriminating too much" (*shakaiteki ni kyōyō shiuru gendo o koete iru sabetsu*). The GOJ neglects to mention that the CERD was ruled by the Sapporo District and High Courts as immaterial to the case, and that the Otaru City Government was not held responsible under it. The Supreme Court of Japan, moreover, ruled that the case was not "a Constitutional issue" as well, so citing this case as an effective means of redress under the CERD is disingenuous.

Elsewhere within this report, the GOJ cited eleven other racial discrimination cases involving the following claims and outcomes: racist prison treatment (plaintiff's claim partially affirmed against the individual, not the state), a cancelled housing contract (plaintiff's claim affirmed because the contract was legally binding), Ainu defamation in a publication (plaintiff's claim dismissed due to a lack of tort liability for members of an ethnic minority), a bank loan refusal (plaintiff's claim dismissed due to lack of tort liability), a golf membership refusal (plaintiff's claim dismissed due to freedom of assembly), a denied national pension (plaintiff's claim dismissed as inapplicable to international treaty), rejection from housing (plaintiff's claim dismissed as inapplicable under the CERD), three contract nullifications (plaintiffs' claims dismissed as unrelated to nationality or race), harsh working conditions (plaintiff's claim partially affirmed tort liability). Hence even by the GOJ's own reports, the CERD is not being enforced in Japan's judiciary.

THE 2010 DEBATES BETWEEN THE GOJ AND THE HUMAN RIGHTS COUNCIL REACH AN IMPASSE

On February 24 and 25, 2010, the GOJ and the CERD Human Rights Council met in Geneva for a review of Japan's human rights record in its 76th Session. Although attended by a large Japanese delegation (fourteen representatives of five GOJ ministries), the contents were again basically a retread of the previous CERD sessions. In oral arguments, the GOJ stressed again, illogically, "[I]f the present circumstances in Japan cannot effectively suppress the act of discrimination under the existing legal system, I don't think that the current situation [necessitates] legislating a law in particular for racial discrimination." The UN scolded again, "I think it would be difficult to say that the views of CERD and of the Japanese government have converged in any substantial degree since the time when we last considered the Japanese periodic report." "There has been no real change between 2001 and today." "It seems that [Japan] prefers to avoid [racism or racial discrimination] as a term."[71]

The exchanges in this meeting mostly focused upon, if not became bogged down in, complicated minority issues, including the definition and distinction of the Burakumin, the complicated taxation status of Korean ethnic schools, whether the Ryūkyūans were a genuine ethnic minority, and whether the Ainu's political position in society had been advanced with their new ethnic minority status recently granted by the GOJ. Significantly less mention was made of the CERD's nonenforcement in Japan's judiciary and criminal code. Almost no mention was made of the "Japanese Only" signs extant nationwide around Japan—arguably the most undeniable violation of the CERD.

Moreover, the Human Rights Council overlooked a perennial "blind spot" in both parties' perception of Japan's "minorities." Noncitizen residents were never couched as residents of or immigrants to Japan, but rather as "foreign migrants." This belied embedded and unconscious assumptions that (1) "Oldcomers" (e.g., the Zainichi) were more worthy of attention than "Newcomers" (e.g., residents from overseas), (2) "foreign migrants" have a "temporary status" in Japan (particularly when the GOJ portrayed Japan's ethnic schools as for "foreign children which are in Japan only for the short stay"), and (3) Japan has few biologically or ethnically diverse Japanese citizens, who might also be visually identified and treated adversely by Japanese society as "foreign."

In other words, similar to the academic analysis discussed in chapter 2, both the UN and the GOJ are blind to the existence of Visible Minorities in Japan.

THE 2018 HUMAN RIGHTS COUNCIL CERD COMMITTEE REPORT ON JAPAN

For this Second Edition, Japan submitted another combined tenth and eleventh periodic report for Universal Periodic Review in March 2018, with the UN issuing a final report (CERD/C/JPN/CO/10-11) on September 26, 2018. The debates[72] and final report[73] are again instructive. The March discussion focused on rights for women and children and did not mention discrimination by race, ethnicity, or nationality. When this was pointed out by NGO IMADR, the GOJ reiterated previous arguments that minorities (as citizens, and only mentioning the Okinawans and Ainu) enjoy equal rights under the law. Thus, once again the more subtle issues of racial discrimination raised in this research were completely ignored.

Regarding those issues, 2018's final report once again repeated the UN's previous criticisms: "The Committee regrets that, despite its previous recommendations, the definition of racial discrimination in the Constitution is still not in line with article 1 of the Convention [which includes the grounds of national or ethnic origin, color, and descent], and that there is still no comprehensive legislation prohibiting racial discrimination in the State party." It also pointed out issues brought up throughout part III of this book: "Hate speech through the Internet and the media, and the use of hate speech and discriminatory statements by public officials, continue; Such crimes are not consistently investigated and prosecuted, and public officials and private individuals remain unaccountable for racist hate speech and hate crimes."

The UN also addressed other issues brought up passim in this research, including Foreigner Suffrage, the Nationality Clause in employment, GOJ targeted surveillance of Muslims, exclusionary housing, the systemic disenfranchisement of Zainichi and noncitizens, unstable visa statuses (particularly for "Trainees"), and poignantly:

> 33(b) The Committee is concerned that . . . [f]oreign nationals and individuals with a foreign appearance have reportedly been denied entry to and services of certain privately owned facilities like hotels and restaurants that otherwise serve the public, including through the posting of signage reading "Japanese only."

The report once again urged Japan to inter alia, "adopt specific comprehensive legislation prohibiting direct and indirect racial discrimination," and "establish a national human rights institution with a broad mandate to promote and protect human rights."

After these decades of embarrassing official intransigence toward international human rights bodies, I remain unoptimistic that the situation will change, especially in light of the persistent invisibility of minorities in GOJ arguments. Let us now consider how minorities are invisible in GOJ domestic enforcement of human rights practices, particularly through official oversight agencies:

OFFICIAL ADMINISTRATIVE NEGLIGENCE TOWARD NONCITIZENS AND VISIBLE MINORITIES: THE MANDATE OF THE MOJ, BUREAU OF HUMAN RIGHTS

In cases of human rights violations, the MOJ has an oversight organ called the Bureau of Human Rights (*jinken yōgobu*, or BOHR), which the GOJ frequently cites in reports to the UN as evidence that Japan is respecting its international treaty obligations.[74] Consider an excerpt of the BOHR's official mandate for overseas consumption (*English original*)[75]:

> The activities of the human rights organs of the Ministry of Justice can be divided into the following areas: human rights promotion, human rights counseling, investigation and resolution of human rights infringement cases, and the civil legal aid system.

(1) Human Rights Promotion

The human rights organs of the Ministry of Justice have been carrying out various activities to improve each citizen's awareness and understanding of human rights . . .

(2) Human Rights Counseling

Human Rights Counseling Offices have been established by the human rights organs of the Ministry of Justice as places of consultation where questions in daily life over whether an issue is a human rights problem or whether legal measures are possible can be asked without reservation . . .

In addition, for foreign nationals who cannot speak Japanese fluently, Human Rights Counseling Offices for Foreigners are held in the legal affairs bureaus and district legal affairs bureaus in Tokyo, Osaka, Kobe, Nagoya, Hiroshima, Fukuoka, Takamatsu, and Matsuyama, where interpreters proficient in English and Chinese [and other languages][76] are posted. Other legal affairs bureaus and district legal affairs bureaus open special human rights counseling offices for foreigners whenever necessary, such as during Human Rights Week [each year, the week ending on December 10, the U.N.-designated "Human Rights Day"].

(3) Human Rights Infringement Cases

1) Investigation and Resolution of Human Rights Infringement Cases

. . . If human rights infringement is confirmed as a result of investigation, one of seven relief measures is taken, which include legal advice as "assistance," "conciliation" to conciliate the discussions of the parties concerned, and strict measures against the perpetrator such as an accusation or warning. Among the relief measures, assistance and conciliation may be carried out during an investigation, taking effective timing into consideration. In addition, depending on the case, human rights promotion is carried out for the parties concerned.

In regard to "activities for human rights promotion," Item 1 within the BOHR's mandate mentions "Human Rights Week" (*jinken shūkan*) to raise public awareness about human rights. The sixtieth Human Rights Week focused on issues including human rights for women, children, elderly, disabled, Burakumin, Ainu, foreigners, AIDs and leprosy patients, formerly incarcerated criminals, LGBT, homeless, and DPRK victims.[77]

For the purposes of this research, consider how the BOHR represented the issue of discrimination against "foreigners" (translation and notations by the author):[78]

LET'S RESPECT THE HUMAN RIGHTS OF FOREIGNERS

Reflecting the era of Japan's Internationalization in recent years, every year the number of foreigners (*gaikokujin*) staying (*zairyū*—[i.e., not "resident" *zaijū* or *kyojū*]) in our country (*wagakuni*) has been increasing. According to the Constitution, and by the nature of the rights of man, and leaving out the interpretation that the Constitution only applies to Japanese citizens [*sic*], foreigners staying in our country also are guaranteed fundamental human rights. However, in practice, our country has had issues originating in history towards the Zainichi North and South Koreans [*sic—Chinese/Taiwanese etc. are not included*]. There are also various incidents of human-rights problems with foreigners facing discrimination in the workplace, as well as being refused apartments, entry into eating and drinking establishments, and public baths. This is due to differences in language, religion, and lifestyle customs [*sic—not also race*].

Our country effected the United Nations Convention on the Elimination of All Forms of Racial Discrimination in January 1996, which demands that we take further action towards the elimination of racial discrimination and discrimination by nationality.

As Japan's internationalization is anticipated to further proceed from now on, it is desirable that we respect the customs of foreigners, and as a member of the international society we accept diversity.

The Ministry of Justice Bureau of Human Rights as an organization will develop enlightenment activities that will cultivate an awareness of human rights suitable for Japan's international era, where all citizens (*kokumin*) here or abroad will deepen their understanding and awareness of all human rights problems.

Interpreting the Mandate of the BOHR

There are three embedded discursive issues relating to the national narrative discussed earlier in this chapter. First, the BOHR still couches discrimination in terms of *nationality*, not as race or national origin. Second, the issue is still couched in terms of "us" and "them": our citizens and then those foreigners with embedded "differences in language, religion, and lifestyle customs." Semantically, it is not clear that foreigners are residents of Japan, as they are only "staying" (*zairyū*) as opposed to "residing" (*zaijū*). Third, there is still no call from the BOHR for an actual law outlawing racial discrimination—calling only for the "respect" for "foreigners" by "citizens." This official statement thus differentiates the audience into Insider and Outsider, with the intended audience the Self, not the Other. In terms of obligations, it also calls for the Self to grant their respect to the Other, not to empower the Other to claim their rights. Also note that it shifts responsibility to the Self as individuals to respect human rights, implicitly absolving the government of any responsibility of enforcement.[79]

Now let us consider issues of enforcement of the BOHR's mandate. Also not clearly mentioned in the English version of the BOHR write-up (the original Japanese is clearer) is that although the BOHR has the mandate to "survey" (*chōsa*) the situation to recommend "relief measures" (*kyūsai*), these have amounted to little more than contacting the alleged discriminator, hearing his or her side of the story, and then carrying out "enlightenment" (*keihatsu*), that is, advising them to stop discriminating (see below). However, the BOHR has no teeth: Its official mandate stops at "explaining to" (*setsuji*) or "advising" (*kankoku*) adjudged discriminators to stop discriminating. As officials will tell applicants immediately and clearly during "consultations" (*sōdan*),[80] it has no "power to compel" (*kyōsei ryoku*) discriminators to stop discriminating—no policing power backed up by criminal law that could include fines, suspension of operating license, or arrest (the highest "relief" the BOHR can undertake is to "expose" (*kokuhatsu*) a case to a criminal court).[81]

The UN is aware of this. In its November 1998 report on Japan, the Committee on Civil and Political Rights (CCPR/C/79/Add.102) stated:

> 9. The Committee is concerned about the lack of institutional mechanisms available for investigating violations of human rights and for providing redress to the complainants. Effective institutional mechanisms are required to ensure that the authorities do not abuse their power and that they respect the rights of individuals in practice. The Committee is of the view that the Civil Liberties Commission [i.e., the BOHR] is not such a mechanism, since it is supervised by the Ministry of Justice and its powers are strictly limited to issuing recommendations. The Committee strongly recommends to the State party to set up an independent mechanism for investigating complaints of violations of human rights.
>
> 10. The Committee is concerned that there is no independent authority to which complaints of ill-treatment by police or immigration can be addressed . . .
>
> 32. The Committee is concerned that there is no provision for training of judges, prosecutors and administrative officers in human rights under the Covenant.

The Performative Ineffectiveness of the BOHR

Let us consider two cases where the BOHR demonstrated clear ineffectiveness. First, the BOHR Asahikawa Division took up the Monbetsu Case (see chapter 3) of more than 100 exclusionary businesses in 2000, issuing the following letter in endnotes.[82] However, despite this caution, it took more than *twenty years* for the "Japanese Only" signs to come down,[83] and no exclusionary establishment has been further contacted, has lost their operating license, or been threatened with "exposure" to criminal court.

As further evidence of its ineffectuality—in fact, complicity with discriminators—consider the case when the BOHR advised a local government that it has no legal obligation to pass an ordinance against racial discrimination, only suggesting that the city make such ordinance if it considers it necessary. It warrants a close reading, as it is a rare document substantiating a closed-door intragovernmental collaboration, uncovered only because a court case required it as evidence (figure 8.1).

According to figure 8.1, during the Otaru Onsens Case, Otaru City representatives "consulted" (*sōdan*) with BOHR representatives between 11 a.m. and noon on November 11, 1999. According to the underscored portions (handwritten by officials), the BOHR advised the city government that establishing a local ordinance (*jōrei*) against racial discrimination was "okay if necessary" (*hitsuyō de areba tsukureba yoi*), but "even if there is no administrative guidance, then legally there is no penalty" (*gyōsei ga shidō o nani mo shinakute mo sore ni taishi penaruti o hatasareru koto wa hōseijō nai*), and "there is nothing in particular that requires this degree of administrative guidance on the part of local governing bodies" (*jichitai to shite no gyōsei shidō no teido ni tsuite wa toku ne sadame ga nai*). It also indicates that it does not know whether there will be any legal grounds for damages if sued for "negligence" (*fusaku'i*) in court. (This prediction turned out to be correct. See chapter 3.)

This advisement also states clearly that the BOHR's powers are limited only to "enlightenment" and "asking for improvements" (*kaizen it suite yōsei*). This may be a mere statement of fact, that is, that there are no legal obligations to legislate either on the part of the city or the BOHR. Nevertheless, this document contains an unorthodox interpretation of the UN CERD by a GOJ organ specifically entrusted to advise and enforce issues of human rights.[84]

This was a different outcome from my requests for reports from the local BOHRs dealing with exclusionary establishments in Misawa and Monbetsu (see chapter 3), both of whom gave me follow-up reports on their "enlightenment" activities. It suggests, in light of the Sapporo BOHR's advice to Otaru that they need not pass a law against racial discrimination, that the BOHR's

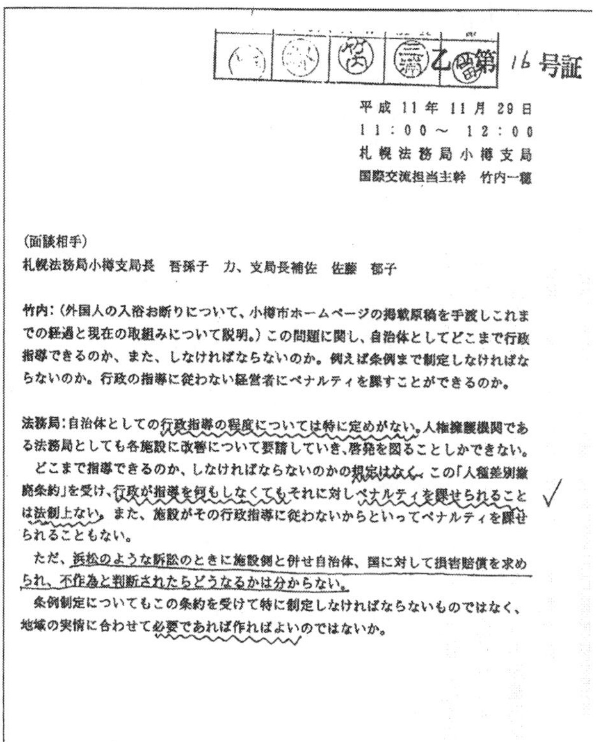

乙第 16 号証

平成 11 年 11 月 29 日
11：00～ 12：00
札幌法務局小樽支局
国際交流担当主幹　竹内一[illegible]

（面談相手）
札幌法務局小樽支局長　吾孫子　力、支局長補佐　佐藤　郁子

竹内：（外国人の入浴お断りについて、小樽市ホームページの掲載原稿を手渡しこれまでの経過と現在の取組みについて説明。）この問題に関し、自治体としてどこまで行政指導できるのか、また、しなければならないのか。例えば条例まで制定しなければならないのか。行政の指導に従わない経営者にペナルティを課すことができるのか。

法務局：自治体としての行政指導の程度については特に定めがない。人権擁護機関である法務局としても各施設に改善について要請していき、啓発を図ることしかできない。
　どこまで指導できるのか、しなければならないのかの規定はなく、この「人種差別撤廃条約」を受け、行政が指導を何もしなくてもそれに対しペナルティを課せられることは法制上ない。また、施設がその行政指導に従わないからといってペナルティを課せられることもない。
　ただ、浜松のような訴訟のときに施設側と併せ自治体、国に対して損害賠償を求められ、不作為と判断されたらどうなるかは分からない。
　条例制定についてもこの条約を受けて特に制定しなければならないものではなく、地域の実情に合わせて必要であれば作ればよいのではないか。

Figure 8.1 Full Text of the Report from the Otaru City Government/Legal Affairs Bureau Otaru Branch, with Signature Seals by Otaru City Government Bureaucrats in the Otaru International Communications Desk. Notations by Otaru City bureaucrats. *Source:* Courtesy of Sapporo District Court records and lawyer Itō Hideko.

oversight mechanisms are only ineffectual, but also insufficiently independent of other government organs to interpret and enforce human rights treaties.[85]

THE GOJ'S HISTORICAL "LACK OF NATIONAL STAKE" IN THE WORLD NARRATIVE ON RACIAL DISCRIMINATION

In fact, Japan has a long history of lack of initiative regarding its obligations under UN agreements vis-à-vis human rights. Peek (1992) notes, "Tokyo holds that human rights issues are a domestic matter and, therefore, beyond the mandate of the UN . . . [Japan] has generally responded defensively to human rights proposals at variance with Japanese law or practice."[86]

In Peek's view, Japan's lack of participation in the incipient stages of the UN's formation (including the Universal Declaration of Human Rights in 1948) led to the lack of "significant national stake in the UN's existing principles and structures," a relative inattention in the political sphere, and an understaffing in the relevant domestic bureaucratic organs. The high-profile tenure of Ogata Sadako as the UN High Commissioner for Refugees notwithstanding, for decades Japan refused to join the UNHCR in the 1960s and 1970s, despite several direct appeals from other countries. Peek argues that the GOJ "feared being drawn into a public denunciation of the human rights policies of any particular state." Even after joining the UNHCR, Japan's interest was in "protecting itself from unwanted or highly politicized criticism," keeping its participation "low-key" and abstemious from ruling on the majority of resolutions within its mandate.

In 1979, after Japan ratified the ICCPR and the International Covenant on Economic, Social, and Cultural Rights, the GOJ continued to oppose (as it had since the 1960s) the establishment of a specific high commissioner to review issues of human rights, arguing the office would be "highly politicized" and lead to bureaucratic inefficiency. Peek noted, "At the core of Japan's position was its objection to any further encroachment on the internal affairs of sovereign nation-states." It also added "reservations" to parts of the covenants (such as the review powers of the ICCPR's Human Rights Committee (HRC)), expressed objections to individuals being able to report claims directly to the HRC (arguing that UN relations are state-to-state), and emphasized the need for "further study" of contentious issues.

The conclusion: Postwar Japan's leadership could not, and most likely (given their UN arguments above) still cannot, accept a fundamental tenet of the UN Charter—that there exists a "universal set of human rights." This cultural relativism at first led to an attitude of "you leave us alone, we'll leave you alone." However, this became less tenable with Japan's ascendancy to the second-largest world economy by the 1980s. As Kashiwazaki notes, Japan coming into prominence "as major player in the world economy . . . with demands from both within and abroad to open, to take a leadership role, . . . to assume international responsibility [and] assume a greater role in international cooperation, and to increase its legitimacy as a competent, advanced Western democracy." However, Kashiwazaki concludes that only with this responsibility came the requirement for Japan to accept a set of international legal norms, the most relevant being "the UN conventions on human rights and the rights of migrant workers and noncitizen residents."[87]

Thus, arguments have been made that many of Japan's human rights reforms were not as a result of bottom-up grassroots-level activism and human rights social movements, but rather created top-down as a matter of opportunistic timing due to outside international pressure (*gaiatsu*) and a geopolitical convergence of interests. For example, Peek mentions the Equal Employment Opportunity Law (*danjo koyō kikai kintō hō*), passed in 1984, which legally guaranteed equal pay for equal work regardless of gender. It was passed into law despite the opposition of women's groups and the opposition parties, who objected to its unenforceability (i.e., no criminal penalties for violators). Peek writes, "The intent of the law seems to have been little more than a symbolic bone tossed to domestic and international critics in anticipation of the upcoming 1985 world conference ending the UN Decade for Women." Peek also notes the revised Nationality Law (granting citizenship through mother as well as father), the ratified Convention on the Elimination of All Forms of Discrimination Against Women as other GOJ "symbolic bones."

Kashiwazaki (2000) adds that *gaiatsu* has profoundly influenced the rights of noncitizens:

> As the only Asian country admitted to membership in the [first G7 Summit in 1975], Japan was obliged to take some steps to accommodate refugees. . . . Although the number of refugees settled in Japan was small, their arrival had a strong impact on the social rights of resident aliens. With the acceptance of refugees, the Japanese government was compelled to join relevant international conventions. Japan acceded to the International Covenant on Civil and Political Rights as well as the International Covenant on Economic, Social, and Cultural, Rights in 1979, and then ratified the Convention relating to the Status of Refugees in 1981. Provisions in these conventions required that resident aliens be treated equally with the citizens of the country in the areas of social security and welfare. Consequently, several legal changes removed eligibility restrictions based on nationality in such areas as national pension and public housing. Furthermore, the creation of a new residential status for refugees in 1981 contributed to improvement in the legal status of preexisting long-term resident aliens.[88]

Even the landmark recognition in 2008 of the Ainu as an indigenous people (and the only recognized ethnic minority in an officially "homogeneous" Japan) is said to have a cynical underpinning. According to Uemura Hideaki, professor of indigenous people's rights at Keisen University, "Japan modernized itself while denying its diversity and multiculturalism. However, the nation, which aspires to a permanent seat on the United Nations Security Council, has already risen to an international stage where they have to acknowledge it."[89] He noted that although Japan was among the 144 nations that supported the Declaration on the Rights of Indigenous Peoples adopted by the UN General Assembly in September 2007, the GOJ stopped short of recognizing the Ainu, claiming that an "official" definition of indigenous people did not exist. Uemura pointed out that it was no coincidence that the 2008 resolution recognizing the Ainu came "just weeks before the Hokkaidō G8 Summit . . . as Japan does not want any protests to detract from the high-profile gathering."

Thus from a historical perspective, the GOJ works on its own timetable in regard to international issues of human rights, joining international agreements when there is "interest convergence" (see appendix 2) due to *gaiatsu*, but makes reforms that do not overwhelmingly affect Japan's "sovereignty" as Japan's governing elites determine it. As Peek notes, the GOJ "has used the defensive tactics of denial of legitimacy, special interpretations, reservations, and symbolic change. It seeks to justify its tactics on the basis of cultural differences. In essence, the Japanese government portrays its policy in terms of protecting the traditional ethic of harmonious human relations against the impersonal ethic of universalism contained in the covenants."[90]

Therefore, to return to our research question, the inevitable conclusion is that a law against racial discrimination in Japan will not be passed in the foreseeable future. And even if one is, it will lack enforcement mechanisms like so many other civil rights laws passed in response to GOJ geopolitical opportunism. Essentially, Japan signs international human rights treaties but finds ways not to enforce them.[91]

CONCLUSIONS

Japan's strong binary narratives on Self (Japanese) and Other (foreigners) have been overtly challenged by peoples, interest groups, and official bodies inside and outside of Japan. Although some concessions have been made to empower outsiders in Japan, the GOJ has successfully managed these challenges to avoid the possibility of "interest convergence" and actual enfranchisement of Non-Wajin, essentially arguing repeatedly before international audiences such as the UN (in tones of obfuscatory exceptionalism) that the Wajin-dominated power structure must be perpetuated to maintain Japan's social order. This has been accomplished in part due to (in ways similar to the worldwide scholarship on Japan discussed passim in this book) the "blind spots" that the GOJ and international bodies have toward hundreds of thousands of disenfranchised residents of Japan. They are blind not only toward Japan's "migrant worker" population (i.e., not viewing them as "immigrants") but also toward the existence of Japan's Visible Minorities.

Chapter 9 will now take this research's concept of Embedded Racism for a test drive, showing how its use as a methodological lens will better enable scholars to see how Japan's racialization processes have been overlooked in Japanese Studies.

NOTES

1. "UN independent investigator raps Japan for Discrimination." *Voice of America*, July 11, 2005; "Japan racism 'deep and profound.'" *BBC News*, July 11, 2005; "U.N. calls for antidiscrimination law." *Japan Times*, July 12, 2005; "Antidiscrimination law needed: Racism rapporteur repeats criticism." *Japan Times*, May 18, 2006.

2. *See*, for example, "Sour Strawberries" (2008); "NOVA fallout." *Asahi Weekly*, November 8, 2007; "The decline and fall of NOVA: Japan's largest employer of foreigners comes to an ignominious end." *Metropolis Magazine*, November 9, 2007; "Talks drag on, teachers fired in Berlitz case." *Japan Times*, July 27, 2010; "Courts back workers' rock-solid right to strike." *Japan Times*, July 17, 2012; "Berlitz union wins raise, bonus in suit settlement." *Japan Times*, January 1, 2013; "Nova founder ordered to pay damages to former students." *Kyōdō News*, February 28, 2014.

3. *See*, for example, "An NGO reaches out to bullied foreign kids." *Japan Times*, November 28, 2008; "Group drawing on long-term foreign residents to help newcomers navigate life in Japan." *Japan Times*, January 10, 2017; *Ijūren's Living Together with Migrants and Ethnic Minorities in Japan: NGO Policy Proposals*, English and Japanese (2007); an example of free legal consultations in Sapporo archived at www.debito.org/?p=2400, and in Tōkyō at www.debito.org/?p=1683.

4. *See*, for example, O'Day 2015. That said, SEALDs disbanded soon after its core leadership graduated from elite colleges, due in part to internal ideological disagreements, but also because its core leadership was entering the job market and was unwilling to hand the brand name down to a younger generation. This had the unfortunate effect of making the movement look more like it was manned by hobbyists than dedicated long-term activists. *See* "Should SEALDs student activists worry about not getting hired?" *Japan Times*, August 30, 2015, commentary at www.debito.org/?p=13768. "Anti-war student organization to close shop after Upper House poll." *Japan Times*, October 28, 2015, commentary at www.debito.org/?p=13663.

5. *See*, for example, "Info on Black Lives Matter demos in Japan in response to excessive police force towards a Kurdish Resident." *Debito.org*, June 7, 2020, www.debito.org/?p=16105; "Black Lives Matter spreads to Tokyo as 3,500 people march to protest racism." *Japan Times*, June 14, 2020; "A summer of solidarity: Looking back on the Black Lives Matter marches in Japan." *Japan Times*, December 21, 2020; and so on.

6. *See*, for example, "*Gaikokujin rōdōsha no taigū kaizen no yukue wa*?" [What is the direction of improved treatment for foreign workers?]. *Tōkyō Shinbun*, December 3, 2006; "Gifu firms warned on Brazilian child labor." *Kyodo News*, December 30, 2006; "Government split over foreign trainee program." *Yomiuri Shinbun*, May 19, 2007; and so on.

7. Text of the *Hamamatsu Sengen* (2001) and analysis archived at www.debito.org/hamamatsusengen.html.

8. *See*, for example, "Grants eyed to help foreigners settle." *Asahi Shinbun*, March 9, 2007.

9. Diene's reports and analysis at www.debito.org/rapporteur.html.

10. Human Rights Council, Working Group on the Universal Periodic Review, Second Session, Geneva, May 5–19, 2008, draft report A/HRC/WG.6/2/L.10, May 14, 2008, www.upr-info.org/IMG/pdf/UPR-_Japan_WG_report__text.pdf [dead link].

11. *See*, for example, "US State Department 2018 Country Reports on Human Rights Practices, Japan: Highlights for Debito.org Readers." *Debito.org*, July 9, 2019, www.debito.org/?p=15599; "UN: Committee on the Elimination of Racial Discrimination considers report of Japan 2014: Little progress made." *Debito.org*, August 31, 2014, www.debito.org/?p=12611; "United Nations demands Tokyo introduce anti-discrimination law to counter hate speech (HRC report CCPR/C/JPN/CO/6 text included in full, citing 'Japanese Only' signs)." *Debito.org*, August 22, 2014, www.debito.org/?p=12598; "UN News: 'Independent UN experts seriously concerned about Japan's Special Secrets Bill.' Fine, but too late." *Debito.org*, November 22, 2013, www.debito.org/?p=11989; "Kyodo: UN HRC prods Japan on sex slaves, gallows. But the elephant in the room still remains no law against racial discrimination in Japan." *Debito.org*, November 26, 2012, www.debito.org/?p=10730; "GOJ wants seat on the UN Human Rights Council for 2013–2015. Here's MOFA's formal pledge of Japan's commitments to human rights. Note what's missing." *Debito.org*, October 16, 2011, www.debito.org/?p=9534; and so on.

12. "Japanese U.N. diplomat's shouts of 'shut up' to fellow delegates go viral, inflame." *Japan Times*, June 13, 2013, archived with video at www.debito.org/?p=11549.

13. *See*, for example, "'No foreigners' (and no women) Capsule inn Omiya hotel in Saitama withdraws 'Japanese Only' rule." *Debito.org*, August 17, 2014, at www.debito.org/?p=12590; "Japanese Only nightclubs 'W' in Nagoya and newly-opening 'CLUB Leopard' in Hiroshima." *Debito.org*, November 25, 2014, at www.debito.org/?p=12846, and so on. Other places on Debito.org's *Rogues' Gallery of Exclusionary Establishments* also have some cases of signs being removed, at www.debito.org/roguesgallery.html.

On a related note, Takeda Pharmaceuticals Co., Japan's largest drug maker, successfully appointed French citizen Christophe Weber as CEO in 2014 despite objections from shareholders and the Takeda family wanting the leadership roster to be Japanese only. Their objections are by now familiar memes, including putative threats of a "takeover by foreign capital" and "technological transfer overseas," security problems with entrusting "finances or research and development" to a foreigner, damage to the "morale of the Japanese employees," and Weber's purported ignorance of "traditions and corporate culture." *See* "Takeda family protests putting foreigner at drug maker's helm." *Yomiuri Shinbun*, June 22, 2014.

14. *See*, for example, Kobayashi (2009, 2012).

15. *See* inter alia "JAPANESE ONLY J1 *de sabetsu ōdanmaku ka*" [Is the Japanese Only banner at a J1 game really discrimination?]. *Asahi Shinbun*, March 9, 2014; "*Urawa: Gēto de sabetsu teki ōdanmaku ka*" [Urawa Case: Was the banner at the gate discriminatory?]. *Yomiuri Shinbun*, March 9, 2014; "Japanese club remove banner: The Urawa Red Diamonds remove a banner from their home stadium over fears the

sign could be considered racist." *Al-Jazeera* from *AP* and *AFP*, March 9, 2014; "Reds remove banner seen as racist." *Kyodo News*, March 9, 2014; "J.League and media must show red card to racism." *Japan Times*, March 13, 2014; "Urawa Japanese Only soccer banner case: Conclusions and lessons I learned from it." *Debito.org*, March 14, 2014, www.debito.org/?p=12179; "*Sabetsu ōdanmaku: Urawa ni mukankyaku shiai: J riigu hatsu no shobun*" [The discriminatory banner: J-League's first punishment of a game without spectators to Urawa]. *Mainichi Shinbun*, March 13, 2014; "Japanese Only sign sparks bigotry debate." *Reuters*, April 16, 2014; "*Japanese Only ten ni mo, harigami ni kizu zuku gaikokujin.*" [Japanese Only at [tempura] shop too; foreigners hurt by sign]. *Asahi Shinbun*, April 28, 2014; and its significantly different English version: "Japanese Only banner at soccer stadium a microcosm of discrimination in Japan." *Asahi Shinbun*, May 2, 2014; "*Zainichi Korian, Zainichi Chūgokujin to no kyōsei o buchikowasu: Senshinkoku to shite hazukashii heito supīchi*" [Destroying the community of Zainichi Koreans and Chinese: Hate speech that is the shame of a developed country]. *SAPIO*, June 2014; "Japanese football authorities to take no action over racist tweet." *Guardian*, December 2, 2015; and so on.

16. "J.League players to take anti-discrimination classes after racist banner." *Asahi Shinbun*, May 30, 2014, and "J3 player handed three-game ban for racist comments." *Kyodo News*, May 30, 2014, both archived at www.debito.org/?p=12433.

Another good example is Konshō Gakuen, a culinary technical college in Saitama, which had refused all "foreign" students entry since its founding in 1976. Although authorities had been notified since 2012 by rejected students, media pressure in the wake of the "Japanese Only" Urawa Reds match allegedly forced the school to officially repeal its exclusionary rule. *See* "School axes policy of barring foreigners." *Japan Times*, May 23, 2014; "'No foreigners allowed' cooking school backtracks, will accept foreign applicants."/ "*Saitama no senmon gakkō: Gaikokujin nyūgaku kyohi 'kairitsu irai no hōshin'*" [A technical college in Saitama: Refusing admission to foreigners "a policy since the school's founding"]. *Mainichi Shinbun*, both May 23, 2014; "*Saitama no senmon gakkō ga gaikokujin nyūgaku kyohi*" [Saitama technical college refuses foreign entrants]. NHK, May 23, 2014.

17. "Japan Soccer League 2: Did referee Takayama use discriminatory language towards [Japanese-German player] Avispa Fukuoka's Sakai Noriyoshi? Outrage on the Internet." *AOL News*, June 10, 2015, archived at www.debito.org/?p=13354.

18. For example, similar racism happened in a 2015 tweet from an Urawa Reds fan that resulted in no disciplinary action from authorities; without that "official confirmation" of the nature of the incident, media avoided using *jinshu sabetsu* as a term. Or consider how *Mainichi Shinbun*, reporting on a 2018 court victory for a Zainichi Korean against hate speech, did mention *jinshu sabetsu* as a fact of the case in the Japanese version, but then translated it as "ethnic discrimination" in the English version. As noted in the main text, Japanese already has an established word for "ethnic discrimination"—*minzoku sabetsu*—so it is unclear why this editorial change happened. *See* "*Ri Shin'e san, songen kaifuku no tatakai*" [Lee Sin Hae san's battle to restore her dignity]. *Mainichi Shinbun*, March 9, 2018; and "Korean resident of Japan's legal battle for dignity ends in her favor but problems remain." *Mainichi Shinbun*, March 20, 2018, both archived at www.debito.org/?p=14973.

19. *See*, for example, the following articles archived with analysis: "23 percent of Japan's top firms eager to employ more foreigners: survey." *Mainichi Shinbun*, January 4, 2012, www.debito.org/?p=9850; Menjū Toshihiro, "Analysis: Accepting Immigrants: Japan's Last Opportunity for Economic Revival." East-West Center's *Asia Pacific Bulletin*, No. 169. June 27, 2012, www.debito.org/?p=10373; "'Only immigrants can save Japan,'" quoting activist Sakanaka Hidenori. *Japan Times*, October 21, 2012, www.debito.org/?p=10690; "Poll: 81 percent welcome foreigners of Japanese descent." *Kyodo News*, March 2, 2013, www.debito.org/?p=11213; "Japanese Permanent Resident Status to be Awarded to Overseas Students? A New Appeal by the [Governor] of Kyoto." *RocketNews24*, April 15, 2013, www.debito.org/?p=11371; "Japan's public baths hope foreign tourists will help keep the taps running." *Japan Times*, January 5, 2016, www.debito.org/?p=13740; "Japan eyes more foreign workers, stealthily challenging immigration taboo." *Reuters*, April 25, 2016, www.debito.org/?p=13969; "Foreign workers in Japan hit the 1 million mark for the first time last autumn: Ministry." *Japan Times/Reuters*, January 27, 2017, www.debito.org/?p=14474; "Trainee program, small firms drive rise in Japan's foreign worker numbers." *Japan Times/Kyodo News*, February 7, 2017, www.debito.org/?p=14484; "As Japan looks for river of foreign talent, landlords erect a dam: Discrimination could hinder companies hiring more from overseas."

Nikkei Asian Review, August 23, 2017, which notes, "Almost nine of 10 private housing units in Tokyo do not allow foreign tenants"; "Japan sees foreign workers climb to record 1.28 million as labor crunch continues." *Japan Times/Kyodo News*, January 27, 2018, www.debito.org/?p=14879; "Setagaya Ward plans to battle racial, ethnic discrimination." *Asahi Shinbun*, February 28, 2018, www.debito.org/?p=14902; "In rural Japan, immigrants spark a rebirth: Newcomers fill the labor and tax void as young Japanese bolt to Tokyo." *Nikkei Asian Review*, March 21, 2018; "Japan faces challenges as it moves to accept more foreign workers." *Kyodo News*, July 25, 2018, www.debito.org/?p=15107; "*Shukurō Gaikokujin: Tamenteki na yakuwari: Shohisha, nōzeisha to shite mo*" [Editorial: Foreign workers would also serve roles as consumers, taxpayers]. *Mainichi Shinbun*, November 9, 2018, www.debito.org/?p=15206; "Surprising survey results from Pew Research Center: Japan supportive of 'immigration.'" *Debito.org*, January 7, 2019, www.debito.org/?p=15465; "Nike Japan ads featuring Japan's Minorities and Visible Minorities taking solace and courage from doing sports." *Debito.org*, December 2, 2020, www.debito.org/?p=16328; "Nike Japan Does Some Good." *Shingetsu News Agency*, December 21, 2020; and so on.

20. "Author dismisses government's fear mongering myth of crime wave by foreigners." *Mainichi Daily News*, December 21, 2006; "*Gaikokujin, shōnen hanzai wa fuete inai!?*" *Sunday Mainichi*, December 31, 2006.

21. *See*, for example, "In landmark move, Japan to recognize indigenous people." *AFP*, June 4, 2008.

22. *See*, for example, "Gaffe-prone Nakayama quits Cabinet." *Japan Times*, September 29, 2008.

23. "Aso apologizes if 'single-race nation' remark misunderstood." *Asahi Shinbun*, January 14, 2020, archived at www.debito.org/?p=15900.

24. "Tokyo Olympics: dance by Japan's indigenous people dropped from opening ceremony: Move raises questions about status of Ainu ethnic minority, whose cultural identity Japan is legally obliged to protect." *Guardian*, February 21, 2020.

25. *See* the archives of five Cabinet hearings, "*Gaikokujin to no Kyōsei Shakai Jitsugen Kentō Kaigi*" [Meetings to Deliberate the Realization of a Society in Co-Existence with Foreigners], May 24, June 1 and 15, July 3, and August 27, 2012, at the Cabinet Secretariat website at www.cas.go.jp/jp/seisaku/kyousei/index.html (last accessed May 28, 2021).

26. www.tfemploy.go.jp/en/coun/cont_2.html. Unfortunately, the link is dead.

27. *See*, for example, "Allegations that GOJ's Hello Work refuses NJ applicants, as evidenced by 'Japanese Only' employer Zeus Enterprise of Tokyo Ginza." *Debito .org*, October 26, 2010, www.debito.org/?p=7661.

28. "Japan Cabinet minister wary of opening 'Pandora's box' of immigration." *Bloomberg*, May 12, 2015, archived with commentary at www.debito.org/?p=13314.

29. "*Byōdō ni mazushiku narō*" [Let's all become equally impoverished together]. *Chūnichi Shinbun*, February 13, 2017, www.debito.org/?p=14486.

30. "Japan will overhaul Immigration Bureau to create agency for expected surge of blue-collar workers under new status." *Japan Times/Kyodo*, August 28, 2018, with commentary at www.debito.org/?p=15129.

31. "Immigration reforms spell Big Brother, Japan Federation of Bar Associations warns." *Japan Times*, March 26, 2009; "Drawing a bead on illegal residents: New law would tighten up oversight of foreigners." *Japan Times*, June 27, 2009. *See also* Higuchi & Arudou (2013), chapters 1 and 2.

32. "*'Gaikokujin kanshi ni shimin o dōin': Nyukanchō ga zairyū kaado shingi yomitori apuri o ippan kōkai; nanminkon ga mondaishi*" ["Mobilizing citizens to surveil foreigners": Immigration Agency releases to the public an app that can test the validity of Zairyū Cards; refugee support groups see this as problematic]. *Tōkyō Shinbun*, June 15, 2021, archived with commentary at www.debito.org/?p=16688.

33. *See*, for example, "Osaka sign saying 'Stop Scrawling Discriminatory Graffiti.'" *Debito.org*, May 21, 2013, www.debito.org/?p=11496; "Counterdemos against hate speech in Japan, now supported by Olympic fever": *Debito.org*, September 22, 2013, at www.debito.org/?p=11855; "Volunteers remove anti-Korea graffiti in Tokyo's Shinjuku." *Asahi Shinbun*, March 3, 2014; "Hate speech protests spreading to smaller cities around Japan." *Asahi Shinbun*, November 7, 2013, archived at www.debito.org/?p=11968; "Scrubbing anti-foreigner scribbling from Tokyo's streets." *BBC World Service*, March 16, 2014, minute 14:45, at www.bbc .co.uk/programmes/p01v2y22; "Neo-Nazis march in Tokyo Edogawa-ku March 23, 2014, bearing swastika flags!" *Debito.org*, March 24, 2014, at www.debito.org/?p =12218; "Counterdemos against racist rally by Zaitokukai in Osaka Nanba May 11, 2014." *Debito.org*, May 19, 2014, www.debito.org/?p=12399; "Thousands of anti-hate demonstrators take to Tokyo streets." *Mainichi Shinbun*, November 3, 2014, archived at www.debito.org/?p=12794.

34. "Japan needs to get tough on hate speech: UN experts." *Jiji Press*, July 16, 2014; Eric Johnston, "Time for legislation to prevent spread of hate speech." *Japan Times*, July 18, 2014; "Japanese high court upholds ruling against anti-Korean

activists' hate speech." *Kyodo News*, July 8, 2014; "Asahi & Mainichi: 'No Hate,' 'No Racism,' 'Refugees Welcome' say protesters at Tokyo anti-discrimination rally." *Debito.org*, November 25, 2015, www.debito.org/?p=13675.

35. "Osaka mayor gets into shouting match with head of anti-Korean group." *Kyodo News*, October 21, 2014, with commentary at www.debito.org/?p=12772.

36. "JDP: Abe criticizes rise of hate speech in Japan, calls it 'dishonorable' and counter to 'The Japanese Way of thinking.'" *Debito.org*, May 9, 2013, www.debito.org/?p=11443.

37. "Diet passes Japan's first law to curb hate speech." *Japan Times*, May 24, 2016.

38. "Editorial: To end hate speech, Japan must face its deep-rooted discriminatory thinking." *Mainichi Shinbun*, June 8, 2017; "Make hate speech law stronger." Editorial, *Japan Times*, June 10, 2017. Here is a more thorough translation, from Higashikawa (2017: 19), of the definition from Article 2 of the Hate Speech Act:

> The term "unjust discriminatory words and deeds against people from outside Japan" as used in this Act means unjust words and deeds used to incite exclusion of people who are from a country or a region outside Japan or their descendants who live in Japan legally (hereinafter referred to as People from Outside Japan) from their local community because of their origin by intimidating them in public through a threat to their life, body, liberty, reputation, or property, or by severely insulting them, with the main purpose of boosting or inducing a sense of discrimination against them.

39. "One month after anti-hate speech law adopted, marches down, language softened." *Mainichi Shinbun*, July 24, 2016, archived at www.debito.org/?p=14139; *Japan Times*, June 10, 2017, ibid. "A year after enactment of hate speech law, xenophobic rallies down by nearly half." *Kyodo News/Japan Times*, May 22, 2017; "Ex-hate speech group core member regretful on anniversary of clampdown law." *Mainichi Shinbun*, June 6, 2017, archived with commentary at www.debito.org/?p=14648.

40. "Editorial: Japan needs effective hate speech law to stamp out racist marches." *Mainichi Shinbun*, April 11, 2016, archived at www.debito.org/?p=13933; "Japan's laws against hate speech piecemeal, lack teeth." *Japan Times/Kyodo News*, October 12, 2016.

41. "Kyoto District Court orders anti-Korean Zaitokukai to pay damages in first J court decision recognizing hate speech as an illegal form of racial discrimination." *Debito.org*, October 8, 2013, www.debito.org/?p=11890.

42. "Ministry issues hate speech advisory to ex-leader of Zaitokukai." *Asahi Shinbun*, December 23, 2015, archived at www.debito.org/?p=13720; "NPA to crack down on hate speech demonstrators through existing legislation." *Mainichi Shinbun*, June 3, 2016; "Court bans planned anti-Korean hate speech rally in Kawasaki." *Mainichi Shinbun*, June 3, 2016; "Effect of new anti-hate speech law spreads to executive, judicial branches." *Mainichi Shinbun*, June 6, 2016.

43. "Police in Japan place anti-Korean extremist group Zaitokukai on watchlist." *Guardian*, December 4, 2014.

44. Debito Arudou, "Sealing the deal on public meetings: Outdoor gatherings are wrapped in red tape." *Japan Times*, March 4, 2003.

45. *Japan Times*, May 24, 2016, ibid.; *Japan Times/Kyodo News*, October 12, 2016, ibid.

46. Sources for this section include "Anti-Korean racism blemishes beauty brand DHC." *Shingetsu News Agency*, March 22, 2021; "*'NHK wa Nihon no teki desu' DHC kaichō ga seimei, zainichi korian e no sabetsu teki hatsugen hōdō ni hanron*" [NHK is the enemy of Japan, DHC CEO declares, argues against any "discriminatory statements" against Zainichi Koreans]. *Yahoo News Japan/BuzzFeed Japan*, April 9, 2021; "DHC chairman's racist posts lead cities to end partnerships." *Asahi Shinbun*, May 24, 2021, and so on.

47. *See*, for example, "In tough economic times, tourism boss finds visitor boost a tall order." *Japan Times*, November 11, 2008.

48. http://yokosojapan.co.jp.

49. "Cool Japan campaign at a crossroads 10 years after setting sights abroad." *Japan Times*, May 31, 2021.

50. https://webunwto.s3.eu-west-1.amazonaws.com/s3fs-public/2020-10/japan.pdf; and https://asset.japan.travel/image/upload/v1579653938/pdf/Number_of_visitor_arrivals_to_Japan_Annual_total_reaches_31.882_million.pdf.

51. *See*, for example, "Tokyo bathhouses scrub up to lure visitors." *Yomiuri Shinbun*, October 22, 2010, www.debito.org/?p=7654; "Japan's public baths hope foreign tourists will help keep the taps running." *Japan Times*, January 5, 2016, www.debito.org/?p=13740; "More baths OK tattooed visitors; stickers needed [for foreign tourists]"; *Yomiuri Shinbun*, August 25, 2015, www.debito.org/?p=13498, which notes, "With the Olympics and Paralympics scheduled for Tokyo in 2020, some facilities are calling for greater understanding of cultural differences." My, how the worm turns.

52. *See* Takigawa's performance at www.youtube.com/watch?v=6hggygKWwhg&t=15s (accessed May 26, 2021), and the text of her IOC speech in English at www.japanbullet.com/news/speeches-by-tokyo-bid-committee-members-during-final-presentation-to-ioc.

53. "Japan at Expo Milano 2015: Official display claims Japan is a land of 'harmonious diversity' (in English). Seriously? Yep. Let's parse." *Debito.org*, May 7, 2015, www.debito.org/?p=13296; "GOJ's 'We are Tomodachi' Newsletter Vol. 4, June 2014 offers fascinating insights into PM Abe Admin mindsets." *Debito.org*, June 9, 2014, www.debito.org/?p=12448.

54. *See*, for example, "*Chūgokujin kyaku sen'yō hoteru . . . Sapporo ni kyō kaigyō*" [Hotel exclusively for Chinese customers opens today in Sapporo]. *Yomiuri Shinbun*, June 1, 2010, www.debito.org/?p=6864; "Maori woman refused entry to bath due to traditional tattoos." *Kyodo News*, September 12, 2013, www.debito.org/?p=11858; "Tokyo bathhouses look to tap foreigners but ensure they behave." *Kyodo News*, December 30, 2013, www.debito.org/?p=12041; "Mainichi: Discrimination against NJ in housing rentals highlighted in Tokyo Govt survey; like 'Tokyo Sharehouse' with its new Tokyo-wide system of Japanese-Only rentals?" *Debito.org*,

April 14, 2014, www.debito.org/?p=12282; "Kyoto taxis specializing in foreign tourists begin one-year trial." *Kyodo News/Japan Times*, March 1, 2016, www.debito.org/?p=13844; "Overseas online info site Traveloco.jp's 'Japanese Only' rules: 'People with foreign-sounding names refused service.'" *Debito.org*, July 5, 2016, www.debito.org/?p=14078; "Train conductor warned after apologizing for crowding due to 'many foreign passengers.'" *Mainichi Shinbun*, October 11, 2016, and "Japanese train conductor blames foreign tourists for overcrowding: Rail company reprimands conductor who made announcement blaming foreigners for inconveniencing Japanese passengers." *Guardian*, October 11, 2016, both archived at www.debito.org/?p=14257; "'Japanese Only' tourist information booth in JR Beppu Station." *Debito.org*, April 11, 2018, www.debito.org/?p=14954; "Japan's reaction to coronavirus: Bigots excluding NJ residents from restaurants. Saitama Korean schools denied protective mask distribution because they might 'sell off' the masks." *Debito.org*, March 22, 2020, www.debito.org/?p=15975; and so on.

55. "Now-boastful Japan not really in tune with what visitors want, foreign expert warns." *Japan Times*, December 25, 2014, which notes,

> Japan's self-professed "omotenashi" (spirit of selfless hospitality) is often misinterpreted to force predetermined services on foreign visitors, says one longtime observer. Cultural services expert David Atkinson, 49, says the nation's confidence in what it offers the world is misplaced: Many foreigners who visit leave unfulfilled. . . . Atkinson says it is troubling to see Japanese increasingly lauding their own culture and that the trend could even become an obstacle to the government's goal of getting 30 million tourists to visit annually by 2030. . . . "Originally, omotenashi means leaving the choices to the guests, not forcing foreigners with a different set of values to behave the way Japanese people expect."

56. *See*, for example, "GOJ busybodies hard at work alienating: Shinjuku Foreign Residents Manual assumes NJ criminal tendencies; Kyoto public notices 'cultivate foreign tourist manners.'" *Debito.org*, May 13, 2016; and "Picture signboards to cultivate manners of foreign tourists." *Yomiuri Shinbun*, May 11, 2016, both archived at www.debito.org/?p=13959; "Kyoto Nakagyou-ku issues comic book on local street safety to grade schoolers, created by Kyoto Seika University and Kyoto International Manga Museum, portraying 'foreigners' as unintelligible ill-mannered tourists!" *Debito.org*, April 28, 2020, www.debito.org/?p=16041.

57. *Japan Times*, June 3, 2003, ibid. This model law, however, stalled in *Nichibenren* committees. *See also "Fuetsuzukeru jinshu sabetsu soshō. Nani ga towarete iru no ka." JCLU Jinken Shinbun* (341:2), March 28, 2003.

58. *See*, for example, my report on the *Nichibenren* Annual Meeting in Miyazaki, October 7–8, 2004, which I attended as a representative of an NGO. The keynote plenary session was on "Establishing a Basic Law of Human Rights for Non-Japanese" (*gaikokujin no jinken kihon hō*), which began with describing the problems well (treating noncitizens not as outsiders but as taxpayers, educating their children properly), but then got bogged down in chicken-and-egg discussions about which should be done first: pass a law, or raise public consciousness sufficiently so people do not discriminate anymore. Indicatively, *Kyodo News*'s write-up on the event did not mention this panel at all. *See* "Group seeks death sentence moratorium." *Japan*

Times/Kyodo News, October 8, 2004. My eyewitness report on the event is archived at www.debito.org/nichibenren2004.html.

59. *See*, for example, "*Shimin wa gaikokujin to no kyōsei o kentō*" [Considering how citizens and foreigners should coexist]. *Yomiuri Shinbun*, February 10, 2008; Debito Arudou, "Public forums, spinning wheels." *Japan Times*, April 1, 2008.

60. *See*, for example, Mark Schreiber, "Motley crew of foreigners backing Japan's revisionists basks in media glare." *Japan Times*, March 22, 2014, on the activities of veteran British journalist Henry Scott-Stokes, naturalized Japanese academic Oh Seon-Hwa, authors Huang Wen-Hsiung and Shi Ping, and tabloid feature "Texas Oyaji" Tony Marano. *See also* columns by naturalized Japanese academic Earl Kinmonth in right-wing online tabloid Japan Forward; TV *tarento* Kent Gilbert has numerous Japan nationalist books for sale on Amazon Japan, and YouTube videos including "Japanese still brainwashed by the War Guilt Information Program" (www.youtube.com/watch?v=fpmFSn2d5x4), and "Who are the revisionists? Check the facts" (www.youtube.com/watch?v=qwumVaUQi2M); the latter is critical of the McGraw-Hill world history textbook treatment of the "Comfort Women" issue (*see* chapter 7), which he calls "anti-Japanese." *See also* David McNeill, "The revenge of history." FCCJ's *Number 1 Shimbun*, April 1, 2014.

61. *See*, for example, columnist Gregory Clark articles about the Bortz and Otaru Onsens lawsuits mentioned in chapter 3: "Problematic Global Standards." *Japan Times*, November 1, 1999; "Japan's particular racism." *Japan Times*, December 25, 1999; and "Antiforeigner discrimination is a right for Japanese people." *Japan Times*, January 15, 2009, where he steadfastly gets fundamental facts of the cases, including the name of the bathhouse being sued, wrong. *See also* the Donald Keene and Daniel Kahl sections of Komisarof (2012) for similar erroneous and under-researched claims; book review at www.debito.org/?p=11042.

62. *See*, for example, the case of Malian-Japanese Oussouby Sacko, president of Kyōto Seika University, who was quoted in the *New York Times* as follows: "Dr. Sacko, a citizen of Japan for 16 years, says he is treated differently because he does not look Japanese. But he distinguished that from racism. 'It's not because you're black.'" *See* "In Homogeneous Japan, an African-Born University President." *New York Times*, April 13, 2018, with commentary at www.debito.org/?p=14968. More on this phenomenon in general at Debito Arudou, "The Guestists and the Collaborators." *Shingetsu News Agency*, May 18, 2020. Ironically, Dr. Sacko's university collaborated in the official Kyōto City comic book mentioned in endnote 56 that portrayed foreign tourists as noisy rulebreakers—in violation of his university's statement of principles which he undersigned. More at www.debito.org/?p=16066 and www.debito.org/?p=15827.

63. *See*, for example, Debito Arudou, "Why Japan's Right keeps leaving the Left in the dust." *Japan Times*, September 7, 2015.

64. As this research focuses upon issues of racial discrimination, this section will focus more upon the CERD instead of other treaties.

65. The reason for the GOJ's egregious tardiness, as told to me by NGO activists, human rights lawyers, and the occasional candid bureaucrat, is that coordination across siloed ministries to present human rights reports on their field is difficult to do in a timely manner. My opinion is that writing up UN reports devoid of content the

UN wants to hear is not a high priority for several of the ministries, and there is no penalty at the UN for submitting late.

66. "Japan disputes racism allegations at UN panel." *Associated Press*, February 25, 2010; "Japan faces UN racism criticism." *Japan Times*, February 26, 2010.

67. Full text archived at www.debito.org/japanvsun.html.

68. Under the governing 1969 Vienna Convention on the Law of Treaties, a "reservation" is defined as "a unilateral statement, however phrased or named, made by a State, when signing, ratifying, accepting, approving or acceding to a treaty, whereby it purports to exclude or to modify the legal effect of certain provisions of the treaty in their application to that State" (Article 2 (1)(d)).

69. Excerpts archived at www.debito.org/?p=1927, with links to primary source materials. GOJ text archived at www.mofa.go.jp/policy/human/race_rep3.pdf.

70. *Hokkaidō Shinbun*, October 6, 1999, translated in Arudou (2006b: 47–49).

71. Full transcript and analysis of the spoken proceedings archived at www.debito.org/?p=6145.

72. www.ohchr.org/EN/NewsEvents/Pages/DisplayNews.aspx?NewsID=22847&LangID=E.

73. https://tbinternet.ohchr.org/_layouts/15/treatybodyexternal/Download.aspx?symbolno=CERD/C/JPN/CO/10-11&Lang=En.

74. *See*, for example, "Opening Statement by H.E. Mr. Hideaki Ueda, Ambassador in Charge of Human Rights and Humanitarian Affairs, on the occasion of the Examination of the Third to Sixth Periodic Reports of the Government of Japan for the International Convention on the Elimination of All Forms of Racial Discrimination (ICERD)," dated February 24, 2010, at www.mofa.go.jp/policy/human/pdfs/state_race_rep3.pdf. This is the same Mr. Ueda (mentioned above) who was later filmed shouting "Shut up!" for occasioning laughter in a meeting about Japan's human rights record.

75. www.moj.go.jp/ENGLISH/HB/hb-02.html, Japanese version www.moj.go.jp/JINKEN/index.html, accessed September 24, 2012 [dead link].

76. www.moj.go.jp/JINKEN/jinken21.html (accessed May 28, 2021).

77. Courtesy www.moj.go.jp/JINKEN/jinken03.html [link revised every year].

78. Courtesy www.moj.go.jp/JINKEN/jinken03-01.html [dead link].

79. This salient point was raised by a legal scholar friend (who wishes to remain anonymous):

> To be honest I think the MOJ would be perfectly happy to advocate non-discrimination against Non-Japanese, because anything that strengthens their ability to characterize human rights violations as something committed by Japanese people (even school children!) rather than then the government, the more they can be seen as a part of the human rights solution rather than the principal source of violations. The complete reversal of what human rights mean, into something the government asserts against its people as a way to badger them into acting properly, is far creepier than whatever they say or don't say about NJ rights, or the laundry list of other forms of discrimination they have summoned out of thin air. (Ever wonder what the statutory or case law basis for this list is? Hard to tell from the home page, isn't it?)

See "Ministry of Justice Bureau of Human Rights 2014 on raising public awareness of NJ human rights (full site scanned with analysis: it's underwhelming business as usual)." *Debito.org*, November 29, 2014, comment 3, at www.debito.org/?p=12144.

80. Interviews, November 1999 and February 2000, as well as January 8, March 27, April 15, and May 22, 2003, with BOHR Sapporo, both during the Otaru Onsens Case and during my consultations for police racial profiling at Sapporo Chitose Airport, December 11, 2002.

81. www.moj.go.jp/JINKEN/index_chousa.html (accessed May 29, 2021).

82. Archived at www.debito.org/jinkenyougobu070400.jpg is the full text of the notice from the BOHR, Monbetsu Bureau of the Asahikawa Legal Affairs Bureau, sent to restaurants and bars (*inshokuten*) in Monbetsu City, Hokkaidō, politely requesting (*onegai*) them to take down their signs saying "Store only for Japanese" dated July 4, 2000. Fax courtesy of the Asahikawa BOHR, July 13, 2000.

83. "'Japanese Only' signs come down in Monbetsu, Hokkaido. Finally. It only took 22 years." *Debito.org*, August 30, 2017, www.debito.org/?p=14726. Local resident James Eriksson confirms that he still saw one sign up as of March 2021.

84. My personal experience with consulting the BOHR has also been disappointing. When I brought a recorded case of racial profiling by police in Chitose Airport to the Sapporo Bureau of Human Rights on January 8, 2003, I was told after nearly six months of deliberations (June 27) that my case of human rights violation (*jinken shinhan*) "had not been recognized" (*mitomerarenakatta*). As the BOHR must create a record of all cases brought before them, I then asked the Sapporo BOHR for my file on this case recording the investigative and "enlightenment" proceedings between the Chitose Police and the BOHR. I had been told on March 27 by Mr. Tashiro at the Sapporo BOHR that this request would have to go through the Freedom of Information Act (*jōhō kōkai hō*). After making said FOIA application on April 15, I was told by the Legal Affairs Bureau on May 13 that my request was denied due to laws protecting "matters about specific individuals reporting human rights violations" (*tokutei no kojin ga jinken shinhan no shinkoku o shita to iu jijitsu*). In other words, the BOHR was protecting my records from myself for the sake of my privacy.

Background and proceedings of this series of negotiations with the Sapporo BOHR archived at www.debito.org/chitosecopcheckpoint.html, www.debito.org/policeapology.html, MOJ (2003b), and also Debito Arudou, "Watching the detectives: Japan's human rights bureau falls woefully short of meeting its own job specifications." *Japan Times*, July 8, 2003.

85. *See also* "Kyodo: Ryukoku University exchange student denied 'No Foreigner' Kyoto apartment in 2013; MOJ in 2015 decides it's not a violation of human rights!" *Debito.org*, April 12, 2015, with several news articles archived at www.debito.org/?p=13185.

86. Peek (1992: 219–224).

87. Kashiwazaki (2000: 448).

88. Ibid.: 448–449.

89. "Japan's Ainu hope new identity leads to more rights." *Christian Science Monitor*, June 9, 2008.

90. Peek (1991: 10).

91. This attitude can also be found within Japan's general reluctance to enforce the Hague Convention on International Child Abductions, mentioned in chapter 7,

endnote 45, where foreign parents are repeatedly portrayed in an official GOJ publication as violent child abusers. This was reflected in a Sakura TV online broadcast which portrays the Hague Convention as a means for White men to exploit women from "uncivilized countries." *See* "Japan Supreme Court enforces Hague Convention on Int'l Child Abductions (for Japanese claimants). Yet Sakura TV claims Hague is for 'selfish White men' trying to entrap women from 'uncivilized countries' as 'babysitters.'" *Debito.org*, March 29, 2018, www.debito.org/?p=14937. In sum, like so many other treaties, the GOJ has generally caveated Japan's way out of applying the Hague. *See* "Good news: GOJ signs Hague Child Abductions Treaty. Bad news: GOJ will probably caveat its way out of ever following it." *Debito.org*, May 24, 2013, www.debito.org/?p=11508.

Part V

DISCUSSIONS AND CONCLUSIONS

Chapter 9

Putting the Concept of "Embedded Racism" to Work

INTRODUCTION: WHY THIS CHAPTER

This shorter chapter is intended for the academic reader, taking the concept of "Embedded Racism" out for a quick test drive. As this book describes the first deep research project applying Critical Race Theory (see appendix 2; more below) to a *non-White-majority society* and finding CRT's principles universally applicable, this section will offer the field of Japanese Studies a different way of looking at how "Japaneseness" is determined. If academic theory and modeling is not something you find interesting, please skip to chapter 10.

This book has focused on Japan's racialization process: how nation-states innately create communities for themselves by deciding who is "a member" (a citizen) and who is not (a foreigner)—as viewed through the racialization process (i.e., how people are officially differentiated, "othered," and subordinated) in Japan's dominant discourse.

Let us briefly review: Chapter 1 gave brief examples of what kind of racial discrimination exists in Japan, and asked why Japan cannot fulfill its constitutional and treaty obligations to pass laws against it. The Introduction and chapter 2 showed how analyses of Japanese society (both from within and without) have been blind to the issue, often denying that Japan's forms of discrimination are "racialized" or visually based, thereby overlooking the very existence of Japan's Visible Minorities. Chapter 3 gave specific case studies of discrimination against Visible Minorities in the form of "Japanese Only" establishments, and surveyed how and why excluders exclude. Chapters 4–8 demonstrated how their exclusionary mindsets are underpinned in and justified by Japan's national narratives, which claim one must "look Japanese" to be treated as "Japanese," generating an "Embedded Racism" behind membership in Japanese society perpetually normalized and reinforced as the inevitable status quo.

This chapter will generate a matrix of four different factors introduced in previous chapters, grouped into (a) the nationality basis (i.e., citizen vs. noncitizen, or *kokumin* vs. *gaikokujin*), and (b) the visual identification basis (i.e., someone who "looks Japanese" vs. someone who does not, or Wajin vs. Gaijin). Then it will demonstrate how this model offers a comparatively more accurate analysis for determining how people will be socially categorized and treated in Japan.

CONCEPTUAL MAPS OF *KOKUMIN* VS. *GAIKOKUJIN, WAJIN* VS. *GAIJIN*

First, consider as categorical boxes (figure 9.1) the concepts of *kokumin* (citizen) and *gaikokujin* (noncitizen) in a strictly legal sense.

People who are Japanese citizens would fall within the darker Kokumin Box, while people who are not Japanese citizens would fall within the lighter Gaikokujin Box. This is how the GOJ and oversimplified versions of the

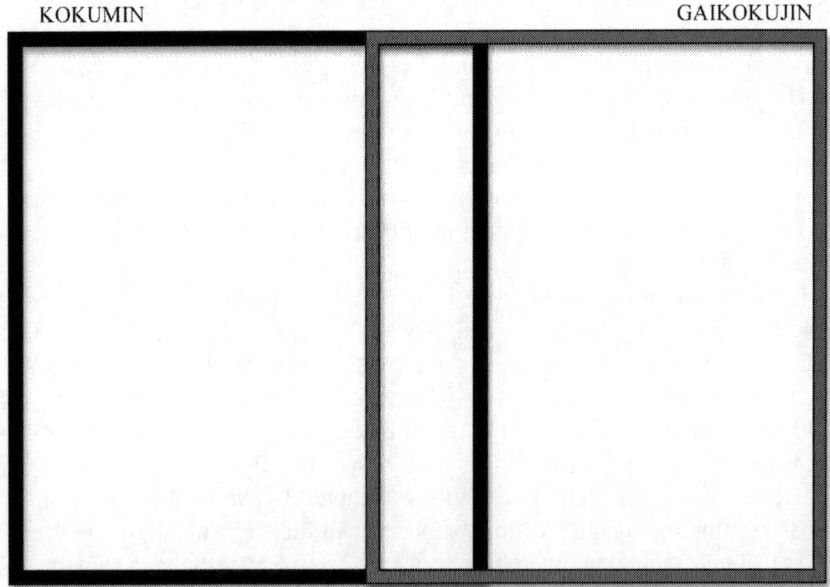

Figure 9.1 Categorical Boxes of "Citizen" (Kokumin) and "Noncitizen" (Gaikokujin), with Overlap to Allow for the Existence of Dual Nationals. N.B.: Boxes are not rendered to scale of population numbers—the equal size is for ease of conceptualization. *Source*: Created by author.

national discourse tend to see Japanese society when suggesting that Japan is monoethnic and homogeneous. Note that there is officially no overlap due to laws against dual nationality. However, in practice there is some overlap, since under the Nationality Law (see chapter 4), children of international unions may maintain their dual nationality until age twenty-two (when they will—officially—be required to conform to the duality above). Therefore, the overlap in this conceptual map would be Japanese citizens with more than one nationality, making them simultaneously Kokumin and Gaikokujin.

Now let us bring in two more categories: the first category is Wajin, that is, people who belong to the "Dominant Majority Group of Japanese" (as defined by Aoki and Sugimoto 2009; see chapter 2) by dint of having "Japanese blood," therefore also qualifying for Japanese citizenship under *jus sanguinis* requirements in the Nationality Law. However, not every Japanese citizen has "Japanese blood" (due to ethnicity or naturalization, meaning the spatial field between Wajin and Kokumin is not an exact fit), and not everyone who has "Japanese blood" has Japanese citizenship (such as the Nikkei diaspora).

The second category is Gaijin, that is, people who do not "look Japanese," as visually identified by people in gatekeeping positions in Japanese society. These people will of course be predominantly Gaikokujin, but again the Gaikokujin and Gaijin boxes are not an exact spatial fit, because in practice some Gaikokujin visually "pass" as Kokumin, and some Kokumin do not "look Japanese." So let us conceptualize these overlaps in figure 9.2.

By viewing this spatial representation as a situational map, it is possible to visualize how conceits of bloodline and physical appearance complicate the determination of a person's relationship to Japanese society, with no fewer than eleven different "types" of "Japanese" and "foreigner." Let us label each overlapping zone within the boxes and see what people are represented by these racialized categories in figure 9.3. (This is quite complicated, but the determination of "Japaneseness" is a complicated process; please bear with me as I walk you through each category.)

Zone A represents people who have Japanese citizenship and "Japanese blood." Representing the majority of Japan's population, they been apportioned the largest space within the Kokumin and Wajin boxes. This zone can, of course, include naturalized Nikkei who have given up their previous citizenship and can visibly "pass" as "Japanese."[1] These people are, as Aoki and Sugimoto (2009) categorize, "the Dominant Japanese" or "most Japanese" in Japanese society.

On the other extreme, *Zone B represents those people who do not have Japanese citizenship and do not "look Japanese."* This would include visibly identifiable Caucasians, Hispanics, Africans, South-East Asians, and so on and the stateless who cannot "pass." One famous person in Zone B would be TV personality Dave Spector.[2]

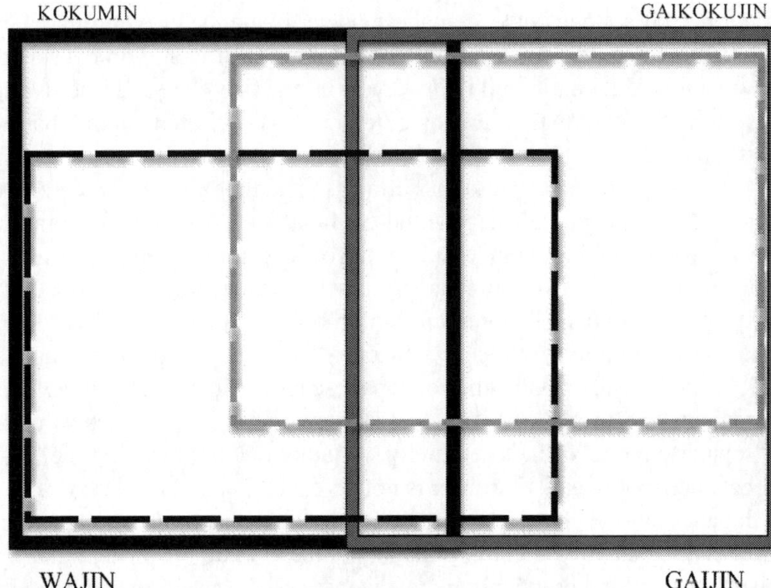

Figure 9.2 Categorical Boxes Revised from Figure 9.1 Spatially Overlaying a Wajin Box (Highlighted Dark Dotted at Bottom Left) and a Gaijin Box (Highlighted Light Dotted at Top Right). Note that these boxes are dotted because the borders of the category are porous, given the subjective judgments, personal advancements within Japan's power structure (see below), and bloodline dilution over generations.*Source*: Created by author.

Zone C represents Japan's people with Japanese citizenship, one or more foreign citizenships, who have "Japanese blood" but cannot visibly "pass" as "Japanese." These would be known in the vernacular as Haafu, "doubles," "quarters," "mixed-blood children," and so on. People in Zone C would be my younger Japanese daughter who "looks foreign" (see chapter 1), beauty queens Miyamoto Ariana and Yoshikawa Priyanka, and Japan Olympics bid ambassador Takigawa Christel.

Zone D represents people with Japanese citizenship and "Japanese blood" who cannot visibly "pass" as "Japanese." These also can include former multinational children who chose Japanese citizenship solely at adulthood, and Japan's "war orphans" (*zanryū koji*) from Wajin=Non-Wajin unions under the Japanese Empire (who have been granted Japanese citizenship and surrendered their Chinese citizenship). A person in Zone C would be Japanese model Umemiya Anna, who has a Japanese father, an American mother, and exclusively Japanese citizenship; it would probably also include tennis champ Ōsaka Naomi who, despite spending most of her life outside Japan, reportedly elected to keep only her Japanese citizenship and forfeit other nationalities as an adult.

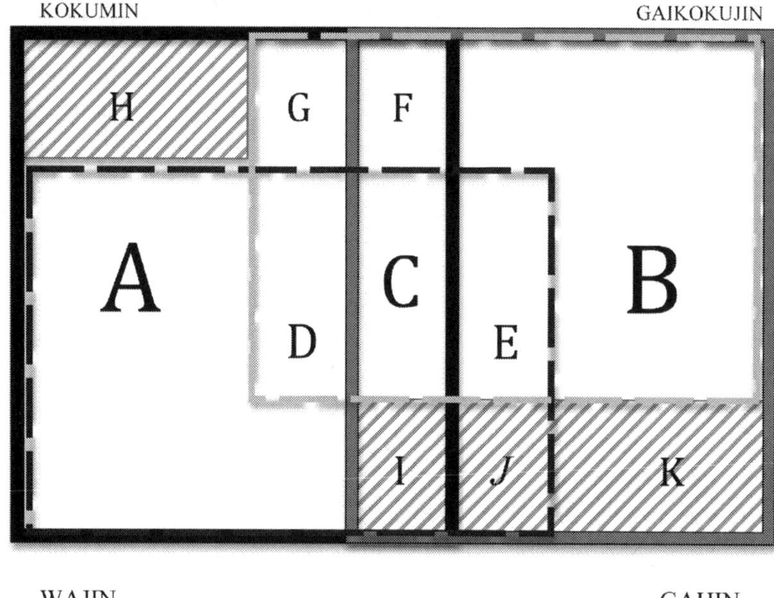

Figure 9.3 Annotated Categorical Boxes Revised from Figure 9.2 Categorizing Each Subdivision and Overlap Within the Four Variables. *Source*: Created by author.

Zone E represents people of international unions without Japanese citizenship but with "Japanese blood" (i.e., Nikkei ancestry), who cannot visibly "pass" as "Japanese" because their phenotype "favors" a Non-Wajin ancestor in their family. This also includes children of Wajin=Non-Wajin unions who did not register their child's birth with Japan's authorities properly (see chapter 4), and Japan's "war orphans" (*zanryū koji*) from Wajin=Non-Wajin unions under the Japanese Empire who have yet to be granted Japanese citizenship.

Zone F represents people with Japanese citizenship and one or more foreign citizenships, who cannot visibly "pass" as "Japanese." People in Zone F are naturalized citizens who are visually identifiable as Gaijin who have not given up their foreign citizenship, such as activist Christopher Savoie.[3]

Zone G represents those people with Japanese citizenship only who cannot visibly "pass" as "Japanese." People in Zone G are naturalized citizens who are visually identifiable as Gaijin, such as former MP Tsurunen Marutei, scholar Donald Keene, or the author.

Zone H represents people with Japanese citizenship who can visibly "pass" as "Japanese," but are minorities disenfranchised from the Wajin dominant majority power structure. This may be due to bloodline conceits (e.g., the Ainu and Ryūkyū ethnic minorities) or historical or social origin (i.e., the Burakumin historical underclass). People in Zone H would be Ainu activist Kayano Shiro or Buraku leader Matsumoto Ji'ichirō.

Zone I represents people with Japanese citizenship, one or more foreign citizenships, who can visibly "pass" as "Japanese." This would include first-generation Haafu/"double" children who are visibly identifiable as "Japanese," and "war orphans" (*zanryū koji*) from Wajin=Non-Wajin unions under the Japanese Empire granted Japanese citizenship upon application but who have not surrendered their Chinese citizenship. A person in Zone I would be my older Japanese daughter who "looks Japanese" (see chapter 1).

Zone J represents people without Japanese citizenship who can visibly "pass" as "Japanese" due to the phenotypical expression of their bloodline. This would include Nikkei Brazilians and Peruvians, and other peoples with "Japanese blood" including children of citizen–noncitizen unions who did not successfully register their child's birth with Japan's authorities. A person in Zone J would be Nikkei Brazilian Japanese TV personality Marcia Kazue Nishi'ie (stage name Marushia).

Zone K represents people without Japanese citizenship who might be able to "pass" as "Japanese" (such as peoples from Asian countries, since, as seen in chapter 5, the Gaijin identification is visually applied to non-Asians in general). This would include Chinese, Koreans, the stateless, and the Zainichi.

PERFORMATIVE INTERPRETATIONS AND POWER RELATIONS

Let us further annotate the map to show performative effects of "looking Japanese" (i.e., the visual identification of nationality) on Japan's Visible and Invisible Minorities. Refer back to figure 9.3 and note the stripes in Zones H, I, J, and K.

Striped Zones H, I, J, and K represent Japan's Invisible Minorities. In terms of power relations and the ability to "pass" as a Wajin in Japanese society, Zone H (Japan's *kokumin* minorities: the Ainu, Ryūkyūans, and Burakumin), Zone I (Haafu children whose phenotype favors the Wajin bloodline), Zone J (foreign Nikkei, who were for their bloodline granted special visa statuses), and Zone K (some foreigners from Asian countries) all allow for people to, prima facie, be treated as "Japanese," and, as seen in chapter 4, to "pass" into Japan's "Japanese Only" exclusionary establishments.

But "passing" is not merely the ability to be left alone and seen as "normal" by a society—some people are able to negotiate the liminal spaces, crossing the porous borders of the Wajin Box and become influential members of the power structure. Examples include Ainu former MP Kayano Shigeru, former Zainichi MP Murata Renhō, former Zainichi and Softbank head Son Masayoshi, and Burakumin such as Ōsaka governor Hashimoto Tōru and former LDP head Nonaka Hiromu (who was denied his chance at becoming prime minister when Wajin in power brought up his ancestry).[4]

Visible Minorities Ōsaka Naomi and Takigawa Christel have also become part of the Wajin power structure, but on a contingency basis, for example, if they win at their assigned tasks of sports champions or international ambassadors. Again, the phenomenon of "They'll claim us if we're famous" (see chapter 5) allows passage through the porous borders into the Wajin sphere of influence; it also means passage outside again, as has sadly happened to once-famous and since-disenfranchised former beauty queens Miyamoto Ariana and Yoshikawa Priyanka (who did not become world champions and achieve lifetime fame). In other words, once these Visible Minorities are no longer famous, try applying the "Yunohana Test" (see chapter 1) and see if a "Japanese Only" establishment would let them in (especially in the case of Ōsaka Naomi who is not fluent in the Japanese language).[5] Back they may go in into the Gaijin Box.

Of course, gaining influence within the Wajin power structure is also possible for people irretrievably in the Gaijin Box due to their lack of Wajin blood, including Dave Spector, Donald Keene, and Tsurunen Marutei. But without the bloodline the barriers are significantly higher, because passage will often require decades of cultural study on their part, constant proving of themselves as "Japanese enough," and dealing with the constant microaggressions that come with differentiation and "othering" that are more likely to target people in the Non-Pass Zones. (Tsurunen and Spector, as do many *gaijin tarento*, performatively Gaijinize themselves constantly as part of their public appeal; see chapter 7.) Comparatively, being part of the Pass Zones thus makes personal advancement in Japan significantly easier, and this is where the structural Embedded Racism in Japan takes hold to differentiate and govern people's life potential by phenotype.

Thus, this situational map conceptualizes the performative aspect of racialized differentiation in Japanese society. If one wishes to "pass" as a "Japanese" without the application of racialized conceits as a "foreigner," one must be within, find oneself within, or find ways to enter the Wajin Box. However, this option is more difficult for people falling within the Gaijin Box—as they have been "differentiated" if not "othered" phenotypically as "not Japanese" under most circumstances. The process is subtle, however, and the odd overlaps and exclusions within the four variables (two of them based upon legal status, one based upon bloodline rules that do not always influence phenotype, and another based solely upon visual identification of phenotype) thus make the conceits and applications of Japan's Embedded Racism very complex.

Caveats

There is one more variable mentioned in the literature review in chapter 2 that has not been included in this situational map: "Acculturation," for example, Japanese language ability, familiarity with Japan's lifestyles, cultural norms and customs, primary and secondary education in Japan, and duration of time living in Japan. For example, where would the multicultural "returnee children" (*kikoku shijo*) fall? (Technically, within Zone D, but "Acculturation" is not a phenotypical issue.) What of the foreign-born and/or naturalized citizens (such as TV personality Wada Akiko), or the naturalized Nikkei or Zainichi (such as Softbank head Son Masayoshi) who are able to "pass" yet have self-proclaimed diverse backgrounds? (Technically, within Zone D again, if not Zones C or I if dual nationals, but again, "Acculturation" is not a phenotypical issue.) One must make a problematic assumption that people who are suitably "acculturated" are not only able to "pass," but also able to completely subsume their Non-Wajin roots. Moreover, since "Acculturation" is extremely difficult to define (compared to the other categories, which are determined in part or in whole by legal status or first-impression indicators—enabling the instant refusals of the "Yunohana Test"), I decided not to include this vague category in an already complicated four-variable map.

HOW THE LENS OF EMBEDDED RACISM ENHANCES ANALYTICAL FOCUS

Clearly there are contradictions and cognitive dissonances within the performative racialization of Japanese society, and they are allowed to exist without being problematized to the degree of necessitating preventive legislation. How are these contradictions managed? It depends on the definition of "Japanese." Let us now apply the concept of Embedded Racism to established concepts within Japanese Studies.

Viewing Fukuoka's Typology of "Japaneseness" through the Lens of Embedded Racism

First, let us reconsider Fukuoka's amended typology of "Japaneseness" from chapter 2. Under a more sophisticated analysis of power structures using the Wajin paradigm provided by this research, an amended typology can include more people in Japan, and more accurately predict if they will be treated as "Japanese" at the simplest legally sanctioned test of "Japaneseness" possible: "Japanese Only" establishments (see table 9.1).

Table 9.1 A Revision of Fukuoka's Typological Framework of "Japanese" and "non-Japanese" Attributes, Using "Wajin" and "Non-Wajin" as Qualifiers

Types	*Zone A: Fukuoka's "Pure" Japanese*	*Zone B: Fukuoka's "Pure" Non-Japanese*	*Zone C: Nikkei Dual Citizens Who Cannot "Pass"*	*Zone D: Nikkei Citizens Who Cannot "Pass"*	*Zone E: Nikkei Non-citizens Who Cannot "Pass"*	*Zone F: Dual Citizens Who Cannot "Pass"*
Japanese citizenship	Yes	No	Yes	Yes	No	Yes
Looks "Japanese"	*Yes*	*No*	*No*	*No*	*No*	*No*
May enter "Japanese Only" establishment	*Yes*	*No*	*No*	*No*	*No*	*No*

Types	*Zone G: Naturalized Citizens Who Cannot "Pass"*	*Zone H: Non-Wajin Citizen Minorities Who Can "Pass"*	*Zone I: Nikkei Dual Citizens Who Can "Pass"*	*Zone J: Non-citizen Nikkei Who Can "Pass"*	*Zone K: Non-citizens Who Can "Pass"*
Japanese citizenship	Yes	Yes	Yes	No	No
Looks "Japanese"	*No*	*Yes*	*Yes*	*Yes*	*Yes*
May enter "Japanese Only" establishment	*No*	*Yes*	*Yes*	*Yes*	*Yes*

Note that Fukuoka's research question has been reframed: "Will these people *be treated* as 'Japanese' by people in gatekeeping positions?"). An emphasis on congruency of reactions is in italics. *Sources* are formal and informal interviews by the author over the course of twenty-five years with all of these "types" of people, and with managers of exclusionary businesses who chose their clientele based upon visual identification of their customer base.

Thus, as per the sections enhanced in italics, there is a direct and positive correlation between visual identification and treatment as a valid customer at "Japanese Only" establishments. Other factors, such as acculturation, language ability, and nationality, were irrelevant: even when proof of Japanese citizenship, language ability, and acculturation was presented, the Gaijin was almost always refused entry. Conversely, noncitizen minorities who looked Wajin, even in cases of displaying proof of foreignness (an ARC), were let in.

The conclusion is that how you are treated in Japan is, again, essentially based on an Embedded Racism: It depends on how you look. Look like a member of Japan's dominant majority Wajin group and you will be entitled to service. Look like a member of an outsider or minority group and you will be denied service.

Thus, in scholarship on Japanese racialization processes, social hierarchies, and power structures, the term "Japanese" (or *Nihonjin*, or *kokumin*, all of which confuse the issue by bringing in irrelevant issues of legal status) is problematic: The more accurate dichotomy is not "Japanese" vs. "foreign," it is "Wajin" vs. "Gaijin." Through this dichotomy it becomes clear that in Japanese society, discrimination based upon a "color stigmata" exists and can be enforced at any time regardless of the rule of law or public policy.

Viewing the "Konketsuji Problem" through the Lens of Embedded Racism

Next, let's revisit Robert Fish's outstanding historical research on the Konketsuji mixed-blood children in Postwar Japan (covered in the Introduction and chapter 2). Fish concluded (55) that "'race' *per se* did not create consistent problems" for the Konketsuji, instead attributing the problems to social reactions both by and toward the people being stigmatized. I would call that a confusion of cause and effect. When Fish's data set is viewed through the lens of Embedded Racism, one can better see the daisy chain of policy drives normalizing the official typologies, and problematizing the existence of an allegedly newfound Visible Minority in society. Let us now reconsider the structural interplays of power and its effects over the dominant discourse and mindsets in Japanese society:

First, consider the assumptions of the Postwar "peaceful homogeneous Japan" narrative as noted by Oguma: the converse association implicitly became that "heterogeneity" (as seen in the Konketsuji) would not be peaceful or tranquil, that is, that "nonhomogeneous" people would be "trouble" and create "problems" for assimilation due to their obvious and unquestioned "differences."

Second, without any scientific basis or evidence, overcautious policymakers made an a priori assumption that phenotypical differences would automatically result in different behavior and treatment on both sides. In other words, contrary to Spickard's argument that "races are not types," and confirming Freire's argument that, "In order to exist, one must be named. . . . Saying *haafu* existed meant this group existed," the GOJ officially created and named a "mixed-blood *type* of Japanese."[6] This gained immediate public legitimacy and hegemony in the national narrative because it came from the Ministry of Education.

Third, the phenotypical difference itself then became entangled in public narratives of shame, pity, and parental irresponsibility, which also made it impossible for people visually identified as Konketsuji who were *not* products of unions of prostitutes and soldiers to escape the stigma.

Fourth, although official claims were that Konketsuji were the same as "Japanese," it was still a differentiation as a "type" of Japanese—a "sameness" with an asterisk: Konketsuji were *supposed* to be the same, but were, due to unfortunate birth-determined circumstances beyond their control, *not* the same. This then became folded into a national narrative of pity and victimization that made asterisking these children not an act of scorn or hatred, but *an act of kindness*. That made it difficult for anyone to protest this differentiated treatment as unnecessary or ill-intentioned (for who would be so unkind as to pretend that putative differences did not exist?).

Fifth, although there was positive enforcement of publicly stated equality for Konketsuji, there is no clear indication in the historical record of an enforcement mechanism in cases of people (such as bullies) who would not respect that equality—to deter or punish racists found in every society. Because there is no law specifically against racial discrimination in Japan, there was then, as now, no protection for these children—for they were, like everyone else, not officially a minority in Japan. They were supposed to be "Japanese" (albeit with caveats and asterisks), even if their asterisked status was as clear as the "foreignness" of their face.

Thus, by being differentiated by even well-meaning authorities, Konketsuji could neither "pass" due to blood conceits, nor were they allowed "multiple identifications" due to the binary nature of "Japaneseness" under the "homogeneous Japan" narrative also being reinforced by a new Postwar *jus sanguinis* Nationality Law (see chapter 4).

In sum, the policymaking apparatus for dealing with Postwar Konketsuji Japanese *further embedded* restrictions in the concept of "Japanese"—to not only *jus sanguinis* blood ties to citizenship, but also "pure-blooded" ties.[7] This official treatment of a generation of Konketsuji who could not "pass" as "Japanese" during the during the 1950s, 1960s, and 1970s set the tone for treatment of foreign nationals who came to Japan during the 1980s,

1990s, 2000s, and 2010s. These future workers and immigrants including people of color would be visually identified, typified, and "othered" as full Gaijin without even the asterisk of Japanese blood. Thus unlike many of the Konketsuji, they were placed in an even more powerless situation in Japanese society, as they lacked official government policies protecting them as Japanese citizens, or from the straightforward bigotry of a "Yunohana Test."

Thus, "race" (and racialization processes) did in fact create consistent (and permanent) problems for Japan's Visible Minorities. Viewing Fish's research through the lens of Embedded Racism provides a different and more powerful insight into an array of structural power relations, coupled with a more effective analysis of the dynamics of public policy that enfranchised racist mindsets toward "foreigners" in Japanese society.

CONCLUSION: RAMIFICATIONS OF CHAPTER 9: WHITENESS STUDIES AND "WAJIN PRIVILEGE"

Several schools of thought analyze dominant majorities in societies based upon inherently racialized structures of privilege. This research is particularly indebted to CRT and Whiteness Studies (see appendix 2), as they are increasingly being applied to countries other than their country of origin (the United States).[8] This research finds that that their analytical paradigms have universal applications to societies without a White majority.

The social construction of "race" (as defined in the letter and the enforcement of Japan's laws) has systematically differentiated, "othered," and subordinated minorities in Japan to the point of invisibility in putatively "monoethnic Japan." However, CRT focuses upon White-dominated societies, whereas Embedded Racism (as a methodological lens polished by CRT) focuses on Japan as a non-White dominated society engaging in the same racialization processes. The difference in Japan's case, given its allegedly "homogeneous society," is that Japan is so dominated by one racialized majority that minorities are rendered invisible. Consequently, racism is embedded to the point of being a "normal" and endemic part of Japan (where even the rigorous academic analyses covered in the Introduction and chapter 2 sometimes deny the very existence of racialized discrimination in Japan). The prejudicial discourses about human categorization, alterity, and subordinating treatment of "The Other" are so hegemonic in Japan that questioning the boundaries of what defines "Japanese" and "foreign" is tantamount to questioning "Japanese identity" itself.

In ways similar to the performative aspects of CRT's "White Privilege," Japan's racializing processes have created and normalized "Wajin Privilege," both (a) as a definition of "who belongs to" and "who is a member within" the modern nation-state, and (b) as a definition of "Japanese identity" that goes beyond legal status. As discussed in chapter 7, Japanese society has created a birth-and-bloodline-based caste system that "walls in the Wajin" within a normalized national discourse of perpetual "uniqueness" and "difference with outsiders." It has reached a point where it becomes exceptionally difficult for "The Other" to ever traverse the wall and become part of "The Self." This has made "race" the central, endemic, and permanent driving force in Japan behind organizing the scaffolding of human interaction, categorization, and regulation both at the individual and (more importantly) the legal, legislative, and media level.

As discussed in chapter 2, this has a history: Japan switched its national discourse from Prewar multicultural "Pan-Asianism" under Japan's Greater East-Asian Co-Prosperity Sphere to "monocultural, homogeneous Japan" in the postwar period. Subsequently, the laws and policies that (at least officially) ethnically cleansed Japan utilized "race" as a fundamental influence, which was factored into the formation, enforcement, and amendment processes of future laws and administrative policies.

This dynamic has become so normalized over several generations that Japan's Embedded Racism has become difficult to decode. Fortunately, because this research was undertaken by the rare Non-Wajin Visible Minority citizen, crucial minority narratives were uncovered. This provided alternative voices and insights that exposed realities present for the Non-Wajin unprivileged and underprivileged.

This system has long become self-sustaining, not only because Wajin Privilege by definition disenfranchises Non-Wajin minorities from ever having a significant voice in Japan's societal power structures, but also because it blinds (or disenfranchises) the most well-intentioned Wajin from giving up their privilege (or from seeing it as privilege at all—more as a natural, "normal" part of the political and social order in Japanese society). For as CRT's theory of "structural determinism" argues, the milieu in which people have been raised and live their lives makes them blind to the viewpoints and needs of people who have not been born and raised in the same milieu.

Pundits have asserted that as "Japanese people" travel more, and have more contact and mind-broadening experiences with peoples outside their "island society," they will change Japan by being more open and welcoming to outsiders. However, I do not think that fits within Japan's societal power structure. I concur with CRT when it argues that nothing can fundamentally change without "interest convergence," that is, where both Wajin and Non-Wajin interests converge, and where both parties stand to gain from a change in the power structure. This means that the occasional Wajin visitor to Hawai'i will neither feel any incentive to open Japan up to the idea of enfranchising outsiders within Japan. It is not in their interest. Nor is it "normal" because, according to the dominant discourse, it has never happened. As repeatedly noted in chapter 7, it would be the "end of Japan" as "we" know it.

This answers the original research question as to why Japan has not created (in fact, has official elements successfully working against the creation of) a law against racial discrimination: Very few people in the dominant power Wajin majority stand to gain from one, and alarmist strands of the dominant discourse in Japan assert that Wajin will lose power (if not lose Japan as a nation entirely) if one is established. Equality is impossible because inequality (in Japan's case, a racialized inequality) as a mindset is so embedded.

Now let us turn to the final chapter of this book, and discuss how Japan's Embedded Racism is having detrimental effects on its future both socially and financially. The headline: Japan is strangling itself demographically and economically because it cannot create "new Japanese." After that comes a new chapter 11 to this Second Edition, where I argue that Japan's unaddressed Embedded Racism has become an inspirational template for the rise of the global far right.

NOTES

1. This chart will assume that naturalized people who have a Wajin bloodline and a phenotype that enables them to "pass" as Japanese also have the ability to subsume their foreign cultural roots. This is of course a problematic assumption, but this situational map is already complicated enough without introducing another variable, such as "linguistic ability" and "acculturation." More in the Caveats section below.

2. NB: This map is again not drawn to scale as a proportion of population. The majority of registered foreigners in Japan are from Asian countries such as China and Korea, meaning they could possibly "pass" in Japan, but when the rubric is expanded to the remaining 95 percent of the world's population, the majority is not from Asian countries and probably could not "pass" as Wajin. Never mind. For ease of reference, I chose the opposite extremes of qualifiers (with citizenship and bloodline vs. without) as Zone A and Zone B.

3. "How did Japan become a haven for child abductions?" *TIME Magazine*, March 7, 2011.

4. "Japan's outcasts still wait for acceptance." *New York Times*, January 15, 2009.

5. Ōsaka's lack of Japanese language ability is sourced from the Wajin press within "Naomi Osaka's US Open victory over Serena Williams: Congratulations, but I don't think you know what you're getting yourself into." *Debito.org*, September 10, 2018, www.debito.org/?p=15145.

6. Spickard (1992: 20–2). Friere, quoted in Williams (1992: 302).

7. Also note that because Japan's Nationality Law was not amended to allow Japanese citizenship to pass through the Japanese mother until 1985, this had the effect of compounding issues of blood ties with gender. Until 1985, liaisons between Japanese women and non-Japanese men could not produce Japanese citizens. Not only did this inconveniently associate Japanese mothers of international unions with prostitutes, but it also denied the civil rights afforded by citizenship to their otherwise "Japanese" children.

8. Cf. Möschel (2011).

Chapter 10

"So What?"

Why Japan's Embedded Racism Matters

The previous chapter was one for the academics. It compared a theory of Embedded Racism to other popular theories in Japanese Studies about how "Japaneseness," that is, the status of "Insider" or "Outsider," is determined within Japanese society. It concluded that Embedded Racism as an analytical lens was more insightful and predictive of inclusionary and exclusionary behavior.

This chapter is one for the policymakers. Why should the community of nation-states be concerned about Japan's Embedded Racism? If Japan wishes to mold itself into a Wajin-dominated ethnostate, so what? The conclusion below is because racism hurts Japan and the Japanese people as a whole—economically, demographically, and socially.

But ethnostatism has repercussions outside Japan too; as chapter 11 will discuss, the outside world's constant forbearance in meaningfully challenging Japan's Embedded Racism allows Japan to be used as template for racial supremacists worldwide, damaging liberal democracies in general.

QUICK REVIEW OF THE BOOK FOR READERS WHO SKIPPED TO THE CONCLUDING CHAPTER

This book's first research question was, "Why are there 'Japanese Only' signs on businesses open to the public in Japan?" The answer is because "Japanese Only" signs and exclusions of people by physical appearance are not illegal—Japan has no law in its civil or criminal code against racial discrimination.

The second, more complicated research question was, "Despite a provision in Japan's Constitution outlawing discrimination by race, why does Japan not have a law against racial discrimination?" In other words, why is racial discrimination in Japan unconstitutional yet not illegal? These two questions—one grounded within a Micro-level individual business decision, the other grounded within a Macro-level governmental decision regarding the rule of law within a sovereign nation-state—occasioned this book.

Part of the answer to each question is based upon how the Japanese government (GOJ) defines "race." According to its testimony to the UN in chapter 8, the GOJ interprets the UN CERD in a way that means it does not cover anyone in Japan: All people in Japan who are citizens are members of the "Japanese race," therefore discrimination against them cannot be "racial." On the other hand, all people who are not citizens automatically do not have the same rights as citizens because they are not citizens, therefore discrimination toward them is also not covered by the CERD.

Thus, the issue becomes how the GOJ defines "citizen" and "noncitizen"—not only in the strict legal sense, but also as a performative process of differentiation and "othering" to create a sense of membership and community. This is not a Japan-specific phenomenon: all nation-states do this. As discussed in the Introduction and chapter 2, differentiation necessarily leads to "othering" (separating noncitizen "Others" from the citizenry "Self") and "subordination" (treating noncitizens in a subordinate manner to citizens).

Where "racism" becomes a factor is that in some societies, this differentiation process involves biological issues. In Japan, you have to "look" like a "Japanese" in order to be perceived as and treated as a citizen by society. This was clearly evident in how "Japanese Only" shopkeepers treated certain customers in chapter 3, that is, the "Yunohana Test": excluding with impunity those who did not "look Japanese" and accepting those who did, regardless of the individual's verifiable legal or social status.

This book next investigated how biological conceits are explicitly encoded in Japan's laws (e.g., a *jus sanguinis* bloodline requirement for citizenship), performatively embedded in the interpretation and enforcement of those laws (e.g., Nationality Clauses in public- and private-sector work), reinforced through public policies, the legislative process (e.g., GOJ "illegal foreigners" and "foreign crime" campaigns), jurisprudence (i.e., court decisions favoring Japanese over "foreigners"), and finally disseminated in media messages (e.g., the public "othering" and commodification of "foreigners" as "evil," "strange," or visually different). This research traced the contours of societal definitions of "Japanese" and a "foreigner," and how they influenced individual behaviors by gatekeeping "Japanese Only" establishments as they visually defined a "foreigner" for exclusion.

This has been a tough narrative to parse because it is so embedded. The Postwar-generated national discourse of Japan as a "homogeneous society" without minorities or races has become so normalized that even rigorous academic research on Japan worldwide is blind to racial discrimination in

Japan. It has (1) assessed Japan's variant as different (e.g., "ethnic discrimination") or immaterial (e.g., "an epiphenomenon"); (2) assessed it as nonexistent (resulting in an underemphasis or reactionary overemphasis of Japan's diversity); or (3) ignored clear evidence of racially discriminatory behavior as lacking in degree or sufficient example. Other research overlooks the fundamental power dynamic that is quite special to Japan: a society where a social majority is so dominant that it denies it has any minorities.

Japan's dominant majority maintains this power structure and insulates it from outside pressure through obfuscation—by entangling the debate in legal issues (citizen vs. noncitizen, Japanese vs. foreigner, *Nihonjin* vs. *Gaikokujin*), while defining itself through racialized conceits to differentiate itself from the rest of the world (e.g., *yamato minzoku*, "the Japanese Race"). At the same time, it quietly enforces domestically embedded social constructions to differentiate, "other," and subordinate peoples who should not belong to the dominant majority, no matter how many generations they live in Japan (e.g., the Burakumin, Ainu, Ryūkyūans, and Zainichi—as well as Japan's rarely studied Visible Minorities). As seen in its arguments to the UN, the GOJ switches between these arguments (racial, legal, and/or social) whenever it wishes to confuse outside observers as to who really holds the power in Japan.

To uncover the interrelationships between the enfranchised and disenfranchised peoples in Japanese society, this research has defined the dominant majority with a special term—"Wajin"—and contrasted it with the term "Gaijin" to introduce the dimension of physical appearance when deciding national membership. As described in chapter 9, inclusion as a "Japanese" in Japanese society is a very complicated matter, but it goes beyond mere citizenship and legal status and into less-porous categories involving bloodline and phenotype.

The point of this chapter is that Embedded Racism augurs ill for Japan's future.

EMBEDDED RACISM AND DEMOGRAPHIC SELF-STRANGULATION

The problem with Japan's Wajin-dominated system is that it is, as are all social systems based upon bloodline and its phenotypical expression, inflexible when it comes to accepting new entrants. As will be described below, Japan's birthrates have been long below replacement levels, meaning that Japan's population is aging and shrinking, and it faces an enormous economic and demographic crisis. Yet due to racialized concepts of "Japaneseness," Japanese society cannot accept people who do not *look* "Japanese" to *be*

"Japanese." Hence the polar dichotomy is, again, not "Japanese vs. foreign" (terminology which entangles the debate in racial and legal issues), but rather enfranchised vs. disenfranchised, "Wajin vs. Gaijin," that is, the people who will always be "Japanese" in positions of power, vs. the people who by definition and dint of birth can never be.

This situation is not sustainable. First, consider Japan's "lost quarter century" of negative or underperforming economic growth that has been significant in a comparative perspective (see figures 10.1 and 10.2).

Figure 10.1 shows data from the First Edition, which indicated Japan's economy had, from the bursting of its economic "bubble" in 1993 through the year 2011, *shrunk* by nearly half a percent *every year on average* compared to its developed-country or regional brethren. As of this Second Edition, now incorporating twenty-six years of data from 1993 to 2019 (before the COVID Pandemic hit), figure 10.2 shows that Japan is no longer in an average economic contraction, but its GDP per capita has grown on average by less than a percent per year, still easily underperforming most of the same select countries. (I surmise that Japan's major growth industry, tourism to Japan, has significantly affected these numbers; as noted in chapter 8, tourism's

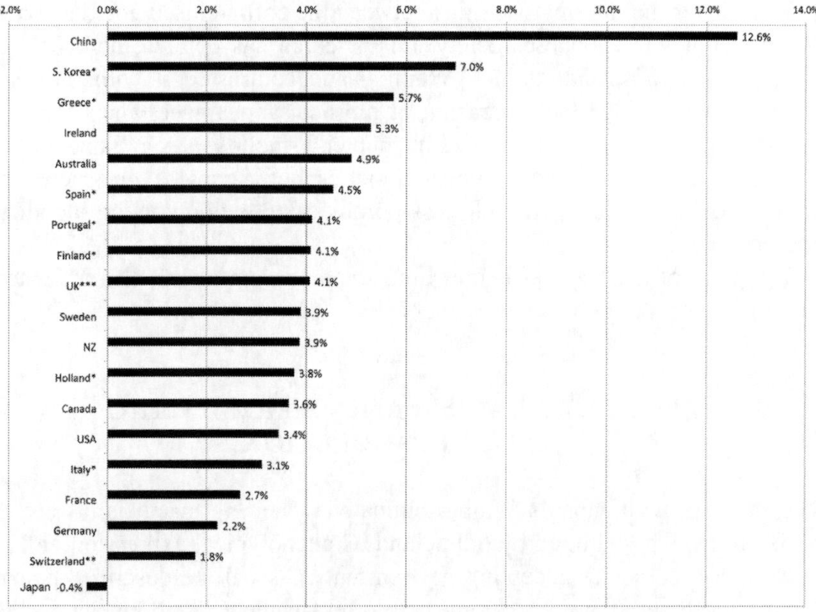

Figure 10.1 Average GDP Growth Per Capita for Select Countries Year-on-Year 1993–2011, in 2015 Local Currency Values (Includes Forecasts Where Indicated). *Source*: Data from IMF, http://www.econstats.com/weo/V003.htm. Created by author.

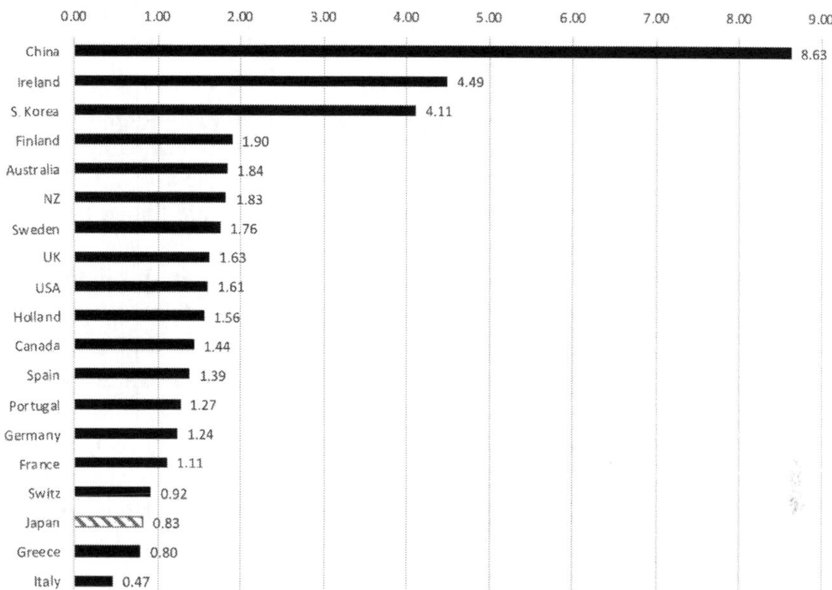

Figure 10.2 Updated for This Second Edition: Average GDP Growth for Select Countries Year-on-Year 1993–2019. *Source*: Data from World Bank, http://data.worldbank.org. Created by the author.

contribution to Japan's total GDP has expanded from 1.7 to 2 percent since 2010. This underscores Japan's need to avoid "Japanese Only" signs and rules.)

It is not clear that even these low growth rates are sustainable, given Japan's perpetual demographic crisis. According to the most recent GOJ figures as this book went to press (June 30, 2021), Japan's population continues to decrease, as its birthrate has long been below replacement levels, reaching the lowest on record in 2019 before being further worsened by the 2020 COVID Pandemic.[1] The number of (Japanese citizen—*sic*) children under age fifteen has dropped to record lows for forty consecutive years, representing the lowest population percentage among major countries with populations of at least 40 million.[2] Japan's population has also been shrinking since 2011, and from the current level of 125.3 million (including the rising number of foreign residents),[3] dropping by close to one million per year; at this rate it is projected to drop below 100 million by 2049.[4]

Meanwhile, Japan's working-age population is forecast to fall by nearly half from 81.7 million in 2010 to 44.2 million by 2060.[5] In terms of people above a "reasonable working age" of sixty-five, the projected elderly but not yet infirm (ages 65–74) are projected to be at around 22 percent of Japan's population; if you include all elderly and infirm (sixty-five and up), this will comprise nearly 36 percent of Japan's total population by 2050.[6] Thus, with Japan's demographic pyramid being top heavy and projected to have one of the world's highest median ages,[7] the elderly and pensioners will soon outnumber young pension contributors, putting the solvency of Japan's social security pension plans into jeopardy.[8] (Note that this is not unexpected: the GOJ and the UN both forecast this happening as early as the year 2000, when the UN advised Japan to immediately start bringing in more than a half million foreign residents *per year*.)[9]

Further, Japan's goal of self-sufficiency in terms of food and industry is also unsustainable.[10] For example, the farming sector as of 2019 has workers with an average age of 66.6—already beyond a "reasonable working age"—and by 2030 nearly three-quarters of all of Japan's farmers will be aged sixty-five.[11] Unless people move to rural areas to take their place, Japan will need to increase its imports of food and labor, becoming more dependent on the same global forces that the GOJ resists when refusing to revitalize its workforce with permanent imports of labor (see chapter 5). However, this is unlikely to happen, as economic opportunities in the countryside have diminished to the degree where some villages have become ghost towns (the National Institution of Population and Social Security Research projects that 896 Japanese cities, towns, and villages will be *extinct* by 2040),[12] while power and population continue to crowd and centralize into urban metropolises.[13]

Again, to replace its elderly, Japan needs to create "new Japanese" to revitalize its economy. This means either more babies being born, or more people being let in, that is, immigration. Given the low birthrate, the first option is infeasible. So how about importing people and making them Japanese?

As this book covered at length, the barriers are too high, and in my personal experience as a Caucasian naturalized Japanese citizen, becoming a Wajin is currently not possible for people categorized as Gaijin. Due to the embedded national discourse on Japan's "uniqueness" (with its stress on "differences" regarding outsiders rather than "similarities"), Wajin are intellectually and sociologically "walled in" to believe that "foreigners" *must by definition be different* than "Japanese" (see chapter 7). This means that Gaijin will have immense difficulty becoming "Japanese" through other means at their disposal, such as individual study and acculturation, familiarity with Japan, duration of time in Japan, Japanese language ability, or even naturalization.

This is of course before we get to the issue of Japanese citizens who are *hāfu* ("half-Japanese," or children of mixed roots mentioned passim), whose numbers are increasing by about 20,000 (one in fifty) children born in Japan every year.[14] Yet they are often socially othered into feeling they are not "real Japanese"—again, policed by Wajin into Gaijin status (see chapters 5, 7, and 8). All of this is the effect of Japan's Embedded Racism, and overcoming it will require significant revisions to Japan's national discourse and landmark policymaking.

This chapter will now discuss: (1) what Japan ought to do in future, and (2) why the GOJ will probably fail to do it. Then the book will conclude with a vignette.

WHAT JAPAN MUST DO TO AVOID ECONOMIC CRISIS: IMMIGRATION AND ASSIMILATION

Let us now consider Japan's future through the lens of one of Japan's most vocal supporters of a law against racial discrimination, who states quite unambiguously, "Japan as we know it is doomed. Only a revolution can save it. What kind of revolution? Japan must become a nation of immigrants."[15]

Sakanaka's "Big Japan" vs. "Small Japan"

Sakanaka Hidenori, director of the Japan Immigration Policy Institute think tank,[16] and former director of the Tōkyō Immigration Bureau, described Japan in 2009 as at a crossroads with a choice between "Big Japan" and "Small Japan."

> From the standpoint of accepting foreign immigrants, one can examine how Japan could address population decline by considering the following two extreme options. One option is to go along completely with the natural population decline and create a "Small Japan." The other option is to compensate for the natural population decrease by accepting immigrants and maintaining Japan's current position as an economic powerhouse or "Big Japan." Put another way, the former requires maintaining the current status quo in which native Japanese account for the vast majority of the population. The latter option requires changing the composition of Japan's population through accelerated growth in the proportion of people who are not ethnically Japanese. Whichever option is chosen, Japanese citizens living through the process of natural population decline will have to overcome difficult obstacles.[17]

Sakanaka's summary of how Big or Small Japan would actually look is included in appendix 1. It is one of the few proposals that seriously considers a future of immigration positively—the alternative of actually *welcoming* immigrants—and offers sophisticated and non-alarmist predictions on immigration's effects on Japanese society. Sakanaka has also advocated that the GOJ shift from its "worker training" (*ikusei kei*) paradigm for importing temporary foreign workers to embracing "immigration" (*imin*), a word at this writing rarely found in GOJ policy proposals. He also demands the establishment of a specialized "Immigration Agency" (*Imin-chō*),[18] which would guide potential immigrants to productive lives within their new homeland.

However, Sakanaka's hopes have dimmed since he first came out in favor of immigration in 2005. As of 2012, he revised his target of 20 million immigrants downward to 10 million by 2050, with the caveat, "I can't exactly say that the plan I've been advocating over the past three years has generated much enthusiasm. Intellectuals and politicians basically ignore me."[19] A septuagenarian, it is unclear whether Sakanaka will see his ideas come to policy fruition within his lifetime. My belief at this writing (perhaps Sakanaka's as well) is that the "Small Japan" scenario is more likely to be Japan's future for another reason that goes beyond egregious racialization processes: The GOJ has been negligent in its fundamental duty to ensure its survival as a nation-state—the creation of a sense of community and legitimacy for *all* of its residents. This can only result in inevitable policy failure.

How Non-Wajin Are Deprived of a Sense of "Belonging" to Japan

Everybody needs to belong somewhere—and this is a feeling fostered by the modern nation-state. Iida (2002) sensibly argues that to ensure its own survival, every country must convince its people that the nation-state they live in is legitimate.[20] They must get their population to accept that (a) there is a country that they are members of, and (b) that there are rules they have to follow in order to be members (e.g., obeying the laws, paying taxes, potentially giving up one's life to defend it, etc.). In other words, denizens must give up some of their power as individuals to society and the State in order to receive the benefits of membership. When power granted to the state becomes unquestioned, it is normal enough to be invisible and generally accepted by the individual. Almost all people on this planet have been born into a nation-state and accept that they are members of one country or another (by dint of having a passport, a tax home, accountability before the law, etc.), playing by the rules because that is how they were socialized.

However, there is still a give-and-take. According to Iida, a nation-state must give its members four things in order for the latter to adopt the rules of play and pass them down to the next generation:

1) A shared memory of the past (i.e., a national narrative) that links them,
2) A sense of community, with moral obligations to it,
3) A worldview that makes sense, and
4) Hope for the future that other people share.

However, what do Japan's "foreigners" (i.e., the *gaikokujin*, the Gaijin, the Invisible and Visible Minorities) in Japan get from Japan as a nation-state?

1) A shared memory of the past? I would argue no. What "foreigners" generally hear in the national narrative is how foreigners, if granted any influence at all in Japanese society, are generally exogenous influences, if not largely ignored and/or overwritten (see vignette below). Thus, "foreigners" are rarely if ever seen as part of Japan's past or legacies, as generally only Wajin figure into the history of Japan as "Japanese."[21]

2) A sense of community? I would argue no. Notwithstanding a few scattered clusters of Chinese, Koreans, and Nikkei South Americans in a few cities, "foreign communities" are generally not acknowledged in Japan's "homogeneous society" and national discourse. It is also difficult for them to form communities in Japan: populations of noncitizen residents both in terms of physical space and absolute numbers are not near a "critical mass." It is also hard for many nationalities to come together due to a lack of commonality in interests: If anything, "foreigners" are linked by who they are *not* (i.e., not "Japanese"), rather than by who they *are*. Although the independent Zainichi, Nikkei, and English-language media have tried to establish ways to link themselves outside the Wajin-dominated media, they still have limited audience and influence in Japanese society.

3) A worldview that makes sense? I would argue no. A dominant discourse that sees minorities as nonexistent or insignificant cannot make sense to those minorities. This is further exacerbated, as documented in chapters 4–8, by official exclusivist propaganda and xenophobic dehumanization—meaning that if a minority existence is even acknowledged, it is generally to target and blame them for social ills.

4) Hope for the future that other people share? I would argue no. Peoples who are constantly "othered" and subordinated in society not only cannot share communal life experiences (e.g., share a bath at a "Japanese Only" establishment, rent living spaces, or buy consumer goods as one chooses), but will also eventually lose hope for a future of equal treatment in society. Constant alienation will prevent many people from a sense of "belonging" to Japan, or from accepting Japan as an entity with hegemonic power over their lives. This is why some potential immigrants ultimately feel little affinity with Japan and will, once a threshold is reached, leave. Moreover, even if some "foreigners" do make the investment and commitment to Japan (e.g., family, home, loans, language and acculturation, even permanent residency/citizenship), they are still generally not included in Japan's national or historical narrative, or even in official population tallies! (see chapter 4).

This is a fatal flaw in Japan's nation-state maintenance. By design, if "foreigners" will never feel "Japanese," then "foreigners" will not keep coming to and staying in a depopulating Japan.

SUGGESTIONS FOR THE GOJ TO MAKE JAPAN MORE APPEALING TO OUTSIDERS

As I have argued elsewhere,[22] there are several ways the GOJ could increase Japan's openness to outsiders.

The first thing is to acknowledge Japan's minorities and their contributions. Many foreigners are here at the GOJ's behest for work (the Chinese, Nikkei Brazilians, Peruvians, Filipinas, Vietnamese, etc.), others for intellectual, cultural, and economic transfer (educators, businesspeople, JICA, JET, etc.); and of course the Zainichi and offspring of noncitizens by dint of birth. Most pay into Japan's pension system, and all pay some form of taxes.

Second, the GOJ must recognize that there is a quid pro quo: Residents must be rewarded for their contributions by defending their civil, political, economic, and cultural rights, that is, the right to maintain a standard of living, spend wages, and avail themselves of the fruits of society like any other resident of Japan. What follows are some specific policies I suggest the GOJ adopt:

1. Passing punitive criminal laws covering all levels of government outlawing discrimination by race, appearance, nationality, and national and social origin.
2. Empowering the MOJ's BOHR with stronger investigative and punitive powers.
3. Creating regional human rights ombudsmen, with appropriate oversight and punitive powers.
4. Abolishing *both de facto* and *de jure* Nationality Clauses from public- and private-sector employment, and allow noncitizens to sit meritocratic administrative advancement examinations. This includes the abolishment of full-time untenured contracted positions for foreign educators at universities, and employment on the same tenured terms and processes as Japanese full-time faculty.
5. Creating family registry systems to register non-Japanese equally with citizens.
6. Making visa renewal and naturalization more transparent, with avenues for investigation and appeal of the processes.
7. Legalizing dual nationality (as this is the increasing trend of the future for modern nation-states).[23]
8. Granting citizenship from birth, as in jus soli.
9. Shortening the time period for qualifying for Permanent Residency.
10. Easing restrictions on granting credit to international residents, including government loans to homeowners based on individual merit, not solely Permanent Residency.

11. Granting national and/or local suffrage to Permanent Residents (as half of them would already be citizens in OECD countries with jus soli requirements for citizenship).
12. Creating an Immigration Ministry independent from the MOJ, with policy priorities that prioritize welcoming noncitizens instead of policing them.
13. Adding enforceable criminal penalties to the new Hate Speech Act.
14. Publicly promoting as a national campaign the idea that in twenty-first-century Japan, "Japaneseness" can no longer be a matter of blood or appearance. It is instead a matter of legal status—for the sake of Japan's hundreds of thousands of Japanese children with international roots.
15. Publicly promoting as a national campaign the idea that foreigners are not temporary guests, but rather are residents, taxpayers, and immigrants, worthy of most privileges and immunities of citizens. Foreign residents are a social boon, not a bane.

To its credit, the GOJ has carried out some reforms, as mentioned in chapter 8. Once reforms are made, they must stick well enough to weather public backlash and claims of, for example, "reverse discrimination." How is this done? Komai (1999, 2001) argues that including noncitizens in these policy-making processes is crucial[24]:

> In order to acknowledge the sociopolitical and cultural rights of minority groups, it is indispensible to establish the public sphere, as emphasized by Habermas [1962]. Here, the public sphere refers to an interest among the members of the society in forming a social consensus, through critical discourse, in opposition to public authority. The public sphere, in this case, can only be established with the participation of the members of the society. It is an absolute precondition for the recognition of various rights and tolerance for other cultures.
>
> From this point of view, we can shed new light on the charge of reverse discrimination, which is often used as a critique of multiculturalism. This claim, which is often made in the United States, charges that affirmative action policies (preferential quotas for certain ethnic groups) represent discrimination in reverse as they take away opportunities from members of the majority group. One can recognize, indeed, that when the decisions on these preferential quotas are made by public authorities, there is no guarantee of real fairness. Only a public sphere established through the participation of all parties with an interest in the issue can guarantee decision-making which contains real fairness.
>
> From this perspective, the responses towards resident Koreans in Japan can be seen in a positive light. The refusal of local governments to uphold the

> "Nationality Clause" carries not only the passive significance of upholding rights, but also opens the door for participation of members of minority groups as residents in local governments, which are organized as providers of service to residents. It thus has the positive significance of contributing to the establishment of the social public sphere. In the same way, for example, allowing citizen foreigners [*Komai's term for local foreign residents*] to participate in decision-making meetings will, from the position of a public sphere divorced from bureaucratic discretion, contribute to the establishment of broad socioeconomic as well as cultural rights for citizen foreigners.

Unfortunately, I remain pessimistic that Japan's minorities will be included and co-opted in Japan's future policymaking processes, given GOJ's past behaviors and mindsets:

Why These Suggestions May Not Be Adopted: The Mindsets of Japan's Bureaucratic Ruling Elite

Who governs in Japan? Although a thorough debate on this topic would take too much space, I subscribe to two probable outcomes in any case: (1) Politics in Japan's aging society will reflect the needs of an increasing-majority elderly voter population and their increasingly conservative values;[25] and (2) What Japan's voters support is generally mooted by the primacy of Japan's ruling bureaucratic elite. I subscribe to Chalmers Johnson's position of "who governs is Japan's elite state bureaucracy."[26] In support of this claim, this book has provided concrete examples of the Japanese bureaucracy's extralegal powers to create and enforce laws without consulting Japan's legislature (see chapters 4 and 5).

Therefore, it is important to understand what attitudes Japan's bureaucrats have (and likely will continue to have) toward "foreigners." Will they ever create policy to grant more rights to "foreigners," and finally the perpetual "Other" to become part of the "Self"? Sadly, I conclude that the GOJ will not for the foreseeable future. Evidence for that conclusion is not only visible in GOJ arguments made to international bodies monitoring racial discrimination worldwide, but also grounded in a long institutional memory of GOJ noncooperation with global standards and neglect of international promises (see chapter 8). Let's consider the likelihood of a positive outcome:

How a Racial Discrimination Law Might Happen: Elements of a Geopolitical-GOJ Elite "Interest Convergence"

As discussed in chapters 8 and 9, several examples of GOJ "progressive policies" could be instances of "interest convergence." Japan's ruling bureaucratic elite found their interests (e.g., of gaining perks and privileges within the club of rich countries) converging with the outside world's interests (e.g., of ensuring that fellow rich country club members abide by the same rules). However, this did not result in reforms actually doing anything meaningful for minorities, that is, creating a fundamental reordering of Japan's power base, since the laws and resolutions were either symbolic or unenforceable. This apparent convergence of "interests" thus bypassed Japan's domestic minorities themselves and converged only on a geopolitical level.

Moreover, when there is an issue that may affect Japan's international reputation (such as the photogenic "Japanese Only" signs of the Otaru Onsens Case; see chapter 3), the GOJ often intervenes as a buffer[27] (e.g., in an ambassadorial or consular form in the international media, or when ministerial officials appear before international bodies such as the UN, etc.) to insulate Japan's polity. Informally referred to as "gaijin handling,"[28] GOJ officials then speak directly to the "outside world" to explain (often in a monocultural manner with a standardized "cultural" narrative) and justify the behavior of an entire nation despite the diverse plurality of individuals within.[29] (These campaigns are so effective that even Non-Japanese abroad enforce Japan's racialized attitudes toward outsiders.)[30]

The two external forces probably offering the most promise of interest convergence have been global media and international human rights oversight bodies. In addition to the examples cited above, they have also had some effect on Japan's media (e.g., overseas articles reprinted with widely quoted interpretations in Japan's print and TV media),[31] laws (e.g., *New York Times* articles shaming Japan in 1998 for fingerprinting foreigners, leading to the (temporary) abolition of fingerprinting),[32] its judiciary (with references made to the inclusion or exclusion of international treaty in its judicial decisions; see chapter 3), and bureaucrats (who have drafted laws under international pressure).[33]

Therefore, for interests to converge enough for Japan to pass a law against racial discrimination, the GOJ would need a high-profile event (such as a UN Decade against Racism or an International Conference for Migrants being held within Japan) or a geopolitical quid pro quo (such as a UN Security Council seat for Japan) to occasion it. However, even then, this author anticipates that any antidiscrimination law will contain built-in safeguards (such as a lack of fines or incarceration for miscreants; see chapter 8) to ensure that it allays international criticism but does not have statutes for enforcement.

In conclusion, a law against racial discrimination in Japan will not occur because "interest convergence" will not occur—because minorities (particularly the noncitizen and Non-Wajin minorities) have no "interests" within Japan's power structure. Minority "interests" may be represented due to *gaiatsu* of international bodies on Japan's ruling elite, but it will not result in a "convergence" of mutual benefits. Instead, as history indicates, revisions of laws will effect cosmetic changes but not empower the disenfranchised. Even in cases mentioned in this research where "foreigners" would be given additional human rights (e.g., Permanent-Resident local suffrage, human rights bills both at the national and prefectural level—see chapter 7), powerful domestic Wajin interests quickly portrayed *the very presence of "foreigners" in Japan* as a form of interest *divergence*, quickly defeated the proposals through alarmism, and reestablished the primacy of Wajin.[34]

It should be noted that with the unrelenting demographic pressure on Japan (a very intractable form of *gaiatsu* indeed), there have been high-profile efforts by Japan's bureaucracy to draft policy that could countermand this embedded exclusionary public discourse. This deserves a mention at this juncture, as a detailed look at the discourse reveals the fatal flaws dooming public policy reform once again to failure.

Elements of Perpetual Policy Failure in Microcosm: 2012 Deliberation Councils on "Coexisting with Foreigners"

In a development that pleasantly surprised this author, the Cabinet Office of Japan in 2012 set up a committee composed of the vice-ministers of the Cabinet Secretariat, and several ministries, including Internal Affairs and Communications, Justice, Foreign Affairs, Finance, Education, Health and Welfare, Trade and Industry, Transport and Tourism, Forest and Fisheries, and the NPA to investigate and recommend public policy for a "co-existence society with foreigners"[35] (*gaikokujin to no kyōsei shakai jitsugen kentō kaigi*). It met five times between May and August, with their hearings archived online for public view.[36] Significantly, attendees acknowledged Japan's interests in having "foreigners" revitalize its future economy. A fuller analysis is elsewhere,[37] but positive proposals included:

- State-supported Japanese language education for all noncitizens.
- State-supported education for all noncitizens' children.
- More multilingual information online and in public access areas.
- Proper enrollment for noncitizens in Japan's health, unemployment, and social welfare systems.
- More assistance with finding noncitizens employment and with resolving unemployment.
- Some attention to "cultural sensitivity" and "mutual respect" issues.
- Better coordination between all levels of government for more comprehensive policies, and so on.

However, there were some fundamental flaws in the program. First, definitions were unclear. What did "coexistence" (*kyōsei*) and "acceptance" (*uke'ire*) mean? Would it go as far as official recognition of ethnic minorities, acceptance of ethnic differences as also "Japanese," or did it stop at simply allowing people into the country and policing them?

Second, embedded in the proceedings was a continued narrative that "othered" "foreigners." As Herbert (1995) uncovered in his analysis of public policies toward "foreigners" three decades ago, *plus ça change*: current policies still had the invective of "our country" (*wagakuni*), and the issue under discussion was couched negatively as "the foreign laborer *problem*" (*gaikokujin rōdōsha mondai*). Thus, if "foreigners" were not being treated as intruders, then they were being portrayed as "guests" being indulgently granted privileges from above.

Third, the ministries were considering vague "environmental preparations" (*kankyō seibi*) before more "foreigners" arrived, as if "foreigners" who needed assistance were not already living in Japan. Minority residents were once again being treated as invisible.

In sum, there was a failure of imagination. Of course, one cannot expect that policymakers, who cannot envision a Japan with minorities at all, would be capable of devising policy welcoming minorities. But this blindness was systemwide, as seen in each attending ministry's proposal and their embedded mindsets toward "foreigners." They sum up nicely the interests and narratives of Japan's power brokers we have covered throughout this book:

The Justice Ministry expressed trepidation that they could not "administer" (*kanri*) "foreigners" properly once they crossed the border. But this problem would be taken care of thanks to July 2012's reforms to registration systems that tightened policing. Thus, policing, not integration, was the Justice Ministry's primary concern.

The Health Ministry suggested important improvements to welfare and employment systems. However, they stated that no fundamental legislative reforms (as part of the "environmental preparations") were necessary, as discrimination against "foreign workers" is allegedly already forbidden (*kinshi*) by law.

The Cabinet talked exclusively about assisting Nikkei entrants—explicitly prioritizing only people with Wajin bloodlines in GOJ public policy. Residents from Japan's largest and then-fourth-largest Newcomer nationalities, that is, China and The Philippines, were not mentioned anywhere.

The Education Ministry recycled old ideas, saying little more than Japan needs to teach "foreigners" the Japanese language.

The Ministries of Foreign Affairs, Finance, Trade and Industry, Transport and Tourism, or Forest and Fisheries offered no suggestions whatsoever in initial meetings.

The most characteristic report was from the NPA, who, with a single page of statistics once again claiming a foreign crime *rise* (despite a dramatic *fall* across the board since 2007 that was *clearly visible in the statistics it presented*), advocated more policing.

The biggest blind spot within this series of meetings was the lack of diversity in its attendees. Most were older Wajin male bureaucrats with approximately the same socioeconomic status and life experience. People with experience (*yūshikisha*) were invited as guest speakers (including a head bureaucrat of Tōkyō Shinjuku-ku, the mayor of Hamamatsu City, two leaders of NGOs that deal in Nikkei issues, and four academics of culture, labor migration, and language teaching), but they too were all Wajin. Only one noncitizen attended—Nikkei Brazilian Angelo Ishi of Musashi University—meaning there were no Visible Minorities present whatsoever. Even their briefings were couched as third-party "reports from the field" (*genba de*), as if "foreigners" were exotic animals studied with binoculars in their habitat.

Thus, the "structural determinism" behind Japan's Embedded Racism had again interfered with a well-intentioned GOJ series of policy meetings, despite considerable time, coordination, and expense. Important questions were not raised: Where is a proposed amendment to the Basic Education Law to ensure that schools can no longer refuse "foreign" children an education? Where are the anti-bullying proposals in primary and secondary education? Where is a proposed punishment for the employer who treats his "foreign" workers unequally and illegally? Where is that law against racial discrimination?

There was also no proposal to publicly promote immigrants as members of Japanese society and as minority "Japanese." Indicatively, the word "immigration" (*imin*) appeared nowhere in written conclusions at the end of the meetings.[38]

Thus, once again the Wajin had been "walled in." Japan's reflexive maintenance of Wajin group dominance by differentiating, "othering," and subordinating Non-Wajin was still systemically unable to create public policy that reflects—not dictates—what Non-Wajin residents want. Despite embryonic policy explicitly stating that Japan's future interests involve "coexistence" with "foreigners," even the highest levels of the GOJ lacked the presence of mind to get input from the long-term Non-Wajin already in Japan. The GOJ, like most of the dominant discourse on Japan's minorities both domestically and worldwide, still treats Non-Wajin as an exogenous force.[39]

FINAL THOUGHTS: JAPAN'S BLEAK FUTURE ON ITS PRESENT COURSE

We opened this book with a quote from an exclusionary public bathhouse owner denying entry to a Caucasian Japanese citizen due to his "foreign" appearance. Let us now close this book with an exchange that concludes how the exclusionism fostered by Japan's Embedded Racism is hurting Japan as a whole.

"Japan must welcome 10 million immigrants between now and 2050," said the abovementioned Sakanaka Hidenori in an article for the *Japan Times*, October 21, 2012. When I posted about that article on my archive, Debito.org, two days later a reader commented:

> Not a hope in hell. I brought this up with two Japanese company presidents over dinner tonight, and they just looked at me blankly in silence.
>
> Then one of them said, "Ah, he means as cheap labor." I said, "No, for the children," to which they replied, "But what help is that? Japan needs more Japanese children."

To gauge how open Japan might ever become toward accepting "foreign" children as "Japanese," even if they were born and raised in Japan, consider this case.

On June 10, 2012, the *New York Times* ran an article entitled "A Western outpost shrinks on a remote island now in Japanese hands." It talked about a chain of islands called the Ogasawaras (Bonins), located 600 miles south of Metropolitan Tōkyō (which administers the islands). Historically active as a stopover point for Non-Wajin travelers (including Commodore Matthew C. Perry and author Jack London) and self-governed until 1875, the Ogasawaras were appropriated by a fledgling Japanese nation-state securing its borders for territorial integrity and imperial expansion.

The Non-Wajin Visible Minority residents there, known as *Ōbeikei*, were treated with "benign neglect" until World War II, when they as subjects of the emperor were forced to take Japanese names, and either serve in a defensive garrison on the island, or, in case they were spies, face deportation to the Japanese mainland. After the war, the Ogasawaras were administered by the US Navy, and the *Ōbeikei* returned to their island as American citizens. When the islands were returned to Japan in 1968, the few hundred *Ōbeikei* residents were offered a choice to retain, adopt, or forfeit Japanese nationality. As of 2012, about two hundred elderly *Ōbeikei* remained on the islands as Non-Wajin citizens, with Japanese and English names, and an uncertain future—outnumbered by Wajin migration from the mainland.

The past is currently being overwritten to suit Wajin interests. The local village-run visitor center on the main island, Chichijima, presents an official history that according to the *New York Times* "plays down the Westerners' role in settling the island," depicting them as "little more than squatters who occupied what officials say was already Japanese territory." The island's vice-mayor reportedly said that "no efforts are being made to preserve the

Westerners' culture." After the Ogasawaras were listed as a World Heritage Site in 2011, tourism and relocation from mainland Japan increased the Wajin residents to around 1,800 souls. They reportedly "have little knowledge of or interest in the Westerners."

In the article, sixty-three-year-old Chichijima resident John Washington worried that the Ogasawara's Non-Wajin history will die out with his generation. "They don't teach the history of the Bonin Islands to kids, don't teach about Nathaniel Savory" (the adventurer who settled lawless Chichijima in 1830, and is John Washington's great-great-great grandfather). "The Japanese hide these things."

A tour guide named Sutanrii Minami (aka Stanley Gilley), sixty-four, a Visible Minority with Polynesian features, also added, "They call me foreigner. I'm not a foreigner. I was born on this island."[40]

What is reportedly happening in Chichijima is another example in microcosm of how Japan as a nation-state enforces its national discourse of "homogeneity" within its territorial mandate: by neglecting, ignoring, and even erasing examples of diversity. The ethnic cleansing of history within the Ogasawaras has many precedents in Japan's past, and is evidence that even present-day Japan has not changed its habit of eradicating Non-Wajin influences from its borders. (It will probably treat resident Russians the same way if the GOJ is ever granted sovereignty over the Northern Territories off Hokkaidō.)

In sum, the under-researched Visible Minorities in Japan warrant more scholarly attention because they are the metaphorical "canary in the coal mine": How visually identified "outsiders" are treated in Japan is a bellwether of Japan's future economic and societal vitality. To hope that Japan's Embedded Racism will ever allow for "new Japanese" who cannot "pass" as Wajin is to misunderstand how "Japanese" view themselves as racialized entities. What Japan cannot phenotypically embrace, it will seek to erase.

It is how Japan as a nation-state is hardwired to preserve its own sense of community and identity. Without a revolution in thinking and self-concept, Japan will not for the foreseeable future have the conditions or mindset to create an effective law against racial discrimination. It will also not succeed in effectively stopping embedded processes of racialization from differentiating, "othering," and subordinating other people—including Japanese citizens—for looking "foreign." It is incumbent not only upon the GOJ, but also upon scholars of Japan and nation-states in general, to consider the prospect that Japan's extremely strong national narratives may be too exclusive for its own good.

Until Japan takes the first steps of removing bloodline as a prerequisite for legally based citizenship status, and makes clear in the national narrative that people do not have to "look Japanese" in order to be "Japanese," then the

Wajin dominant majority, even as it demographically ages and shrinks, will through its reflexive control over a sovereign nation-state perpetually retain a suffocating and self-strangulating dominance over the Japanese archipelago. If not properly analyzed and addressed, Japan's Embedded Racism will be its undoing.

NOTES

1. "An uphill battle to reverse the falling birthrate." *Japan Times*, June 4, 2020; "The COVID-19 Pandemic is Accelerating Japan's Population Decline: A Statistical Analysis." *Nippon.com*, May 25, 2021.

2. "Japan's child population falls to record low 16.17 million." *Japan Times/ Jiji Press*, May 4, 2015; "Japan's child population hits record low after 40 years of decline." *Kyodo News*, May 4, 2021.

3. www.stat.go.jp/english/data/jinsui/tsuki/index.html.

4. "The COVID-19 Pandemic is Accelerating Japan's Population Decline: A Statistical Analysis." *Nippon.com*, May 25, 2021.

5. "Japan Cabinet minister wary of opening 'Pandora's Box' of immigration." *Japan Times*, May 13, 2015; "Japan's Population Falls for Ninth Straight Year." *Nippon.com*, April 30, 2020.

6. "*Kōreisha jinkō (65–74, 75 ijō) to sono wariai*" [Population and proportion of elderly (65–74, 75+)]. *Shūkan Ekonomisuto*, January 15, 2008: 16.

7. "A declining Japan loses its once-hopeful champions." *Washington Post*, October 27, 2012, particularly the graphic "As Japan's population ages, optimism wanes." More current statistics show that South Korea may overtake Japan in terms of highest median age by 2050, but Japan will still remain in second place. *See* www.statista.com/statistics/673014/top-ten-countries-with-highest-projected-median-age/ (accessed June 2, 2021).

8. One often-touted solution to the demographic crisis is automation, that is, getting robots into fields that require elderly care, such as hospitals and care centers. *See*, for example, GOJ policy trial balloons floated at "Better than people: Why the Japanese want their robots to act more like humans." *Economist* (London), December 20, 2005; "Government tackles population decline." *Yomiuri Shinbun*, August 26, 2014, archived at www.debito.org/?p=12609; "Aging Japan: Robots may have role in future of elder care." *Reuters*, March 27, 2018; and so on. However, robots do not pay taxes, so without young people paying into pension plans for the current elderly, I do not see how automation will make up the financial shortfall when the young taxpayers reach retirement.

9. Arudou (2006c), which notes, "As far back as 2000, under the Obuchi Administration, 'The Prime Minister's Commission on Japan's Goals in the 21st Century' (as well as the UN) famously advised Japan to import *around 600,000 people per annum*. This would maintain Japan's tax base and ameliorate the effects of record-high longevities and record-low birthrates contributing to an aging population" (emphasis added).

10. Examples of Japan's policy of self-sufficiency (*jikyū jisoku*), particularly in terms of energy and "food security," are abundant in Japan's policy writings. *See*, for example, the Ministry of Agriculture, Forestry, and Fisheries brief on the subject at www.maff.go.jp/j/zyukyu/zikyu_ritu/011.html. A good example of the mysticism this evokes can be found in Emiko Ohnuki-Tierney, "Rice as self: Japanese identities through time." *Education about Asia* 9(3) Winter 2004, adapted from an eponymous book by Princeton University Press, 1993.

11. "Trade talks pit Japanese farmers against industry." *BBC News*, November 1, 2011; "Takako Yoshino's growing community of farmers." *Japan Times*, September 7, 2019.

12. "Is Japan becoming extinct?" *Japan Times*, May 16, 2015.

13. *See* inter alia "Village writes its epitaph: Victim of a graying Japan," and "Japan's rice farmers fear their future is shrinking." *New York Times*, April 30, 2006 and March 28, 2009, respectively; Menju Toshihiro, "Accepting immigrants: Japan's last opportunity for Economic Revival." *Asia Pacific Bulletin* No. 169, June 27, 2012. Related to Japan's regional depopulation: According to the Internal Affairs and Communications Ministry, as of 2008, 13.1 percent of all homes in Japan are already vacant or abandoned; that figure is expected to increase to 23.7 percent by 2028. *See* "National tax loophole ensures unused, dilapidated firetraps stay standing, till they fall: Abandoned homes a growing menace." *Japan Times*, January 7, 2014.

14. Chapter 5 in particular focuses on the treatment of multiethnic beauty queens Miyamoto Ariana and Yoshikawa Priyanka as "not real Japanese." *See also* documentaries by Reggie Life, "Doubles: Japan and America's Intercultural Children" (1995); and Megumi Nishikura and Lara Perez Takagi, "Hāfu: The Mixed-Race Experience in Japan" (2013), at http://hafufilm.com. *See also* "Coming of age: 1 in 8 new adults in Tokyo are not Japanese, ward figures show." *Japan Times*, January 10, 2018.

15. "Only immigrants can save Japan." *Japan Times*, October 21, 2012.

16. JIPI's website is at www.jipi.gr.jp/.

17. "A new framework for Japan's Immigration policies," translated specially for Debito.org by Andrew J. I. Taylor and archived at www.debito.org/sakanakaonimmigration.htm.

18. *Ekonomisuto*, January 15, 2008, 22–24.

19. Ibid., *Japan Times*, October 21, 2012.

20. Iida (2002: 264–265).

21. This is substantiated within the worldwide discourse of scholarship and punditry on Japan: for example, Japan takes any foreign influence and makes it "Japanese," and that is what makes Japan "unique." As Befu (2001: 84) observes, predicating "Japan's national identity" on "the primordial homogeneity of the ethnic Japanese" automatically and necessarily excludes other ethnicities from existing not only in Japan's past (by "ignor[ing] their contributions"), but also in Japan's present and future (as we shall see in this chapter).

22. Arudou (2001).

23. Anderson (2012).

24. Komai (1999); English version 2001.

25. Amid copious commentary on the Japan's resurgent nationalism elsewhere, I have written at length about Japan's "right-wing swing" before and after the reelection of Abe Shinzō in 2012. *See*, for example, "Revisionists marching Japan back to a dangerous place." *Japan Times*, October 2, 2012; "The year for NJ in 2012: A top 10." *Japan Times*, January 1, 2013; "Keep Abe's hawks in check or Japan will suffer." *Japan Times*, February 4, 2013; "The empire strikes back: The top 10 issues for NJ in 2013." *Japan Times*, January 7, 2014; and so on.

26. *See* Chalmers Johnson (1975, 1982); citation from (1995: 13).

27. *See*, for example, Kawamura Yasuhisa, director of International Press Division, MOFA, in a Letter to the Editor of the *New York Times* regarding the Otaru Onsens Case, as quoted in Arudou (2006b: 88–89).

28. *See*, for example, Johnson (1995: 88); "Dr. Kitaoka Shinichi, Chair of Council on Security and Defense Capabilities, speaks at UH East-West Center October 11, 2013, on Japan's need to remilitarize." *Debito.org*, October 12, 2013, www.debito.org/?p=11896; Debito Arudou, "Japan brings out big guns to sell remilitarization in US." *Japan Times*, November 7, 2013; "Another Gaijin Handler speaks at East-West Center: Dr. Nakayama Toshihiro, ahistorically snake-charming about how Japan's warlike past led to Japan's stability today." *Debito.org*, September 23, 2015, www.debito.org/?p=13529; "Abe Admin backlashes against UN Rapporteur criticism against Conspiracy Bill, overseas Gaijin Handlers kick into gear." *Debito.org*, June 1, 2017, www.debito.org/?p=14641; and so on.

29. Of course, national image control and outreach is a practice that viable nation-states engage in. But in connection with this research, this is part of the GOJ and ruling elite's attempt to project power by controlling Japan's image abroad. Much research has been done on Japan's "buying power" through PR campaigns overseas, including endowing chairs in universities, funding academic scholarships, conducting lobbying efforts in overseas media and through government offices, and plying other kinds of pressure through mass media campaigns, government organs, foreign aid structures, overseas corporate branches, and embassies/consular missions abroad. *See*, for example, Pat Choate, *Agents of Influence.* Knopf: 1990; Clyde Prestowitz, *Trading Places.* Basic Books: 1993; David Arase, *Buying Power: The Political Economy of Japan's Foreign Aid.* Lynne Reinner: 1995; Hall (1998); "Reuters reports GOJ reinvestment in overseas universities, claims 'no strings attached.'" *Debito.org*, March 19, 2015, www.debito.org/?p=13045; and so on.

30. Japan's ability to control its own narrative overseas has extended to racializing foreigners abroad. The most common reaction to my saying just about anywhere in the world (including at the US border) that I am a Japanese citizen is, "But you don't *look* Japanese" (*see also* the opening of chapter 4). The converse, of someone saying, for example, to a person of color, "But you don't *look* American (Canadian, etc.)," might elicit a quick reaction of surprise if not a job-endangering charge of racism. Thus, the discourse linking physical appearance to Japanese nationality is so hegemonic, even worldwide, that my phenotype is reflexively contested by most people outside Japan with whom I have had this conversation, without any apparent cognitive dissonance on their part whatsoever.

31. Arudou (2006b: 90–93).

32. Cf. Morikawa (1998).

33. There are other avenues for *gaiatsu*, of course, such as geopolitical forces, lateral negotiations, and international trade relations. Although these forces naturally have an influence over Japan's policies and laws, it is unlikely they will have much influence over how "foreigners" are treated in Japan in terms of human rights. It is hard to conceive of countries resorting to trade wars with or placing international sanctions on Japan, a staunch geopolitical ally in Asia, on behalf of the civil and political rights of a few of their resident countrymen. Civil and political rights tend to be seen, again, as the domain of international human rights bodies, subordinated to issues involving international movements of goods and money. *See*, for example, Hall (1998: Introduction and chapter 3) on failed intergovernmental negotiations over job stability for noncitizen educators in Japan. For another example, my personal negotiations with the US Embassy and consulates during the Otaru Onsens Case resulted in no meaningful pressure placed on the GOJ whatsoever; activists and plaintiffs were told on numerous occasions that American residents of Japan were to follow Japanese laws under all circumstances, and since "Japanese Only" signs and rules are not illegal under Japanese law, they said there is nothing the US government could do.

34. *See* "Overseas work, study seen as negative point for anyone handling state secrets." *Kyōdō News*, December 8, 2014. Even the further erosion of civil and political rights within the 2013 promulgation of the problematic "State Secrets Law" (The Act on the Protection of Specially Designated Secrets, or *Tokutei Himitsu Hogo ni kansuru Hōritsu*), empowering the GOJ to declare arbitrary types of government information as secret and severely punish leakers, reportedly had special provisions to address "foreign influences" by screening Wajin for "overseas experiences":

> The documents presented by the intelligence and research office at a meeting with other government bodies in November 2011 state that the experience of attending schools overseas or foreign schools in Japan as well as working abroad or working for foreign companies "could be an opportunity to nurture a special feeling about foreign countries." The papers said such people "tend to be influenced by" approaches from foreign countries and there is a "risk" that they "prioritize the benefits of foreign countries and voluntarily leak secrets."

How this will be put into effect is unclear, but this would explicitly single out if not disqualify Japan's Non-Wajin or Wajin with Non-Wajin roots from positions of authority. How this would be applied to, for example, many of Japan's Wajin elite politicians who have studied abroad (including Abe Shinzō himself, who studied at USC) is as yet unclear. In any case, it may well discourage some ambitious Wajin from venturing overseas or even having "foreign" friends. More in chapter 5.

35. Debito Arudou, "In formulating immigration policy, no seat at the table for non-Japanese." *Japan Times*, July 3, 2012.

36. www.cas.go.jp/jp/seisaku/kyousei/index.html.

37. "GOJ embryonic policymaking reboot for 'co-existence with foreigners:' Some good stuff, but once again, policy about Non-Japanese without any input from them." *Debito.org*, June 10, 2012, at www.debito.org/?p=10271.

38. Cabinet Secretariat, "*Gaikokujin to no kyōsei shakai no jitsugen ni mukete (chūkanteki seiri)*," dated August 27, 2012. The word *imin* has since surfaced in GOJ debates in 2014 dealing for the first time with immigration as a potential panacea for Japan's long-term demographic decline. However, once again, the debate did not include any Visible Minorities (almost all pundits were elite right-wing Wajin, including essayist Sakurai Yoshiko and former Tōkyō Governor Ishihara Shintarō): *See* "*Imin to Zainichi gaikokujin*" [Immigration and the Zainichis]. *SAPIO*, June 2014, special cover issue. The debate was soon drawn into issues of Zainichi discrimination (which does not involve new immigrants, as these are "Oldcomers"), ignoring discrimination toward Japan's "Newcomers," and derailing the debate once again with rightist fears of granting any rights or privileges to potentially subversive North Koreans and Chinese residents. *See* Debito Arudou, "Humanize the dry debate about immigration." *Japan Times*, June 5, 2014.

39. This inability to grasp the reality of what noncitizens need from Japan's visa regimes was soon reflected in the "Points System," a visa regime appraised by these 2012 GOJ deliberations as an attempt to lure "high-skilled foreigners" with fast-tracking to Permanent Residency. Poorly designed, it failed within two years and was phased out. *See* chapter 5.

40. For more information, *see* Long (2002a, b); *see also* Scott Kramer and Hanae Kurihara Kramer, "The Other Islands of Aloha." *Hawaiian Journal of History* 47, 2013: 1–26. *See also* Asakawa (2007: 43–51) for a discussion on how the naturalization of Non-Wajin on the Ogasawaras was one factor in how Meiji-Era Japan eventually drafted its naturalization laws.

Chapter 11

Conclusions for the Second Edition

Japan's Embedded Racism Undermines the World's Democracies

I have had six years to think about this book's thesis since the First Edition, and I have come to the conclusion that the effects of Japan's Embedded Racism are not limited to Japan.

One of my axioms after three decades studying racialization processes is, "If you don't stop racial discrimination, it spreads." I witnessed this firsthand during the Otaru Onsens Case,[1] where one exclusionary bathhouse emboldened others to put up their own "Japanese Only" signs. Then once bigots realized nobody in the government was going to stop them, signs appeared in other cities around Hokkaidō, and then in other prefectures, as businesses nationwide copycatted Otaru's exclusionary signs, sometimes down to the very font.

Discrimination spreads because it can. Prejudice and bigotry, as described in the Introduction and chapter 2, exist in every society, and the difference in how freely prejudice translates into discrimination depends upon the government's will to stop it. That is why the UN has multiple treaties to deal with multiple types of discrimination, and why rich, developed countries are expected to sign and enforce them if they want to be seen as a "civilized" society within the community of nation-states. Japan, however, signs but does not enforce its human rights treaties, and that matters. As covered in chapter 8, the fact that Japan faces no meaningful sanctions for breaking international promises has not just advantaged Wajin and disadvantaged Japan's minorities—it has inspired racial supremacists worldwide.

Japan is a viable model of an ethnostate. Chapters 4–7 covered Japan's official policies that refuse refugees, abuse foreign detainees, offer foreign residents revolving door visas with arbitrary and extralegal barriers to becoming immigrants, prop up domestic industry by lethally exploiting cheap foreign labor, feed propaganda to a compliant and complicit media in order to scare citizens and demonize outsiders, selectively ignore and glorify a brutal colonial and wartime past, and encourage prominent political actors who routinely make racist statements and promote nativist public policies. Despite all of this, Japan remains one of the world's most well-respected countries. That offers succor to racial supremacists in other countries, who ask why "we" can't similarly retool "our" society into having a "pure" monoethnic outlook toward our "real" countrymen. They see Japan as the only developed country successfully avoiding internationalization, immigration, and multiculturalism—scourges of the more liberal, tolerant societies allegedly being "overrun" by people with different skin colors, intolerant religions, and unassimilable value systems.[2] By sticking to its ethnostatism, Japan apparently "saved" its "unique" society, and racists pedestal it as a template.

This is not my imagination. As I argued in a 2018 *Japan Times* article,[3] prominent White supremacists have direct connections to Japan and cite it as an inspiration. Jared Taylor, author and guru of America's so-called alt-right (and, according to the Southern Poverty Law Center, a "modern-day version of the refined but racist colonialist of old"),[4] is a fluent speaker of Japanese and frequent commentator on Japanese TV, born in Kobe to missionary parents and schooled in Japan until high school. A self-described White separatist, Taylor expressly believes Japan will be more successful this century than mongrel America due to its "racial and cultural homogeneity."[5] Richard Spencer, the White supremacist head of the "National Policy Institute" who coined the term "alt-right" (and, according to the SPLC, "a suit-and-tie version of the white supremacists of old, a kind of professional racist in khakis"),[6] advocates America's "peaceful ethnic cleansing" into a "white ethnostate"; cloaking ethnosuperiority as "identitarianism" (which means, "you identify with your race, with your people, with your culture"), Spencer's spokesman claimed, "Everyone in Japan is an identitarian."[7] William Daniel Johnson, chairman of the White nationalist American Freedom Party, wrote a book (and a proposed constitutional amendment) advocating the deportation of all non-Whites from America. Majoring in Japanese in college, Johnson is fluent in the language after his Mormon mission in Tōhoku, and prospers under what the *Guardian* calls "an uncanny connection between Japan and white nationalism in America."[8] Even mass murderer Anders Behring Breivik, the Norwegian Neo-Nazi who massacred sixty-nine people at a Labour Party island youth retreat in 2011, is an ardent Japanophile; in his manifesto, he specifically praised Japan as "a model country" for avoiding multiculturalism.[9]

But another template Japan has offered the world is the environment for online harassment, hate speech, and mobilization of violent fringe groups. Japan's internet "free speech" haven 2chan (or *2channeru*, "Channel 2") since 1999 has been a haven for Japan's *Netto Uyoku* (internet far-rightists), and a cesspool for anonymous bullying, trolling, doxxing of adversaries, and summoning xenophobic public rallies. They have accomplished this without any real legal repercussions for disseminating libel or causing social damage.[10] The creator of 2chan then created the English version 4chan in the same mold, and since the end of 2020, according to the *Guardian*, "more than 136 channels in English, German, Japanese, Korean and Italian have sprung up, adding tens of thousands of followers on a daily basis."[11] The most visible damage has been the conspiracy theories gaining currency and promoting violence against democratic institutions. The most devastating of them, QAnon, has its roots in 8chan and 8kun, which are offshoots of 4chan. Their site administrator and disseminator of inflammatory falsehoods, Ron Watkins, has since reportedly been unmasked as Q.[12] (Watkins, for the record, currently lives in Japan.)

Japan has also offered templates for the Global Far Right[13] to gain real political power. PM Abe recognized the influence and reach of the Netto Uyoku early on, netting a wide audience on ultraconservative outlets like Sakura TV, and this has provided instructional paths for alt-right Americans. Steve Bannon, the engineer of Donald Trump's successful 2016 presidential election strategy, visited Japan in 2017 as a guest of the Japanese Conservative Political Action Conference, and proclaimed Abe the pioneer of Trumpism—"Trump before Trump."[14] According to Joshua Green, author of book *Devil's Bargain*, Bannon harnessed the power of online white male hate, "a rolling tumbleweed of wounded male id and aggression."[15] Recruiting "rootless white males" from the online gaming community into propaganda outlet Breitbart (the "crown jewel of the alt-right's media universe"),[16] Bannon continues to this day, after Trump's presidential pardon in 2021, to spearhead an international social movement of intolerance.[17] Thus, thanks to the lessons of effective mobilization learned from Japan, online hate helped elect a racist to the American presidency in 2016.

Further, if one looks at the tone of governance under the Trump administration, we can see parallels to Japan's policy goals covered in this book, including indefinite border detention under abusive conditions, official narratives demonizing specific ethnicities (e.g., Mexicans in America vs. Chinese/North Koreans in Japan), policies targeting Muslims, racialized preferences for migration, the dissemination of false and distorted propaganda through the news media, the weaponized meme of "fake news" to dispel negative press coverage, online trolling and coded "dog-whistle" messaging to appeal to a nativist base, telling critics of color to "go back" to where they came from, and an overall reactionary playbook that seeks to take the nation back to a halcyon day when the country was "great." These strategies have all been beta-tested in Japan for decades.[18]

However, Japan's political mobilization playbooks are no longer limited to the international mutual-appreciation societies of neoconservatives working within doctrinaire anticommunist ideologies.[19] Given their racialized nature, Japan's strategies have been easily co-opted by White supremacists worldwide, who are now eschewing liberal democracy in favor of authoritarian means to ethnically cleanse their societies. Consequently, we are seeing "nativist" parties, "populist" movements, and authoritarian regimes springing up with degrees of viability worldwide, including Great Britain, Hungary, Poland, The Philippines, Brazil, Hong Kong, Turkey, and India.

Even the United States has come up with a nativist "America First Caucus," sponsored by "hard right, Trump won in 2020"-elected Congresspeople raising record amounts of campaign donations. Their major plank is to protect "uniquely Anglo-Saxon political traditions." This concept has a long history, as it was used as a policy to "control the racial makeup of America" to ban non-European immigrants for more than a century until 1965. As author Jia Lynn Yang (MSNBC Interview, 2021) notes, "Anglo-Saxon political identity is what makes America 'America,' and anyone who is not isn't properly American." However, America would face singular challenges returning to "Anglo-Saxonism," as a quarter of Americans are now either an immigrant or a child of an immigrant who has come in since 1965,[20] but that is why White supremacists advocate authoritarianism to overcome the pluralism of diversity. This ideology is fundamentally grounded in a mindset, still alive and widely practiced in Japan, that only certain people, based upon their birth, bloodline, and physical attributes, are entitled to hold power in a society.

This book has been an effort to make Japan take responsibility for the codified racism it has fostered, and for the damage to democracy it has inspired worldwide. For too long Japan has gotten a free pass thanks to its position as a staunch geopolitical ally, that is, East Asia's anticommunist "unsinkable aircraft carrier"[21] for the United States during the Cold War (which has since evolved into Japan as Asian counterweight to an ascendant China). As discussed in chapter 2, Japan has never been meaningfully called to account for its overt nativism and racial discrimination. Escaping a postcolonial reckoning, Japan was able to take Prewar policies that subordinated its colonials and apply them to its Postwar minorities. Generations later, that template is a genie out of its bottle.

What can be done? Unlike the general imperviousness of China toward international shaming, Japan's policymakers respond definitively to *gaiatsu*, that is, "outside pressure." Japan's bureaucrats wield so much power that something as simple as an embarrassing newspaper article in the *New York Times* can eventually result in surprising policy reversals (e.g., the abolition of fingerprinting for all foreigners in 1998; the "Tonegawa Shock"). But it will take concerted pressure from prominent allies and organizations, particularly the United States and the United Nations, to ensure Japan keeps its international promises made under the treaties it has signed, backed up with potential sanctions that Japan's influential business leaders care about—access to overseas markets.

Linking business interests with universal human rights issues is generally frowned upon by people who only care about the profitability of international trade. But once constrained by law (e.g., the United States' International Anti-Bribery and Fair Competition Act of 1998, in conjunction with the OECD's Convention on Combating Bribery of Foreign Public Officials in International Business Transactions, designed to keep foreign exchange from corrupting overseas institutions) the business community can be compelled to engage in ethically sound practices.

It is time for the rest of the developed world to reassess Japan's place in their world, and acknowledge that it has been a fast-breeder reactor of racism, irradiating discriminatory policy templates into the civil societies of liberal democracies. If it wants to remain a member of that club, Japan must carry out some fundamental reforms to protect the lives and livelihoods of the minorities in its society. This will inevitably mean Japan doing something it promised in 1996 when it effected the UN CERD: passing a national law, with criminal penalties, against racial discrimination.

A quarter-century of waiting for that to happen is long enough, and this book has spent the past 500 pages describing why Japan will not do so on its own. Friends must help friends break bad habits, especially before those bad habits spread. If one is to see Japan truly begin to amend its ways, that is the place to start. It is fundamental for giving minorities, particularly the Visible Minorities, the ability to have a stake in Japan's polity.

Debito Arudou, PhD
July 1, 2021

NOTES

1. Arudou (2006a, b).

2. Debito.org has not been exempt from this line of criticism. When I critiqued an article talking about the increasing multiculturalism of Japan's youth ("'JT: Coming of age: 1 in 8 new adults in Tokyo are not Japanese'; underanalyzed stats posing as media peg." *Debito.org*, January 22, 2018, www.debito.org/?p=14860), an anonymous poster commented:

> Why is this a good thing? Japan needs to stay Japanese. Keep your Leftist, neo-Marxist ideology out of Japan. Japan does not want to go down the same Leftist road as Canada,

UK, Europe, etc. Japan must remain an ethnostate. Keep the poz [HIV-positive] out. We see how that it's destroying the West. Multiculturalism and diversity are a cancer, and I hope to never see it in Japan.

3. Debito Arudou, "White supremacists and Japan: A love story." *Japan Times*, March 7, 2018. As also discussed in this article, Japan tends to attract a type of intolerant person (I call them "White Samurai") disillusioned with diversity in their country of origin; they actively argue against "importing Western morals" into Japan (and conveniently try to leverage Leftist arguments about "cultural imperialism" to their advantage).

4. www.splcenter.org/fighting-hate/extremist-files/individual/jared-taylor.

5. "'Call me a racist, but don't say I'm a Buddhist': meet America's alt right" "They present themselves as modern thinkers of extremism. But the US far right have the same white supremacist obsessions." *Guardian*, October 9, 2016; *see also* https://www.splcenter.org/fighting-hate/extremist-files/individual/jared-taylor. White separatist, homogeneity: "Allerlei Interviews Jared Taylor." *American Renaissance blog*, undated, https://www.amren.com/archives/interviews-appearances/allerlei-interviews-jared-taylor/.

6. www.splcenter.org/fighting-hate/extremist-files/individual/richard-bertrand-spencer-0.

7. "Meet the White Nationalist trying to ride the Trump train to lasting power: Alt-right architect Richard Spencer aims to make racism cool again." *Mother Jones*, October 27, 2016; "He's not a racist, he says, just an 'identitarian,' and he books Richard Spencer's campus talks." *Miami Herald*, October 19, 2017.

8. An uncanny connection: *Guardian*, October 9, 2016, ibid. The *New York Times* has even opined that "exclusively dating Asian women is practically a white-nationalist rite of passage." *See* Audrea Lim, "The Alt-Right's Asian Fetish." *New York Times*, January 6, 2018.

9. "Norway attack killer praises Japan as model country." *Telegraph* (London), July 26, 2011.

10. For example, I won a libel lawsuit against 2chan in 2006, but my court damages went unrequited because the authorities could not track down their bank accounts. *See* www.debito.org/2channelsojou.html#english; Debito Arudou, "2channel: the bullies' forum." *Japan Times*, February 3, 2009.

11. "Unmasked: Man behind cult set to replace QAnon." *Guardian*, March 20, 2021.

12. "Q: Into the Storm" *HBO*, March 2021. Trailer at www.youtube.com/watch?v=rK_Gf9H2CWI&t=118s. *See also* "Leader of QAnon conspiracy group unmasked, new documentary claims: 'Q'—the mysterious leader of the bizarre QAnon conspiracy movement—has been unmasked, a new documentary claims." *News.com.au*, March 17, 2021.

13. This term is from Miller-Idriss, Cynthia. (2020). *Hate in the Homeland: The New Global Far Right*. Princeton University Press.

14. Trump before Trump: "Former Trump strategist Steve Bannon praises Abe's nationalist agenda." *Japan Times*, December 17, 2017. Pioneer of Trumpism: William

Pesek, "Why Bannon showing Abe love is cringeworthy." *Japan Times*, December 19, 2017. Indicatively, Abe was the first foreign leader to visit President-Elect Trump one week after the 2016 election, and remained throughout Trump's presidency a frequent visitor and staunch supporter at international summits.

15. Green: 142, 145–146. This is also substantiated within an interview with Joshua Green, "Inside the 'Shakespearean irony' of Trump and Bannon's Relationship." *NPR*, July 18, 2017, transcript at https://www.npr.org/templates/transcript/transcript.php?storyId=537885042.

16. *Mother Jones*, October 27, 2016, ibid.

17. *See*, for example, "Steve Bannon drafting curriculum for right-wing Catholic institute in Italy." *Reuters*, September 14, 2018, and so on.

18. Debito Arudou, "'Love it or leave it' is not a real choice." *Japan Times*, July 24, 2019.

19. For example, consider how the ultraconservative interest group, "Japan Institute for National Fundamentals" (see chapter 7), funds conservative scholarship and has "Guest Researchers" on its rolls (http://en.jinf.jp/about/officer)—one of whom, a Dr. Kevin Doak of Georgetown University, was presented with a special JINF "Japan Study Award" in 2014 for his research arguing that Japan's nationalism is not racialized. *See* "US professor honored for Japan studies." *Yomiuri Shinbun*, July 14, 2014; and John Breen, "Popes, Bishops and War Criminals: reflections on Catholics and Yasukuni in post-war Japan." *Asia-Pacific Journal—Japan Focus*, 8(9)3, March 1, 2010. Similarly, US neocon think tank Hudson Institute in 2013 awarded a Herman Kahn Award to PM Abe, joining what the *Wall Street Journal* called "an elite group of right-leaning leaders like Ronald Reagan, Henry Kissinger, and Dick Cheney." *See* "Abe First Non-American to Win Conservative Hudson Institute Award." *Wall Street Journal*, September 23, 2013, archived with commentary at www.debito.org/?p=13679.

20. Cribbed from "Why Republicans won't give up the Big Lie" and "Nativist Dog Whistles" segments, MSNBC, *All In With Chris Hayes*, April 16, 2021, minute 0:00 to 7:30, and 52:15 to 59:59. Other sources for this section include "Hard-right Republicans forming new caucus to protect 'Anglo-Saxon political traditions.'" *NBC News*, April 16, 2020; Adam Serwer, "Restoring the 'Soul of the Nation' means taking in Refugees." *The Atlantic*, April 16, 2021; Yang, Jia Lynn (2021). *One Mighty and Irresistible Tide: The Epic Struggle Over American Immigration, 1924–1965.* W.W. Norton; and the "America First Caucus" platform archived at https://punchbowl.news/wp-content/uploads/America-First-Caucus-Policy-Platform-FINAL-2.pdf.

21. Quote is from former PM Nakasone. *See* "Yasuhiro Nakasone, Japanese Leader Who Revived Postwar Military, Dies: Former WWII Navy officer forged closer ties with the U.S. under President Reagan and oversaw Japan's development into a global economic power." *Wall Street Journal*, November 29, 2019.

Glossary

DEFINITIONS OF TERMS NOT DISCUSSED ELSEWHERE IN THE TEXT (IN ALPHABETICAL ORDER)

Citizenship and Nationality: As acknowledged by specialists in the field,[1] this research uses "citizenship" and "nationality" interchangeably purely as a legal status. Many academics divide them into two separate concepts due to the historical roots of the words,[2] that is, where "citizenship" has been cited to mean "a bundle of rights and duties the state confers or imposes upon individuals," while "nationality" has been defined more vaguely in scholarship on Japan as "formal membership in a state in the sense of international law"[3] and "a civil status."[4] However, as distinctions over time within modern nation-states between nationality and citizenship have decreased to the point of full overlap, Kashiwazaki (2000) acknowledges, "In scholarly works as well as in ordinary English usage of the term, 'citizenship' is used interchangeably with the term 'nationality.'"[5] Therefore, for the purposes of this research, "Citizenship" and "Nationality" are used as equivalents, meaning that if you have a Japanese passport, you are a Japanese citizen or a Japanese national—irrespective of race, ethnicity, or national origin.

Ethnicity (in regard to Race): I define "ethnicity" as "a geographic heritage distinction among peoples who have otherwise been racialized into a single group."[6] However, when this term is transposed onto the Japanese language and context, discussion under this term runs into problems. As discussed in the Introduction and chapter 2, discussions about "race" in Japan lead to ill-defined entanglements about ethnicity and *jinshu* ("race," as defined under the translation of the *jinshu sabetsu teppai jōyaku*, or United Nations Convention on the Elimination of *Racial* Discrimination) and *minzoku* (translated as "ethnicity" when referring to minorities in Japan—the exception being *yamato minzoku* being translated as "the Japanese Race" due to historical conceits).[7] For the context of this research, I use "ethnicity" in Japan to refer to people with a geographic origin or heritage distinct from what has historically referred to as *naichi*, or "Japan proper," including ethnic Ainu, ethnic Ryūkyūans, ethnic Koreans, ethnic Chinese, and so on.

Gaijin: Although most dictionaries define this word simply as "foreigner" or "outsider" (as a contraction of *gaikokujin*, extranational), this research will use the word "Gaijin" as a term in contrast with the word "Wajin," to refer to a person who is visually identifiable as "different" from "Japanese," who is then often "othered" and subordinated in Japanese society. Note that for the purposes of this research, the term Gaijin is not restricted to the stereotypical *aoi-me no gaijin*, the "blond-haired blue-eyed Caucasian." It is applied to anyone considered to be "not Japanese" due to how they look, as evidenced by the performance of "Japanese Only" establishments in chapter 3 visually identifying who qualifies as "not Japanese" to exclude.

Japan and Japanese: When referring to "Japan" and in any form, this research is not assigning characteristics to all Japanese as a people or as individuals. Its critique focuses on the structural, institutional organs of state, meaning the government of Japan, its judiciary, its media, its bureaucracy, and any other domestic institutions which influence Japan's national narrative regarding concepts of "Self" and "Other," creating a pervasive mindset that "others" people as "Gaijin" through visual identification. The fieldwork, however, surveys expressly xenophobic "Japanese Only" business owners on an individual level to find out who they visually identify as "Japanese," so analysis on this level, although not representative of Japanese society as a whole, may provide insights into an established exclusionary mindset toward the "Gaijin" in society.

Othering: For the purposes of this research, this is the second stage of the "racial formation process" of racialization and racial discrimination.[8] After "differentiation" (the act of saying or demonstrating that people are different in terms of types, traits, tendencies, and characteristics),[9] "othering" is the act of constructing an "Other" within a nation-state, comparing and offsetting people with differences with those who are "Us" (the Self) in order to create a "Them."[10] This is often done with the political purpose of creating a sense of "belonging" and "entitlement" for the "Us," while for the "Them" it creates a socially acceptable logic for denying equal access to public and private facilities, or denying equal civil, political, or even human rights within the same society. This leads to the third stage in the process, "subordination" (or to use Goldberg's terms: subjection, exclusion, and subjugation).[11]

Passing: To scholars of racism, "passing" refers to "a deception that enables a person to adopt specific roles or identities from which he or she would otherwise be barred by prevailing social standards [towards race, phenotype, or social origin],"[12] with the purpose of "shedding the identity of an oppressed group to gain access to social and economic opportunities"[13] to move "from the lower to the higher caste."[14] Scholars of the theory note that this is a conscious act, not merely being mistaken or lacking knowledge about one's own ethnic, racial, or historically based identity, and it is done "to enjoy the privileges of the dominant [racial] community."[15] Although this term traditionally refers to racialized situations toward African Americans in North America,[16] it has also been applied to beyond the black-white racial binary to other ethnicities.[17]

However, this research narrows the focus of "passing" down to the performative identification of physical characteristics, meaning that it involves a conscious act on the person being viewed by society to cover up visually identifiable Gaijin roots so as to "pass" as a Wajin in Japanese society. This is an attempt to gain equivalent privilege with the dominant Wajin community, or to avoid the stigmas and racialized treatment afforded those people assigned to Gaijin status in Japan.

Race: This research wishes to avoid a lengthy biological discussion of what constitutes a "race," except to note that on a performative level that it is a collection of biological traits that are used as visual markers by people and governmental systems to identify people as "similar" or "different" to oneself. This is not to say that "race" has no meaning: As a means of visual identification, "race" is often used as a social construct to differentiate, "other," and subordinate people into socially constructed categories, predetermined groups, and/or social statuses within a social order. More discussion in the Introduction.

Racism: Current scholars of racism (see Introduction) generally converge on the definitions of racism as an application of belief—conscious or unconscious[18]—that results in material differences between people (e.g., material wealth and societal opportunity),[19] and further acknowledges that those who are in a socially disadvantaged position under racist practices are in the best position to understand and articulate racism's existence and effects.[20] The UN, under the CERD, defines racism, expressed as the creed that underscores "racial discrimination," as "any distinction, exclusion, restriction or preference based on race, colour, descent, or national or ethnic origin which has the purpose or effect of nullifying or impairing the recognition, enjoyment or exercise, on an equal footing, of human rights and fundamental freedoms in the political, economic, social, cultural or any other field of public life" (Article 1(1)). As Japan has been a signatory to the CERD since 1995, it has therefore agreed to these rules, definitions, and applications for the scope of this debate. This research will attempt to synthesize these definitions both under UN rubric and within its analytical concept of Embedded Racism. The concise version that will be used throughout this research is as follows:

"Racism is the act of differentiating, 'othering', and subordinating people into a predetermined group within a social order through criteria established sociologically and legally in a society."

Zainichis, Oldcomers, and Newcomers: *Zainichi* refers to the former citizens of the Japanese Empire and their descendants born in Japan who have the legal status of residence of "Special Permanent Resident" (*tokubetsu eijūsha*). They are mostly ethnic Koreans and Chinese with respective nationalities and, despite being born in Japan, do not have Japanese citizenship under Japan's blood-based Nationality Law. They are also referred to in Japanese as the "Oldcomers" (*ōrudokamā*)[21] due to their long history in Japan. The "Newcomers" (*nyūkamā*), however, are non-Japanese who have come to Japan to stay for an indefinite period, possibly for the long term or a lifetime. For this research, I generally say that the "Newcomers" are the people with the legal status of residence of "Regular Permanent Resident" (*ippan eijūsha*)—as they, like the *Zainichis*, have indefinite permission to remain in Japan.

NOTES

1. Cf. Kashiwazaki (2000).
2. For example, where "nationals" of a state once lacked full citizenship, such as suffrage, because they were not male landowners. Cf. Wetherall (2008) and Kashiwazaki (2000, 2009).
3. Kashiwazaki (2000: 14).
4. Wetherall (2008: 281).
5. Kashiwazaki (2000: 14).
6. Levin (2008).
7. Oguma (2000: 350).
8. Winant (2003: 51, 56).
9. Appiah in Goldberg ed. (1990: 4–5).
10. Miles 1993, Saïd 1998, and so on.
11. Goldberg (1990: 298).
12. Kennedy (2004: 283).
13. Ginsberg (1996), cited in Belluscio ed. (2006: 1).
14. Myrdal (1944), cited ibid.; see also Kennedy (2008), and so on.
15. Daniel, in Root ed. (1992: 92).
16. Cf. Myrdal; Belluscio; Ginsberg, all ibid.
17. Cf. Belluscio; Daniel, both ibid.
18. "[A] set of beliefs whereby we irrationally attach significance to something called race." *See*, for example, Lawrence (1987), Greenwald and Krieger (2006), and Sue and Rivera (2010), all of whom offer what may be groundbreaking insights into the degree of unconscious bias regarding "race" and favoritism.

19. “[A] means by which society allocates privilege, status, and wealth.” *See* Delgado (2001).

20. “[T]hose who lack material wealth or political power still have access to thought and language, and their development of these tools will differ from that of the more privileged.” *See* Matsuda (1987).

21. Cf. Weiner (2009: xvii).

Appendix 1

Sakanaka's "Big Japan" vs. "Small Japan"

Caveats: Sakanaka's thoughtful paradigm falls into a tendency to attribute behavior and ability to culture and nationality, and in my opinion excessively compartmentalizes peoples into jobs by ethnicity. Sakanaka also unproblematically sees the "Small Japan" as too calm and the "Big Japan" as overly fractious and full of strife. Nevertheless, it is a well-intentioned attempt to overcome several of Japan's hegemonic discourses and deserves an audience in the canon.

Appendix Table 1 Japan in 2050

<u>SMALL JAPAN</u> *Population 100 million* *(Immigrant population of 3 million)*		<u>BIG JAPAN</u> *Population 120 million* *(Immigrant population of 20 million)*
The number of Japanese citizens falls. Japan maintains strict immigration policies that as a rule do not permit the immigration or entry of foreign workers and as a result the foreign population stays within 3 million. Japan remains an essentially homogenous society.	*State of the Nation*	The decline in native Japanese is offset by a rise in the population of other ethnic groups. The ethnic balance of Japan's citizenry changes but the total population remains the same. Japan becomes a multiethnic nation, a nation of immigrants.
Three million foreigners live in Japan, mainly in urban areas. Most are either married to native Japanese or are long-term or permanent residents.	*Foreign Residents*	Fifteen million immigrants live in urban areas and another 5 million in the countryside (including those with Japanese citizenship). Several towns and villages have a majority immigrant population. Many immigrants are from neighboring Asian countries. The largest single number is from China followed by India, Vietnam, the Philippines, and Indonesia.
Income per person rises. People lead rich lives with a three-day working week. Lifestyles are diverse with an emphasis on the slow and simple. Houses are larger and income disparities reduced. An idle rich class emerges with plenty of time and money. An increasing number of people favor living a quiet, retired life.	*National Lifestyle*	Living standards increase and society is competitive. Income disparities increase. Lifestyles are conspicuously different depending on social class. People continue to desire a materially rich lifestyle.

Society is quiet and leisurely. Society is ordered and stable and made up mostly of native Japanese. People are generally satisfied. However, all aspects of society from citizens' lifestyles through to social systems and industrial composition need modification to operate on a premise of population decline rather than population growth. For example, people will need to change their lifestyles from the pursuit of material richness to the pursuit of actual living quality. They will also have to bear increased payments and reduced benefits to support the social security system as the birthrate falls and the population grays.	*Society*	Society is multiethnic and vibrant. Various ethnic groups are active in social life. People have strong material desires. A new class system develops. Large groups of minority ethnic groups settle in certain regions. Conflict between ethnic groups is a daily occurrence. Problems of discrimination by native Japanese remain unresolved. A true multiethnic society that values the contributions of immigrants is yet to be achieved.
The social security system is supported by high payments (taxes at 50 percent of income). There is a chronic shortage of caregivers.	*Social Security*	Immigrants play an important role in supporting the social security system. Around 2 million ethnic Filipinos work as nurses and caregivers.
The economy is in decline and taxes are higher. Savings rates are lower, as is the asset value of land. Land is no longer seen as a guaranteed investment. The consumer market as a whole is smaller but the elderly consumer market is larger. The economy is led by consumption. Japan's food self-sufficiency ratio is higher. There is greater use of natural energy sources to raise Japan's energy self-sufficiency. The economy is more self-contained but massive financial assets are invested overseas. Domestic investment and spending on public works have declined massively. Large general construction contractors have disbanded. Robotics has grown into one of Japan's leading industries.	*Economy*	The economy is growing. Japan is a major economic power. The income gap is wider and the country faces energy crisis. The economy is led by investment based on processing and trade. The fundamental economic structure emphasizing industrial production remains unchanged. Immigrants support the service industry, IT industry, and construction industry. However, problems, including the social cost of accepting a large number of immigrants, environmental problems, and urgent problems appear, likely to slow future growth.

(*Continued*)

Appendix Table 1 Japan in 2050 *(Continued)*

SMALL JAPAN Population 100 million (Immigrant population of 3 million)		*BIG JAPAN* Population 120 million (Immigrant population of 20 million)
The robotization of simple tasks is taken as far as possible, making Japan a country of robots. The retirement age has risen to seventy and many elderly people remain hard at work.	*Labor*	Simple jobs that native Japanese will not do are handled by immigrants. Discrimination against foreign workers occurs regularly.
Education centers around the development of native Japanese personnel. Integration of elementary, junior high, and high schools continues. Universities that cannot attract students are closing. Cram schools no longer exist. But many people dream of remaining a student for life and studying just for the pleasure of it.	*Education*	Japanese language education is emphasized as a means of integrating the multiethnic population. Native Japanese and a range of other ethnic groups learn Japanese together at elementary and junior high school. The elementary and junior high curriculum includes self-development classes that promote a multiethnic society. Many schools are established to teach minorities their ancestral native languages.
A new, mature Japanese culture has arrived. Kabuki, Noh, Japanese literature, Japanese painting, animations, and Japanese cinema are all enjoying a renaissance.	*Culture*	A new, diverse Japanese culture has been created. Minority group cultures and native Japanese culture fuse. Multinational and international cuisine is popular as are various different types of sports. People from various minorities are active in the world of sports and entertainment, including as newscasters and television presenters.
Sumo and professional baseball are enjoying a popularity rebound. Domestic tourism is flourishing.	*Entertainment*	Soccer's J-League has a fanatical following. Each minority group backs a specific team, and battles on the pitch are hard. Two-thirds of the sumo wrestlers in the senior division belong to an ethnic minority. The diverse range of wrestlers contributes to the continuing popularity of the sport.

Cultural values emphasize substance, spirituality, and respect for traditional Japanese culture.	*Value System*	Cultural values emphasize quantity, material value, and cultural diversity.
Native Japanese of various religious persuasions form the bulk of the population, but the role of religion in society is not prominent.	*Religion*	Many people of various religions including Islam, Christianity, and Hinduism reside in Japan and religion as a whole takes a more prominent role.
Society, composed chiefly of native Japanese, is stable, as long as strict immigration policies can stem the flow of migration.	*Public Security*	An Immigration Agency oversees social integration in Japan's multiethnic society. Interethnic conflicts are affecting public security. Social integration and security maintenance require a massive social cost.
Rice fields and forests in depopulated areas have fallen into ruin. Energy consumption is lower as is the concentration of atmospheric pollution.	*Environment*	Destruction of the natural environment continues. Severe damage results from natural disasters in overcrowded cities.
Overcrowding problems are resolved. Commuters now have breathing space. More people own their own homes and living environment has improved. Elderly people are concentrated in urban areas.	*Urban Areas*	Overcrowding continues. Ethnic minorities for the most part concentrated in cities, but living environments for ethnic minorities are deteriorating. Many people are calling for improvements.
The importance of agriculture has risen with the need to secure a stable food supply and the revitalization of rural society is underway.	*Rural Areas*	The acceptance of immigrants has put the brakes on depopulation. Immigrants employed by food production companies are supporting the agricultural industry. The introduction of immigrants has accelerated the reform of rural society. Agricultural production is higher and food self-sufficiency levels are vastly improved.

(*Continued*)

Appendix Table 1 Japan in 2050 (*Continued*)

SMALL JAPAN *Population 100 million* *(Immigrant population of 3 million)*		*BIG JAPAN* *Population 120 million* *(Immigrant population of 20 million)*
There are now more elderly people who have never married. Many people live with their parents as the number of single people who have never left home is high. The number of households is higher, mainly due to one-person households, and the average number of persons per household has shrunk to around two. For married couples, it is common for both the husband and wife to work.	*Family*	Later marriages and low birthrates continue. New arrivals in Japan also choose to have few children. Interethnic marriage is common and there are more multicultural children.
A conservative political party is in office backed by urban residents and the elderly. Their policies favor stability. There is intergenerational political conflict over the payments and benefit levels required to support the social security system.	*Politics*	Numerous different political parties are supported by various ethnic minorities. There are many ethnic minority politicians. Their policies favor reform. There is conflict among citizens over whether to accept new immigrants.
Japan maintains its current defense capability by using advances in equipment to compensate for declining troop numbers.	*National Security*	Japan's defense capability improves as troop numbers rise and equipment improves. Japan enjoys strong relationships with the countries from which it has accepted immigrants.
International relationships destabilize and the balance of power in international society changes with population decline in the developed world and population growth in the developing world. The international community is reassured by Japan's population decline. Although the international influence of developed countries declines as the population falls, Japan, with a population of 100 million, remains as a major player and economic power, and enjoys a certain degree of influence.	*International Relations*	The international community is wary of Japan's tenacious maintenance of its population, but Japan's open attitude to immigration is praised in some quarters, particularly by the developing countries from which the immigrants come.

Source: Courtesy Sakanaka (2005). Translated by Andrew J. I. Taylor, used with permission.

Appendix 2

This Research's Debt to Critical Race Theory

This research owes a great debt of gratitude to the deconstructing influences of Critical Theory, particularly Postmodernism and Postcolonialism. There is a postmodernist critique that deconstructs racism into structural power relations called Critical Race Theory (CRT), which deserves a longer description in this appendix.

CRT sees racism above all as a study of power relations within a society, and of how people are rendered into categories of power, influence, and wealth acquisition. Fundamental theories synthesizing economic and postcolonial arguments are said to go back to W. E. B. Du Bois (1905: 233–234), where he linked the abolition of American slavery with the convergence of White economic and postcolonial interests, rather than by American society being convinced by "moral good" and "just society" arguments. CRT in its current form first appeared in legal studies within American academia in the 1970s in response to perceived shortcomings within the American Civil Rights Movement, grounded in minority frustrations at underrepresented voices within American public discourse and academia (Crenshaw 1995: xxii–xxvii). Incorporating various criticisms from Ethnic Studies, Women's Studies, Cultural Nationalism, Critical Legal Studies, Marxism and Neo-Marxism, and Internal Colonial models (Solorzano & Yosso 2001: 474), CRT has expanded out of deconstructing legal and judicial processes and into other fields, including deconstructions of education, public discourse, gender, ethnicity, class and poverty, globalization, immigration and international labor migration, hate speech, the meritocracy, and identity politics. It has also been expanded beyond America's borders to examine postcolonialism and power structures in other societies, including Great Britain, Israel, and Europe (cf. Delgado 2012; Möschel 2011; Sakata 2012), but not yet Japan. That is the goal of this book.

CRT starts from the fundamental standpoints (cf. Delgado & Stefancic 2001, 2012; Matsuda in Crenshaw et al. eds. 1995) that, inter alia, (1) "race" is purely a social construct without inherent physiological or biological meaning, so it is open to the same perceptional distortions and manipulations as any other social convention or ideology; (2) the prejudicial discourses about human categorization and treatment are so hegemonic that they become part of the "normal" in society; that is to say, so embedded in the everyday workings of society that they give rise to discriminatory actions (both conscious and unconscious), resulting in discriminatory public policies and laws regardless of policymaker intentions; (3) "race" is in fact the central, endemic, and permanent driving force behind organizing the scaffolding of human interaction, categorization, and regulation both at the individual and more poignantly the legislative level; (4) "race" thus fundamentally influences, even grounds, the formation, enforcement, and amendment process of a society's laws; (5) those who best understand this dynamic and its effects are the people disadvantaged within the racialized structure of power and privilege, and thus are necessarily excluded from the discourse regarding the organization of society; and, consequently, (6) one must also recognize the power of minority narratives as a means to allow more minority voices and alternative insights into the discussion, to expose the realities present for the unprivileged and underprivileged.[1] These standpoints are the foundation of this research's theory of Embedded Racism.

The dynamic of racism under CRT is one of power and self-perpetuation of the status quo. Racism is seen as necessarily existing to advance and promote, both materially and psychologically, the interests and privileges of members within the dominant power structure. In America's case, CRT helped foster "Whiteness Studies" to examine the power and preference (e.g., material wealth, prestige, privilege, opportunity, etc.) that both naturally and not-so-naturally accrues to the "White" majority or elite. Due to the "normalization" of this dynamic, it becomes self-perpetuating due to "structural determinism," where even the most well-intentioned members of the elite will have little awareness or incentive to eliminate this system. The only time there may be power concessions granted to the nondominant people is when there is "interest convergence," that is, when both the Whites and the minorities stand to gain from a policy shift; then current racial paradigms will be discarded and shifted instead to disfavor another weakened, easily targeted disenfranchised minority. In this sense, racisms and racialisms will shift over time, but they will nevertheless continue to exist and remain a fundamental ordering force within a society (Miles 1997).

Although these analytical paradigms have been applied primarily to the American example, this dissertation argues the same dynamics can be seen in the Japanese example, by substituting "White" with "Japanese."[2] CRT's shortcoming, however, is that it has yet to escape the milieu of the study of "White dominance." It has not been applied to a non-White society (such as Japan) to study universal racialized social majority dominance. I believe there are two reasons for this: One is because CRT's postmodernist/postcolonialist roots peg it to the study of world historical domination by one particular race. The other is because scholarship on racism in Japan tends to see Japan's racism as "different" in tone and content compared to racism worldwide. However, this research argues in the Introduction and chapter 2 that racism in Japan is not "unique" and should be studied like any other.

Fortunately, CRT, and by extension Embedded Racism, enable the scholar to understand contexts grounded in "political events, personal histories, societal norms, and laws and policies that affect the primary setting" (Chapman: 157), while avoiding "culturally based" explanations of behavior and policy outcomes (i.e., "Japanese do this because they are Japanese"); that is to say, by putting contexts in a mysterious "culture box," one tends to ignore universal paradigms of the racialization process in favor of treating Japan's racism as "exceptional" or "unique" (therefore exempt from analysis under universal concepts of human rights).

In sum, Japan is no exception from postmodernist critique, and this book applies that critique to Japan in unprecedented ways.

NOTES

1. There are, naturally, other tenets in CRT's very broad spectrum of disciplines, but the above are the tenets germane to this research. Given its roots in dissent and diversity, CRT as a multidisciplinary umbrella theory is flexible enough in its application within academic disciplines to allow for a selection of approaches.
2. Levin (2008: 14–21).

References

Abe, Shinzō. 2013. *Atarashii Kuni E, Utsukushii Kuni E* [Towards a Beautiful New Country]. Tōkyō: Bunshun Shinsho.

Amazon Japan Website. 2010. Searches in Japanese to Show the Lack of Books with "*jinshu sabetsu*" and "*Nihon*" [Racial Discrimination and Japan] in the Title. February 5.

Amos, Timothy. 2011. *Embodying Difference: The Making of Burakumin in Modern Japan*. University of Hawai'i Press.

Amos, Timothy. 2019. *Caste in Early Modern Japan: Danzaemon and the Edo Outcaste Order*. Routledge.

Anderson, Benedict. 1993. *Imagined Communities: Reflections on the Origin and Spread of Nationalism*. New York: Verso.

Anderson, Benedict. 2012. "Nationalism: Change in Consciousness or Fiction?" *Lecture*, University of Hawai'i at Mānoa Campus, November 5.

Anderson, Kent, and Okuda Yasuhiro. 2003. "Issues Raised under Japanese Nationality Law and International Criminal Law" by the Case of Former Peruvian President Alberto Fujimori." *Hokkaido Law Review* 54(3): 334–289.

Anonymous. 1995. *Joshi Gakusei Daraku Manyuaru* [Manual for Women Students Regarding Depravity]. Tōkyō: Hikō Mondai Kenkyūkai.

Anonymous. 2001. *Kanji Gakushū Nōto 2-Nen Shita*. Kyōiku Dōshinsha.

Anonymous. 2007. *Gaijin Hanzai Ura Fairu 2007* [The Underground Files of Foreign Crime 2007]. Tōkyō: Eichi Shuppan.

Aoki, Hideo. 2009. "*Buraku* Culture." In Sugimoto Yoshio, Ed., *The Cambridge Companion to Modern Japanese Culture*, 182–198. Cambridge: Cambridge University Press.

Appiah, Kwame Anthony. 1990. "Racisms." In Goldberg, David Theo, Ed., *Anatomy of Racism*, 3–17. Minneapolis: University of Minnesota.

Árnason, Johann P., and Yoshio Sugimoto. 1995. *Japanese Encounters with Postmodernity*. New York: Kegan Paul International.

Arudou, Debito. 2001. "*'Kokusai Jūmin' ni Taishi 21 Seiki no Nihon, Hokkaidō no Arubeki Sugata" Fōramu Jinbun Dai 3-Gō, Tokushū, Dai 20 Kai Hokkaidō Bunkaron. Sōgō Teima: "Hokkaidō to Kokusai Kōryū—Sono Jisseki to Tamesareru Rinen* [Proceedings: "The 20th Hokkaidō Culture Lecture Series—Hokkaidō and Intercultural Exchange—Achievements and Ideas on Trial"]. Published by Sapporo Gakuin University, February.

Arudou, Debito. 2004. "Foreign Crime in Japan: More to the Issue that Meets the Eye." Presentation, Peace as a Global Language Conference, Tōkyō, September 26.

Arudou, Debito. 2005a. "On Racism and Xenophobia in Japan." Report submitted to United Nations Special Rapporteur Doudou Diene on July 6, Tōkyō.

Arudou, Debito. 2005b. "*'Gaikokujin' Nyūten Kinshi to iu Jinshu Sabetsu.*" In Okamoto Masataka, Ed., *Nihon no Minzoku Sabetsu: Jinshu Sabetsu Teppai Jōyaku kara Mita Kadai*, 218–229. Tōkyō: Akashi Shoten.

Arudou, Debito. 2006a. *Japanīzu Onrī: Otaru Onsen Nyūyoku Kyohi Mondai to Jinshu Sabetsu.* 2nd ed. Tōkyō: Akashi Shoten.

Arudou, Debito. 2006b. *Japanese Only: The Otaru Hot Springs Case and Racial Discrimination in Japan.* 2nd ed. Tōkyō: Akashi Shoten.

Arudou, Debito. 2006c. "The Coming Internationalization: Can Japan Assimilate Its Immigrants?" *Asia-Pacific Journal—Japan Focus*, January 12.

Arudou, Debito. 2007. "*Gaijin Hanzai* Magazine and Hate Speech in Japan: The Newfound Power of Japan's International Residents." *Asia-Pacific Journal—Japan Focus*, March 20.

Arudou, Debito. 2009. Otaru Lawsuit Website Archive, Specifically the Exhaustive Vault of All Collectable Non-Tabloid (and Some Tabloid) Media Regarding the Otaru Onsens Case from its Inception on September 19, 1999 to its end on April 8, 2005, www.debito.org/lawsuitbackground.html and www.debito.org/nihongo-timeline.html#keii.

Arudou, Debito. 2010a. "Chapter 2: Race and Nationality-based Entrance Refusals at Private and Quasi-Public Establishments." NGO report submitted with NGO Solidarity with Migrants Japan, International Human Rights Division, to United Nations CERD Committee February 2010 meeting, dated January 20, 2010.

Arudou, Debito. 2010b. "Propaganda in Japan's Media: Manufacturing Consent for National Goals at the Expense of NJ Residents." Linguapax Asia: A Retrospective Edition of Language and Human Rights Issues. Collected Proceedings of Linguapax Asia Symposia, 2004–2009. Linguapax Institute, Pubs. November, 2010.

Arudou, Debito. 2011. "Rogues' Gallery of Exclusionary Establishments." *Debito .org*, www.debito.org/roguesgallery.html.

Arudou, Debito. 2013a. "Japan's Rightward Swing and the Tottori Prefecture Human Rights Ordinance." *The Asia-Pacific Journal* 11(9)3, March 4.

Arudou, Debito. 2013b. "An Introduction to Japanese Society's Attitudes toward Race and Skin Color." In Ronald E. Hall, Ed., *The Melanin Millennium: Skin Color as 21st Century International Discourse* , 49–70. Heidelberg: Springer.

Arudou, Debito. 2015. "Japanese Government Pressures American Publisher to Delete Textbook Treatment of Wartime Sexual Slavery: An Interview with Herbert Ziegler." *Asia-Pacific Journal—Japan Focus* 13(10)3, March 9.

Asakawa, Akihiro. 2007. *Kindai Nihon to Kika Seido* [Naturalization in the (*sic*) Modern Japan]. Hiroshima: Keisuisha.

Ashikari, Mikiko. 2005. "Cultivating Japanese Whiteness: The 'Whitening' Cosmetics Boom and the Japanese Identity." *Journal of Material Culture* 10(1): 73–91.

Assogba, Jöel. 2012. "Book is behind Bullying of Mixed-Race Children." *Japan Times*, April 10.

Atkins, E. Taylor. 2001. *Blue Nippon: Authenticating Jazz in Japan*. Durham: Duke University Press.

Balibar, Etienne, and Immanuel Wallerstein. 1991. *Race, Nation, Class: Ambiguous Identities*. New York: Verso.

Bannerman, Helen. 1899 [2005]. *Chibi Kuro Sanbo* [Japanese translation of *Little Black Sambo*]. Tōkyō, Zui'unsha.

Bannerman, Helen. 2002. *The Story of Little Babaji*. New York: HarperCollins.

Beard, Henry, and Christopher Cerf. 1994. *Sex and Dating: The Official Politically Correct Guide*. New York: HarperCollins.

Becker, Ernest. 1973. *The Denial of Death*. New York: The Free Press.

Befu, Harumi. 2001. *The Hegemony of Homogeneity*. Melbourne: Trans Pacific Press.

Bell, Derrick A. 1980. "*Brown v. Board of Education* and the Interest Convergence Dilemma." *Harvard Law Review* 93: 518–533.

Belluscio, Steven J., ed. 2006. *To Be Suddenly White: Literary Realism and Racial Passing*. Columbia, MO: University of Missouri Press.

Beoku-Betts, Josephine. 1994. "When Black is Not Enough: Doing Field Research among Gullah Women." *NWSA Journal* 6(3): 413–433.

Bernal, Delores Delgado. 1998. "Using a Chicana Feminist Epistemology in Educational Research." *Harvard Educational Review* 68(4): 555–582.

Besnier, Niko. 2012. "The Athlete's Body and the Global Condition." *American Ethnologist* 39(3): 491–510.

Bishop, Claire Hutchet, 1938 [1995]. *Shina No Gonin Kyōdai* [Japanese translation of *The Five Chinese Brothers*]. Tōkyō, Zui'unsha.

Bortz, Ana. 1998. "Brazilians that were Victims of Discrimination in Japan." Press Conference at the Foreign Correspondents Club of Japan, October 1.

Bryant, Taimie L. 1991. "For the Sake of the Country, for the Sake of the Family: The Oppressive Impact of Family Registration on Women and Minorities in Japan." *UCLA Law Review* 39(1): 109–168.

Cabinet of Japan (*Naikaku*). 1999, 2003, and 2007. "Public Survey on the Defense of Human Rights" (*jinken yōgo ni kansuru yoron chōsa*).

Cabinet of Japan. 2012. "*Gaikokujin to no Kyōsei Shakai Jitsugen Kentō Kaigi*" [Meetings to Deliberate on the Realization of a Society in Co-existence with Foreigners], May 24, June 1 and 15, July 3, and August 27, 2012. Archived at the Cabinet Secretariat website at www.cas.go.jp/jp/seisaku/kyousei/index.html (last accessed May 14, 2021).

Cabinet of Japan. 2013. "*Nikkei Teijū Gaikokujin ni kan suru Tokubetsu Yoron Chōsa*" [Special public opinion survey on Nikkei Long-Term Residents]. February 28. Archived at the Cabinet Secretariat website at www8.cao.go.jp/survey/tokubetu/h24/h24-nikkei.pdf (last accessed March 31, 2013).

Cabinet Secretariat of Japan. 2012. "*Gaikokujin to no kyōsei shakai no jitsugen ni mukete (chūkanteki seiri).*" [Towards the realization of a society coexisting with foreigners: Intermediate Summary]. August 27.

Cary, Ann B. 2000. "Affiliation, Not Assimilation: Resident Koreans and Ethnic Education." In Mary Goebel Noguchi and Sandra Fotos, Eds., *Studies in Japanese Bilingualism*, 98–132. Clevedon, UK: Multilingual Matters Ltd.

Central Intelligence Agency. 2012. CIA Factbook on Japan's National Statistics (accessed April 1, 2012).

Chapman, Thandeka. 2007. "Looking from Points of Strength: Using Portraiture and Critical Race Theory in Educational Research." *Educational Researcher* 36(3): 156–162.

Chapman, William. 1991. *Inventing Japan: The Making of a Postwar Civilization.* New York: Prentice Hall Press.

Charmaz, Kathleen. 2006. *Constructing Grounded Theory*. London: Sage.

Chen, Edward I-te. 1984. "The Attempt to Integrate the Empire: Legal Perspectives." In Ramon H. Myers and Mark R. Peattie, Eds., *The Japanese Colonial Empire 1895–1945*, 240–274. New Jersey: Princeton University Press.

Ching, Leo T. S. 2001. *Becoming Japanese: Colonial Taiwan and the Politics of Identity Formation*. Berkeley: University of California Press.

Chomsky, Noam, and Edward S. Herman. 2002. *Manufacturing Consent: The Political Economy of the Mass Media*. New York: Pantheon.

Chung, Erin Aeran. 2000. "Korean Voluntary Associations in Japanese Civil Society." *Japan Policy Research Institute*, Working Paper No. 69, July.

City of Hamamatsu. 2001. *Gaikokujin shūchūtoshi kaigi; Hamamatsu sengen oyobi teigen* [Meeting of Cities with Concentrated Communities of Non-Japanese. Hamamatsu Declaration and Proposal]. October 19.

City of Otaru. 2000. *Kōhō Otaru* [Monthly Public Newsletter], No. 620, April.

Clammer, John. 1995. *Difference and Modernity: Social Theory and Contemporary Japanese Society*. London: Routledge.

Clammer, John. 2001. *Japan and Its Others*. Melbourne: Trans Pacific Press.

Cleveland, Kyle. 2014. "Hiding in Plain Sight: Minority Issues in Japan." In Jeff Kingston, Ed., *Critical Issues in Contemporary Japan*. 213–222, Oxford: Routledge.

Condry, Ian. 2006. *Hip-Hop Japan*. Durham: Duke University Press.

Corbin, Juliet, and Anselm L. Strauss. 2008. *Basics of Qualitative Research: Grounded Theory Procedures and Techniques*. 3rd ed. London: Sage.

Crenshaw, Kimberle, Neil Gotanda, Garry Peller, Kendall Thomas, eds. 1995. *Critical Race Theory: The Key Writings that Formed the Movement*. New York: The New Press.

Dahl, Roger. 2001. "Otaru Onsen and City in Hot Water." Political Cartoon with the Express Word "Racist" Within the Discourse. *The Japan Times*, February 14.

Daniel, Reginald G. 1992. "Passers and Pluralists: Subverting the Racial Divide." In Maria P. P. Root, Ed., *Racially Mixed People in America*, 91–107. Newbury Park, CA: Sage Publications.

Delgado, Richard. 2001. "Two Ways to Think About Race: Reflections on the Id, the Ego, and Other Reformist Theories on Equal Protection." *Georgetown Law Journal* 89: 2279–2296.

Delgado, Richard, and Jean Stefancic. 1997. *Critical White Studies: Looking Behind the Mirror*. Philadelphia: Temple University Press.

Delgado, Richard, and Jean Stefancic. 2001. *Critical Race Theory: An Introduction*. 1st Ed. New York: New York University Press.

Delgado, Richard, and Jean Stefancic. 2012. *Critical Race Theory: An Introduction*. 2nd Ed. New York: New York University Press.

Demel, Walter. 2013. "How the Mongoloid Race Came into Being: Late Eighteenth-Century Constructions of East Asians in Europe." In Rotem Kowner and Walter Demel, Eds., *Race and Racism in Modern East Asia: Western and Eastern Constructions*. Leiden, The Netherlands: Brill.

Denoon, Donald, ed. 1996. *Multicultural Japan: Paleolithic to Postmodern*. New York: Cambridge University Press.

Dikötter, Frank, ed. 1997. *The Construction of Racial Identities in China and Japan*. Honolulu: University of Hawai'i Press.

Dilworth, David A. et al. trans. 2009. *Yukichi Fukuzawa: An Outline of a Theory of Civilization*. New York: Columbia University Press.

Dixon, John, and Kevin Durrheim. 2000. "Displacing Place-Identity: A Discursive Approach to Locating Self and Other." *British Journal of Social Psychology* 39(1): 27–44. March.

Drifte, Reinhard. 2014. "The Japan-China Confrontation over the Senkaku/Diaoyu Islands—Between 'Shelving' and 'Dispute Escalation'." *Asia-Pacific Journal—Japan Focus* 12(30)3, July 27.

Doak, Kevin M. 2001. "Building National Identity through Ethnicity: Ethnology in Wartime Japan and After." *Journal of Japanese Studies* 27(1): 1–39.

Dower, John W. 1999. *Embracing Defeat: Japan in the Wake of World War II*. New York: W.W. Norton.

Du Bois, W. E. B. 1905 [2011]. *The Negro*. CreateSpace Independent Publishing Platform.

Eades, J. S., Tom Gill, and Harumi Befu. 2000. *Globalization and Social Change in Contemporary Japan*. Melbourne: Trans Pacific Press.

Economist, The. 2005. *Pocket World in Figures 2006*. London: Profile Books.

Eskildsen, Robert. 2002. "Of Civilization and Savages: the Mimetic Imperialism of Japan's 1874 Expedition to Taiwan." *American Historical Review* 107(2): 388–418.

Essed, Philomena. 1994. "Contradictory Positions, Ambivalent Perceptions: A Case Study of a Black Woman Entrepreneur." *Feminism and Psychology* (special issue entitled *Shifting Identities, Shifting Racisms*): 4(1): 99–118.

Essed, Philomena. 2002. "Everyday Racism: A New Approach to the Study of Racism." In P. Essed and D. Goldberg, Eds., *Race Critical Theories: Text and Context*, 176–194. Oxford: Blackwell Publishers.

Farber, Daniel A., and Suzanna Sherry. 1997. *Beyond All Reason: The Radical Assault on Truth in American Law*. New York: Oxford University Press.

Fish, Robert A. 2009. "'Mixed-Blood' Japanese: A Reconsideration of Race and Purity in Japan." In Michael Weiner, Ed., *Japan's Minorities: The Illusion of Homogeneity*, 40–58, 2nd ed. Sheffield: Routledge.

Foote, Daniel H. 1992. "The Benevolent Paternalism of Japanese Criminal Justice." *California Law Review* 80(2): 317–390. March. As cited in Johnson (2002).

Foucault, Michel. 1970. *The Order of Things: An Archaeology of the Human Sciences*. New York: Pantheon.

Freeman, Laurie A. 1996. "Japan's Press Clubs as Information Cartels." *Japan Policy Research Institute*, Working Paper No. 18: April.

Frühstück, Sabine, 2000. "Treating the Body as a Commodity: 'Body Projects' in Contemporary Japan." In Michael Ashkenazi and John Clammer, Eds., *Consumption and Material Culture in Contemporary Japan*, 143–161. London: Kegan Paul International.

Fuess, Harald. 2004. *Divorce in Japan: Family, Gender and the State 1600–2000*. Stanford: Stanford University Press.

Fukuoka, Yasunori. 2000. *Lives of Young Koreans in Japan*. Melbourne: Trans Pacific Press.

Fukushima Prefectural Government. 2007–9. Tourist Information Website Sponsored by the Fukushima Tourist Information Agency, at www.tif.ne.jp/jp/spot/cat_search.php; enter 外国人の受入：不可 into the キーワード section. Last accessed July 2012.

Fukuzawa, Yūkichi. 1875 [2009]. *An Outline of a Theory of Civilization (Bunmei-ron no Gairyaku)*, David A. Dilworth trans. New York: Columbia University Press.

Gamble, Adam, and Watanabe Takesato. 2004. *A Public Betrayed: An Inside Look at Japanese Media Atrocities and their Warnings to the West*. Washington, DC: Regnery Publishing Inc.

Gellner, Ernest. 1983. *Nations and Nationalism*. Ithaca: Cornell University Press.

Gibson, Mary. 2002. *Born to Crime: Cesare Lombroso and the Origins of Biological Criminology*. Santa Barbara, CA: Praeger.

Gill, Thomas P. 2001. "Review of Multiethnic Japan by John Lie." *Monumenta Nipponica* 56(4): 571.

Ginsberg, Elaine K. 1996. *Passing and the Fictions of Identity*. North Carolina: Duke University Press.

Glaser, Barney G. 2001. *The Grounded Theory Perspective: Conceptualization Contrasted with Description*. Mill Valley, CA: The Sociology Press.

Glaser, Barney G., and Anselm L. Strauss. 1967. *The Discovery of Grounded Theory: Strategies for Qualitative Research*. Chicago: Aldine.

Gluck, Carol. 1985. *Japan's Modern Myths: Ideology in the Late Meiji Period*. New Jersey: Princeton University Press.

Goldberg, David Theo, ed. 1990. *Anatomy of Racism*. Minneapolis: University of Minnesota.

Gould, Stephen J. 1981. *The Mismeasure of Man*. New York: W.W. Norton.

Greenwald, Anthony G., and Linda Hamilton Krieger. 2006. "Implicit Bias: Scientific Foundations." *California Law Review* 94(4), July.

Greenwald, Robert (Director). 2004. *Outfoxed: Rupert Murdoch's War on Journalism* (documentary). Carolina Productions, University of South Carolina.

Habermas, Jürgen. 1962. *The Structural Transformation of the Public Sphere: An Inquiry into a Category of Bourgeois Society*. Translated by Thomas Burger. Cambridge, MA: The MIT Press.

Habermas, Jürgen. 1993. "Citizenship and National Identity: Some Reflections on the Future of Europe." *Praxis International* 12(1): 1–19.

Hall, Ivan P. 1998. *Cartels of the Mind: Japan's Intellectual Closed Shop.* New York: W.W. Norton.

Hamai, Koichi, and Thomas Ellis. 2006. "Crime and Criminal Justice in Modern Japan: From Re-integrative Shaming to Popular Punitivism." *International Journal of the Sociology of Law*, 34(3): 157–178.

Hammar, Tomas. 1990. *Democracy and the Nation State: Aliens, Denizens, and Citizens in a World of International Migration.* Aldershot: Gower.

Hanami, Tadashi. 1998. "Japanese Policies on the Rights and Benefits Granted to Foreign Workers, Residents, Refugees, and Illegals." In Myron Weiner and Hanami Tadashi, Eds., *Temporary Workers of Future Citizens: Japanese and U.S. Migration Policies*, 211–237. New York: New York University Press.

Hane, Mikiso. 1972. *Japan: A Historical Survey.* New York: Charles Scribner's Sons.

Hardacre, Helen, and Adam Kern, eds. 1997. *New Directions in the Study of Meiji Japan.* Boston: Brill Academic Publishers.

Hayes, Declan. 2005. *The Japanese Disease: Sex and Sleaze in Modern Japan.* iUniverse.

Hepburn, Stephanie, and Rita J. Simon. 2013. *Human Trafficking around the World: Hidden in Plain Sight.* Columbia University Press.

Herbert, Wolfgang. 1996. *Foreign Workers and Law Enforcement in Japan.* London: Kegan Paul International.

Higashikawa, Kōji. 2017. "Japan's Hate Speech Laws: Translations of the Osaka City Ordinance and the National Act to Curb Hate Speech in Japan." *Asian-Pacific Law and Policy Journal* 19(1): 1–12.

Higashizawa, Yasushi. 2005. "*Jinshu Sabetsu Soshō o Meguru Hanrei Hōri no Hatten to Kadai.*" In Okamoto, Masataka, Ed., *Nihon no Minzoku Sabetsu: Jinshu Sabetsu Teppai Jōyaku kara Mita Kadai*, 322–337. Tōkyō: Akashi Shoten.

Higuchi, Akira. 2007–8. Interviews on visa Statuses in Japan.

Higuchi, Akira, and Arudou Debito. 2008. *Handbook for Newcomers, Migrants and Immigrants to Japan.* 1st ed. Tōkyō: Akashi Shoten Inc.

Higuchi, Akira, and Arudou Debito. 2012. *Handbook for Newcomers, Migrants and Immigrants to Japan.* 2nd ed. Tōkyō: Akashi Shoten Inc.

Higuchi, Naoto, and Kiyoko Tannō. 2003. "What's driving Brazil-Japan migration? The making and remaking of the Brazilian niche in Japan." *International Journal of Japanese Sociology*, 12: 33–47.

Hobsbawm, Eric, and Terence Ranger, eds. 1983. *The Invention of Tradition.* Cambridge, Cambridge University Press.

Huang, Chun-Chieh. 2010. *Humanism in East Asian Confucian Contexts.* Wiesbaden: Verlag.

Ichihashi, Tatsuya. 2011. *Taiho sareru made: Kūhaku no 2 nen 7 kagetsu no Kiroku* ["Until I was arrested: a record of a blank 2 years and 7 months"]. Tōkyō: Gentōsha, Inc.

Iida, Yumiko. 2002. *Rethinking Identity in Modern Japan.* London: Routledge.

Irish, Ann B. 2009. *Hokkaido: A History of Ethnic Transition and Development on Japan's Northern Island.* Jefferson, NC: McFarland & Co.

Ishihara, Shintarō. 2002. *Nihon Yo.* Tōkyō: Sankei Shinbun Shuppansha.

Ishii, Kōta. 2012. *Nippon ikoku kikō: Zainichi gaikokujin no kane, seiai, shi.* [Journey through Foreign Japan: The Money, Love, Sex, and Death of Foreigners in Japan]. NHK Shuppan Shinsho 368, January.

Iwasawa, Yūji. 1998. *International Law, Human Rights, and Japanese Law. The Impact of International Law on Japanese Law.* Oxford: Clarendon Press.

Johnson, Chalmers. 1975. "Japan: Who Governs? An Essay on Official Bureaucracy." *Journal of Japanese Studies* 2(1): 1–28. Autumn.

Johnson, Chalmers. 1982. *MITI and the Japanese Miracle.* Stanford: Stanford University Press.

Johnson, Chalmers. 1995. *Japan: Who Governs? The Rise of the Developmental State.* New York: W.W. Norton.

Johnson, David T. 2002. *The Japanese Way of Justice: Prosecuting Crime in Japan.* Oxford: Oxford University Press.

Kajita, Takamichi. 1994. *Gaikokujin Rōdōsha to Nihon* [Foreign Workers and Japan]. Tōkyō: Nihon Hōsō Shuppan Kyōkai.

Kajita, Takamichi. 1998. "The Challenge of Incorporating Foreigners in Japan: 'Ethnic Japanese' and 'Sociological Japanese.'" In Myron Weiner and Hanami Tadashi, Eds., *Temporary Workers of Future Citizens: Japanese and U.S. Migration Policies*, 120–47. New York: New York University Press.

Kashiwazaki, Chikako. 1998. "*Jus Sanguinis* in Japan: The Origin of Citizenship in a Comparative Perspective." *International Journal of Comparative Sociology* 39(3): 278–300.

Kashiwazaki, Chikako. 2000. "Citizenship in Japan: Legal Practice and Contemporary Development." In T. Alexander Aleinikoff, and Douglas Klusmeyer, Eds., *From Migrants to Citizens: Membership in a Changing World*, 434–474. Washington, DC: Carnegie Endowment for International Peace.

Kashiwazaki, Chikako. 2009. "The Politics of Legal Status: The Equation of Nationality with Ethnonational Identity." In Sonia Ryang and John Lie, Eds., *Diaspora Without Homeland: Being Korean in Japan*, 121–146. Berkeley: University of California Press.

Kawai, Yūko. 2015. "Deracialised Race, Obscured Racism: Japaneseness, Western and Japanese Concepts of Race, and Modalities of Racism." *Japanese Studies*, May 6. London: Routledge.

Kayano, Shigeru, Iijima Shun'ichi, and David T. Suzuki. 2003. *The Ainu: A Story of Japan's Original People.* Hong Kong: Periplus Editions.

Kearney, R. 1998. *African American Views of Japanese: Solidarity or Sedition?* Albany: State University of New York Press.

Kelsky, Karen. 2001. *Women on the Verge: Japanese Women, Western Dreams.* Durham: Duke University Press.

Kennedy, Randall. 2004. *Interracial Intimacies: Sex, Marriage, Identity, and Adoption.* New York: Vintage.

Kennedy, Randall. 2008. *Sellout: The Politics of Racial Betrayal.* New York: Pantheon.

King, J. C. 1981. *The Biology of Race.* Berkeley: University of California Press.

Kingston, Jeff. "Exploring the Pathologies of Japan's Youth." In Roger Goodman, Yuki Imoto and Tuukka Toivonen, Eds., Book Review of *A Sociology of Japanese Youth: From Returnees to NEETs. The Japan Times*, May 20, 2012.

Klusmeyer, Douglas. 2000. "Introduction." In Aleinikoff, T. Alexander and Douglas Klusmeyer, Eds., *From Migrants to Citizens: Membership in a Changing World*, 1–25. Washington, DC: Carnegie Endowment for International Peace.

Kobayashi Masao. 2009. "*Nihon no Chiiki Shakai ni okeru Tai Gaikokujin Ishiki ni kansuru Shakaigakuteki Kōsatsu: Hokkaidō Wakkanai shi to Tōyama ken kyū Minato shi chiiki o jirei to shite.*" [A Sociological Study of Awareness towards Foreigners in Japan's Regional Societies: Using Hokkaido Wakkanai City and Toyama Prefecture's former Minato City as examples]. Doctoral dissertation successfully defended at the Waseda University Institute of Asia-Pacific Studies.

Kobayashi Masao. 2012. *Nihon no Chiiki Shakai ni okeru Tai Gaikokujin Ishiki* [Awareness towards Foreigners in Japan's Regional Societies]. Tōkyō: Fukumura Shuppan, 2012.

Kobayashi, Yoshinori. 1992. *Gōmanizumu Sengen.* Tōkyō: Gentōsha Inc.

Komai, Hiroshi. 1993. *Gaikokujin Rōdōsha Teijū e no Michi* [The Path to Foreign Worker Settlement]. Tōkyō: Akashi Shoten Inc.

Komai, Hiroshi. 1995. *Migrant Workers in Japan.* Translated by Jens Wilkinson. London: Kegan Paul International.

Komai, Hiroshi. 1999. *Nihon no Gaikokujin Imin* [Japan's Foreign Immigrants]. Tōkyō: Akashi Shoten Inc.

Komai, Hiroshi. 2001. *Foreign Migrants in Contemporary Japan.* Translated by Jens Wilkinson. Victoria, Australia: Trans Pacific Press.

Komisarof, Adam. 2012. *At Home Abroad: The Contemporary Western Experience in Japan.* Tōkyō: Reitaku University Press.

Kondō, Atsushi. 1996. *"Gaikokujin" no Sanseiken: Denizunshippu no Hikaku Kenkyū* [Suffrage for "Foreigners": Comparative Studies of Denizenship]. Tōkyō: Akashi Shoten.

Koshiro, Yukiko. 2013. "East Asia's 'Melting Pot': Re-evaluating Race Relations in Japan's Colonial Empire." In Kowner, Rotem, and Walter Demel, Eds., *Race and Racism in Modern East Asia: Western and Eastern Constructions*, 475–498. Leiden, The Netherlands: Brill.

Kowner, Rotem. 2013. "Between Contempt and Fear: Western Racial Constructions of East Asians since 1800." In Kowner, Rotem, and Walter Demel, Eds., *Race and Racism in Modern East Asia: Western and Eastern Constructions*, 87–125. Leiden, The Netherlands: Brill.

Kowner, Rotem, and Walter Demel. 2013. "Modern East Asia and the Rise of Racial Thought: Possible Links, Unique Features and Unsettled Issues." In Kowner and Demel, Eds. *Race and Racism in Modern East Asia: Western and Eastern Constructions*, 1–37. Leiden, The Netherlands: Brill.

Kramer, Eric Mark, ed. 2003. *The Emerging Monoculture: Assimilation and the "Model Minority."* Westport, CT: Praeger Publishers.

Krauss, Ellis S. 2000. *Broadcasting Politics in Japan: NHK and Television News.* Ithaca: Cornell University Press.

Kublin, Hyman, and Michael Kublin. 1990. *World Regional Studies: Japan.* New York: Houghton Mifflin.

Kubo Hiroshi. 2006. *Chian wa Hontou ni Akka shiteiru no ka?* [Is Public Safety Really Getting Worse?]. Tōkyō: Kōjinsha.

Kushner, Barak. 2007. "Cannibalizing Japanese Media: The Case of Issei Sagawa." *Journal of Popular Culture* 31(3): 56.

Kyōdō Tsūshin, eds. 2003. *Takokuseki Jipangu no Shuyaku Tachi* [The Main Characters of Multinational Japan]. Tōkyō: Akashi Shoten Inc.

Lawrence III, Charles. 1987. "The Id, The Ego, and Equal Protection: Reckoning with Unconscious Racism." *Stanford Law Review*, 39: 317–88.

Lauren, Paul Gordon. 1988. *Power And Prejudice: The Politics And Diplomacy Of Racial Discrimination.* Boulder, CO: Westview Press.

League of Nations, 1919. Covenant.

Lebowitz, Adam, and David McNeill. 2007. "Hammering Down the Educational Nail: Abe Revises the Fundamental Law of Education." *Asia-Pacific Journal—Japan Focus*, July 9.

Lee, Soo Im, Stephen Murphy-Shigematsu, and Harumi Befu, eds. 2006. *Japan's Diversity Dilemmas: Ethnicity, Citizenship, and Education.* Lincoln, NE: iUniverse.

Levin, Mark. 2001. "Essential Commodities and Racial Justice: Using Constitutional Protection of Japan's Indigenous Ainu People to Inform Understandings of the United States and Japan." *New York University Journal of International Law and Politics* 33(2): 419–526, Winter.

Levin, Mark. 2008. "The Wajin's Whiteness: Law and Race and Privilege in Japan." *Hōritsu Jihō* 80(2) February.

Lesser, Jeffrey, ed. 2003. *Searching for Home Abroad: Japanese Brazilians and Transnationalism.* Durham: Duke University Press.

Lester, Julius. 1996. *Sam and the Tigers.* New York: Dial/Penguin Young Readers.

Lie, John. 1998. "Review of 'Japan's Minorities: The Illusion of Homogeneity' by Michael Weiner." *Monumenta Nipponica* 53(3, Autumn), 419–420.

Lie, John. 2004. *Multiethnic Japan.* Cambridge, MA: Harvard University Press.

Linger, Daniel Touro. 2001. *No One Home: Brazilian Selves Remade in Japan.* Stanford: Stanford University Press.

Long, Daniel. 2002a. *English on the Bonin (Ogasawara) Islands.* Durham: Duke University Press.

Long, Daniel. 2002b. "Disappearing English Language and Culture of the 'Westerners' of the Bonin (Ogasawara) Islands." *Endangered Languages of the Pacific Rim, Vol. 15.* Tōkyō: Nakanishi.

Lopez, Geraldo R., and Laurence Parker, eds. 2003. *Interrogating Racism in Qualitative Research Methodology.* New York: Peter Lang.

Lopez, Ian Haney. 1997. *White by Law: The Legal Construction of Race.* New York: New York University Press.

Mabuchi, Ryōgo. 2003. *Shinbun Hanzai Hōdo ni okeru Yōgisha no Kokuseki* [Newspaper crime reportage by nationality of suspects]. Currently out of print.

Mabuchi, Ryōgo. 2003. "*Shinbun Hanzai Hōdo ni okeru Yōgisha no Kokuseki*" [Newspaper Crime Reportage by Nationality of Suspects]. Lecture at Nara University, online notes last updated March 27, 2003, available at www.k3.dion .ne.jp/~mabuchi/lectures_nara/nwsppr_ntnlty.htm (accessed November 9, 2012).

Maher, John. C., and Gaynor Macdonald, eds. 1995. *Diversity in Japanese Culture and Language*. London: Kegan Paul International.

Majima, Ayu. 2013. "Skin Color Melancholy in Modern Japan: Male Elites' Racial Experiences Abroad, 1880s–1950s." In Kowner, Rotem, and Walter Demel, Eds., *Race and Racism in Modern East Asia: Western and Eastern Constructions*, 391–410. Leiden, The Netherlands: Brill.

Malagon, Maria C., Lindsay Perez Huber, and Veronica N. Velez. 2012. "Our Experiences, Our Methods: Using Grounded Theory to Inform a Critical Race Theory Methodology." *Seattle Journal for Social Justice* 8: (1) Article 10.

Marx, Karl. 1867 [1976]. *Capital, Volume 1*. Harmondsworth: Penguin.

Matsuda, Mari. 1987. "Looking to the Bottom: Critical Legal Studies and Reparations." *Harvard Civil Rights - Civil Liberties Law Review* 22: 323–399.

Matsutani, Miyoko. 1989. *Ninjin-san ga Akai Wake* [The Reason Why the Carrot is Red]. Tōkyō: Dōshinsha.

McChesney, Robert W. 2004. *The Problem of the Media: U.S. Communication Politics in the 21st Century*. New York: Monthly Review Press.

McCormack, Gavan, and Julia Yonetani. 2000. "The Okinawan Summit Seen from Below." *Japan Policy Research Institute*, Working Paper 71, September.

McNeill, David. 2015. "*Nippon Kaigi* and the Radical Conservative Project to Take Back Japan." *Asia-Pacific Journal—Japan Focus*, 13(50)4, December 14.

McNeill, David and Justin McCurry. 2019. "Reinventing the Japan Times: How Japan's Oldest English-language Newspaper Tacked Right." *Asia-Pacific Journal—Japan Focus* 17(7)4, April 1.

McVeigh, Brian J. 2000. "Education Reform in Japan: Fixing Education or Fostering Economic Nation-Statism?" In J. S. Eades, Tom Gill, and Harumi Befu, Eds., *Globalization and Social Change in Contemporary Japan*, 76–92. Melbourne: Trans Pacific Press.

McVeigh, Brian J. 2001. "Postwar Japan's Hard and Soft Nationalism." *Japan Policy Research Institute*, Working Paper No. 73, January.

Menton, Linda K., Noren W. Lush, Eileen H. Tamura, and Chance I. Gusukuma. 2003. *The Rise of Modern Japan*. Honolulu: Curriculum Research and Development Group University of Hawai'i, and University of Hawai'i Press.

Miles, Robert. 1993. *Racism after "Race Relations."* London: Routledge.

Minear, Richard H. 1980. "Orientalism and the Study of Japan." *The Journal of Asian Studies* 39(3): 507–517.

Ministry of Foreign Affairs. 1999. "Japan's First and Second Periodical Report on Human Rights, Submitted to the International Convention on Racial Discrimination, Geneva, Switzerland." June.

Ministry of Foreign Affairs. 2001. "Comments of the Japanese Government on the Concluding Observations adopted by the Committee on the Elimination of Racial Discrimination." October.

Ministry of Foreign Affairs. 2005. Embassy of Japan Washington D.C. website, "Registration Procedure at lodging facilities in Japan to be changed as of April 1, 2005." Dated March 2005, accessed July 31, 2012.

Ministry of Foreign Affairs. 2008. "Third, Fourth, Fifth and Sixth Combined Periodic Report on the Implementation of the International Convention on Elimination of Racial Discrimination, Japan." March.

Ministry of Justice. 1998. "Interview with Officials for Citizenship Qualifications and Requirements." August 7.

Ministry of Justice. 2003a. "*Gaikokujin fuhō taizai no tōkei*" [Statistics for foreign illegal overstays]. Immigration Bureau pamphlet.

Ministry of Justice. 2003b. "Interviews with Officials of the Bureau of Human Rights Regarding their "Enlightenment" Procedures Towards Racially-Profiling Police at Sapporo Chitose Airport." January 8, April 15, May 13, and June 27.

Ministry of Justice. 2009. Bureau of Human Rights. "*H.21 Keihatsu katsudō nenkan kyōchō jikō*" [Points of emphasis for 2009's "enlightenment" activities], downloaded September 15, 2012.

Ministry of Justice. 2012a. "Bureau of Human Rights." *Dai-64 Jinken Shūkan* Human Rights Week events. Downloaded from www.moj.go.jp/JINKEN/jinken03.html November 8, 2012.

Ministry of Justice. 2012b. *Kika kyoka shinseisha tō no sui'i* [Statistics for applicants and successful recipients for naturalization.] Online resource accessed July 31, 2012.

Miyagi Prefectural Assembly. 2000. "Assemblyman Konno Takayoshi Comments on Possibility of Rapes by Foreigners During World Cup 2002." *Miyagi Kengikai Teireikai* 283, June 27.

Miyajima, Takashi. 1997. "Immigration and the Redefinition of 'Citizenship' in Japan: 'One People-One Nation' in Question." In T. K. Oommen, Ed., *Citizen and National Identity: From Colonialism to Globalism*, 121–141. New Delhi: Sage.

Mizohata, Sachie. 2016. "*Nippon Kaigi*: Empire, Contradiction, and Japan's Future." *Asia-Pacific Journal—Japan Focus*, 14(1)4, November 1.

Montagu, Ashley. 1942. *Man's Most Dangerous Myth: The Fallacy of Race*. Whitley Press.

Mori, Kazuo. 2005. "A Comparison of Amusingness for Japanese Children and Senior Citizens of *The Story of Little Black Sambo* in the Traditional Version and a Nonracist Version." *Social Behavior and Responsibility* 33(5): 455–466.

Morikawa, Kathy. 1998. "Presentation on Her Protests Towards Fingerprinting of Foreigners." Presented at the Hokkaido International Business Association, November 5.

Morley, Jeremy D. 2006. "Interview with the Canadian Broadcasting Company." March 31, 2006, as cited in Higuchi & Arudou 2008: 266–267.

Mone, M. 2008. "Structural Determinism." In S. Clegg and J. Bailey, Eds., *International Encyclopedia of Organization Studies*, 1478–1480. Thousand Oaks, CA: Sage.

Moro'oka, Jun'ya. 2006. "The Rhetoric of the Foreign Worker Problem in Contemporary Japan." Doctoral dissertation, Faculty of Arts and Sciences, University of Pittsburgh, February 22.

Morton, W. Scott, and J. Kenneth Olenik. 2004. *Japan History and Culture*. New York: McGraw Hill Professional.

Morris, Steven. 2007. "Issei Sagawa: Celebrity Cannibal." *New Criminologist*, September 20.

Morris-Suzuki, Tessa. 2010. *Borderline Japan: Foreigners and Frontier Controls in the Postwar Era*. Cambridge: Cambridge University Press.

Morris-Suzuki, Tessa. 2012. "Out With Human Rights, in With Government-Authored History: The Comfort Women and the Hashimoto Prescription for a 'New Japan'." *The Asia-Pacific Journal*, 10(36)1, September 3.

Morris-Suzuki, Tessa. 2015. "Beyond Racism: Semi-Citizenship and Marginality in Modern Japan." *Japanese Studies*, March 25. London: Routledge.

Möschel , Mathias. 2011. "Race in Mainland European Legal Analysis: Towards a European Critical Race Theory." *Ethnic and Racial Studies* 34(10) October, 1648–1664.

Murphy-Shigematsu, Stephen. 1993. "Multiethnic Japan and the Monoethnic Myth." *MELUS* 18(4): 63–80.

Myers, Ramon H. and Mark R. Peattie, eds. 1987. *The Japanese Colonial Empire 1895–1945*. New Jersey. Princeton University Press.

Myrdal, Gunnar. 1944. *An American Dilemma: The Negro Problem and Modern Democracy*. Cited in Belluscio, Steven J. 2006, ed. *To Be Suddenly White: Literary Realism and Racial Passing*. Columbia, MO: University of Missouri Press.

Nakashima, Cynthia L. 1992. "An Invisible Monster: The Creation and Denial of Mixed-Race People in America." In Maria P. P. Root, Ed., *Racially Mixed People in America*, 162–80. Newbury Park, CA: Sage Publications.

Nantais, Simon. 2011. "Koreans and the Politics of Nationality and Race During the Allied Occupation of Japan, 1945–1952." PhD Dissertation defended August 2011 at the Department of History, University of Victoria, British Columbia, Canada.

National Police Agency. 2009. "*Heisei 20 nen no soshiki hanzai no jōsei*" [The status of organized crime for 2008]. *Keisatsuchō Soshiki Hanzai Taisaku-bu, Kikaku Bunseki-ka*, February.

National Research Institute of Police Science, 2001. "*Gaikokujin hanzai o kyūmei suru tame no seitai shiryō o mochiita shihyō no kaihatsu*" [Development of an Index Using Biological Materials to Uncover Foreign Crime]. August.

Neary, Ian J. 2009. "Burakumin in Contemporary Japan." In Michael Weiner, ed., *Japan's Minorities: The Illusion of Homogeneity*, 59–83, 2nd ed. Sheffield: Routledge.

Neumann, Iver R. 1996. "Self and Other in International Relations." *European Journal of International Relations* 2(2): 139–174, June.

O'Day, Robin. 2015. "Differentiating SEALDs from Freeters, and Precariats: The politics of youth movements in contemporary Japan." *Asia-Pacific Journal—Japan Focus* 13(37)2, September 14.

Oguma, Eiji. 1995. *Tan'itsu Minzoku Shinwa no Kigen*. Tōkyō: Shin'yōsha.

Oguma, Eiji. 2002. *A Genealogy of "Japanese" Self-Images*. Melbourne: Trans Pacific Press.

Okamoto Masataka, ed. 2005. *Nihon no Minzoku Sabetsu: Jinshu Sabetsu Teppai Jōyaku kara Mita Kadai* [Japan's Ethnic Discrimination: Issues vis-à-vis the UN Convention on the Elimination of Racial Discrimination]. Tōkyō: Akashi Shoten.

Ōkubo, Yūko. 2005. "'Visible' Minorities and 'Invisible' Minorities: An Ethnographic Study of Multicultural Education and the Production of Ethnic 'Others' in Japan." PhD Dissertation, Department of Anthropology, University of California, Berkeley.

Omi, Michael, and Howard Winant. 1986. *Racial Formation in the United States: From the 1960s to the 1990s*. Sheffield: Routledge.

Osada, Masako. 2002. *Sanctions and Honorary Whites: Domestic Policies and Economic Realities in Relations between Japan and South Africa*. Westport, CT: Praeger Publishers.

Ōsaka District Court. 2006. H.16 (Wa) 11926–Gō, *Songai Baishō Seikyū Jiken Hanketsu Bun Steve McGowan vs. G.Style*. Court ruling January 30.

Outlaw, Lucius. 1990. "Toward a Critical Theory of Race." In Goldberg, David Theo, ed. *Anatomy of Racism*, 58–82. Minneapolis: University of Minnesota.

Parry, Richard Lloyd. 2011. *People Who Eat Darkness: The Fate of Lucie Blackman*. London: Jonathan Cape.

Peek, J. M. 1991. "Japan and the International Bill of Rights." *Journal of Northeast Asian Studies*, Fall 10(3): 3–16.

Peek, J. M. 1992. "Japan, The United Nations, and Human Rights." *Asian Survey* 32(3): 217–229.

Pekkanen, Robert. 2006. *Japan's Dual Civil Society: Members Without Advocates*. Stanford: Stanford University Press.

Pillow, Wanda. 2003. "Race-Based Methodologies: Multicultural Methods or Epistemological Shifts?" In G. R. Lopez and Laurence Parker, Eds., *Interrogating Racism in Qualitative Research Methodology*, 181–202. New York: Peter Lang.

Prieler, Michael. 2006. "Japanese Advertising's Foreign Obsession." In Lutum, Peter, Ed., *Japanizing: The Structure of Culture and Thinking in Japan*, 239–266. Berlin: LIT Verlag.

Reischauer, Edwin O. 1970. *Japan: The Story of a Nation*. New York: Knopf.

Reischauer, Edwin O. 1995. *The Japanese Today*. Cambridge: Harvard Belknap.

Repeta, Lawrence. 2013. "Japan's Democracy at Risk: The LDP's Ten Most Dangerous Proposals for Constitutional Change." *Asia-Pacific Journal—Japan Focus* 11(28)3, July 14.

Root, Maria P. P., ed. 1992. *Racially Mixed People in America*. Newbury Park, CA: Sage Publications.

Roth, Joshua Hotaka. 2002. *Brokered Homeland: Japanese Brazilian Migrants in Japan*. Ithaca: Cornell University Press.

Russell, John G. 1991. "Race and Reflexivity: The Black Other in Contemporary Japanese Mass Culture. *Cultural Anthropology* 6(1): 3–25. February.

Russell, John G. 2009. "The Other Other: The Black Presence in the Japanese Experience." In Michael Weiner, Ed., *Japan's Minorities: The Illusion of Homogeneity*, 84–115, 2nd ed. Sheffield: Routledge.

Ryang, Sonia and John Lie, eds. 2009. *Diaspora Without Homeland: Being Korean in Japan*. Berkeley: University of California Press.

Saaler, Sven, and J. Victor Koschmann, eds. 2007. *Pan-Asianism in Modern Japanese History: Colonialism, Regionalism, and Borders*. Abingdon, UK: Routledge.

Saïd, Edward. 1978. *Orientalism*. New York: Random House.

Sakanaka, Hidenori. 2005. *Nyūkan Senki* [Immigration Bureau Battle Diary]. Tōkyō: Kōdansha.

Sakanaka, Hidenori. 2007. *A New Framework for Japan's Immigration Policies*. Tōkyō: Japan Immigration Policy Institute.

Sakata, Fumi. 2012. "A Critique of Critical Race Theory: A Textual Analysis of the 'Mr. Gaijin' Mask." Master's Thesis, Queens University, Kingston, Ontario, Canada. Successfully defended August.

Sakurai, Yoshiko et al. 2006. *Kinkyū Shuppan: Abunai! Jinken Yōgo Hōan: Semari kuru Senshinkoku-kei Zentai Shugi no Kyōfu.* [Urgent Publication: Danger! The Protection of Human Rights Bill: The Imminent Threat of the Totalitarianism of the Developed Countries.] Tōkyō: Tentensha.

Sapporo District Court. 2002. *Songai Baishō Tō Seikyū Jiken Hanketsu Bun, Karthaus et al. vs. Earthcure KK* [parent company of Otaru Onsen Yunohana] *and City of Otaru, Heisei 13 (Wa) Dai 206* [The Otaru Onsens Case Initial Decision], November 11.

Sapporo High Court. 2004. *Dai Futai Kōso Jiken, Karthaus et al. vs. Earthcure KK and City of Otaru, Heisei 14 (Ne) Dai 498* [The Otaru Onsens Case Appeal Decision], September 16.

Sasagase, Yūji, Hayashi Keita and Sato Kei. 2015. "Japan's Largest Rightwing Organization: An Introduction to *Nippon Kaigi*." *Asia-Pacific Journal—Japan Focus*, 13(50)5, December 14.

Schreiber, Mark. 1996. *Shocking Crimes of Postwar Japan*. Tōkyō: Yenbooks.

Seidensticker, Edward. 1991. *Tokyo Rising: The City Since the Great Earthquake*. Cambridge: Harvard University Press.

Sharma, Nandita Rama. 2006. *Home Economics: Nationalism and the Making of "Migrant Workers" in Canada*. Toronto: University of Toronto Press.

Sheftall, M. G. 2008. "Kamikaze Ethos: The Rise, Fall, and Revitalization of a Modern Japanese Hero-System." Doctoral Dissertation successfully defended at the Graduate School of Asia-Pacific Studies, Waseda University.

Sheftall, M. G. Forthcoming. "*Kyōsei*: Cultural Space, Multiculturalism, and the Prospect of a 'Post-Homogeneous' Japan." (*working title*). Currently in editing stages.

Shih, Fang-Long. 2008. *Re-writing Culture in Taiwan*. London: Routledge.

Shin, Hwaji. 2010. "Colonial Legacy of Ethno-racial Inequality in Japan." *Theory & Society* 39: 327–342.

Shipper, Apichai A. 2008. *Fighting for Foreigners: Immigration and its Impact on Japanese Democracy*. Ithaca: Cornell University Press.

Shizuoka District Court. 1999. *Bortz v. Suzuki*, judgment of October 12, Hamamatsu Branch. *1718 Hanrei Jihō 92.*

Shizuoka Prefectural Police. 2000. "*Rainichi gaikokujin hanzai no tokuchō*" Handbook [Characteristics of Crimes Committed by Foreigners Coming to Japan]. *Shizuoka Ken Bōhan Kyōkai Rengōkai*, February.

Siddle, Richard M. 1996. *Race, Resistance, and the Ainu of Japan.* Abingdon, UK: Routledge.

Siddle, Richard M. 1997. "The Ainu: Indigenous people of Japan." In Michael Weiner, Ed., *Japan's Minorities: The Illusion of Homogeneity.* 1st ed. Sheffield: Routledge.

Sjöberg, Katarina. 1993. *Return of the Ainu: Cultural Mobilization and the Practice of Ethnicity in Japan.* Amsterdam: Harwood Academic Publishers.

Solorzano, Daniel G. and Tara J. Yosso. 2001. "Critical Race and LatCrit Theory and Method: Counter-storytelling." *Qualitative Studies in Education* 14(4): 471–495.

Sour Strawberries: Japan's Hidden "Guest Workers" 2008. Documentary by Tilman König and Daniel Kremers. Leipzig: Cinemabstruso.

Spickard, Paul. R. 1992. "The Illogic of American Racial Categories." In Maria P. P. Root, Ed., *Racially Mixed People in America*, 12–23. Newbury Park, CA: Sage Publications.

Stafford, Mai, Bruce K. Newbold, and Nancy A. Ross. 2010. "Psychological Distress Among Immigrants and Visible Minorities in Canada: A Contextual Analysis." *International Journal of Social Psychiatry* 57: 428, April.

Stanfield II, John H., and Rutledge M. Dennis, eds. 1993. *Race and Ethnicity in Research Methods.* Newbury Park: Sage.

Sterling, Marvin D. 2010. *Babylon East: Performing Dancehall, Roots Reggae, and Rastafari in Japan.* Durham: Duke University Press.

Stoler, Ann Laura. 1995. *Race and the Education of Desire: Foucault's History of Sexuality and the Colonial Order of Things.* Durham: Duke University Press.

Strauss, Anselm L., and Juliet Corbin. 1990. *Basics of Qualitative Research: Grounded Theory Procedures and Techniques.* London: Sage.

Strauss, Anselm L., and Juliet Corbin. 1998. *Basics of Qualitative Research: Grounded Theory Procedures and Techniques*, 2nd ed. London: Sage.

Sue, Derald Wing, and David Rivera. 2010. "Racial Microaggressions in Everyday Life." *Psychology Today*, October 5.

Sugimoto, Yoshio. 1997. *An Introduction to Japanese Society.* Cambridge: Cambridge University Press.

Sugimoto, Yoshio. 2009. *The Cambridge Companion to Modern Japanese Culture.* Cambridge: Cambridge University Press.

Supreme Court of Japan. 1985. Judgment of November 21. *Minshū 39 Kan 7*, at 1512.

Supreme Court of Japan. 2005. *Heisei 17 (O) Dai 448.* Judgment of April 7 on the Otaru Onsen Case.

Tajfel, Henri, and John Turner. 1979. "An Integrative Theory of Intergroup Conflict." In W. G. Austin and S. Worchel, Eds., *The Social Psychology of Intergroup Relations*, 33–47. Monterey, CA: Brooks-Cole.

Takenaka, Akiko. 2016. "Japanese Memories of the Asia-Pacific War: Analyzing the Revisionist Turn Post-1995." *Asia-Pacific Journal—Japan Focus* 14(20)8, October 15.

Takezawa, Yasuko, ed. 2011. *Racial Representations in Asia*. Melbourne: Trans-Pacific Press.

Tamanoi, Mariko Asano. 2000. "Knowledge, Power, and Racial Classification: The 'Japanese' in 'Manchuria.'" *The Journal of Asian Studies* 59(2, May), 248–276.

Tamogami, Toshio et al. 2010. *Kinkyū Shuppan: "Gaikokujin Sanseiken" de Nihon ga Nakunaru Hi* [Urgent Publication: Doomsday for Japan due to Foreign Suffrage]. Tōkyō: Bessetsu Takarajima.

Tanaka, Hiroshi. 2006. In Kim Geduk, ed. *Nichi/Kan "Kyōsei Shakai" no Tenbō* [A view to a Japanese/Korean "Coexistence Society"]. Tōkyō: Shakansha.

Teikoku Databank. 2007. Bankruptcy records for Eichi Shuppan Inc. April 5.

Thomas, Jim. 1993. *Doing Critical Ethnography*. Newberry Park, CA: Sage Publications.

Tōkyō District Court. 2007. *Heisei 17 (Wa) Dai 17658*, on the Valentine Case, decision handed down March 29.

Tsuda, Takeyuki. 2003. *Strangers in the Ethnic Homeland*. New York: Columbia University Press.

TV Asahi. 1996a. *News Station*, October 14, 10 P.M. Ten-minute segment on the different permutations of McDonald's food across Asia (regarding the Kume Hiroshi "*gaijin ga katakoto ga ii*" gaffe).

TV Asahi. 1996b. *News Station*, November 18, around 11 P.M. "*History Special, looking back on the 20th Century, a time when the word 'gaijin' still existed*" segment.

TV Asahi. 1999. *News Station*, October 12, 10 P.M. Ten-Minute Segment on the *Ana Bortz vs. Sebido* lawsuit verdict.

Twine, France Winddance, and Jonathan W. Warren, eds. 2000. *Racing Research, Researching Race: Methodological Dilemmas in Critical Race Studies*. New York: New York University Press.

United Nations. 2012. Country Profiles, Japan. www.data.un.org, downloaded March 1, 2012.

United Nations. Committee against Torture. 2007. CAT/C/JPN/CO/1, May 18.

United Nations. Office of the High Commissioner for Human Rights, Committee on Civil and Political Rights. 1998. Report CCPR/C/79/Add.102, November 19.

United Nations. Office of the High Commissioner for Human Rights, Committee on the Elimination of Racial Discrimination. 2001. Report CERD/A/56/18, March.

United Nations. Office of the High Commissioner for Human Rights. 2006. Report by Dr. Doudou Diene, Special Rapporteur on Contemporary Forms of Racism, Racial Discrimination, Xenophobia, and Related Intolerance, E/CN.4/2006/16/Add.2, January 24.

United Nations. Human Rights Council. 2008. Working Group on the Universal Periodic Review, Second session, Geneva, May 5–19, 2008, draft report A/HRC/WG.6/2/L.10, May 14.

United Nations. Human Rights Council. 2010. "Transcription of the Japanese Government CERD Review (76th Session)." February 24–25, Geneva, Switzerland.

United States US Citizenship and Immigration Services. 2012. *Welcome to the United States: A Guide for New Immigrants*. Pamphlet given to all new Permanent Residents. Received November 2012.

United States Department of State. 2001–2008. Country Reports on Human Rights, Japan.

Vlastos, Stephen. 1998. *Mirror of Modernity: Invented Traditions of Modern Japan*. Berkeley: University of California Press.

Wagatsuma, Hiroshi. 1967. "The Social Perception of Skin Color in Japan." *Daedalus* 96(2): 407–443.

Wagatsuma, Hiroshi, and George DeVos. 1967. *Japan's Invisible Race: Caste in Culture and Personality*. Berkeley: University of California Press.

Wald, Gale. 2000. *Crossing the Line: Racial Passing in Twentieth-Century U.S. Literature and Culture*. Durham: Duke University Press.

Webster, Timothy. 2007a. "Bortz. v. Suzuki (Translation and Commentary)." *Pacific Rim Law and Policy Journal* 16: 631.

Webster, Timothy. 2007b. "Arudou v. Earth Cure: Judgment of November 11, 2002, Sapporo District Court." *Asian-Pacific Law & Policy Journal* 9: 297.

Webster, Timothy. 2007c. "McGowan v Narita, Case Note and Commentary." *Australian Journal of Asian Law* 9: 346.

Weiner, Michael. 1995. *Race and Migration in Imperial Japan*. London: Routledge.

Weiner, Michael, ed. 1997. *Japan's Minorities: The Illusion of Homogeneity*. 1st ed. Sheffield: Routledge.

Weiner, Michael, ed. 2009. *Japan's Minorities: The Illusion of Homogeneity*. 2nd ed. Sheffield: Routledge.

Wetherall, William. 2008. "The Racialization of Japan." In David Blake Willis and Stephen Murphy-Shigematsu, Eds., *Transcultural Japan: At the Borderlands of Race, Gender and Identity*, 264–281. London: Routledge.

Whiting, Robert. 1990. *You've Gotta Have Wa*. New York: Vintage.

Williams, Theresa K. 1992. "Prism Lives: Identity of Binational Amerasians." In Maria P. P. Root, Ed., *Racially Mixed People in America*, 280–303. Newbury Park, CA: Sage Publications.

Winant, Howard. 2003. "The Theoretical Status of the Concept of Race." In Coco Fusco and Brian Wallis, Eds., *Only Skin Deep: Changing Visions of the American Self*, 51–62. New York: Harry N. Abrams.

Witherspoon, D. J. et al. 2007. "Genetic Similarities Within and Between Human Populations." *Genetics*, 176(1), May, 351–359.

Wodak, Ruth and Michael Meyer, Eds. 2009. *Methods for Critical Discourse Analysis*. London: Sage.

World Bank. 2012. Worldbank.org Statistics on Japan's Economic Indicators (accessed March 1, 2012).

XENE Magazine. 2002. "Apology" (On Their Creation of Exclusionary Signs for World Cup 2002 in Sapporo). October-December issue 2002, page 16.

XENE Magazine. 2012. XENEnet.com (accessed July 1, 2012).

Yamaguchi, Tomomi. 2017. "The 'Japan Is Great!' Boom, Historical Revisionism, and the Government." *Asia-Pacific Journal—Japan Focus* 15(6)3, March 15.

Yoshino, Kōsaku. 1992. *Cultural Nationalism in Contemporary Japan.* London: London School of Economics.

Yoshino, Kōsaku. 1997. "The Discourse on Blood and Racial Identity in Contemporary Japan." In Frank Dikötter, Ed., *The Construction of Racial Identities in China and Japan*, 199–211. Honolulu: University of Hawai'i Press.

Zachmann, Urs Matthias. 2013. "Race and International Law in Japan's New Order in East Asia, 1938–1945." In Kowner, Rotem, and Walter Demel, Eds., *Race and Racism in Modern East Asia: Western and Eastern Constructions*, 453–473. Leiden, The Netherlands: Brill.

Zinn, Howard. 2005. *A People's History of the United States.* New York: Harper Perennial Modern Classics.

Zolberg, Aristide R. 2000. "Introduction." In T. Alexander Aleinikoff, and Douglas Klusmeyer, Eds., *From Migrants to Citizens: Membership in a Changing World*, 383–385. Washington, DC: Carnegie Endowment for International Peace.

Index

Figure page numbers are in Italics

About the Author

Debito Arudou, PhD, has been a scholar of Japan for more than three decades, a Japan resident for a quarter-century, and a naturalized Japanese citizen since 2000. A graduate of Cornell University, University of California, San Diego, and Meiji Gakuin University, he is the author of several books in English and Japanese, including *Japanese Only: The Otaru Hot Springs Case and Racial Discrimination in Japan* and *Handbook for Newcomers, Migrants, and Immigrants to Japan*. He also writes the monthly "Visible Minorities" column for the Shingetsu News Agency and the "Just Be Cause" column for the *Japan Times*. His award-winning archive of essays, articles, and reference materials for life and human rights in Japan, established in 1996 and updated weekly, can be found at www.debito.org.